Success in

EUROPEAN HISTORY 1815–1941

Success Studybooks

Advertising and Promotion
Book-keeping and Accounts
Business Calculations
Chemistry
Commerce
Commerce: West African Edition
Communication
Electronics
European History 1815-1941
Information Processing
Insurance
Investment
Law
Managing People
Marketing
Politics
Principles of Accounting
Principles of Accounting: Answer Book
Principles of Catering
Statistics
Twentieth Century World Affairs
World History since 1945

Success in
EUROPEAN HISTORY
1815 – 1941

Jack B. Watson, M.A.

JOHN MURRAY

The cover illustration shows an artist's (Carl Wagner's) impression of Bismarck dictating terms of peace to Thiers and Favre at Versailles in February 1871, after the fall of Paris (see Unit 7.3(c)). 'If you don't make haste,' Bismarck is reported to have exclaimed, 'I shall begin to speak in German.' He had hitherto been using the language of diplomacy – French.

© Margaret Watson 1981, 1985

First published 1981
by John Murray (Publishers) Ltd
50 Albemarle Street, London W1X 4BD

Reprinted 1985 (revised), 1988, 1991, 1993, 1995, 1997

Printed in Great Britain by
Athenæum Press Ltd, Gateshead, Tyne & Wear

British Library Cataloguing in Publication Data

Watson, Jack Brierley
    Success in European history, 1815–1941.
    – (Success study books).
    1. Europe – History
    I. Title   II. Series
    940.2'8
ISBN 0–7195–3794–0

Foreword

This book aims to provide a basic and comprehensive survey of the development of Europe in the period 1815–1941. It is essentially concerned with the political framework within which the development took place, and it also deals with economic and social change, developments in thought, and international relations. Its subject is the whole of continental Europe, and it emphasizes the differences between western Europe and eastern Europe – political, economic, social and ideological. Comparisons are made with developments in Britain, and the book includes coverage of Britain's role in European affairs, but does not attempt to deal as fully with Britain's internal affairs as with those of the major countries on the continent.

The study of history should not, at any level, be limited simply to the accumulation of facts. Factual material is essential but modern history is a matter for controversy and differing opinions: students must not only be well-informed, they must also acquire a degree of critical awareness that enables them to develop their own powers of independent thought. It is vital that students in present-day public examinations should have learned to think for themselves.

Success in European History, therefore, has the aim of providing essential factual material while, at the same time, suggesting interpretations and stimulating readers' individual responses. Each Unit of study ends with exercises which challenge the student to make active use of the text, maps, diagrams and illustrations. With practice, the student can become skilled in the use of such aids to study as the many cross-references, the Glossary, and the Index, and can approach each new Unit with a growing appreciation of the important differences between evidence and assertion, generalization and example. The suggestions for Further Reading at the end of each Unit, and the Bibliography on page 437, will assist the student to achieve a deeper understanding of those aspects of European history in which he has a special interest.

This book is particularly useful for students of O Level and equivalents overseas, also as introductory reading for students of A Level, first-year degree courses, or similar examinations in further or higher education. For the general reader, the book provides an account of European history during a period which was of great importance in the evolution of present-day Europe – an age of undoubted progress in many ways, but also an age which, towards its close, produced a measure of barbarism which was without precedent.

The better to determine where it is going, each generation needs to know where previous generations have already been. The years 1815–1941 saw enormous changes in Europe as it moved from the age of Metternich and Alexander I to the age of Hitler and Stalin; and this book ends with the Second World War, a suitable point for looking back on the European development, both noble and ignoble, and for looking forward to present-day Europe, when Europeans have perhaps at last begun to see their history in perspective, and to recognize not only its achievements but also its follies and crimes.

J.B.W.

Acknowledgments

During the many years in which this book has been maturing I have had the benefit and privilege of working with teachers, examiners and students, too numerous to name in this brief note but to whom I owe gratitude and thanks for influence which has been invaluable. I would particularly like to mention among them W.W. Davies, whose eye for accuracy and detail never once failed his colleagues. In writing the book, I have had especially valuable assistance once again from Ed Rayner, who gives so generously of his time and so unselfishly of his advice to try to ensure that what is written is both accurate and balanced. I have also been fortunate to be advised, and sometimes admonished, by Bernard Seaman, whose historical insight is matched by an elegance of expression which few of us can hope to emulate.

My colleagues have undoubtedly made this a better book than it might otherwise have been, and I am happy to acknowledge my debt to them. I would also wish to thank Rosemarie Burston for her work in preparing the book for publication and especially for her enthusiasm and achievement in searching out the illustrations, and Carolyn Nichols who helped with vital editorial work at the later stages. I must thank my wife for her vigorous work on the Index and for her general advice and encouragement. And finally, I owe thanks to Irene Slade who has so unfailingly encouraged, guided and stimulated to ensure that what was begun was also completed.

J.B.W.

We are grateful to the following for their kind assistance in providing illustrations:

Barnaby's Picture Library (Figs. 18.5, 24.4, 25.2); BBC Hulton Picture Library (Figs. 2.1, 3.2, 5.3, 6.1, 7.4, 11.4, 13.3, 15.3, 20.6, 21.1, 22.2); Bibliothèque Nationale Paris (Fig. 1.2, 4.4, 11.1); Bilderdienst Süddeutscher Verlag (Figs. 22.4, 23.5); the British Library (Figs. 4.6, 5.1, 16.2, 18.7); the Trustees of the British Museum (Fig. 4.2); Deutsches Museum, Munich (Fig. 3.3); Eupra Press Service, Munich (Fig. 19.6); Fotomas Index (Figs. 13.1, 19.1); Fox Photos Ltd. (Fig. 21.4); Photographie Giraudon, Musée Palais, Versailles (Fig 1.6); Robert Harding Picture Library/Victor Kennett (Fig. 4.7); the *Illustrated London News* (Figs. 9.4, 11.2); Imperial War Museum (Figs. 17.3, 18.4, 24.2, 25.4); Keystone Press Agency (Figs. 12.3, 14.6, 22.1, 22.6); Krupp

(Fig. 10.3); the London *Evening Standard* and the Low Trustees (Figs. 22.3, 24.5); the Mansell Collection (Figs. 4.5, 6.3, 6.4, 7.6, 7.7, 16.1); Mary Evans Picture Library (Figs. 9.5, 17.2); Märkisches Museum, East Berlin (Fig. 5.4); Moro/Rome, Museo San Martino (Figs. 9.3, 12.2); National Army Museum (Fig. 8.3); National Film Archive Stills Library (Fig. 14.4); Novosti Press Agency (Figs. 14.1, 14.5, 19.2, 19.3, 19.5); Bild-Archiv der Österreichischen Nationalbibliothek, Vienna (Figs. 1.3, 2.5, 5.6, 13.4); Popperfoto (Figs. 21.7, 22.7); *Punch* (Figs. 4.3, 6.2, 7.2, 8.1, 8.4, 9.6, 10.2, 15.1, 15.4, 17.4, 18.2, 20.7, 23.2, 25.1); Royal Commonwealth Society (Figs. 16.3, 25.3); Snark International (Figs. 11.3, 12.1, 15.5, 16.5, 16.6, 23.7); Thomson Organization (Fig. 20.1); TUC Library (Fig. 3.4); Ullstein Bilderdienst (Figs. 10.4, 23.3, 24.7). We should also like to thank Miss Elizabeth Clark of Thames and Hudson who was very helpful in tracing several illustrations.

Contents

Unit 1   Europe in 1815
  1.1 European Societies and Economies   1
  1.2 1814–15 and the Conflict of Ideas   3
  1.3 The Peace Settlement of 1814–15   6
  1.4 The Reconstructed Europe   13
  1.5 Appendix: Summary of the Principal Terms of the
         Treaty of Vienna (June 1815)   15
  Further Reading   15
  Exercises   15

Unit 2   The Defence of the Existing Order 1815–48
  2.1 The Conservatism of the Age of Metternich   17
  2.2 The Congress Period   19
  2.3 Austrian Spheres of Influence   24
  2.4 Elsewhere in Europe   33
  Further Reading   34
  Documentary   34
  Exercises   34

Unit 3   The Challenge to the Existing Order 1815–48
  3.1 Change and Protest   35
  3.2 The Demand for Constitutional Liberties   36
  3.3 The Demand for National Independence   40
  3.4 The Search for National Identity   49
  3.5 The Conflicts in the Existing Order by 1848   53
  Further Reading   54
  Exercises   54

Unit 4   Western Liberalism and Eastern Autocracy
  4.1 France and Russia: Contrasts in Development   55
  4.2 France 1814–48   58
  4.3 Russia 1801–55   67
  Further Reading   72
  Documentary   72
  Exercises   72

Unit 5   Revolutionary Upheaval 1848–9
  5.1 Revolutionary Forces   73

5.2   The Revolutions: a Regional Survey   74
5.3   The Failure of the Revolutions   88
Further Reading   89
Exercises   89

Unit 6   France 1848–71: The Revival of Republicanism and Bonapartism
6.1   The Second Republic   91
6.2   The Second Empire   96
Further Reading   104
Documentary   104
Exercises   104

Unit 7   The Renewed Attack on the Existing Order 1848–71
7.1   Disillusionment after 1848   105
7.2   The Creation of a United Italy   106
7.3   The Creation of a United Germany   115˙
Further Reading   124
Documentary   124
Exercises   124

Unit 8   The Great Powers 1815–71 and the Eastern Question
8.1   National Policies and the Balance of Power   125
8.2   French Foreign Policy   125
8.3   Russian Foreign Policy and the Eastern Question   127
8.4   Russian Foreign Policy and the Crimean War   130
Further Reading   135
Documentary   136
Exercises   136

Unit 9   Europe in 1871 and the Quickening Pace: A Survey
9.1   Nation States and Empires   137
9.2   European Economies   138
9.3   European Societies   144
9.4   The Papacy   147
Further Reading   148
Exercises   149

Unit 10   The German Reich 1871–1918
10.1   The Chancellorship of Bismarck   150
10.2   Wilhelmine Germany   156
Further Reading   163
Exercises   163

Unit 11   The French Third Republic to 1914
11.1   The Economy and Society   165

11.2   Post-Imperial Confusion   166
11.3   The Third Republic from 1875 to 1914   171
Further Reading   180
Documentary   180
Exercises   180

Unit 12   Liberal Italy 1861–1922
12.1   The Economy and Society   181
12.2   The Years before 1914   182
12.3   The First World War and the Rise of Fascism ✓   187
Further Reading   191
Exercises   191

Unit 13   The Habsburg Empire 1867–1918
13.1   The Ausgleich   193
13.2   The Non-Hungarian Empire   196
13.3   Hungary   200
13.4   The Foreign Policy of Austria-Hungary   201
13.5   The First World War and the End of the Empire   203
Further Reading   205
Exercises   205

Unit 14   Imperial Russia 1855–1917
14.1   The Economy and Society   206
14.2   The Reign of Alexander II 1855–81   209
14.3   The Reign of Alexander III 1881–94   214
14.4   The Reign of Nicholas II 1894–1917   215
14.5   Russian Foreign Policy 1855–1917   226
Further Reading   229
Exercises   229

Unit 15   The Eastern Question 1871–1913 and the Balance of Power
15.1   The Diplomacy of Bismarck 1871–90   230
15.2   The Bulgarian Crisis   235
15.3   The Ottoman Empire after 1878   242
15.4   Ferment in the Balkans 1908–13   243
Further Reading   248
Documentary   248
Exercises   248

Unit 16   Overseas Empires and European Imperialism
16.1   Empires Old and New   249
16.2   The Expansion of Empires after 1871   255
16.3   Colonial Conflicts   260
Further Reading   263

Documentary   264
Exercises   264

Unit 17   The Great Powers 1890–1914
17.1   Alliances and Ententes   265
17.2   Killing Power   268
17.3   A Crescendo of Crises   270
17.4   From Sarajevo into the Abyss   272
17.5   Why was there a War? War Aims   274
Further Reading   277
Documentary   277
Exercises   277

Unit 18   The First World War
18.1   The Failure of the Schlieffen Plan   279
18.2   The Eastern Front and the Defeat of Russia   282
18.3   The Western Front and the Defeat of Germany   284
18.4   The Land War in Other Theatres   289
18.5   The War at Sea and in the Air   290
18.6   Defeat without Victory   291
18.7   Appendix: British War Aims; Wilson's Fourteen Points;
       The Dead   293
Further Reading   294
Documentary and Maps   294
Exercises   294

Unit 19   Russia 1917–41: Marxism-Leninism and Stalinism
19.1   Russia in 1917   295
19.2   Russia under Lenin 1917-24   301
19.3   The Power Struggle   309
19.4   Russia under Stalin   311
Further Reading   316
Documentary   316
Exercises   316

Unit 20   Europe after the First World War
20.1   The Peace Settlement   317
20.2   European Society and the Economy   331
20.3   Appendix: Summaries of the Peace Treaties   336
Further Reading   337
Documentary and Miscellaneous   338
Exercises   338

Unit 21   The Struggle for Democracy
21.1   Optimism and Obstacles   339

21.2 The French Third Republic 1918–40   342
21.3 Weimar Germany   346
21.4 The Lesser Democracies   355
Further Reading   358
Documentary   359
Exercises   359

Unit 22 The Dictatorships
22.1 Nationalism and Fascism   360
22.2 Fascist Italy   361
22.3 The Turkish Republic and Mustapha Kemal   365
22.4 Nazi Germany   367
22.5 The See-Saw in Spain   372
22.6 The Lesser Dictatorships   376
Further Reading   379
Documentary   379
Exercises   380

Unit 23 The Struggle for International Co-operation and Peace
23.1 Before the First World War   381
23.2 The League of Nations   382
23.3 The 1920s: Decade of Hope   388
23.4 The Early 1930s: Years of Setback   394
23.5 Appendix: Summary of the Covenant of the
      League of Nations   401
Further Reading   402
Documentary   402
Exercises   402

Unit 24 The Coming of the Second World War
24.1 The Anti-Comintern Pacts   403
24.2 The Anschluss   404
24.3 The Failure of Appeasement   406
24.4 The Unsuccessful Threat   411
24.5 The Second World War   415
Further Reading   421
Miscellaneous   421
Exercises   421

Unit 25 Europe 1815–1941: Retrospect
25.1 Revolution and Evolution   423
25.2 European Civilization   430

Glossary   433
Bibliography   437
Index   440

List of Maps

Poland 1772–1815   9
Europe in 1815   11
The Multi-racial Austrian Empire after 1815   26
The German Confederation after 1815   28
Italy in 1815   32
The Break-up of the Ottoman Empire in the Balkans (Phase I)   42
Revolutions and Upheaval 1848–9   75
The Making of Italy 1859–70   113
The Making of the German Reich 1864–71   116
The Crimean War 1854–6   131
Europe in 1871   139
The Austro-Hungarian Empire in 1914   195
Russia's Expansion in Asia   227
The Break-up of the Ottoman Empire in the Balkans (Phase II):
  (a) 1877–8: to the Treaty of San Stefano; (b) 1878: The Treaty
  of Berlin   238
The Break-up of the Ottoman Empire in the Balkans (Phase III)   247
The Division of Africa by 1914   258
Europe in 1914   275
The Western Front (a) The Failure of the Schlieffen Plan;
  (b) The War of Attrition: some major engagements   280
The Theatres of War in Eastern Europe   283
Civil War and the Wars of Intervention in Russia 1918–21   304
Germany: the Treaty of Versailles   323
The Former Austro-Hungarian Empire: the Treaties of St Germain
  and Trianon   325
The Balkan and Turkish Settlement 1919–23   327
The Eclipse of Democracy in Europe 1918–39   356
The Making of Italian East Africa   398
The Expansion of Nazi Germany 1935–9   409
The Soviet Union's European Frontier 1939–42   416

Unit One

Europe in 1815

1.1 European Societies and Economies

About two hundred million people lived in Europe in 1815. Medical science had already begun to reduce the death rate, and the population was growing steadily. From 1815 to 1914 Europe's population more than doubled. In the two hundred years from 1750 to 1950, indeed, it increased by almost 400 per cent. Such an expansion inevitably had far-reaching consequences, affecting societies, economies and political systems.

The great majority of Europeans still worked on the land in 1815. This was true even in Britain, where the agricultural and industrial revolutions had begun some two generations earlier. The medieval system of serfdom had already been eroded in western Europe, but millions of peasants in central and eastern Europe were still bound to the soil and to their masters. Even in 1848, a generation later, only about a quarter of the populations of France and Germany lived in towns, though these areas were among the most advanced in continental Europe. Western Europe, in fact, developed far more quickly than the east. Agriculture was modernized, and the introduction of scientific farming improved crop yields and the quality of the livestock. In Russia, on the other hand, the serfs were not emancipated until 1861, and the output of Russian peasants remained dismally low well into the twentieth century, since their farming techniques remained almost medieval. Where progress was faster, however, more scientific agriculture not only produced more food to support the growing population, but this food was produced by a smaller labour force, thus freeing workers for industry.

Industry was the key to rising standards of living, although working conditions were harsh during the early stages of industrialization, and life in the early industrial towns was squalid and unhealthy. James Watt patented his steam-engine in 1769, and its application brought more efficient mining, increased factory-production and, eventually, led to the development of the railways. Railway construction spread rapidly from Britain to the continent of Europe in the late 1820s and 1830s, revolutionizing transport and encouraging further economic growth and social change. Growth brought increased wealth, which not only sustained a larger population (although the unequal distribution of wealth left millions in want and squalor), but also brought a challenge to the traditional ruling classes from prospering manufacturers and businessmen.

Social change, like improvements in agriculture and developing industrialization, occurred more rapidly in western than in eastern Europe. By 1815 the rising middle classes in Britain and France were already challenging the traditional landed interest. The defence of the old order rested mainly with monarchies, aristocracies and the Church. The French Revolution of 1789 had been, to a large extent, an assault on the privileges of the aristocracy and the Catholic Church, but it had developed into an assault on the French monarchy as well. Nevertheless, monarchies, aristocracies and the Church remained powerful in 1815 across almost the entire continent. Aristocrats, like Prince Metternich (the Chancellor of Austria from 1821), still tended to think more in terms of preserving the status of their international class rather than of advancing the interests of their own nations; and the Church (Catholic in western and central Europe, Greek Orthodox in countries such as Russia) had a similar conservative and international concern. Monarchs, aristocrats and churchmen had a vested interest in preserving the *status quo* and their own privileges. It was on these privileges that society rested, but it was a society which was ill-fitted to cope with rapid change, and which was soon to appear out of step in a Europe where mines, factories and railways were spreading.

In the first instance, the challenge to existing authority and to privilege was likely to come from a minority of intellectuals and from those new rich whose wealth was derived not from landed estates but from the profits of industry and trade – from those groups whom the French identified as the *bourgeoisie*. It was to these middle classes that the ideas of liberalism and nationalism most readily appealed. Most members of the bourgeoisie were concerned above all with their own advancement. They could appreciate the injustice of serfdom in Europe and of Negro slavery in Europe's colonies, and they pressed for their abolition, but they tended to see constitutional reform as a device to replace the authority of landowners with their own authority, and they saw social reform as a device to enlarge their own opportunities rather than to lift up the labouring poor. Marxists were later to envisage a sequence of historical

Fig. 1.1 Gneisenau and Blücher – Prussian military leaders who contributed to the overthrow of Napoleon I. An East German stamp of 1963 commemorating the defeat of Napoleon at the Battle of Leipzig, 1813

changes whereby feudalism and the rule of landowners would give way to bourgeois democracy and the rule of the middle classes; and bourgeois democracy would give way in turn to people's democracy and the rule of the *proletariat*, the industrial working classes. In 1815, however, Europe had comparatively few industrial workers, and the impending struggle at that time was between the landed interest and the growing bourgeoisie. The priorities of the latter were to remove the restrictions which hampered their own profit-making activities, and to seize the authority which had long been monopolized by landowners and noblemen. But landowners and noblemen were unlikely to abandon their ancient privileges without a struggle. Indeed, with the final defeat of Napoleon I in 1815, the forces of tradition were looking for the restoration, rather than for the abolition, of ancient privilege.

1.2 1814–15 and the Conflict of Ideas

Napoleon I abdicated in April 1814, having ruled the French as their Emperor for some ten years. The combined opposition of most of Europe had at last proved too strong for him, and he had no alternative but to accept the terms his enemies offered. They allowed him to continue to call himself an emperor, but he could no longer rule France: he was now to rule only an empire in miniature, the tiny island of Elba, to which he was banished. Hardly surprisingly, the island interested him for less than a year, and Napoleon escaped and returned to Paris in March 1815. Having only just recovered the throne of France, Louis XVIII again had to flee.

The divisions in France were in some ways similar to divisions elsewhere in Europe. Those who welcomed Napoleon's return saw him as a son of the people and as a far more convincing heir to the French Revolution of 1789 than was Louis XVIII, whose elder brother (Louis XVI) had been executed by the revolutionaries. Louis XVIII had been willing to guarantee at least some of the fruits of the Revolution in a Charter (see page 55) but, like kings and noblemen elsewhere in Europe, he recalled the Revolution with horror. The Revolution had not only tried to destroy the *ancien régime* in France, it had shaken many of the foundations on which eighteenth-century society had rested throughout Europe. Kings, noblemen and churchmen saw the Revolution as a dangerous poison. For more than twenty years, there had been war between many of the states of Europe and the French. That war had helped to bring Napoleon Bonaparte to the forefront of French politics, first as Consul and then as Emperor; if he embodied the French Revolution for his supporters, he also embodied the threat of the Revolution for those who hated it. There was little chance in 1815 that France's neighbours would allow Napoleon to remain at large, and there was even less chance that they would again permit him to rule the French.

The end came swiftly. In June 1815 Napoleon's hastily-collected forces were defeated at Waterloo in Belgium by the British and the Prussians under

Wellington and Blücher. Retiring from the battlefield, the Emperor thought of escape to the USA but, as had happened so often in the past, the British navy frustrated his plans. Napoleon surrendered himself to the captain of HMS *Bellerophon*, the victim – he claimed – of 'the factions which divide my country and . . . the hostility of the greatest powers of Europe'. Writing to the Prince Regent in Britain, Napoleon went on:

> I have ended my political career and I am going . . . to seat myself at the hearth of the British people. I put myself under the protection of its laws, which I ask from Your Royal Highness, as from the most powerful, the most constant, and the most generous of my enemies.

British generosity did not extend to allowing Napoleon to remain as close to France as a British 'hearth'. This time, he was dispatched to a more remote and even smaller island than Elba – to St Helena in the south Atlantic – and he died there six years later, in lonely exile.

The years 1814–15 settled the personal fate of Napoleon. At the same time European statesmen were also attempting to settle the future of the continent, reconstructing Europe after the many years of upheaval and conflict (see Section 1.3). Napoleon himself had in many ways personified that upheaval, but his defeat and exile would not halt the changes which were taking place in societies, in economies and in the realm of ideas. Nineteenth-century Europe

Fig. 1.2 The Allied Entry into Paris, March 1814 – an English print. Many of the French were less enthusiastic than the artist

was likely to be markedly different from the Europe of the previous century, especially from the Europe which had existed before 1789. 'Liberty, Equality and Fraternity' (the heady slogan of the French revolutionaries) had no very precise meaning, but it summarized something of the challenge to the old order about which eighteenth-century philosophers had written, and which more practical men had tried to translate into action. Idealists and radicals still hoped that major changes would come about, to make the world a more just place. Most of the statesmen of 1814–15, however, had had enough of change. They looked back nostalgically to the pre-revolutionary society in which everyone, it seemed, had known his place. They preferred *conservatism* to the philosophies of modernization. They believed that society could be destroyed by the appeal to 'reason', which had become fashionable among intellectuals in the later eighteenth century, and which questioned the very foundations of authority and privilege. The statesmen were all conservative enough to have an instinctive fear of liberalism, and many of them were extreme reactionaries, to whom even Louis XVIII's Charter could seem dangerously radical.

The forces of change, on the other hand, were particularly strong among the middle classes, although there was no universal agreement about the sort of changes which were desirable. One of the main objectives was *liberalism*, but the term was flexible enough to embrace a variety of aims. For some it meant 'Liberty' which had been advocated by the French revolutionaries. 'Liberty' was likely to mean social liberty – the attainment of certain civil rights such as the freedom of speech and of religion, trial by jury, and the ending of serfdom. Others extended it also to mean political liberty, with the right to participate in some sort of representative government rather than to remain subject to the arbitrary whims of a despot. Liberals also came to be associated with the cause of free trade, as an alternative to tariffs and to the hampering regulations of mercantilism. Liberal ideas in general appealed strongly to the growing numbers of businessmen, professional men, financiers and manufacturers, who swelled the ranks of the middle classes. To such men, the 'Equality' of which the French revolutionaries had spoken meant their own equality with the landowners and the governing classes. It could be defined more precisely, for example, as equality of opportunity, equality before the law, and equal burdens of taxation. But few members of the middle classes wanted to recognize the lower orders of society as their equals. Liberalism in the nineteenth century seldom meant thoroughgoing egalitarianism. In 1815 the labouring poor had few spokesmen at all.

Meanwhile, the conservatives were not only alarmed about the fashion for liberalism; they also frowned on the developing fashion in the arts for *romanticism*. Romanticism encouraged a disturbing emotional idealism, and it seemed to threaten to undermine more traditional and more orderly artistic forms. Composers, poets and artists alike were beginning to be less concerned with established forms and more concerned with moods and with self-expression; less concerned with the rigid ordering of traditional society and more concerned with youth and with dreamers who might wish to change that society. By 1815 Beethoven had passionately explored the themes of freedom and injustice in his opera, *Fidelio*. In his *Pastoral* Symphony he had shown the romantic's concern not with artificial high society but with the countryside and the lives of peasants. Soon after 1815 Beethoven composed his *Choral* Symphony, setting to music the words of Schiller, with an exuberant vision of a new society, 'pleasanter and more joyful'. Such innovations added, it seemed, to the general attack which was being mounted on the old order.

Another threat to the old order came from the rising tide of *nationalism*. French armies had marched across Europe, and Napoleon had even reached Moscow in 1812. The French had played havoc with existing international boundaries, which would always be examined more critically in future. Napoleon himself was defeated partly by an upsurge of nationalism, when European nationalities were fired by a hatred of the domination of the French. But when the French had been forced to retreat, nationalist dislike of alien rule continued to smoulder. The statesmen of 1814–15, seeking to restore much of the old order, left many peoples with unfulfilled ambitions for national freedom, a sure recipe for outbursts of protest by those such as Belgians, Poles, Italians and the nationalities of the Balkans (see Section 3.3). Nor were these ambitions confined to Europe. During the recent wars, the Portuguese and Spanish colonies in the Americas had begun to clamour for their freedom, doubtless influenced by the example of the USA, which had already successfully broken free from British rule.

Europe's statesmen were accused by some of trying to put back the clock in their re-making of constitutions and re-drawing of boundaries, when Napoleon had been defeated. It was impossible to pretend that nothing much had happened since 1789, to ignore the new forces which were at work in Europe, but the statesmen faced the problem of combining the old and the new, in order to provide a basis for future European development. Since they associated the new with revolution and war, they not surprisingly looked back with nostalgia to the Europe of the years before 1789, the Europe into which they had been born. Francis I, the Emperor of Austria from 1792 to 1835, declared:

> My nation is like a worm-eaten house; if one part is moved one cannot tell how much of it will fall.

The statesmen of 1814–15 suspected that the same was true of Europe as a whole and, in their work of reconstruction, they showed a strong preference for erring on the side of conservatism rather than on the side of liberalism and nationalism.

1.3 The Peace Settlement of 1814–15

The Treaty of Vienna, which was signed in June 1815, was the centrepiece of the peace settlement after the French Revolutionary and Napoleonic Wars.

Two treaties with the French were signed by the Allies in Paris, before and after Napoleon's return from Elba. Miscellaneous other agreements completed the general settlement.

The universal desire for a peace which would be lasting was expressed in the *First Treaty of Paris* in May 1814:

> Article I: There shall be from this day forward perpetual Peace and Friendship between His Britannic Majesty and his Allies on the one part, and His Majesty the King of France . . . on the other. . . . The High Contracting Parties shall devote their best attention to maintain . . . between all the States of Europe, that harmony and good understanding which are so necessary for their tranquillity.

The Bourbon monarchy had already been restored in France and the intention was to treat France leniently. The boundaries were to be those of January 1792 save for some minor additions of territory. Many French colonies were restored, but, in Europe, the French could no longer claim lands in Belgium, Holland, Germany and Italy. There was to be no indemnity, no army of occupation and no reduction in the French armed forces.

The *Second Treaty of Paris* was made in November 1815 and it took account of the further support the French had given to Napoleon during his Hundred Days after his escape from Elba. French frontiers were put back to those of 1790. An indemnity of 700 million francs was imposed and France was to suffer, and pay for, an army of occupation for not less than three years.

Delegates to the *Congress of Vienna* began to assemble in September 1814. Like the Treaties of Paris, the Treaty of Vienna would be mainly the outcome of decisions taken by representatives of the four major powers (Britain, Austria, Prussia and Russia) which had brought about the defeat of France. But the restored Louis XVIII was a brother-monarch to the other rulers of Europe and he was allowed to send Talleyrand to Vienna as the representative of France. Talleyrand had already shown a remarkable talent for survival. Born an aristocrat, he had sided with the revolutionaries in France, ingratiated himself with Napoleon, and craftily switched his support by 1814 to King Louis, and the Allies. At Vienna he quickly exploited divisions between the Allies to secure for himself a place in their deliberations which was denied to lesser European powers. Representatives of the lesser powers were sometimes allowed a voice in general and minor decision-making, but for them the Congress of Vienna was less a congress than a festival. At great expense to the Austrian government, which the Habsburg monarchy could hardly afford, months were spent in celebrating – a little prematurely as it turned out – the overthrow of the Emperor Napoleon. The Treaty of Vienna was eventually signed a couple of weeks before the Battle of Waterloo.

The representatives of the major powers combined business with pleasure. In spite of the distractions, a comprehensive European settlement took shape. The Tsar, Alexander I, led the Russian delegation, bringing to Vienna a strange mixture of liberal and reactionary ideas in pursuit of an equally strange combination of Christian and expansionist objectives. Other rulers left the

Fig. 1.3 Emperor Francis I, the host of the Congress of Vienna, welcomes Tsar Alexander I and Frederick William III of Prussia to the city, September 1814 – a contemporary print. The three rulers expressed their 'fraternity and affection' in the Holy Alliance

diplomacy more to their ministers. Metternich represented Francis II of Austria, the host to the Congress. Metternich found considerable common ground with Viscount Castlereagh, the British Foreign Secretary, and with the Duke of Wellington, who supported Castlereagh. All three were essentially conservative. It hardly occurred to them to consult the wishes of peoples, but they honestly sought peace and stability with only moderate rewards for the victors of the recent wars. Prince Hardenberg, the chief representative of Frederick William III of Prussia, was also willing to moderate his country's demands in order to achieve a lasting settlement.

Poland gave rise to the fiercest controversies between the statesmen at Vienna. Poland had vanished from the map of Europe in 1795 when the last of what then remained of it had been divided between Austria, Prussia and Russia. Something of the country was reconstructed when Napoleon created the Grand Duchy of Warsaw, but it was under French control. At Vienna Alexander I hoped to turn the Grand Duchy into the Kingdom of Poland, with himself as king (see Fig. 1.4). What had to be agreed, in effect, was a new partition of what had been known in the eighteenth century as Poland and, to ensure the lion's share for Russia, Alexander suggested that Austria and Prussia should seek compensation elsewhere. Prussia, he suggested, should take Saxony, but that would involve deposing Frederick Augustus, the King of Saxony. The King of Prussia was inclined to support the Tsar's plan and to

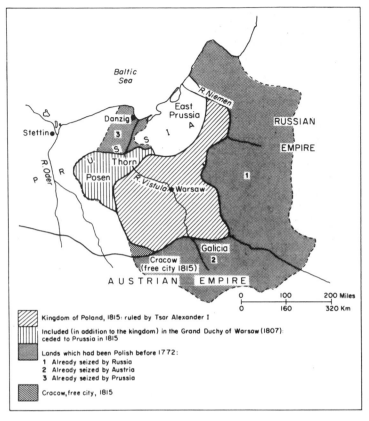

Fig. 1.4 Poland 1772–1815

override the better judgment of Hardenberg. Frederick Augustus, it was pointed out, had more than once supported Napoleon, and so deserved to be punished.

Alexander's control of Poland would bring Russian influence well to the west of the River Vistula, a prospect that caused general disquiet. Metternich, Castlereagh and Talleyrand went as far as to make a secret treaty in January 1815, prepared at least to resist Prussian designs on Saxony. But eventually the issue was resolved around the conference table. The Tsar made concessions giving Thorn (in what had been the north-west corner of the Grand Duchy of Warsaw) to Prussia, Galicia (in the south) to Austria, and making Cracow a free city, but he could be well pleased with what remained to his new Kingdom of Poland. He laid his hand on the map, covering Poland with a broad palm, and said 'C'est a moi' – 'That's mine'. Prussia then settled for two-fifths of Saxony and left the rest to Frederick Augustus. Prussia also received territories elsewhere, much extending its possessions in the Rhineland and taking over what had been Swedish Pomerania on the Baltic. Meanwhile, Tsar Alexander was also confirmed as the overlord of Finland.

Several of the principles on which the statesmen based their decisions at Vienna are illustrated in this account of the outcome for Russia and Prussia. As the victors in the recent struggle, the Allies believed that they were entitled to rewards. They felt no obligation to consult the wishes of the peoples, such as the Poles, who were involved in their territorial rearrangements. But they bore in mind the question of the balance of power, to ensure that no one state was rewarded more richly than the others and made excessively strong. They also intended to keep a watch on France and by strengthening Prussia's presence along the Rhine they were strengthening the barriers against further French aggression, which Castlereagh especially wished to do. France itself was dealt with in the Treaties of Paris, but those, like Frederick Augustus, who had supported France in the recent conflict, could be punished as the settlement took shape. That settlement, the statesmen hoped, would bring stability and peace to Europe for generations to come. Now that he had become converted to the support of the restored Bourbon monarchy in France, Talleyrand urged a further principle – that 'legitimate' rulers should be restored to the lands and thrones they had lost. This was a popular principle among kings, princes and noblemen. But it was less popular with the people of Naples, where Ferdinand I returned as the representative of the legitimate House of Bourbon, and with the people in other states of Europe where returning legitimate rulers brought with them a passion for stamping out all forms of dissent.

Liberal and nationalist aspirations had little influence on the statesmen at Vienna. Wherever possible, they wished to restore the traditional ruling classes, and they saw their task not as one of pleasing their subjects but as one of making:

> the arrangements rendered necessary by the state in which Europe was left at the termination of the last war.

Above all, the statesmen wanted to avoid future wars. In this context, they were willing to make certain modest changes. Some attempt was made to rationalize the political divisions of Italy, and the states of Germany were reduced to thirty-nine in number, linked together in a loose Confederation. Switzerland was given a new constitution and pledged to permanent neutrality. The Treaty of Vienna also included incidental clauses to safeguard the rights of minorities such as the people of Genoa, who were now made the subjects of the King of Piedmont-Sardinia. There were agreements about the free navigation of Europe's international rivers, and a declaration of support for the abolition of the trade in slaves.

Britain wanted no new possessions in continental Europe. In 1714, the Elector of Hanover had become King of Britain and it now seemed fitting that Hanover should be raised to the status of a kingdom, enabling George III to style himself King of Hanover. (In 1837, as a female, Queen Victoria was unable to succeed to Hanover and Hanover passed to her uncle, Georg Ernest.) Britain was confirmed in possession of a variety of off-shore islands which it seemed might be useful: Malta and Ionian Islands in the Mediterranean, and Heligoland in the North Sea. The settlement of 1814–15, however, enlarged Britain's empire overseas, and it was here that Britain looked for its rewards for the years of persistent opposition to the French. In the West Indies, St Lucia and Tobago had been seized from France and Trinidad from Spain, and the British retained these. They also secured Guiana from the Dutch, along with the Cape of Good Hope and Ceylon, which were important to navigation across the Indian Ocean. (For the loss of these colonies the Dutch received financial compensation and were allowed to unite with Belgium, making a stronger barrier on the north-east frontier of France in the process.) Mauritius and the Seychelles, further booty from the French, provided the British with ports of call east of Africa.

The Appendix on page 15 shows the principal decisions which were made at Vienna, and the map (Fig. 1.5) on page 12 shows the political divisions of Europe that resulted.

In November 1815 Britain, Austria, Prussia and Russia signed a Treaty of Alliance and Friendship 'to prevent the general Tranquillity . . . from being again disturbed' and 'to guarantee Europe from dangers by which she may still be menaced.' This *Quadruple Alliance* was essentially concerned with policing the settlement with France and preventing the return of Napoleon, but the Treaty went on:

> the High Contracting Parties have agreed to renew their Meetings at fixed periods . . . for the purpose of consulting upon their common interests, and for the consideration of the measures which at each of those periods shall be considered the most salutary for the repose and prosperity of Nations.

The Alliance thus looked forward to further congresses (see Section 2.2). It was vague about the details of such congresses, but they were clearly intended 'for the maintenance of peace in Europe'.

Two months earlier Francis, Frederick William and Alexander had signed the *Holy Alliance*, recording the 'fraternity and affection' which existed between the rulers of Austria, Prussia and Russia. The Alliance was promoted enthusiastically by Tsar Alexander, under the influence of Baroness von Krüdener, the wife of a Russian diplomat and a revered holy woman. Inspired by 'the blessings which it has pleased Divine Providence to shower down upon' them, the three monarchs pledged that their relations, henceforth, would be governed by 'the sublime truths which the Holy Religion of our Saviour teaches'. They took it for granted that this would help to preserve their status. 'As fellow countrymen' (or rather, as fellow sovereigns) they aimed 'to protect Religion, Peace and Justice', and they recommended their subjects 'to strengthen themselves every day more and more in the principles and exercise of the duties which the Divine Saviour has taught to mankind'. Metternich thought

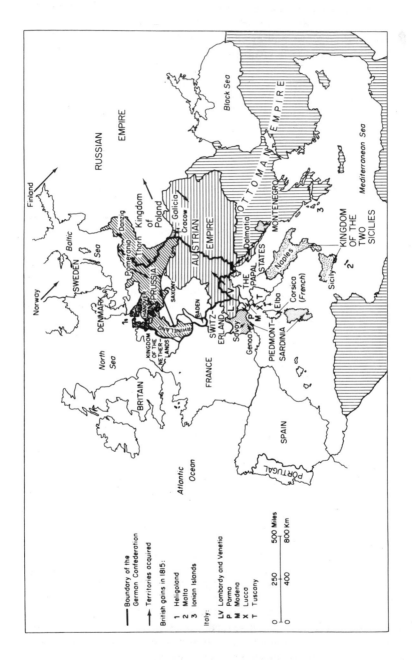

Fig. 1.5 Europe in 1815

the whole thing 'a loud-sounding nothing', but the Alliance was eventually signed by most of the rulers of Europe with three exceptions: the Sultan of the Ottoman Empire, a Moslem, who could not possibly support Christian objectives; the Pope who could hardly support an Alliance with non-Catholic Christians; and the Prince Regent of Britain who expressed his support for the 'sacred maxims' of the Alliance, but found signature incompatible with 'the British constitution'. Castlereagh considered the Treaty was 'a piece of sublime mysticism and nonsense'; and the monarchy in Britain was no longer free to act except on the advice of its ministers. Some Englishmen had in any case noted that the Treaty referred to *duties*, but omitted to refer to *rights*.

1.4   The Reconstructed Europe

The Prince Regent's refusal to join the Holy Alliance was evidence of the gap which already existed between Britain and the major powers on the continent. Britain was not democratic in 1815 but parliament had already taken to itself much of the authority of the monarchy. The influence of Castlereagh, as Foreign Secretary, was greater than that of the Prince Regent, who was acting on behalf of the ailing George III. When Louis XVIII returned to the throne of France he had to sign a Charter (see page 55) which imposed mild restrictions on royal authority in that country too. But other European kings and emperors were accustomed to rule without such restrictions, and the Tsar of Russia was perhaps the most autocratic of all. In general, royal power was strongest where societies and economies had as yet changed least, and where the bourgeoisie was comparatively weak.

Fig. 1.5 (opposite) shows that Europe in 1815 was dominated by three large, multi-racial empires: the Russian, the Austrian and the Ottoman (Turkish). The Tsar, the Austrian Emperor and the Sultan ruled vast areas of land and controlled the destinies of people of many different races. Among the subjects of the Austrian Empire were many who were German-speaking and many others who were Italian-speaking. In northern Germany the strong Kingdom of Prussia existed, but Germany at this time, like Italy, was little more than a geographical expression. Within both Germany and Italy there were numerous states of varying sizes and with varying systems of government, the majority of which were authoritarian. Adjoining the Austrian Empire was the Ottoman Empire, under a government which was Moslem, authoritarian and often inefficient, and which was already resented widely. Ottoman rule was resented in the Balkans for its cruelties, and because the peoples of the Balkans were different from the Turks in race and also, in many cases, in religion. The Ottoman Empire formed a barrier between Russia and the Mediterranean, and a crumbling Ottoman Empire seemed likely to endanger the balance of power as well as to threaten the stability of the neighbouring Austrian Empire, which similarly held subject races captive. Thus, looking misleadingly orderly on the map of 1815, the Balkans threatened to become an

Fig. 1.6 Louis XVIII, restored to the French throne with some mild restrictions on his authority – a painting by F. Gérard, 1823

area of considerable turbulence, and the focus of a nineteenth-century problem which Europeans referred to as the *Eastern Question* (see Sections 8.3 and 8.4 and Unit Fifteen).

There was no similar international conflict in Europe on the scale of the Revolutionary and Napoleonic Wars for almost a century after the Congress of Vienna. Although the peace settlement of 1814–15 began to be adjusted within a short time of the ending of the Congress, the statesmen could justifiably have claimed that they had brought to Europe the peace at which they aimed. By 1914 Europe changed substantially from the re-constructed Europe of 1815, but the change was piecemeal and much of it was gradual. During the nineteenth century Europe was comparatively free from dramatic convulsions. The First World War, however, was to release many pent-up forces and to bring to the continent a far more turbulent era than much of it had so far known.

The revolutionary tradition meanwhile survived in France, in spite of the setbacks of 1815. Monarchism and Bonapartism had eventually to give way to republicanism during the course of the nineteenth century. In the Netherlands and Scandinavia, however, monarchies were to develop comparatively peacefully into constitutional monarchies on something like the British pattern. The monarchies of the Iberian Peninsula (Portugal and Spain) were less successful and, after a stormy history in the nineteenth century, they disappeared in the twentieth century as the result of long conflicts with their subjects which began very soon after 1815. (The monarchy was restored in Spain in 1975.)

1.5   Appendix: Summary of the Principal Terms of the Treaty of Vienna (June 1815)

Rearrangements which strengthened the barriers against French aggression:
>   The Austrian Netherlands (Belgium) merged with Holland in the Kingdom of the Netherlands
>   Rhineland states ceded to Prussia: the Prussian Rhineland
>   Austrian Swabia ceded to Baden
>   Savoy and Genoa annexed to Piedmont-Sardinia
>   Switzerland, new constitution and permanent neutrality

Rearrangements which rewarded the major Allies and further strengthened future resistance against France:
>   The states of Germany reduced to 39 within the German Bund (Confederation) under the presidency of Austria
>   The Austrian Empire enlarged with Lombardy and Venetia, Salzburg, Galicia and Dalmatia
>   Prussia enlarged with two-fifths of Saxony, Swedish Pomerania, Thorn and Danzig (as well as the Rhineland)
>   The Russian Empire enlarged with authority over Finland and the Kingdom of Poland

Legitimate rulers were restored where this was consistent with the objectives referred to above:
>   e.g. Italy: Habsburg rulers restored in Tuscany and Modena; the Papal States restored; the Bourbon monarchy restored in Naples; Marie-Louise (Austrian-born wife of Napoleon I) given a life-interest in the rule of Parma

Additional provisions:
>   Cracow, a free city
>   Norway, transferred from Denmark to Sweden
(For the colonial gains made by Britain in the settlement of 1814–15, see page 11.)

Further Reading
Nicolson, H.: *The Congress of Vienna*. Methuen (London, 1946).

Exercises

1.   Describe some of the ways in which (*a*) as one of the labouring poor and (*b*) as a member of the middle classes, you would have found life in western Europe in 1815 very different from life there today.

2.   What can you learn from a study of Section 1.3 above of 'the principles on which the statesmen based their decisions at Vienna' (page 10)?

3.   Study Sections 1.3 and 1.5 and Fig. 1.5 and work out which countries benefited most extensively from the peace settlement of 1814–15. In what ways did *each* of the countries you have selected benefit?

4.   Refer to the definitions in the Glossary of *liberalism* and *nationalism* (pages 434–5). For what reason were (*a*) liberals and (*b*) nationalists, likely to have been dissatisfied with the peace settlement of 1814–15, which has been discussed in this Unit?

Unit Two

The Defence of the Existing Order 1815–48

2.1 The Conservatism of the Age of Metternich

The settlement of 1814–15 was fundamentally conservative. It laid the foundations for a general peace but it made few concessions to those who wanted rádical changes; so it soon became necessary to defend it. There was dissatisfaction in many states with social systems which kept alive old privileges and old inequalities, and with political systems which left power in the hands of aristocratic élites, who were more anxious to defend their class interests than to promote national well-being. The result was unrest. The specific reasons for the unrest varied from one state to another (as will be examined further in Units Three and Four) and there was little agreement among Europeans about the exact nature of the changes they wished to see. There was much more unity, on the other hand, between governments and ruling classes about their common interest in preserving the existing system, though it was a unity in which cracks were soon to appear.

The representatives of the major powers who met after 1815 in congresses 'for the purpose of consulting upon their common interests' (see page 11) found themselves frequently having to respond to the revolutionary initiatives taken by those who were dissatisfied. It was soon clear that Britain took a different and more liberal view of these revolutions than did the monarchies of Europe, to whom every revolutionary outbreak seemed to be a serious threat to the existing order. The continental monarchies therefore favoured repression, and used the 'Congress System' to co-operate to put down the uprisings (see Section 2.2). The Greek rebellion against the Ottoman Empire, however, undermined their unity. The Russian monarchy rather reluctantly realized that there could be advantage for Russia in encouraging the Greek revolutionaries, and Greece eventually won its freedom from the Turks with Russian assistance (see Section 3.3(b)). After that the Belgians also had foreign help when Britain and France assisted them to achieve their independence from Holland (see Section 3.3(d)). Such divisions among the powers, though they were careful not to quarrel openly, ensured that the Congress Period was short-lived.

Each monarchy nevertheless went on resisting the major changes which might be demanded by its own subjects. The changes made in the years 1815 to 1848 were by no means extensive, and such changes as there were were usually grudgingly conceded. One result of this tenacious defence of the existing order was a plague of rebellions which were widespread in Europe in 1848–9 (see

Unit Five). When Nicholas I of Russia then sent troops to assist the Habsburgs in Hungary, he showed that the brotherhood of kings was even then by no means dead.

Prince Metternich was removed from power by the revolution of 1848 in Vienna. He had become the symbol of repression in Europe and seemed to personify the defence of the existing order. As Foreign Minister of Austria from 1809 he had been one of the main architects of the defeat of Napoleon and of the peace settlement of 1814–15. After 1815 he aimed to preserve that settlement and he outlined his philosophy in a memorandum to Alexander I in 1820:

> The revolutionary seed [has] penetrated into every country and spread. . . . The evil exists and it is enormous. We do not think we can better define it and its cause at all times and in all places than . . . by the word *presumption*, that inseparable companion of the half-educated, that spring of unmeasured ambition. . . . It is principally the middle class of society which this moral gangrene has affected.

Metternich fought strenuously against the 'presumption' of the middle classes, aiming to keep them away from political activities which could destroy the supremacy of the nobility, both in the Austrian Empire and further afield. From 1821 he was the Chancellor of the Empire as well as its Foreign Minister and he also aimed to keep the Empire intact and to suppress the nationalist groups which might wish to break away. His influence extended far beyond the limits of the Empire, however. The settlement of 1814–15 gave the Austrians special influence in Germany and Italy. In Germany Metternich kept watch over the German Confederation, of which the Habsburg Emperor was the President (see Section 2.3(*b*)). In Italy he set himself to police the peninsula against revolutionary change, with Austria exercising direct rule over Lombardy and Venetia, while members of the Habsburg family ruled in the Duchies (Parma, Modena and Tuscany) (see Section 2.3(*c*)). He also thought at first that he could use international congresses to police the whole of Europe, but the Congress Period did not last (see Section 2.2). With its passing, Metternich became less dominant.

Even in Austria Metternich was less influential after 1826 (see Section 2.3(*a*)). The royal family preferred to listen to the advice of his rival, Count Kolowrat, a narrow-minded and unimaginative administrator. Metternich's plans for developing the provincial diets went largely unheeded. The plans were intended to improve the image of Habsburg rule, but the diets would still have been scarcely more than ornamental, allowing little genuine participation in government to their members. Metternich planned them as an instrument to resist social upheaval, by giving the mere appearance of change. His greatest influence had passed by the late 1820s, however, and he became one of Europe's elder statesmen, a symbol rather than a continuing powerful force. He helped to shield the Austrian Empire, Germany and Italy from the liberalism which was shaping developments in western Europe in the first half of

Fig. 2.1 Prince Klemens Metternich (1773–1859), the Austrian Foreign Minister from 1809 and Chancellor from 1821, resigned in 1848

the nineteenth century, but he built nothing for the future. He saw himself as 'the physician of sick governments in the entire world', and he helped to keep many of them alive. But he did little to cure them; even his principal 'patient', the Austrian Empire, continued to be sick, in spite of its apparent strength at the time of the Congress of Vienna. When Metternich fell in 1848 the Empire was still the 'worm-eaten house' which Francis I had described (see page 6).

2.2   The Congress Period

(a) The Congress of Aix-la-Chapelle

The ministers of the Quadruple Alliance met in the Congress of Aix-la-Chapelle in 1818, the only congress after 1815 in which they were able to achieve anything like total unity of purpose, and about which Metternich commented, 'a prettier little Congress never met'. The Congress was part of the process 'of completing the Pacification of Europe' which had begun in 1814, and the main business was to consider 'the internal state of France'. The ministers:

> recognized with satisfaction, that the order of things happily established in France, by the restoration of the legitimate and constitutional Monarchy . . . fully [justified] the hope of a progressive consolidation of that order.

France had almost paid off the indemnity and it was agreed to withdraw the army of occupation immediately. The Duke of Richelieu was welcomed to the Congress as the representative of Louis XVIII, and France was admitted to the Quadruple Alliance, making it a Quintuple Alliance of the powers of Britain, Austria, Prussia, Russia and France. Richelieu signed a Protocol in November 1818 part of which declared:

> that France, associated with other Powers by the restoration of the legitimate Monarchial and Constitutional Power, engages henceforth to concur in the maintenance and consolidation of a System which has given Peace to Europe, and which can alone insure its duration.

Further minor agreements were reached at Aix-la-Chapelle – concerning the safe custody of Napoleon, the rights of Jews in Germany, and money which was owed by Denmark. But, with the French problem settled, the Allies began to differ. Prussia and Russia wanted to set up an international army to guarantee all rulers their thrones. Tsar Alexander also wanted collective action to force the rebellious Spanish colonies in the Americas to abandon their claims to independence, and he proposed joint action in the Mediterranean against the pirates of the Barbary Coast. Castlereagh and Metternich had no enthusiasm for any of these schemes. They shared a suspicion that one result of them would be the extension of Russian influence to the west, and Castlereagh was particularly unwilling to commit Britain to the support of rulers whom their subjects regarded as intolerable. The differences between the Allies were not settled, but they were partly hidden under a vague declaration of support for 'moral solidarity' and the postponement of specific action for the time being. Nevertheless, a fundamental conflict was beginning to emerge about what was to be the future role of the 'System which has given Peace to Europe'.

(b) The Congress of Troppau

The Congress of Troppau, which met in 1820, showed that the great powers were deeply divided on this question. They were so divided that, although Tsar Alexander demanded a congress to discuss the outbreak of revolutions first in Spain and then in Naples and Portugal (see Section 3.2), Castlereagh thought a congress unnecessary. Britain and France sent only observers so they were not fully represented when Russia, Austria and Prussia met at Troppau. Metternich drafted a Protocol to express the views of the three founder-members of the Holy Alliance:

> States which have undergone a change of Government due to revolution, the result of which threatens other States, *ipso facto* cease to be members of the European Alliance. . . . If . . . immediate danger threatens other States, the Powers bind themselves, by peaceful means, or if need be by arms, to bring back the guilty into the bosom of the Great Alliance.

The emphasis of this Protocol of Troppau on the threat of revolutions to 'other States' did not appease Castlereagh. He felt obliged to 'disavow and even protest against' it as likely to involve interference in a country's internal affairs. The British were loudly cheered in Naples – prematurely, as it turned out, for Castlereagh soon agreed that, because Austria had a special interest in Italy, Metternich had a right to put down rebellions there. The signatories of the Protocol were not deterred when Castlereagh found it 'destitute of common sense'. They were determined to rescue their fellow-kings and they adjourned from Troppau to Laibach.

(c) The Congress of Laibach

When the Congress of Laibach opened in January 1821, Metternich had already assembled 80,000 troops to deal with the rebellious Neapolitans whose 'wickedness' was described to the Congress by King Ferdinand. The Austrian troops put down the rising in Naples and another which suddenly broke out in Piedmont, and then hunted down troublemakers in Lombardy. The French were now massing troops on the Spanish border, ready to undertake similar repression in Spain and perhaps Portugal. Alexander too declared his readiness to send Russians to wherever there were rebels to suppress. But a new rebellion confused the issue when the Greeks rose against their Ottoman government in March 1821. Even Alexander was torn between enthusiasm for suppressing rebels and Russian strategic ambitions to smash the Ottoman Empire. Metternich was reluctant to see the Russians going to war with the Ottoman Empire, and since the British were not properly represented at Laibach but were known to have interests in Greece, it seemed wise to defer decisions about Spain and Greece to some further meeting. It was eventually arranged at Verona, in October 1822.

(d) The Congress of Verona

Before the Congress of Verona met Castlereagh committed suicide and Britain had a new Foreign Secretary, George Canning. Canning sent Wellington to the Congress in a last British attempt to restrain the Europeans. Wellington condemned the idea of interfering in Spain. It was also made clear that Britain was opposed to interference in Greece and, perhaps even more so, to any interference with the claims for independence in the Americas. With the division now wide between Britain and the major powers of Europe, Wellington returned home from Verona.

(e) Conflicting Interests

There were, of course, many later international conferences, but the Congress of Verona was the last of the meetings which had been foreshadowed when the Quadruple Alliance was signed in 1815, at which the four Allies would come together to preserve the European peace. Austria, Prussia and Russia held a further congress in St Petersburg in 1825, but by then it was apparent that the Congress System was dead. At St Petersburg, there was further division between Austria and Russia concerning the Greek problem. Metternich recognized that there was no longer a 'System' by which international relations could be controlled, and by the end of 1825 Tsar Alexander, who had so much wanted a 'System' which was rigid in its opposition to revolutionaries, was also dead. Nicholas I, the new Tsar, quickly decided that the Greek revolution was a cause worthy of help (see Section 3.3(b)).

When the First World War ended in 1918 a further attempt was made to set up international machinery for the preservation of peace, the League of Nations (see Section 23.2). At that time the Congress Period was remembered as an early and rather crude attempt at peace-keeping. The League had more in common with Castlereagh's views than with those of Alexander I, and it was generally accepted by members of the League that they would not concern themselves with the internal politics of any country: the non-intervention which Castlereagh had preached had become a basic principle. The British dislike of intervention after 1815 stemmed mainly from the belief that countries should be free to develop in their own ways if they did not threaten their neighbours. Britain itself had had revolutionary upheavals in the past and the British were convinced that their country was all the better for them. Nor did the British share the obsession of continental rulers with the welfare of kings: the British monarchy had already been put in its place as a part – but no longer the dominant part – of the constitution. There was sympathy in Britain with those revolutionaries who aimed at some sort of parliamentary government and some recognition of a subject's rights. But the British were not radical idealists. They were deeply suspicious that, when foreign troops suppressed revolutionaries, they might plant foreign influence. When the French invaded Spain in 1823 in order to restore the Spanish crown and crush those of its subjects who wanted parliamentary government Canning was indignant. He felt that a counter-move was justified and in 1826 he sent British forces to Portugal, to forestall foreign interference in that country (see page 39). The great powers were now acting individually again, with no pretence that there was an organized Congress 'System'. Things were getting back, as Canning himself had put it, to 'a wholesome state . . . every nation for itself and God for us all'.

Markets for British goods were vitally important to Britain. The wars before

1815 had disrupted traditional trade patterns and Britain had won new markets in the colonies in the Americas which belonged to Spain. If Spanish authority were restored in these colonies it seemed likely that attempts would be made to exclude British traders, as had happened in the past. But the colonies did not want Spanish authority to be restored. Both Castlereagh and Canning resisted suggestions that the Congress powers should subdue them, but when the French helped Ferdinand VII to put down revolutionaries in Spain itself in 1823 the matter became more urgent. Ferdinand and those who might have assisted him in restoring his authority in the Americas were forestalled when President Monroe of the USA issued the Monroe Doctrine. Henceforth, any European interference in the Americas other than by colonial powers in their existing colonies, would be taken as showing 'an unfriendly disposition to the United States'. Without help Ferdinand was too weak to reconquer Spain's colonies and their independence was virtually assured. One after another, the states on the American mainland and Santo Domingo in the West Indies repudiated Spanish rule. In 1825 Canning recognized the independent governments of Argentina, Colombia and Mexico. Portuguese Brazil also established its independence (see page 38). Canning had warned the French against extending their support of Ferdinand across the Atlantic and he made clear his support of Monroe. But it was Monroe who had finally settled the issue, though Canning jubilantly told an audience a few years later:

I called the New World into existence to redress the balance of the Old.

In the 'Old' World the unity of the continental powers was destroyed by the revolution in Greece, and it was this which finally wrecked the Congress 'System'. There had been considerable common ground between the three central and eastern powers in their hostility to all revolutions and, under the influence of Charles of Artois, France had also begun to favour repression after 1820. But the Greek revolt against the overlordship of the Turks occurred in an area where the great powers had rival national interests. Trade in the Mediterranean was important to both Britain and France, and the Ottoman Empire not only formed a traditional barrier against Russian expansion into the Balkans and the Mediterranean, it also adjoined the Austrian Empire. Disturbances in Greece, therefore, touched several sensitive nerves. Only Metternich (and the Prussians, from whom the area was remote) could afford to be consistent in wishing to see order and the *status quo* restored. The British had to weigh their sympathy for the Greeks against the possible effects of weakening the Ottoman Empire. On the other hand, Tsar Alexander could no longer think only in the simple terms of repressing revolution: a weakening of the Ottoman Empire could well be to the advantage of Russia, and he therefore hesitated. It was thus the final weakness of the Congresses that national self-interest eventually became more important than the unity of the 'System'. A new alignment came into being in 1827 when Britain, France and Russia joined together in the Treaty of London to tackle the Greek problem pragmatically rather than on the basis of rigid doctrines (see Section 3.3(*b*)). Defeated by the USA and Britain over the American colonies, Metternich found that he could no longer rely on Russia and France in the suppression of rebellions in Europe.

2.3   Austrian Spheres of Influence

The existing order was nevertheless stoutly defended after 1815 wherever Austrian influence was strong. Metternich expected that his influence would be particularly effective in three areas: the Austrian Empire itself, the German Confederation, and Italy.

(*a*) The Austrian Empire

The Habsburg Emperor Joseph II, who died in 1790, attempted without much success to make sweeping reforms in the Austrian Empire on the basis of a benevolent paternalism. By 1815, however, the Habsburgs had little interest in reform and the principal ambition of Francis I seemed to be to increase the efficiency of the police system. In 1835 Francis was succeeded by his son Ferdinand I. The father had been unimaginatively stubborn; the son was a near imbecile, and Metternich manoeuvred Archduke Louis into office as the regent. Louis was Ferdinand's uncle, but he appealed to Metternich not so much for his abilities as for his lack of them. He seemed likely to be a man who could be manipulated. But Metternich had not foreseen that Louis would also be manipulated by other and more strong-minded uncles who supported Metternich's rival, Count Kolowrat. From 1835 until the revolutions of 1848, therefore, the Habsburg government was weakened by political intrigues. The mild administrative reforms which Metternich had hoped to implement, to foster the illusion of popular consent, were not implemented, and Kolowrat continued to rely for his reputation on the fact that he had once actually managed to balance the government's budget, in 1831.

Metternich later complained that he had given his life 'to propping up the mouldering edifice' of the Austrian Empire. It was an empire of many races. In the north, in Bohemia and Galicia, there were Germans, Czechs, Slovaks and Poles. The Austrians themselves were German-speaking. In the centre of the Empire the majority of people were Magyars. In the east there were Ruthenians and Rumanians, and the gains in the south and south-west, made in the settlement of 1814–15, increased the numbers of Italians, Slovenes, Serbs and Croats in the Empire. It would be disastrous for the Habsburg Empire if these various nationalities became infected with dangerous new ideas about national independence, but sooner or later it seemed inevitable that subject races would ask by what right the Habsburgs ruled them. Past wars and marriage alliances would not provide a convincing answer, especially if Habsburg rule was unprogressive and inefficient.

It was both. If anything, there was too much governmental machinery and there were too many officials. The officials re-did the jobs that others had already done; they opened and read letters, searching for evidence of sedition, and they tried by censorship and the control of education to stifle liberal and nationalist thought; but they seldom even considered making improvements. Changes in the economy and in society – railways were introduced into Austria in the 1830s – meant that the subjects of the Empire had rising expectations of reforms, while the Habsburg government remained unimaginative. Middle-class ambitions for a parliamentary system and liberal freedoms, peasant ambitions for the end of labour rents and for freedom of movement, and the ambitions of industrial workers (growing in number, though chiefly in Vienna) for improved conditions, were all regarded as dangerously radical and disruptive.

Metternich did, however, encourage some provincial diets in the hope of pacifying the various races within the Empire. These local assemblies were not democratic. When the Hungarian Diet was revived in 1825 it represented mainly the Magyar landowners. Metternich himself believed that the common interests of landowners, noblemen and the ruling classes would form a defence against local nationalism and local opposition to Habsburg supremacy. But the diets frequently became centres of that opposition. By 1848 the Diets of Hungary, Bohemia and Croatia were all giving voice to nationalist feelings and challenging outside authority. It is not likely that this opposition would have been less if Metternich's further plans for the development of the administration had been implemented. His plans for setting up a *Reichsrat* were rather vague: it would be a council to assist in the central government of the Empire and the diets would be allowed to send representatives. But the powers of the Reichsrat would be negligible, its influence on the haphazard administrative system in Vienna minimal. The representatives of the diets were hardly likely to become more enthusiastic about Habsburg government as a result of their opportunities to watch the fumbling officialdom of the Empire at its very centre.

Among his contemporaries Metternich was sometimes known as 'the Grand Inquisitor of Europe'. At the Congress of Aix-la-Chapelle he met and fell in love with Madame de Lieven, the wife of the Russian ambassador in London. For some years, she wrote to him at frequent intervals, recording in 1823 a conversation she had had with George IV. George claimed that Canning had insisted that Metternich:

> wanted to rule the whole world, to wipe out every constitution from the surface of the globe. 'No harm in that,' said the King, 'as long as our constitution is among them.'

Yet Metternich himself asserted that he had never really been able to rule the Austrian Empire. His influence was perhaps greater outside it than within it. Within the Empire he had to contend with an unhelpful monarchy, a ramshackle administrative apparatus, and a racial hotchpotch, and the Empire was

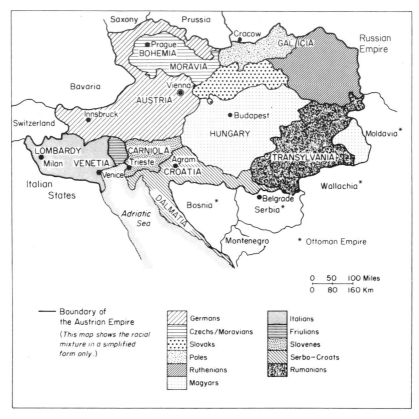

Fig. 2.2 The Multi-racial Austrian Empire after 1815

always tottering on the edge of bankruptcy. What was principally lacking, however, was positive leadership. All too often Metternich seemed content with the rather negative role of 'Grand Inquisitor', seeking only to root out those who threatened that which existed. The nobility kept their privileges, protected from the burdens of taxation, military service and punishment in the common courts. The lower orders were kept in their place, the peasantry still shackled by feudal obligations. Although the government was less vicious than many governments elsewhere in Europe it was still a tyranny. In 1848 Louis Kossuth, a Hungarian patriot (see page 85), spoke bitterly of 'a cursed inheritance' bequeathed to Hungarians by 'the policy of Metternich', but it may be doubted whether Metternich had much of a 'policy' at all within the Austrian Empire. To prop up a 'mouldering edifice' was hardly a policy in the eyes of those who thought the Empire should move with the times, in the century after the French Revolution of 1789. Understandably, revolutions broke out almost everywhere in the Austrian Empire in 1848 (see Section 5.2(*d*)).

(*b*) The German Confederation

When the German Confederation was set up in 1815 it finally reduced the 300 German states of 1790 to 39. The *Bund* (Confederation) seemed to bring a new and imaginative orderliness to Germany, but it can be argued that this too was a Metternichian recipe for stagnation. Representatives of its members met in Vienna in 1820 to put the finishing touches to the Bund's organization, aiming to 'unite the whole of the States of Germany in peace and harmony', but without giving the Bund any real power. The *Bundestag* (Confederation Diet) had very little power to levy taxes or raise troops. Metternich was confident that, although decisions were usually by majority vote, the princes would vote according to self-interest, to preserve the independence of their states and their own authority. Neither existing social distinctions nor the balance of power in Germany and Europe as a whole were likely to be disturbed. Austria and Prussia, with others such as Bavaria, were the main powers within the Bund, but none would be strong enough to dominate it. The few liberal-minded princes, such as the Duke of Saxe-Weimar, would always be outvoted and the Bundestag seemed likely to be little more than a useful forum for co-ordinating resistance to change. It would also co-ordinate German resistance to any attack on its members by a foreign power. Thus it would help to deter future French aggression without threatening the Austrian Empire, as a truly united Germany might have done. In 1820 it was confirmed that:

> The independence guaranteed by the Federal Act [of 1815] to the individual states of the Confederation certainly excludes in general all interference of the Confederation in the internal organization and administration of those States.

It was Metternich's calculation that most of the rulers of the German states would be very willing to suppress the forces for change.

Metternich also hoped that the setting up of the Bund would quieten those who thought there should be a united Germany. Such people were not numerous in 1815, but it was an idea which appealed to intellectuals, among whom there was an awareness of a distinctive German culture (see Section 3.4). They thought it logical that German culture should flourish in a German nation state, as French culture flourished in France. Student societies (the *Burschenschaften*) spread rapidly in universities such as that at Jena. Romanticism, liberalism and nationalism made an intoxicating brew for young Germans who had received some education, and they agitated for liberal reforms and national unity. Metternich thought their political passions as absurd as their passion for fighting duels and flaunting their sword scars.

By 1819, Metternich was convinced that the authorities must act. Two years earlier, the Burschenschaften had organized a demonstration at Wartburg

Fig. 2.3 The German Confederation after 1815

in Saxony to commemorate glorious events in German history – Luther's resistance to the Papacy, and the defeat of Napoleon at Leipzig in 1813. The Wartburg Festival became more concerned with the present and future, and the students burned on a bonfire such various symbols of repression as books they thought reactionary, and some of the equipment, including the corset, of a Prussian cavalryman. In March 1819 a student assassinated von Kotzebue, a writer violently opposed to liberalism and an agent of the Russian government. Metternich summoned representatives of the German princes to Carlsbad and

Fig. 2.4 German students protested vigorously against the reactionary policies of the authorities: an East German stamp of 1953 commemorating the Wartburg Festival of 1817, and its place in the Kampf für Nationale Einheit, *Fight for National Unity*

assured Alexander I that this indiscipline would be checked.

The Carlsbad Decrees were welcomed by most of the German princes and especially by Frederick William III of Prussia, who shared Metternich's hatred of liberalism and remembered the insult to his cavalry at Wartburg. There was no difficulty in getting them approved by the Bundestag in September 1819. It was then up to each of the princes to enforce them in his own state and, as Metternich had expected, the majority of the rulers enforced them vigorously, if not always efficiently. The key elements in the Carlsbad Decrees were censorship, the banning of political meetings, the control of universities and a witch-hunt for revolutionaries. The Burschenschaften were outlawed, and university teachers and students who criticized the existing order were purged. For most of the 1820s the German Confederation achieved 'peace and harmony', but at the expense of freedom of thought.

By 1830 cracks were again appearing in the system. The revolution in France in that year (see Section 4.2(*b*)) set off risings in various minor German states, and the rebels won some concessions. The Burschenschaften began to form again, and there was a new movement, *Young Germany*, which, like Young Italy (see page 33) dreamed of freedom and national unity. Reform and unity were loudly demanded at the Hambach Festival in 1832 and a year later an attempt was made to invade and break up the Bundestag. The Bundestag had just accepted more directives from Metternich, the Six Articles; it had even accepted a cautious measure to permit federal intervention in states where repression was not fierce enough. The new wave of repression included further bans on student organizations and further censorship. The writings of the poet Heinrich Heine were outlawed, since his romanticism was alleged to have inspired the Young Germany movement. Even Metternich must have felt, however, that he was trying to sweep back the tide.

Fig. 2.5 A Frankfurt cartoon of 1819: after the Carlsbad Decrees German liberalism was bound, doped and poisoned

The effectiveness of the repression still depended mainly on the individual German princes. In 1837 the Duke of Cumberland succeeded to Hanover when his niece became Queen Victoria in Britain. He purged the University of Göttingen and rejoiced in his new authority to crush dissent. But Metternich lost an enthusiastic supporter in 1840 when Frederick William III of Prussia died. The new King, Frederick William IV, relaxed the censorship and even began to listen to the demands of the emerging middle classes for a parliament, though when a Prussian Diet was allowed to meet in 1847 the King was quickly frightened into dismissing it. By that time restlessness was widespread in the German Bund and the existing order was about to be tested in the upheavals of 1848 (see Section 5.2(c)).

(c) Italy

Italy, like Germany, was made up of separate states in 1815 (see Fig. 2.6) but there was no Italian Confederation to match the German Bund. There was, however, a strong Austrian presence in Italy which would help to protect the peninsula against any renewal of French ambitions there. It would also enable Metternich to curb any Italians who wished to challenge the existing order. Like German liberals and nationalists, progressive Italians faced formidable odds after 1815. The Italian middle classes were few in number and they had little contact with the masses. The interests of the latter were narrow and localized. Italian peasants were generally apathetic even about their own poverty and they often devoted what energies they had to their religion, which alone brought colour and spectacle into their lives. The leaders of the Catholic Church opposed reform: they taught that a good Catholic had to be an obedient Catholic. The more enterprising of the lower orders in Italy tended to take not to political activity but to banditry. In any case, the existing order was zealously supported not only by the Austrians but by Ferdinand I in the Two Sicilies and by Pope Pius VII in the Papal States, and there was little reason to believe that Victor Emmanuel I, King of Piedmont-Sardinia, was any more favourable to liberal and nationalist aspirations.

The first resistance to the established order in Italy centred on secret societies with mysterious rituals. Groups of *Carbonari* began to develop in Italy before 1810, meeting in the isolated huts of charcoal-burners. There was little unity between the groups themselves and with similar societies such as the *Federati* in Piedmont. There was certainly no grand plan for political freedoms and national unity, but Carbonari had in common a romantic belief that plots and revolutions could bring about change and they attracted recruits among Italian intellectuals, conscience-stricken clergymen and those with a taste for adventure, perhaps even for crime. It was the Carbonari and societies similar to them who made Italy appear revolutionary in 1820–1 and again in 1831 (see pages 39–40).

Austrian troops were authorized by the Congress of Laibach to suppress the early uprisings in Italy (see page 21). Ferdinand in the Two Sicilies and Charles Felix, the new king in Piedmont-Sardinia, then celebrated the recovery of their powers by hunting down and savagely punishing all forms of dissent. The repression was so effective that when new revolutionary outbreaks occurred in 1831 in the Papal States, Parma and Modena, there were no similar risings in the south and north. Austrian troops again crushed the rebels. Louis Philippe, who had come to the throne of France as the result of revolution in Paris in 1830, sent French troops to Ancona in the Papal States, but they came not to assist the rebels but to remind the Pope that the French too, like the Austrians, were loyal Catholics. Pope Gregory XVI felt that he could quite safely ignore a tentative note from the major powers suggesting that he might make some reforms in the Papal States, where much remained that was still medieval.

Isolated rebellions had no chance of success while the Austrians kept close watch on Italy. It was also unrealistic to expect that, at this time, the Italians could unite to expel the Austrians. When Charles Albert succeeded to the throne of Piedmont-Sardinia in 1831 there were some Italians who thought he

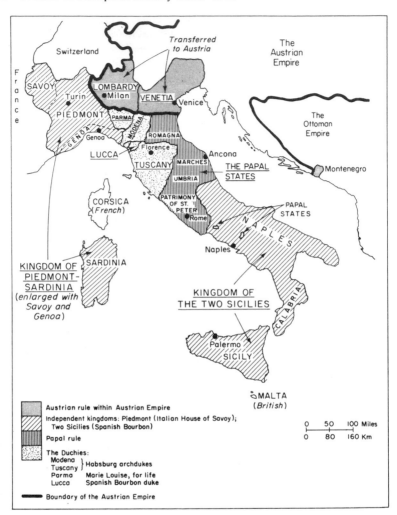

Fig. 2.6 Italy in 1815

might lead a crusade to unite the peninsula, since he had earlier shown signs of being anti-Austrian. The ardent republican, Giuseppe Mazzini, quickly tested him with an open letter, inviting him to lead. Mazzini was neither surprised nor dismayed when Charles Albert, fully aware of the size of the Austrian forces, did nothing. Mazzini was convinced that there needed to be more unity in Italy both of purpose and action, and that Italians had to be educated to become more aware of their nationality and of Italy's backwardness. He therefore founded *Young Italy* and defined its philosophy:

Young Italy is a brotherhood of Italians who believe in a law of progress and duty, and are convinced that Italy is destined to become one nation. . . . The aim of the association is revolution, but its labours will be essentially educational. . . . From [education] alone Italy may hope for safety and regeneration.

Like the Carbonari, however, the members who rallied to Young Italy were middle class and the movement hardly touched the masses. It did something 'to educate the under-thirties' for rebellion and to spread awareness among the Italian bourgeoisie, and Mazzini himself, a prolific writer and propagandist, was later remembered as a prophet; but Young Italy was as unsuccessful in revolution as the Carbonari had been. Its leaders were arrested when they planned a coup in Piedmont in 1832 and further scattered uprisings, as unco-ordinated as those previously, were easily crushed. Until 1848 (see Section 5.2(*b*)) Italian revolutions continued to be little more than romantic splutterings of protest, like the attempt in 1844 of the Bandiera brothers, Attilio and Emilio, to seize Calabria. As often happened, the brothers had been betrayed even before their expedition arrived and the Neapolitan government had no need to summon Metternich's assistance.

2.4   Elsewhere in Europe

The influence of Metternich and Austria was important in the defence of the existing order in central Europe and in Italy in the years 1815 to 1848, but Metternich's love for the existing order was shared by almost all the rulers and ruling classes of those areas. To the east, meanwhile, the dead hand of Russian tsardom kept a stranglehold on almost all forms of progress. In Unit Four we will examine the stark contrast between France, which continued to revolt against autocracy after 1815, and Russia, where autocracy reigned supreme. But France was not the only western state in which change went on. Belgium began a successful revolt against the Dutch in 1830 (see Section 3.3(*d*)). Portugal and Spain hovered uncertainly between authoritarianism and liberalism, but Denmark and Sweden, in Scandinavia, made constitutional changes to keep up with the times. Provincial diets were introduced into Denmark in 1834 and a liberal constitution was adopted in 1849. Bernadotte, once one of Napoleon's Marshals, became King Charles XIV of Sweden in 1818, and a constitution was adopted which, with subsequent amendments, ensured liberal political systems for both Swedes and Norwegians. Norway moved on to complete independence in 1905, without the need for conflict. Meanwhile, William I was forced to abdicate in the Netherlands in 1840, making way for a more liberal ruler. In none of these areas had Metternich been able to exert the influence he held in the heartlands of Europe. Wherever his influence had been strong, however, explosions occurred in 1848 (see Unit Five). France still insisted in that year on being more radical than the rest of Europe, and the French monarchy was again overthrown. But in the east

Nicholas I remained undisturbed, and not even his unfortunate Polish subjects could manage more than a brief flicker of protest. The gulf between western and eastern Europe grew wider. By the time that Nicholas II came to the Russian throne in 1894, it was clear that the price of autocracy for the Russian Empire had been to fall far behind the rest of Europe in almost every aspect of economic and social development.

Further Reading

Holbraad, C.: *The Concert of Europe: German and British International Theory 1815-1914*. Longman (Harlow, 1970).
Kohn, H.: *Absolutism and Democracy, 1814-52*. Anvil (Dublin, 1965).
Kohn, H.: *The Habsburg Empire, 1804-1918*. Anvil (Dublin, 1961).
Milne, A.: *Metternich*. Hodder and Stoughton (London, 1975).

Documentary

Walker, M.: *Metternich's Europe, 1813-48*. Harper Torchbooks (London, 1968).

Exercises

1. (*a*) Study Figs. 1.5, 2.3 and 2.6. How do these maps help to explain why the Austrian Empire was so important after 1815 in (*i*) Germany, (*ii*) Italy, and (*iii*) Europe?
   (*b*) Study Fig. 2.2. Explain how this map shows that the Austrian Empire was multi-racial.
   (*c*) How do Fig. 2.2 and Section 2.3(*a*) help to explain why Francis I referred to the Austrian Empire as 'a worm-eaten house' (page 6)?
2. (*a*) What were the aims of (*i*) the Quadruple Alliance (page 11), and (*ii*) the Holy Alliance (pages 11–13)?
   (*b*) Which of these Alliances was the more influential in *each* of the Congresses described in Section 2.2?
3. What evidence can you find (*i*) in Section 2.3(*b*) of a conflict between young Germans and the authorities, and (*ii*) in Section 2.3(*c*) of a similar conflict between young Italians and the authorities?
4. 'The influence of Metternich and Austria was important in the defenc of the existing order in central Europe and in Italy in the years 1815 to 1848' (page 33). How far does Unit Two show that this was true?

The Challenge to the Existing Order 1815–48

3.1 Change and Protest

The existing order which Metternich was anxious to preserve was based to a large extent on agricultural economies. European noblemen were almost always landowners: land gave them their wealth; it also provided a living for the great majority of the people. In past centuries only a tiny minority of Europeans had inhabited the towns, worked as craftsmen and engaged in manufacturing for the market, or worked as traders and engaged in trafficking in goods. But the growth of industry led to the development of larger and more numerous towns. By 1848 London had a population of more than three million and Paris was about half the size of London. Vienna had a population of about half a million and Berlin was not far behind. New ideas spread more rapidly where people lived close to one another in towns, and new ideas were especially likely to influence those who travelled and broadened their horizons. Thus the spread of railways, which brought an unprecedented mobility to society, helped to undermine the existing order. The first European railways were built in Britain where modern industrialization began: the Stockton–Darlington Railway was opened in 1825, and the Liverpool–Manchester Railway in 1830. By 1848 France had some 3200 kilometres of railway, Prussia about 2400 with another 2400 in other parts of Germany, and 1600 kilometres in Austria. In eastern Europe and the south, however, railway-construction proceeded much more slowly – evidence of the slower pace of industrialization and of the less urgent need for transportation in areas such as Russia and Italy.

Industrialization produced social change. A new-rich class developed, made up of capitalist employers and increasing numbers of merchants and financiers. A new class of labouring poor also grew: the workers in industry, the proleteriat. Neither economic nor social change occurred overnight and its exact nature and pace varied from country to country, but the new classes had little enthusiasm for preserving the existing order which their own existence was tearing apart. Government by landowners was often remote from the problems of industrialists, merchants and the labouring poor, and the traditional privileges of landowners and hereditary noblemen aroused jealousy and resentment. But life in the countryside was also changing, under pressure from the need to produce more food for growing populations. In 1800 Europe had about 18 people per square kilometre, and by 1850 the number had risen to 26. In 1815 there were nearly 30 million people in France and almost as many in the states of Germany, 18 million in Italy and over 10 million in Austria. The production of more food required more efficient farming. This meant the adoption of more scientific techniques, which demanded more expert management and the investment of capital with which to buy equipment and stock. Such changes were bound to affect both landowners and peasants. Landowners began to wonder whether they could continue to afford the luxury of a life at court, remote from their estates. And even in Russia, in the late 1850s, Alexander II debated whether a downtrodden and servile peasantry was making a worthwhile contribution to the country's development, and what more progressive social system was needed in the Russian countryside.

From such economic and social change stemmed the protest movements against the existing order after 1815. Progress demanded the removal of old obstacles, and there was now a widespread belief in 'progress'. Writing in 1841, Robert Owen declared:

> The decree has gone forth from the almighty energies of the universe, that man shall be put in the right path now, to become good and wise and happy; and every obstacle in the way of his progress to this advent of his existence shall prove unavailing and powerless.

Owen was a mill-owner, but he was also a socialist whose vision included a better life for the masses. Before 1848, however, the socialist challenge was barely beginning. More usually, the challenge to the existing order was that of liberalism, which expressed itself in the demand for constitutional liberties mainly for the new rich. There was also a developing nationalist challenge which, in some cases, took the form of a demand for national independence from foreign rule and, in others, of the search for a national identity. Few of these demands achieved complete success in the first half of the nineteenth century. They were seldom widely supported and the existing order was well entrenched, but ideas were taking root and in later generations it would not be possible to continue to frustrate them.

3.2   The Demand for Constitutional Liberties

The Charter, which Louis XVIII granted to the French at the time of his restoration, recognized the impossibility of totally denying to Frenchmen in the future many of the liberties they had already fought for by revolution. But few elected assemblies existed elsewhere in Europe and, even where there were assemblies, their powers were few and their members were unrepresentative. (For diets in the Austrian Empire, see Section 2.3(a), and for the German Bundestag, see Section 2.3(b).) The British parliament was almost unique in 1815, but the British House of Commons and the French Assembly provided inspiration for all those in Europe who believed that kings, in government, should consult the elected representatives of at least some of their subjects. This was an idea which appealed to the educated and to those who were growing in prosperity and economic importance, but who remained outside the traditional ruling classes. Such people wanted recognition of their importance by being able to influence government, and they wanted reforms to guarantee their personal liberties, protect their economic interests and remove the barriers between themselves and the privileged few. They often found themselves frustrated by blinkered rulers.

(a) Spain

Ferdinand VII, King of Spain, was as blinkered as any. He arrived in Spain in 1814 to reclaim the throne when French troops had been expelled in the closing stages of the Napoleonic Wars. During the confusion of that time, Spanish liberals had drafted the constitution of 1812 which went a long way towards transferring power in Spain to the bourgeoisie through their representatives in the Cortes, an assembly to which ministers would be answerable. Ferdinand had no intention of reigning as a constitutional monarch. In his view government was for the king and the royal favourites. He rejected the constitution and savagely punished those who upheld it, relying on the fact that the Spanish nobility, the Catholic Church, and the mass of the people, were also hostile to the bourgeoisie and their ambitions. He could also, for the moment, count on the army. The liberals were routed and their feeble attempts to rebel were quickly suppressed. In 1820, however, Ferdinand's ambition outran his capability. Eager to recover possession of Spain's American colonies, most of which were rejecting Spanish control (see page 23), army units were ordered to prepare to cross the Atlantic; but the army mutinied, already disillusioned by the King's cruelties and incompetence. The constitution of 1812 was reintroduced.

For three years Ferdinand was virtually a prisoner of his own subjects. His plight was discussed at the Congresses (see Section 2.2), but it was 1823 before a French army came to his rescue and forced the Cortes to submit. Ferdinand celebrated his release and the recovery of his absolutism by cancelling the amnesty he had promised, and by slaughtering his opponents. Again the masses offered no resistance. For the next ten years, until his death in 1833, Ferdinand ruled unhampered by any nonsense about a constitution.

A watered-down constitution, which preserved for the crown more powers than that of 1812, was granted in 1837. Ferdinand had left the throne to his infant daughter Isabella II on whose behalf his widow, Maria Cristina, acted as regent. Maria Cristina was driven to make concessions to the liberals, many of whom returned from exile, in order to resist Don Carlos, Ferdinand's reactionary younger brother who coveted the throne for himself. But the new constitution was granted grudgingly and when Isabella came of age and herself ruled from 1843, there was a continuing struggle between despotism and liberalism. The constitution was several times amended, and Spanish history was complicated by several intertwined conflicts. Rural poverty led to peasant uprisings at frequent intervals in Isabella's reign. Supporters of Don Carlos, although they had admitted defeat in 1839, went on disputing the succession. Disputes occurred about the rights of the Catholic Church and about regional privileges, and factions developed among army officers who were caught up in the political quarrels. But the middle classes remained weak and Spain remained backward by the standards of western Europe generally. Opposition represented separate interest groups and was not co-ordinated, so that the European revolutions of 1848 left Spain untouched. Not until 1868 did the Spaniards achieve sufficient unity to overthrow Isabella and drive her across the border into France. Even then, opinion was divided between republicanism and support for a new monarchy.

Occasionally Spanish affairs involved other powers. Britain and France were caught up in the Carlist problem in the 1830s when, superficially, Spain seemed to be at a crossroads between despotism and liberalism, and they became involved again when Isabella married in 1846 (see pages 126–7). When she was overthrown, confusion about the Spanish crown helped to bring about the Franco-Prussian War (see page 120). But Spain after 1815 was almost as irrelevant to the rest of Europe as European economic and social development seemed to be irrelevant to the majority of Spaniards.

(b) Portugal

Portugal, like Spain, suffered from the absence of a substantial educated bourgeoisie. Like Spain, it had been invaded by the forces of Napoleon who brought with them some of the ideas of the French Revolution, and the years after the French were expelled were years of confusion. John VI succeeded to the Portuguese throne in 1816, but he preferred to remain in the Portuguese colony of Brazil and to leave the British officers, who had remained in Portugal after the French defeat, to put down liberal agitators in Lisbon. Viscount Beresford did the job well for several years but decided in 1820 that it was time to bring John back from Brazil. As soon as Beresford set out for America, the liberals revolted and drafted a new constitution with which to confront their King. John reached Portugal in July 1821. Without any immediate assistance from the powers who had met at Troppau and Laibach, he had no alternative but to accept the constitution, to the disgust of his younger son Dom Miguel.

John's elder son, Dom Pedro, was less hostile to liberalism than Miguel, but Pedro had remained in Brazil. Coming to terms with those Brazilians who demanded national independence, Pedro became the Emperor of a Brazil whose independence John VI recognized in 1825. The loss of Brazil and constitutional rule in Portugal itself infuriated the conservatives. In spite of their support, however, Miguel failed in a bid to seize power in 1824 and went off to Vienna to tell Metternich of his troubles. Two years later, the death of King John plunged Portugal into new confusion.

Pedro was the rightful heir and the hope of the liberals, but Pedro was ruling in Brazil. He suggested a somewhat unworkable solution to Portugal's problems: that his daughter Maria, who was seven years old, should become queen and marry her uncle Miguel, and that Miguel should agree to a new constitution, less democratic than the old. It was at this point that Canning sent British troops to Lisbon (see page 22) to make certain that neither Spain nor France intervened there to support anti-liberal forces. Canning told the House of Commons:

> We go to Portugal, not to rule, not to dictate, not to prescribe constitutions, but . . . to preserve the independence of an ally. We go to plant the standard of England on the well-known heights of Lisbon. Where that standard is planted, foreign dominion shall not come.

The British could prevent 'foreign dominion' but they were not prepared to do more than that. Miguel did not intend to accept any constitution, and within a short time of his return to Portugal the liberals were routed. He was not dislodged until 1834, several years after Pedro had abdicated in Brazil to lead the resistance against him. Pedro died in 1834, leaving the throne to Maria. She was able to preserve some elements of her father's cautious liberalism during the next nineteen years, seeking to keep a balance between the supporters of authoritarianism and those who demanded more radical reforms. Social change took place only slowly in an economy dominated by the export of port wine, and Portugal, like Spain, remained one of the backwaters of nineteenth-century Europe.

(c) Italy

Liberals in Italy were even less successful before 1848 than in Spain and Portugal. Only in Piedmont-Sardinia, nearer France than the rest of Italy and in closer touch with economic development, and in Lombardy and Venetia, which were rich enough to provide a quarter of the revenue of the Austrian Empire, did a substantial bourgeoisie exist. But here, as elsewhere in Italy, demands for reform came up against the stone wall of repression. The first major outbreak of protest occurred in Naples where troops mutinied in 1820, inspired by the uprising in Spain (see page 37) against the Spanish House of Bourbon, to which Ferdinand I of the Two Sicilies was related. Carbonari joined in the rebellion and demanded a constitution like the Spanish one of 1812. Ferdinand gained time with a pretence of agreement, and he regained his despotic power when Austrian troops arrived to crush the revolution. Successive rulers then kept the Two Sicilies in an iron grip, Ferdinand II (who came to the throne in 1830) eventually earning for himself the nickname 'King Bomba' when he enthusiastically bombarded his Sicilian subjects into submission during the revolutions of 1848. Meanwhile, there was a momentary flicker of liberalism in Piedmont-Sardinia in 1821, and again rebellion started with army mutinies. Piedmontese noblemen and middle classes took the opportunity to demand a constitution and so demoralized Victor Emmanuel I that he abdicated. His successor, Charles Felix, was out of the country and, acting as regent, Charles Albert thought it best to agree to a constitutional government, subject to the new King's approval. Charles Felix refused such approval, and Austrian troops again crushed all protest. When Charles Albert himself succeeded to the throne in 1831, he too was determined to have no restrictions on royal power.

Demands for constitutional liberties similarly came to nothing when there were risings in central Italy in 1831 (see page 31). Austrian troops again overwhelmed the liberals, and restored threatened rulers to their full powers. In Modena, Francis IV, one of the Habsburg archdukes who ruled in the Duchies and an arch-reactionary, was restored. Both in the Duchies and in Lombardy-Venetia, Habsburg rule was comparatively efficient by Italian standards. It was always despotic but sometimes, as in Tuscany, it was an easy-going despotism, which Tuscans recognized in 1831 by refusing to join in the risings. There was nothing easy-going about the Papal despotism, however. Successive Popes took their cue from Pius VII who abolished street lighting in the Papal States as something not only dangerously modern but also French. The Popes believed that ignorant subjects were the most obedient subjects, and every new idea was suppressed ruthlessly. Not until Giovanni Mastai-Ferretti became Pope in 1846, as Pius IX, was even the mildest reform possible; but Pius IX, too, soon convinced himself that liberalism and nationalism were inventions of the Devil. His conception of reform fell far short of that of enlightened nineteenth-century opinion.

(d) Germany

Germany differed somewhat from Italy in having not only more radical universities (see page 27) but in producing a tiny handful of liberal-minded rulers. Frederick William III of Prussia toyed with the idea of granting a constitution in the years after 1815, until frightened by student demonstrations and persuaded otherwise by Metternich. But not all the German princes were so timid. Diets were permitted in several states, among them Baden and Bavaria, and oases of free thought survived even in the darkest days of Metternich's repression. One such oasis was at Weimar, at this time a centre of German intellectual life. Schiller had written his romantic dramas there, and Goethe, the outstanding German poet, dramatist and philosopher, worked there until his death in 1832. But the existence of a few oases did not make Germany as a whole less of a desert. The majority of the princes in the German Confederation were well satisfied with the existing order, and the few who were not had no more power than had Germans in general to change the system. Not until 1848 were German liberals strong enough to mount a real challenge (see Section 5.2(c)).

3.3   The Demand for National Independence

Government by a foreign power sometimes provoked more determined opposition in the years 1815–48 than government which was merely despotic.

In creating an international crisis a revolution which aimed at independence might gain outside support, although the example of Poland will show this was not always the case. Spain's colonies in south and central America became independent after 1815 with assistance from the USA and Britain (see page 23), and Brazil gained independence from Portugal in 1825 (see page 38). The success of these independence movements was partly due to the weakness of the governments in Madrid and Lisbon. There was also a weak government in Constantinople, the capital of the Ottoman Empire, where Mahmud II ruled as Sultan from 1808 to 1839. The extent of the Sultan's weakness was tested by both the Serbs and the Greeks as well as by Mehemet Ali, once an Albanian tobacco-merchant, who from 1805 ruled Egypt for the Sultan. By the time of his death, Mahmud had been forced to make concessions to all of them.

(a) The Serbian Revolution

The rebellion of Serbian patriots in 1804 was led by a swarthy dealer in pigs known as Karadjordje (Karageorge, 'Black George'). It was not the first attempt by the Serbs to regain the independence which they had lost to the Turks nearly three hundred years earlier. Turkish rule was alien, brutal and inefficient, but Karadjordje was successful only for as long as he had support from Russia. When Russian support was withdrawn the Turks were strong enough to crush the rebellion in 1813. They confirmed their barbarous reputation by a fortnight's killing in Belgrade and by herding Serbian women and children into slavery. Milos Obrenovic, a Serbian patriot who refused to follow Karadjordje into exile, launched a new assault on Turkish authority in 1815, and this time the Serbs consolidated their grip on several hundred square miles of territory south of Belgrade. Obrenovic made himself the Prince of Serbia and he ruthlessly eliminated all rivals including Karadjordje, who was assassinated in 1817. An assembly of the Prince's nominees and of Serbia's principal citizens accepted Obrenovic's title in that year, and demanded his recognition by the Sultan.

Serbia lay on the northern edge of Mahmud's Balkan territories, remote from Constantinople. It was also cushioned from direct Russian intervention by the Turkish provinces of Moldavia and Wallachia. For the moment, Russia was not inclined to interfere and the Sultan was powerless to do so. Not until revolution in Greece precipitated a crisis of greater interest to the outside world and led to war between Russia and the Ottoman Empire, however, did the Sultan recognize Obrenovic. In 1830 Serbia was granted what amounted to independence, although still subject in theory to Turkish overlordship. Lest the Sultan should change his mind, Serbia's security was guaranteed by Russia. Three years later Obrenovic almost doubled the size of his country by freeing more of Serbia from the Turks, when Mahmud was preoccupied with the challenge to his authority by Mehemet Ali of Egypt. The total independence of Serbia was not recognized by the Turks until 1878 (see Section 15.2), but from 1817 onwards Turkish overlordship had had very little reality in Serbia. The example of the Serbs inspired other Balkan peoples to seek their freedom from the Turks and, by 1914, little remained of the Ottoman Empire in the Balkans. In 1914, however, Serbia was attacked by Austria (see Section 17.5). As Metternich always feared, a disintegrating Ottoman Empire threatened the Austrian Empire with a similar collapse and, by 1914, Metternich's successors in Vienna had finally persuaded themselves that an independent Serbia, supported by Russia, was a challenge they could no longer ignore.

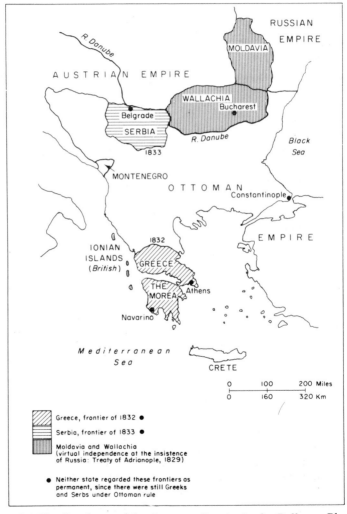

Fig. 3.1 The Break-up of the Ottoman Empire in the Balkans, Phase I

(b) The Greek Revolution

Metternich did nothing to suppress the Serbs and nothing to suppress the Greeks, who followed the Serbian example and rebelled against Turkish rule in 1821. Russia's hostility to the Turkish Empire was always a complicating factor (see page 23), but it was difficult for any Christian to condone the savage rule of the Sultan. Tsar Alexander I, however, found it equally difficult to condone rebellion. The first uprising of the Greeks was therefore left to run its course and to be crushed by the Turks. It took place not in Greece but in Moldavia and Wallachia, where *Philike Hetaireia*, a secret society of Greek nationalists, hoped their rebellion would attract Russian support. They also hoped to rouse Rumanian nationalists in a joint crusade against the Moslem Turks. They chose as their leader Prince Ypsilanti, who had seen service in the Russian Imperial Guard and whose noble birth might win the Tsar's approval. Neither the Tsar nor the Rumanians responded to appeals for support, however, and when Ypsilanti fled to the Austrian Empire, Metternich put him in prison.

Almost at once, a new Greek uprising began in the Morea and on various Greek islands. The Sultan found his forces seriously over-stretched. Apart from the Greeks, he also had to contend with rebellion in Albania. Like the Serbs, the Greeks began to drive the Turks from their country but this conflict was fought with horrifying savagery, becoming something of a holy war between the Greek Orthodox Christians and the Moslems, as well as a war of national liberation. There were numerous atrocities on both sides, which dismayed the great powers. Alexander broke off diplomatic relations with the Sultan and international opinion seemed to favour the Greeks rather than the Turks, but no European power wished to be the first to intervene. Control of the seas by the Greeks was a major factor in ensuring their success and, in 1823, Canning recognized a Greek government. For a time the powers manoeuvred for influence in the new Greek state where the war for independence degenerated into a civil war. Lord Byron, the English poet, went to Greece to campaign not only for national independence but for constitutional liberties, and his death attracted even more support for the Greeks from romantics who yearned for freedom. But the Greeks themselves, their unofficial advisers, and idealist supporters, were severely tested when Mahmud enlisted Egyptian support for the Turkish cause.

Mehemet Ali expressed a willingness to provide the Sultan with both naval and military forces in return for a wider authority. It was an offer Mahmud could not resist, and he promised Crete and Syria. Mehemet sent his son Ibrahim to subdue the Greeks and the tide was turned. During 1825 and 1826 Ibrahim steadily reconquered the Morea, and the Greeks were only saved from eventual surrender by international rivalries. The death of Alexander I in 1825 brought his brother Nicholas to the Russian throne, a new Tsar who seemed unlikely to tolerate any revival of Turkish power. Canning suspected that Russian assistance to the Greeks might fundamentally alter the balance of power in the eastern Mediterranean, but it was unthinkable for Canning to support the Turks when the Greek cause was so popular in Britain. He decided to rely on diplomacy, and to co-operate with the Russians if only to prevent them seeking their own advantage. Wellington was sent to St Petersburg to agree a formula for settling the Greek problem, and a joint Protocol was signed in April 1826. It committed Britain and Russia to trying to secure the virtual independence of Greece while leaving it, like Serbia, nominally under Turkish overlordship, but Canning thought Clause V of the Protocol equally important:

> His Britannic Majesty and His Imperial Majesty will not seek, in this Arrangement, any increase of Territory, nor any exclusive influence, nor advantage in commerce . . . which shall not be equally attainable by all other nations.

First, however, they intended to secure the goodwill of other powers, not least that of Metternich.

France thought it best not to be left out, and the Protocol was followed by the *Treaty of London* in July 1827. Britain, Russia and France agreed to try to implement the terms of the agreement of 1826 and, as a preliminary, to stop the fighting in Greece within a month. They expressed their concern at:

> the state of things which has, for six years, existed in the East.

Their concern arose:

> no less by sentiments of humanity, than by interests for the tranquillity of Europe.

But the Treaty also showed clearly that what particularly concerned them was the interruption of trade, obstacles to commerce, and 'acts of Piracy'. A joint fleet assembled in the Mediterranean but no specific instructions were given as to what it should do. The fighting in Greece went on until, in October 1827, the Allied fleet came up with the Egyptian-Turkish fleet at Navarino. The Turks were foolish enough to open fire, and Admiral Codrington replied to such effect that some sixty Moslem ships were sunk and the Sultan's transport system was thus destroyed. Astonished politicians could think of no better description of the engagement than that of the Duke of Wellington, who considered it to be 'an untoward event'. With no hope now of further supplies, Ibrahim abandoned his campaign and Greek freedom was won.

Mahmud blamed the Russians and, by closing the Dardanelles to all Russian shipping and by similar provocative actions, he found himself involved in a war with Russia which had little to do with Greece (see Section 8.3). The war ended in the *Treaty of Adrianople* in 1829 and, as part of the settlement, the Sultan was forced to agree to both 'the tranquillity of Serbia' and the abandonment of his ambitions in Greece. Since the Battle of Navarino (and the death of Canning shortly before it) Wellington and other European statesmen

Fig. 3.2 An artist's impression published soon after the Battle of Navarino, which ensured the freedom of Greece from Ottoman rule

had been busy settling the Greek frontiers and finding the Greeks a king. Palmerston was the Foreign Secretary in Britain before all the issues were finally settled. The Sultan gave formal agreement to the total independence of Greece in 1832 and, in the same year, Prince Otto of Bavaria accepted the Greek crown after Leopold of Saxe-Coburg had rejected it. Like Serbia, however, Greece was considered to be incomplete in 1832. Its inhabitants had still to liberate fellow-countrymen beyond the existing boundaries. The British ceded the Ionian Islands to Greece in 1864, but many Greeks were still under Turkish rule. The European powers would not permit further extension of Greek boundaries in 1832, since the idea persisted that the Ottoman Empire was important to the balance of power, but the Ottoman Empire had been gravely weakened and its further decay seemed inevitable.

(c) The Revolt of Mehemet Ali

Mehemet Ali received the island of Crete for his efforts against the Greeks. The Sultan argued that Greece had not in the end been reconquered and so no more was due. The result was further disruption when Mehemet decided to take Syria by force. By 1833 the Ottoman Empire was again tottering – and again the great powers became involved in its affairs (see Section 8.3). The problems caused by Mehemet were not settled until 1841, by which time he had lost everything but Egypt, though he was allowed the consolation of hereditary rule there, and he thus became the founder of the Egyptian dynasty which lasted until the overthrow of King Farouk in 1952.

(d) The Belgian Revolution

The Kingdom of the Netherlands, which came into existence in 1815 (see page 11) uniting the former Austrian Netherlands (Belgium) with Holland, was not a union of equals. There were three and a half million Belgians and only two million Dutch; but the Dutch considered that they had been allowed to annex Belgium. The Belgians for their part resented the union. They seemed to have passed, within a single generation, from conqueror to conqueror – from the Austrians to the French, and now from the French to the Dutch. In 1815 they hoped in vain for independence. By 1830 they were ready to fight for it, protesting that almost alone of the peoples of western Europe, save for the Irish and the Norwegians, Belgians were denied their right to nationhood.

Already Belgium was developing an industrial economy with a significant output of textiles, coal and sugar produced from beet. Middle-class Belgians had tasted administrative modernization during the recent French occupation. They hated French control but they could at least understand the French language. When Dutch was made the official language of the union with Holland the Belgians were bitterly resentful. They also resented their equal representation in the States-General, the Netherlands assembly, arguing that the larger Belgian population entitled them to more seats. Worse than that, they complained that the States-General had little power and that all real authority lay with the Dutch King William I and his ministers. They were not inclined to count the benefits of the union, such as the markets for Belgian exports in the Dutch colonies and the few constitutional liberties, which included religious toleration and an independent judicial system.

Instead, the Belgians counted and brooded on their grievances. They were saddled with an equal share of the national debt, though over 95 per cent of it had been accumulated by the Dutch. Partly because of the language problem, Belgians gained few state offices and government appointments, and few of the higher ranks in the army. Commercial law favoured Dutch merchants, who had a traditional belief in free trade, but the Belgian industrialists wanted tariffs, to protect their industries from foreign competition. Revenue was raised by a tax on bread, a staple food in Belgium, whereas there was no similar tax on the potatoes the Dutch preferred. Even religious toleration gave rise to protest. The Belgians were devout Catholics, to many of whom religious toleration seemed to be an encouragement of heresy. Belgian Catholics detested the puritanical fervour of Dutch Calvinists, and they were deeply suspicious of William's policy of freeing education from religious control. State control of the universities and secondary schools, and state inspection of religious schools offended the Church, and they were also seen as a threat to Belgian culture. Both liberals and conservatives became united in a common determination to break the union. The King's attempt to ban all seditious literature only increased the Belgian anger.

The revolution in Paris which brought Louis Philippe to the French throne in 1830 (see Section 4.2(b)) excited the Belgians, but their own revolution began in August that year with little more than street-shouting, following a performance in Brussels, of Auber's opera, *La Muette de Portici*, which romanticized rebellion in Naples. The demonstrations were not checked and, within little more than a week, government troops were withdrawn from Brussels. A month later, after easily defeating a weak Dutch attempt to reoccupy the city, the Belgians declared their country independent. Support for national freedom spread rapidly but William I, in the meantime, had appealed to the major powers to subdue his rebellious subjects. A conference of European ambassadors met in London.

Austria, Prussia and Russia were in favour of restoring the union, but the Tsar had troubles of his own in Poland (see Section 3.3(*e*)). The French welcomed the uprising: an independent Belgium would demolish one of the barriers erected in the settlement of 1814–15, and Louis Philippe thought it presented him with an opportunity to extend French influence and to delight his subjects with a lively foreign policy. Britain's attitude was the important one, however. The British had a traditional interest in the Belgian coastline, close enough for the launching of an invasion of the British Isles, and Palmerston, the Foreign Secretary, was determined to keep it out of the hands of France or any other powerful European state. Palmerston also recognized that the union between Belgium and Holland had proved unworkable. By January 1831 the powers agreed in principle that Belgium should be independent. But that was not what the Dutch government wanted.

It took some time to make Belgium truly independent. One problem concerned the Belgian crown. The powers suggested that the Belgians should accept the Prince of Orange, a Dutchman, as their king. The Belgian reply was to choose the Duc de Nemours, son of Louis Philippe. That alarmed Palmerston, and the French King was persuaded to withdraw his son's candidature. There was then general agreement that Leopold of Saxe-Coburg (the uncle of the future Queen Victoria) should be the King of the Belgians, and he took the oath in July 1831 to respect constitutional government in Belgium.

A second problem was the refusal of William I to accept the loss of his Belgian territories. He launched an invasion in August 1831, and was driven back only by French troops whom the great powers had authorized to act on their behalf. But William still refused to agree to the Treaty of London of November 1831. The great powers set down in detail in this Treaty 'certain modifications in the transactions of the year 1815', and in Article XXV they guaranteed Belgium's independence. They saw this revision of the settlement of 1814–15 as a 'necessity' for preserving 'the general Peace'; and they offered to restore Luxemburg and part of Limburg to William, if only he would accept the loss of Belgium. He remained obstinate. The French drove his troops out of Antwerp and the British blockaded his ports, but the most that he would agree to in 1833 was to refrain from launching new invasions of Belgium. He continued to refuse to recognize Belgian independence until 1838, and only then was a final settlement possible. This settlement was made in further *Treaties of London* during 1839:

> The Union which has existed between Holland and Belgium, in virtue of the Treaty of Vienna of . . . 1815, is acknowledged by His Majesty the King of the Netherlands, Grand Duke of Luxemburg, to be dissolved.

William was now able to regain possession of Luxemburg (except for the Walloon area) and to rule it as the 'Grand Duke'. He also recovered the Dutch share of Limburg.

The 1839 Treaties also stated that Belgium:

> shall form an Independent and perpetually Neutral State. It shall be bound to observe such Neutrality towards all other States.

This was a less clear-cut undertaking to protect Belgium than that given in Article XXV of the Treaty of 1831, but when Belgium was invaded by Germany in 1914 (see Section 17.5) the British government argued that the defence of Belgium remained a binding obligation.

The immediate consequence of the Belgian revolution was an economic crisis in the early 1830s, but Belgium became a country where, after early teething troubles, constitutional liberties were well protected and economic development proceeded steadily, to the satisfaction of the middle classes. Leopold I founded a dynasty which was prepared to adapt itself to change. There was therefore no revolution in Belgium in 1848, though industrialization led to clashes between the authorities and the working classes later in the century. Holland also moved towards a more liberal system with constitutional reform in 1840, which William I found so distasteful that, having conceded it, he promptly abdicated. His son, William II (the Prince of Orange), made further concessions in 1848, swiftly enough to prevent the spread into Holland of the European revolutions. Such concessions to middle-class liberals were in contrast to the harder line to which ancient monarchies tried to cling elsewhere in Europe.

(e) The Polish Revolution

Alexander I was willing to give a veneer of liberalism to his rule of the new Congress Kingdom of Poland (see page 9) and Poles were later to look back on his rule from 1815 to 1825 as comparatively benevolent. The Poles kept their national flag, a national army (under Russian control), and the Polish language in much of the administration. They were promised civil liberties including some freedom for the press. Catholicism was made the official religion and other faiths were tolerated. There was even a constitutional assembly in two houses, where Polish opinion could be heard. Alexander invested state money in economic enterprises and gave protection to the developing Polish industries. His rule was nevertheless foreign, and his apparent leaning towards liberalism was no more than flirtation. It was soon obvious to the Poles that the assembly was toothless, and that civil liberties did not extend to the freedom to undermine the system. Like students in

Germany, Polish students had a romantic longing for all sorts of freedom, including national freedom from Russia; and, like Italy, Poland had a scattering of secret societies. But opposition to Alexander was not broadly based and he had little difficulty in containing it, subduing disruptive students and conspirators, and frustrating all protest in the assembly.

Alexander's successor, Nicholas I, was crowned in Warsaw as King of Poland in 1829. In November 1830, an army mutiny began in that city. Polish soldiers were angered by a rumour that Nicholas intended to send them to put down the recent revolutions in France and Belgium. The military uprising quickly turned into a national revolution. With the examples before them of Serbia, Greece and now Belgium, the Poles aimed at independence and, unrealistically, imagined that the more liberal governments of western Europe might help them to achieve it. They were encouraged by the flight of the Tsar's brother, Constantine, whose job it was to command the Polish army. Nicholas was declared deposed and a national Polish government was set up. But the government was largely aristocratic, divided by class from the Polish masses and divided within itself by factions. Its energies were wasted in internal disputes, and it could not make up its mind whether to concentrate on military operations or to try to bargain with the Tsar. In February 1831 Nicholas sent an army of over 100 000 men to crush the revolution and, by the autumn, the Poles had been overwhelmed. No outside help was forthcoming.

With the Poles at his mercy, Nicholas determined to root out the surviving traces of Alexander's liberalism. One result was an exodus of thousands of Poles to the west, there to plan further revolutions for the freeing of Poland and to keep alive a romantic national literature. In Poland itself there was military government and severe repression. The University of Warsaw was closed and free thought was stifled. Efforts were made to deprive Poles of their national identity by ending the use of the Polish language in official business, suppressing Polish literature and harassing their Catholic Church. The Polish economy was no longer assisted and, as in Russia itself, the peasant masses remained an ill-treated and impoverished section of the population, often apathetic, and divided from the landed nobility of Poland by rigid social barriers. Thus Nicholas broke the Polish spirit for at least a generation. No significant uprising occurred in Poland in 1848, but exiles in the west and conspirators within Poland itself kept alive the idea of rebellion until it was strong enough to launch a new uprising in 1863 (see Section 14.2(c)).

3.4 The Search for National Identity

In Poland the main problem for nationalists was to break free from foreign rule. In Italy and Germany fragmentation into small states produced a barrier to the development of national consciousness. It seemed more natural to consider oneself a Neapolitan rather than an Italian, or a Bavarian rather than a German. But a common language and a slowly developing awareness among the educated of a common culture helped to prepare the way for the later unification of Italy and Germany, even though, for the moment, formidable obstacles prevented much progress. Sections 2.3 and 3.2 showed the strength of the existing authorities and the weakness of the forces for change in both Italy and Germany.

(a) Italy

Silvio Pellico, a Milanese dramatist, spent many years in prison as the result of his part in the disturbances of 1821 in Italy. In 1832 he published an account of his sufferings in *My Imprisonment*, adding to Italy's revolutionary literature. The very title was revealing, for Italian nationalists were almost certain to finish up in gaol or in exile. Splutters of protest by the Carbonari and later by Young Italy (see Section 2.3(c)) produced martyrs and won converts to the causes of liberalism and nationalism, but it was optimism rather than realism which caused Mazzini to claim that 'ideas grow quickly when watered with the blood of martyrs'. Aware and educated Italians were a small minority before 1848, and it was of the Catholic Church that Italian peasants were most likely to think, not of a united Italy, if they lifted their eyes beyond their own immediate environment. Even among those who had a vision of a united Italy, opinion was divided, not only as to how it could be achieved but as to what they meant by a united Italy. There were those in Piedmont who thought their king could lead a national movement, an idea from which Charles Albert shrank back in 1831. Mazzini's followers wanted a liberal republic. Others thought the Pope was the natural leader of Italians and among these was Vincenzo Gioberti, who published his *Spiritual Pre-eminence of the Italians* in 1843 and followed it with other works, urging Italians to unite behind the Pope, and the Pope to lead Italians in getting rid of the Austrians. Gregory XVI was content enough with things as they were and Pius IX, his successor, soon concluded that even paltry reforms in the Papal States could be dangerously disruptive. Pius gave his blessing to continued Austrian influence and the *status quo* in general, when he explained that he 'regarded with equal affection all peoples, races and nations'. Other Italians showed more imagination, and mixed together a love of freedom, a vision of a united Italy and a thirst for adventure. One such was Giuseppe Garibaldi, but before 1848 Garibaldi spent more time fighting for the freedom of Uruguay against the Argentians than fighting for the unity of Italians. By 1848, however, there were many Italians to whom patriotism now appealed, and there were widespread uprisings in the peninsula in that year.

(b) Germany

In Germany, patriotism was also encouraged by writers. Much of the writing was anti-French, a protest first against French aggression in the years of Napoleon I and then a protest against French culture, which seemed to threaten Germanic culture. Germans tended to regard the French as frivolous, and German philosophers developed a heavy-handed concept of the powerful nation state, obeyed by its subjects and preserving its national culture. Hegel lectured in Berlin in the 1820s and told his audience:

> In the history of the World, only those peoples can come under our notice which form a state. . . . The State is the Divine Idea as it exists on Earth.

But Germany's problem was that there were too many states and, though students were fired with the ideal of a united Germany, the *status quo* was defended by too many vested interests, which included thirty-nine 'princes', most of them anxious to preserve their separate authorities. Intellectuals might read the philosophy of Kant and Hegel, the patriotic writings of Fichte and Arndt, and the elegant works of Schiller and Goethe, rejoicing that all were German, but this alone would not bring about unification. The political weakness of intellectuals was revealed in the Frankfurt Parliament of 1848–9, a parliament which it was hoped would unite Germany but which included only one peasant (see page 80).

Economic pressures, on the other hand, produced a degree of inter-state co-operation which won new converts to the ideal of a united Germany. Friedrich List advocated the building of a German railway network as early as 1833. The first German railway was opened in 1835, linking Nuremberg and Fürth, and by 1848, the German states led all Europe except for Britain (see page 35). By the 1880s Germany had more track than any other European country. Railways helped Germans to travel, and they also helped to entwine the economies of the individual German states. List also advocated the protection of developing industries by tariffs. In 1841 he published his *National System of Political Economy*, to show that a nation's industry would benefit if foreign competition were shut out. Such a policy made more sense if the state was big enough to supply many of its own needs, and Germans had already begun to look enviously at nations like Britain, France and even Belgium, which were not fragmented.

Prussia had begun, shortly after 1815, to weld into a single economic unit the various territories which had accumulated under the rule from Berlin of Frederick William III. They were linked together in a customs union, the *Zollverein*, which permitted unrestricted trade within the union and could enforce a common policy towards competition from outside it. At first the main aim was merely to simplify administration, and free commercial exchanges from the delays and expense of local toll barriers. But the Prussians were then able to impose levies on all goods which passed through their territories, from which it was only a small step to imposing tariffs on goods which entered Prussia from 'foreign' states. Other German states began to make similar unions among themselves, copying the Prussian example. In 1828 a union was set up in south Germany between Bavaria and Württemberg, and in the north another Zollverein centred on Hanover. Hesse-Darmstadt, however, chose in 1828 to join the Prussian Zollverein, recognizing the

Fig. 3.3 A Silesian iron foundry, from a painting of 1841. Industrialization led to the organization of workers in protest against the existing order and their hardships

advantage of being within the largest union. Three years later Saxony and Hesse-Cassel deserted Hanover to join Prussia and, by 1836, Bavaria and the southern states merged their union with the Prussian one. Influenced by Britain, which feared for its German markets, Hanover resisted the trend for some time longer, but Hanover too joined the Prussian Zollverein in 1851.

The customs union did not involve political unification but it encouraged Germans to think increasingly in national terms. In 1844 the Zollverein was able to begin to sign commercial treaties with foreign powers on behalf of most of the German states. It also boosted the prestige of Prussia. Austria played no part in the Zollverein and continued to resist any closer ties between Germans than those which existed in the hollow German Bund. The Austrian Empire included many races who were not German, and the idea seemed bound to grow that Prussia rather than Austria might be the real leader of a future German nation.

Prussia's response to such an idea was extremely cautious. Baron Stein who, as the chief minister of Prussia in 1807–8, had emancipated Prussian serfs and introduced administrative improvements, urged, at the end of the Napoleonic Wars, that there should be a united Germany, but Metternich frustrated his plans. Other Prussians did not press the plans, and Frederick William III, until his death in 1840, showed no ambition to challenge Austria and to lead Germany. Although Prussia had played a major part in freeing Germany from the domination of Napoleon, the Prussian authorities seem to have regarded

Fig. 3.4 Workers' organizations, however, were unpopular with the authorities and were often ridiculed. This cartoon of c.1830 casts doubts on the workers' ability to organize successfully, scornful of a 'union meeting'

the Zollverein as nothing more than an instrument of economic policy. All the same, Prussia was obviously the most important north German state, and it would be natural to look to Prussia for leadership when Germans became convinced that unity was not only desirable but necessary. That stage was not reached in the first half of the nineteenth century. By 1860, however, the industrial power of Britain and France was beginning to dwarf that of a disunited Germany. By that time the German production of iron was only a fifteenth of the three million tons produced annually in France. To the defence of German culture against that of France, nationalists could now add the argument that, to achieve comparable economic strength, Germany must become one state.

3.5   The Conflicts in the Existing Order by 1848

On the surface not much had changed in Europe in the years 1815 to 1848. Except in western Europe, few concessions had been made to liberalism, and European nationalists had freed only Serbia, Greece and Belgium. More often than not in this period the challenge to the existing order seemed to come only from intellectuals, the middle classes, and enlightened noblemen, seldom enlisting the masses in support of liberal and nationalist objectives. But other conflicts were developing. In Britain, France and in isolated pockets elsewhere, the labouring poor were beginning to make their grievances known. From time to time outbreaks of peasant fury disturbed the tranquillity of rural life, but it was in the industrial areas that organizations of workers began to form. By strikes and rioting, and sometimes in more ambitious movements such as that of the Chartists in Britain, the workers served notice that there were more issues to be settled than those involving the aspirations of middle-class liberals and nationalists. The response of the authorities was usually repression in one form or another. The middle-class response was also often hostile or, at best, indifferent. In the 1840s, hardship drove Silesian weavers to rioting and machine-breaking, in a protest like that of earlier English Luddites against machinery which took away their work. But such protests also challenged their middle-class employers who, to the workers, seemed a part of the existing order.

The revolutions of 1848 began on a tide of economic discontent which produced, for the moment, an apparent unity of purpose among the revolutionaries and which helped to win some temporary successes (see Unit Five). But the middle classes refused to see the workers as allies, except where they could be persuaded to pursue middle-class objectives. This conflict of interests between the revolutionaries was to be seen most clearly in 1848 in France (see Section 6.1(a)), but where the revolutions were defeated – which was almost everywhere – defeat was due not just to the continuing strength of the existing order but to the continuing weakness of the resistance movements. It was the divided interests between the middle classes and the workers which, as much as anything, enabled the traditional ruling classes to preserve much of the existing order even beyond 1848.

Further Reading

See **Further Reading** for Unit Two.
Lamb, M.: *Nationalism*. Heinemann (London, 1974).
Perry, K. R.: *The Bourgeois Century, 1780–1870*. Macmillan (London, 1972).
Talmon, J. L.: *Romanticism and Revolt, 1815–48*. Thames and Hudson (London, 1967).

Exercises

1. What reasons can you find in Section 3.2 for the discontent after 1815 of Spaniards, Portuguese, Italians and Germans? Why was this discontent largely confined to the middle classes?
2. Study Section 3.3(b). Explain why, as a Greek, you would be likely to have supported rebellion against the Turks in the 1820s, and to have looked for foreign help in your struggle.
3. 'Belgians counted and brooded on their grievances' (page 46). Explain this statement, and show how the Belgians won their independence.
4. Making use of the Index in this book and Fig. 1.5, trace the history of Poland in the years before 1848.
5. What evidence can you find in this Unit that the governments of Britain and France
· sometimes pursued 'liberal' foreign policies?

Western Liberalism and Eastern Autocracy

4.1 France and Russia: Contrasts in Development

France

Louis XVIII reckoned the year 1814 as the nineteenth of his reign as King of France. He had assumed what was then an empty title on the death of Louis XVII in 1795. At that time, he was in exile in Verona, and he had to wait until 1814 to gain the throne. In the interim France had managed without the Bourbons for more than 20 years – since the execution in 1793 of Louis XVI, Louis XVIII's elder brother. The Allies restored the Bourbons to the French throne in 1814, and had to restore them again in 1815 after Napoleon's Hundred Days, but it was up to Louis XVIII to come to terms with his subjects and to ensure that the monarchy lasted. He therefore agreed to the Charter in June 1814, making what were probably the minimum concessions which would reconcile the French middle classes to the restoration.

The Charter guaranteed certain basic rights and a measure of constitutional government. However much Louis might refer to his ancient royal prerogatives in the preamble to the Charter, its signing showed that he was prepared to bargain for his throne. He was almost 60 and he preferred to spend his remaining years as the ruling King of France rather than as a pretender in exile. He therefore agreed in the Charter to various concessions to liberalism, among them freedom from arbitrary imprisonment, equality before the law, fair trials and religious toleration. The Charter also put considerable emphasis on property. It pledged the King to respect the security of property, including any bought during the years since 1789; and property was made the key to representation in the Assembly, to which the royal ministers were to be answerable. The right to vote rested on a property qualification so high, that only one in three hundred of the French population of almost 30 million was able to achieve it. In effect, Louis was agreeing to share power with the landowners and the most prosperous of the bourgeoisie, classes whose property gave them a stake in the stability of the country. It was not surprising that the first elections returned an Assembly which was both royalist and extremely conservative. The restoration thus divided French society between an elite, whom the Charter admitted to a share in government, and a restless majority.

The continuing development of French industry in the years after 1815 increased the pressures for further change. The bourgeoisie demanded that the franchise be widened and that more extensive liberties be granted. The proletariat demanded improved conditions and better opportunities. Frenchmen remembered that revolution had already brought changes in the country, destroying what had remained of feudal privileges in the late eighteenth century, and even toppling the monarchy for a lengthy period. Future governments would need to adapt themselves to the changing society, if they themselves were not to be toppled. In 1814 the French were weary of upheaval and war, and the Charter was enough to reconcile most of them to the restoration. But further concessions would be needed if the monarchy were to survive for any length of time.

Charles of Artois, who succeeded his brother Louis XVIII as King Charles X in 1824, believed that even the Charter was too radical, and the result was that his reign ended in another revolution in 1830. This revolution gave a new impetus to the lusty singing of the *Marseillaise*, composed by Rouget de Lisle. The Marseillaise had been adopted as the national anthem in 1795, and was a symbol of the revolutionary spirit. Hector Berlioz had in 1830 just completed a new and extravagant setting of this romantic anthem 'for full orchestra and double chorus', and the composer led the Paris crowds in its singing:

> Irate at their apparent coldness, I roared out, 'Confound it all! *Sing!*' And they sang.
> Remember, those four or five thousand tightly packed people were – men, women and children – hot from the barricades, inflamed with lust for combat, and imagine how their *Aux armes, citoyens!* rolled out.

They manned barricades again in 1848 when Louis Philippe, who had become King of the French in 1830, was overthrown; once more the Marseillaise rolled out.

Russia

There were few such excitements in the streets of St Petersburg, however. Russian tsars ruled with no charter, no assembly, and very few civil liberties. Millions of peasants in the Russian Empire were still bound by serfdom to the soil and to their masters, and a vast gulf divided the ruling classes from the masses. The monarchy, the nobility, the army, and the Orthodox Church, presented an impenetrable barrier against change. Russia lacked a substantial middle class and the Empire was almost untouched by the industrialization which was proceeding in western Europe; Russian technology was typified in the primitive methods used in manufacturing sugar. Renegade noblemen, intellectuals and army officers managed an occasional splutter of protest, but it was yet too early for barricades to appear in St Petersburg and Moscow with the regularity and enthusiasm with which they appeared in Paris. The more usual insurrections in Russia were the hopeless uprisings of the tormented peasantry, provoked by hunger, cruelty and injustice.

Alexander I became the Tsar in 1801. He stepped out of the murky shadows of the Romanov court when his half-mad father, Paul I, was murdered. Alexander changed little in Russia, and he, too, died in mysterious circum-

Fig. 4.1 A French stamp of 1936 commemorating the centenary of the death of Rouget de Lisle, whose Marseillaise *has provided inspiration for generations of Frenchmen*

stances. Intrigue and mystery were as much a part of the Russian court as formality and etiquette were a part of the Habsburg court in Vienna, and the rumour spread that Alexander was not dead but had gone off to indulge his fanatical devotion to his religion, as a hermit. His successor, Nicholas I, had a fanatical devotion to autocracy, which he preserved zealously until his death in 1855. The untroubled security of Nicholas in 1848 was in sharp contrast to the turbulence which ended the monarchy in France in that year.

A similar contrast existed between the economic and social development of the two countries. In 1850 the population of European Russia was about sixty million, of whom some forty million were serfs and only 300 000 were workers in industry. The first railway in Russia had been built in 1836 – from St Petersburg to the Tsar's summer palace – but there were still fewer than a thousand miles of track in the country, only half that which existed in the much smaller France. St Petersburg, the Russian capital, and Moscow trailed far behind Paris in size. But one should not exaggerate French development at this time. Three-quarters of Frenchmen still lived and worked in rural areas rather than in the town, though they worked as free men and, like Frenchmen in industry, they made use of new technology, accumulating capital which could be reinvested. Their output was considerably higher than that of their counterparts in Russia, for Russia remained almost medieval, lacking capital, rigidly divided into social classes between which there was little mobility, and vigorously protected against almost all new ideas by the Tsar's autocracy. Thus Russia dropped further behind most of Europe as the nineteenth century went on.

4.2   France 1814–48

(a) The Restored Bourbons

Louis XVIII

The first elections of the reign of Louis XVIII took place only a short time after Napoleon's defeat at Waterloo. Napoleon's Hundred Days had deepened the divisions in France, and his return from Elba had forced Louis to flee from Paris almost as soon as he had accepted the Charter. Now that Louis was restored for the second time, the royalists clamoured for revenge against the Bonapartists. The elections returned an Assembly which was dominated by the ultras (right-wing extremists) who paid more heed to Charles of Artois than to the King. Towards the end of 1815 the ultras carried out a purge known as the White Terror. Thousands were imprisoned and Marshal Ney, hero of Napoleon's Moscow expedition of 1812, was shot after a summary court martial. It seemed that the fury of the ultras might quickly put the Bourbon restoration in jeopardy again, but Louis gradually asserted his authority and toned down their excesses. Advised by the liberal-minded Decazes, he dissolved the Assembly in 1816, and he was relieved when the new elections returned many more moderate deputies. Louis and Decazes were able to embark on four years of constructive government, during which the ultras were restrained.

These years, 1816–20, saw a genuine effort to make a success of Bourbon constitutional rule. The economy and French finances were put on a sound footing, and the indemnity was paid, so that at the Congress of Aix-la-Chapelle the occupation forces were withdrawn and France was admitted to the Quintuple Alliance (see Section 2.2). With his prestige rising Louis felt confident enough to relax the censorship of the press in 1819. The constitution remained narrowly based, but France was still more liberal at this time than most of the states of Europe. The ultras made a comeback, however, in 1820. The French bourgeoisie were clamouring for further reform, the King's health was failing, and revolutions elsewhere in Europe created a climate of fear which was favourable to the ultras. Moreover, the King's nephew, the Duc de Berri, was assassinated, and the ultras demanded stronger government. Louis was forced to dismiss Decazes and to appoint a more right-wing administration under Richelieu. There was some tinkering with the electoral system, which helped to produce a more right-wing Assembly in 1821, and Richelieu too was dismissed in favour of Villèle, who strongly favoured the ultras. Louis now found it difficult during the rest of his reign to restrain Artois and the forces of reaction. The electoral laws were altered again. Protest was savagely suppressed, secret societies such as the *Charbonnerie* (French Carbonari) were rooted out and, in 1823, a French army was sent into Spain to restore royal absolutism there (see page 37). By 1824 the Assembly favoured the ultras as strongly as in 1815. In September 1824 Louis died.

Charles X

Artois succeeded to the throne as Charles X. At his accession, he took the uncharacteristic step of abolishing censorship, but more typical of his reactionary views was the religious and traditional ceremony with which he was crowned. Charles quickly encouraged Villèle to set about restoring the ancient authority of the Catholic Church, which had strongly supported royal despotism in the years before the Revolution of 1789. Sacrilege was made punishable by death, and the Church again tightened its grip on education after the years of lay control under Napoleon. Jesuits returned to France, and the growing influence of churchmen generally infuriated the strong anti-clerical forces in French society. The *émigrés* (see Glossary) received compensation for their lost lands, and it was strongly suspected that those who had gained the lands of the nobility and of the Church might soon lose them, in spite of the guarantee in the Charter. Middle-class opinion was further alienated when Villèle reduced the interest payable on government stock and angered investors. By 1827 attempts were again being made to censor the press to stifle the criticisms of the government. Even the Assembly, royalist as it was, was restless, and so Charles dissolved it. The new elections returned a majority hostile to Villèle, and Charles replaced him with the more moderate Martignac in January 1828. For just over a year it appeared that Charles was settling after all for the sensible and mild liberalism which Louis XVIII had pursued in the period 1816 to 1820.

The illusion was shattered in August 1829 when Charles appointed Prince Polignac to be his chief minister. There could be no pretence that Polignac had majority support in the Assembly, and his appointment roused new fears that the King meant to overturn the constitution. Charles had claimed:

I would rather hew wood than be a king under the conditions of the king of England.

He now seemed to be set on a collision course with his subjects. Polignac was not only an ultra, hated by the liberals; he claimed to have visions of the Virgin Mary, guiding his policy – and that was certain to inflame the anti-clericals. When the Assembly met early in 1830 it demanded Polignac's dismissal. Instead, Charles dismissed the Assembly. The new elections merely confirmed how much Charles and Polignac were out of touch even with the small electorate of propertied voters: 49 more opposition deputies were elected to the new Assembly. But the Assembly was not allowed to meet. Charles suspended the constitution and set down his intended solution to his difficulties in the *Ordinances of St Cloud* in July 1830 – stricter censorship and yet another new Assembly, to be elected this time by a tiny group of landowners who would be fewer than 0.1 per cent of the population. Even then there would be no guarantee that Charles would appoint ministers whom the Assembly supported. Such contempt for the constitution was intolerable to Frenchmen. Charles made virtually no attempt to organize the army in defence of his throne, and he abdicated scarcely more than a week after issuing the Ordinances. He retired to spend the rest of his life in religious devotion, settling in Prague in his closing years.

(b) The July Revolution of 1830

What persuaded Charles to abdicate was not so much the criticisms of middle-class liberals but the activities of the Paris working classes: they threw up barricades, waved the tricolour again and sang the Marseillaise. In three days they routed the army, which was weakened by mutinies and had no great enthusiasm for Bourbon rule anyway. At the last minute Charles offered to dismiss Polignac, but the gesture was now irrelevant. It was equally irrelevant that Charles went on to proclaim his grandson, the Count of Chambord, as the new King Henry V. Hardly anyone in Paris now wanted a Bourbon monarchy. Many of the workers were demanding a republic, remembering the First Republic of 1792, which had been set up when Louis XVI was deposed.

Memories of the 1790s alarmed the propertied. The bourgeoisie wanted a constitution, but they were uneasy about republicanism and they wanted no 'Equality' with the masses. It was also possible that the monarchies of Europe would intervene to restore the Bourbons if France were again to turn republican. On 30 July 1830 members of the bourgeoisie including Adolphe Thiers, at that time a newspaper editor, mounted a campaign to make Louis Philippe King of the French. He was willing to rule as a constitutional monarch and his aristocratic background as the Duke of Orleans would please foreign powers and right-wing opinion. To pacify the working classes he could also claim something of a revolutionary background. His father had called himself Philippe Égalité and joined the Jacobins soon after 1789 (though that had not saved him from the guillotine), and Louis himself had become a Jacobin and fought (briefly) against the Austrians in 1793. Since that time his fortunes had fluctuated, but he had always kept at least one foot on the side of liberalism. He had benefited from Charles X's compensation to the émigrés but he had remained a known critic of the ultras. Louis Philippe's strength in 1830 was that he was widely acceptable, though nowhere did he rouse any great enthusiasm. He won the consent, if not the hearts, of the Paris workers when he wrapped himself in the tricolour and received an embrace from Lafayette, a veteran of the American War of Independence and of the first French Revolution. Promising constitutional rule, Louis was sworn in as 'King of the French by the grace of God and the will of the people'. Thus the revolution of 1830 stopped in midstream. Louis Philippe's July Monarchy was a

Fig. 4.2 Honoré Daumier's representation of a Revolutionary Grocer *in France in 1830. Daumier welcomed the accession of Louis Philippe and so too, likely as not, did the Grocer*

compromise between royalism and republicanism, and between the objectives of various social groups. It was also a contradiction: Louis Philippe was 'Citizen King', half man of the people and half royalty. He would need all his skills in balancing to keep his new throne.

(c) Louis Philippe

The Assembly insisted that Louis Philippe should agree to an amended version of the Charter. It was not vastly different from that of 1814, but the number of voters was doubled. That still left the electorate extremely narrow, well below one per cent of the population and made up mainly of landowners and rich industrialists. The King was expected to choose ministers whom the Assembly supported, but support was often won by bribery rather than by genuine agreement on policy. Many of those who served Louis were motivated only by self-interest. They showed little interest in the problems of the masses, and their refusal to enlarge the electorate angered many of the middle classes too.

But there was no return to the extremism of Charles X and the influence of the Church grew much weaker, to the satisfaction of anti-clericals. The latter, and liberals generally, were pleased by Guizot's educational law of 1833, which provided for a network of state-aided primary and secondary schools which was among the most extensive in Europe. It was soon evident, however, that the government was sadly lacking in ideas for further reforms.

There were many uprisings during the reign of Louis Philippe, before the revolution of 1848 which overthrew him. Some were the attempts of dissenting groups to change the political system. Legitimists, the supporters of the Bourbons, regarded the King as a usurper, and as early as 1832 they attempted to raise a revolt in La Vendée. Disciples of Napoleon wanted a more exciting ruler and the Emperor's nephew, Louis Napoleon, twice tried to seize power in 1836 and 1840 (see page 94). Determined republicans opposed any monarchy and kept up a chorus of dissent. Their outbursts sometimes assumed dangerous proportions, as they did in 1834 in Lyons and Paris when they were fiercely put down by Thiers, at that time Minister of the Interior. Such uprisings were dangerous when they coincided with mass unrest, brought about by harsh social conditions in the industrial areas. Louis Philippe had had to face the first serious rioting of workers in 1831 when an economic recession and unemployment caused bitterness, especially in Lyons. But his response and that of his ministers to the social problems of industrialization was essentially negative. Disturbances were put down, but hardly anything was done to improve the conditions which had provoked them. A feeble factory law of 1841 had little effect since it included no provisions for inspecting the factories. In general the government based its policy on *laisser-faire* – not interfering with the activities of employers, businessmen and speculators. There was admiration for the calm with which Louis Philippe endured the frequent attempts to assassinate him, but in his unconcern about France's social problems his calm amounted to inertia.

Like many of his contemporaries, the King thought that the answer to problems and to unrest was repression. Censorship returned in 1834. Trade unions were hampered, political clubs harassed and demands for a larger electorate and social reform stifled. From 1840 Francois Guizot was the King's most influential minister and he dedicated himself to a policy of laisser-faire combined with repression. This permitted economic development. The first French railway dated from 1828 and there was vigorous railway-construction in Louis Philippe's reign and vigorous expansion in industry. But the lack of government supervision led to financial speculation, corrupt dealings and the collapse of the stock exchange in 1847. It also led to exploitation, brutality and squalor in the industrial centres. And it led to mounting anger against a government which had nothing to offer to the mass of its subjects.

Louis Philippe's personal interest seemed to lie mainly in accumulating money and estates. Other Frenchmen supplied the ideas in which the government was conspicuously lacking. The Count of St Simon emphasized the importance of productive labour and of industrialization, and he deplored the

PUNCH TURNED OUT OF FRANCE!

"I have this moment, in a half-tempest, arrived from Boulogne—thrust from the port by the point of the sword. Yes ; it is true— *Punch* is no longer to be admitted into France."

Fig. 4.3 Louis Philippe soon brought back censorship. In 1843, Louis Philippe's government banned copies of Punch

regime of Louis Philippe which was based on the upper middle classes and the nobility. St Simon's goal was, he said, 'the founding of social organization in the interest of the majority'. These ideas were part of a developing socialist movement. Louis Blanc, a writer and socialist, asserted that human beings had a right to work, and in *L'Organisation du Travail* (1839) argued in favour of the state control of industry, to guarantee employment and a fitting dignity for labour. Many more French writers developed these and other socialist ideas, preaching to the deaf ears of the government the need for a social conscience, a social policy and a more democratic political system. Louis Napoleon managed to combine elements of socialism and democracy with memories of imperial grandeur, suggesting (though not perhaps convincingly) that a new Napoleonic regime would fulfil all aspirations. He wrote in *Des Idées Napoléoniennes* (1839):

The Napoleonic Idea is not one of war, but a social, industrial, commercial idea, and one which concerns all mankind.

Louis Napoleon had genuine proposals to make for curing unemployment, improving the lives of the working classes and spreading prosperity more widely, but doubts remained when he argued that Bonapartists were lovers of parliamentary rule. The working classes were impressed by his concern for their welfare but not yet to the point of fighting for his cause. Louis Philippe managed to draw the wrong conclusions from the Bonapartist propaganda. Instead of developing a reforming social policy he completed the building of the Arc de Triomphe and had Napoleon I's remains brought home to France. Writing his Memoirs twenty years later, Guizot showed a similar inability to grasp the point that what was needed was a progressive social policy. He insisted that Louis Philippe's government had been a liberal custodian of freedom:

The policy which we . . . adopted and adhered to was principally supported by the preponderating influence of the middle classes; an influence recognized and accepted in the general interest of the country, and subjected to all the tests and all the influences of the general liberty.

It seemed by 1848 that the King and his ministers were living in a different world from that of the majority of Frenchmen.

An English traveller in France wrote in 1849:

Fig. 4.4 The return to France in 1840 of the remains of Napoleon I did nothing to help Louis Philippe's régime. Louis Philippe was not a ruler of the stature of Napoleon. A contemporary print

A thirst of military renown and acquisition by force of arms is strong in the minds of a large section of the population . . . who have the recollection of the brilliant career of Napoleon.

Lamartine, a poet and moderate member of the Assembly, had remarked of Louis Philippe's foreign policy, some ten years earlier, that France was 'bored'. Although the King had helped the Belgians to consolidate their independence shortly after his accession (see Section 3.3(*d*)), his foreign policy aroused little excitement and it produced little 'renown' or 'acquisition'. He disappointed his romantic subjects by prudently refusing to help Polish and Italian rebels in 1831, and when he gave cautious support to liberalism in Portugal and Spain in 1834 (see Section 8.2) he did so, as in Belgium, under what appeared to be British supervision. Worse was to follow in the eyes of those who thirsted for glory. Having encouraged Mehemet Ali, the French deserted him (see pages 129–30) and, at the same time, lost British goodwill. Louis Phillippe quarrelled with Britain again in 1843 over Tahiti, having first allowed French missionaries to go there to compete with British missionaries, and then having made Tahiti a French protectorate. The French went on to arrest the British consul, only to be forced to release him and pay compensation. In 1846 Louis seemed at last to have outwitted the British over the affair of the marriage of Isabella of Spain (see Section 8.2) but the circumstances hardly fitted in with the French concept of honour. There was a certain shabbiness about the King's foreign policy which was in line with the corruption at home. Lovers of 'military renown' thought the policy dull, and liberals were alarmed that the quarrels with Britain pushed France towards the despotic monarchies to the east. But above all Louis Philippe seemed to have no grand strategy, as if his foreign policy was as lacking in ideas as his domestic policy. It was small consolation for Frenchmen that he defeated the Algerians and began the colonization of north Africa, following up an initiative begun shortly before he became king.

Inglorious as it was, Louis Philippe's foreign policy would not in itself have brought about his downfall. The majority of Frenchmen had more immediate interests. Crop failures in 1846 led to expensive food, and they helped to bring about a recession in industry since there was less money to spend on buying factory-made goods. The recession coincided with a financial crisis and scandals about corruption. Middle-class liberals redoubled their efforts to enlarge the electorate and to improve the quality of government. During 1847 they held reform banquets – substantial dinners followed by political speeches – combining pleasure with business. As the year went on the speeches became more radical, and some began to include demands for universal suffrage and for a republic. Alexandre Ledru-Rollin, a spokesman for popular democracy and sweeping reform, became involved in them, and newspapers defied the censorship to add to the mounting excitement. By the beginning of 1848 both Guizot and those who had begun the banquets feared that things were getting out of hand. Guizot banned the banquet which had been arranged in Paris for

Fig. 4.5 Daumier soon became disillusioned with Louis Philippe, representing him in this cartoon as showering his people with coins. The King's interest in money was no substitute for reform and for progressive ideas

22 February, but he was unable to stop the crowds who gathered in the streets on that day. They built a few barricades and shouted for reform, and Guizot resigned on 23 February. Later that day troops fired on the crowds outside the ministry for foreign affairs, and the street demonstrations which had begun light-heartedly at once turned ugly. Faced with what appeared to be an armed uprising, Louis Philippe abdicated without a struggle on 24 February. He left the throne to his grandson, the Count of Paris, who was ten years old. Before the day was out, the Count was swept aside in a wave of republican enthusiasm and a provisional government was proclaimed:

> A reactionary and oligarchical government has just been overthrown by the heroism of the people of Paris. The government has fled, leaving behind it a trail of blood that forbids it ever to retrace its steps. . . . The provisional government wishes to establish a republic.

There was no movement either in Paris or in the provinces to support the monarchy. Louis Philippe retired quietly to England and died in Surrey a couple of years later. Narrowly based and insensitive to change, his govern-

Fig. 4.6 Caricatures of Louis Philippe by Charles Philippon. The King became a pear – to the French the symbol of a dullard

ment had certainly been 'reactionary and oligarchical'. The King himself had commanded little respect: lighting his own fire, dressing like the middle classes, complete with umbrella, and shaking hands in the streets, he was mercilessly caricatured in *Punch* as a sort of pear. But his main fault was neglect rather than cruelty. Although he had for eighteen years put down all uprisings, sometimes ruthlessly, he abdicated to avoid further bloodshed when he at last recognized that France was outgrowing a political system based only on a tiny minority of wealthy conservatives. But the King's abdication was not the end of France's problems. Power would now be shared more widely, but it remained to be decided how widely (see Section 6.1).

4.3 Russia 1801–55

(a) Alexander I

The nearest that Russia came to any sort of elected assembly in the first half of the nineteenth century was in a programme for reform, which was drawn up by Michael Speransky, one of Alexander I's advisers. The programme roused such an outcry that the Tsar dismissed Speransky in 1812 and forced him to spend some time in exile. 1812 was the year when Napoleon occupied Moscow and when the city went up in flames. Alexander considered this event a turning-point in his life:

> The fire of Moscow lit up my soul. I then got to know God and became another man.

The Tsar meant that his enthusiasm for Christianity was reinforced, but it seemed that his enthusiasm for repression was similarly boosted. At the beginning of his reign, he had made administrative reforms, encouraged education and opened three new universities, and he had considered the abolition of serfdom. The serfs were not freed, however. Alexander got no further than to issue a modest *ukase* (decree) in 1803, to permit landowners to free their serfs if they felt so inclined. Very few did. There was little political change and little social change in Russia during the Tsar's reign from 1801 to 1825. He showed something of his alleged leanings towards liberalism in his rule of Finland, where he was the Grand Duke from 1809, in his rule of Poland, where he was the King from 1815 (see Section 3.3(*e*)), and in some lightening of the burden on the serfs in the Baltic provinces, but the Russian people saw little of his liberalism. He himself complained that the obstacles to change were too great in Russia. The vested interests of noblemen and the Church, administrative weaknesses, the size of the Empire and the ignorance of its subjects, were certainly formidable obstacles, but Alexander himself was irresolute. In any case, having dismissed Speransky, he began to equate Christianity with preserving the existing system, and he relied increasingly on the most reactionary advisers, such as General Arakcheyev.

Much of the earlier part of the reign was spent in wars against the French. At the peace settlement of 1814–15 Alexander was one of the leading European statesmen and the author of the Holy Alliance (see Section 1.3). He devoted much of his energy after 1815 to trying to preserve the existing order in Europe by means of the Congress 'System' (see Section 2.2), but he had energy to spare for suppressing dissent in Russia too. French revolutionary ideas had reached Russia, brought back by soldiers who had fought in Europe and learned about constitutions and even republicanism. The injustices, cruelties, the primitive divisions of Russian society, and the mass ignorance of the people, now seemed intolerable compared with other parts of Europe. A few secret societies were founded to work for the end of serfdom and for a constitution in Russia, but membership was extremely small and they caused few problems for the government. Colonel Pavel Pestel was one of the most dedicated rebels, who became convinced that an armed uprising to set up a republic was the only solution to Russia's problems. He later took part in the Decembrist conspiracy. But others hoped that Alexander could be persuaded to grant representative government. They were wrong.

In pursuit of holiness rather than constitutionalism Alexander set up a Ministry for Spiritual Affairs. This Ministry, searching out ideas which were not consistent with the scriptures, closed universities and harassed liberal-minded teachers in the same way that liberals were rooted out in Germany as the result of the Carlsbad Decrees. Alexander thus settled for stagnation and the opposition was much too weak to overthrow him. When he died he left Russia much as he had found it, with a tottering economy, a creaking administration, a feudal society and a Church sunk in medieval ritual and superstition.

(b) The Decembrist Conspiracy, 1825

The death of Alexander I in December 1825 encouraged a rising of army officers and disgruntled noblemen, known as the Decembrists. They took advantage of confusion about the succession to put into operation the plans they had been making for a coup in the following spring. Alexander's brother Constantine had already renounced the throne in order to marry beneath his rank, though a younger brother, Nicholas, seemed in no hurry to take his place. In the interval between Alexander's death and the oath of allegiance to Nicholas the Decembrists hastily planned their military uprising. They were divided about their aims. Some, like Pestel, were expecting to assassinate Nicholas and set up a republic. Others, like Nikita Muravyov, expected to force the Tsar to agree to constitutional government. They were betrayed by informers, but might still have succeeded in achieving something had their mutiny not been handicapped by last-minute desertions and muddled orders. In St Petersburg, the mutineers were dispersed by loyal troops. Elsewhere, an attempt to seize Kiev ended equally ingloriously. Pestel and four others were hanged and many of the conspirators went to prison or to exile in Siberia.

Reporting to Canning, the British representative in St Petersburg observed:

> The late conspiracy failed for want of management, and want of head to direct it, and was too premature to answer any good purpose, but I think the seeds are sown which one day will produce important consequences.

The short-term consequence of the Decembrist revolt was to convince Nicholas, if conviction were needed, that liberal ideas were dangerous and must be suppressed. In the long term the revolt helped to inspire new dissenting movements in Russia and eventually to persuade some revolutionaries, among them Lenin, that revolution was work for professionals, not amateurs, and that it needed thorough preparation.

(c) Nicholas I

Alexander Herzen left Russia in 1847, one of many of the country's intellectuals who fled to the west. In *The Development of Revolutionary Ideas in Russia*, he described the Russia of Nicholas I:

> Russia always seems so tranquil that one has difficulty in believing that something is happening there. Few people know what happens beneath the shroud with which the

Fig. 4.7 The Winter Palace, St Petersburg. Though Russia was in many ways backward, the tsars more than matched other European rulers in the grandeur of their surroundings. An early-nineteenth-century print

government covers the corpses, the stains of blood, the military executions, while maintaining hypocritically and arrogantly that there is neither blood nor corpse beneath the shroud.

Almost all the achievements of Nicholas I within his Empire were concerned with strengthening his despotism. Chief among them was the development of the Personal Chancellory of His Imperial Majesty, the Third Section of which was a ferocious police system under General Benckendorff. What little progress had been made in education under Alexander I was checked by reorganization of schools, to ensure that the few children of the masses who received an education should not receive more than an elementary one. More advanced education was confined to the children of landowners and officials, but since this continued to produce critics of the government, Nicholas embarked on a new purge of the universities after 1848. Count Uvarov, the Tsar's Minister of Education, who once remarked – so it was alleged – that he would only sleep peacefully when literature ceased to be written, was found to be too liberal and was dismissed. It was Uvarov who had given the regime a slogan: 'Orthodoxy, Autocracy, Nationality'. Each word provided good reason for persecuting some dissenting group – religious freethinkers, political freethinkers and those, like Poles and Jews, who were not adequately Russian.

Perhaps because there were more than seven hundred peasant uprisings during his reign, Nicholas made some small changes with regard to serfdom. In 1842, he forbade the breaking up of families of serfs and declared it illegal to sell serfs except as part of the property of an estate. (A peasant in 1917 recollected to a revolutionary assembly that, during serfdom, his grandfather had once been exchanged for a greyhound.) At the same time, serfs on royal estates received more equal shares of the lands set aside for them, and some local services were begun, to protect their health, improve their knowledge of agriculture and give a basic education to some of their children. But Nicholas made few other concessions to the nineteenth century, and serfdom itself remained.

In foreign policy, Nicholas combined a negative enthusiasm for preserving existing monarchies with a more ambiguous enthusiasm for meddling in the affairs of the Ottoman Empire. He was powerless to suppress the revolutions of 1830 in France and in Belgium, in the way that he suppressed that in Poland (see Section 3.3(e)), but he met Metternich at Münchengrätz in 1833 to agree on a course of joint action if the Poles should give any further trouble. A month later they both signed an agreement with Frederick William III of Prussia, to assist any ruler who asked for their help against liberal rebels – a pledge which Nicholas stood ready to fulfil in 1848. The Münchengrätz agreement also committed the Tsar and Metternich to seeking the survival of the Ottoman Empire, although Nicholas had already been at war with the Turks in 1828–9 and was to go to war with them again in 1853. On the surface it seemed inconsistent that Nicholas should have helped Greeks (see Section 3.3(b)), Serbs and the people of Moldavia and Wallachia to break away from the Ottoman Empire, and yet in 1833 to have been supporting that Empire. Just before the meeting at Münchengrätz he had indeed signed the Treaty of Unkiar Skelessi with the Sultan, pledging help against Mehemet Ali. But we will consider the problems of the Ottoman Empire and the Tsar's involvement in them in a later Unit (see Sections 8.3 and 8.4).

The European revolutions of 1848, one of the earliest of which had ousted Louis Philippe, did not extend to the Russian Empire. A few Russian romantics eagerly made unrealistic plans to raise a great rebellion among the country's apathetic peasants, and Nicholas Speshnev, a young landowner, dreamed of a force of almost half a million men with which to overthrow the system. From the outset spies kept the authorities informed and the plot failed miserably. The Russian masses were capable of sudden outbursts of anger as the numerous disturbances of the reign showed, but organized revolution was out of the question. For generations still to come, the Russian peasantry remained largely unresponsive to the efforts of revolutionaries to increase their political understanding. Russia's intellectuals, on the other hand, were aware and critical of the country's shortcomings. The young Fedor Dostoievsky, later to become one of the world's foremost novelists, was one of Speshnev's fellow-conspirators in 1848 and he was exiled to Siberia for four years in punishment. Dostoievsky became a supporter of the tsarist system in the reign of Alexander II, but his early liberalism was typical of that of many educated Russians. They eagerly debated Russia's past, present and future, and many went to prison or into exile. They kept alive the spirit of protest throughout Nicholas I's autocratic reign, and they still defied him when he intensified his campaign against independent thought after 1848. But it was only the romantics among them, like the young Dostoievsky, who believed there could be any immediate solution to Russia's problems. Nicholas himself, however, began to suspect that his negative policy could not endure for ever. When he died in 1855 Russia's feeble showing in the Crimean War (see Section 8.4) was already revealing the bankruptcy of his system, and expectation was growing that a new tsar would have to make changes. Writing of Russian history soon after Nicholas had become the Tsar, Peter Tchadayev observed:

> Nothing of what was happening in Europe reached us. . . . While the whole world was building anew, we created nothing: we remained crouched in our hovels of log and thatch. In a word, we had no part in the new destinies of mankind.

The authorities declared Tchadayev insane, yet there was still much truth in what he had written when Nicholas I died, a generation later. Except in the studies and private rooms of writers and of intellectuals generally, there was little evidence in Russia that the economic, social and political forces which caused regular upheavals in France, and which were spreading elsewhere in Europe, had yet penetrated into the realms of the Romanovs.

Further Reading

Almedingen, E. M.: *The Emperor Alexander I.* Bodley Head (London, 1964).
Lincoln, W. B.: *Nicholas I, Emperor and Autocrat.* Allen Lane (Harmondsworth, 1977).
Randell, K.: *Monarchy, Republic and Empire, 1814–70.* Edward Arnold (London, 1986).

Documentary

Collins, I.: *Government and Society in France 1814–48.* Edward Arnold (London, 1970).

Exercises

1. Using Section 4.1, list the main differences between France and Russia in the years 1815 to 1850 under the following headings: The Economy; The Society; The Political System; The Activities of Revolutionaries.
2. 'The illusion was shattered in August 1829' (page 59). What is meant here by 'the illusion'? Why, and how, did Charles X then lose his throne?
3. Study the cartoons in this Unit which concern Louis Philippe. State what opinion of the King *each* cartoon expresses, and explain why Louis Philippe was depicted in this way.
4. 'Inglorious as it was, Louis Philippe's foreign policy would not in itself have brought about his downfall' (page 65). Why then did Louis Philippe's downfall occur?
5. Referring to the definitions in the Glossary, explain how far it would be fitting to describe (*a*) Alexander I as 'a liberal', and (*b*) Nicholas I as 'a reactionary'.
6. Explain in your own words what Peter Tchadayev meant by the words quoted on this page and show how well they described Russia in the years 1815 to 1855.
7. How far does this Unit suggest that the masses were as much neglected by the authorities in France as they were in Russia?

Revolutionary Upheaval 1848–9

5.1 Revolutionary Forces

The upheavals which caused 1848 to become known as the Year of Revolutions began in Sicily in January. The map on page 75 shows that revolutionary outbreaks followed during the next twenty months in many parts of Europe, and the last flames of revolt were not extinguished until the end of August 1849, when the Austrians reconquered Venice.

Various factors combined to bring about the widespread upheavals of 1848–9. The labouring poor were embittered by economic distress (see Section 3.5). A succession of poor harvests led to hunger among the peasants, and the scarcity of food led to higher prices which ill-paid industrial workers could hardly afford. The price of food left less money available to buy the products of the factories, and this led to increased unemployment. Peasants and workers seldom had reserves on which to fall back in times of crop failure and depression. They were already resentful against a system which kept them in conditions of permanent hardship, and further distress inflamed their anger. They demanded changes which would lessen their misery, but there was little agreement among the masses as to what those changes should be or as to how they would be achieved. Rebellion for the masses was a matter of protesting against hardship, and for making a variety of miscellaneous demands which varied from one locality to another. Industrial workers wanted better pay, shorter hours, and less squalid living conditions. Peasants wanted the removal of feudal obligations, where they still survived, more land, and a better quality of life. Middle-class liberals and nationalists, on the other hand, had more specific political objectives (see Unit Three). They wanted a share in political power, and the removal of foreign authority. They were still inspired by a romantic belief in revolution as a means for bringing about change. They looked back to the French Revolution of 1789, and they were further excited when the French again overthrew a king in February 1848 (see page 66 and Section 6.1). Each revolutionary outbreak tended to encourage another and, in the first months of 1848, it seemed that the existing order was crumbling fast.

The strength of the revolutions of 1848–9 lay in their number. Rulers seemed to have no alternative but hastily to grant concessions. But it soon became clear that the revolutions were unco-ordinated, and this was their weakness. Not only was there a lack of co-ordination between the various revolutionary areas: there was often a lack of co-ordination between the

Fig. 5.1 A caricature of German society by W. Scholz, 1849. From bottom to top: the workers, the middle classes, the nobility, the princes – each pressed down by those above. It was a weakness of the revolutions of 1848 that the middle classes had little enthusiasm for enlisting the support of the workers

revolutionaries even within a single area. Within individual cities, such as Paris, Berlin and Vienna, the revolutionaries were commonly disunited. The aims of the workers were not the aims of the middle classes, and opinion within each protest group was often divided. Thus, the challenge to the existing order rapidly became a fragmented, almost haphazard, collection of challenges. For this reason, and above all because armies generally remained loyal to existing governments, the outcome of the revolutions was bitterly disappointing to Italians, Germans and the subjects of the Austrian Empire.

5.2 The Revolutions: a Regional Survey

(a) France

Although Louis Philippe lost his throne in February 1848, the outcome of the revolution did not fulfil the ambitions of many of the Paris workers. The Second Republic was set up, but before its constitution was published in

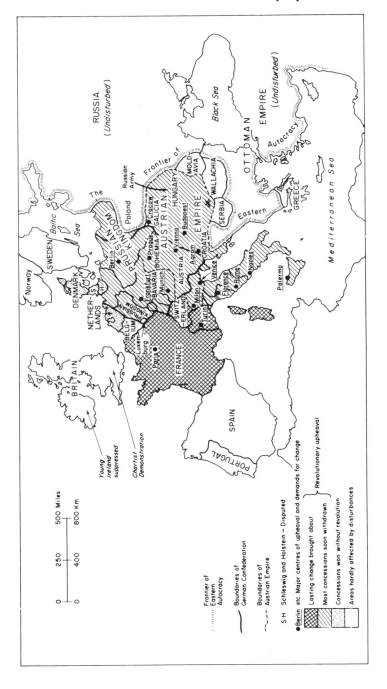

Fig. 5.2 Revolutions and Upheaval 1848–9

November, the workers had been routed in a fierce struggle for power which left the propertied classes in control of France. In December Louis Napoleon was elected the Prince-President of the Republic. Four years later he proclaimed himself the Emperor. (The history of France from 1848 to 1871 will be considered in Unit Six.)

(b) Italy

On New Year's Day 1848 the citizens of Milan made a resolution to give up smoking. Their intention was to strike a blow at the finances of the Austrian administration of Lombardy, which relied on revenue from the sales of tobacco. Austrian troops were promptly issued with cigars, to puff smoke into the faces of the Milanese patriots. The Milanese called the soldiers 'German pigs' and tobacco riots broke out. They were easily suppressed, but blood was shed and Radetsky, the Austrian commander, took the precaution of increasing the military garrison. For the moment order was restored in Lombardy, but the first blows of 1848 had been struck.

A week later, there was a more serious uprising in Sicily against the repressive and neglectful government of Ferdinand II, King of the Two Sicilies. The demand of the Sicilians was for a constitution, but the rebellion was supported by bandits and impoverished peasants. Fearful that the rebellion would spread to the mainland, Ferdinand agreed to constitutional reform, but he haggled about the details and Sicily declared itself independent in April. For a time Ferdinand ruled Naples with an assembly and Sicily ruled itself, but the tide eventually turned and, by May 1849, the King was able to dismiss the Neapolitan parliament and reconquer the Sicilians. Ruthlessly bombarding Messina, Ferdinand earned the nickname 'King Bomba'. Having won the military victory he committed himself to the work he did best, hounding and punishing those subjects who had dared to challenge his autocracy.

The experience of other Italians was similar to that of the subjects of Ferdinand II. Revolts occurred in quick succession, prompted by the news of the rising of the Sicilians, the fall of Louis Philippe, and the resignation of Metternich in Vienna (13 March 1848). Staggering under the shock, rulers granted constitutions – Leopold of Tuscany in February, Charles Albert of Piedmont-Sardinia and Pius IX in the Papal States in March. These three rulers had already moved cautiously towards reform in 1847, whetting the appetite of the liberals who now wanted more. The rulers of Parma and Modena, however, preferred to flee rather than make concessions. All these changes now focused attention on Austria, which was still seen as the main barrier to progress throughout Italy. Before the end of March 1848 the Milanese took revenge on Radetsky and drove his troops from the city; at the same time Daniele Manin led a revolt to drive the Austrians from Venice, where he proclaimed the Republic of St Mark. It now began to seem that nationalist aims could be achieved as well as those of the liberals, and that the Austrians could be expelled from Italian soil. Charles Albert declared war on

Austria and marched into Lombardy. Early in April the Piedmontese won their first victory against the Austrians, at Goito.

Enthusiasm for the crusade against Austria brought Charles Albert volunteers from all over Italy. Regular troops were also sent from Tuscany and Naples, where the rulers were forced by their subjects to declare war on the Habsburgs. Charles Albert hoped for the blessing of Pius IX, and praised the Pope whom God had given to Italy. But Pius asserted that war against the Catholic Austrians was:

> altogether alien from our counsels, inasmuch as We, albeit unworthy, are upon earth the viceregent of Him that is the Author of Peace and the Lover of Charity.

Even so, Pius allowed both Papal troops and civilian volunteers to join the Piedmontese. His refusal to give more positive support, however, discredited him in the eyes of those who had hoped for an Italy united under Papal leadership (see page 50). It seemed that a union of Italians, at least in northern Italy, would now be achieved under the leadership of Piedmont-Sardinia. Charles Albert had forces which were at least the equal in manpower of those of Radetsky. Radetsky, in the meantime, had retreated to the Quadrilateral (four fortresses, on the border of Lombardy-Venetia: Peschiera and Mantua on the River Mincio; Verona and Legnago on the River Adige). It was this obstacle which Charles Albert attacked at the end of May, capturing Peschiera.

That was the Piedmontese King's last major success. Charles Albert was hesitant. His forces were a patchwork collection of various units, and – apart from fighting the Austrians – the aims of the campaign were far from clear. In July Radetsky hit back and routed the Piedmontese at Custozza. Charles Albert retreated, considered for a moment trying to hold Milan, but then abandoned it and asked for peace. The superficial unity of purpose, which the Italians had achieved only a short time earlier, now vanished. Except in Venice, where Manin held out, the Austrian rule of Lombardy-Venetia was restored, and Italians were left to argue about who was to blame for their frustration. Much criticism, especially that made by republicans, was heaped on Charles Albert. With little hope of success he again declared war on Austria in March 1849, entrusting command of Piedmont's troops to a Polish officer, Adalbert Chrzanowsky. The campaign lasted less than a fortnight, and when his army was routed at Novara, unable to free even Milan from the Austrians, Charles Albert abdicated in favour of his son, Victor Emmanuel II.

In November 1848, Pius IX was forced to flee from Rome by a new popular uprising, which was triggered off by the assassination of his chief minister, Count Rossi. The Pope took refuge at Gaeta, in Naples. In February 1849 the Roman assembly declared the city a republic, and in March the Romans welcomed the veteran republican Mazzini to lead them. The revolutionary spirit was thus kept alive a little longer in Rome and in Venice, but elsewhere the old rulers and the old systems were steadily restored. Constitutional rule survived only in

Piedmont. Without foreign help Italians had proved no match for the professional Austrian army, led by Radetsky. But the outcome of the revolutions had also revealed the weakness which came from disunity. Italians not only lacked the unity to free and unite their country; they lacked the unity to force anything but temporary concessions from the rulers of the individual states.

For several months, the Roman Republic was defended heroically by Garibaldi, who had returned to Italy in 1848 (see page 50). The first attack came from King Bomba, who was now full of enthusiasm for the restoration of the old order. A more dangerous threat to the Republic came from France, where Louis Napoleon sought to win popularity with the Catholics by restoring the Pope and, by persuading the Pope to agree to a constitution, hoped to retain the goodwill of French liberals. Louis Napoleon's mind, Palmerston was later to comment, was 'as full of schemes as a warren is full of rabbits'.

Louis Napoleon had taken part in an anti-papal rebellion in 1831, but his accession to power in France seemed to have made him forgetful of youthful romanticism. Garibaldi fought off the first French attack on Rome and forced General Oudinot to send for reinforcements, and he continued to keep the Neapolitans at bay. But eventual defeat was unavoidable, and the further defence of the city became impossible at the end of June 1849. Pius IX returned, comforted by the protection of a French garrison. Whatever might have been Louis Napoleon's original intentions, Pius saw no reason to restrict his own despotism now that the opposition had been crushed, and no constitution was granted. Garibaldi had made a fighting withdrawal from Rome, leading what was left of his forces northwards, and intending to join Manin in the continuing defence of the Republic in Venice. He was too late. There too the republicans were overwhelmed and forced to surrender to a siege by the Austrians. Mazzini, Garibaldi and Manin were all driven into exile, to await new opportunities to battle for the freedom of their oppressed native land.

(c) The German Confederation

It seemed, at the end of 1847, that Metternich's grip on the German Confederation, and that of the princes on the individual states within it, were still fairly secure (see Section 2.3(b) and pages 40 and 50–53). Frederick William IV permitted a Prussian Diet to meet early in 1847, but dismissed it almost at once (see page 30). Elsewhere economic distress caused rioting during the year, and there was spasmodic pressure in several states for liberal reform and for some movement towards national unity, but there were still only few concessions. In Bavaria protest was mainly concerned with the ageing King Ludwig's relations with the dancer and adventuress, Lola Montez, whom he created Countess Landsfeld. Ludwig was forced to abdicate in March 1848.

Baden was the first German state to respond in 1848 to the revolutions in Italy and in France. A diet already existed in the state, and new liberal concessions, including trial by jury, were quickly extracted from the Grand Duke. Nationalists in Baden then made preparations for setting up a

FIRST ATTACK OF THE FRENCH TROOPS AT ROME NEAR THE PORTA CAVELLEGIERE.

Fig. 5.3 French troops marching on Rome, 1849. The French intervention on behalf of Pius IX proved too much even for Garibaldi

parliament for the whole of Germany. Events were now moving quickly in the Bund. The fall of Metternich in Vienna (see page 83) encouraged all German liberals and nationalists. There was a rising in Berlin and Frederick William rapidly made concessions. With disturbances in almost all of the German capitals, princes everywhere scrambled to pacify their subjects. Constitutions suddenly became fashionable, and hardly any prince dared to obstruct the preparations for a new all-German parliament.

The events in Berlin provide an example of the mood of March 1848. Open-air meetings, abuse hurled at the troops of the city garrison, and a mounting clamour for reform, frightened Frederick William into agreeing to summon a new Prussian Diet. But the demonstrations went on and, on 16 March, the troops killed several rioters outside the Opera House. The King declared his cautious commitment to an examination of the German question and national unity, but the clashes increased in violence on 18 March and barricades were erected. The King appealed to his people:

> Return to peace; remove the barricades which are still standing; and send to me men filled with the genuine ancient spirit of Berlin, speaking words which are seemly to your King. . . . Listen to the paternal voice of your King, ye inhabitants of my true and beautiful Berlin; and forget the past . . . for the sake of that great future . . . which is dawning upon Prussia, and through Prussia on all Germany.

The Berliners were not impressed and Frederick William had to watch a

Fig. 5.4 A cartoonist's comment on the behaviour of Frederick William IV, the King of Prussia. His appeal to his beloved Berliners in March 1848 soon gave way to a more traditional hostility towards those who demanded reform

parade of the bodies of the dead beneath his balcony. On 21 March, imitating Louis Philippe in 1830, he walked in the streets, wearing the black, red and gold sash of a united Germany. But a few days later he retired to Potsdam, weary of this unusual contact with his people. Like other princes in 1848, Frederick William then waited for the storm to pass, and in December he was able to dismiss the Prussian Diet and regain most of his former authority, while preserving the semblance of a constitution in a much weakened form.

On 31 March 1848, however, a preliminary meeting of German liberals began in Frankfurt. This was the *Vorparlament*, whose members, from many German states, intended to arrange for the meeting of an all-German parliament. They busied themselves with answering the question of what was 'Germany', and drew boundaries which included Austria and Bohemia. They arranged constituencies and gave the vote to all adult males, and generally prepared the way for a meeting in May of a German parliament of over 800 members. When that parliament met it quickly drafted a German constitution and nominated Archduke John, an Austrian Habsburg, as head of state. John then proceeded to appoint a government, answerable to himself, for the new Germany. It seemed that, on paper, a united Germany now existed, but a vast number of problems remained unsolved. Although the German princes either accepted or ignored these developments at Frankfurt, they felt no commitment to them.

The Frankfurt Parliament was dominated by professional men and the middle classes. Its members included over two hundred lawyers but only one peasant, a representative from Silesia. Trade was well represented, but there were few industrialists and farmers in the Parliament, and there were hardly any representatives at all from the lower classes. Long-winded speeches and academic debate consumed valuable time, although what was urgent was to consolidate the Parliament's authority, and to settle key questions about the relationships between a united democratic Germany and the power of its individual princes. Vital decisions were postponed, while many liberal theories were debated and a general Declaration of Rights was drafted. Archduke John and his government could be no more than stop-gaps, but the parliamentarians were baffled as to what should come next. A republic would be unlikely to survive the anger of Habsburgs, Hohenzollerns and the princes in general. But the others would be jealous if one prince were chosen to lead Germany, even if such a prince could be found. The Austrian Habsburgs showed no enthusiasm for a united Germany, and they themselves ruled an Empire, much of which was non-German. Frederick William of Prussia seemed to be the obvious choice as the German leader, Prussia being second only to Austria in power, but the Prussian King inspired little confidence in anybody. The dilemma remained at the end of 1848, and by then it was already too late. Reaction had set in in almost every state, and the princes were busy dismantling constitutions and restoring their own authority. Almost in desperation, the Frankfurt Parliament took the plunge in the last days of March 1849; they invited Frederick William to become the Emperor of the Germans.

Fig. 5.5 An East German stamp of 1953, commemorating the German patriots of the Revolution of 1848

Frederick William had shown his hostility to liberalism by watering down the Prussian constitution several months earlier. He had also shown his limitations as a German nationalist over the affair of Schleswig and Holstein. Frederick VII, the King of Denmark, ruled these northern states as their Duke. Anxious to avoid complications about the succession when he died, he proposed to incorporate them in the Kingdom of Denmark. Schleswig had a partly German population, and the population of Holstein was wholly German; Frederick's German subjects rebelled in March 1848. At that time, Frederick William was eager to please his Prussian subjects. He appointed himself the protector of German interests in the Duchies, and Prussia went to war with Denmark. When it met in May, the Frankfurt Parliament confirmed Frederick William as the agent of German nationalism. The Prussian King was already worried about international disapproval of his activities, and he felt no commitment to being the agent of the Frankfurt Parliament. In August 1848, he abandoned the war, and the problem of Schleswig and Holstein was left to drag on (see Section 7.3(*b*)). Now that he had the chance to become the German emperor, Frederick William again failed to rise to the occasion. In a vague reply, he suggested that he could not accept the crown without the approval of his fellow-princes, a crown 'from the gutter'. The Parliament took this to be a refusal, as indeed it was. Some weeks later, Frederick William clarified his attitude in a proclamation which was uncompromising:

> I was not able to return a favourable reply to the offer of a crown . . . because the Assembly has not the right, without the consent of German governments, to bestow the crown . . . and . . . because they offered the crown upon condition that I would accept a constitution.

He went on to declare the members of the Assembly:

> in league with the terrorists . . . fighting the battle of godlessness, perjury and robbery, and kindling a war against monarchy.

This was the real voice of Frederick William IV.

The Frankfurt Parliament could go no further. It had little support from the masses, no army, and no solution for the insuperable problems of how Germany was to be organized. The Habsburg government ordered the Austrian representatives to withdraw from the Parliament in April 1849. Prussians were ordered home a month later. Some members of the Parliament moved to Stuttgart, but most went home in disillusionment, and those who persisted in meeting were chased away by soldiers. The experiment was over and the old German Bund was restored shortly afterwards. A few splutterings of protest still occurred during 1849. There was a revolt in Saxony in May, quickly followed by another in Baden. These and other outbreaks were put down by Prussian troops. Prussian troops were also involved in another brief and inconclusive conflict with Denmark about Schleswig and Holstein. But the principal conflict which followed the disturbances in Germany in 1848–9 took the form of a diplomatic tussle between Prussia and Austria.

In May 1849 Frederick William, perhaps prompted by the possibilities which the offer of the German crown had revealed to him, set up a League of Princes (a *Fürstenbund* or *Dreikönigenbund*) with the rulers of Hanover and Saxony. The apparent intention was to create a union of German states at least in north Germany. A few other princes, including the Elector of Hesse-Cassel, joined the League. Austria disapproved, making it clear that the Habsburgs still preferred the weak German Bund. Saxony and Hanover withdrew. The Prussian King persisted, however, and summoned a new German assembly at

Erfurt in March 1850, to devise a Prussian version of a united Germany. Both Prussia and Austria manoeuvred for support, but a rebellion in Hesse-Cassel in September brought a more direct confrontation. The Elector asked for help against his troublesome subjects and, with the support of Austria, the Confederation Diet sent troops to assist him. Prussia sent troops to support the rebels, a somersault in Frederick William's usual policy towards rebels, which not only infuriated the Austrians but alarmed Tsar Nicholas I. The outcome was a meeting at Olmütz in November 1850. Frederick William backed away from what had now begun to seem possible, a war against both Austria and Russia. He agreed to abandon his Erfurt Union, his support of the rebels in Hesse-Cassel, and his opposition to the Austrian-dominated German Bund. With Frederick William's 'humiliation' at Olmütz, stability again returned to the Confederation. For all the upheavals of 1848–50, the Germans who wanted to make changes had achieved hardly anything.

(d) The Austrian Empire

There were five major centres of revolution in the Austrian Empire in 1848. In Austria itself, a liberal uprising in Vienna began on 12 March. About the same time there were outbreaks in Bohemia and Hungary, and in the Austrian provinces in Italy (see Section (b) above). A fifth revolt was that in Croatia, where the aim was not so much to break free from Habsburg rule as to avoid a takeover by the Magyars of Hungary.

The subjects of the Austrian Empire had long nursed a variety of grievances. There was peasant resentment against the continuation of many feudal duties and restrictions on personal liberty. In the growing industrial areas, especially in Vienna, there was discontent with primitive conditions. Among educated and middle-class liberals there was frustration with the absolutism of the Habsburgs. And, among the subject peoples of the Empire (see Fig. 2.2), there were nationalist discontents and resentment of foreign control. The rising in Vienna began among the university students and, within a matter of days, Metternich was forced to resign and an Austrian parliament was promised. In common with the other revolutionary areas of Europe, it seemed that the rebels would sweep everything before them. Throughout the·Empire the government had to make concessions. But Ferdinand I, like other European rulers, was also waiting for the tide to turn. In May 1848 he retired to Innsbruck, leaving his ministers to grapple with revolutionary demands, and his generals to organize the counter-attack.

Bohemia was the first part of the Empire to be subdued. Demands for equality between Czechs and Germans led to a Slav Congress in Prague in June 1848, organized by the Czech patriot, Francis Palacky. The Congress excited rioters in the city and Prince Windischgrätz, the local military commander, seized the opportunity to occupy the city. This show of military strength, and the earlier abolition of feudal duties and restrictions in Galicia, quietened the north of the Austrian Empire. In July Ferdinand received news of Radetsky's

Fig. 5.6 Revolutionary students at the University of Vienna, 1848, painted by F. Schams. There was no lasting co-operation between the various classes of revolutionaries

victory at Custozza (see page 77). His fortunes were beginning to revive.

Austria, especially Vienna, took longer to subdue. From the outset the government was helped by the distrust which existed between the middle classes and the workers, but Ferdinand had to appoint more liberal ministers than he would have preferred, to agree to a constitution, and to allow an Austrian Reichstag to meet in July. His subjects even forced the Emperor to return for a short time to Vienna, and in September he signed the Emancipation Law which ended serfdom throughout the Empire. The emancipation was not just a concession to social change and civilization. It was also an effective political manoeuvre, for the peasants of the Empire now had little further interest in revolution. The revolutionaries were further weakened by differences of opinion about the future of the Empire and the nationalities within it. The Austrian Reichstag voted approval of the Emperor's efforts to prevent the Hungarians breaking away from the Empire, and there was a new uprising in Vienna in October by radicals who now disapproved of the Reichstag. Ferdinand fled to Olmütz, but a Hungarian attempt to join forces with the Viennese radicals was blocked by Josip Jellacic, the Governor of Croatia, near what is now Vienna Airport. This allowed Windischgrätz to crush the Viennese, and their rebellion was over. Ferdinand, however, abdicated in favour of his nephew, Franz Joseph, and a new chief minister was appointed, Prince Schwarzenberg. This was a formidable combination. Schwarzenberg was a believer in strong government and Franz Joseph had a strong sense of duty, not least of his duty to preserve the Empire and its traditional values.

The Austrian Empire had thus been brought to heel by the end of 1848, except for the continuing problems to the south which centred upon Hungary, and the unfinished business to the south-west in Venice (see page 78). The Hungarian Diet (see page 25) had quickly responded to the revolutions of 1848 by demanding self-government and a reduction of Austrian influence in Hungarian affairs. Louis Kossuth, a lifelong Hungarian nationalist and the editor of the Magyar newspaper *Pesti Hirlap*, led the movement. The Diet passed the March Laws, effectively establishing Hungary as a separate state under the control of Magyar landowners, and linked to the Austrian Empire by little more than personal allegiance to the Emperor. The Laws also included the emancipation of the serfs and the setting up of a parliament in Budapest. But they defined the limits of Hungary as including Croatia and Transylvania. This was hotly disputed by the Serbo-Croats and Rumanians (see Fig. 2.2). The Croats in particular had no wish to exchange Austrian rule for that of the Magyars. They raised the standard of revolt at Agram (now Zagreb), aiming to keep out the Magyars but to have their own self-government within the Habsburg Empire. The Emperor appointed Jellacic, a Croatian patriot, to be their Governor, but he was forced to dismiss him under pressure from the Hungarians. Jellacic remained, nevertheless, the adopted leader of the Croatian resistance.

In July 1848, Kossuth called upon the Hungarians to defend their nation. 'Croatia,' he asserted, 'is in open rebellion.'

> The Viennese ministers have thought proper in the name of the Austrian Emperor, to declare to the cabinet of the King of Hungary, that, unless we make peace with the Croats at any price, they will act in opposition to us. This is as much as to say, that the Austrian Emperor declares war to the King of Hungary, or to his own self.

The Emperor of Austria saw no such confusion in the problem. The Hungarians were in rebellion against the Empire, and the Croats were willing to side with Austria against them. The Viennese were crushed in October 1848, with some help from Jellacic and the Croats (see opposite). The Hungarians were now without support, and Austrian and Croatian forces could be sent against them. The task of organizing the defeat of the Magyars was left to Schwarzenberg. In March 1849 he devised a new constitution for the whole Austrian Empire, with a central diet and administration but leaving open the possibility of some limited self-government in Hungary, as long as Hungary did not include Croatia and Transylvania. A month later, Hungary proclaimed its total independence with Kossuth as its president. Windischgrätz was successfully resisted and Hungary remained defiant. But Schwarzenberg had one further card to play. If the Austrians and their Croat allies could not overthrow Kossuth, Nicholas I was ready to send a Russian army. The Magyars made their last stand at Vilagos in August 1849, far to the south. When they were

Table 5.1   The Upheavals of 1848–9

Date	France	The Austrian Empire				Non-Austrian Italy	Germany			Elsewhere
		Austria	Bohemia	Hungary/Croatia	Lombardy/Venetia		Prussia	German States	Frankfurt	
1848 January						Revolution in Sicily				
February	Louis Philippe abdicated: Second Republic				Tobacco Riots	Constitutions granted				
March		Revolution in Vienna: fall of Metternich	Revolution in Prague	March Laws in Hungary	Revolution in Lombardy. Republic in Venice —Austro-Piedmont War—	Constitution in Piedmont-Sardinia	Revolution in Berlin. Constitution granted	Ludwig of Bavaria abdicated. Many uprisings	Vor-parliament met	
April		Constitution granted								Cracow crushed
May		Emperor Ferdinand withdrew to Innsbruck				Naples and Sicily crushed	Prussian War against Denmark		All-German Parliament met	Warsaw crushed
June	'June Days' in Paris		Czech Revolution crushed						Archduke John appointed	
July		Austrian Reichstag met		Anti-Magyar rising in Croatia	—————— Piedmont defeated —————— Lombardy crushed					
August							Danish war ended			
September		Serfs emancipated in Austrian Empire								New constitution in Switzerland
October		Viennese radical uprising crushed								

Month	France	Austrian Empire	Central Europe	Germany (Parliament)	German states	Italy	Venice	Hungary	Netherlands / Denmark
November	Constitution of Second Republic					Pius IX fled from Rome			More liberal constitution in Holland
December	Louis Napoleon elected President	Abdication of Ferdinand I: Franz Joseph	Constitution modified	Declaration of Rights					
1849 January									
February						Roman Republic set up. Duke of Tuscany expelled			
March		Modified Constitution for the Empire				Austro-Piedmont War — Piedmont defeated. Abdication of Charles Albert			
April				German crown rejected by Frederick William		Duke of Tuscany restored		Hungary proclaimed independent	
May					Further revolts crushed				
June				End of Frankfurt Parliament					
July					Rebellion in Baden crushed	Roman Republic crushed: Pius IX restored			Constitution in Denmark
August							Republic in Venice crushed	Hungarians crushed by Russia	

routed, Kossuth fled into the neighbouring Ottoman Empire and spent the rest of his life in exile. Two weeks later Venice surrendered and the Austrian Empire was again intact.

(e) Elsewhere

In Switzerland, a new democratic constitution was drawn up in 1848. Since 1815 Switzerland had had a national Diet in which the Swiss cantons were represented, similar in many ways to the weak diet of the German Bund. Pressures to increase the powers of the Diet and liberalize the country, perhaps unleashing anti-clericalism, had alarmed Catholic and conservative opinion, and resulted in 1845 in the creation of the *Sonderbund*, a league of Catholic cantons. This led to civil war in 1847, when federal forces sought to break up the Sonderbund, which they regarded as a threat to national unity. The French and the Austrians were inclined to support their fellow-Catholics, but were deterred by Palmerston who favoured the federalists. The main importance to Switzerland of the European revolutions of 1848 was that they distracted the foreign powers, leaving the Swiss to settle their own affairs.

No such good fortune befell the Poles, or the people of Cracow. A flicker of revolt in Warsaw was quickly extinguished in May 1848, and the Austrians had by that time already crushed a protest in Cracow. This earlier protest sprang from the Austrian annexation of the free city of Cracow in 1846. In western Europe, on the other hand, the threat of revolution was often enough to prod governments into concessions. This was the case in the Netherlands (see page 48), and in Denmark where a new constitution was introduced in 1849.

5.3   The Failure of the Revolutions

It can be argued that the revolutions of 1848–9 marked the end of the romantic movement in politics. Except in Russia, people found it difficult to go on believing that governments and societies could be changed by a sudden uprising of students, conspirators, literary and professional men. The reality of 1848–9 was that they had nowhere proved a match for armies which remained loyal to the governments. The lasting concessions which had been won were very few. The surviving constitutions, like those in Prussia, Piedmont and the Austrian Empire, did little to undermine royal authority or to change the balance of power in society. Only the desires of the most cautious liberals had been satisfied, and that in only a handful of states. The demand for social reform had been even less successful, except for the emancipation of the serfs in the Austrian Empire. Nationalists had also been frustrated and, when the revolutions were over, not a single national frontier had been changed. The Austrian Empire was intact, and Italy and Germany remained divided.

The disunity of the revolutionaries was a major factor in their failure. There was hardly any co-operation between classes. In the Austrian Empire there was division between races. In Italy there was division between differing views as to what kind of united Italy was wanted, and much the same was true in Germany. In any case, the masses saw no great relevance to their own problems in unification. Nor were the revolutions co-ordinated. Their early effectiveness came from the multiplicity of revolutions which bewildered the authorities, but by the summer of 1848 the authorities were able to deal with them individually, to isolate each uprising. Thus Windischgrätz could move from Prague to Vienna, and from Vienna to Budapest, while Prussian troops moved similarly around Germany.

Inevitably, and often in exile, the revolutionaries tried to learn lessons from the events of 1848–9. For Italians it seemed that there was a need for a more united aim, and probably for foreign assistance to overcome the Austrians. Manin concluded that republicanism could not succeed against the Austrians, and that Italians must look to the leadership of Piedmont-Sardinia. Germans questioned whether liberalism and nationalism could succeed simultaneously, and they pondered the choice between seeking to liberalize individual states and seeking union under a strong and authoritarian state such as Prussia. Others considered the narrowness of bourgeois objectives and the weakness of middle-class revolutionaries. Early in 1848, Marx and Engels had issued their *Communist Manifesto*, designed partly to be a programme for that year for Germans and west Europeans, and partly to be a programme for social change in the interests of the masses. It had little effect on the events of 1848, but its ideas for a proletarian revolution and the 'overthrow of all existing social conditions' were to be developed massively by Marx in the years ahead. Marx claimed a scientific basis for his ideas, not a romantic one. Revolutions in future would hardly be able to disregard the interests of the masses, and the time would come when Lenin would argue that revolutions must be planned scientifically and led professionally. Marx and Engels wrote:

> Let the ruling classes tremble at a Communist revolution. The proletarians have nothing to lose but their chains. They have a world to win. Working men of all countries, unite!

Here were the seeds of powerful new conflicts which would be very different in character from the hopeful tilts at authority by the educated bourgeoisie and by the romantic revolutionaries of 1848–9.

Further Reading

Bruun, G.: *Revolution and Reaction, 1848–52*. Anvil Books (Dublin, 1958).
Eyck, F.: *The Revolutions of 1848–49*. Oliver and Boyd (Edinburgh, 1972).
Langer, W. L.: *The Revolutions of 1848*. Harper Torchbooks (London, 1971).

Exercises

1. Use Fig. 5.2 to make a list of the revolutionary outbreaks in Europe in 1848–9. Alongside each outbreak, state briefly its outcome. What generalizations can you

then make about revolutionary outbreaks in *each* of the following areas: western Europe; central Europe; eastern Europe?

2. 'The strength of the revolutions of 1848–9 lay in their number. Rulers seemed to have no alternative but hastily to grant concessions' (page 73). How does Table 5.1 on pages 86–7 show that this was true in the early months of 1848?

3. How does Section 5.2(*b*) show that Italian rebels were no match in 1848–9 for the Austrians, the French and the Pope?

4. How did the composition of the Frankfurt Parliament, which is described on page 80, help to explain why eventually most 'went home in disillusionment' (page 82)?

5. Use Table 5.1 and Section 5.2(*d*) to show how, and why, the various uprisings in the Austrian Empire were all suppressed.

6. How did the *Communist Manifesto* (page 89) suggest that Europe after 1848 would differ from that before 1848, and what is meant by 'the end of the romantic movement in politics' (page 88)?

Unit Six

France 1848–71: The Revival of Republicanism and Bonapartism

6.1 The Second Republic

(a) France in 1848

The Second Republic in France lasted from the overthrow of Louis Philippe (see pages 66 and 74) to the proclamation of the Second Empire by Louis Napoleon in December 1852. The Republic began with high-sounding radical oratory, and with a bold declaration on 26 February 1848:

> Citizens: royalty, under whatever form, is abolished; no more legitimism, no more Bonapartism, no regency. . . . The republic is proclaimed. The people are united.

But it soon became evident that the people were *not* united and, by the end of 1848, it was also clear that Bonapartism would not be abolished merely by words.

The inauguration of the Republic was the work of Paris, and a provisional government was set up before the end of February. Among its members were Alphonse de Lamartine, a poet and orator and a moderately radical politician, and Louis Blanc, a writer and socialist (see page 63). In *L'Organisation du Travail*, Blanc had advocated equal pay and the abolition of unemployment, and had become a fierce critic of Louis Philippe's government. He had also advocated the establishment of national workshops, in which workers would share in the profits of their labours. With the support of the Paris workers in 1848 Blanc persuaded the provisional government to proclaim 'the right to work', and he set about the introduction of national workshops. It was typical of the prevailing confusion, however, that the workshops were managed by Emile Thomas, who did not share Blanc's socialist ambitions. They became little more than relief agencies for the unemployed, produced hardly anything, and were a drain on the government's finances. Blanc himself referred to those whom the workshops collected together as 'a rabble of paupers' and 'battalions of paid idlers'. Far from being a constructive experiment in socialist co-operation, the workshops became a source of grievance to the propertied classes whose taxes supported them. In May 1848 almost 100 000 Frenchmen drew their 'pay' from the workshops.

The upper and middle classes were not prepared to see the benefits of the revolution go to the masses, and they were even less prepared to see them go to the unemployed. Moreover, the provinces were not prepared to allow Paris alone to determine the outcome of the revolution. One of the first acts of the provisional government had been to arrange for new elections to the Assembly. All adult males were permitted to vote, and the elections were held in April. The voters seized the opportunity to defeat the radicals and socialists, thus expressing their alarm at what they had heard of the national workshops, and of sporadic clashes in Paris between the authorities and the forces of the left. About seven and a half million Frenchmen voted. The Assembly they elected was overwhelmingly moderate and conservative, although the voters confirmed their support for a republic rather than for the restoration of monarchy. Radicals and socialists gained fewer than 12 per cent of the seats. When a new government, responsible to the Assembly, took office, Lamartine kept his place, but Blanc was excluded. Almost at once, on 15 May, an attempt was made to overthrow the government, and the mob invaded the Assembly. But it was driven off by the recently created *Garde-mobile*, which had been recruited in the defence of property, and by the National Guard (a voluntary militia, originally dating from 1789, mainly for the defence of middle-class interests).

The propertied classes were now determined that the forces of the left should be weakened further. The government tried to deal with the problem of the national workshops, and there was tension in Paris for several weeks. An effort was made to remove from the workshops all those who were not Parisians, and payment, it was proposed, should be made only for work which

Fig. 6.1 Revolutionary Paris, 1848: a barricade on the Boulevard, Montmartre – a contemporary drawing

had been accomplished. This would stop 'inactivity pay', a 'dole' paid when no work was available. But the numbers in the workshops went on increasing, climbing above 100 000. The decision to close the workshops provoked a showdown, inflamed all the more when the Assembly voted on 21 June to draft idle young men into the army. Within 48 hours there was a new uprising in Paris. The government was ready, however, and professional troops advanced on the city under the command of General Cavaignac.

Cavaignac had served in Algeria and returned to Paris early in 1848. As a soldier he was ruthless; as a politician he was a staunch republican, but a determined enemy of socialism. He used the railway to bring extra forces to Paris, and he was given the supreme power to deal with the emergency which he demanded. For four days ('the June Days'), the fighting in the capital was ferocious, until those who resisted were overwhelmed by Cavaignac's army and its supporters in the National Guard and the Garde-mobile. When the fighting was over more than 10 000 prisoners were summarily tried. Many of them were executed, and many more were transported overseas. Louis Blanc fled to England and did not return to France until 1871. But Cavaignac did not prosper: he played little further part in public affairs after 1848. Nevertheless, it was his victory in the June Days which ensured the triumph of the propertied classes over the working classes. Lamartine observed that 'the Republic is dead', but it lingered in name for a further four years.

(b) The Presidential Election, 1848

Details of the new constitution were agreed in November 1848. The Assembly was to be elected by adult males, and executive power was to be entrusted to a President, whom they would also elect. From the outset presidential power would be considerable, and the presidential election in December 1848 attracted four principal candidates. Neither Lamartine nor Ledru-Rollin attracted more than a handful of supporters. General Cavaignac did better, with a million and a half votes, but in the eyes of the masses he was now a blood-stained figure. Some 75 per cent of the voters chose instead Louis Napoleon Bonaparte, giving him a convincing vote of five and a half million. Louis Napoleon thus became the President of the Second Republic, entitled, by the terms of the constitution, to serve for four years, but not to be re-elected.

Undoubtedly, the name 'Napoleon' appealed to the French electors. Indeed it is likely that there were illiterate voters who thought they were voting for Napoleon I himself. But the elections to the Assembly in the spring of 1849 confirmed that France had moved to the right since the overthrow of Louis Philippe. There was a substantial royalist majority in the new Assembly, although the royalists were divided between the supporters of the Bourbon house and the supporters of the Orleanists. Between the royalists and Bonapartists, however, little room was left for loyalty to the Republic, and its days seemed to be numbered.

Three factors combined to secure the election of Louis Napoleon as

President, or Prince-President as he preferred to be called. In the first place, the propertied classes wanted orderly government which would guarantee them against the further activities of Paris radicals and socialists. The name 'Napoleon' stood for order and the rule of law in France, more so than did the name of Cavaignac, who was now associated with confrontation. For moderate conservatives Louis Napoleon seemed at least to have the right pedigree. More than that, however, he appealed to a broad band of Frenchmen, and the Napoleonic Legend worked to his advantage. Now remote from the rule of Napoleon I, Frenchmen remembered his reign as some sort of golden age, when French foreign policy had been glorious and the reputation of France had stood high.

The nostalgia for these past glories was increased by the Napoleonic Legend, which blurred the past and made it more attractive. The Legend began with Napoleon I himself re-writing history during his exile in St Helena. The Empire, he argued, had sought peace, though war had been forced upon it. His own dictatorship, if not actually a democracy, had been a liberal government which safeguarded the gains of the Revolution of 1789. And, above all, the Empire had been truly French, which was what Frenchmen most readily remembered of it.

The third factor which helped Louis Napoleon was his own history. For years, he had sought to win fame and popularity by methods which ranged from the shrewdly constructive to the fatuously bizarre. He was the nephew of Napoleon I and the son of Louis Bonaparte, whom the Emperor had made King of Holland for a time. Louis Napoleon had been brought up with a passionate belief in his own destiny, and he became the heir of Napoleon I when the latter's only son (the Duke of Reichstadt, in theory Napoleon II) died in 1832. In 1839 he published *Des Idées Napoléoniennes*, further expanding the Legend that his uncle had been a friend of true liberty and a man of peace, on whom the British made war (see pages 63–4). In 1844 he wrote *L'Extinction du Paupérisme*, and advocated public works to help reduce unemployment, and economic reforms to increase French wealth. He managed to suggest that he had a programme to better the lives of most Frenchmen, and that he was a thinker. On the other hand, though he had been offered a government post in Ecuador, his career before 1848 had been spectacularly unsuccessful.

Most of Louis Napoleon's early life was spent in exile. He backed lost causes, such as that of the Carbonari in Italy. He took part in a rebellion against the Papacy in 1831, and he longed to lead a Bonapartist uprising against Louis Philippe in France. In 1836, therefore, he arrived in Strasbourg, and requested the garrison there to follow him to Paris. Within a couple of hours, he was under arrest, and Louis Philippe packed him off to the USA, although he returned to Europe almost immediately. In 1840 he attempted a seaborne invasion of France, coming ashore at Boulogne from a hired pleasure-steamer. He had a mixed army of about 50 Frenchmen and Poles, together with a tame vulture that represented the Napoleonic eagle to the best of its ability. The Boulogne garrison, like that in Strasbourg, failed to respond to his call to arms, and he was eventually fished abjectly from the sea. This time Louis Philippe imprisoned him, and the would-be emperor spent some years in reasonable comfort in the medieval fortress at Ham. Ever resourceful, he walked out of the fortress in 1846, disguised as one of the workmen making repairs. He was thus able to return to the life he loved in fashionable society, flitting from banquets and balls to the theatre, and beloved by the girls of the ballet. But he continued to dream of becoming l'Empereur. The French revolution of 1848 excited him, but the revolutionaries quickly requested him to leave when he once more arrived in France. In April he offered to help the British government to disperse the London Chartists, now posing as the man of law and order; and two months later he was admitted to France, this time to stay. His band-wagon began to roll when he won election to the republican Assembly, not in one constituency but in nine, so that his name might be better known. By the end of the year the men of property, but more particularly the mass votes of the peasants, had made him the Prince-President. He was on the way to becoming the Emperor, but he had little of an organized party in the Assembly, and he had only four years of office in which to tighten his hold on power. His record suggested that he was likely to be too incompetent to stage a coup and overthrow the constitution.

(c) The Presidency of Louis Napoleon

The constitution of the Second Republic put together – perhaps even set against each other – an elected President and an elected Assembly. The French people went some way towards making the system unworkable, by electing a Bonapartist President and a royalist Assembly. Conflict between them seemed unavoidable. It was a conflict which Louis Napoleon used to his own advantage, posing as the friend of the people against an Assembly bent on betraying them. His greatest opportunity came when the Assembly voted to change the electoral laws in May 1850, in effect robbing three million Frenchmen of their votes. The President soon declared himself the champion of the original wider franchise. It was on this issue that Louis Napoleon staged his first coup d'état in December 1851. Because the Assembly would not restore the lost votes, he dissolved it. At the same time he proclaimed himself President for ten more years with extended powers, and he appealed for the support of the nation in a plebiscite. Thousands of likely political opponents were put under arrest, among them Cavaignac, and for the purposes of the plebiscite the vote was restored to all adult males. Frenchmen approved. Seven and a half million voted their support for Louis Napoleon, and only 650 000 voted in opposition. A few barricades went up in Paris, however, and some blood was shed. It was not until the spring of 1852 that the President had all his enemies safely in detention or in exile; over 10 000 Frenchmen were deported, mainly to Algeria and to Devil's Island in French Guiana.

Louis Napoleon showed a certain ruthlessness in carrying through the coup of 1851, but the plebiscite showed that he was also popular. He had worked tirelessly since 1848 to achieve this popularity, touring the provinces, advertising his plans for various social and economic reforms, and undermining his political rivals. Those who, like Thiers, had believed in 1848 that he would be a President whom they could manipulate, found that he could neither be manipulated nor stopped. The President's nominees steadily took over key positions such as commands in the army. But Louis Napoleon still lacked a personal party and strong support in the Assembly. He had to try to be all things to all men: a man of order to please the conservatives, a man of reform to please the liberals, a friend of the poor to please at least some of the socialists, and a good Catholic to please the Church. To please them all at the same time required a remarkable feat of juggling, which even a man with the name 'Napoleon' was unlikely to be able to sustain for long. The Catholics were undoubtedly pleased when he sent a French garrison to Rome in 1849 (see page 78), but French liberals were angered by this support for the reactionary Pius IX. The *Loi Falloux* of 1850 again pleased the Church but displeased the left, since it extended Catholic control over French education and allocated state funds to the running of Catholic schools. After the coup of 1851 Louis Napoleon now concentrated on winning liberal opinion, and a stream of presidential decrees abolished Sunday labour, reduced interest rates, launched an attack on slums, and encouraged developments in sanitation and communications. But alongside the reforms, censorship was brought back, and the amended constitution of 1852 disguised the President's dictatorial powers only thinly.

Louis Napoleon was helped by the recovery of the French economy, both from the depression which had begun in 1846 and from the upheavals of 1848. He also profited from the widespread disillusionment with the constitution of the Second Republic and with the Assembly it had produced. It was comparatively easy for him to make another change in December 1852, when he declared himself Emperor Napoleon III, replacing the Second Republic with the Second Empire. (Napoleon III is sometimes referred to as 'The Man of December' because of the fateful Decembers of 1848, 1851 and 1852.) Frenchmen dutifully voted their approval in a new plebiscite, in which they gave the Emperor several hundred thousand more votes than he had won a year earlier. The opposition vote was only a quarter of a million. Louis Napoleon had at last reached the top of the greasy pole, and he celebrated in 1853 by marrying Eugénie de Montijo, a Spanish countess who added brilliance to his court.

6.2   The Second Empire

(a) The Contradictions

All the contradictions of the Napoleonic Legend were evident in the reign of Napoleon III; and they were heightened both by his own enigmatic character,

TERRIFIC ASCENT OF THE HERO OF
A HUNDRED FÊTES.

Fig. 6.2 A Punch *view of the upwards progress of Louis Napoleon. The fiascos of Strasbourg and Boulogne were behind him but, having become the French President, Louis Napoleon would need to keep all his wits about him to become the Emperor*

and by his need to take account of a society more complex than that of the First Empire. Forecasting the desire of France 'to revert to the empire', Napoleon III told an audience in October 1852:

> A spirit of distrust leads certain persons to say that the empire means war. I say, the empire means peace. France longs for peace. . . . Glory is rightly handed down hereditarily, but not war.

He seemed thus to recognize the problem he faced in satisfying a French expectation of Napoleonic glory without resorting to war, and his foreign policy was to see some strange twists before it ended in total disaster in 1871 (see Section 6.2(*d*) below). But when Napoleon went on, in the speech of October 1852, he seemed to anticipate something of twentieth-century fascism. His aim, he claimed, was 'the good of our common country', and he intended to:

> conquer, for the sake of harmony, the warring parties, and bring into the great popular current the wasteful and conflicting eddies.

Here was a cry for national unity, but perhaps only a dictator could impose such a unity on French society with its existing social divisions and political antagonisms. Napoleon held virtually dictatorial powers in 1852, but he shared the respect of his subjects for constitutionalism and, in later years, he was to pursue the apparent political contradiction of a 'Liberal Empire', which would be in accordance with the fantasies of the Napoleonic Legend and with the search for constitutional rule in the revolutions of 1830 and 1848. If Napoleon was to remain Emperor by consent, he would have to continue to be all things to all men. Thus, in 1852, he contrived to suggest in a single paragraph that he would promote Christianity, develop communications – especially the railway system – and extend 'the primary necessities of life'. Glory and peace, national unity and liberty, social reforms and an economic policy which would please all sections of the community – these were the goals which Napoleon III had apparently set himself, and which those who supported him in the plebiscites expected him to achieve. The Emperor had shown himself to be a skilled politician in the years 1848 to 1852, but there nevertheless seemed to be reason to doubt whether the musical-comedy character of Strasbourg and Boulogne was the man to accomplish such ambitious aims.

(*b*) Dictatorship and Constitutionalism

The constitution of 1852 gave Napoleon III almost unlimited power. His nominees sat in the Senate, the upper house of the French parliament. The lower house, the 'Corps Legislatif' (Assembly), was elected at six-year intervals and had very little authority. The press was tightly controlled; political opponents risked arrest, and elections were rigged, not least by the use of 'the Irish vote' whereby voters who were dead mysteriously cast their votes for supporters of the Emperor. It was hardly surprising that the Assembly was usually obedient to Napoleon's wishes. But the Emperor seemed to want most of all a freer parliamentary system, which would somehow ensure to him permanent support and permanent power. He pardoned some political opponents on the occasion of his marriage; and he granted a more general amnesty in 1859 which allowed exiles to return, while at the same time he relaxed the restrictions on the press and permitted more influence to the Assembly.

The result of the Emperor's shift towards liberalism was an increase in the criticisms of his rule. Further concessions were demanded. Both in foreign policy and domestic policy, Napoleon searched desperately for those achievements which would strengthen his support. By 1867 conservatives had been alienated by his failures in foreign policy, in Italy, in Mexico and in his dealings with Bismarck over the Austro-Prussian War (see Section 6.2(*d*) below). Industrialists were angered by the Cobden Treaty (see page 100), and the rapid progress of the industrial revolution in France left the urban masses unenthusiastic about the Empire in spite of its social reform (see Section 6.2(*c*)).

In an attempt to appease the liberals further, Napoleon extended the freedom of the press and of public meetings, and ministers were ordered to answer questions in the Assembly. Two years later, in 1869, three and a quarter million votes were cast in the elections for opposition groups, and the supporters of the Empire won only a million more. Paris and the industrial centres returned opposition deputies. Napoleon decided to make a bold bid for renewed popularity. The powers of the Assembly were increased, and the liberal Emile Ollivier was appointed chief minister, charged with forming a government which would be responsible to the Assembly. For the first time Napoleon's Empire seemed to be truly constitutional. The 'Liberal Empire' had been achieved. At the same time, however, Napoleon made another appeal to the people in a plebiscite to confirm his own position along with the revised constitution. More than seven million Frenchmen gave their approval, only a million and a half voting against the new arrangements.

It was a remarkable achievement, that Napoleon had moved from an almost naked dictatorship to what appeared to be rule by parliamentary consent based on manhood suffrage. Whether the system would have worked, or whether there would have been unendurable conflict between the parliamentary government and Napoleon himself, there was not time to prove. Seven months after Ollivier formed his government, France went to war with Prussia, and Napoleon was defeated and captured at Sedan in September 1870. A republic was instantly demanded in Paris. Napoleon abdicated, retired to England and, already a sick man from a painful disease of the bladder, he died there in 1873.

(c) The Reforming Empire

Napoleon's health had to some extent been undermined by over-indulgence and by the burden of responsibility he carried. Before the appointment of Ollivier, the ministers of the Empire were usually men of limited ability, chosen in part to be the pawns of the Emperor. But whatever the freedoms which were denied to Frenchmen in the 1850s and 1860s, there were material benefits to be had from Napoleon's reign. The Emperor aimed to combine economic advancement with social reform. Most of the economic advancement was achieved by private enterprise, but Napoleon sought to provide the necessary support for expansion. Banking developed with joint-stock banks such as the *Société Générale*. Credit was made available through institutions such as the *Crédit Mobilier*. Trade fairs were held, such as the

Exhibitions of 1855 and 1867. French overseas trade expanded almost 400 per cent during the years of the Empire, helped by the introduction of new steamship services; and at home, the growth of industry was assisted by the massive development of the railway system, climbing from about 3200 kilometres of track to over 16 000 kilometres. It was an age of technological innovation when steam-power boosted the output of the factories, and sewers and gas-lighting improved the quality of life in the cities. Financial, commercial and industrial empires grew, but Napoleon nevertheless antagonized French industrialists and brought fears of unemployment, when he negotiated the Anglo-French Commercial Treaty (the Cobden Treaty) in 1860. By arranging mutual tariff reductions, the Treaty enabled French agriculturalists to sell more wine and brandy in Britain, but it exposed French industry to British competition.

Nineteenth-century industrial and urban development often brought misery to the labouring poor, but Napoleon was not indifferent to their problems. In 1864 trade unions were made legal, though their rights were limited. Trade boards were also set up, to bring together employers and workmen and government officials, for the settlement of disputes and for the improvement of working conditions. Public works provided employment, and the high level of economic activity during the years of the Empire helped to cushion the poor against unemployment and poverty. Napoleon also sought to persuade local authorities to improve living conditions, to clear the slums, to extend water supplies and to lay drains. The most spectacular results of the concern of the Empire for the environment were those achieved in Paris, where Baron Haussmann, the Prefect of the Seine, effected both slum-clearance and the construction of tree-lined and gas-lit boulevards. Paris became a European showpiece during Napoleon III's reign. Its population was almost doubled from the million or so of 1848. The city administration was reorganized; many of the workers were re-housed, and grand new buildings appeared, among them department stores and a new opera house. Yet Napoleon still failed to win the support of the Paris proletariat, which preferred socialism to Bonapartism and brooded on the defeats of the June Days.

No one criticized the Empire more fiercely than Victor Hugo, the poet and novelist, who exiled himself from France until 1870 in protest against the Emperor's dictatorship, and kept up a constant attack from the Channel Islands. But Napoleon was a patron of the arts to those who were less critical, and he aimed to make Paris the cultural centre of the continent. The Empire glittered, its magnificent court presided over by Eugénie and visited regularly by men as prominent as Pasteur and Verdi. The city resounded to the lilting music of Offenbach and, after his return from Rome in 1860, to the operas of Bizet. Spectacle, often involving the army, helped to establish Paris and the Empire as high in the itinerary of tourists, especially those from Britain where the court sparkled much less brightly. Yet, with his humiliation at Sedan, the Empire of Napoleon III crumbled into nothing almost overnight and, with the death of the Emperor's son in 1879, Bonapartism ceased to be a significant force in French politics.

Fig. 6.3 The rebuilding of Paris, from a drawing of 1860. Napoleon III and Baron Haussmann made great improvements in the city

(d) The Foreign Policy of the Second Empire

In his youth, Louis Napoleon had written:

> The Napoleonic Idea is not an idea of war, but a social, industrial, commercial, humanitarian idea.

But Frenchmen expected a Napoleonic regime to be influential in the world. Napoleon III himself intended that France should be influential, and he was often under pressure from Eugénie to achieve international distinction, ultimately with disastrous results when she encouraged him to declare war on Prussia in 1870. However much he might claim that the Empire stood for peace, Napoleon III was nevertheless involved in war with Russia in 1854, with Austria in 1859, with Mexicans and almost with the USA in the mid-1860s, and with Germans in 1870. There was little to show for these wars by the end of the Emperor's reign, but he had on the other hand continued the penetration of Algeria and begun an empire in the Far East when he annexed Cochin China in 1862.

Napoleon's policy in Europe will be considered further in other Units. His involvement in the Crimean War against Russia (see Section 8.4) stemmed from a variety of causes, among which were a genuine concern to prevent Russian expansion, a desire to please the Church by upholding Catholic rights in the Holy Land, a desire to please the liberals by confronting a power notoriously autocratic, a willingness to co-operate with the British and, perhaps, a personal hostility to Nicholas I who refused to address him as 'brother' and as a fellow-emperor. It may still be doubted whether the war served any useful purpose and whether, indeed, there was justification for it but – after considerable bungling – the war ended in victory and a triumphal peace conference in Paris. At this stage, Frenchmen seemed well satisfied with their Emperor.

In his youth, Louis Napoleon had shown interest in the liberation of Italy, an area where the first Napoleon had won great victories. In 1849 he seemed to have changed his policy by rescuing Rome for the Pope, but ten years later he went to war with Austria in an attempt to free at least parts of northern Italy from Habsburg control (see Section 7.2(b)). From the Italian point of view the Emperor won considerable success, and France was duly rewarded with the territories of Savoy and Nice. But opinion in France was divided. Catholics were alarmed by the developments which Napoleon had triggered off in Italy, which deprived the Pope of part of his possessions. Liberals criticized the Emperor for leaving Venetia in Austrian hands, and militarists deplored the fact that he had shrunk from an attack on the Habsburg fortresses in the Quadrilateral, where glory might have been won.

It was the 1860s, however, which brought a mounting number of setbacks in foreign policy. In Italy the Emperor had shown some signs of idealism in trying to free subject peoples from the Habsburgs. Unrealistically, French liberals wanted him to assist the Poles in a similar way when they rebelled against the Russians in 1863, but Napoleon gave no such assistance. He had turned instead to a rather squalid enterprise in Mexico, which began when the French collaborated with Britain and Spain in a debt-collecting expedition. Hard-pressed by civil war, the Mexican republican government of Benito Juarez had suspended repayments to its European creditors. Palmerston in Britain wanted the money back, and the mission in 1861 duly collected it. Napoleon now schemed to keep a French presence in Mexico, adding to the French empire in the West Indies and Guiana. He also intended to protect the interests of Mexican Catholics (and please the Church in France), and at the same time he could recover Austrian goodwill by enthroning a Habsburg archduke as the client emperor of Mexico. With a lack of common sense, Archduke Maximilian, the brother of Franz Joseph, agreed to accept the crown: it would relieve his boredom since he had lost an earlier appointment in Lombardy, and he too could serve the Church. The snag was that the Mexicans wanted neither the French nor Maximilian. French troops became involved in a war of conquest, which dragged on longer than Napoleon's European wars. In 1865 the Civil War in the USA ended, and President Johnson quickly reminded Napoleon of the Monroe Doctrine. If Napoleon continued to meddle in Mexico, he would risk conflict with the USA. By 1867 French troops were withdrawn. Maximilian remained and showed some sense of loyalty to those Mexicans who had supported him, but he was taken by Juarez and shot. For Napoleon, the affair had turned out to be a total disaster, which left him to face the anger of liberals, Catholics, the army, and the Austrians.

By this time, however, events were moving quickly in Germany where

Prussia, under the leadership of Bismarck, was growing in strength. Napoleon's main concern was to protect the interests of France, since the balance of power in central Europe was shifting rapidly. But he found himself out of his depth, and his defeat in the Franco-Prussian War was the final humiliation (see Section 7.3). After his comparative successes in the Crimean War, the Emperor had lost control of events in Italy, had bitten off more than he could chew in Mexico, had been left behind by events in Germany, and had – finally, and in desperation – embarked on a war he could not win against the most dangerous army in Europe.

Fig. 6.4 Defeat in the Franco-Prussian War cost Napoleon III his Empire. A sketch of the Prussian shelling of Paris, which left the city 'by balloon post'

Like so much else in his career, Napoleon III's foreign policy was enigmatic. Occasionally he showed vision, as in his attempt to free Italians. Yet he insisted on extracting Savoy and Nice from the Italians, as the reward for French services. In his discussions with Bismarck in the 1860s he sometimes seemed only to be interested in French aggrandisement; and this angered the British. Aware, no doubt, that British hostility had helped to ruin his uncle, he tried to co-operate with the British on other occasions, and the two fought as allies in the Crimean War. But Napoleon's ambitions in Mexico went far beyond those of Palmerston and were somewhat absurd, although they were not entirely ignoble, since the civil war in which he meddled had begun partly as a result of attacks on the Catholic Church. In fact, the Emperor in the end was a prisoner of the name 'Napoleon' and a victim of his own desire to be loved by Frenchmen. It was his misfortune that Frenchmen were divided in their expectations, and in his attempt to win their hearts, his foreign policy became as varied as a patchwork quilt. It was finally reduced merely to a search for success – any success which might enhance Napoleon III's prestige.

Further Reading

Bury, J. P. T.; *Napoleon III and the Second Empire*. Hodder and Stoughton (London, 1970).
MacIntyre, D.: *Napoleon, the Legend and the Reality*. Blackie (Glasgow, 1976).
Randell, K.: *Monarchy, Republic and Empire, 1814–70*. Edward Arnold (London, 1986).
Thompson, J. M.: *Louis Napoleon and the Second Empire*. Blackwell (Oxford, 1954).

Documentary

Patrick, A.: *The Empire of the Third Napoleon*. Edward Arnold (London, 1973).
Price, R.: *1848 in France*. Thames and Hudson (London, 1975).

Exercises

1. Why, in 1848, did Louis Blanc lose popularity and Louis Napoleon gain popularity?
2. Study Sections 6.1(*a*) and (*b*), and state, with reasons, whether you, as a citizen of France, would have voted for Louis Napoleon or for some other candidate in the presidential election of 1848.
3. Explain what the cartoon on page 97 suggests about the past, present, and future, of Louis Napoleon. Where do you think the sympathies of the cartoonist lay?
4. How far do you agree that the Second Empire was full of 'contradictions' (Section 6.2(*a*))?
5. How did Frenchmen benefit from the domestic policy of Louis Napoleon, as President and as Emperor, and what grievances did he fail to remedy?
6. What can you learn of the history of Paris and of France in the years 1848 to 1871 from the study of the illustrations in this Unit?
7. After studying the later Units of this book referred to in Section 6.2(*d*), explain what is meant by, and consider the truth of, the assertion that Napoleon III's foreign policy was 'finally reduced merely to a search for success' (above).

The Renewed Attack on the Existing Order 1848–71

7.1 Disillusionment after·1848

Carl Schurz took part as a student in the attempts in 1848–9 to create a united and liberal Germany based on the Frankfurt Parliament. He later described the frustration which came with failure:

> A feeling of profound shame overcame us. Our enterprise had not only come to an unfortunate, but to a ridiculous and disgraceful end. . . . And this after the big words with which many had pledged themselves to the cause of German liberty and unity.

Unit Five showed that the failures of the revolutionaries of 1848–9 were widespread; and Unit Six showed that, even in France, a movement to the right quickly followed the overthrow of Louis Philippe, leading to the authoritarian rule of Napoleon III. Such progress as there was, in Europe, towards liberalism and constitutionalism during the 25 years after 1848, did not result from dramatic revolutions. Liberals were often disillusioned and pessimistic, reduced once more to theoretical discussion, like the Russian liberals who could see no way in which to overcome tsarist power. The comparatively few changes which were made were piecemeal and peaceful, like the Second Reform Act in Britain in 1867 and the concessions made by Napoleon III in his later years.

Nationalists, on the other hand, achieved rather more spectacular success, for both Italy and Germany became nation states before the end of 1871. In both cases unification brought with it some constitutional development, but each new country was under the rule of a monarchy, and neither brought much joy to republicans and socialists. The new Italy and the new Germany were created less by the people at large than by rather narrow interest groups. To put it in the simplest terms, Piedmont-Sardinia took over the rest of Italy, and Prussia took over the rest of Germany. Italy, and even more so Germany, were the creations of power-politics. Called to office in Prussia in 1862, Otto von Bismarck asserted:

> The great questions of the day will not be decided by speeches and the resolutions of majorities – that was the blunder of 1848 and 1849 – but by blood and iron.

Armies united Germany, not the revolutionary declarations of liberal amateurs. The same was true to some extent in Italy, although there, in the events of 1859–60, there was still some part to be played by the voice of the people and by the romantic exploits of Garibaldi's red-shirted followers.

7.2 The Creation of a United Italy

(a) Foundations: Piedmont-Sardinia

Italians had little to show for their revolutionary efforts by the end of 1849 (see Section 5.2(b)). Nevertheless, Charles Albert left Piedmont-Sardinia with a constitution, when he abdicated in favour of Victor Emmanuel II in March 1849. The constitution had similarities to that of the Second Empire in France: Article 3 stated that 'the executive power is vested in the king alone', and the upper house of parliament was made up of royal nominees. The constitution went on, however, to guarantee individual liberties, and it was favourable to the freedom of the press. Much would depend on the king and on the ministers he appointed. When Victor Emmanuel appointed Camillo de Cavour as Prime Minister of the Kingdom in 1852, a partnership began which was to prove of outstanding importance. Cavour was a nobleman, but he brought a reforming zeal to his office. He had liberal inclinations and he was ambitious. His first aim was to make Piedmont-Sardinia an efficient and forward-looking state. He had entered the Assembly as a member for Turin and, at the same time, he had founded a newspaper, *Il Risorgimento*, to campaign for liberal and nationalist ideals. (*Risorgimento*, literally 'resurrection', was the term applied to the movement for Italian unification after 1815.) Cavour had earlier shown an interest in scientific farming, which led to his appointment as Minister of Agriculture and Commerce in 1850. A short time later, he took charge of the Navy as well. His rapid political advancement was evidence of his energy and ability.

Cavour's modernization of Piedmont bore similarities to the work of Napoleon III in France. Both men showed an interest in railways and steamships, in the expansion of trade, often by free-trade treaties, and in the establishment of sound financial institutions. Cavour was also an admirer of Britain, both of its constitution and of its economic development. Piedmont was already the most developed state in Italy, and it pulled further ahead of the rest under Cavour's leadership. Cavour claimed to believe in 'a free Church in a free state', but he might better have said that he believed in a subordinate Church in a dominant state. D'Azeglio had already, when Prime Minister in 1850, introduced the Siccardi Laws in Piedmont, eroding the authority of the Pope. The Church lost its special courts and exemptions. It could no longer monopolize marriage ceremonies, and it was subjected to control over its accumulation of property. Cavour now went further. The Law of Convents was issued in 1855, abolishing the religious orders which made no practical contribution to society, and narrowing the income gap between the princes of the Church and the humble clergy. Pius IX angrily stigmatized the Law as 'greatly adverse to the good of human society', but it increased the admiration for Piedmont of liberals and anti-clericals. The reputation of Piedmont was further enhanced when Victor Emmanuel declared war on Russia, and joined Britain and France in the Crimean War. The 15 000 Piedmontese troops showed that they were at least as competent as other armies involved in the Crimea, and they made their mark at Tchernaya. The troops gained experience; Cavour became more closely associated with the liberal powers of western Europe, and he was able to attend the peace conference at Paris in 1856 and speak about Italy's sad condition. He came to regard the war as an investment in Piedmont's future, but his country's taxpayers doubted whether the publicity was worth the expense.

Cavour had become Prime Minister partly through intrigue and political manoeuvring; throughout his career he had something of a reputation for duplicity. He was always an opportunist. Although long associated with propaganda for a united Italy, it seems likely that his practical goals were more limited; but it was logical that Piedmont should be extended as well as modernized. From about the time of the Crimean War he began to consider reviving the ambitions of Charles Albert of moving eastwards into the Italian provinces which bitterly resented Austrian rule. Charles Albert, however, had proved that the Piedmontese alone were no match for the Austrian whitecoats. It would be necessary to secure an ally and, at Paris in 1856, Cavour sought to interest Napoleon III.

Fig. 7.1 An Italian Stamp of 1959 commemorating the struggle for independence a century earlier. Victor Emmanuel II, Garibaldi, Cavour and Mazzini

(b) The North and Centre: Napoleon III

There were few tangible results before 1858 of Napoleon III's fascination with Italy (see pages 78 and 102). In January 1858 Felice Orsini, an Italian patriot who had once followed Mazzini, threw a bomb at Napoleon as he made his way by carriage to the Paris Opera. It killed eight bystanders, and spattered the Emperor and Empress with mud. Napoleon was furious and had Orsini executed. The French demanded that revolutionary activities in Piedmont should be suppressed, and they also complained angrily to Palmerston, when it was discovered the bomb had been made in England. For once in his career Palmerston was apologetic, but Victor Emmanuel vigorously defended his country's independent rights. The unpredictable Napoleon was impressed, and his mind began to work on the problem of what he might achieve in Italy.

The outcome was a surreptitious meeting at Plombières in the Vosges in July 1858, between Napoleon and Cavour. The essence of what they agreed was that if Piedmont were involved in a war with Austria within a year, and if Austria appeared to be the aggressor, France would supply 200 000 men to drive the Austrians back to the Adriatic. Piedmont could then annex Lombardy, Venetia and some northern parts of the Papal States, and perhaps also Parma and Modena; and the French would be paid for their services with Savoy and Nice. Southern Italy would remain untouched, but other parts of the Papal States would be transferred to Tuscany. The Pope would be compensated by becoming the president of an Italian Federation, made up of the enlarged Piedmont, the enlarged Tuscany, the remaining Papal States and the Kingdom of the Two Sicilies in the south. With a personal touch that seemed almost medieval, the bargain was to be sealed with a marriage between Napoleon's ageing cousin and the young Princess Clothilde, daughter of Victor Emmanuel. The couple married in January 1859 and, in April, Austria obligingly attacked Piedmont, provoked into war by a series of threats and insults, orchestrated by Cavour. French troops rushed to Piedmont's assistance, and Napoleon poured out a verbal smokescreen, allegedly to explain his policy:

> Frenchmen! Austria in ordering her army to invade the territory of the King of Sardinia, our ally, has declared war upon us. . . . The purpose of this war is . . . to restore Italy to herself. . . . We shall have upon our frontiers a friendly people who will owe their independence to us.

The Emperor was particularly anxious to reassure the French Catholics that it was not the intention 'to disturb the authority of the Holy Father', though this seemed to be not wholly consistent with what had been discussed at Plombières.

Two major and bloody battles were fought in June 1859, the first at Magenta, the second at Solferino. The battles freed Lombardy from the Austrians but, if they were to go on to free Venetia, the French had now to assault the Quadrilateral. It was a daunting prospect, and Napoleon was already disturbed by the lives the war had cost. He was also disturbed by Catholic criticisms of the war: the Empress Eugénie herself feared for the Holy Father. Rebellions had broken out in the Duchies, including Tuscany, and it seemed highly likely that events in Italy might soon be out of control. The mobilization of Prussian and other German troops added a new element of uncertainty in European affairs, though their intentions were not necessarily hostile to France. Anxious now to stop that which he had helped to start, Napoleon met Franz Joseph at Villafranca, near Verona, early in July, and arranged a Franco-Austrian armistice. Preliminary terms were agreed, which were confirmed before the end of the year in the Treaty of Zürich. Austria surrendered Lombardy except for the forts of the Quadrilateral, and Napoleon undertook to hand Lombardy to Piedmont, which was also to abandon the war. Elsewhere in Italy, Napoleon and the Austrian Emperor hoped to restore the *status quo*, although they agreed to encourage the setting up of an Italian Federation:

> under the honorary presidency of the Holy Father, . . . the object of which will be to uphold the Independence and Inviolability of the Confederated States.

The Treaty of Zürich went on to suggest that the Pope should also make reforms in the Papal States.

Cavour resigned after the Truce of Villafranca, loud in condemning Napoleon's treachery. But his own good faith was by no means certain. He was in touch with the recently-founded National Society, whose slogan was 'Unity, Independence and Victor Emmanuel'. He seemed to encourage the movements which drove out the rulers of Tuscany, Parma and Modena and which led to fighting in the Papal States, and it was not clear what his ultimate intentions were, once Lombardy and Venetia had been freed. For the moment he was angered by Victor Emmanuel's good sense in refusing to continue to fight Austria without French help. The main problem now, however, was to settle things in the Duchies. It seemed possible that an Austrian army would again restore their rulers, if Napoleon were to agree. At present they were under virtually dictatorial rule by men like Baron Ricasoli in Tuscany and Luigi Farini in Parma and Modena, both of whom favoured some sort of association with Piedmont. Palmerston was not in favour of the return of the Habsburgs, but the decisive factor for Napoleon was that he had not yet earned his reward, Savoy and Nice. He therefore used his influence to support the holding of plebiscites in the Duchies to determine the people's wishes, which was enough to encourage Cavour to return to office at the beginning of 1860, and to cede Savoy and Nice to the French.

Voting in the plebiscites was decisive. They were held in March 1860, and they gave overwhelming support to union with Piedmont, by about 25 to 1 in Tuscany, and by about 400 to 1 in Parma, Modena and the Romagna, which had by now been collected together under the leadership of Farini. When Victor Emmanuel's new parliament opened in April, it included representatives not only of Sardinia and Piedmont, but also of Lombardy, Tuscany, Parma, Modena and the Romagna. Except for the failure to wrest Venetia from the Austrians, Cavour could be well satisfied with this development of the Kingdom of Piedmont, though many of his supporters were far from pleased by his surrender of Savoy and Nice.

(c) The South: Garibaldi

Garibaldi had fought his own campaign against the Austrians in 1859, harassing them with his guerillas around Lake Como. He was no enthusiast for monarchy, but he was always in favour of freeing Italians from Austrians. He got little pleasure from the expansion of Piedmont, and complained bitterly when his native Nice was ceded to France: 'They have made me a stranger in the land of my birth'.

He sought consolation in May 1860 when he sailed from Genoa with a thousand revolutionaries, their officers clad in red shirts like those Garibaldi's men had previously worn in South America and Rome (see page 78). They were supported and armed by the National Society, and their objective was to help the rebellion which had broken out in Sicily. Mazzini and Francesco Crispi had prodded the Sicilians into rising against Francis II, who had succeeded Ferdinand II (Bomba) as the King of the Two Sicilies in 1859. For some Sicilians, it was a movement towards a united Italy and they drank the toast *Viva Verdi*, ostensibly honouring the Italian composer, himself a radical, but also subscribing to the slogan 'Viva Vittorio Emanuele Re D'Italia'. For most Sicilians, however, it was a renewed protest against poverty and brutal government. For Garibaldi it was an opportunity again to challenge tyranny, and perhaps to renew his allegiance to Mazzini. Cavour remained aloof from the venture. If it failed there could be no repercussions against Piedmont. If it succeeded there would be time enough to see what new opportunities it offered.

In fact the expedition was dramatically successful, though a diversionary landing of 60 volunteers to raid the Papal States proved a very damp squib. The main force landed in Sicily at Marsala, where two British warships mysteriously turned up and unnerved the King's defences while the redshirts disembarked. Joining with the local rebels, Garibaldi's Thousand proceeded to rout the government troops at Calatafimi, and to defeat them again to take Palermo. Victories brought volunteers flocking to join Garibaldi. He was the uncrowned king of Sicily and, by the end of July, Neapolitan troops had been expelled from the island. Cavour thought it was worthwhile to send his representatives to Sicily to explore the possibility of a union with Piedmont, but for Garibaldi the higher priority was to attack the mainland. He crossed the Straits of Messina in August and, supported by a new flood of volunteers, he entered the city of Naples within a month. By now Cavour was alarmed. Garibaldi's soaring prestige threatened to outstrip that of Victor Emmanuel and, even worse, the veteran warrior 'with the brains of an ox and the heart of a lion' (as Mazzini put it) might well march on to Rome and provoke the Catholic powers throughout Europe.

Cavour's immediate interest centred on the Papal States. They still separated the north of Italy from the south. Even if Garibaldi could be persuaded to unite his conquests with Piedmont, there would be no land bridge between them, and Pius IX seemed determined not to concede one. With the

GARIBALDI THE LIBERATOR

Fig. 7.2 A Punch *view of Garibaldi's expedition to Sicily, and to the rescue of the island from 'Bomba Junior' (King Francis II)*

agreement of Victor Emmanuel, Cavour decided to gamble. A Piedmontese army was sent to fight its way south through the Marches and Umbria, keeping well away from Rome, and Papal mercenaries were defeated in a number of engagements, including that at Castelfidardo. The army thus reached the Neapolitan border and entered the territory of Francis II. Francis, meanwhile, instructed his army to re-take Naples, and Garibaldi confronted the Neapolitan troops to the north of the city, on the River Volturno. In a two-day battle Garibaldi's lines were held but, with Francis's forces barring his way, there was no possibility that the guerilla leader could march on Rome. Garibaldi was now rapidly outmanoeuvred by the politicians. In Turin the parliament voted to incorporate in the northern kingdom the Marches and Umbria and the Two Sicilies, provided that this was the will of the people expressed in plebiscites. Cavour wasted no time in having the plebiscites conducted, and a massive vote was recorded in favour of the union: 200 to 1 in the Papal States and well over 100 to 1 in the Two Sicilies. It was little more than a formality when Garibaldi met Victor Emmanuel near the Volturno on 26 October 1860. The King was now at the head of the Piedmontese army. Garibaldi declared: 'I salute the first king of Italy'. Victor Emmanuel inquired politely as to his health – and told the old campaigner that his services were no longer needed. The two of them made a joint public appearance in Naples a few days later, and then Garibaldi sailed for the island of Caprera with a bag of seed-corn.

(d) Venetia and Rome: Bismarck

Victor Emmanuel was 'the first king' of a united Italy, but he retained the title he had in Piedmont, Victor Emmanuel II. As the result of the train of events which had begun at Plombières and of Cavour's quick-witted opportunism, he now reigned in all of Italy except Austrian Venetia and the Papal Patrimony of St Peter around Rome. Cavour told the Italian parliament in Turin that Rome must eventually be the nation's capital, but there was little hope of this for the present while Pius continued to be protected by a French garrison. In any case there were problems enough already, for there were great diversities within the new nation, and there was far more to nation-building than the mere attainment of a common government. The King and Cavour had ensured that Italy had been created as a constitutional monarchy, but many parts of the country had no tradition of constitutional government. Catholics were unsettled by the Pope's condemnation of the national movement, and it was certain that many difficulties lay ahead – difficulties which were increased when Cavour died suddenly in June 1861. (The history of united Italy will be continued in Unit Twelve.)

Both Venetia and Rome were incorporated in Italy when Cavour's successors were able to take advantage of developments elsewhere in Europe. Garibaldi favoured more direct methods and twice left Caprera, intending to march into Rome. In 1862 he landed in the toe of Italy, hoping to raise support among the Neapolitans, but he was quickly arrested by the Italian authorities at Aspromonte, before he could reach the French. In 1867, when the Italian capital had been moved to Florence and the French garrison had been removed from Rome, which Napoleon thought was no longer in danger, Garibaldi landed in the Patrimony and defeated the Papal army. His success was short-lived. The French hastily returned and Garibaldi's guerillas were routed at Mentana. Napoleon III was too sensitive to Catholic opinion in France to let Garibaldi solve the Roman problem so simply.

It was Bismarck, pursuing his own policy for Germany, who provided the answer for Italians both in Venetia and Rome. Prussia went to war with Austria in 1866, and Bismarck was willing enough for the Italians to have Venetia in return for their military assistance. Garibaldi's guerillas harassed their old enemy in the Alps, but the official Italian army under La Marmora was routed in a new engagement at Custozza. The war was won elsewhere by the Prussians, and Italy's acquisition of Venetia by the Treaty of Prague was no more than a side-issue for Bismarck. When the Franco-Prussian War began in

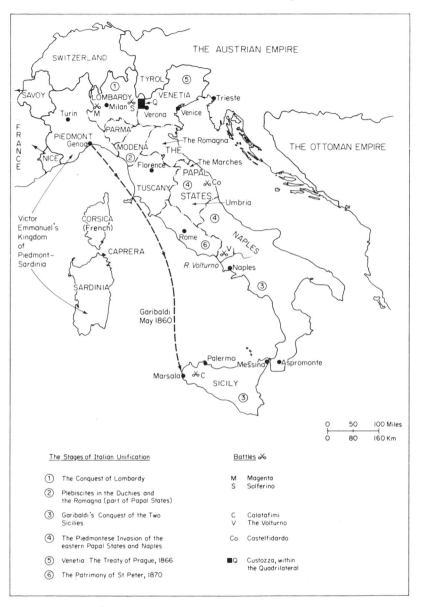

Fig. 7.3 The Making of Italy 1859–70

1870 Napoleon III was forced to recall his troops from Rome. Rome was of little interest to Bismarck. In any case, Pius IX tended to alienate European governments from the Papacy by making an untimely declaration of Papal Infallibility in 1870 (see Section 9.4). At last the way was open, and Victor Emmanuel ordered his army to seize the city. Italy now had its capital, and the Pope retired to the Vatican. But there was no triumphal entry into Rome for Garibaldi. He had gone to help the French against the Prussians, a typically quixotic and generous gesture, but also a shrewd recognition of the fact that the romantic Europe of Garibaldi's youth was finally being buried by the scientific German war machine and by Bismarck's policy of 'blood and iron'. Nor did Garibaldi rejoice in the completion of the unification of Italy. Like Mazzini, he had wanted a republican Italy. Mazzini chose to remain in exile from his native land, and Garibaldi again retired to Caprera. Italy had been united on Piedmontese terms, which was enough for some Italian nationalists

Fig. 7.4 Giuseppe Garibaldi (1807–82), photographed on the island of Caprera, 1865. No lover of monarchy, he held no political office in the Italy he had helped to create

but it did not satisfy the romantics. Nor did it wholly satisfy the most ardent nationalists, for they still laid claim to *Italia Irredenta*, those Italian-speaking areas in the Tyrol and around Trieste which were still in the Austrian Empire, and even to Corsica, which was part of France.

7.3   The Creation of a United Germany

(*a*) Foundations: Prussia

Stability returned to Germany after the upheavals of 1848–9 when Frederick William IV of Prussia made his submission at Olmütz (see page 83). The German Bund was restored and, with it, the authority of Austria. Frederick William lost his reason in 1858, and his brother William became the Regent in Prussia, assuming the crown as William I when Frederick William died in 1861. William had the traditional Hohenzollern sense of duty to the state and, though by no means a liberal himself, he tried to work with his brother's weak parliamentary system by appointing a liberal ministry. But William also had the traditional Hohenzollern respect for a strong army. Like Count von Roon, his War Minister, he was ambitious to modernize and to enlarge the Prussian forces. Young Prussians were traditionally required to do military service, and the growing population was itself enough to demand a larger army. William and Roon proposed almost to double it, to about 400 000 men. The result was a constitutional crisis. Liberals in the Landtag (the Prussian Assembly) objected to additional military expenditure. In 1862 they refused to approve the budget while it included clauses for longer military service and for increased spending. The taxes could not be collected until such financial approval was given, and the King's government could hardly continue in office. It became a matter of honour for William: should he allow himself to be dictated to by parliament? He prepared to abdicate:

> I will not reign, if I cannot do so in such a way as to be responsible to God, my conscience, and my subjects. I cannot do that . . . if I cannot find any ministers . . . willing to conduct my government without subordinating themselves and me to the parliamentary majority.

This was William's view, according to what Bismarck later wrote in his Memoirs. But the King was saved from abdication by Roon's suggestion that he should send for Bismarck.

Otto von Bismarck gave every appearance of being a hard-bitten *Junker* (see Glossary). (Bismarck's father was a Junker, but his mother was the daughter of a Prussian bureaucrat, a man without a title, so in fact Bismarck himself was only half a Junker by descent.) From 1851 he had been a Prussian delegate to the Diet of the German Bund and, more recently, he had served in the Prussian embassies in St Petersburg and Paris. He was not a man to be intimidated by parliamentary majorities, and his ambitions were to serve the

Prussian monarchy and the interests of his father's Junker class. When he accepted appointment as William's Minister-President (chief minister) in September 1862 there began in Prussia a partnership similar to that of Victor Emmanuel and Cavour in Piedmont, though Cavour was considerably more liberal in his attitudes than was Bismarck. The programme for Prussia's military development was continued and, unconstitutionally but effectively, the necessary taxes were collected. Some years later the Prussian Landtag passed an Indemnity Act to legalize what Bismarck had done. In the end it was not Bismarck who had been overawed by the parliament, but the parliament which had been overawed by Bismarck.

Nor was Bismarck overawed by Austria. In his view, Prussia rather than Austria should be the dominant power in Germany and, in 1863, he obstructed Austrian proposals for a reform of the Bund which would have increased

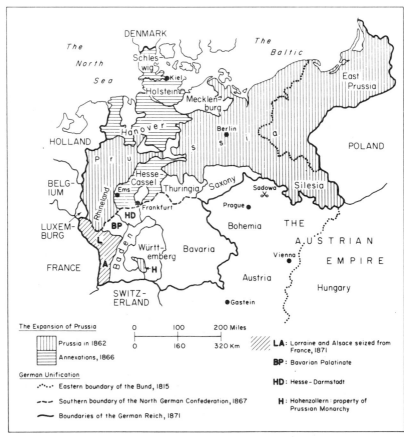

Fig. 7.5 The Making of the German Reich 1864–71

Habsburg authority. In the same year he won favour with Alexander II of Russia, though with hardly anyone else. Palmerston, Napoleon III and even the Austrians were sympathetic to Polish nationalists, who rebelled against the Russians in 1863 and were savagely punished. Bismarck was not prepared to risk nationalist unrest among the Poles who were under Prussian rule, and he was also interested in securing a friendly Russian neighbour and in demonstrating Prussian independence of Austria. He sent General Alvensleben to the Tsar, assuring him of Prussian support, and he warned Napoleon against any attempt to interfere in Poland. Alexander was left with a free hand to crush the rebellion, and the rebels who fled into Prussia were rounded up and returned to him.

(b) The North German Confederation

Frederick William IV had already briefly made the Prussian army the agent of German nationalism in the tangled affairs of Schleswig-Holstein in 1848 (see pages 81–2). Bismarck seized a similar opportunity in 1864 and pressed ahead with it with a great deal more enthusiasm than the earlier King. The affairs of Schleswig-Holstein had been settled for a time in the Treaty of London of 1852. The Duchy of Schleswig, with its largely Danish population, and that of Holstein, largely German, remained under the rule of the king of Denmark, though separate from the Danish kingdom; and the German claimant to part of the territories, the Duke of Augustenburg, received financial compensation. In 1863 the question of Schleswig-Holstein arose again when the Danes proposed to incorporate Schleswig into Denmark. At the same time the Danish throne was inherited by Christian IX. Christian's inheritance came to him through the female line of succession, which was no inheritance at all in German eyes. Germans observed the Salic Law, which denied inheritance through females. A new Duke of Augustenburg, who had recently succeeded to his title, promptly revived his family's old claims. The Diet of the German Confederation supported Augustenburg, and Hanover and Saxony provided him with troops. Bismarck intended to exploit the situation to the advantage of Prussia: Prussia would lead the campaign of the German nationalists. Austria, however, also wished to lead, unwilling to be left behind by Prussia, so the two powers co-operated in insisting that Denmark abide by the Treaty of London and, in declaring war in 1864, to increase the pressure.

It was a one-sided war, soon over. In October 1864 the Treaty of Vienna was signed, whereby:

> His Majesty the King of Denmark renounces all his Rights over the Duchies of Schleswig, Holstein, and Lauenburg in favour of their Majesties the King of Prussia and the Emperor of Austria, engaging to recognize the dispositions which their said Majesties shall make with reference to those Duchies.

The victory was Bismarck's. Palmerston, who sympathized with the Danes, had not dared to interfere, and Napoleon III had not wished to; the interests of the Duke of Augustenburg were quickly forgotten, and the Treaty of Vienna handed the Duchies not to the Confederation Diet but to Prussia and Austria. By the Convention of Gastein in August 1865, Austria agreed to administer Holstein while Prussia administered Schleswig, and tiny Lauenburg was incorporated into Prussia. Prussia also obtained the right to cut a canal through Holstein, to link the North Sea with the Baltic.

Increasingly confident, Bismarck moved nearer to a confrontation with Austria, whose prestige had been severely damaged in recent years – driven out of Italy except for Venetia, ignored during the Polish rebellion, and less respected now in the German Bund for repudiating Augustenburg and agreeing to separate the Duchies at Gastein. The moment seemed to be near when Prussia might replace Austria as the leader of the Bund. Bismarck was a believer in *Realpolitik*, conducting his diplomacy with meticulous attention to detail and taking care to negotiate from strength. The Prussian army, organized by Roon from the War Ministry and by Helmuth von Moltke as the Chief of Staff, was a powerful weapon, but Bismarck also wished to make sure that Austria would be stripped of allies. It was easy enough to win Italian co-operation with the promise of Venetia. Tsar Alexander was already pro-Prussian. Napoleon III was a greater problem. The French were likely to be hostile to the further growth of Prussian power, which would alter the balance of power in Europe, and it was at least possible that Britain might collaborate with France to prevent major changes in spite of Britain's limited involvement in continental affairs. A shadowy meeting therefore took place in October 1865 at Biarritz, where Bismarck talked with Napoleon III. The Prussian concluded that he had nothing to fear from the French at least in the short term. Napoleon, for his part, appears to have returned home half-expecting that France would be compensated in western Europe for any changes in the balance of power, but believing that whatever happened any conflict between Prussia and Austria was bound to weaken both of them and leave France all the stronger. Napoleon was not a master of *Realpolitik*.

Austro-Prussian relations deteriorated rapidly early in 1866. The Prussians governed Schleswig with an iron hand, but Austrian rule in Holstein was lax enough for the supporters of Augustenburg to be active there. In response to Prussian criticisms Austria proposed to refer the future of the Duchies to the Confederation Diet; and the Prussians invaded Holstein. The Prussians then declared war on Austria on 18 June, after proposal and counter-proposal had been made in the Confederation Diet, and the majority of German opinion had sided with Austria. It was evident that the only way to destroy Habsburg authority in Germany was now on the battlefield.

William I excitedly addressed the Prussian people:

> I have done all I could to spare Prussia the burden and sacrifices of war; many people know this; God, who searches all hearts, knows it. . . . We must fight for our very existence. . . . Let us petition Almighty God, the director of the history of nations, the disposer of battles, to bless our arms.

Moltke proceeded ruthlessly to destroy the enemy. Within days, Prussian forces occupied Saxony, Hesse and Hanover, crushing their armies before they could unite. Austrian troops were driven back into Bohemia when they tried to invade Silesia and, on 3 July, they were smashed at Sadowa (Königgrätz) under the eyes of William I and Bismarck. The Austrian supremacy in Germany was ended and the way to Vienna was open. William was enthusiastic about making a triumphal entry into the Habsburg capital and obliterating once and for all the Hohenzollern memories of Olmütz. But Bismarck had other ideas. He had achieved what he wanted: to exclude Austria from Germany. To advance further would cause international alarm and perhaps embitter the Austrians irrevocably. He later recollected:

> We had to avoid wounding Austria too severely. . . . We were not there to sit in judgment, but to pursue the German policy. . . . Our task was the establishment . . . of German national unity.

He persuaded William to agree to a truce at Nikolsburg, and to confirm it in August at the *Treaty of Prague*, of which Article IV was the keynote:

> His Majesty the Emperor of Austria acknowledges the dissolution of the Germanic Confederation as hitherto constituted, and gives his consent to a new organization in Germany without the participation of the Imperial Austrian State.

Alongside this the other Articles were merely bonuses: Austria surrendered its rights in Schleswig-Holstein, ceded Venetia (to Napoleon III to be handed to Italy, as had been agreed at Biarritz), and paid 40 million thalers to help to finance Prussia's war effort.

Austria was in any case not the only defeated state. In addition to Schleswig-Holstein, Prussia grabbed Hanover, much of Hesse, and the city of Frankfurt, where the mayor hanged himself. The remaining states of north Germany were dragged into the North German Confederation, leaving outside it only the mainly Catholic states of south Germany. The constitution of the North German Confederation was drafted quickly but carefully, to invest real power in the partnership of William and Bismarck, but to provide a constitutional framework which might appease German liberals. The King of Prussia was to be the President of the Confederation, in control of its army and foreign policy. The King would appoint the Federal Chancellor (Bismarck), and the Chancellor was responsible to the President, not to the Confederation parliament. The latter had two houses. The upper house, the Bundesrat, had 43 representatives who were chosen by the governments of member-states, 17 of them by the government of Prussia. The lower house, the Reichstag, was elected by manhood suffrage, but the powers of the Reichstag were limited to much the same way as those of the Landtag in Prussia. Cavour had once said that his aim was 'the aggrandisement of Piedmont'. Bismarck's aim, it seemed, was the aggrandisement of Prussia.

(c) The German Reich

Before the North German Confederation was transformed into an Empire which also included south Germany, a third war was fought, this time against France. Napoleon III viewed with dismay the brief Austro-Prussian War and the events which followed it. The European balance of power was so changed, that it could be said that it was France that was defeated at Sadowa, faced as it now was with a far more powerful neighbour. No compensation was forthcoming and, when Napoleon fumblingly raised the issue, trying to buy Luxemburg from Holland and expressing ambitions in Belgium and the Palatinate, he only alarmed the south Germans and upset the British. Bismarck made defence treaties with the south German states, and left Napoleon to flounder. A threat from France was the likeliest incentive for south Germans to seek association with Prussia, and anti-French feeling was a useful cement with which to bind Germans together. Prodded by propaganda, German public opinion became gradually more enthusiastic about nationhood.

An affair only slightly less obscure than that of Schleswig-Holstein brought matters to a head. Queen Isabella of Spain was overthrown in 1868 (see page 38). Spaniards quickly rejected republicanism and looked for another monarch. With Bismarck's connivance the crown was offered to Prince Leopold of Hohenzollern-Sigmaringen, a relative of William I. Bismarck had to work hard to persuade Leopold and the King to accept it. News of the secret manoeuvring leaked out, and reached Paris at the beginning of July 1870. It was promptly assumed that Hohenzollerns to the south as well as to the east would be a further threat to the balance of power, and to France. Napoleon III felt unable to endure another diplomatic setback, and he sent his ambassador, Vincent Benedetti, to ask William I to veto the candidature. William was holidaying at Ems. He had no great interest in the Spanish throne and no desire to confront France, and the candidature was withdrawn. There the matter would have ended but for the incredible folly of the French.

Benedetti was ordered to see William again, to obtain a guarantee that the Hohenzollerns would never again seek the Spanish throne. William broke off the interview: he had already given his word. But he reported the events to Bismarck by telegram from Ems to Berlin – the *Ems Telegram*. Bismarck received the Telegram while dining with Roon and Moltke. William had casually mentioned that the Chancellor might publish the Telegram if he wished. Determined now to provoke war with France, Bismarck not only published, he edited. In its much shortened form Bismarck's version was insultingly terse, ending:

> His Majesty, the King, thereupon decided not to receive the French Ambassador again, and sent the aide-de-camp on duty to tell him that his Majesty had nothing further to communicate to the ambassador.

This apparent rebuff was calculated to anger the French. The earlier part of Bismarck's version, referring to the French demand for an all-time guarantee, was calculated to anger Germans. Bismarck later boasted, accurately, that he had not altered a single word. But Moltke jubilantly noted of Bismarck's editing:

> Now that has another sound; before, it sounded like a signal for retreat; now, like a fanfare in response to a challenge.

The press, including that in France, carried Bismarck's text. Napoleon considered there was no alternative but to go to war to retrieve his tottering reputation. Germans were equally belligerent. When hostilities began, other nations declared their neutrality, with the British warning both sides to respect Belgian neutrality. The war was therefore certain to be fought around the French provinces of Alsace-Lorraine, whose borders were mainly with south German states. While German armies were routing the French, Bismarck busied himself with the diplomatic arrangements which brought the south German states into the Confederation, and transformed it into the German Reich.

Directed by Moltke, the German armies with their superior artillery had virtually won the war by October 1870. Troops were moved quickly to the front by rail, and the German command was far superior to that of the French. Napoleon took the field himself, but he was inexperienced and in poor health.

Fig. 7.6 Napoleon III, the defeated, and Bismarck, the victorious, shortly after the Battle of Sedan, September 1870 – a painting by W. Camphausen

Marshal Bazaine was defeated at Gravelotte, retired to Metz, and was besieged there. Other French forces marched with Napoleon to relieve him, only to be cut to pieces at Sedan. 20 000 Frenchmen were killed and 80 000, among them the Emperor, were taken prisoner. That was on 1 September. Two months later Bazaine surrendered Metz. By that time the Germans were besieging Paris and, although various efforts had been made to organize further French resistance, the city surrendered late in January 1871. Napoleon III had abdicated at Sedan and France was in new political turmoil (see Section 11.2), but Bismarck was making progress in creating the new Germany, rubbing salt into the wounds of the French by establishing his headquarters at Versailles.

The German Reich was proclaimed at Versailles on 18 January 1871.

Fig. 7.7 William I proclaimed the Kaiser of the German Reich at Versailles, January 1871. This contemporary engraving with its uniforms and flags captures the martial spirit of the occasion

Special concessions were made to Bavaria, to persuade the Bavarians to join the Reich. They kept certain legal privileges, their own postal system and railways, and control of Bavarian troops in peacetime. Baden and Hesse-Darmstadt joined the Reich more eagerly, and the Grand-Duke of Württemberg was pushed into the Reich by his subjects. It was a simple matter to change the constitution of the North German Confederation to that of the Reich, with William I as Kaiser rather than President, and Bismarck the Imperial rather than the Federal Chancellor. Basically the constitution remained unchanged. William showed some reluctance to take the title of Kaiser, but the King of Bavaria was persuaded to offer him the dignity: this was no crown from the gutter. In a grand ceremony at Versailles, the Empire was proclaimed:

> A choir consisting of men of the Seventh, Forty-Seventh and Fifty-Eighth regiments intoned the choral, 'Let all the world rejoice in the Lord'. . . . A sermon [was] preached by the Reverend A. Rogge . . . [and] the grand-duke of Baden stepped forth and exclaimed, 'Long live His Majesty the Emperor'.

The Franco-German Peace Treaty was signed at Frankfurt in May 1871. Carried along by popular pressures, Bismarck agreed to terms which were more savage than he would have wished, and which left France with a rooted desire for revenge. Alsace and much of Lorraine were incorporated into Germany. Parts of France were to be occupied by German troops until 5000 million francs had been paid to Germany. In the interval between January and May the Germans had insisted on a triumphal entry into Paris. All the seeds for future conflict had now been sown. But in the immediate future France faced grave internal problems and, in Germany as in Italy, the unification had to be consolidated by the fostering of national consciousness.

(d) Kleindeutschland

The German Empire of 1871 did not include all the German-speaking people of Europe. It was *Kleindeutschland* (Little Germany) rather than *Grossdeutschland* (Large Germany), but it was part of Bismarck's mastery of *Realpolitik* to know that he had gone to the limits of what was possible at the time. Other German-speaking people were within the Austrian Empire, most of them in Austria itself. A *Grossdeutschland* which included these Germans was not possible until the Austrian Empire had disintegrated, and it was created eventually, though only briefly, by Adolf Hitler in the late 1930s (see Section 24.2). Meanwhile, the Habsburgs saved their Empire by a measure of reorganization. Driven from Italy and deprived of influence in Germany, it had become essential for the Austrian government to take greater care of what was left, and the most important change was that of 1867, the *Ausgleich*, which set up the Austro-Hungarian Dual Monarchy (see Section 13.1). *Kleindeutschland*, however, was a very substantial state in the heartland of Europe. It had a population of 41 million, almost all of them German-speaking, although the acquisition of Alsace-Lorraine dragged in a million who were French, and it already outstripped France both in population and in coal production. It was Bismarck's intention now to build upon these foundations, and to make Germany the leading power on the continent, not by further territorial expansion, but by economic development (see Section 10.1).

Further Reading

Holt, E.: *Risorgimento*. Macmillan (London, 1970).
Holt, E.: *Giuseppe Mazzini, the Great Conspirator*. Dobson (London, 1968).
Moses, J.: *Germany 1848–1879*. Heinemann (London, 1973).
Sellman, R. R.: *Bismarck and the Unification of Germany*. Methuen (London, 1974).
Sellman, R. R.: *Garibaldi and the Unification of Italy*. Methuen (London, 1974).
Woolf, S. J.: *The Italian Risorgimento*. Longman (Harlow, 1969).

Documentary

Garibaldi and the Risorgimento (Jackdaw Wallet). Cape.
Hewison, A.: *Bismarck and the Unification of Germany*. Edward Arnold (London, 1970).
Leeds, C.: *The Unification of Italy*. Wayland (Hove, 1974).
Lloyd, R. L. H.: *Cavour and Italian Unification*, 1854–60. Edward Arnold (London, 1975).
Smith, D. Mack: *The Making of Italy, 1796–1870*. Macmillan (London, 1968).

Exercises

1. Compare the divisions which existed in Germany and Italy in the mid-1850s, making use of Figs. 7.3 and 7.5. What further divisions existed in German and Italian society, not shown on the maps?
2. What part was played in the unification of Italy by *each* of the men shown on the Italian stamp on page 107? Which man, in your opinion, played the most important part?
3. Explain to what the cartoon on page 111 refers, and consider how fitting was the title, 'Garibaldi the Liberator', which was given to it.
4. Why did the Prussians think it necessary that there should be 'a confrontation with Austria' (page 118), and how did this confrontation result in the birth of the North German Confederation?
5. What key steps in the unification of Germany are depicted in the illustrations on pages 121 and 122?
6. 'Bismarck's aim, it seemed, was the aggrandisement of Prussia' (page 119). Explain this view of Bismarck's policy from 1862 to 1871.
7. Show how Napoleon III helped to promote the unification of Italy, but tried to obstruct the unification of Germany.
8. Making use where necessary of the Index and cross-references, define *each* of the following terms: *Italia Irredenta* (page 115); *Realpolitik* (page 118); *Grossdeutschland* (page 123); *Kleindeutschland* (page 123); *Ausgleich* (page 123).

The Great Powers 1815–71 and the Eastern Question

8.1 National Policies and the Balance of Power

The settlement of 1814–15 produced a balance of power in Europe which was not seriously disturbed until Italy and Germany were created (see Unit Seven). The powers in general remained cautious. They pursued their national interests zealously, but only occasionally violently. In the years 1815 to 1871, the longest war in which the great powers were involved was that in the Crimea. It was a product of the Eastern Question, and a conflict which remained localized. But even localized and short wars became increasingly bloody, and the carnage at Solferino (see page 108) was such that the International Red Cross was founded soon afterwards (see Section 23.1). The bayonet was particularly deadly, but weaponry in general was continuously developed to increase its killing-power. The armies of Roon and Moltke fought devastating campaigns with their breech-loading rifles and thunderous artillery. Moreover, it was a part of the new *Realpolitik* (see Glossary) after 1850, that men like Cavour and Bismarck were ready to unleash war in pursuit of their diplomatic ambitions.

British policy in the years after 1815 was to avoid involvement in European affairs, as far as that was consistent with the country's commercial interests and its security. Prussian policy, before the arrival of Bismarck, was somewhat parochial, essentially concerned to preserve the *status quo* in central Europe. Austrian policy favoured the *status quo* generally, since the Habsburgs and Metternich were only too well aware that the Austrian Empire was a rickety structure, ill-fitted to withstand storms. The other great European powers were France and Russia. Although French policy still bore traces of the ambitiousness of Louis XIV and Napoleon I, it was much affected by political changes within France, while the Russian policy of the tsars was much entangled in the Eastern Question.

8.2 French Foreign Policy

Bourbon foreign policy was cautious and undistinguished at a time when the powers were still deeply suspicious of the country which had produced Napoleon I. Internationally the reign of Louis XVIII coincided with the Congress Period, during which France was admitted to the Quintuple Alliance (see

Section 2.2). An early flirtation with Britain and with liberalism did not last. France remained aloof from the Congress of Troppau but, by 1823, Artois was influential in France, and French troops went to suppress rebellion in Spain. Any further intervention to restore the old order, which Artois might have contemplated in Portugal and Latin America, was frustrated by Canning and President Monroe of the USA. The French nevertheless co-operated with Canning in the matter of Greek independence (see Section 3.3(b)).

Louis Philippe was cautious too (see Section 4.2(c)). As the heir of a liberal revolution he felt some obligation to pursue liberal policies abroad, often in conjunction with Britain. He was thus instrumental in securing the independence of Belgium (see Section 3.3(d)). But he was also ready to promote French influence when opportunity occurred, especially when he was criticized in France for apparently acting in Belgium only under Palmerston's supervision, and for not persisting in making a Frenchman King of the Belgians. Ambition, however, led to setbacks in two areas. Half-hearted support for Mehemet Ali involved him in the Eastern Question (see Section 8.3). The other area was Spain.

French policy in Spain began promisingly enough. In 1834 Louis Philippe joined Palmerston in the Treaty of London, for the preservation of constitutionalism in Spain and Portugal. The Treaty even seemed chivalrous, since Palmerston and the French King were going to the aid of ladies in distress. Isabella II had just inherited the Spanish crown, Maria II, the crown of Portugal – and each was threatened by a reactionary uncle (see Section 3.2). The young Queens were assisted by regents and, in the Treaty of London, the regents, Palmerston and Louis Philippe, undertook to co-operate in:

restoring to the subjects of each [Queen] the blessings of internal Peace.

Britain would send a naval force, Louis Philippe any necessary additional help. In fact they did very little and a civil war dragged on in Spain until 1839, though the Queens survived. The question of Isabella's marriage arose in 1846. The British obstructed a French candidature, but Louis Philippe arranged for his son Antoine to marry the Queen's younger sister, in the hope that some day a Frenchman might inherit the Spanish throne. Palmerston obtained his promise to delay the marriage until the Queen herself had an heir. In what he thought was a master-stroke, however, the French King arranged for his son to marry Isabella's sister on the very same day that Isabella married an ageing Spaniard who was thought to be incapable of fathering children. Nothing came of Louis Philippe's scheming, except the fury of Palmerston. Although she soon lived in separation from her husband, Isabella somehow gave birth to nine children, one of whom, Alfonso XII, gained the throne in 1875. The marriages were almost the last of Louis Philippe's achievements in foreign policy. He contrived to support the Sonderbund, the losing side in the Swiss Civil War (see page 88), and thus to annoy Palmerston again, but his own throne had been lost before the Swiss settled their differences.

YE TOURNAMENT

Fig. 8.1 A Punch *view of his old enemy, Louis Philippe (see Fig. 4.3), the cloth of the King's horse suitably decorated with money bags. At first sight it seemed that Louis Philippe had outwitted the British (lion) over the affair of the Spanish Marriages of Queen Isabella and her younger sister, shown here in the centre of the spectators. Von Coburg was an unsuccessful suitor favoured by the British*

Louis Philippe's foreign policy was as shabby as much else in his reign. If he had any visions at all of French glory, they were less in evidence than those of Louis Napoleon who succeeded him. But Napoleon's foreign policy achieved no more than Louis Philippe had achieved, and its history after the Crimean War was chiefly a tale of disaster (see Section 6.2(*d*)). In the years 1830 to 1871 the French achieved some expansion of their overseas empire, but their foreign policy as a whole served their national interests far less effectively than did British policy, which reinforced Britain's economic supremacy. Perhaps one of Napoleon III's most useful services to France was to co-operate with Palmerston in bullying the Chinese. The Chinese were forced to sign the Treaties of Tientsin in 1858 and a series of Peking Conventions, which admitted Europeans to their ports and allowed them to establish diplomatic missions. France thus received a share of a profitable Far Eastern trade. In Europe, however, Napoleon III merely gained Savoy and Nice while losing Alsace-Lorraine and, when he abdicated, a powerful new Germany was emerging to the east of France, which was to be a serious threat to France until after the Second World War.

8.3 Russian Foreign Policy and the Eastern Question

The Eastern Question was essentially the question of the future of the Balkan and eastern Mediterranean territories. They were under the control of the

Ottoman Empire (see Figs. 1.5 and 3.1), which barred Russia's path into the Mediterranean. The Turks were Moslem, whereas the Russians, like many inhabitants of the Balkans, were Orthodox Christian and the Russians resented the harsh treatment of the Balkan peoples by the Turks, especially since many of those peoples were, like the Russians, Slavs. A long history of Russian-Turkish conflict already existed before 1815, and both sides remembered past injustices and atrocities. In western Europe it was taken for granted that Russia's policy was to smash the Ottoman Empire, and the Ottoman Empire seemed to grow ever less capable of resisting such a threat. Yet the British and French preferred the Turkish Empire to remain intact, as a safeguard for their profitable commercial interests in the eastern Mediterranean. On the other hand, they could hardly condone Turkish misgovernment, which was an affront to liberals and Christians everywhere.

There were, therefore, two dilemmas in the Eastern Question. One was that of the British and French, who feared Russian expansion, but found it difficult to uphold an outdated Empire in order to prevent it. The other was that of the Russians, who were tempted to support nationalist and even liberal uprisings against a legitimate government, in order to advance their own national interests. Of the two the Russians were the less worried by their dilemma: a campaign against the Turks could always be passed off as a religious and moral crusade. The Austrians also had an interest in the Eastern Question since the Austrian Empire adjoined that of the Turks. They were like a pair of semi-detached houses: it was in the interest of the Austrians that the Turkish house should neither catch fire, nor simply fall down.

Anti-Turk revolutions in Serbia and Greece provided the first indications after 1815 that the Ottoman Empire was far from stable (see Sections 3.3(*a*) and (*b*)). Both Serbia and Greece were effectively free by 1832 but, especially in the case of Greece, the major powers had been caught up in the turmoil. Greek Independence was virtually certain after the naval engagement at Navarino, a setback for the Turks which so infuriated the Sultan, Mahmud II, that in his rage he repudiated past agreements with Russia, and closed the Dardanelles to Russia's trade. Nicholas I and Mahmud had only recently settled some outstanding differences in the Convention of Akkerman of 1826:

> wishing to consolidate the relations of the two Empires, by giving them as bases a perfect harmony and an entire reciprocal confidence.

The Sultan had promised to respect certain rights of his subjects in Serbia, Wallachia and Moldavia, and similarly to respect Russia's freedom of the seas. The withdrawal of these promises provoked Russia into declaring war in April 1828. By September 1829 Mahmud sought peace, and the *Treaty of Adrianople* was signed. Near-independence was conceded to Greece, Serbia, Wallachia and Moldavia; and the Sultan paid an indemnity and made a minor cession of territory in Asia to the Tsar. The Treaty also stated that:

Russian subjects shall enjoy, throughout the whole extent of the Ottoman Empire, as well by land as by sea, the full and entire freedom of trade secured to them by the Treaties concluded heretofore.

Mahmud had scarcely recovered from this blow before he suffered another. His Egyptian vassal, Mehemet Ali, attacked Syria, demanding reward for his earlier services to the Sultan in Greece (see Sections 3.3(*b*) and (*c*)). Turkish armies were routed at the Beilan Pass and at Konia. Mehemet's army had been trained by the French, who had continued to be fascinated by Egypt since Napoleon I fought there in the 1790s. The French also had interests to protect in Egypt, and Louis Philippe was therefore unwilling to save the Sultan. Fresh from settling the problem of the Greek constitution, Palmerston showed no inclination to become involved. In desperation Mahmud turned to Russia, and Nicholas I jumped at the opportunity to send naval and land forces into the Ottoman Empire. The British and French were now alarmed at what the Russians might get out of this, and they pressed the Sultan to come to terms with Mehemet and to send the Russians home. In the Convention of Kutaya, the Egyptian renewed his acknowledgment of the Sultan's overlordship and was given control of Syria. The Russians withdrew, but not before Nicholas extracted another agreement from the Turks, the *Treaty of Unkiar Skelessi* of 1833. In a promise of mutual aid the Tsar reserved the right to 'assist' the Sultan again, when necessary, and there was a secret definition of how Turkey was to:

confine its action in favour of the Imperial Court of Russia to closing the Strait of the Dardanelles . . . to not allowing any Foreign Vessels of War to enter therein under any pretext whatsoever.

The secret leaked out. It seemed possible that the Dardanelles would become a private channel for the Russian navy, and Palmerston was even more alarmed. The Treaty of Unkiar Skelessi was to be reviewed after eight years, however, and the British were sure to be quicker off the mark next time there was a crisis in the area. Mehemet Ali precipitated a new crisis in 1839.

Mehemet wanted to be completely independent of the Sultan, and relations so deteriorated that a new conflict broke out between them. The Turkish army again suffered defeat, at Nezib. Mahmud died a week later, leaving his throne to Abdul Mejid, a mere youngster of sixteen. With that disloyalty which was typical of the chaotic affairs of the Ottoman Empire, the Turkish navy sailed for Egypt where its admiral surrendered it to Mehemet Ali. And with the complications which were typical of the Eastern Question, Russia, Britain and France were soon meddling in the affair. Nicholas I was conciliatory and he was willing to reach some agreement with Palmerston. The French were out of step, however. While Russia and Britain supported the Turks, the French supported Mehemet, thinking to extend their influence throughout his flourishing empire. Thiers returned to office in 1840 as Louis Philippe's chief minister, and he trumpeted his intention of helping the Egyptian. The powers

were not impressed: in the *Convention of London* of July 1840, Russia and
Britain agreed with Austria and Prussia that terms should be imposed on
Mehemet. The Sultan was advised to offer him hereditary rights in Egypt and
lifetime control of southern Syria, but northern Syria and Crete were to be
returned to the Turks. Led to expect French assistance, Mehemet refused to
agree. The British navy arrived, but not that of the French. While the British
were subduing the Egyptians, with some assistance from the Austrians, Louis
Philippe dismissed Thiers and appointed more cautious ministers. Mehemet
was driven out of Syria and left with nothing but hereditary rights in Egypt.
The French meekly accepted the settlement.

The question of the Dardanelles, which had irked Palmerston since 1833,
was settled in a further Convention of London in July 1841 (the *Straits
Convention*), when Nicholas I again proved conciliatory. The major powers
were now joined by France and the Convention expressed their:

> unanimous determination to conform to the ancient rule of the Ottoman Empire,
> according to which the passage of the Straits of the Dardanelles and of the Bosphorus
> is always to be closed to Foreign Ships of War, as long as the Porte [Turkish
> government] is at peace.

The Russian advantages of Unkiar Skelessi were thus cancelled. There was
now a lull in the Eastern Question, giving Abdul Mejid a breathing-space. But
in spite of Nicholas I's moderation, the belief persisted in the west that it was
Russian policy to destroy the Ottoman Empire. In Britain, Russia was persistently seen as an ugly bear with long claws.

8.4   Russian Foreign Policy and the Crimean War

(a) The Origins of the War

Nicholas I paid a visit to Britain in 1844 while the cordial relations of 1841 still
lasted; but he merely confirmed his reputation in Britain as a tyrant when the
European revolutions of 1848 occurred. Palmerston heartily disapproved of
the use of Russian troops in Hungary. Louis Napoleon disapproved too, and
soon had his own further reasons for an anti-Russian policy (see pages 101-2).
The Ottoman Empire, meanwhile, staggered along and, during conversations
with the British about disturbances there, Nicholas observed in 1853: 'We
have a sick man, a seriously sick man, on our hands'. The Turkish sickness was
evident for all to see, and Nicholas seems to have intended nothing more than
co-operation with Britain if some new crisis arose. But he mentioned the word
'partition' and British suspicions were aroused again.

A new problem was already beginning to bubble, in which Napoleon III
chose to involve the honour of France. There was rivalry between Catholics
and the Orthodox Church in the Holy Land, where both wanted the keys to

Christian shrines in Bethlehem and Jerusalem. Napoleon III saw an opportunity to please French Catholics in this, and to recover some of the French
influence in the eastern Mediterranean which Louis Philippe had lost in 1840.
He backed the Catholics. Nicholas backed the Orthodox Church and reminded the Sultan that Russia had old treaty rights to protect Christians in the
Ottoman Empire. Some Russian forces were mobilized, further to remind the
Sultan that Turkey was too weak to resist. The British view was that Nicholas
was being unreasonable, and the British ambassador in Constantinople, Stratford de Redcliffe, encouraged the Sultan to reject the demands of the Menshekov mission from the Tsar, which sought a confirmation of Russia's treaty
rights. Lord Aberdeen was now Prime Minister in Britain and, in June 1853,
he sent a British fleet to Besika Bay. Not to be left behind, Napoleon sent a
French fleet too. Before the end of the month, the Tsar ordered Russian troops
to occupy Moldavia and Wallachia, to underline his military strength. Thus
began a tale of diplomatic incompetence which led to the Crimean War.

   Britain, France, Austria and Prussia drew up the Vienna Note, hopefully
advising the Sultan to abide by the ancient treaties – which was what Nicholas I
wanted him to do. Abdul Mejid assumed this meant he should defy the
Russians, and he declared that the Turks themselves would protect their

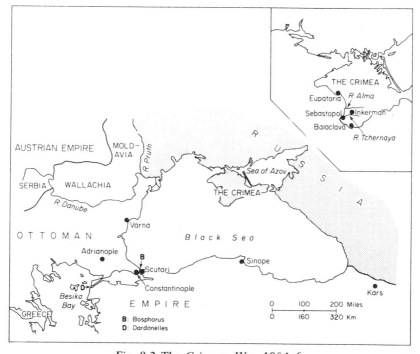

Fig. 8.2 The Crimean War 1854–6

Christian subjects – which brought no comfort at all to the Christian subjects! Nicholas was ready to negotiate some face-saving formula, but the British and French were merely negative. The Sultan was allowed to follow his own crazy path. He declared war on Russia in October and engaged the Russians in Wallachia. Apart from moving their fleets to Constantinople and appealing for peace, the British and French seemed spellbound. British policy might have been more decisive had Palmerston not been dismissed from the Foreign Office in 1851 but, as it was, the British government simply watched events – the most spectacular of which was the destruction of a Turkish fleet by the Russians off Sinope at the end of November.

This was Russian aggression in western eyes. Public opinion – the press anyway – demanded resolute action. The British and French fleets entered the Black Sea regardless of treaty commitments, and the Russians were ordered to withdraw from Wallachia and Moldavia. This time, the Russians did nothing, and Britain and France declared war on the Tsar in March 1854. Troops were

Fig. 8.3 An artist's impression of the dashing Lord Cardigan, who led the Charge of the Light Brigade at the Battle of Balaclava. Cardigan was one of the few who survived this encounter in the Valley of Death

landed at Varna where they quickly fell prey to cholera. Under diplomatic pressure from Austria, which bordered Wallachia and Moldavia, the Russians then withdrew from these principalities, and so there was nowhere left to fight in the Balkans. Both the British and the French, however, were determined to fight the Russians somewhere. A master-plan was conceived: they would invade the Crimea and destroy the Russian naval base at Sebastopol. They arrived at Eupatoria in September 1854, setting themselves to make a triumphal march of almost a hundred miles to the port. At this point the generals showed themselves a match for the politicians in incompetence.

(b) The Events of the War

Almost no preparations had been made for a Crimean campaign. The Russian winter was already approaching when the campaign began, and Nicholas could console himself that 'Generals January and February' were likely to make good the deficiencies of such commanders as Menshekov. The Allied forces were commanded by Lord Raglan and St Arnaud, a dual control which left plenty of scope for Anglo-French bickering, not least because, aged and confused, Raglan sometimes imagined that this was still the Napoleonic War against the French. Both of them died during the war and there was some limited improvement in command under their successors, Generals Simpson and Canrobert. There was also some improvement in supply after the first deadly winter, and after Palmerston became Prime Minister in Britain in February 1855. Nevertheless, Sebastopol was not taken until September 1855 and there was no peace until February 1856. By that time the despatches of William Russell, correspondent of *The Times*, had made the British public fully aware of the whole sorry story of the Crimean campaign.

After landing at Eupatoria the Allies had struggled southwards to the River Alma, where Menshekov was beaten back. By mid-October 1854 Sebastopol was under bombardment. It was hardly a secure fortress, but the Allies decided to besiege it rather than make a direct attack. This gave time for Count Todleben, a Russian engineer, to strengthen Sebastopol's defences. Before the winter set in the Russians made two counter-attacks, at Balaclava and Inkerman; and on both occasions the incompetence of the commanders took a heavy toll of the soldiers. The winter took a further heavy toll, at least of the Allies. Supply ships sank in storms, and the death toll from wounds and disease would have been even more horrifying but for the work of Florence Nightingale and her nurses at Scutari, where the more fortunate casualties were sent. Cavour's Piedmontese arrived to give support to the Allies, and the bitter struggle continued around Sebastopol for much of 1855. The naval base was finally taken; the French were delighted that it was they who first broke through the defences. When the War ended half a million lives had been lost, more than half of them Russian. The French had lost 100 000 men, the British 60 000. Between them, politicians and generals had made a remarkably costly series of blunders in one of the most useless of all wars. 'The Crimea,' said Bright – 'a Crime.'

(c) The Peace of Paris

It was never clear what the Allies were fighting for, although a military success at Sebastopol became almost an obsession with the French. Diplomacy continued during much of the war and the Austrians played a prominent part in it, anxious to secure a settlement for Wallachia and Moldavia and the free navigation of the River Danube. One result of this was a rift between Austria and Russia, which was later to weaken the Habsburgs when they had to deal with Cavour and Bismarck. Before the end of 1855 Austria was threatening to join the war unless Russia agreed to end it. A new Tsar, Alexander II, was now on the Russian throne, and the capture of Kars from the Turks gave Russia something with which to bargain. Mutual suspicions between Palmerston and Napoleon III helped to persuade Britain, and France too, that a treaty should

"GENERAL FÉVRIER" TURNED TRAITOR.
"RUSSIA HAS TWO GENERALS IN WHOM SHE CAN CONFIDE—GENERALS JANVIER AND FÉVRIER."—*Speech of the late Emperor of Russia.*

Fig. 8.4 The Russian winter of January and February traditionally took a heavy toll of those who invaded Russia, and the Allies in the Crimea suffered severely. A patriotic Punch *took some satisfaction from the fact that Tsar Nicholas I died too in February – actually 2 March, but still February by the Russian calendar*

be negotiated. Fighting ended on 1 February 1856, and the peacemakers assembled in Paris.

The Treaty of Paris was signed in March 1856. The Allies evacuated the Crimea, and the Russians returned Kars to the Sultan. The Black Sea was neutralized: there were to be no warships on its waters and no naval bases on its shores. Freedom of navigation on the Danube was guaranteed, and Russia withdrew from the mouth of the River by transferring a small part of Bessarabia to Moldavia. With Wallachia, Moldavia kept near-independence under the overlordship of the Sultan, and Russia gave up all claims to special authority in the principalities. Much else, such as commercial privileges, were restored to the pre-war situation, with the Sultan making another of his many promises to treat his Christian subjects decently:

> having, in his constant solicitude for the welfare of his subjects, issued a Firman [decree], which while ameliorating their condition without distinction of Religion or of Race, records his generous intentions towards the Christian population of his Empire.

The Straits Convention was renewed, closing the Straits to all warships when the Ottoman Empire was at peace.

The most important clause of the Treaty was perhaps that neutralizing the Black Sea. It was repudiated by Alexander II when Europe was occupied with the Franco-Prussian War in 1870. Other parts of the Treaty crumbled rapidly too. In 1862 Wallachia and Moldavia united to become Rumania, and fifteen years later they shook off the last remaining authority of the Sultan. The Sultan for his part showed very little 'solicitude for the welfare of his subjects' and, by 1875, there was a new explosion in his Empire (see Section 15.1). It was a fundamental weakness of the Treaty of Paris that no one had been left with the right to protect Turkey's Christians, the very issue on which the war had begun. Indeed, the peacemakers had specifically rejected the right to interfere in Turkey's internal affairs. The Crimean War and the Treaty of Paris were therefore merely milestones along the dreary road to the settlement of the Eastern Question. Almost nothing had been settled. The western powers were satisfied that a setback had been administered to the ambitions of the Russians, but the biggest setback was that which had been administered, unwittingly, to the unfortunate subjects of the Ottoman Empire. Even if the intentions of Abdul Mejid were good, a new Sultan came to power in 1861, Abdul Aziz, who combined great extravagance with the traditional Turkish inability to control brutal regional officials.

Further Reading

Anderson, M. S.: *The Eastern Question, 1774-1923.* Macmillan (London, 1966).
Hearder, H.: *Europe in the Nineteenth Century, 1830-80.* Longman (Harlow, 1966).

Documentary

The Crimean War (Jackdaw Wallet). Cape.

Exercises

1. Explain how the cartoonist illustrates various aspects of the affair of the Spanish marriages in the cartoon on page 127, and consider whether the cartoonist seemed to be hostile to Louis Philippe.
2. What do you understand by 'the Eastern Question'? Making use of Section 8.3 and the references contained in it, show how the Ottoman Empire had already declined before 1853.
3. 'We have a sick man, a seriously sick man, on our hands' (page 130). In what ways was the Ottoman Empire sick, and why were 'British suspicions' of Nicholas I so easily 'aroused' (page 130)?
4. How would you make use of Fig. 8.2 in explaining the purposes of the Allies in fighting the Crimean War?
5. 'Almost nothing had been settled' (page 135). Is this a fitting verdict on the Crimean War and on the Treaty of Paris?

Europe in 1871 and the Quickening Pace: A Survey

9.1 Nation States and Empires

Several nation states existed in Europe in 1871 which had not existed in 1815 (compare Figs 1.5 and 3.1). Belgium and Greece had shaken off foreign control; the divided states of Germany had come together in one Reich; and Italians had both shaken off foreign control and united into one parliamentary state. By 1871 all the nation states of west and central Europe had adopted some sort of constitutional system, but the mere existence of parliaments did not in itself provide evidence of democracy. Almost everywhere power still rested with privileged groups, though it was usually shared more widely than had formerly been the case: the commercial and industrialist classes had made inroads into the privileges of the landowners. Nor was a wide franchise necessarily evidence of the wider distribution of power. In Germany in 1871 the vote was available to all adult males (at the age of 25), and secret ballot existed. But power in Germany remained in the tight grasp of the Kaiser and his nominees, many of whom had narrowly aristocratic traditions. This was in contrast to Britain, where ministers were responsible to the House of Commons, and were thus dependent upon securing the support of the nation's voters. But the franchise in Britain was still comparatively narrow in 1871. All over Europe there were still battles to be fought for true democracy – battles to extend the vote, to enfranchise women, and to make governments more genuinely representative of the people as a whole, and responsible to the people.

The contrast nevertheless remained between western liberalism and eastern autocracy. The three ancient Empires of Russia, Austria and the Turks still survived in eastern Europe, although there were signs that at least the latter two were weakening. The Habsburgs had been forced to reorganize the Austrian Empire and to create the Dual Monarchy of Austria-Hungary in 1867 (see Section 13.1). The Sultan had lost Greece, and he had had to make such concessions to Serbia and Rumania that they stood on the threshold of independence by 1871. There were spasmodic attempts to reform the Ottoman Empire. When Abdul Mejid drank himself to death in 1861, he was succeeded to the Sultanate by Abdul Aziz, who made some effort to modernize his realm. Nevertheless, the regime of Abdul Aziz was so despotic that he was challenged by the reforming group of Young Ottomans, and he abdicated and committed suicide in 1876. The new Sultan, Abdul Hamid, agreed to

Turkey's first constitution, borrowing ideas for it from France. But it was short-lived, and Turkey had to wait for its revival until the rebellion of the Young Turks in 1908 (see Section 15.3). The subject peoples of the Russian Empire, meanwhile, remained under tight supervision, though even St Petersburg had begun to feel the shock-waves of change. There was still no parliament in Russia in 1871, but Alexander II had legislated to emancipate Russian serfs ten years earlier, and he made a few tentative efforts to narrow the gap between a Russia which remained almost medieval, and a Europe which was leaving Russia behind (see Sections 14.1 and 14.2). Alexander's Polish subjects, however, had been suppressed as recently as 1863, and change occurred in eastern Europe with painful slowness.

9.2   European Economies

In 1871 Britain still had a substantial lead over the countries on the continent, both in industrial output and in the volume of trade. The volume of British trade was more than double that of any continental rival, and free trade was still the prevailing economic doctrine in Europe. The gap between Britain and the continental countries narrowed in the period 1871–1914 and, well before the end of this period, protection for native industries was widely adopted in Europe, though not yet by Britain. Almost all the European countries were increasing in wealth, mainly as the result of industrialization, and the growing output of metal industries in particular. Table 9.1 gives some of the indicators of economic development. It shows the remarkable progress which was made by Germany in the years after 1871, especially in comparison with France; and it shows how Britain's lead was eroded. Russia was beginning to develop, rather belatedly, but it still lagged behind other states. Development was not confined to the countries listed in the Table, of course. Belgium produced 23 million tons of coal in 1901, and Belgium's external trade before 1914 was as great as that of Russia, in spite of the fact that the population was little more than five million. Austria and Italy had five times the population of Belgium, but they both became industrialized at a comparatively leisurely pace. Both developed their industrial regions, and Austria's output of coal ran only slightly behind that of France, but Austria and Italy were far outstripped by Germany. By 1911, however, the Austro-Hungarian Empire had developed a substantial railway network, with more than 41 000 kilometres of track. Italy again lagged behind, with little over 17 000 kilometres.

Industrial output added dramatically to the material possessions of Europeans, though great inequalities of wealth remained between the classes. Many were left in poverty by fluctuations in employment, and by wages which were often low. The societies which remained predominantly agricultural – the pattern in eastern Europe – remained less wealthy generally, and poor harvests almost always meant severe hardship, but these societies were often nevertheless more stable than the industrialized and urbanized communities. As a

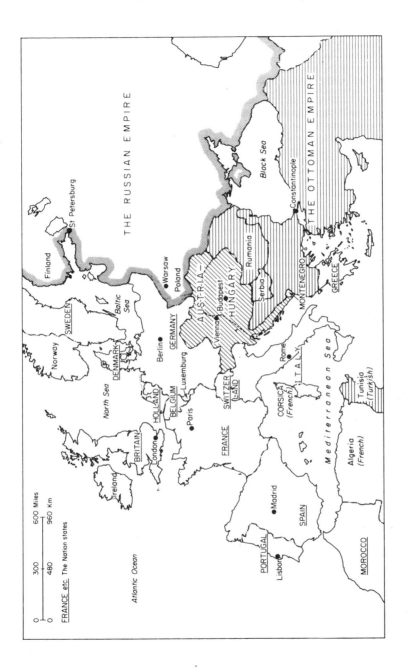

Fig. 9.1 Europe in 1871

whole, Europe was richer in material goods than in any previous age, and it was richer than any other area of the world except the United States, which rapidly outran its rivals in the years before 1914.

Table 9.1   Industrialization 1871–1911

	Population (millions)	Coal output (million metric tons)	Pig Iron (million metric tons)	Steel output (million metric tons)	Railways (kilometres of track)
Britain*					
1871	32	118	6.5	3.5†	26 000
1911	45	269	10	7.5	38 000
France					
1871	37	13	2.5	1.5†	18 000
1911	39	40	4	3	50 000
Germany					
1871	41	30	1.5	1.5†	21 000
1911	65	222	15	13	61 000
Russia					
1871	80	0.9	0.3	0.2†	13 000
1911	168	26	3.5	3	75 700

* including Ireland
† 1880: steel production was still in its infancy in 1871; but technological developments in the 1870s, especially the perfecting of the improvements to Bessemer's process for steel-manufacture by Thomas and Gilchrist in 1878, opened the way to the manufacture of steel on a massive scale, both for peaceful and military purposes.

Steam-power was the basis for much of the increased wealth. In 1871, the combined capacity of European steam-engines has been put at about 12 million horse-power, rising to over 40 million by 1896 (see Table 9.2). Steam-power became even more versatile. Not only railways but iron steamships were built, and the first screw-propelled steamship crossed the Atlantic in 1839. Steam powered the steamroller, and it was also used in agriculture, for example in the further development of McCormick's reaping machine. It was used in the factories for an ever-increasing list of new processes which boosted production, like the power loom for making carpets. By 1871, however, the dynamo had been invented, and the way was opened to the age of electricity. One after another, new industrial processes meanwhile made possible the manufacture of a greater variety of products, from cement to celluloid, and from tin cans to ball bearings. There were new items to buy, for those who had the purchasing power, from Lucifers (matches) to carpet sweepers. By 1871,

Fig. 9.2 A German Stamp of 1935 commemorating the first German railway in 1835 and 'The Eagle'

sewing-machines, refrigerators, and even an electric washing-machine, had been invented, along with typewriters, bicycles and cameras, and their mass-production followed, as their designs were improved. Gas street lighting and horse-drawn omnibuses were introduced into Europe's cities. Anaesthetics began to be used in surgery. Lifts were installed in buildings and, in the open air, men began to ascend in balloons. Communications were quickened by the electric telegraph, and by developments in printing which facilitated the cheaper production of newspapers. With increasing literacy, people became

Table 9.2   Steam-power: capacity of all steam-engines (million horse-power)

	1870	1896
World	18.46	66.10
Europe	11.57	40.30
Britain	4.04	13.70
Germany	2.48	8.08
France	1.85	5.92
Russia	0.92	3.10
Austria	0.80	2.52
Belgium	0.35	1.18
Italy	0.33	1.52
USA	5.59	18.06

(Quoted in D. S. Landes, *The Unbound Prometheus*. C.U.P. (Cambridge, 1970).)

Fig. 9.3 A painting by S. Fergola of the opening of the new railway between Naples and Portici in 1849

more aware of the world in which they lived but, at the same time and as Bismarck realized, propaganda became an increasingly powerful weapon.

The years between 1871 and 1914 saw even more dramatic advances, with the invention of the internal combustion engine and the coming of motor vehicles. And electricity was explored for its uses, as steampower had been explored. London had some electric street lighting as early as 1878, although

Fig. 9.4 Switchboards at the London Telephone Exchange, 1883 – a contemporary print. Telephones were not only part of the new technology. They contributed to the social revolution in extending the employment opportunities for women. (Note the gas lighting)

Fig. 9.5 An electric tram in Paris, sketched in 1898

gas was still being extended to the lighting of houses. Electricity was applied to production in industry, and to the powering of railway locomotives. The electric telegraph was followed by the telephone, and wireless telegraphy led to the development of the radio. In the shops, a new variety of products was added to improved versions of old ones: artificial silk and rayon, which widened the choice of fabrics; refrigerated and tinned foods which widened the choice for the table; zip fasteners and safety razors; phonographs and bicycles. The invention of the cinematograph prepared the way for a new popular entertainment. Only the rich could afford motor cars and motor bicycles, but the first public motor buses appeared in London in 1905. Meanwhile, Count Zeppelin had designed a German airship in 1898, and the development of aeroplanes enabled Bleriot to fly across the Channel in 1909. The technology of heavy industry also developed throughout the period, producing increasing quantities of capital goods as well as consumer goods. But not all the progress was for the betterment of man since, inevitably, technological advancement was also being put into service to perfect the weapons of war (see Section 17.2).

Almost 300 million people lived in Europe in 1871, and by 1914 the number increased again by over 50 per cent. Advances in medicine steadily increased the expectation of life: Louis Pasteur was a pioneer of bacteriology; Joseph Lister worked in the field of antiseptics, and Marie and Pierre Curie developed the uses of radium. Industry helped to support the growing population by generating additional wealth, but – particularly in the west – Europeans also searched for new techniques and additional output in agriculture. Land was reclaimed from waste; artificial fertilizers were developed, and farm machinery was improved. The most industrialized countries often imported food from those where agriculture remained more central to the economy, though none wished to be utterly dependent on others for its supplies. British and German farmers pursued agricultural efficiency, making more expert use of agricultural manpower. Denmark, Holland and Switzerland made dairy-farming pay handsome dividends, and Russia, Poland, Rumania and Hungary exported grain. After 1871 grain was imported into Europe in substantial quantity from the USA and Canada, and Britain in particular made use of refrigeration to import meat from Australasia and Argentina. By 1914, the gap which had existed in 1871 between the industrialized west of Europe and the agricultural east was widening, however, and it was typical of the eastern states – Russia especially – that even agriculture had stagnated in comparison with western modernization.

9.3   European Societies

(a) Social Change

In 1871 only 24 per cent of Germans lived in towns. Twenty years later the figure had risen to 35 per cent and, by 1914, to approximately 60 per cent. This provides a rough indication of Germany's movement towards an economy based on industry, and towards a society predominantly engaged in manufacturing, trade and administration. At the same time, however, 40 per cent of Germans in 1914 were still rural, and yet Germany was the most industrialized state on the continent. Europe as a whole had remained predominantly agricultural since 1871. Fifty per cent of the French population were urbanized by 1914, but the peasant-farmer remained the backbone of the nation. The same was even more true in Austria-Hungary and Italy, and Russia remained overwhelmingly a land of peasants. By 1871, however, Europe's vast peasant population was free from legal shackles, since serfdom had been abolished everywhere, at least in name.

In central and eastern Europe, a good deal remained in 1871 of the traditional influence of landed noblemen. Prussia's military victories had reinforced the prestige in Germany of the Junkers, and of the army, especially of its officer class. In Russia the tsar continued to depend on the nobility to support his antiquated system of government; and in Austria-Hungary the Habsburgs and their attendant nobility went on cherishing tradition. Franz Joseph could see nothing that was attractive in government by the soberly-dressed and often middle-class politicians, who manoeuvred for the party support of other soberly-dressed, middle-class politicians, in the parliaments of France and Italy and Britain. But almost everywhere, except in Russia, the bourgeoisie were becoming too influential to be ignored. Even Bismarck had to concern himself with parliamentary majorities after 1871, though it was not until after the First World War that the old uniforms, the titles, and the power that went with them, disappeared from Europe. They were already condemned by radicals in 1871. Cavour had given a lead in Italy, resting his own authority not on his title and ancient privilege but on service and, at least to some extent, on support in parliament. In France the splendours of the Second Empire proved to be only an interlude. In the 1870s the royalists failed to restore the monarchy, and a succession of soberly-dressed presidents and prime ministers confirmed that power had now been irrevocably transferred to the bourgeoisie.

(b) The Proletariat and Socialism

According to Marx the next struggle after the landed aristocrats had been routed by the bourgeoisie, would be between the bourgeoisie and the proletariat of wage-earners in industry. The proletariat erupted from time to time in Europe's industrial cities and, in 1871, they briefly set up the Paris Commune (see Section 11.2(b)), but the working classes had little organization as yet. Even when mass votes were held (for example, in Napoleon III's plebiscites and in elections to the German Reichstag), the radical and socialist

Fig. 9.6 Some thoughts by Punch *on the hesitant development of technology*

elements in the proletariat were invariably swamped by more conservative interests: by the conservative peasantry, the bourgeoisie, and those others of the proletariat, whom Marxists would have regarded as politically uneducated. Millions of Europeans worked in industry in 1871, but almost nothing suggested that they were near to obtaining power. Even in Britain, in the forefront of trade-union development, the workers had not yet secured the right to picket in support of strike action. They had little unity and little strength to improve their own conditions, let alone to take control of government.

But the foundations of future working-class influence were being laid. Marx had worked steadily to develop his philosophy since the publication of the *Communist Manifesto* in 1848, and in 1867 he completed the first volume of *Das Kapital*. Earlier socialists were often vaguely and romantically optimistic, believing in human goodness and co-operation, but without a clear programme for action. Marx himself was hardly precise about how the transition to a communist society was to be brought about, but he claimed to prove by scientific analysis that such a society would be the inevitable outcome of industrialization and of the pre-eminence of the bourgeoisie. By exploiting the proletariat, the bourgeoisie would produce further social upheaval and a revolution, out of which equality and justice would be born. Impressing his audiences with his personal magnetism and huge physique, and impressing his readers – if not by the intellectual arguments which comparatively few could follow in detail, then by the sheer volume of his writing – Marx gave his followers great confidence. Some, like Lenin, believed that it was essential to prepare for confrontation and revolution. Others believed that pressures could be organized to win concessions by constitutional means, to transform society by reform. Yet others were less concerned with transforming society than with the piecemeal improvement of conditions, especially by shortening the hours and improving the wages of working men. They all agreed, however, that organization was essential. Those who organized revolutionary cells were comparatively few. The development of political parties of Social(ist) Democrats, seeking votes in elections, was more evident after 1871 than the plotting of revolutions – provided that governments were sensible enough to allow elections to be held. Alongside this political activity, there also developed trade unionism, to wrest concessions from employers.

With the encouragement of Marx, the (First) International Workingmen's Association was founded in London in 1864, to try to co-ordinate the activities of socialists and workers throughout Europe. All its members were to recognize:

truth, right, and morality as the basis of their conduct towards one another and their fellow-men, without respect to colour, creed, or nationality . . . and the duty of man to demand the rights of a man and citizen, not only for themselves, but for everyone who does his duty. No rights without duties; no duties without rights.

The Association was not without its problems. It was hampered by differences of opinion about how goals were to be attained, and especially by conflicts between Marx and Mikhail Bakunin. Bakunin was a Russian anarchist, who was committed to making violent protest against existing society, in the belief that 'the passion for destruction is also a constructive passion'. Until his death in 1876 Bakunin was typical of many Russian revolutionaries, but he was untypical of the majority of European Social Democrats, who preferred more peaceful methods.

The Second International Workingmen's Association was founded in Paris in 1889. It survived even the outbreak of the First World War, when 'nationality' proved stronger than international socialism, and when only the Social Democrats of Serbia, and the Bolsheviks in Russia, unequivocally condemned the War and emphasized duty to one's fellow-men instead of duty to one's country. After they came to power in Russia, the Bolsheviks organized the setting up of a Third International in 1919 (the Comintern) to pursue the path of revolution, rather than the constitutional path of most of the western Social Democrats. Meanwhile the international socialist movement got its anthems. Eugene Pottier, a Communard of 1871, wrote the text of the *Internationale*, which Paul Degeyter set to music in an unmistakably French style in 1888. About the same time, Jim Connell, an Irish revolutionary, wrote the words of *The Red Flag*, which was set to more traditional European music. Such anthems expressed the clear intent of the more militant working classes and of European socialists, to campaign for a society far more equal than that of 1871.

9.4 The Papacy

Nineteenth-century Europeans experienced far-reaching consequences of economic change, social transition, political upheaval, and the progress of science and technology. Many old beliefs were re-examined, religious beliefs among them. In 1859 Charles Darwin published *The Origin of Species*, asserting that species evolve through the natural selection of those best suited to the environment. He went on to claim, in *The Descent of Man* (1871), that man was descended from animals. This seemed to contradict the Christian account of the origins of man in the Book of *Genesis*, and it helped to weaken the faith of Europeans in Christianity. Moreover, Marxism went hand-in-hand with atheism, seeking scientific explanations of the human experience. To many nineteenth-century Europeans, it appeared to be an act of faith bordering on superstition to continue to believe in that which could not be explained. It seemed that men were everywhere discovering natural and scientific laws and, in learning them, were becoming the masters of their own environment. As the Holy Father of the Catholic religion, the Pope seemed to be doubly exposed: he was the high priest of a faith which many began to doubt, and he claimed for himself, as the basis of his authority, a mystical succession from St Peter, which could not conclusively be proved and which Protestants had long since rejected. The Pope also suffered at the hands of governments who were eager to reduce the influence of the Church. This was the case in Piedmont in the 1850s (see Section 7.2 (*a*)). During the unifying of Italy the Pope also lost his temporal possessions.

Pius IX fought back. He worked hard after 1848 to strengthen the organization of the Church in Britain and in Holland, and to secure the goodwill towards the Church of the governments of Catholic states such as France, Spain and the Habsburg Empire. But organization was not enough. Roman Catholicism was an authoritarian religion, which required its followers to accept unquestioningly the decrees of their leaders, and Pius concerned himself with doctrine. He propounded the dogma of the Immaculate Conception, defying the scepticism of those who demanded scientific explanation. He drew up the Syllabus of Errors in 1864, vigorously condemning many current ideas which were held by Darwinists, Marxists, socialists, liberals and nationalists, and aiming to alienate Catholics from them. To give further guidance to Catholics, the Vatican Decrees were published in 1870. The most important of these Decrees was that of Papal Infallibility:

> When he discharges the office of Pastor and Teacher of all Christians by defining . . . a doctrine regarding faith or morals . . . by that divine assistance promised to him in Blessed Peter possessed of that infallibility which the Divine Redeemer wished to bestow . . . such definitions by the Roman Pontiff [Pope] are in their nature, apart from the consent of the Church, irreformable.

It was not easy to draw the line between politics and 'faith or morals', and the Pope put himself on a collision course with European governments. The Syllabus of Errors suggested that Pius himself would interpret 'faith or morals' widely. Even the staunch Catholics of Austria-Hungary were disturbed by the Pope's new pronouncement, though they deeply respected the Papal descent, and a tooth of the Blessed Peter was treasured among the Habsburgs' holy relics. Protest groups among Catholics formed almost everywhere, and the secular governments of Italy, Germany and France viewed the Papacy with heightened suspicion. How further conflicts developed between national governments and the Vatican will be seen in Units Ten, Eleven and Twelve.

Pius IX was succeeded by a more flexible Pope, Leo XIII, in 1878. Leo was prepared to work with the new ideas, rather than merely confront them. While preserving the traditional beliefs, he encouraged the Church to befriend the working classes, to support trade unions, and to seek parliamentary representation. Papal encyclicals (circular letters) now moved with the times, and that of 1891, *Rerum Novarum*, earned Leo the name of 'the working man's Pope', since it supported improvements in working conditions and better wages. Partly through the work of Pope Leo, the Catholic Church came to co-exist not unharmoniously with socialism, the new scientific discoveries, and a Europe which seemed to grow increasingly materialistic.

Further Reading

Jackson, J. H.: *Marx, Proudhon and European Socialism*. Hodder and Stoughton (London, 1970).

Kettle, A.: *Karl Marx.* Weidenfeld and Nicolson (London, 1963).

Mosse, W. E.: *Liberal Europe, the Age of Bourgeois Realism 1858–75.* Thames and Hudson (London, 1974).

Seaward, C.: *Karl Marx.* Wayland (Hove, 1974).

Exercises

1. Study Fig. 9.1, and list (*a*) the nation states, and (*b*) the empires, which existed in Europe in 1871. Alongside *each*, write either 'liberal' *or* 'autocratic', whichever you consider the more appropriate. Check your selections later, after reading Units Ten to Fifteen. Why is it difficult to choose between these two words in the case of Germany?

2. What were the major differences in the economies and societies of European states in 1871 (Sections 9.2 and 9.3), compared with those which existed in 1815 (Section 1.1)?

3. Study Tables 9.1 and 9.2. What do these Tables show of the ways in which European economies expanded in the period 1871–1911? Which individual countries achieved the largest percentage growth in this period in *each* of the five areas shown in the column headings of Table 9.1?

4. Referring to Section 9.4 and to the Index, write a summary of the career of Pope Pius IX. Compare what you have written with such a summary in a good encyclopaedia.

Unit Ten

The German Reich 1871–1918

10.1 The Chancellorship of Bismarck

(a) Consolidation and Constitutional Management

The successful partnership between William I and Bismarck, which led to the setting up of the German Empire in 1871 (see Section 7.3), continued until the death of the Kaiser in 1888, and Bismarck remained the Chancellor of the German Empire until 1890. The continuity of government ensured that the Empire was founded on secure beginnings, and it also ensured that Germany was extensively Prussianized. Bismarck missed no opportunity to develop German national feeling but he made certain that, as far as possible, the values of the Empire were those of Prussia and its Junkers. Germany was nevertheless a federal state. It embraced three free cities, four kingdoms and eighteen grand-duchies, duchies and other princedoms, each of which retained its own state government and tried to retain something of its own identity. Skills in management were needed to make Germany into a thriving nation state.

A variety of factors combined to assist the development of unity. The Zollverein had prepared the way for economic unity (see pages 51–3). Goods were already moving freely about Germany, promoting the development of a network of communications. In the 1860s all German-speaking states were members of the Zollverein, except Austria and the free cities of Bremen and Hamburg. From 1863 they adopted a common policy of low tariffs towards the outside world, although the south German states would have preferred more protectionism. It was a small step in 1871 to move to a single German economic policy. A common language and a common culture also assisted the process of unification, and Bismarck placed great importance on the construction of railways to break down barriers. He did not go so far as to nationalize the German railways, but he insisted on supervising their development to serve the national interest. He seized every opportunity to display the imperial symbol, and to apply the adjectival '*Reichs-*'. A Reichsbank was set up, with a Reichs-currency, and the imperial arms appeared on coins and banknotes. There was a Reichspost, and the humble postage stamp became a messenger of imperial unity. A start was made on a common code of German law, and court procedures were made uniform. Similarly, administrative systems were modelled on a common German pattern. Educational institutions developed national coherence, and compulsory service in the German army encouraged both discipline and national pride.

(The 'army' was divided in peacetime into the four armies of Prussia, Bavaria, Saxony and Württemberg, but they were organized on a common German pattern.) In most cases German meant Prussian, and states such as Bavaria had to struggle to retain the privileges which they had made a condition of their joining the Reich.

The German constitution gave the Reichstag some power to obstruct the Kaiser's ministers, but not to control them (see pages 119 and 123). As early as 1871 Bismarck had difficulty in persuading the Reichstag to approve the Army Bill. The German Reichstag could not be overawed as easily as the Prussian Landtag, so that Bismarck from the outset tried to secure majority support whenever possible. In the 1870s this meant the support of the National Liberals, whose views were usually conservative, and who were usually opposed to the Catholics. Bismarck was essentially the servant of the Kaiser and of the state, and he was not a party politician. When his relations with the National Liberals became strained in the late 1870s he began to rely more on the Catholic Centre Party. The National Liberals had shown signs of wanting to develop the constitution towards more genuinely parliamentary government, where a majority in the Reichstag would determine the appointment of ministers. To this end, they also wanted tax reforms, with more direct taxes over which the Reichstag could exercise control. Bismarck preferred indirect taxation, which he himself could control and vary from time to time – for example the taxes on tobacco.

The split between Bismarck and the National Liberals actually occurred on the question of tariffs, however. German industrialists had begun to clamour for tariffs to protect their enterprises against foreign competition, especially from Britain; and agriculturalists also demanded protection when they were hit by economic recession. Bismarck sympathized. Tariffs would be useful for raising revenue; and they would also help to make the Reich self-sufficient, independent of supplies from potential enemies if those supplies were home-produced. Like liberals generally, however, the National Liberals clung to free trade. Only a section of the National Liberals were willing to vote for the general protective tariff for Germany which was introduced in 1879, and Bismarck had to bargain with the Centre Party to ensure its acceptance. The price the Centre Party demanded was the ending of the government's conflict with the Catholic Church, which was known as the *Kulturkampf* (see (*b*) below). Bismarck emerged from the wrangling more successfully than did the National Liberals. The latter were now split, and they lost support from the voters in subsequent elections. In the 1880s Bismarck continued to gain majorities in the Reichstag, even though he now faced a new opposition from the rising group of Social Democrats in the house. He claimed constantly to personify the national interest, and he urged German electors to return to the Reichstag those who would support him. Without personal enthusiasm for overseas adventures, he pandered to German national pride by joining the scramble for colonies in Africa, in the 1880s. In 1887 he made use of an alleged external threat from the French to enlist nationalist support in the elections.

But he could not successfully manage the constitution for ever. The election of 1890 returned fewer of his supporters among the Conservatives and National Liberals, and it seemed likely that he would be obstructed seriously by a coalition of Social Democrats, Radicals and the Centre Party. What was even more ominous for him, however, was that by that time he relied for his Chancellorship on a new Kaiser, with whom he was on poor terms.

Fig. 10.1 A West German stamp of 1965, commemorating the 150th anniversary of Bismarck's birth

The successful launching of the German Empire had been largely Bismarck's work, supported by William I. Bismarck had shown considerable skill in his management of German affairs, working within the constitution with its facade of democracy. Time had been given for the growth of a strong German national consciousness. But in his dealings with the Catholic Church Bismarck had shown that he underestimated the strength of organized religion; and in his dealings with the Social Democrats, he showed that there was little mutual sympathy between himself and the German working classes.

(b) The Catholic Church

About a third of the German population in 1871 was Roman Catholic. Most of the Catholics lived in southern Germany and along the Rhine; Prussia and much of north Germany had long ago adopted Protestantism. Bismarck would have been content to disregard the religious differences of Germans, which could add nothing to national unity, but he was aware of the international nature of the Catholic Church, and the danger that Catholics might be more obedient to the Papacy than to the German government. A struggle was already in the making when the German Empire was set up. The Declaration of Papal Infallibility in 1870 had meant that the first shot had been fired from Rome (see Section 9.4). It divided the Catholics themselves. In Germany the historian von Döllinger campaigned against the Papal claims, and groups of 'Old Catholics' were formed, mainly among intellectuals, who opposed the doctrine of Infallibility. Pius IX branded them as heretics, for which the punishment was excommunication. Many 'Old Catholics' held state appointments in Germany, in education and administration. They looked to the new German government for protection, and it was a challenge Bismarck felt unable to ignore. The stage was thus set for the *Kulturkampf*, the struggle of two cultures, between the international Church and the national state. Bismarck was mistaken, however, if he thought such a struggle would unite all Germans in a common cause against the Vatican.

On Bismarck's side the struggle was conducted at two levels. Anti-Papal regulations were imposed on Prussia, biting hard in the Rhineland, where Catholics were numerous. Some of these regulations were also applied to the German Empire as a whole. But there was a substantial Catholic Centre Party in the Reichstag, led by Ludwig Windthorst, which championed the Papacy, and Bismarck had to work with the National Liberals to outmanoeuvre them. German priests were forbidden to use their religious appointments to interfere in politics. German education was brought under the supervision of the state rather than of the Church, and all Jesuits were expelled from Germany in 1872. With the assistance of Adalbert Falk at the Prussian Ministry of Culture, further measures were taken against Prussian Catholics in the May Laws of 1873. Seminaries for the training of priests were placed under state control; priests had to graduate in German, not foreign, universities; religious appointments were made subject to government approval, and the state could stop the payment of stipends to unsatisfactory priests. Further laws followed in Prussia, threatening the loss of all civil rights to obstructive priests, dissolving most religious orders, and making civil marriage compulsory. Civil marriage was imposed on the whole of Germany in 1875.

Loyal Catholics were prepared to suffer, and many priests were suspended, fined and imprisoned. More ominously for Bismarck, the Centre Party won additional seats in the Reichstag elections of 1874. The Catholics were winning sympathy even among Protestants, and the struggle was dividing Germany rather than uniting it. It became more urgent for Bismarck to find a way out of the conflict as his relations deteriorated with the National Liberals (see page 151), and the death of Pius IX in 1878 offered the opportunity of a compromise with the new Pope. Neither side won outright victory. Bismarck shifted much of the blame on to Falk, and dismissed him. Both in Prussia and Germany, many of the restrictions were lifted gradually, but civil marriage remained compulsory, the state continued to supervise education, the Jesuits were not allowed back (until 1917), and priests were still forbidden to meddle in politics. In the Reichstag, Bismarck secured Windthorst's support, for a time. The Old Catholics, even if they had wished to, had not succeeded in creating an independent German Church, and the vast majority of German Catholics remained loyal to the Pope. But with some reason Bismarck himself denied that he had suffered a defeat.

(c) The Social Democrats

The combination of industrialization, the writings of Marx, and manhood suffrage, led to increasing support for socialism in the Reichstag. Numerous groups helped to spread Marxist ideas in Germany. Ferdinand Lassalle was a pioneer of German socialism and, soon after his death, a Workers' Party was founded in 1869. The Party won ten seats in the Reichstag in the elections of 1874, and it joined hands with other Marxists a year later, uniting behind the Gotha Programma and founding a new party which came to be known as the Social Democrats. The Social Democrats polled almost half a million votes in 1877, and they won thirteen seats in the Reichstag. Theirs was the first Social Democratic Party in Europe, and their first allegiance was to the working classes. They maintained contacts with Marx and with other European socialists through the International, and Bismarck regarded them as a threat not only to Germany's social system but even to the nation state. The brotherhood of working men offered an international loyalty, like that of the Catholic Church, rather than a loyalty to the Reich, and Bismarck decided to strike before they became too powerful. An anti-socialist law was introduced in 1878:

> Associations which aim, by social-democratic, socialistic, or communistic agitation, at the destruction of the existing order in State or society, are forbidden.

The law went on to restrict the rights of members of such associations to publish literature, to collect funds, and even to meet. The Social Democratic Party was driven underground, while many of its supporters fled into exile. While Bismarck remained in office the law was renewed from time to time. But after the initial shock had been administered, it was by no means tightly enforced. Although 1500 Germans were imprisoned in the 1880s, the Social Democrats continued both to contest elections and to win seats in the Reichstag. The law was simply a useful weapon in Bismarck's armoury, which he could use when necessary against those socialists who offered a revolutionary threat. That was as much as the Chancellor needed. The socialist scare helped to increase support for his conservative policies and, in the elections of 1881, there was a marked swing away from the Social Democrats and the left generally.

Bismarck had no wish to create martyrs by persecuting the socialists too fiercely. By 1883 he decided that it might be better to attempt to kill socialism by kindness, to steal enough of their policies to win over their working-class supporters. The result was that, having already given a lead with a manhood suffrage, Germany gave a lead to Europe in the field of state insurance. National insurance schemes were introduced against sickness (1883), industrial injuries (1884) and old age (1889). When Lloyd George introduced similar insurance against sickness into Britain in 1911, he studied Bismarck's system. At the same time, Bismarck made concessions to trade unionism. Such reforms undoubtedly improved the quality of life of Germans, and they put a brake on the development of Social Democratic opposition. By 1890 the socialist vote had risen to nearly a million and a half, and the Social Democrats had 24 seats in the Reichstag; but it was only after Bismarck's resignation that the Party achieved a real breakthrough. At no time, however, did Bismarck and the Social Democrats regard each other with anything but hostility.

(d) Bismarck's Foreign Policy

Bismarck saw no clear distinction between internal policy and foreign policy. His aims were always the security of the German Reich, and the retention of his own authority and that of the Kaiser within the Reich. He regarded it as essential after 1871 to ensure that Germany was not involved in war, and Section 15.1 will show how he constantly worked to build friendly alliances, and to isolate France. But Bismarck's foreign policy was part of his general policy of developing German national consciousness. Both in 1875 and 1887 he used alleged threats from France to help unite Germans behind the Imperial government, and it may also be argued that the Kulturkampf went hand in hand with a policy of befriending Russia and Britain, non-Catholic European powers. The Kulturkampf was abandoned when he decided to make a close alliance with Catholic Austria-Hungary in 1879. There was a period of peace in Europe after 1871 which owed at least something to Bismarck's diplomacy, and even the ever-threatening Eastern Question was successfully damped down again in the Congress of Berlin in 1878 (see Section 15.2). On the other hand, Bismarck left Europe with a tangled system of alliances which played some part in entangling the continent in war in 1914.

The focus of Bismarck's attention was always on Germany and its immediate surroundings in Europe. By the time he retired Germany had begun to acquire an overseas empire (see Section 16.2), but Bismarck remained unconvinced that such an empire was desirable. To possess colonies meant the need to develop a navy to protect them, and the development of a German navy would bring the risk of arguments with Britain, which Bismarck preferred to avoid. Later German leaders showed far less caution, both with regard to empire and to navies.

(e) 1890: A Turning Point

In 1890 Bismarck faced a newly-elected Reichstag, more hostile to him than any previous one. He considered reverting to the tactics of 1862, and ruling by the Kaiser's decree. But William II was the German Kaiser now. He had succeeded his father Frederick, whose brief reign had lasted for only three months in 1888, when Frederick's death had quickly followed that of William I. William II was comparatively young – he had been born in 1859 – and he was ambitious. He had no wish to be overshadowed by his veteran Chancellor who, he believed, had mishandled the problem of socialism and had put too much effort into pleasing the Russians and the British. The personality clash between William and Bismarck left the old Chancellor isolated. To cope with the Reichstag he would need to rely on the Kaiser and the army. The Kaiser no longer wanted him, and even the army could not be relied on to give political support since the death of Roon in 1879 and the retirement of the aged Moltke in 1888. Bismarck quarrelled violently with the Kaiser, and when he offered his resignation William readily accepted it. From March 1890 the German Reich was under new management.

Before it collapsed in 1918 the Reich had a variety of different chancellors, chief among them Bernhard von Bülow, from 1900 to 1909, and Theobald Bethmann-Hollweg, from 1909 to 1917. But none achieved the great distinction of Bismarck. A *Punch* cartoon of 1890 suggested that in the retirement of Bismarck, the German ship had dropped its pilot (Fig. 10.2). In his own skilful but ruthless way, Bismarck had piloted Germany through two comparatively peaceful decades. In the next twenty-five years Germany's economic development was to accelerate strikingly, but neither the Kaiser nor his ministers matched the stature of Bismarck. Particularly in international affairs, the course they steered was often erratic, and 1890 marked a turning point between Bismarckian navigation, which was always purposeful, and the Wilhelmine steersmanship which was often unpredictable.

Table 10.1 Germany's growing share of world trade

	Total World Trade (£s million)	Percentage shares of World Trade			
		Britain	France	Germany	USA
1840	600	32	10	—	8
1880	1 400	25	11	9	10
1900	4 000	21	8	12	11
1913	8 000	17	7	12	11

(Adapted from H. Heaton, *Economic History of Europe*. Harper and Row (London, 1963).)

10.2 Wilhelmine Germany

(a) The Economy and Society

By 1914 Germany had outstripped Britain in the building of railways and in the production of pig-iron and steel, and it had almost caught up in the output of coal from the coalfields of the Saar, the Ruhr, Saxony and Silesia (see Table 9.1, page 140). The volume of German trade was three times what it had been in 1890, and the Reich towered above its rivals on the continent. Great combines and large family firms dominated German industry. Siemens-Schuckert and the German Edison Company (later AEG) produced vast quantities of electrical equipment. Krupp and Thyssen developed steel empires, and the German iron industry benefited enormously from the technology developed in 1878 by Thomas and Gilchrist, which enabled it to use the phosphoric ores of Lorraine. Chemical industries were also growing, later to be merged in 1925 into the gigantic I. G. Farben. Such development provided a powerful base for Wilhelmine Germany and, for the Kaiser, it seemed only logical that it should be matched by a great overseas empire and a huge iron navy. Economically and politically it appeared to be Germany's destiny to

DROPPING THE PILOT.

Fig. 10.2 Bismarck resigned in 1890. This **Punch** *cartoon saw him as the pilot of the Reich who now left the German 'ship of state' to Kaiser William II*

Fig. 10.3 The Krupp steelworks at Essen, 1912 – part of Germany's developing industrial strength

dominate Europe. Its capital, Berlin, grew rapidly. By 1900 its population had overtaken that of Vienna and was threatening to catch up with that of Paris; and in Germany as a whole a bigger percentage of the population now lived in towns than in any rival country, such as France.

The industrialization brought further support for socialism and the Social Democrats, but power still rested with the traditional aristocracy, both in the state and in the armed forces. Most of William's chancellors recognized, however, that majorities needed to be won in the Reichstag, and that meant at least something of a partnership with the conservative elements of the bourgeoisie and the prosperous leaders of the nation's industry and trade. Wilhelmine Germany, therefore, continued to bear many of the imprints of Bismarck's Germany and, indeed, of the Prussia out of which it had grown. Only when Germany was defeated in the First World War was there upheaval, when the Kaiser was driven to abdicate in 1918, and Germany followed the French example and set up a republic.

(b) The Chancellors and the Reichstag

Bismarck's successor as the Chancellor of the Reich in 1890 was Leo von *Caprivi*, who balanced on the tightrope until 1894, when William dismissed him. Caprivi seemed to be in harmony with the Kaiser when he first took office. The anti-socialist law was abandoned, and an attempt was made to please the masses with factory reform and further welfare measures. Caprivi pleased the Kaiser as well as the political left by abandoning Bismarck's alliance with Russia. But none of this won over the Social Democrats in the Reichstag, and the Chancellor's further ideas created more enemies than friends. He reduced tariffs, upsetting both industrial and farming interests, and he had to abandon a plan to restore some control of education to the Catholics, which might have won over the Centre Party. He had to work very hard indeed in 1893 to persuade the Reichstag to approve the army grant, and he even conceded a reduction in the interval at which that approval was needed, from the seven years on which Bismarck had always insisted, to five. The elections of 1893 returned 44 Social Democrats, as hostile as ever. Caprivi's leanings towards liberalism had by now upset the Prussian Junkers, and the Kaiser himself was swinging towards more traditional attitudes. He dismissed Caprivi in 1894, and handed the Chancellorship to an aged Bavarian, *Hohenlohe-Schillingfürst*, a stop-gap, whose sympathies with Catholicism enabled him to pacify the Centre Party, and whose conservatism was generally agreeable to the Junkers.

Meanwhile, William II had begun to promote von *Bülow*. Bülow took care to ingratiate himself with the Junkers, and did his best to keep up with the Kaiser, who looked for glory abroad. A new generation of Germans could now be distracted from internal conflicts by excitements in foreign policy, the pursuit of overseas empire and the building of a formidable navy. The Centre Party was so well pleased with the work of Alfred von Tirpitz, who became Minister of Marine in 1897 and set himself to expand the fleet, that when Bülow replaced Hohenlohe in 1900, the Party continued to support the government. Not until 1906 did Bülow encounter serious problems in the Reichstag. Losing the Centre in that year, when the Party demanded more ministerial offices, he patched together support from the Conservatives and the Radicals, only to anger the Conservatives when he proposed to raise revenue by death duties. The logic of the German constitution was that governments would eventually become responsible to the Reichstag, as had long been the custom in Britain, where the government was responsible to the House of Commons. It required constant manoeuvring to win parliamentary majorities for government measures, and all chancellors faced the problem of walking a tightrope between the Reichstag and the Kaiser. By 1909 Bülow had no options left but to fall off. Except for the Conservatives, the parties in the Reichstag wanted genuinely parliamentary government: ministers to be appointed on the basis of their parliamentary support, and direct taxation which the Reichstag could control. The Kaiser would not permit this, since it would reduce his own status and strike at the social foundations of the Reich. Like Bismarck in 1890, therefore, Bülow thought the only way out was to rule without the Reichstag; but William II would not agree to that either. He was also displeased with Bülow's conduct of foreign policy, and he now saw an opportunity to dismiss him. *Bethmann-Hollweg* became the new Chancellor, a man conveniently lacking in ideas for a domestic policy, other than to survive from day to day.

In 1912 the Social Democrats received four and a quarter million votes, and won 110 seats to become the largest single party in the Reichstag. Bethmann's weak position was starkly revealed a year later, but so too was the constitutional stalemate. The Reichstag carried a massive vote of censure on the Chancellor, when he defended the bullying tactics of the military in Alsace. He simply ignored the vote and continued his negative government and, as long as he kept the favour of the Kaiser, there was nothing that parliament could do to remove him.

1914, however, showed that national feeling in Germany was far stronger than constitutional ambitions. The Reichstag rallied behind the government to fight the First World War. The necessary finances for the military were approved, and even the Social Democrats supported the war effort. Bismarck and nationalist propagandists had done their work well. Germans were above all now fiercely German. The historian Heinrich von Treitschke had expounded the philosophy of the Reich:

> If [the State] neglects its strength in order to promote the idealistic aspirations of man, it repudiates its own nature and perishes. . . . The masses must for ever remain the masses. There would be no culture without kitchen-maids. . . . Let us hear no claptrap about the disinherited. No doubt there have been times when those in possession have grossly abused their power, but as a rule the social balance is kept. . . . The individual should feel himself a member of the State, and as such have courage to take its errors upon him.

Germans united behind the Kaiser, whatever his 'errors', and when Bethmann resigned in 1917, it was under pressure from the military high command for his weak wartime leadership, rather than the result of constitutional ambitions in the Reichstag.

Further chancellors tried, with little success, to please the Kaiser, the army and the Reichstag, and to win the war. 1918 brought military defeats. By the end of September General Ludendorff was recommending the Kaiser to sue for peace, and to try to save the regime with concessions to democracy. *Prince Max* of Baden, renowned for his liberalism, was appointed the Chancellor on 3 October, and William agreed that his future governments would be based on the wishes of the Reichstag. It was too late. William had yielded only at the moment of defeat in war. In 1914 war united the German nation; but in 1918 defeat divided it. Early in November the Kaiser was forced to abdicate and to flee to Holland to escape a mass explosion of anger against the Imperial system. Prince Max resigned, and the First World War ended in the armistice of 11 November, while Germany hovered on the brink of revolution.

The Reich had been born in the military victory of 1871. It crumbled to extinction in the military defeat of 1918. From the outset the constitution had married together two opposites: Prussian authoritarianism and a parliament elected on manhood suffrage. The system had always threatened to become unworkable. Once the conduct of affairs had passed from the hands of William I and Bismarck into those of William II and his mediocre chancellors, the threat became a reality. But it was in their conduct of foreign policy that William II and his chancellors had finally determined the fate of the German Reich and shattered the national cohesion. Out of the ruins the Weimar Republic was born (see Section 21.3).

(c) German Foreign Policy after 1890

Writing his Memoirs in the interval between his resignation and his death in 1898, Bismarck summed up the foreign policy he had pursued as Chancellor of the Reich:

> Germany is perhaps the single Great Power in Europe which is not tempted by any objects obtainable only by a successful war. It is our interest to maintain peace.

William II had no desire for war either, but he brought a new recklessness to German foreign policy in a pursuit of glory that was almost Napoleonic. He believed along with Treitschke that:

> up to the present, Germany has always had too small a share of the spoils in the partition of non-European territories among the Powers of Europe.

In William's words, Germany was entitled to 'a place in the sun'. It was almost inevitable that the pursuit of a colonialist policy would bring Germany into conflict with other Europeans, which Bismarck had sought to avoid. It also required the development of the German navy and, as Bismarck had foreseen, German naval expansion antagonized the British. Bülow, however, argued that Germany needed a larger navy to protect its growing overseas trade, quite apart from the protection of colonies. Building up the navy became an obsession with the Kaiser but it was also a rallying flag for the German nation. Bülow saw that it was possible:

> to rouse public opinion by harping on nationalism, and waking the people to consciousness.

For him, naval expansion and adventures overseas were a way of uniting the people behind the government, and reducing the government's difficulties with the Reichstag.

Admiral von Tirpitz took charge of the navy in 1897. His ambition was to build a great battle fleet. Its development was planned in the navy laws of 1898 and 1900. Mighty new battleships were part of the plan, similar to what the British later called 'dreadnoughts'. Once committed to the plan, the Germans found it difficult to draw back and, within a few years, a furious naval race began between them and the British. By 1914 Britain had 19 dreadnoughts and Germany 13, with both of them busily building more. Britain had a mystical belief in the Two-Power Standard, defined in 1889 as the right to have a navy the equal in strength to the combined navies of any two other powers.

William II was infuriated by this British arrogance, and was determined to show that Germany was just as great a power as Britain. But he wanted, at the same time, to have a vast army, far greater than that of Britain. General von Schlieffen, who was the German Chief of Staff until 1905, devised a master plan for defeating Germany's enemies in Europe, if war were to break out. By the beginning of the twentieth century, therefore, Germany was busy rattling the sabre while a fast-growing iron and steel industry built up its formidable military and naval weaponry.

Bismarck had always taken care to negotiate from strength, and the Prussian tradition was a military one. But the real danger lay in the combination of military strength with erratic diplomacy. William II knew how to bluster, but he had limited understanding of where such blustering might lead. Since he seemed always ready to take offence and to imagine that Germany was being robbed of its entitlements as a great power, *Punch* depicted him as an irresponsible clown, leaping about in the diplomatic rowing-boat, and threatening to pitch the states of Europe (and himself) into the water. It was in sharp contrast to the *Punch* view of Bismarck, the sober pilot. In 1896 William sent a telegram (the Kruger Telegram) to President Kruger of the Transvaal, congratulating him on the efficient way in which he had dealt with the raid into his country by Starr Jameson and a party of British adventurers from Bechuanaland. In the eyes of the British government, the telegram was nothing but meddling and, since the Boers of the Transvaal now got the the impression that they had likely German support, it perhaps played some part in bringing about

Fig. 10.4 A visit by Kaiser William II (helmeted) to the Krupp works in 1912, to mark the firm's centenary. The Kaiser took considerable pride in Germany's industrial and military strength

the Boer War of 1899–1902, during which the Kaiser criticized the British but did nothing more effective. There were many other occasions on which William rocked the diplomatic boat, and contributed to the international crises which preceded the First World War (see Sections 16.3 and 17.3). But he also helped to undermine Bismarck's system of alliances in Europe and, in doing so, contributed to the emergence of two antagonistic camps. Bismarck always worked to retain the goodwill of Russia, to ensure that he would always have a friend to the east. The moment he retired, William and Caprivi chose not to renew the Russian alliance. Russia was allowed to move into an alliance with France, confronting Germany with potential enemies both to east and west (see Section 17.1). The Kaiser later complained bitterly that the Reich was being encircled and, rather than reflect on his own responsibility for this, he chose to associate it with an alleged plot by his uncle, the British King, Edward VII. The pair of them feuded constantly until Edward died in 1910. Even then, William persisted in the belief that Edward's influence lived on, to plague him, and he complained: 'The dead Edward is stronger than the living I.'

William was obsessed with strength, with proof of virility. He had suffered an accident at birth which left him with a withered arm, and he seemed to find a constant need to prove himself. It was a combination which proved deadly for Europe when a recklessly ambitious Kaiser came together with weak ministers, a thwarted Reichstag, strong armed forces, a powerful economy, a conservative and Prussianized society and, above all, a fierce German national consciousness. In part this was the legacy of Bismarck. But the problem for Europe in the years 1890 to 1914 was that Bismarck was no longer present to control his legacy.

Further Reading

Baker, F.: *Bismarck*. Hutchinson (London, 1967).
Balfour, M.: *The Kaiser and His Times*. Cresset (London, 1964).
Elliott, B. J.: *Bismarck, the Kaiser and Germany*. Longman (Harlow, 1972).
Evans, R. J.: *Society and Politics in Wilhelmine Germany*. Croom Helm (London, 1978).
Kisch, R.: *Bismarck*. Wayland (Hove, 1976).
Medlicott, W. N.: *Bismarck and Modern Germany*. Hodder and Stoughton (London, 1975).
Röhl, J. C. G.: *From Bismarck to Hitler*. Longman (Harlow, 1970).
Simon, W. M.: *Germany in the Age of Bismarck*. Allen and Unwin (London, 1968).
Waller, B.: *Bismarck*. Blackwell (Oxford, 1985).

Exercises

1. Divide a sheet of paper into three columns. List in one column the factors which favoured 'the development of unity' (page 150) in Germany after 1871. List in the second column the factors which hindered such development. List in the third column the policies Bismarck adopted after 1871 to encourage German national feeling.
2. What do you understand by the word *Kulturkampf* (Section 10.1(*b*))? Was Bismarck right to deny 'that he had suffered a defeat' (page 154) in this struggle?

3. Study the *Punch* cartoon on page 157. What might well have been the thoughts at the time to which the cartoon refers of (a) Bismarck, and (b) the Kaiser? How fitting a comment was this cartoon on the event to which it referred?

4. What can you learn from this Unit of the ways in which socialism developed in Germany in the years 1871–1914? Why did support for socialist ideas grow? Why did socialists have only limited political power in Germany before 1914?

5. State in your own words the ideas of von Treitschke which are quoted on page 160. What are your own opinions about such ideas? Why do you think such ideas appealed to many Germans before 1914?

6. How can it be argued that (a) Bismarck pursued a different foreign policy after 1871 from the one he had pursued before that year, and (b) William II pursued a different foreign policy after 1890 from the one Bismarck had pursued from 1871 to 1890?

7. Making use of the Index to this book, write a short paragraph about *each* of the following: Roon; the elder Moltke; Schlieffen; Tirpitz. Why were such military men prominent in German affairs?

Unit Eleven

The French Third Republic to 1914

11.1 The Economy and Society

Compared with the German Reich the French economy grew slowly in the period from 1871 to 1914, and the population hardly increased at all (see Table 9.1, page 140 and Table 10.1, page 156). Nevertheless the French volume of trade remained twice that of Russia throughout the period, and it continued in its turn to run at almost half that of Britain. The last decade of the Second Empire had been one of considerable economic expansion in France, generating a prosperity which made it possible to pay off remarkably quickly the indemnity imposed in the Treaty of Frankfurt (see page 123). Thereafter, though the loss of Alsace-Lorraine struck a blow at the French economy as well as at French pride, industrialization proceeded steadily if not strikingly. France's urban population almost doubled between 1871 and 1914, bringing a corresponding interest in labour organizations and socialism, but still less than half of the population as a whole lived in towns. This strong rural element in French society strengthened the forces of conservatism, although long before 1914 the French had lost the awe of titles and uniforms which survived in the German Reich. After some hesitation in the 1870s, the idea of restoring a monarchy was rejected. Republicanism took a firm hold, and it was left to the conflict of social and political forces to determine the direction the Republic would take. So fierce was the conflict, and such was the nature of the constitution of 1875, that when René Viviani took office as Prime Minister on the eve of the outbreak of war in 1914, his was the fifty-second administration in France since the fall of Napoleon III.

Short-lived governments were not simply the product of fierce political debate. Their experience of the Republic and its politicians was such that many Frenchmen became apathetic or deeply sceptical about their country's political life. There was much political in-fighting. Many French politicians seemed to represent only local or other vested interests, or to be motivated solely by self-interest. Governments were often manoeuvred out of office before they could effect changes. Frenchmen found it easier to unite in opposition than to unite for more constructive work. The Republic itself, it seemed, existed mainly because, compared with a monarchy or a Bonapartist regime, it divided Frenchmen least. From 1789 onwards Frenchmen had often given a lead to Europe in protesting against outdated systems. They found it far less easy to agree on the sort of France they wished to create.

Fig. 11.1 The Palace of Electricity at the Paris Exhibition of 1900 – a spectacular display in the style of the eighteenth century, in a France where industrialization and technological progress were now proceeding steadily

11.2   Post-Imperial Confusion

(a) The Caretakers

The collapse of the Second Empire at Sedan promptly revived French republicanism, especially in Paris (see page 99). A provisional Government of National Defence was set up in Paris under General Trochu, chosen mainly from Parisian anti-Bonapartists in the Assembly; and a new republic was proclaimed. But Paris was besieged by the Germans within three weeks of the disaster at Sedan. Cut off by German forces the city and the Government could communicate with the rest of France only by carrier pigeon or balloon. A balloon enabled Leon Gambetta to float over the German lines to raise new forces to resist the enemy but, although he collected raw and untrained enthusiasts, they were no match for the professional troops of Roon and Moltke. After Christmas 1870 the Germans began the shelling of Paris, and the stranglehold tightened. Food shortages began to take their toll in the city, and the inhabitants had to resort to eating animals from the zoo. One Parisian wrote:

> I must say that one finds it almost easier to become accustomed to shells (which, like railway locomotives, whistle before arriving at their destination) than to eating

horse-flesh. I cannot get any more used to eating horse than dog or rat. I dined last night on camel. . . . Tonight there will be porcupine and a piece of elephant trunk.

By the end of January the artillery bombardment and starvation left Paris with no alternative but to surrender. An armistice was arranged with Bismarck: the Germans would make a triumphal march into the city, and the French would elect a new Assembly to provide a government which was authorized to sign a peace treaty.

The elections were held in February 1871 and the new Assembly met at Bordeaux, away from the emotionalism of Paris. Gambetta would have nothing to do with the making of the peace, but Thiers re-emerged, to act for a time as the head of state. The new Assembly included only 30 Bonapartists, but it was strongly conservative, much more inclined to the restoration of some sort of monarchy than to a republic. The first task was to sign the Treaty of Frankfurt. As 'Head of the Executive Power' Thiers was, in effect, both president and prime minister, and he piloted the French through the humiliation of making peace with the Germans. Before the Treaty of Frankfurt was signed, however, the 'Government of Thiers' faced a new problem, the uprising in Paris of the Paris Commune. The Treaty of Frankfurt was eventually signed on 10 May 1871, and the Paris Commune was suppressed with much bloodshed by the end of that month.

In August 1871 Thiers was named 'President of the French Republic'. It was too soon yet to draft a new constitution amid the upheaval which had followed the fall of Napoleon III, but Thiers was an efficient caretaker, well in tune with the national conservatism. Already, however, France was beginning to swing back towards republicanism. Republicans were beginning to win by-elections, encouraged by an energetic campaign conducted by Gambetta against all forms of monarchism. Thiers would have preferred the restoration of an Orleanist monarchy, but his first concern was the nation's unity and reconstruction. In 1872 French pride was set on the road to recovery by the introduction of a limited measure of conscription for military service. The indemnity was paid off and German troops left France in 1873. Thiers continued to govern until May 1873, when he was defeated by the royalist forces still strong in the Assembly. He promptly resigned and the Assembly named a new President, Patrice de MacMahon, whose royalist sympathies were well known. Until his death in 1877 Thiers continued to work with Gambetta to unite the Republicans, sensing that it was with them rather than with the Bourbons or the Orleanists that the best hopes of uniting France lay. That France recovered so quickly from the Franco-Prussian War was due in no small part to the skilful caretaking of Thiers.

(b) The Paris Commune

The election of a royalist Assembly in February 1971, its location in Bordeaux, and its consent to German military display in Paris, were not to the liking of Parisians. A clash occurred in March 1871 between the citizens of Paris and military forces under the command of 'Bordeaux', when the military tried to collect the artillery at Montmartre, which had been used to defend the city against the Germans. Thiers withdrew the government troops and the Parisians set up the Commune. The red flag was hoisted and the government of the city was entrusted to a revolutionary council.

It was a confused protest. It was partly a radical Parisian protest against the conservatism of the rest of France. The Communards envisaged a chain of communes across France for vigorous and democratic local government, loosely federated within a national republic, and a few other cities like Lyons and Marseilles tried to follow the Parisian example. The Manifesto of the Commune in April 1871 declared that:

> Political unity as Paris desires it is the voluntary association of all local initiatives.

But it was also a nationalist rebellion, a protest against surrender to the Germans, from which developed the Communards' desire to reconstruct France. That reconstruction should be in the interests of the masses. A proclamation of the Central Committee of the National Guard, whose pay had been stopped by 'Bordeaux', declared:

> Workers, do not be deceived: it is the great struggle. . . . If you want your children to be men gaining the reward of their labour, not a sort of animal trained for the workshop and for war, fertilizing with their sweat the fortune of an exploiter or pouring out their blood for a despot . . . be intelligent, arise. . . . Long live the Republic! Long live the Commune!

It was thus to some extent a socialist protest, a workers' movement, reaching back to the June Days of 1848, and beyond them to the events of 1793. Karl Marx gave the Commune his blessing, and Marxists since have tended to regard it as a communist revolution. But it was more than that: it was essentially Parisian and essentially French, a consequence of the city's humiliation at the hands of the Germans, and the Communards included not only socialists and communists, but petit-bourgeois radicals.

Thiers regarded the Paris Commune as a threat to national unity. A proclamation by his government was addressed to Parisians:

> France, freely consulted by universal [manhood] suffrage, has elected a government, which is the only legal one. . . . In spite of this government, the Commune . . . presumes to impose its will upon France. . . . It violates property . . . arrests the prosperity which was about to revive.

In the view of Thiers Paris had to be made to submit, to preserve both unity and the social system. There was little real unity within Paris itself. For a second time the city was virtually besieged, this time by French troops, while interest groups jockeyed for position within it. In the middle of May 1871 the troops began to fight their way into the city. As the Communards retreated they burned buildings such as the Tuileries, executed hostages and butchered traitors. But the government troops outmatched them in violence, routing an enemy which it was easier than the Germans to defeat. In a single week of killing, about 20 000 Parisians perished: 20 Parisians for every soldier of the government. Getting on for 40 000 more Parisians were arrested, of whom more than a quarter were imprisoned and more than 7000 exiled, while two dozen ringleaders were shot by a firing-squad. A brooding hostility to the Republic survived in Paris, but the Commune marked the end of Parisian efforts to dictate the system of government in France.

(c) Monarchism

The Assembly which was elected in February 1871 had a majority of royalists, but there was no agreement among them as to who should be king. Thiers concluded that monarchy was 'impossible, because there are three claimants but only one throne'.

But there was a clear front-runner among the claimants. Henry, the Comte de Chambord, was the grandson of Charles X and, in the eyes of the Bourbon supporters, should become Henry V. It was Henry's narrow-mindedness and political ineptitude which most decided the French that monarchy could not be restored. Chambord was honest to the extent of insisting that the Bourbon white flag must replace the tricolour, as the symbol of the monarchy, and this gave every indication that the monarchy would try to restore the royal prerogatives from which Frenchmen had broken free. Chambord seemed certain to divide the nation rather than to unite it. But the other candidates were even

Fig. 11.2 Paris, May 1871 – a scene of carnage and devastation, published in the Illustrated London News

weaker. The hope of the Orleanists was Philippe Albert, the grandson of Louis Philippe, but his chances were so poor that some of his supporters even tried to do a deal with the Bourbons, whereby Henry V would reign but would bequeath the throne to Philippe Albert's son. Louis Napoleon's son, the Bonapartist candidate, had far fewer supporters. When Thiers resigned in 1873 monarchism was already fading fast.

MacMahon was himself a monarchist, but he was also cautious. As the French President, he co-operated with the Assembly. Only in 1877 did he threaten to ignore constitutional practices, when he dismissed Jules Simon, a Republican prime minister, and appointed his own nominee, the Duc de Broglie, an Orleanist. To try to obtain a parliamentary majority for de Broglie elections were held. But the results were unfavourable. De Broglie was forced to resign before the end of 1877, and MacMahon also resigned at the beginning of 1879, to be replaced with a Republican President, Jules Grévy. By this time it was clear that monarchism had become too weak for any restoration of a king. Indeed, the constitution of the Third Republic had been agreed in 1875.

(d) The Constitution of the Third Republic

The constitution was the result of various piecemeal decisions rather than the product of a single draft, as was the case in Germany. The Chamber of Deputies was elected by manhood suffrage. This was the lower house of the French parliament (the National Assembly), elected at four-year intervals. The upper house was the Senate, which did not become wholly elective until 1884 and which, even then, because of complicated electoral law, retained a strong rural and conservative bias. The Assembly, Deputies and Senate, was the French law-making body. Together the Deputies and Senate elected a President at intervals of seven years, to serve as the head of state. Among the President's duties was the appointment of ministers to govern. In a sense, the options were left open in 1875, since the President could quite easily be replaced by a king.

Indeed much was left undefined: how the constitution would work in practice was decided more by custom than by rigid rules. After MacMahon's dismissal of Simon in 1877 two such customs were quickly established: that prime ministers and their cabinets should have majority support in the Chamber of Deputies, and without it should resign; and that elections to the Chamber should be at four-year intervals, and not whenever a government resigned. The French system differed, therefore, from that in Germany and also from that in Britain. In Germany ministers were little more than the nominees of the Kaiser. In Britain elections were usually held when a government lost the support of the House of Commons (with a maximum of seven years between elections, until its reduction to five years in 1911). But both Germany and Britain produced longer-lasting governments. The multiplicity of political groupings in France, and electoral laws which required second ballots to ensure that a successful candidate for office eventually secured an overall majority, provided a recipe for a great deal of political manoeuvring. The average life of a French government before 1914 was well below 12 months. This resulted in a lack of continuity, and sometimes in political weakness at a time of international crisis. Safe from their electors until the four-year term expired and elections were due, French Deputies were often far too ready to vote a government out of office. Yet the Third Republic and its 1875 constitution, with only minor amendments, lasted until defeat at the hands of Nazi Germany in 1940.

11.3   The Third Republic from 1875 to 1914

(a) Party Politics and the Procession of Governments

In the 1870s the main political struggle in France was between republicans and monarchists. Of some 10 million electors the majority were rural and conservative. The Republican party which Gambetta did much to create appealed to peasant proprietors and small businessmen. When the battle had been won for a republic rather than a monarchy, the Republicans split. Gambetta and Jules Ferry led the conservative wing, which came to be known as the Opportunists. Another wing, more inclined to reform, was that of the Radicals, who included Georges Clemenceau. Both Opportunists and Radicals appealed essentially to the peasantry and the lower middle classes. On the right, divisions remained between the various monarchists and Bonapartists, but strong support also existed for the Catholic Church: supporters of the Papacy were usually hostile to the Republicans. On the left, a Socialist Labour Party was founded in 1879, seeking support especially among France's three million industrial workers. But this Party also became fragmented, weakening the labour movement, and further complicating French politics. No single group could gain the support given in Britain to Conservatives or Liberals. Not until a left-wing coalition under René Waldeck-Rousseau came to office in 1899, did a French government survive for three years, and many of the shifting coalitions achieved nothing except to survive for a month or two.

The issues in French politics were often those which involved the defence of the Republic. From the right, there seemed to be a threat from those who preferred a more authoritarian system. From the left, there seemed to be a threat from those who cherished memories of the Commune of 1871, and those who wanted a more egalitarian social system. The Republic itself seemed to be accident-prone, inclined to be involved in scandals (see Section 11.3(d)). But there were also fundamental questions to be solved: of the relationships between the Republic and the Catholic Church; of whether, for economic or other reasons, the Republic should seek to expand the overseas empire; and of how the nation should adjust to its defeat by the Germans and the growing strength of Germany in Europe. It was in the nature of the politics of the Third

Republic that coherent solutions to these problems were not easily found. All too often it seemed merely to be living from day to day. The first election to be held after the agreement of the constitution of 1875 returned a secure Republican majority in the Chamber of Deputies. In 1879 the National Assembly returned to Paris. (It had moved from Bordeaux to Versailles in 1871.) But it was the end of the century before there was much coherence in the government of the Third Republic.

(b) The Republic and the Catholic Church

Some coherence was provided until 1885 by Jules Ferry. Ferry was twice Prime Minister and he also held other offices. As Minister of Education he aimed to modernize the French educational system and break the grip on it of the Catholic Church, which had been achieved since the Loi Falloux of 1850 (see page 96). This led to a struggle with the Church similar to the Kulturkampf in Germany. The Jesuits and other teaching orders were banned from teaching, and the Jesuits were expelled from France. In 1882 primary education was made compulsory and free, and controlled by the state. About 40 per cent of French children had been educated by the Church, but it was now possible for the state to supervise the education of all French children. The curriculum placed more emphasis on science and, in the *lycées*, on philosophy. Religious teaching was banned in schools. The general intention was to educate future citizens to support and serve the Republic, and to match the education of Germans which, it was believed, had helped them to win the Franco-Prussian War.

The attack on Church education inevitably involved an attack on the Church. Divorce was permitted and civil marriage was introduced. Catholic influence in hospitals and charities was also reduced. The attack occurring later than the Kulturkampf, the French had to deal not with Pius IX but with the more moderate Leo XIII. To the disappointment of monarchists and the right, who were prepared to support the Church, Leo gave his blessing to the policies of the Republic and, in the 1890s, the two co-existed comparatively comfortably. Nevertheless, the Church was always likely to be associated with the political right-wing in France, and to be discredited in affairs such as that concerning Dreyfus (see Section 11.3(d), below). Waldeck-Rousseau's government of 1899–1902 was a left-wing coalition, which was partly bound together by anti-clericalism as well as by anti-militarism, forces which had grown stronger during the Dreyfus Affair. It made changes in the French army, imposing stricter political control on the high command and officer corps; and it attacked the monastic orders. The Law of Associations of 1901 gave freedom to almost all associations except those which were religious, which required government consent. Waldeck-Rousseau was in poor health, and in 1902 he gave way to Emile Combes, who remained Prime Minister until 1905. Combes was more violently anti-clerical. Only five religious orders were permitted by his government. The rest were disbanded, their members hounded into exile and their property seized by the state. Clashes occurred with the Papacy about the appointment of bishops in France, especially after the accession to the Papacy of Pius X in 1903.

Unlike Pope Leo, Pius X would not compromise. The Papacy and the French Republic were now bitterly estranged, and Combes prepared to end the Concordat of 1801, in which Napoleon I had accepted Catholicism as the religion of the majority of Frenchmen and the official religion of France, the stipends of the clergy being paid by the state. The Law of Separation was carried through in 1905. It disestablished the Church in France: Catholicism was no longer the official religion, and the Church no longer received money from the state. Church properties were placed in the hands of lay committees, the clergy merely being allowed the use of the churches. Officially France was now a Godless country. The remaining monastic houses were dissolved, and it was only by allowing freedom of worship that church services were permitted at all. Many Frenchmen continued, of course, to be devout Catholics, and the Church itself found a new strength in being forced to struggle for its very existence. But the Law of Separation ended the tug-of-war between Church and State, and it ended the influence of the Church in French politics.

Fig. 11.3 An artist's sketch of the assassination of President Carnot, 1894. Carnot was stabbed by an anarchist

(c) The Republic and the Socialist Left

1873 marked the beginning of a period of economic depression in France. It increased the unrest in the industrial areas and, especially with the poor harvests of 1878–9, also in the countryside. The Republic weathered the storms, but the influence of Marxism and other left-wing philosophies was longer lasting than the temporary depressions in the trade cycle, which the whole of Europe had to endure from time to time. It was helpful to the peasant and middle-class Republic that the industrial and socialist left was far from being united. Many socialists were willing to work within the constitution, building up a parliamentary opposition. In 1899 Waldeck-Rousseau included the socialist Alexandre Millerand in his government as the Minister of Commerce, the first socialist in Europe to attain such an appointment, although many other socialists criticized this collaboration with the authorities of the Republic. Outside the National Assembly, revolutionary groups existed, among them the Anarchist descendants of Bakunin, some of whom assassinated President Carnot in 1894. The Republic dealt ruthlessly with such groups, but a more serious threat developed when some Anarchists and Marxists turned to syndicalism (see Glossary) in the belief that bourgeois society and the Republic could be crippled by industrial strikes.

The problem for the socialists in the Chamber of Deputies was to present a common viewpoint. Forty-three socialists were elected to the Chamber of Deputies in 1893, as part of the electorate's protest at the scandal concerning the Panama Canal (see Section 11.3(d), below). In 1889 the socialists had won only seven seats. Jules Guesde was one of those elected in 1893, the leader of a Marxist wing whose goal was the destruction of capitalism.

Jean-Léon Jaurès was also elected in 1893. He had sat in the Chamber in 1885 as a Radical, but was now intent on uniting as many socialists as possible, to work through the parliamentary system to win reforms. By championing Dreyfus (see pages 177–8), he won many more converts to socialism, but fundamental differences remained between his followers and the Guesdists. Jaurès never accepted government office, but he remained the most popular French socialist leader until 1914, and he was the founder of the newspaper, *L'Humanité*. True to his principles, he tried to stem the growing enthusiasm for war in both France and Germany in 1914, and was assassinated.

The dilemma of Jaurès was the dilemma of many European socialists in the years before 1914: to work within the existing economic, social and political systems, to try to improve the lot of the masses, was to risk being branded a traitor. Jaurès nevertheless won over many supporters to his brand of moderate socialism. Aristide Briand was an early follower, although he was expelled from the Socialist Party when he accepted government office in 1906. Léon Blum was another, though he did not obtain a parliamentary seat until 1919. Both Briand and Blum had distinguished political careers. But Guesde too accepted office in wartime when, to the dismay of Lenin and hardline Marxists, most European socialists put their countries before their internationalism.

Reforms which were helpful to the masses were passed during the years 1875 to 1914, partly under socialist pressure. The socialists were in favour of the reforms in education and of the attacks on the Church. They were pleased when child labour was prohibited in 1874 and when, during a general extension of civil rights in 1880s, the press achieved complete freedom and trade unions were legalized in 1884. The introduction of tariffs in 1881 helped to safeguard employment, and piecemeal efforts were made to raise wages and to improve working conditions. The main period of reform came after 1900. Trade unions benefited from the Law of Associations of 1901. But conservatism remained strongly entrenched in France and, although the Radical Clemenceau took office as Prime Minister in 1906 and was followed by Briand in 1909, many of their ideas bore little immediate fruit. Millerand set up a Labour Department and made some progress towards a ten-hour day, and a Public Health Act allocated government money towards improving housing. Nevertheless the introduction of income tax, old-age pensions, workmen's compensation for injury, and the state supervision of labour contracts, proceeded very slowly and were much obstructed in the National Assembly.

Outside the Assembly there were bitter industrial confrontations in the years before 1914. Trade unions banded together in 1895 in the CGT (*Confédération Général du Travail*), and they adopted syndicalist objectives. The syndicalists rejected parliamentary socialism. They expected to achieve power by uniting the working classes in industrial action and a general strike, out of which (somewhat vaguely) would emerge a new order, in which society was organized through democratic trade unions. In 1908 George Sorel published his *Reflections on Violence*, developing the philosophy of syndicalism.

But it was not easy to organize a general strike. Anarchists and anarcho-syndicalists often settled for piecemeal strikes and sabotage instead. Three million working days were lost through industrial action in France in 1893, and the decade as a whole was turbulent in the industrial areas. The twentieth century brought even more bitter clashes. Several years of 'class warfare' began in 1906 with a rash of strikes, when even the vine growers in the southern countryside went on strike. The railways were paralysed, but the syndicalists still did not manage to bring about a general strike. Both Clemenceau, who had already earned the nickname 'The Tiger', and Briand struck back fiercely. Troops were used to break the strikes, and strikers were drafted into the army reserves, to be taught military discipline. France was torn by controversy about the activities of the CGT and about the tactics of the governments. Briand fell from power in 1911 and once again there was political confusion, with seven further administrations before the outbreak of war in 1914. Outside parliament bitter conflict continued between the authorities and strikers, syndicalists and anarchists. War against Germany, however, provided a rallying-call to national unity. As Guesde put it: 'When the house is on fire, it is no time for controversy. The only thing to do is to take a hand with the buckets.'

(*d*) **The 'Scandals'**

The Third Republic still survived in 1914 but there was no great enthusiasm for it. Attention had focused several times not on its achievements but on peculiarly French episodes, which created scepticism and cynicism in France about the Republic's politicians.

(*i*) **The Boulanger Affair.** General Boulanger was at the centre of one such episode in the late 1880s. Boulanger was the Minister for War in 1886, but like most French politicians at this time, he quickly lost office. He attracted the attention of Bismarck, however, who branded him as an obstacle to good Franco-German relations, so set was Boulanger on revenge for the loss of Alsace-Lorraine. He also attracted the attention of French nationalists and won support from Bonapartists and monarchists, and he cashed in on the popular hostility to the authorities, which developed when it was discovered that President Grevy's son-in-law was conducting a thriving business in selling government honours. Boulanger's fame spread when he stood in numerous elections to the Chamber and won them. In 1889 he even succeeded in Paris. He could only occupy one seat, but his electoral victories and the popular demonstrations in his favour made it seem possible that he might seize power, like some latter-day Napoleon III. He toyed with the idea of a coup d'état, but took fright when the government talked of trying him for treason. On 1 April 1889 he fled to Brussels, and two years later he committed suicide on the grave of his mistress. Clemenceau commented: 'He died as he had lived – like a subaltern.'

(*ii*) **The Panama Canal Scandal.** No sooner had Boulanger fled than a new example of political corruption was revealed. Thousands of Frenchmen had invested in the Panama Canal Company. Ferdinand de Lesseps, who had constructed the Suez Canal, and Gustave Eiffel, the builder of the Tower, were cutting the Panama Canal. It seemed a good investment, especially when the French government gave it official support at the end of 1888. In February 1889 the Company went bankrupt. The project had to be abandoned and many Frenchmen lost their savings. Eager to find someone to blame Frenchmen looked for scapegoats. During the next few years the Canal Company was denounced as a swindle organized by Jews and by politicians, whom they were alleged to have bribed to gain the apparent guarantees of the government. The Jewish financier, Baron de Reinach, committed suicide. Another Jewish financier, Cornelius Herz, who was found to have been blackmailing him, fled. The government was forced to set up a committee of inquiry and proceedings were begun against ten politicians, including five ministers and ex-ministers. Rumour fed on rumour, though only one conviction resulted. Clemenceau was known to have been an associate of Herz and it was alleged that he was an agent of the British Foreign Office. For some years his career was blighted. The immediate outcome was a swing to the socialists in

*Fig. 11.4 General Georges Boulanger mounted on 'Tunis', a favourite horse.
Boulanger's bid for power ended in suicide in 1891*

the elections of 1893 but, more important, the scandal helped the latent anti-semitism in France to surface.

(*iii*) **The Dreyfus Case.** Anti-semitism became rampant during the Dreyfus Affair. Captain Alfred Dreyfus was a Jewish officer in the French army. In 1894 he was convicted of selling military secrets to Germany and was sent to Devil's Island for life. His family and friends insisted that he was innocent and, in 1897, Colonel Georges Picquart of the intelligence service asserted that the evidence against Dreyfus was in the handwriting of Major Esterhazy, and that secrets were still being betrayed. Picquart was promptly posted to Tunisia, but a public outcry led to Esterhazy's trial in 1898. He was acquitted. By now, however, Clemenceau was campaigning on behalf of Dreyfus and the novelist, Emile Zola, demanded a thorough inquiry into military corruption, in a powerful article headed *J'Accuse*. Public interest grew steadily during 1898, especially when Colonel Henry of the military intelligence committed suicide. Esterhazy fled the country, yet the authorities still dismissed Picquart for continuing to deny Dreyfus's guilt. Dreyfus was re-tried in 1899, only to be declared guilty again 'but with extenuating circumstances'. He was given a grudging pardon. Such half-measures were still unsatisfactory and, in 1906, the Chamber of Deputies set aside his conviction, restored him to his military appointment, and tried to placate him with the Legion of Honour.

Episodes such as these not only discredited authority in France: they divided the nation even more deeply than it was divided already. Dreyfus himself became almost irrelevant to the furious conflicts between Dreyfusards and anti-Dreyfusards. He became a rallying-flag for liberals, socialists, anti-clericals and anti-militarists, ever ready to criticize the system. Against him were ranged the supporters of the army, the Church, conservatism in general and anti-semitism in particular. That he was a Jew was enough for many of the more bigoted Frenchmen. Thus the Affair revealed the tensions in French society and, like the episodes which went before it, it unsettled the already far from stable political groupings on which French politics were based. The Dreyfus Affair did, however, rally the forces of the left, and it helped to produce the reforming administrations of the early years of the twentieth century, which began with the appointment of Waldeck-Rousseau in 1899.

(e) The Foreign and Colonial Policies of the Republic

Alsace-Lorraine was the burning issue in French foreign relations after 1871. Paris had solemnly draped in black its monument to Strasbourg (in Alsace), since the provinces were seized by the German Reich. Boulanger owed some of his popularity to his demand for revenge, but it was easier to demand revenge than to take it. France alone was no match for Germany, and Bismarck ensured that for twenty years after 1870 France was without allies (see Section 15.1). Moreover, France was still the only important republic in Europe, and other powers, such as Russia, remained suspicious of republicanism. For some time the French sought to compensate themselves for defeats in Europe by the pursuit of empire overseas. The Radicals were not enthusiastic. A rebellion in Algeria in 1871 made empire less attractive generally for a time, but Jules Ferry and the Opportunists encouraged a new interest in imperialism. Tunisia was seized in 1881. Ferry lost office at the end of that year, and his successors abandoned Egypt, where a traditional French interest had been strengthened with the building of the Suez Canal by de Lesseps. On return to office in 1883 Ferry worked busily to lay foundations for the French control of Madagascar, the Congo (French), and other areas of Africa, and to expand the empire in Indochina. He co-operated with Bismarck in the Berlin Conference on Africa in 1884–5. By 1914 the French overseas empire was second in size only to that of Britain, though it continued to create divisions among the politicians of the Republic. (See Sections 16.1 and 16.2. The extent of the French empire in Africa can be seen in Fig. 16.4.)

Colonial expansion also brought clashes with other powers. Italy was angered by the French annexation of Tunisia. The British took exception to the French attempt to penetrate the Sudan, and Germany challenged the extension of French interests in Morocco (see Section 16.3). Germany remained the principal target of French hostility, so much so that after 1900 France drew closer to Britain, another old enemy. By that time, France had already made a Dual Alliance with Russia, something Bismarck had always sought to prevent. In 1904 the Entente Cordiale with Britain was signed, for the settlement of colonial problems. As understanding with the British deepened, France became a key member of the Triple Entente (France, Russia and Britain), which, at least in the Kaiser's eyes, threatened Germany with encirclement (see Section 17.1). When war broke out in 1914 France therefore had allies and, at the end of the war, the Third Republic regained possession of Alsace-Lorraine.

In spite of the great expansion of its overseas empire, and the apparent building of alliances which eventually enabled France to take revenge on Germany, French external policy was nevertheless hardly more coherent in the years 1875 to 1914 than was French internal policy. The same quick changes of ministries handicapped external as much as internal policy. But in general the Republic was cautious. France tried to avoid external problems or, if they arose, to settle them peacefully. On the other hand, the colonial empire helped to raise the prestige of the Republic, and it provided an outlet for the energies of soldiers, adventurers, missionaries and traders, which sometimes seemed to be frustrated at home. In Europe it never seemed likely that France would fight simply to recover Alsace-Lorraine, but the wound was nevertheless deep, and when the opportunity came in 1914, the French were quick to unite for battle. Ramshackle as it was in many ways, the Third Republic then proved strong enough, at least with the help of allies, to stop the advance of the German military machine, which France had been unable to stop in 1870.

(f) French Cultural Achievement

The Republic also had the merit of allowing great individual freedom. The splendours of the Second Empire lived on in the cultural and scientific achievements of the late nineteenth and early twentieth centuries. Among the French artists at this time were Cézanne, Degas, Gauguin, Manet, Monet, Pissarro, Renoir and Toulouse-Lautrec. The French Impressionists held their first exhibition in 1874, profoundly affecting the development of painting with their unique contribution. The names of French composers in the period including Bizet, Debussy, Fauré, Franck, Massenet, Ravel and Saint-Saëns, and they too made a unique contribution to European music. French literature flourished: prose writers included Barrès, Benda, Daudet, France, Maupassant and Zola. Verlaine and others were writing poetry. Sorel and Durkheim contributed to the social sciences, Bergson to philosophy, Pasteur and Curie to medicine. Paris went on growing, topping a population of two and a half million at the beginning of the twentieth century, and continuing to lay claim to the title of the cultural capital of Europe. Like Europe as a whole (and more so than most of it in terms of material devastation), France was to be scarred deeply by the First World War. The Third Republic went on during and after the War, but it was possible in later years to look back on '*La Belle Epoque*', before 1914, as a time of cultural renaissance, imperial expansion, and even of comparative calm.

Further Reading

Anderson, F. D.: *France 1870–1914, Politics and Society.* Routledge and Kegan Paul (London, 1977).

Derfler, L.: *The Third French Republic, 1870–1940.* Anvil (Dublin, 1966).

Holt, E.: *The Tiger: Life of Clemenceau*, 1841–1929. Hamish Hamilton (London, 1975).

Johnson, D.: *France and the Dreyfus Affair.* Blandford (Poole, 1966).

Kedward, R.: *The Dreyfus Affair.* Longman (Harlow, 1965).

Randell, K.: *France: The Third Republic, 1870–1914.* Edward Arnold (London, 1986).

Documentary

The Siege of Paris and the Commune (Jackdaw Wallet). Cape.

Edwards, S.: *The Communards of Paris, 1871.* Thames and Hudson (London, 1973).

Exercises

1. Explain why 'a brooding hostility to the Republic survived in Paris' (page 169).
2. Making use of the Index to this book as well as of this Unit, construct accounts of (*a*) the life of Adolphe Thiers, (*b*) the activities of Boulanger, (*c*) the Dreyfus Case, and (*d*) Syndicalism. Compare what you have written with the entries in A. W. Palmer's *Dictionary of Modern History, 1789–1945* (Penguin).
3. Compare the Constitution of the Third Republic (Section 11.2(*d*)) with that of the German Reich (see Index).
4. In what ways does Section 11.3(*b*) show that French governments faced (a) similar, and (b) different, problems in its relations with the Catholic Church, compared with those faced by Bismarck in the *Kulturkampf*?
5. How were the years before 1914 in France years of growing industrial unrest? Why did most French workmen agree with the opinion of Guesde which is quoted on page 175?
6. Write an account to show whether, as a French peasant born about 1850, you would have supported the Third Republic in the early years of the twentieth century, or would have demanded a different system of government.

Unit Twelve
Liberal Italy 1861–1922

12.1 The Economy and Society

Most of Italy was united under a single government in 1861 (see Section 7.2). That was the legacy of Cavour whose death in that year deprived Italy of his much-needed leadership. He had pointed the way for Italy – towards a secularized state, a parliamentary system, industrialization, and free trade. But he left the new nation beset with problems, of which the completion of unification (by bringing in Venetia and Rome) was almost the simplest to solve. Italians had little experience with which to work the oligarchical political system, in which the members of parliament were elected throughout the country by about two per cent of the population. Pius IX implacably opposed the new Italy, but greater problems were posed by the Italian economy and by Italian society.

The country produced too little wealth to support national prosperity. Almost alone in liberal Europe, Italy could cope with its problems only by encouraging its subjects to emigrate, to check the rising population. There were 25 million Italians in 1861. At the beginning of the twentieth century Italian emigration was running at about half a million annually, but even so the population rose to over 35 million by 1914. The increase in population persistently held down living standards. According to a report circulated in 1906 an Italian in recent years had had an income below 30 per cent that of a Frenchman, and the average Italian was poorer than a subject of the Austro-Hungarian Empire. The report also pointed to the contrast between north and central Italy, on the one hand, and south Italy on the other. The north had industries and fertile farming land, and there were minerals to be worked in Tuscany and Sardinia, so that the hard-pressed peasant could increase his income by seeking work in industry. But, it went on:

> To the south of Tuscany there commences a new world . . . [of] veritable desolation . . . [with an] immense extent of marshy land or land imperfectly cultivated . . . almost everywhere devoid of the necessary farming equipment.

Poverty, superstition and banditry were widespread in what had been the Papal States and the Kingdom of the Two Sicilies. Much of the terrain was mountainous; the soil was poor, and industry was almost non-existent. Italy as a whole lacked capital, so that it was difficult to make farming more efficient and to establish new industries. Moreover, in order to finance government, heavy taxes were imposed on people who could ill afford to pay them. The optimism which accompanied unification soon gave way to disillusionment, and disillusionment with liberal Italy enabled Mussolini in 1922 to begin to fashion an Italy which was thoroughly illiberal.

12.2   The Years before 1914

(a) The Political System

Although based on a narrow property franchise, the constitution which Italy inherited from Piedmont-Sardinia was liberal: Cavour had established the precedent that governments needed to have majority support in parliament, and King Victor Emmanuel had less freedom than the German Kaiser to appoint his own nominees to office. But Cavour also left something of a tradition: that majorities in parliament resulted from intrigue and political deals rather than from the clash of identifiable parties and principles. For some years after his death, the support he had built up for the government enabled his successors to carry on his work. In these years governments were on the whole honest and thrifty. By the mid-1870s they had balanced the government's budget, completed the unification, and laid some foundations for economic development. Among the prime ministers were Ricasoli and Farini although, as men from the Duchies, there was some resentment of them in Piedmont. Cavour's parliamentary majority gradually crumbled, however, as local interests and self-interest began to play more part in parliament. In the later 1870s the system grew debased to the point at which bribery and corruption became notorious. Few of the new generation of politicians showed either a sense of mission or qualities of leadership. There was a similar lack of continuity between governments to that in France, but graft became more pervasive, and the level of competence was often low. With comparatively few voters to worry about, Italian politicians could devote themselves to political horse-trading, peddling offices, honours, personal gifts and local amenities, in return for support. They retained a general loyalty to the constitutional monarchy and the parliamentary system, but there was very little idealism. Agostino Depretis, who became the Prime Minister in 1876, practised *trasformismo*, transforming opponents into supporters, by political deals (and transforming his policies to fit in with what was possible).

The history of Italian politics before 1914 was in many ways the history of individual politicians, jockeying for influence. Governments came and went in bewildering succession, but a number of key figures emerged who were dominant for a decade or so. From 1876 to his death in 1887 Depretis was such a figure. After him came Francesco Crispi, the most forceful Italian politician, whose authoritarianism seemed to threaten the constitution, but who was driven out of politics after a disastrous failure to conquer Abyssinia in 1896 (see page 186). A good deal of the energies of Depretis and Crispi were devoted to political manoeuvring but also to trying to make Italy a great power, though its resources were hardly adequate to justify such a status. King

Humbert, who reigned from 1878 to his assassination in 1900, favoured such ambitions. But the new century brought a greater concern for reform. Both the Church and socialism achieved greater influence in Italian politics. Giovanni Giolitti came to the fore in the early twentieth century and, in 1912, Italy lurched closer to democracy when he introduced what was almost manhood suffrage, and salaries were paid to members of parliament. The result was that Italian politics at last began to concern the masses, and policies rather than personal deals grew in importance.

It should not be thought that governments had made no improvements in Italy, however. The improvement of communications and of public health was carried on by many governments. Illiteracy was slowly eroded, and Depretis quadrupled the franchise in 1882 to take account of improving education and a growing middle class. Crispi imposed tariffs after 1887 to protect Italian producers, although they were so severe that they damaged Italy's trade with France, with whom Italy had made commercial treaties. Crispi also relaxed the penal code and reformed the prisons. Yet government neglect of the masses was such that Sicilian peasants rebelled in 1893, and mismanagement and financial scandals were more commonplace than major reforms. Giolitti found much that needed to be done in the opening years of the twentieth century. With the encouragement of the new King, Victor Emmanuel III, he abolished child labour and improved conditions in factories. Trade unions were recognized and co-operative marketing schemes were promoted. National insurance – a pale imitation of Bismarck's system in Germany – was introduced, against sickness and industrial accidents and to provide old-age pensions. Italians also now secured a weekly rest day. By 1914, therefore, Italy was beginning to come into line with western Europe, although the south remained stubbornly poverty-stricken. By 1914 Italy was also beginning to solve the problem of the hostility of the Church.

(b) The State and the Church

The Pope had been angered by Piedmontese anti-clericalism even before the upheavals of 1859–60 (see Section 7.2(a)). The national government continued Piedmontese policy and, in 1866, all monastic houses in Italy were dissolved. In 1870 the Pope lost the last of his temporal possessions save for the Vatican. Pius IX was then in no mood to negotiate with Victor Emmanuel's government, so the latter produced its own settlement of the Papal problem, in the Law of Guarantees of 1871. It was a not ungenerous settlement. The Pope was allowed the ownership of the Vatican and of almost all his palaces, and he was given an annual payment of over £120 000. Although Italy would permit free religious debate, the state would punish insults to the Catholic faith. The Pope remained free to make all religious appointments in Italy, and the clergy were not required to swear loyalty to the political authorities. Pius was not appeased. To the declaration of Infallibility (see Section 9.4) he added an instruction that all loyal Catholics should avoid participation in Italian politics both as parliamentarians and voters. He rejected the annual payment, and he insisted on regarding himself as 'the prisoner in the Vatican'. When Pius died Leo XIII adopted a similar attitude.

In practice, however, neither the Italian state nor the Church stuck rigidly to the positions adopted in 1870–1. The state meddled in ecclesiastical appointments, and it interfered with Church schools, insisting on inspecting them and encouraging parents to reject religious teaching for their children. It also introduced civil marriage. Catholics, on the other hand, found ways of getting round the Papal veto in order to vote and to sit in parliament, though the country as a whole remained staunchly loyal to the Catholic faith. Over the years the government of the Vatican found that it was impossible not to co-operate with the government of Italy in many day-to-day matters. Nevertheless, the underlying hostility added to the difficulties of the Italian state, and it divided opinion both in the country and in parliament. The tension was not eased until 1905, when Pius X made the concession of allowing Italians to be involved in Italian politics, even though he showed a greater hostility to the state in France than had Leo XIII. Pius recognized that it had been a mistake not to encourage the growth of a Church party in the Italian parliament, and he now hoped that Catholic influence might help to obstruct the development of Italian socialism.

(c) The State and Socialism

Support for socialism in Italy grew out of poverty, squalid conditions and government neglect. Italian socialists in the 1890s were revolutionary, since they had little hope of influencing parliament with its narrow electoral base. But they were not easy to distinguish from the anarchist followers of Bakunin nor from those, like the Sicilian peasants in 1893, who were driven to rebellion less by ideals than by blind despair. The government tried to crush all such violent protest, and Crispi went on, in 1894, to ban all socialist societies and publications, and to arrest the tiny group of eight socialists who had secured election to the parliament. As Bismarck had discovered in Germany, such tactics only increased support for socialism. In 1895 the socialists won 12 parliamentary seats, and they founded the newspaper, *Avanti*, a year later. Open warfare continued between the authorities and the revolutionary left. Anarchists threw bombs and succeeded in killing King Humbert; and syndicalist ideas began to spread rapidly. Repression was achieving little. In 1900 the socialists won 33 seats in parliament, though their opposition was weakened by feuds among themselves. Giolitti followed Bismarck's example, and introduced social reforms to counter the growing interest in Marxism.

Like French socialists Italian socialists became divided. The moderates were willing to co-operate with governments to win further reforms, but they found themselves caught up in the parliamentary horse-trading. The syndicalists preferred industrial action, but they suffered a setback with the collapse of a general strike in Milan in 1904. Improvements in the economy undermined support for socialism among the factory workers, to whom Marxists made their principal appeal since, distressed as they were, the peasants of the south showed little interest in socialist ideology. Nevertheless, there was a general strike in central Italy in the summer of 1914, with the threat to set up a breakaway Marxist Republic. One of its organizers was Benito Mussolini, a socialist agitator and journalist, who had become the editor of *Avanti* in 1912. When war broke out in 1914 *Avanti* thundered against it and demanded peace. But Mussolini quickly changed his mind. Before the end of the year, he was demanding that Italy should declare war on the Austrians, hoping perhaps to give the country a new sense of purpose. His fellow-socialists were shocked, and Mussolini was expelled from the Socialist Party. They in turn were denounced by Mussolini: 'You cannot get rid of me because I am and always will be a Socialist.' But it was as the advocate of dictatorship and fascism that Mussolini was next to make his mark in Italy, and Italian socialism was to prove too weak to bar his way. Mussolini destroyed both socialism and liberal Italy.

(d) Italian Foreign and Colonial Policies

Bismarck observed that Italy had 'a large appetite but poor teeth'. Both Depretis and Crispi wanted international prestige and an overseas empire, and Italians had still to achieve *Italia Irredenta* (see page 115); but Italy lacked the economic strength and a sufficiently strong army to compete with other powers on equal terms. Italian patriots created trouble for the Austrians in the Tyrol and Trieste, but the Italian government was too weak to do much to pursue their claims to be united with Italy. It was impossible for Italy to strike in any area where the great powers had interests, and its attention focused primarily on the Mediterranean and Africa.

In 1882 Italy nevertheless became part of the European alliance system, joining the Triple Alliance with Germany and Austria-Hungary. From the outset the Alliance made little sense for Italians. They had more in common with the liberal states of western Europe. But France had just annexed Tunisia which Italy had hoped to acquire: indeed many Italians had already settled there. The Triple Alliance was a snub to the French and it guaranteed help to Italy in the unlikely event of a French invasion. It also boosted Italy's prestige by its association with major powers. It had few other advantages, and when the First World War began in 1914, Italy hastily abandoned the Alliance. When they joined the War in 1915, Italians fought on the opposite side. Nor was Italy much helped by the Mediterranean Agreements of 1887 with Britain and Austria-Hungary, except for the prestige the negotiations themselves brought. The Agreements were essentially to preserve the status quo in and around the Mediterranean, and they were intended to thwart France and Russia. They lapsed in 1892.

Meanwhile, an early Italian settlement on the Red Sea grew, by 1885, into the colony of Eritrea, and Crispi acquired Italian Somaliland soon afterwards. Like other European powers, Italy was helping to carve up Africa. Bordering both Eritrea and Somaliland, Abyssinia offered a greater prize. Crispi embarked on a war to conquer it. The Emperor Menelek of Abyssinia resisted fiercely, and the Italians were routed at the Battle of Adowa in 1896. It was a humiliation which Crispi's career could not survive, and the memory of it rankled with Italians until Mussolini conquered Abyssinia forty years later. In 1914, however, Abyssinia remained the one area of Africa which had proved strong enough to defy the Europeans (see Fig. 16.4).

Fig. 12.1 One in the eye for King Humbert (1878–1900) and for Italian morale. Alone among Europeans, the Italians grabbed for possession of an African state, only to be defeated at Adowa, 1896. A French cartoon

A war against the Ottoman Empire in 1911 turned out more successfully for Italy. By that time France and Britain had taken charge of all the north African states on the Mediterranean, except for Tripoli and Cyrenaica (Libya), which remained in Turkish hands. The Turks had problems enough in the Balkans, and European attention was focused on a dispute over Morocco (see Section 16.3). Italian public opinion was generally favourable to some new foreign adventure, to win prestige to offset the humiliation at Adowa and a more recent rebuff, when Italy had made no headway in trying to join in the

European infiltration of China. War on the Turks was declared in September 1911, and Italy snatched Rhodes and the Dodecanese Islands, as well as Tripoli and Cyrenaica. That was by no means the end of it, however. Senussi tribesmen in Libya continued to resist Italian authority, and the Italians were confined to little more than the coastline. Their victory over the Turks was only the prelude to a struggle with local tribesmen which went on until 1931. Libya brought little benefit to Italy, and it was a constant drain on the latter's limited resources. In theory the acquisition of Libya made the Italian empire three times larger, and it was a triumph in that Italy had seized one of the last major territories still available for the establishment of empire. But the poor performance of Italy's armed forces, both against the Turks and the Senussi tribesmen, helped to delay the country's involvement in the First World War: it was first necessary to attempt some military reforms.

12.3   The First World War and the Rise of Fascism

(a) The War and Postwar Confusion

Military unreadiness was one reason why Italians remained at peace in 1914. Other reasons were that Italians saw that they had little to gain by honouring the Triple Alliance and fighting alongside Germany and Austria-Hungary, and they were also reluctant to fight against Britain, for whom some of Cavour's admiration still lingered. Nor could Italy afford another war. But British persuasion nevertheless drew Italy into the *Treaty of London* of April 1915, when sweeping promises were made in return for an Italian undertaking to join the Allies. When the war was won Italy would not only receive *Italia Irredenta*, but it would be given Albania, Adalia (in Turkey) and further territories in Africa, and it would share in an indemnity. The Italians thought the offer too good to refuse, and war was declared on Austria-Hungary in May 1915. That satisfied the Allies for a time since it opened another front, but Italy exasperated them by delaying a declaration of war against Germany until August 1916.

The Allies were victorious (see Unit Eighteen) but Italy itself won little glory. As Giolitti had warned, the Italian army was still weak in 1915. It won some early successes, and it managed to set foot on Austrian territory and to cling on grimly during 1916, but it was never able to advance more than a few miles outside Italy. In 1917 it was routed at Caporetto. It seemed possible that the whole of Venetia would be lost as the Italians made a disorderly retreat, but they were rescued by British and French reinforcements. The Austrians were held on the River Piave, just short of Venice, and a late victory for the Italians at Vittorio Veneto, before the War ended, boosted the prestige of Vittorio Orlando, who had become the Prime Minister after Caporetto. The war had cost the lives of 650 000 Italians, and plunged the country deeply into debt.

The Peace Conference at Paris brought few of the expected rewards (see Section 20.1(*d*)). President Wilson of the USA had little sympathy with Italian ambitions, and even less with the Treaty of London, which the USA had not signed and had not originally known about. *Italia Irredenta* was conceded insofar as Italy gained the southern Tyrol, Trentino, and Istria, with Trieste but not Fiume. The Italians wanted Fiume, more of the Tyrol and a stake in Albania, and they were bitter at getting none of the German colonies. The only part of the Ottoman Empire they received was Adalia, and they were chased away from that by Turkish nationalists.

Orlando's reputation could not survive his failure at the Peace Conference. He resigned in June 1919 and Italian politics plunged back into confusion. The election of 1919 returned 156 Socialists and 100 members of a Catholic Popular Party, though neither group was entirely united. Between them were numerous traditional groupings, and forming a government was even more difficult than before 1914. Yet this was the time when Italy had a particular need for stable government and for able leadership. Disillusioned with the war and with the peace, Italians faced a massive national debt. There were shortages even of food, with consequent high prices. (Since 1913 prices in general in Italy had risen by more than 500 per cent, those in Britain by about 125 per cent.) It was difficult to sell exports and there were comparatively few tourists, so that unemployment soared, especially as the soldiers were returning home. In the poverty-stricken south, banditry thrived, the number of brigands swelled by army deserters. Industrial relations resembled a sort of guerilla warfare in the north and centre.

The left wing took their inspiration from the Bolshevik revolution in Russia of 1917. Industrial warfare grew fiercer and a few soviets were established. In 1921 the Communist Party broke away from the Socialists, to pursue more extreme policies for the transformation of society. On the right, there was a demand for strong leadership to restore law and order, to protect property, to discipline the strikers, and to rescue national honour. The right was inspired when Gabriele D'Annunzio, a nationalist poet, led a group of volunteers to seize Fiume, and held it for a year. Giolitti was now back in office. He negotiated with Jugoslavia that Fiume should be a free city rather than a part of Italy – the best deal he could obtain – and then he had to remove D'Annunzio by force, to the anger of many Italians. (Mussolini was to seize Fiume for Italy in 1924.) Giolitti was driven to resign. Meanwhile, the election of 1921 had returned 13 Communists, and 35 Fascists, whom Giolitti had mistakenly encouraged, in the belief that they would support orderly government. Neither was more than a splinter group in an assembly of 535, but they indicated a growing support in Italy for the two extremes. Outside parliament the violence continued. Ivanoe Bonomi put together a government after Giolitti but, when he too resigned in February 1922, it took weeks to find anyone strong enough to form a government at all. When a new Prime Minister, Luigi Facta, was found, his government was virtually paralysed. The political situation was ready-made for the seizure of power by an unscrupulous demagogue.

Fig. 12.2 The two faces of Giovanni Giolitti, the friend of the capitalists and the friend of the workers. Giolitti was Prime Minister of Italy five times, holding the office for some eleven years in the period 1892 to 1921. An Italian cartoon

(b) Mussolini and the Fascists

The 35 Fascists in the Italian parliament were led by Mussolini. Since his expulsion from the Socialist Party in 1914 Mussolini had set up his own newspaper, *Il Popolo d'Italia*, to preach his nationalist ideas. He joined the army in 1915 but was wounded in an accidental explosion and was discharged in 1917, to return to Milan and his newspaper. By 1919 he had collected a miscellaneous rabble of discontented revolutionaries and ex-soldiers who dressed in black shirts and called themselves the *Fasci di Combattimento*. They adopted the Roman salute and carried daggers, and they took as their symbol the *fasces* of ancient Rome, a bundle of rods bound round an axe. They formed the Fascist Party but could win no seats at all in the election of 1919.

The principal policy of Mussolini and his followers was to obtain power. They promised strong government, with a purge of the Communists and the left. They made little secret of their contempt for Italian democracy, but they appealed to industrialists and landowners as the men to protect property, and to nationalists as the men to make Italy great. Mussolini had moved some way

Fig. 12.3 Mussolini photographed at a Fascist meeting in 1932. The Fascists won no parliamentary seats in the election of 1919, yet Mussolini became Italy's Prime Minister in 1922

from the views he had expressed as the editor of *Avanti*. His new beliefs were far from clear, though they could be summarized and daubed on walls in the terse slogan, 'Believe. Obey. Fight.' Portraits of Mussolini were posted up throughout the country, suggesting the coming of a national saviour. The Fasci, meanwhile, practised their thuggery, breaking up Communist meetings and beating up opponents. They claimed that the Fascist Party had a quarter of a million members.

The trade unions were branded as disruptive forces in Italian society, to the delight of many employers. When the unions tried to show their own power in a general strike in 1922 Mussolini seized his chance. Fascists acted as strike-breakers, and helped to keep essential services running. They fought the strikers, and burned the printing presses of *Avanti*; and they constantly ridiculed the ineffectiveness of the government. In October 1922 the Fascists planned a dramatic showdown, threatening to march on Rome if they were not admitted to government. A proclamation was issued:

> Fascists! Italians! The hour of decisive battle has struck. . . . The Fascists march . . . against the political class of feeble, weak-minded men who, in four long years, have not been able to give a true Government to our nation. The bourgeoisie should know that the Fascists want to impose a unique discipline on the nation. . . . The labourers and workmen have nothing to fear from Fascist power.

The Church and the monarchy were also reassured that they were not threatened, in spite of what Fascists had suggested previously. The Fascists appealed to the army not to interfere.

Facta wanted to make a stand and he asked King Victor Emmanuel III for emergency powers. The King refused. He had no desire for further bloodshed, and he was uncertain of the loyalty of the army. It was simpler to give in. No march was needed. The King sent a telegram to Mussolini, and Mussolini came to Rome to be appointed Prime Minister, arriving in a borrowed morning suit, top hat and spats. The Fascist blackshirts followed, in time to hold a victory parade. Mussolini's first cabinet included only four Fascists but, within a month, he had persuaded Parliament to grant him full powers until the end of 1923. The constitution was revised so that the party to win the most votes in an election would have two-thirds of the seats in parliament: the election of 1924 in any case gave the Fascists more than 60 per cent of the votes, the support of four and a half million electors. The figures no doubt exaggerated the true support for the Fascists, but Mussolini had undoubtedly achieved a genuine popularity. His popularity was perhaps more of a comment on the failures and disappointments of liberal Italy than on Mussolini's own qualities or on his policy. He had shown considerable skill in manoeuvring himself into office, but he had also been much assisted by the numerous divisions among his rivals. Having become the Prime Minister of Italy, he was to remain in office for over 20 years (see Sections 22.1 and 22.2).

Further Reading

Absalom, R. N. L.: *Mussolini and the Rise of Italian Fascism*. Methuen (London, 1969).
Barclay, G. St. J.: *The Rise and Fall of the New Roman Empire*. Sidgwick and Jackson (London, 1973).
Seton-Watson, C.: *Italy from Liberalism to Fascism, 1870–1925*. Methuen (London, 1967).
Whyte, A. J.: *The Evolution of Modern Italy, 1715–1922*. Blackwell (Oxford, 1944).

Exercises

1. 'The country produced too little wealth to support national prosperity' (page 181). Explain and illustrate this statement.
2. What does this Unit show to have been the economic, social, and political weaknesses of 'Liberal Italy'?

3. Making use of the Index as well as of this Unit, describe (a) what happened at Adowa in 1896, and (b) in what ways this event was important to Italians.
4. Write an account of Italian foreign policy in the years 1871 to 1919. Why was the policy not more successful?
5. Write *two* views of Mussolini in 1921, one from the point of view of an Italian trade unionist, the other from the point of view of a member of the Fascist Party.
6. (a) What does the illustration on page 190 reveal about Mussolini-ism?
   (b) What did Mussolini mean by 'a unique discipline' (page 191)? Read Section 22.2, and then develop your answer further.

The Habsburg Empire 1867–1918

13.1 The Ausgleich

When the Hungarians surrendered at Vilagos in August 1849 it seemed that normality was fast being restored in the Austrian Empire, and that the revolutions of 1848–9 had changed very little (see Section 5.2(*d*)). General Haynau took a ferocious revenge on the Magyars as he completed the subjection of Hungary, and martial law was not lifted there until 1857. But Franz Joseph, who had become the Austrian Emperor in 1848, intended to go even further than 'normality'. He imposed a new tightness of control on the whole Empire, centralized on Vienna. By the end of 1851, virtually all traces of constitutionalism had been removed, along with all civil liberties. The Emperor held absolute power and, when Schwarzenberg died in 1852, Franz Joseph acted as his own chief minister. Only a feeble advisory council, the *Reichsrat*, remained – in theory, to advise the Emperor on law-making. The Habsburg crown was stronger even than that in Prussia. Its subjects were subordinated to a legion of German-speaking officials under the direction of Alexander Bach, Franz Joseph's Minister of the Interior. The Bach 'system' was disliked even in Austria for its unimaginative rigidity, and it was hated in the non-German-speaking areas of the Empire both for its rigid centralization and its Germanism. The only authority which was strengthened in Franz Joseph's Empire, apart from that of the Emperor and his ministers, was that of the Catholic Church. A Concordat was made with Pius IX in 1855 which guaranteed many privileges to the Church, including the control over education, and which removed such challenges to the Church as ceremonies of civil marriage. No other ruler in Europe worked with a greater sense of dedication to duty than Franz Joseph but, like Metternich before him, he was dedicated to fighting a losing battle. He was trying to preserve an outdated multinational Empire (see Fig. 2.2), and he was trying to preserve a social and political system much closer to that of Russia than to that of France.

The Austrian Empire lost even Russian goodwill during the Crimean War (see Section 8.4). It lost Lombardy, its influence in Italy, and finally Venetia in the period 1859 to 1866 (see Section 7.2); and in 1866, it was routed by Prussia and robbed of influence in Germany (see Section 7.3). The Empire and its influence were shrinking, and such setbacks inevitably had repercussions on the Emperor's government. Bach was succeeded in 1859 by Agenor Goluchowski who, in a brief 16 months before his dismissal, began the painful process of trying to preserve the Empire by granting tiny concessions, making some movement away from Germanism and over-centralization. Provincial diets were set up again, and the Reichsrat was modestly strengthened to become the embryo of an imperial parliament. It was hoped that such concessions would rally aristocrats and landowners to the support of the Emperor. But the middle classes too demanded a role, and the non-German nationalities, especially the Hungarians, wanted greater powers for the diets. Almost as fast as concessions were made, they were withdrawn. But the tide was flowing towards change, and defeat by the Prussians at Sadowa in 1866 made everything more urgent. The Hungarian problem was the most urgent of all.

Fig. 13.1 An Austrian caricature of Count Andrassy, a Hungarian politician who helped to arrange the Ausgleich and, in serving the Dual Monarchy, rushed to and fro between Wien (Vienna) and Pest (Budapest)

The Hungarians wanted independence but they were not strong enough to take it by force. Led by Ferenc Deák and Count Andrassy, Hungarian moderates were willing to compromise on home rule, and the Compromise (*Ausgleich*) was negotiated by Count Beust in 1867 on behalf of Franz Joseph. Hungary received complete internal self-government by a ministry responsible to the Magyar Reichstag, the former Diet. Franz Joseph would be crowned as the King of Hungary, and he would appoint ministers to conduct the foreign and defence policies common to all his territories. The Austro-Hungarian Empire, the Dual Monarchy, would thus retain a common front to the outside world. Provision was made for trade between the two parts of Franz Joseph's Empire, and for such joint finance as was necessary. Sixty members of the

Reichstag in Budapest and sixty members of the Reichsrat in Vienna would meet annually, to discuss matters of common interest, and these members were to be known as the Delegations.

This settlement with Hungary remained in force until 1918, when the whole Empire collapsed. But, in some ways, it was only the starting point for new problems. Other nationalities such as the Czechs wanted similar arrangements to be made, and battles were still to be fought to make the Reichstag and the Reichsrat more representative of the people. Franz Joseph had shown that he could be made to yield, and the moral of that was that further pressure should be put upon him. Two years after the Ausgleich, education became compulsory in the Austro-Hungarian Empire, and that itself was a recipe for social change which would further undermine the old traditions which Franz Joseph always struggled to maintain.

Fig. 13.2 The Austro-Hungarian Empire in 1914

13.2   The Non-Hungarian Empire

(a) Society and Politics

Hungary had its own king and a distinct identity after 1867, but the other half of Franz Joseph's Empire had less coherence. The struggle for constitutional government and for the democratic control of the Reichsrat in Vienna was complicated and handicapped by racial rivalries, as well as by the Emperor's implacable opposition to constitutionalism. A narrow but elaborate electoral system existed, and the aristocracy and some of the middle classes were represented in the Reichsrat. Some provincial diets also existed in 1867, similarly weighted towards an élite. But Franz Joseph continued to believe that parliamentary government was out of place in Austria, although his ministers made some effort to win majority support in the Reichsrat. Indeed the Emperor replaced Count Beust in 1868 with a ministry of bourgeois liberals, and this ministry restored civil marriage, made educational reforms, and introduced universal military service. By the time that Ernst von Körber became the chief minister in 1900, however, ministers relied less on a supporting coalition in the Reichsrat, than on the divisions among their opponents which were likely to prevent their defeat. In any case power now rested much more with civil servants than with politicians, and the traditional bureaucracy of the Empire was again dominant.

The politics of the non-Hungarian half of the Empire were not only concerned with the struggles between conservatism, liberalism and socialism. Germans in the Habsburg Empire were anxious, above all, to preserve German ascendancy. They often preferred to avoid change, rather than promote change which might strengthen the non-German nationalities. The franchise was widened in 1896 but the vote was not given to all adult males (at the age of 24) until 1906, when the electoral system was also simplified. Meanwhile, a Christian Socialist Party was founded in 1887, on a strange platform which combined anti-capitalism and anti-semitism with support for the Emperor and for imperial unity. The Social Democratic Party, founded in 1889, paid lip service to revolutionary Marxism, but it concentrated on winning reforms to help the workers while resisting disruption by non-German minorities. The first election on the basis of manhood suffrage was held in 1907, and the Christian Socialists were returned as the largest single party with 94 of the 516 seats in the Reichsrat. The return of 87 Social Democrats gave some indication of the developing industrialization in Bohemia and in cities such as Vienna. Both parties claimed to be *kaisertreu* (loyal to the Emperor), and they had a greater fear of a coalition of non-Germans against Germans, than of the abuse of power by the Emperor's ministers and officials.

In truth, the Emperor's ministers were often administrators rather than politicians. They carried on the day-to-day running of the Empire; they made improvements when necessary, but they aimed above all to keep the Empire together. The influence of liberals brought educational progress, administrative reform and civil liberties. Socialist influence brought improvements in working conditions and, after 1900, old-age pensions and insurance against sickness (insurance against industrial accidents having been introduced earlier, along with the inspection of factories). But struggles such as those over the control of education, between Church and state, were entangled in the problems of the nationalities, as was almost everything else.

Fig. 13.3 Franz Joseph (left), an ageing and increasingly lonely Emperor, greets Kaiser Wilhelm II on the latter's visit to Vienna, shortly before they became involved in the First World War

Compared with the nation states of Europe, Franz Joseph's Empire developed slowly and ponderously. The population of the non-Hungarian Empire rose from 16 to 26 million in the half century from 1851 to 1901. In 1901 coal production was double that of Russia, but less than a third of that of Germany. Railway development, however, almost kept up with that of France and, by 1914, the Austro-Hungarian Empire had over 41 000 kilometres of track. But Vienna was less renowned as an industrial centre and commercial capital, than as a city of music and continuing imperial splendour. The waltz kings of the age of Johann Strauss lorded over the late nineteenth century. Brahms settled in Vienna in 1863. Mahler became the artistic director of the Vienna Imperial Opera at the beginning of the twentieth century. About the same time, Sigmund Freud added to the fame of Vienna University as the founder of psychoanalysis. But at the heart of the Empire Franz Joseph worked steadily on in the Hofburg Palace. He had an enormous capacity for work, even if very little for original thought. Personally receiving and dealing with their petitions, he won an equally enormous respect from his subjects of all nationalities. In 1908, his subjects celebrated the sixtieth year of his reign:

> Vienna was the scene of a historic and ethnological pageant; deputations from every region in the realm once more presented to the Emperor's sight the various and coloured image of the multiform lands and races over which [he] held sway.

Nothing cemented the Empire more strongly together than the mutual devotion of the Emperor and his subjects. Yet Franz Joseph became an increasingly lonely figure. His brother Maximilian was killed in Mexico (see page 102). His only son, Rudolf, died in 1889, almost certainly by committing suicide, unable to measure up to the demanding standards of the Habsburg court. His wife was murdered by an Anarchist in 1898. His nephew and heir, Franz Ferdinand, was murdered at Sarajevo in 1914 (see page 201). Franz Joseph died in 1916, when the First World War was at its height. He remained to the end a curious survivor of the bygone age of benevolent and hard-working autocrats, to whom duty and honesty were the principal values to be upheld.

(b) The Czech Problem

None of Franz Joseph's subjects struggled more fiercely against German domination than the Czechs. In 1867 they demanded an Ausgleich for Bohemia and Moravia – home rule such as had been conceded to Hungary. They were not strong enough to obtain it. For a time they boycotted the Reichsrat, but found it more profitable to return, and to bargain with ministers who were in need of support. In 1880 they won the right to use the Czech language in the dealings of officials with the Bohemian public. The more radical Young Czechs, who dominated the Bohemian Diet in 1889 and won all the Bohemian seats in the Reichsrat two years later, wanted the Czech language to be equal to German in the entire administration of Bohemia. All educated Czechs understood German, but few Germans understood Czech, so that if this concession could be won, the Czechs would be well on the way to the complete control of Bohemia. Governments were harassed in the Reichsrat, and in 1897 government was almost paralysed when the Czech deputies clattered desk-lids and an inkpot was thrown at the speaker. Both then and on subsequent occasions, Czechs and Germans clashed in the streets. It was rivalries such as these that made constitutional government so difficult in the non-Hungarian part of the Empire: so much so that, by 1914, neither the Reichsrat nor the Bohemian Diet was functioning as an effective parliament, and Franz Joseph's ministers simply carried on as best they could. In their anxiety to outmanoeuvre each other, both Czechs and Germans seemed willing to forfeit the constitutional rights which were fought for so determinedly in other countries.

The Czechs nevertheless preserved their national identity. A Czech university was founded in Prague in 1882. A Czech National Theatre was also opened in the city. Already there was a Czech bank, the *Zivnostenska Banka*.

Fig. 13.4 An artist's view of Czech obstruction in the Reichsrat, on this occasion in June 1900

The Czechs fought for schools in which to teach their language and culture, and they fought their way into administrative appointments and into the professions. In the late nineteenth century a substantial Czech middle class developed. Nationalist writers and composers not only kept a Czech culture alive, but caused it to flourish. The music of Smetana and Dvořák was distinctively Slavonic, matching with a Czech voice the Germanic compositions of Brahms and Mahler, and drawing much of its inspiration from Bohemian folk music. When the Habsburg Empire tottered towards its final collapse during the First World War, the Czechs directed their energies towards securing independence, and towards the creation of a state of Czechs and Slovaks, neighbours with whom they felt they had far more in common than with Germans. Tómàš Masaryk, a Professor of Philosophy at the Czech University of Prague, escaped to London when war began in 1914. There he argued the case for an independent Czechoslovakia, and maintained that the Habsburg Empire was doomed. The Empire, he said, was:

> an aggregate of nine small nations . . . quite an artificial state . . . [where] the dynasty tries to maintain its absolute position by the principle of *divide et impera* [divide and rule], by little concessions now to one nation, now to another; [and where] the Germans – the dynasty is German – and Magyars are the favourites.

An independent Czechoslovakia was born at the end of the First World War (see Section 20.1(*d*)).

13.3 Hungary

The Magyars were certainly 'the favourites' in Hungary. Although only about half of the population, they profited from the division of the rest into different races. But like the Germans in the non-Hungarian Empire, they faced resentment from one race especially, the Croats. The Croats had their own capital in Zagreb, just as the Czechs had Prague, and they resented Magyar rule from Budapest. The Croats had rejected Magyar rule in 1848 (see Section 5.2(*d*)), but many of them found themselves subject to it by the Ausgleich. Magyars dominated the Hungarian Reichstag; they filled almost all official positions, and they even tried to pack the Croatian Diet with nominated Magyar officials. Deák promised fair treatment to the national minorities at the time of the Ausgleich, but the promise was not kept. Magyar was the dominant language, and every effort was made to prevent Croatian and other languages from being used in official matters. In 1907 Magyar was even made the language to be used on Croatian railways. The minorities were not allowed their own schools, in which to teach their languages and culture. A Croat university was nevertheless founded at Zagreb in 1874.

The population of Hungary rose from 13 million to over 19 million during the half century before 1901. A social gulf developed between the owners of vast estates and the peasantry, who found it difficult to rise above subsistence farming. In addition to the rivalries between races, there also developed a rivalry between the great landowners who dominated the country and the mass of Magyars, who sought to extend the narrow franchise and to broaden the interests of Franz Joseph's ministers. The more radical members of the Magyar opposition also wanted to go further than the Ausgleich, to achieve total independence. Controversies centred on trade relations with the rest of Franz Joseph's Empire, and on the Emperor's determination to merge Hungarian regiments in a common army. Arguments about the Ausgleich went on long after it had been accepted in 1867. Such arguments and racial conflicts made the Reichstag in Budapest almost as ineffective as the Reichsrat in Vienna. The conflicts hindered any substantial movement towards genuinely parliamentary government, and diverted attention from the reforms which were much needed to assist the impoverished smallholders and landless labourers in Hungary. Like Italians, many Hungarians sought to relieve their poverty by emigrating. Few Hungarian politicians made a distinguished contribution to the nation's development although, having negotiated the Ausgleich, Andrassy was Hungary's chief minister from 1867 to 1871 and the Austro-Hungarian Foreign Minister from 1871 to 1879. One of the most prominent of the political families in Hungary was that of the Tiszas. Kalman Tisza founded the Liberal Party in 1875, and he was the chief minister from then until 1890, but his energies were devoted to preserving a majority in the Reichstag and to preserving Magyar authority over rival nationalities. Istvan Tisza, his son, was the chief minister in 1904–5 and from 1913 to 1917. On the latter occasion, he ensured that Hungary gave loyal support to the Empire in the First World War.

The Social Democratic Party and the People's Party, founded in 1890 and 1896 respectively, made comparatively little impact on a system of government which remained securely élitist.

Just as the Czechs and Slovaks came together partly under pressure from domineering Germans, so the minorities of Hungary responded to the arrogance of the Magyars. Josef Strossmayer, the Bishop of Zagreb until his death in 1905, encouraged a movement towards unity among the South Slavs – the Catholic Croats, the Slovenes to their north (around Trieste), and the Orthodox Serbs. In 1908 Austria-Hungary annexed Bosnia and Herzegovina, and this brought more South Slavs into the Empire. But there was an essential difference between the South Slav problem and the Czechoslovak problem. Serbia already existed as an independent state on the borders of the Austro-Hungarian Empire (see Fig. 13.2). Like another Piedmont, Serbia might one day lead a war of liberation, and relations worsened between Serbia and the Habsburgs. In Vienna and Budapest the authorities became increasingly exasperated by 'the South Slav question', and the newspapers paid increasing attention to it as Serbo-Croat restlessness mounted. In 1912 the German ambassador in Vienna reported to his government in Berlin:

> On all sides I hear the question ventilated, whether it will be possible – if the Monarchy does not pull itself together and take vigorous measures against Serbian aspirations and pretensions – to keep the seven million South Slavs in the framework of the Monarchy.

The South Slav problem was not the only one by this time. In Transylvania, in eastern Hungary, Rumanians were showing interest in uniting with the independent state of Rumania. But the South Slav question was the most urgent, especially when Serbia blamed the Habsburgs for the creation of the state of Albania in 1913 (see page 245). On 28 June 1914 the Archduke Franz Ferdinand was assassinated by a Slav nationalist at Sarajevo. A showdown was now imminent and from it developed the First World War. When that war ended the South Slavs were united in the independent state of Jugoslavia (see Section 20.1(d)).

13.4 The Foreign Policy of Austria-Hungary

The Prussian war and the Treaty of Prague of 1866 left the Habsburg Empire battered and isolated (see Section 7.3(b)). Bismarck's insistence on the lenient treatment of the Habsburgs paid dividends, however. Austria-Hungary remained neutral in the Franco-Prussian War, and even began to draw closer to Germany again in 1873 in the *Dreikaiserverhältnis* (Three-Emperors-Understanding of Franz Joseph, William I and Alexander II, which later hardened into a League or *Dreikaiserbund*). Six years later, under pressure from events in the Balkans, a close Dual Alliance was made between

Austria-Hungary and Germany, which lasted until both were defeated in the First World War. Defeat in 1866 had not permanently alienated the Habsburgs from the German Reich, but it did help to turn Austrian attention away from Germany and central Europe, towards the Balkans. The Ausgleich was the first result of this looking south-eastwards, the *Drang nach Osten*. Beyond Hungary, however, lay Serbia and Rumania, and the seething discontents of the Balkan subjects of the Ottoman Empire: the entire Eastern Question, in fact (see pages 127–8). The fate of Austria-Hungary became intertwined with the fate of the Ottoman Empire. As Habsburg relations with Serbia worsened, so too did Habsburg relations with Russia; and the more such relations worsened, the more closely Austria-Hungary clung to its alliance with the German Reich (see Units Fifteen and Seventeen).

The Balkan policy of Austria-Hungary was partly defensive, in that it sprang from an anxiety to protect the Empire against the racial discontents of the subjects of the Sultan. The whole thing was aggravated even further, it was suspected, by the Russians. But the Habsburgs were also concerned for their prestige. The years after 1871 were expansionist years, when many European countries enlarged their empires overseas. Austria-Hungary was not a sea-going power. Its only coastline was on the Adriatic Sea, and even its principal river, the Danube, reached the Black Sea through foreign territory. The Habsburgs did not therefore seek overseas colonies, but they saw a modest expansion in the Balkans as an outlet for ambition, even though such expansion could only worsen the racial confusions of their Empire. Franz Joseph and Andrassy profited from Turkish weakness in 1878, by obtaining the right to occupy Bosnia and Herzegovina and when, thirty years later, these provinces were fully incorporated into the Austro-Hungarian Empire, Franz Joseph issued a proclamation:

> Remembering the ties that existed of yore between our glorious ancestors on the Hungarian throne and these lands, we extend our suzerainty over Bosnia and Herzegovina, and it is our will that the order of succession of our House be extended to these lands also.

It was part of the Emperor's devotion to tradition to recover, wherever possible, the long-lost properties of his crowns in a modest pursuit of glory. But Austria-Hungary was too weak, and its rivals were too strong, for the Emperor to achieve much more than Bosnia and Herzegovina. Habsburg foreign policy resulted more in frustration than in aggrandisement, and this led to a dangerous recklessness by 1914 (see Section 17.4).

Franz Joseph's proclamation of 1908 went on to list some of the benefits of Habsburg rule for his new subjects:

> Among the many cares of our throne, solicitude for your material and spiritual welfare shall not be the last. The exalted idea of equal rights for all before the law, a share in the legislation and administration of the provincial affairs, equal protection for all religious creeds, languages, and racial differences, all these high possessions you shall

enjoy in full measure. The freedom of the individual and the welfare of the whole will be the aim of our government in the two lands.

Thus even the Emperor at last showed evidence of having been influenced by liberal ideas. His proclamation was optimistically coloured, but it was not without truth. There would certainly be 'benefits' for his subjects, when compared with their rule by the Turks. Franz Joseph's rule stopped well short of tyranny, but Germans and Magyars made it difficult to fulfil all the good intentions, and the masses as a whole were beginning to want more than an aged Emperor's 'solicitude'. Bosnia and Herzegovina were ruled by a joint Austro-Hungarian administration, but many of its subjects looked forward to liberation by the Serbs, and to the union of independent South Slavs.

13.5   The First World War and the End of the Empire

In spite of the internal strains in the Empire, Habsburg forces fought tenaciously in the First World War. They won early successes, driving southwards through Serbia and Albania; and they won some success against Rumania, when that country joined the Allies in 1916. But Austria-Hungary was itself invaded by the Russians, and its forces were mauled especially in the Brusilov Offensive of 1916. Despite the success at Caporetto, it was not possible to win a convincing victory over Italy. When the conflict ended, the Empire had lost 1 200 000 dead.

Franz Joseph held the Empire together until his death in November 1916. His successor was his grand-nephew, Charles, who inherited formidable problems in keeping the administration going. Almost as soon as the war began there was ferment within the Empire, not least because of rivalry between Germans and Magyars for the control of affairs. The minorities, on the other hand, showed remarkable loyalty to the Empire. Masaryk was exceptional in fleeing to London, and the majority of Czechs supported the war effort. The shallowness of South Slav unity was shown by the fierce attacks on Serbia made by Croatian troops. The masses, it seemed, had not yet been converted by the agitators and politicians to their ideas for secession and independence. But national leaders and politicians continued to manoeuvre vigorously and to advance their new ideas on how the Empire should be reorganized. Charles had to struggle with ever-shifting groupings among ministers and would-be ministers, and the Empire became increasingly subordinate to instructions from Berlin. Charles would have liked to try to pacify the minorities with a federal structure, but he was obstructed by Germans and Magyars and bullied by the government of the German Reich, which insisted that he keep the war going and preserve the privileges of the dominant races.

Defeat in the war brought the disintegration of the Empire. In the autumn of 1918 new governments were proclaimed in Prague, Zagreb and even Budapest, in favour of national independence. In Vienna German socialists

*Fig. 13.5 Austrian stamps of 1916, 1917 and 1919: Emperor Franz Joseph,
Emperor Charles, and the Parliament of the Austrian Republic*

proclaimed a 'German Austria'. Other racial groups such as the Poles declared
their allegiance to external governments, like that in Warsaw. When peace was
made, republics were proclaimed in both Vienna and Budapest. There was
nothing for Charles to do but to go into exile in Switzerland. The Habsburg
Empire had collapsed. Charles refused to abdicate, but he clung only to empty
titles until his death in 1922. Where the Habsburg Empire had existed, there
were now new states.

Further Reading

Dedijer, V.: *The Road to Sarajevo*. MacGibbon and Kee (St Albans, 1967).
Kohn, H.: *The Habsburg Empire, 1804–1918*. Anvil (Dublin, 1961).
Sinor, D.: *History of Hungary*. Allen and Unwin (London, 1959).
Taylor, A. J. P.: *The Habsburg Monarchy, 1809–1918*. Hamish Hamilton (London, 1949).

Exercises

1. Study Figs. 2.2 and 13.2.
   (a) How was the Austro-Hungarian Empire of 1914 different from the Austrian Empire of 1815?
   (b) What racial mixtures existed by 1914 in *each* of the two parts of the Austro-Hungarian Empire?
2. 'Like Metternich before him', 'dedicated to fighting a losing battle' (page 193). Compare the aims of Metternich and Franz Joseph, and explain what is meant by these phrases.
3. Why did Franz Joseph become 'an increasingly lonely figure' (pages 197 and 198)?
4. Show how any *two* nationalities were by 1914 dissatisfied with their membership of the Austro-Hungarian Empire.
5. What do you understand by 'the South Slav question' (page 201)? Read Section 17.4 and explain the connection between the South Slav question and the outbreak of war in 1914 between the Austro-Hungarian Empire and Serbia.
6. How does this Unit help to explain why the Habsburg Empire collapsed after the death of Franz Joseph?

Imperial Russia 1855–1917

14.1 The Economy and Society

Russia's first census of population was held in 1897. It recorded 129 million subjects of the tsar. They inhabited an area of about eight and a half million square miles. Some 55 million of the people were Russians, 22 million Ukrainians, 8 million Poles, and 5 million Jews: in all, the tsar ruled over about a hundred nationalities. What most of them had in common was their poverty. Imperial Russia remained overwhelmingly an agricultural state, a land of peasants, whose low level of production was such that a poor harvest drove them to picking out the seeds from their thatched roofs to feed themselves, and stripping the roofs to feed animals which were often too weak to stand without supporting slings. By 1914 the population had risen to 175 million, of whom only 26 million lived in towns and only 5 million worked in industry – in factories, mines, and oilfields and on the railways. There had been a considerable increase in Russian output as a whole since the reign of Nicholas I (see Section 4.3) – it doubled in the period 1850 to 1890, then increased almost fourfold from 1890 to 1914 – but few benefits were felt by the mass of peasants and by the Russian industrial workers, whose conditions of work still closely resembled those in Britain a hundred years earlier, when industrialization was in its earliest stages. There were vast factories, like the Putilov steelworks in St Petersburg which helped to arm the Russian state, but technology was often primitive in the industrial areas of the capital, of Moscow, of the area east of Moscow, of the Don Valley, and in the Baku oilfields: Russian industry relied heavily on human sweat. In agriculture there was little technology at all other than the wooden plough, and farming methods were primitive. Although Stolypin, before his assassination in 1911, encouraged the consolidation of scattered medieval strips into compact holdings, and tried to end the practice of sub-dividing a peasant's property at his death into ever shrinking smallholdings (shared among his sons), much of Russia remained untouched by such reform in 1914.

The growing population cancelled out what little progress was made in agriculture and, since grain was one of Russia's chief exports, famine was not unusual. Huge areas of land belonged to the nobility. Indeed, the tsar himself had personal estates far larger than France, and the mass of peasants were convinced that their poverty was due in no small part to the existence of such vast estates, from which they could gain no benefit except by serving the landlords for meagre wages. Wages in industry were similarly meagre, and

Russia itself gained only limited profits from its industries, since many were financed by foreign capitalists. French, British, Germans and Belgians invested substantially in Russia's mines and metal industries, and syphoned off a significant proportion of the profits. Russia was short of capital, and the tsar helped to finance his government by foreign borrowing, mainly in France. Moreover, Russia had a comparatively small middle class to bridge the enormous social gulf between the nobility and the masses.

Fig. 14.1 The living conditions of the Putilov steelworkers, St Petersburg, photographed in the 1890s. The workers were 'corner lodgers': they rented corners of rooms for themselves and their families

Social divisions in Russia remained far more rigid than in western Europe. No alliance developed between liberal noblemen and the bourgeoisie to carry Russia forward, to modernize society, and to develop constitutional government. In almost every respect Imperial Russia dragged behind the rest of Europe. Tsarist autocracy was preserved almost intact, in spite of the setting up of a *Duma* (assembly) in 1906. The peasants ceased to be serfs in 1861, but they remained abjectly downtrodden. Only one Russian in five was classed as literate in the census of 1897, and only four per cent of the population received education in 1914, a mere six million children. Mass education was much neglected but, on the other hand, Russian higher education – especially in the sciences – compared favourably with that in many other European countries. To the disappointment of the authorities, this higher education often bred revolutionaries. A substantial part of the Russian intelligentsia was disaffected, driven to protest against the inequalities, injustices and incompetence of the Imperial system. The Romanovs paid little attention; they excluded dissident intellectuals from authority, and relied instead on the support of loyal, unimaginative and often brutal officials to obstruct change.

Table 14.1   Russia's industrial economy

Year	Production (million metric tons)			Railway track (thousand kilometres)	Investment in industrial companies (million roubles, foreign investment in brackets)
	Coal	Pig iron	Steel		
1860	0.3	0.2	–	1.4	–
1890	6.0	1.1	0.4	30.4	443 (114)
1914	26.0*	3.5*	4.0	75.7*	3 400 (1 400)

* 1911 (Compare Table 9.1, page 140)

In 1903, Russia also produced some 47 per cent of the world's output of oil, the world's second producer behind the USA.

Table 14.1 shows that Russia nevertheless increased industrial activity quite markedly after 1890. Tariffs were raised in 1877 from hitherto negligible levels, and were increased in 1881–2. They were raised again in 1891 to levels which were formidable. It was not merely the government's intention to protect Russian industry, however, since tariffs became an important source of government revenue, and the imposition of duties on imported machinery probably hampered expansion. The tariffs also discouraged the introduction of more efficient farming equipment. The government was seldom systematic in anything it did, and even its tyranny was often inefficient. Censorship was erratic, allowing a lively university life to flourish, especially in Moscow, though that was often critical of Russian society. The *Okhrana* (political police) watched out zealously for the 'untrustworthy', kept the prisons well filled, and sent a steady flow of exiles to Siberia; but in spite of the Okhrana's bulky dossiers, there seethed an underworld of revolutionaries, who fed on the failure of the authorities to make sweeping improvements. Many revolutionaries struggled in vain to rouse the peasant masses to organized rebellion. Explosions of anger were frequent and bloody clashes numerous, but the revolutionaries seemed as haphazard in their sedition as the Romanovs were in spasmodic attempts to reform. In 1900 Lenin wrote in *Iskra*, the Marxist newspaper:

> We must train people who will dedicate to the revolution, not a spare evening but the whole of their lives.

Lenin and his fellow-Bolsheviks achieved just such dedication, and strove to unite the industrial workers for revolution. But when the tsarist state collapsed in February 1917, it did so because of its own paralysis and because of universal disaffection and disgust, not because of a planned revolution.

Yet Imperial Russia was distinguished for its music, literature, and science. Music and literature remained distinctively Russian, patriotic and devoted to Mother Russia, though at the same time shot through with melancholy and pessimism. Tchaikovsky lived until 1893, the contemporary of Borodin, Mussorgsky and Rimsky-Korsakov. His '1812 Overture' was a fiercely patriotic celebration of the now historic defeat of Napoleon I's Moscow Campaign; his last completed symphony (the 'Pathétique') was a melancholy testament to his own private agonies, and to those of his country. In St Petersburg, the Imperial Ballet maintained standards of excellence seldom reached in the west at that time, though it was a shock to Nicholas II when even the Ballet joined the general protests against his rule, and went on strike in 1905. The great writers were also often critical, not least of corrupt officialdom and incompetence, which went along with injustice. Russian literature was often a unique blending of high moral purpose and national pessimism, and writers like Chekhov, Tolstoy, and Dostoievsky developed to great heights the country's literary reputation of the earlier generation of Pushkin and Gogol.

14.2 The Reign of Alexander II 1855–81

(a) The Liberator

Alexander II succeeded his father to the Russian throne in 1855. The first major event of his reign was the capture of Sebastopol by the Allies: Alexander had to accept defeat in the Crimean War and to sign the Treaty of Paris (see Section 8.4). Alexander was essentially a Romanov, intent on preserving tsarist authority. He had already outstripped even Nicholas I in his assertion of reactionary opinions on occasions, but defeat in the Crimea pointed to the need for change in Russia. European serfdom now survived only in the Russian Empire, and the Empire had proved too weak to drive off the western powers. Moreover, serfdom led to almost endless peasant uprisings (see pages 70–71). The serfs were tied to the soil and to their lords, but they were sullen and unco-operative; and even among the lords, there were those who thought that wage labour would be more productive and more profitable. It was also argued that, if Russia were to develop industries to compete with the west, labour would need to be more mobile, since an industrial work force in Russia could come only from the mass of peasants. Alexander became convinced that serfdom must be ended, though he remained equally convinced that social change should not be allowed to get out of hand, and that it should not lead to political change. In 1856 he addressed the nobles of Moscow:

> You yourselves are certainly aware that the existing order of serfdom cannot remain unchanged. It is better to abolish serfdom from above than to wait for the time when it will begin to abolish itself from below. I request you, gentlemen, to reflect on how this may be achieved.

The nobles gave the Tsar little positive assistance and, in February 1861, Alexander had himself to abolish serfdom and define the terms for the emancipation in a royal decree, which earned him the title of the 'Tsar Liberator'.

The Edict of Emancipation liberated from serfdom about 40 million peasants, although almost half of these were on royal estates and they were not freed until 1866. The million or so who were personal servants, working in their masters' houses, received no land, and they either continued to work for wages or drifted to the towns in search of work in industry. The majority were allowed to buy land from the landlords with money advanced by the government. The arrangements for this transfer of land attracted almost universal discontent. The peasants argued that the land was theirs by right, already paid for by centuries of service; but they were now saddled with debts, for the purchase money had to be repaid to the government over a period of 49 years. It was the usual practice to collect these 'redemption payments' from the village community, the *mir*, so that the individual peasant often found that he had hardly more personal freedom than before. The mir supervised farming techniques and the allocation of lands, and it prevented peasants from leaving the village lest the financial burden should be all the greater on those who remained. Moreover, the sale and distribution of land in the first place was often left to the landlords. Incessant complaints were made that prices were high, and that the lands transferred were too small and of the poorest quality. Many Russian nobles were themselves in financial difficulties and they seized the opportunity of the emancipation to make as much money as possible. As a result, millions of peasants could hardly scratch enough from the soil to feed their families and to meet their redemption payments. The growing population made the situation worse. Far from feeling gratitude for their emancipation, the peasants were often convinced that it was a fraud. Without capital, with farming techniques which remained primitive, with their lands often scattered in medieval strips and subdivided between sons on a father's death, Russian peasants moved into the twentieth century, impoverished and angry. Those who escaped to seek work in industry were comparatively few. Moreover, fierce social discrimination remained. Peasants needed passes to move outside their villages. They could still be flogged and they were conscripted for military training. Even the mir was controlled much less by the villagers than by government officials and policemen. The freedom of 1861 was hollow, but what rankled most was the peasants' hunger for land. The vast estates which the landlords had kept for themselves remained a source of great provocation, and they added fuel to the discontents which erupted in 1917. In 1861 Alexander had declared:

> And now we confidently hope that the freed serfs . . . will appreciate and recognize the considerable sacrifices which the nobility has made on their behalf.

And he advised the peasants that:

> Only by assiduous labour, a rational expenditure of their strength and resources, a strict economy and, above all, by an upright life – a life constantly inspired by the fear of the Lord – can they hope for prosperity and progress.

The peasants took a more realistic view of his Edict of Emancipation: within four months of its issue there were 647 peasant riots.

(b) The Reformer

Alexander kept up his reforming enthusiasm until 1865. He made changes in the legal code in 1864: trial by jury was introduced and fewer trials were held in secret. Judges were adequately paid, to reduce their dependence on bribes, and they were given security against arbitrary dismissal when they displeased the government. Punishments were made less severe and, in theory, torture was no longer used to extract confessions. At the same time, censorship was relaxed. Alexander encouraged the building of schools and made it possible, again in theory, for Russians of all classes to obtain secondary education, if qualified by an examination. The *zemstva* were also set up in 1864, in an effort to improve local administration and to develop services such as education. These district and provincial councils were elected, but the electoral system was weighted to give the nobility far more influence than the peasants, and far more influence than the townsmen, when the system was extended to urban *dumas* in 1870. Nevertheless the zemstva and dumas provided the first role of any kind in administration for the Russian people. Although the Tsar himself retained all policing powers, the councils did useful and sometimes progressive work in the administration of schools, hospitals and prisons, in developing systems of communication and sanitation, and in relieving the poor. A group of Zemstva Liberals emerged, who pressed for a national parliament and liberal reforms like those in the west, but they made little headway. The zemstva survived although in later years the Imperial government regarded them with suspicion, and it interfered shamelessly in their elections. Peasant representation was virtually eliminated after 1890, and the powers of the zemstva were frequently curtailed.

Alexander II also wanted to improve Russia's economy and to strengthen its army. The Russian state was more active in the expansion of industry and the railways than was usual in western Europe. In 1857 the Tsar set up the Grand

Company of Russian Railways, with assistance from bankers in France, Britain and Holland. In 1860 the Russian State Bank was founded, and it helped to make credit more readily available to finance industrial enterprises. Reforms were also made in the army. The length of service was reduced from 25 to 15 years, and then to six years in 1874, when all classes were made equally liable for military service. The practice of using the army as a dumping ground for criminals was abandoned, and military discipline was made less barbarous. The army was nevertheless routed by the Japanese in the war of 1904–5 (see Section 14.5).

(c) The Romanov

After 1865 not much was left of Alexander's enthusiasm for reform. The Poles had rebelled in 1863. Since their earlier uprising in 1830–1, they had been comparatively quiet (see Section 3.3(e)), and Alexander had made a few concessions, re-admitting the use of the Polish language in official business. The Poles instantly demanded more, but the Tsar was quick to stamp on all nationalist societies. Clashes between Poles and Russians led on to a major uprising. It took almost a year to subdue the rebellion and, as usual, the Poles were savagely punished. All concessions were withdrawn; the Russian language was again used for official business, and the policy of Russification was applied strenuously. Polish ringleaders were driven out to the west, or they were rounded up and herded to Siberia. Alexander was not prepared to tolerate any threat to his authority from subject races, and he was quick to show that he could be every bit as illiberal as Nicholas I had been.

His early concessions had equally disturbing results in Russia. The freed serfs showed no gratitude. The political prisoners, whom he had released, instantly demanded more substantial reforms. The less censored press echoed their criticisms and, in 1866, an attempt was made on his life. Even before 1866 Alexander had begun to tighten his grip on Russia. Ministers who were inclined to reform were replaced with reactionaries. Press freedom was eroded and the 'untrustworthy' were imprisoned. By 1868 the right to a trial by jury was withdrawn for political crimes, and the zemstva were deprived of some of their authority. The traces of freedom which survived in Russia owed more to the inefficiency of the Tsar's police than to Alexander's own intentions. His main anxiety now was to preserve Romanov autocracy and to stabilize Russian society, relying as was customary on the loyalty of a privileged nobility and the blind obedience of a legion of officials.

There was no lack of opposition, but it was divided and not particularly dangerous. The *Narodniks* (Russian populists) put their trust in the romantic notion of a great peasant uprising to bring about some kind of socialist Utopia, in which the essentially good and moral Russian people (the *narod*) would be liberated from the corrupting influences of the tsarist state. It was from the Narodniks that the SRs (Socialist Revolutionaries) were to descend. The peasants seethed with discontent, but they were also apathetic, and they were

Fig. 14.2 A British view of Russian 'Civilisation' in the reign of Alexander II, 1880. Protest and dissent were often punished with exile to Siberia

almost impossible to organize for constructive and united action. Peasant outbreaks therefore remained disunited and localized. A substantial section of the Narodniks (the *Narodnovoltsy*) joined hands with the followers of Bakunin, turning to Anarchism. Along with Nihilists, who believed that almost nothing worthwhile could be achieved, they practised terrorism and destruction, agreeing on little except their aim to destroy the existing system. Tsarist ministers and officials, and the Tsar himself, were among their favourite targets. In 1880, four attempts were made to murder Alexander II, when he had been condemned to death by a group of Narodnovoltsy known as 'The People's Will'.

Alternative opposition forces in Russia developed rather later than the reign of Alexander II. Westernizers, who wanted the liberalism of western Europe, were as yet comparatively few, and many were in exile. Interest in Marxism grew only slowly, and it was itself a protest at the ineffectiveness of the Narodniks. For the moment Alexander had to contend chiefly with the champions of the peasantry, and the greatest danger came from those who practised terrorism. Nevertheless it seemed possible that some sort of constitution might at least blunt the attacks of Alexander's enemies. The Tsar appointed General Loris-Melikov to explore the possibilities, and he signed his approval in March 1881 of the exploratory machinery which the General devised. On the very same day a bomb was thrown at Alexander's carriage. He climbed out into the path of another bomb which blew off his legs, and he died soon afterwards. The verdict of the People's Will had been carried out by a group of Narodnovoltsy led by Sofia Perovskaya. Whatever plans Alexander had had in mind for a revision of the system of government died with him. He had reigned for 26 years. By Russian standards, his first decade had seemed almost liberal, but his reign as a whole showed that Alexander II had a far stronger attachment to the Romanov tradition of government by repression.

14.3   The Reign of Alexander III 1881–94

Alexander III, Alexander II's son, reigned from 1881 to 1894. He was much influenced by Konstantin Pobedonostsev, his former tutor and adviser, who believed whole-heartedly in Romanov autocracy and despised western constitutionalism. Pobedonostsev wrote in 1896:

> In a Democracy, the real rulers are the dexterous manipulators of votes, with their placemen, the mechanics who so skilfully operate the hidden strings which move the puppets in the arena of democratic elections. . . . Such is the Parliamentary institution. . . . It is sad to think that even in Russia there are men who aspire to the establishment of this falsehood.

Alexander III was never one of them. After the assassination of his father, his policy was autocracy and Russification. The assassins of 1881 were hunted down and killed, and relentless war was waged on all terrorists. They were by no means eliminated, but Lenin's elder brother was among the Tsar's victims, hanged in 1886 for allegedly plotting to murder Alexander. Pobedonostsev used his authority as the Procurator of the Holy Synod (the lay supervisor of the Orthodox Church), to crush free thought and to browbeat minority religions, especially the Jews, who were herded into ghettos. The universities, the press and the law courts were strictly supervised. In 1889, Land Captains were imposed on the peasantry: they had wide powers to enforce discipline and they were chosen by the nobility. The Land Captains also sat in the zemstva, which were subjected to greater domination by the landowners. Minority races, such as the Poles and Finns, were also browbeaten and subjected to even greater restrictions in an effort to stamp out every spark of resistance.

The Tsar was not successful. In 1883 Russia's first Marxist group was formed, the 'Emancipation of Labour', under the leadership of Georgi Plekhanov, from which was to descend in the next reign the Social Democrats. The Narodniks and Narodnovoltsy continued their activities, in spite of the Tsar's own terrorism. Interest in western parliamentary institutions grew among the intelligentsia. Industrialization, meanwhile, proceeded, quickening in pace towards the end of the reign, and adding an embittered proletariat to the embittered peasantry. Sergei Witte was appointed Minister of Finance in 1892 to pursue policies of economic advancement, one of the few comparatively able ministers whom tsarism produced, and a descendant of the Baltic Germans over whom the Russians ruled. Witte's work did much to improve the economy, and it was largely his achievement that the Trans-Siberian Railway was virtually completed by 1904. But industrialization imposed new strains on Russian society, and it was typical of the Romanovs that, when Nicholas II most had need of Witte's services after the revolution of 1905, Witte was abruptly dismissed. Witte might well have helped Nicholas II to establish a successful parliamentary government, for which he saw the need. As it was, his financial skill, and the loans he raised in France, merely made the monarchy solvent enough to ignore liberal demands for parliamentary control of taxation.

Such demands would be commonplace in the reign of Nicholas II, but Alexander III rejected all demands upon him by his subjects. The handful of reforms he himself made were handed down from above, and weakly enforced. In 1882 Alexander set up the Peasants' Bank to lend money for improvements in agriculture. Much of the capital had to be borrowed abroad, however, and few loans were made. Redemption payments were eased and the poll-tax was abolished, but these concessions hardly touched the grievances of the peasants. In industry, factory laws were so limited as to be almost useless, yet Alexander vigorously denied to the workers any right to strike. Although factory inspectors were appointed, the results of their activities were minimal. Limitations were imposed on the labour of women and children, but the wages, hours and conditions of all workers remained barely tolerable. Russians gained little consolation, however, when Alexander III died in 1894.

14.4   The Reign of Nicholas II 1894–1917

(a) The First Ten Years

Alexander's son, Nicholas II, promptly asserted his own intentions: 'I shall preserve the principle of autocracy as undeviatingly as my father.' Pobedonostsev remained the Procurator of the Holy Synod until 1905, and he influenced the new Tsar as much as he had influenced the old. Within a year of his accession, Nicholas rebuffed the Zemstva Liberals, dismissing their demands for a constitution as 'senseless dreams'. In 1896 he banned all meetings between representatives of the zemstva. Witte remained in office until 1903 as Minister of Finance, and Count von Plehve served Nicholas as he had served Alexander, keeping zealous watch on the 'untrustworthy' – until they assassinated him in 1904. But Nicholas soon showed his disastrous talent for appointing for himself the worst of ministers: Count Vladimir Meshersky was an early choice, a man with an obsessive faith in the usefulness of flogging. Nicholas was by no means an inhumane man, but he was unimaginatively devoted to Romanov traditions, weak in will, and lacking in even moderate competence. Like Napoleon III, he was not helped by his marriage to an ambitious wife, the German Princess Alexandra of Hesse-Darmstadt, who was forever anxious that her husband should rule as well as reign. It fell to Nicholas to preside over the collapse of the Romanov dynasty.

The first years of his reign were years of considerable economic development, although little changed for the peasantry. They were also years during which there was extensive revolutionary organization, in spite of the vigour of the Okhrana. The Narodniks drew together, in about 1900, as an opposition party of Socialist Revolutionaries, although the SR Party itself was not formally constituted until 1907. Their terrorist wing remained active. They formed a Union of Socialist Revolutionaries in the Volga Valley in 1896, and murdered Bogolepov, the Minister of Education. Other opposition to the government was organized by westernizers, who rejected the Slavophil (devoted to things exclusively Russian or Slavonic) approach of the SRs, and who took their inspiration from European liberalism. Such groups of westernizers banded together in 1904 in the Union of Liberation, to campaign for a parliament and manhood suffrage, and a year later they set up the party of Constitutional Democrats (KDs – Cadets). By this time, a third force had also developed. Marxist ideas spread steadily in Russia after the founding of the Emancipation of Labour in 1883. The divisions between the early Marxists and the Narodniks were sometimes far from clear, but Plekhanov broke with the Narodniks in favour of a more scientific definition of objectives, in accordance with the teachings of Marx, and a more specific appeal to the industrial workers. In 1898 a congress of Marxists met at Minsk, and it lasted for three days before it was raided by the police and many of its members were arrested. The government claimed to have caught eight out of every nine delegates.

By 1898 Vladimir Lenin was already in Siberia. In 1893 he had joined the *Stariki*, a group of St Petersburg Marxists, had attracted the attention of the police, and had been sent to Siberia for three years in 1897. On his release, he felt he could work more effectively outside Russia. With his wife, Krupskaya, he went into exile, and published the first issue of *Iskra* in Leipzig at the end of 1900. *Iskra* became the main mouthpiece of Russian Marxists, but Lenin wrote much more than articles and editorials for the newspaper. In 1902 he produced *What Is to be Done?*, asserting his own belief in a dedicated revolutionary party, strictly disciplined and professional, to lead Russians to a Marxist state. When a new Marxist congress was held in 1903 the Social Democrats (SDs) were divided between Lenin and his followers, with their ideas for an élitist party of dedicated revolutionaries, and the followers of Plekhanov and Martov, who preferred a socialist party with mass support – even the support of those whom Lenin dubbed 'radishes' (red outside but white inside). A vote on an issue concerning *Iskra* gave Lenin's supporters a majority. Henceforth they were known as the *Bolsheviks* (majority men), and Martov's supporters were the *Mensheviks* (minority men); but both continued to call themselves SDs.

Fig. 14.3 shows, in simplified form, something of how the opposition parties to tsarist autocracy developed in Russia. The divisions were not always rigid, however: revolutionaries tended to shift their allegiances, and some kept a foot in two camps. Lenin was almost unique in insisting on a precise identity and rigid discipline for the Bolsheviks.

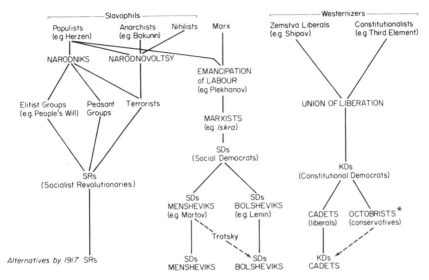

Fig. 14.3 The development of opposition parties in Russia (* Octobrists supported the Tsar after his October Manifesto of 1905, agreeing to set up a Duma. Some drifted back to the Cadets when the Tsar was overthrown. Trotsky felt more sympathy with the Mensheviks in 1903, but he joined Lenin in 1917)

(b) The Revolution of 1905

In 1904 Russia went to war with Japan (see Section 14.5). Humiliating defeats followed, and the war added to the unrest which seethed within Russia. Things were made worse on 'Bloody Sunday' in January 1905. Father Gapon, a priest of peasant origins and a friend of the workers who had set up the St Petersburg Assembly of Factory Workers, led a vast crowd of about 200 000 to the Winter Palace. Much of the city was already on strike following the sacking of some members of the 'Factory Workers'. The demonstration was peaceful, and its purpose was to deliver a petition to the Tsar for such reforms as shorter hours, better pay for women, free medical aid, and for the constitutional demands of the liberals. Not untypically, Nicholas II had left the Palace the previous evening, leaving matters to his officials. Although the crowds sang hymns, and carried crosses and other religious symbols and portraits of the Tsar, the officials and palace guards panicked at the sight of such numbers. An eye witness recorded:

> The Cossacks at first used their knouts [leather-thonged whips], then the flat of their sabres, and finally they fired. . . . The people, seeing the dead and dying carried away in all directions, the snow on the streets and pavements soaked with blood, cried aloud for vengeance. . . . Men, women and children fell at each volley, and were carried

away in ambulances, sledges and carts. The indignation and fury of every class were aroused.

The official figures were that 130 were killed and 300 wounded, an inaccurate and absurdly low estimate. Nicholas wrote in his private diary:

A painful day ... many killed and wounded. ... God, how painful and sad. Mama arrived from town, straight to Mass. ... Went for a walk.

The events of Bloody Sunday destroyed the last lingering respect in Russia for the Tsar, the people's 'Little Father'. Within days half a million workers were on strike in St Petersburg and Moscow, and disorder spread rapidly. Peasant uprisings erupted in the villages; street fighting broke out in the cities. In March Nicholas was forced to promise a constituent assembly, though he reasserted at the same time his right to be an autocrat. The disorders went on; there was a mutiny on the battleship *Potemkin* in the Black Sea, and renewed demands for independence were made in Poland. By September, it seemed that the protests were running out of steam, but they were given new life by a strike of printers in Moscow. Their demands for freedom of expression triggered off a general strike in the city, which spread to the railways and then to St Petersburg, and became almost a general strike throughout the country. Major concessions were needed now, and Nicholas issued the October Manifesto, firmly promising to summon a parliament, and following it with other reforms including the ending of the peasants' redemption payments. During November the country began to return to normal.

The October Manifesto committed Nicholas to summoning a national Duma, elected on a wide franchise and with the power to approve future laws,

Fig. 14.4 A still from Battleship Potemkin, *a film by the Soviet film-maker Eisenstein, recreating the events at Odessa during the Revolution of 1905*

and to preserving civil liberties in Russia. He had been advised by Witte of where the future of his monarchy lay:

> The government must be ready to proceed along constitutional lines. The government must sincerely and openly strive for the well-being of the state. . . . The government must either place itself at the head of the movement which has gripped the country, or it must relinquish it to the elementary forces to tear it to pieces.

For a moment it seemed that Nicholas had learned the lesson. Witte was appointed his chief minister in November 1905, and preparations went ahead for the meeting of the Duma. The day before it met, however, in May 1906, the Tsar had a relapse: with breath-taking foolishness, he dismissed Witte in favour of Goremykin, the vicious opponent of anything progressive.

The October Manifesto had disrupted what little unity there had been in the opposition to the Tsar in 1905. The KDs had supported the workers and peasants, to try to secure civil liberties and a parliament. The Tsar's vague promises of March 1905 had satisfied some KDs, and the rest were sufficiently pleased with the October Manifesto to be willing to co-operate with the government, at least for the time being. Disturbances in the villages were gradually brought under control. The SRs found it increasingly difficult to rouse the peasants in face of the determination of the troops to crush them. Although the Tsar and his ministers had been frightened in 1905, the armed forces remained overwhelmingly loyal so that, in fact, the monarchy retained the trump cards. The *Potemkin* mutiny was an unusual episode, which ended when the battleship was scuttled by the mutineers in a Rumanian harbour. The industrial workers had, meanwhile, set up *soviets* in cities such as St Petersburg, Moscow and Odessa. The soviets were councils to which strikers and rebels sent delegates. They bore some similarity to the Commune in Paris in 1871, although their ultimate purpose was never clear. In the short term, they tried to organize the protest movement, and to formulate the workers' demands. It was they who prolonged the resistance into January 1906. In Moscow the government had to use artillery to smash soviet opposition. But early in 1906 order was restored, and firing-squads and flogging-parties dealt ruthlessly with the Tsar's enemies.

The SRs and SDs had no confidence in the Duma. Their general policy was to boycott it. Both reverted to their underground activities, and an SR assassin during 1906 murdered Father Gapon, who was alleged after all to have been a government agent. In spite of the many preparations for revolution, the Revolution of 1905 had been conspicuous for its lack of leadership. SD leaders in exile were slow to return to Russia, and Lenin and Trotsky put in only belated appearances. At first they underestimated the seriousness of the disturbances, but they also realized that there would be little success while the army was loyal to the government. Lenin saw the Revolution as an opportunity for SDs to practise insurrection and to recruit new members:

> Immediate operations. Some can undertake to assassinate a spy or blow up a police

station; others can attack a bank to expropriate funds for an insurrection. Let every squad learn, if only by beating up police. The dozens of sacrifices will be repaid with interest by producing hundreds of experienced fighters who will lead hundreds of thousands tomorrow.

Later, he pondered the importance of the soviets, and concluded that they had great revolutionary potential. The St Petersburg Soviet had 500 members, elected by some 200 000 workers. It had been created spontaneously by the workers themselves. This, Lenin concluded, was a 'dress rehearsal' for a future revolution.

(c) The Dumas

Witte did not hold office after 1906. Nor did Nicholas appoint ministers on the basis of majorities in the Duma. Four days before the First Duma met, the Tsar once more proclaimed his right to rule as an autocrat. The First Duma lasted for only 73 days in 1906. The Second Duma survived for three months in 1907. There was then a Third Duma from 1907 to 1912, and a Fourth from 1912 to 1917. Rather than fit his government to the Duma and a parliamentary system, Nicholas preferred to try to fit the Duma into his own autocratic system. Constitutional government therefore became something of a farce. The Duma had little power: it could not control the Tsar's finances; it could not select or dismiss his ministers; it could not insist on legislation. The Tsar insisted on an upper chamber, which he packed with his own nominees. But, even then, he was horrified by the speed with which the First Duma arrived at deadlock. The Duma offered an Address to the Throne, demanding a variety of reforms, which Goremykin instantly rejected. It then passed a vote of no confidence in the Tsar's ministers, and Nicholas dismissed it, though a handful of deputies retreated to Finland and sat for a time as an illegal Rump, criticizing the Tsar. Martial law was declared, and some more outspoken rebels were executed, but the promise of another Duma and the appointment to office of the tough Peter Stolypin prevented more serious disturbances.

Stolypin had excelled in 1905 as the Governor of Saratov Province, where he energetically suppressed the peasants. For two months in 1906 he served as the Minister of the Interior, and then became the Tsar's chief minister until he was assassinated in 1911. His first priority was to manage the elections to the Second Duma, to ensure a more docile assembly. In dismissing the First Duma, Nicholas had declared:

A cruel disappointment has befallen our expectations. The representatives of the nation, instead of applying themselves to the work of productive legislation, have strayed into spheres beyond their competence.

But he promised:

In dissolving the Duma we confirm our immutable intention of maintaining the institution, and in conformity with this intention we fix 5 March 1907, as the date of the convocation of a new Duma.

The SRs and SDs were now seeking election. Stolypin tightened censorship, banned some candidates and organizations, and used government money to help favoured candidates – but the Second Duma was worse than the First. The KDs lost seats, dropping to 99 members of the assembly, but 65 SDs and 37 SRs were elected, along with about a hundred radical peasants and various representatives of non-Russian nationalities. The Duma as a whole was in open opposition to the government, a further 'cruel disappointment' for the Tsar. After some stormy sessions, an attempt was made to arrest the SD members, but it only provoked a new storm about parliamentary privilege. The Duma was dissolved in June 1907.

Before a Third Duma was elected, Stolypin changed the electoral laws. The promise of a wide franchise in the October Manifesto had so far been honoured, although the system already diluted the votes of the masses. Many industrial workers were now disfranchised altogether, and an even more complicated system of electoral colleges weakened the vote of the peasants. A German observer calculated that, to get a member elected to the Third Duma required the votes of 230 rich landowners, or 1000 businessmen, or 60 000 peasants, or 125 000 industrial workers. As a result only 14 SDs got into the Duma. The KDs fell to 52, but 120 Octobrists were elected, who were usually willing to support the Tsar and Stolypin, content with the October Manifesto and the existence of even a toothless Duma (see Fig. 14.3). From the government's viewpoint the Duma system was at last workable. The Duma was often critical, but it co-operated in some useful reforms.

Elections were held in 1912 and a Fourth Duma followed the Third. Two years later, the First World War began and, as it dragged on, the Duma became fiercely critical of the mismanagement of the war by the government. It renewed the demand that ministers should be appointed from the leaders of the Duma itself. By 1917 relations with the government were again seriously strained. When Alexander Kerensky asserted in the Duma that the Tsar himself was mismanaging the war, the Tsarina Alexandra demanded – in vain – that Kerensky should be executed.

(d) Reform, Repression and Society

Stolypin aimed to rule with a combination of strict repression and constructive reform. Jews and non-Russian nationalists were fiercely persecuted, and dissent was brutally crushed. Partly because of Stolypin's watchfulness, and partly because of an expanding economy, the years 1907 to 1911 were comparatively peaceful. The zemstva were given support for local improvements, and some modest progress was made in education. Little was done for the industrial workers. Though trade unions had been made legal after the upheaval of 1905, their right to strike was still disputed. Stolypin concentrated on the mass of peasants, however. If they could be pacified, he argued, Russia would have a strong backbone: a contented peasantry would almost certainly be a guarantee of stability. His aim was to develop a class of prosperous peasants (*kulaks*), with a vested interest in preserving the existing structure of society. But the obstacles were enormous. It was necessary to transfer land from the village mir to the individual peasant, to consolidate the scattered strips, to discourage the subdivision of holdings at death, to provide the peasants with capital, and to teach them more efficient farming. If this social transformation could be carried through, the countryside would be prosperous and stable, and a pool of labour would be available for industry as landless younger sons were disinherited.

Fig. 14.5 The search for work in Russia in 1914 at one of the labour exchanges opened during the recent reforming period. Some of these workers (those on the right of the photograph) still wore bark shoes

Such an ambitious plan would take time. Stolypin estimated 20 years, but he was killed in 1911 and his successors showed only spasmodic interest in the reform. By 1914, perhaps half of the peasant lands had become the personal and hereditary possessions of individual holders, but much less than that had been consolidated into compact farms in place of scattered strips. The Peasants' Bank loaned money for development, but that piled up new debts for the peasantry. Above all, the peasant population expanded rapidly, while the lands available to them expanded only slowly. A great land hunger remained, and with it great discontent. Stolypin's successor cut down the loans to the peasants, and the whole project lost its urgency. In the eyes of the peasants, the key to their prosperity lay in seizing the estates of the great landowners. But the great landowners were the allies of the Tsar. When Stolypin died, the nobility was already suspicious of his modest reforms, and Nicholas had begun to turn against him. There were insuperable barriers to major change in Russia, it seemed.

In 1912 some effort was made to pacify the industrial workers with paper schemes for state insurance against sickness and industrial accidents. But, in the same year, the government again roused the people to fury. Workers in the Lena goldfield went on strike in support of modest demands for shorter hours, rest days on holy days, and free lighting in the huts in which they were housed. Troops shot down 170 of them. The result was similar to that of Bloody Sunday, as strikes and protests again erupted across the country. The Bolsheviks struggled to channel the unrest towards political revolution, and they increased their prestige in the towns, but the SRs remained more dominant in the countryside. The Bolsheviks were aware, moreover, that strikes and riots led to arrests, disrupting their own organization. Almost as soon as a Bolshevik won a reputation, he was exiled to Siberia or chased from the country. Although the ferment continued after the shootings in the goldfield through 1913 and into 1914, there was no reason to believe that the collapse of the Romanov state was imminent, and war in 1914 even brought temporary national unity and some show of support for the Tsar. Only the Bolsheviks declared unequivocal opposition to the war, and the dozen Bolsheviks in the Duma were shipped off to Siberia as traitors. Almost all classes of Russian society united to defend Mother Russia, even though that meant rallying to the Tsar's autocracy.

(e) The Collapse of Tsarist Government

The First World War starkly exposed the limitations of Tsarist government. In a desperate effort to find a successful team of ministers, Nicholas, from 1914 to the end of 1916, appointed five chief ministers, seven ministers of the interior, four war ministers and four foreign ministers; and he appointed himself the Commander-in-Chief of the armed forces. In vain the Duma demanded the appointment of talented men from among its own ranks. Such an idea was still too liberal for the Tsar. As the war dragged on and news of defeats arrived more commonly than news of victories, the patriotism of the masses turned to apathy; and the frustrations of the intelligentsia, the middle classes and the KDs produced despair.

Russian armies relied mainly on their manpower. They suffered heavy defeats at the hands of the Germans, but were more successful against the Austrians, especially in the Brusilov Offensive of 1916. By 1917 they were dispirited, badly equipped, and struggling in a war which had become unpopular. The supreme command of the Tsar, and the energy of Orthodox priests in blessing their efforts, no longer roused enthusiasm, and desertion became common. The war also imposed great strains on the Russian economy. Manpower was conscripted indiscriminately, disrupting agriculture, industry and communications. As early as 1915, 573 factories and mills shut down for want of raw materials, fuel and manpower. In 1916, 36 of Russia's blast furnaces stood idle. Sections of the railways were paralysed. The countryside was raided for horses to serve the needs of the army. Shortages caused prices to soar, and inflation was made worse by the government's folly in printing paper money to pay its own debts. Another effect of the war was to change the nature of the army. When the war ended in 1918 Russia had lost 1 700 000 dead, a total exceeded only by Germany. Many of the dead were professional soldiers on whom the Tsar had been able to rely for support against rebels, and the army had become one of peasant and worker conscripts. Trotsky described the army in Petrograd (the new, less Germanic name for St Petersburg):

> Let us recall . . . that the garrison consisted mainly of reserve battalions many thousands strong. . . . These men . . . had the prospect of going to the trenches when the war was lost and the country ruined. They did not want war. They wanted to go home to their farms. They . . . had not the slightest feeling of attachment to the monarchy.

When the masses rebelled in Petrograd in February 1917, the army sympathized with them, and the Tsar could no longer suppress revolution, as he had been able to do in 1905. Even Cossack troops stood idly by. Only a handful of officer cadets and the Petrograd police defended the monarchy, and the mob pelted them with lumps of ice and quickly routed them.

The Tsar's government had become not only chaotically incompetent but even ridiculous. The absences of Nicholas on military affairs left the Tsarina Alexandra in charge of the government, and Alexandra fell under the spell of Gregori Rasputin, a dissolute peasant who claimed to be a holy man, and who seemed able to exercise some hypnotic healing power over Tsarevich Alexei, the haemophiliac heir to the throne. Rasputin's influence at court grew from 1911 to become almost total by the end of 1915. His alcoholic and sexual excesses were so repulsive that he was murdered by members of the nobility at the end of 1916. The Tsarina mourned 'our friend' grievously, convinced that he had 'died to save us'. For a time, Rasputin had been the uncrowned king of Russia, responsible for many changes of ministers, especially for the dismissal of those whose wives rejected the spiritual grace he offered through sexual intercourse. His place at court discredited both the monarchy and the Church, but Rasputin provided only one among the almost innumerable grievances which Russians now nursed against the Romanovs.

The end came suddenly in 1917. Crowds assembled in Petrograd to celebrate International Women's Day on 23 February (the Russian calendar was 13 days behind that of Europe). There were rumours of shortages of bread. Strikes broke out, and crowds continued to throng the streets. On 25 February there was fighting with the police when the police opened fire. The next day 40 workers were killed, but when the crowds appealed to the city's military units, the soldiers joined them. On that day Nicholas dissolved the Duma, though its

Fig. 14.6 Tsar Nicholas II, 1894–1917 – the vast estates of the royal family provided plenty of space and plenty of game, while the peasants coveted them for more productive pursuits

members continued to hang about the Tauride Palace. Anger in the Duma had mounted as Nicholas had proved deaf to every request in recent months. He would not appoint ministers in whom it was possible to have confidence. He would not even soften the persecution of Jews and trade unionists. Instead, as strikes erupted during 1915 and 1916, the authorities had gone on shooting the strikers, merely driving more people – including some members of the Duma – to plotting and to violence. On 27 February the president of the Duma, the Tsar's own nominee, sent the Tsar a stern warning of the need for urgent action. Nicholas commented:

> That fat Rodzianko has sent me some nonsense. I shall not even reply.

It was too late anyway. Nicholas, on his way to the military headquarters, ended up ignominiously at Pskov, his train becalmed by railway workers, and there he abdicated on his own behalf and that of his son, the sickly Tsarevich Alexei, on 2 March. The next day the Tsar's brother, the Grand Duke Michael, haughtily rejected the crown of a parliamentary monarchy. The Romanov dynasty had ended.

In the Tauride Palace, the Duma appointed a provisional government from its own members, headed by Prince Lvov. The Petrograd Soviet was recreated in the same Palace, representing workers, soldiers and peasants. Russia had deposed the Tsar in an almost totally unplanned revolution, which took even the Bolsheviks by surprise. But much more was yet to happen in the eventful year 1917 (see Section 19.1).

14.5   Russian Foreign Policy 1855–1917

Vast as were the territories of the Romanovs, ambition dictated that they should be greater still. The Crimean War checked, but did not end, the rivalry between the Russian and Ottoman Empires, and the tsars continued to be involved deeply in the Eastern Question (see Sections 8.3, 8.4 and Unit Fifteen). To the east of the Caspian Sea, however, there was still room for expansion in areas less sensitive than the Balkans, and in the far east of the Russian Empire there was scope for expansion in Amur (see Fig. 14.7). Amur Province was added to Alexander II's Empire in 1858, and two years later the Russians pushed on to the Pacific Coast, where the city of Vladivostok was founded in 1860. Like all other Russian ports, however, Vladivostok was not ice-free, and the search had to be continued for an outlet to the sea which could be used all the year round.

In Europe, Alexander II co-operated with Bismarck and developed understandings with Germany which lasted until Bismarck's retirement in 1890 (see page 117 and Section 15.1). Bismarck's skill helped to paper over the cracks in Russia's relations with Austria-Hungary, uniting both of them with Germany in the Dreikaiserbund. But Romanov-Habsburg rivalries in the Balkans were deep-seated. After 1890 William II allowed Russia to drift away from both Austria-Hungary and Germany, and a Franco-Russian Alliance was signed, one advantage of which was the access it gave to Alexander III and Nicholas II to French financial aid, some of which was used in the construction of the Trans-Siberian Railway. In the Balkans, Nicholas II became the protector of Serbia and, in 1907, he settled colonial differences with Britain. Thus the sides took shape whereby, in 1914, Russia fought in alliance with Serbia, France and Britain in the First World War (see Units Seventeen and Eighteen).

The Trans-Siberian Railway connected Moscow and European Russia with Vladivostok. Its construction began in 1891, and most of the single-track line was completed by 1904. It did not become a double-track railway until the 1930s. Its building was strongly supported by Witte, who was interested in the economic exploitation of the areas around Vladivostok, including Manchuria, a corner of north-eastern China across which the Railway ran from Chita, near Lake Baikal. After a rebuff in the Balkans in 1878 (see Section 15.2), the Far East and Manchuria seemed to offer alternative prospects for Russian expansion. China was as weak as the Ottoman Empire, hardly capable of defending Manchuria and Korea, and the Russians hoped there would be fewer international complications in the Far East than in the hotbed of the eastern Mediterranean. Manchuria also offered the prospect of an ice-free (warm water) port. Yet Russia was not without a rival. Japan went to war with China in 1894 and, a year later at the Treaty of Shimonoseki, secured the island of Formosa, and the Liaotung Peninsula with the important Port Arthur. Pressure from Russia

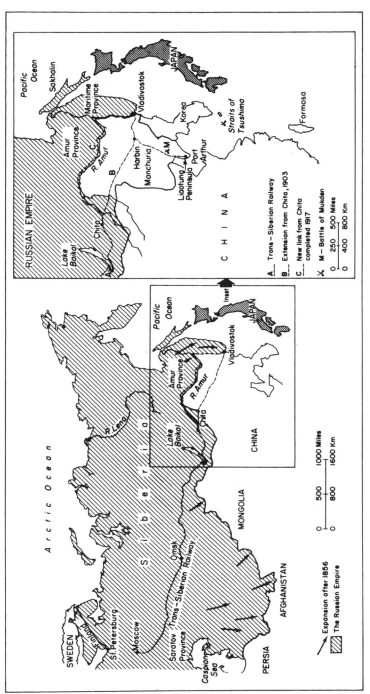

Fig. 14.7 Russia's Expansion in Asia

and other Europeans nevertheless forced the Japanese to leave Port Arthur almost immediately. At Shimonoseki Japan had also agreed to the independence of Korea, but both Japan and Russia were now bent on possessing both Port Arthur and Korea as soon as the moment was ripe.

Russia made the early running. In 1898 China was persuaded to lease the Liaotung Peninsula and Port Arthur to Nicholas II for 25 years and at the same time Russians began to infiltrate into northern Korea. The Tsar used the excuse of the Boxer Rebellion of 1900 (see Section 16.2(*b*)) to occupy the whole of Manchuria. In 1902 the Japanese made an alliance with Britain, guaranteeing that if either was attacked by two enemies, the other would give assistance. This cleared the way for a Japanese conflict with Russia, whose French ally was likely to be deterred by the prospect of involvement with Britain. The Japanese requested that Russian troops should be removed from Korea, but Nicholas took no notice and, in February 1904, Japanese forces launched a surprise attack on Port Arthur. It was this Russo-Japanese War which helped to provoke the Revolution of 1905 in Russia (see Section 14.4(*b*)). Russia's Pacific fleet was routed, and its troops were beaten back both in Korea and Manchuria. Port Arthur withstood a long siege but, like Sebastopol in 1855, it was eventually forced to surrender in January 1905.

It seemed absurd that the vast Russian Empire could not defeat the comparatively tiny state of Japan, but even greater disasters followed. The Russians were routed in the ten-day Battle of Mukden at the beginning of March 1905: 90 000 men were lost, and Japan was left with complete mastery on land. Nicholas II had only one last hope. His Baltic fleet was making an eccentric voyage round Africa, lumbering towards the Pacific under a mighty cloud of black smoke and consuming coal at a prodigious rate, to the delight of the German merchants who shuttled the fuel supplies to it. It took some eight months to arrive off Korea, where it was destroyed in the Straits of Tsushima in a matter of hours. More than 20 Russian warships were sunk with heavy casualties, and hardly any struggled through to Vladivostok. They did not sink a single Japanese vessel. Nicholas accepted the mediation of Theodore Roosevelt, President of the USA, and agreed to the Treaty of Portsmouth (New Hampshire). The Russians had to surrender Port Arthur, the Liaotung Peninsula and the whole of Manchuria, all of which the Japanese proceeded to infiltrate, eventually embarking on the total conquest of Manchuria in 1931. Russia had also to cede to Japan the southern half of the island of Sakhalin. Korea was left for the moment, but Japan annexed it in 1910.

The Russo-Japanese War of 1904–5 shattered the Tsar's ambitions in the Far East. A new rail link had now to be built from Chita to Vladivostok, skirting round Manchuria, and there was no longer any hope of an ice-free port. Except for the defeat of the Italians at Adowa, Russia's defeat was the first major setback for Europeans at the hands of a nation which was totally non-European, a defeat of whites by non-whites. The humiliation for the Tsar was enormous. Hopefully, he returned to the Balkans, only to meet a further rebuff when Austria-Hungary annexed Bosnia and Herzegovina in 1908, and further defeats when Russia embarked on the First World War.

Further Reading

Floyd, D.: *Russia in Revolt, 1905*. Macdonald (London, 1969).
Kennett, J.: *The Growth of Modern Russia*. Blackie (Glasgow, 1979).
Morrow, H. and Black, C. E.: *Russia under the Czars*. Cassell (London, 1962).
Mosse, W. E.: *Alexander II and the Modernisation of Russia*. Hodder and Stoughton (London, 1959).
Roberts, E. M.: *Lenin and the Downfall of Tsarist Russia*. Methuen (London, 1966).
Seton-Watson, H.: *Decline of Imperial Russia, 1855–1914*. Methuen (London, 1964).
Tames, R.: *Last of the Tsars*. Pan Books (London, 1972).
Troyat, H.: *Daily Life in Russia under the Last Tsar*. Allen and Unwin (London, 1961).

Exercises

1. Using Table 14.1 and the information in this Unit, show when and how Russia embarked on an industrial revolution.
2. Which of the headings in Section 14.2 – 'The Liberator', 'The Reformer', 'The Romanov' – in your opinion provides the best overall description of Alexander II?
3. 'We must train people who will dedicate to the revolution . . . the whole of their lives' (page 209). Why did Lenin reach this opinion, and how consistent with it was Lenin's response to the Revolution of 1905 (Section 14.4(*b*))? Use Fig. 14.3 to explain how the Bolsheviks developed before 1914.
4. Use the information in Section 14.4 to write *two* character studies of Nicholas II, one from the point of view of one of his admirers, the other from the point of view of a Russian revolutionary.
5. Why did the Dumas (Section 14.4(*c*)) have only limited influence in Russia?
6. (*a*) What do the illustrations in this Unit show of the life of the Russian lower classes under the tsars?
   (*b*) Explain why, as a Russian peasant, you would have welcomed the February Revolution of 1917.
   (*c*) Read Section 19.1. To what extent, as a Russian peasant, would you also have welcomed the further developments in Russia during 1917?
7. 'It seemed absurd that the vast Russian Empire could not defeat the comparatively tiny state of Japan' (page 228). Why could the Russians not defeat the Japanese?

The Eastern Question 1871–1913 and the Balance of Power

15.1 The Diplomacy of Bismarck 1871–90

(a) The French and Balkan Problems

A German socialist asked the question in 1871:

> How is one reasonably supposed to picture the future relationship of Germany and France, in view of the abyss of irreconcilable hatred which opened up between them . . . while the whole French people passes on its grim thirst for revenge to its children and children's children?

The 'thirst for revenge' focused on the Franco-Prussian War, the Treaty of Frankfurt which ended it, and the loss of Alsace-Lorraine (see Sections 7.3(c) and 11.3(e)). Bismarck had wanted to take Strasbourg, where German was spoken, but Prussian and German nationalists demanded Metz too, and indeed almost all of Alsace-Lorraine, and Bismarck had had to give way. The German Reich would now have to live with French resentment. From 1871 onwards Bismarck aimed to make certain that France would not attack Germany. He had no intention of relinquishing the German military superiority, which had been demonstrated, but he also aimed to establish such good relations with the rest of Europe that the French would be unable to find allies. Germany now had everything to gain from a period of peace in which to consolidate the changes which had taken place, and it was Bismarck's view, later expressed in his Memoirs, that:

> Germany is perhaps the single Great Power in Europe which is not tempted by any objects obtainable only by a successful war. It is our interest to maintain peace. . . . We do not require an increase in our immediate territory. . . . German policy would be just and peaceful.

In short, Bismarck adopted the role of the pacifier after 1871, hoping that Europe would remain tranquil. But he had to balance a variety of forces. His foreign policy and his internal policy were almost always closely linked, because he had to consider the ambitions of German voters (see Section 10.1). At the same time, however, he had to consider the ambitions of other powers, for example in the scramble for colonies (see Unit Sixteen), and in the Eastern Question which still smouldered.

The Ottoman Empire had gained only a temporary reprieve at the end of the Crimean War (see Section 8.4). Three nation states already existed in the Balkans in addition to the tiny state of Montenegro, which had somehow retained its independence since the fourteenth century. Serbia and Rumania (the latter created in 1862 when Alexander Cuza united Wallachia and Moldavia) still had to shake off the last remnants of the Sultan's claim to overlordship, though by 1871 that seemed little more than a formality. There were still other Serbs and Rumanians to be liberated from the Turks, however, when opportunity occurred, and Serbia and Rumania also resented the fact that other Serbs and Rumanians were still locked inside the Habsburg Empire. The third nation state, Greece, already had total independence from the Turks, but the Greeks too had fellow-nationals still to be liberated from the Ottoman Empire. Elsewhere in the Balkans Bulgarians remembered their own long-lost empire, and they stirred restlessly under Turkish rule which had now lasted for five centuries. The Sultan whetted the Bulgarian appetite for freedom in 1870, when he agreed to set up the Bulgarian Exarchate, a national branch of the Orthodox Church. In the same year Tsar Alexander II repudiated the Black Sea clauses of the Treaty of Paris (see Section 8.4(c)).

It always seemed likely that the instability of the Balkans would undermine the tranquillity which Bismarck sought for Europe after 1871. His most difficult problem lay in reconciling the conflicting ambitions in the Balkans of Austria-Hungary and Russia, and in this he enjoyed quite remarkable, though in the end only temporary, success. One device that he used to good effect was the international conference, and in such conferences at Berlin he managed first to smooth feathers which had been ruffled in the Eastern Question in 1878, and then to pave the way for the partitioning of Africa in the 1880s. But he also relied on the building of alliances, sometimes by secret diplomacy, and from these alliances and from the secrecy there grew the later entanglements which overwhelmed the statesmen of Europe in 1914. Bismarck also continued to believe whole-heartedly in military strength. Germany had the largest army in Europe in the mid-1870s, except for that of Russia. The German army was almost seven times the size of the French army and well over twenty times the size of the British. The tradition was continued enthusiastically by Bismarck's successors and, from 1875 to 1906, the army grew from nearly three million to almost eight million. This was Bismarck's legacy. International entanglements, secret diplomacy and military muscle produced an explosive mixture, but perhaps the Chancellor's greatest failure was that his diplomacy did little in the end permanently to tranquillize the Balkans.

(b) The Alliances

Berlin was the setting for a meeting in 1872 of the Three Emperors of the German Reich, Austria-Hungary and Russia, and for the beginning of their Understanding (*Verhältnis*). Franz Joseph and Alexander II signed the Convention of Schönbrunn, Vienna, a year later, and William I was quick to join it.

The Convention put its faith in 'a direct and personal understanding between the Sovereigns', and it recommended collaboration in:

> imposing the maintenance of the peace of Europe against all subversions, from whatever quarter they may come.

The Convention was aimed as much at revolutionaries as at any power such as France, but a natural gulf existed between the Emperors and the French Republic, and Bismarck saw the Understanding as a useful discouragement to any French aggressiveness. France, however, was in no condition to challenge Germany, and a war scare in the German press in 1875, claiming that a French challenge was imminent, had more to do with Germany's internal politics and the Kulturkampf than with international relations. If Bismarck, on the other hand, hoped that the scare would provoke anti-French feelings in Britain, the plan misfired, since the British sent their protests not to Paris but to Berlin.

The Eastern Question gave rise to more serious problems (see Section 15.2). Franz Joseph and Alexander had admitted at Schönbrunn that their interests diverged 'respecting special questions', and Russia's attack on the Ottoman Empire in 1877 caused consternation in Vienna. The best that Bismarck could do was to try to reconcile Austria-Hungary and Russia, and to pacify the British at the same time, in the Congress of Berlin. The Treaty of Berlin produced a compromise, and left the Eastern Question to continue to smoulder. The Tsar was hardly pleased with the Treaty, and Bismarck now had to reckon with a dissatisfied Russia. He persuaded himself that Russia was dangerous, and wrote in September 1879 to King Ludwig II of Bavaria:

> I cannot resist the conclusion that in the future, perhaps even in the near future, the peace is threatened by Russia and by Russia alone.

And he went on to argue that, while trying to preserve the Understanding, a closer alliance was necessary with Austria-Hungary. In October 1879, such a Dual Alliance was negotiated with Andrassy, though it was kept secret:

> Should, contrary to their hope, and against the loyal desire of the two High Contracting Parties, one of the two Empires be attacked by Russia, the High Contracting Parties are bound to come to the assistance one of the other with the whole war strength of their Empires.

Thus Germany became committed to assisting Austria-Hungary since, if any attack were to be made, it was most likely to arise over the Balkans, where Habsburg and Romanov interests conflicted. If an attack were launched by any power other than Russia (such as France), the allies promised only friendly neutrality. The Dual Alliance lasted until 1918, by which time it had drawn Germany into the First World War. Russia had not threatened the peace until 1914 in fact; and even then, it can be argued, Austria-Hungary was at least as much to blame as Russia.

THE THREE EMPERORS;
OR, THE VENTRILOQUIST OF VARZIN!

Fig. 15.1 A Punch *view of Bismarck the Ventriloquist manipulating the Three Emperors of Germany, Austria-Hungary and Russia. Bismarck's private estate was at Varzin. Rivalry in the Balkans made it difficult to keep Austria-Hungary and Russia within a single alliance*

The Dual Alliance was expanded in 1882 into the Triple Alliance, including Italy. Bismarck gave some encouragement to the British to consolidate their grip on Egypt, and to the French to grab Tunisia, perhaps in the hope that this would drive Italy in search of allies though the real initiative for the Alliance came from the Italians (see Section 12.2(*d*)). With many more provisions for secrecy, Germany and Austria-Hungary promised in the Triple Alliance that:

> In case Italy, without direct provocation on her part, should be attacked by France for any reason whatsoever, the two other Contracting Parties shall be bound to lend help and assistance with all their forces. . . . This same obligation shall devolve upon Italy in case of any aggression without direct provocation by France against Germany.

Other Articles dealt with other possible breaches of the peace, and Italy was exempted from war 'against England'.

Meanwhile the web became more complicated. The Understanding was in 1881 turned into a formal League, the *Dreikaiserbund*, subject to renewal after three years. Once again mutual promises of secrecy were made. Germany, Austria-Hungary and Russia agreed to consult one another about any further changes in the Ottoman Empire, and they guaranteed friendly neutrality if one were involved in war with a fourth power. For Bismarck, the League offered the opportunity to mediate in any new quarrel about the Balkans, as well as depriving France of any alliance with Russia. But it involved some double-dealing, since the Dual Alliance of 1879 already existed. The Dreikaiserbund was nevertheless renewed in 1884, and it was due to be renewed again in 1887.

1887 was a difficult year for the great powers. Russia had come into open conflict with Bulgaria, and especially with Stambulov (see pages 240–1). With the Eastern Question bubbling again, Alexander III refused to renew the Dreikaiserbund. But Bismarck encouraged Austria-Hungary to sign the Mediterranean Agreements with other powers (see page 185), and the Triple Alliance of 1882 was renewed. The latter now had additional secret clauses, which mainly provided for a common watch on the Balkans and on north Africa by Germany, Austria-Hungary and Italy. In June 1887 Bismarck personally signed a Reinsurance Treaty with Russia. Germany and Russia promised mutual friendly neutrality in any future war by one of them against a third power, unless Russia were to attack Austria-Hungary or Germany were to attack France. The Treaty also had an 'Additional and Very Secret Protocol'! Germany promised to support Russian interests in Bulgaria and to deny any support to Alexander of Battenberg; Germany further agreed to offer 'moral and diplomatic' support if Russia found it necessary to assume:

the task of defending the entrance to the Black Sea in order to safeguard [its] interests.

Such an agreement would surely have alarmed Britain and Austria-Hungary, had they known of it. Yet Bismarck cynically disregarded his own pledges to secrecy when, in 1888, he published the terms of the Dual Alliance of 1879, hoping further to reassure Russia that it was not an aggressive Alliance. The Reinsurance Treaty was due to be renewed in 1890, but it was allowed to lapse by Caprivi, when William II eagerly accepted Bismarck's resignation. William disliked Alexander III and, in any case, he wanted to pursue his own foreign policy. He had already visited Constantinople with a view to befriending the Sultan.

Bismarck handed on to his successors a firm alliance with Austria-Hungary, and a paper alliance with Italy. He had maintained relations with Britain which were generally cordial, but he had not succeeded in interesting the British in signing an alliance in the late 1880s. On the other hand, he had avoided trampling on British toes, deliberately limiting Germany's colonial expansion and its naval programmes. He always realized that, strong as it was, Germany would be no match for a coalition of other great powers. His aim was security and, unlike William II, he avoided all risks which he considered unnecessary. Bismarck once remarked that the entire Orient was 'not worth the bones of a single Pomeranian grenadier'. The stability of Europe was what was important to him, though his crafty diplomacy and tangled alliances gave him the appearance of a juggler, even of a trickster. France remained quiet on Germany's western frontier, partly because of its isolation by Bismarck's diplomacy, but also because of its own internal problems. It was a greater achievement for Bismarck that he managed for almost 20 years to paper over the cracks between Austria-Hungary and Russia, and to keep them both linked with the German Reich. Such a state of affairs was nevertheless artificial: the Balkans would erupt again, and Habsburg-Romanov rivalry had not been eliminated while Bismarck was in office – it had merely been hidden.

15.2   The Bulgarian Crisis

(a) The Rebellion

The subjects of the Sultan continued to be misgoverned, and nowhere more so than in Bosnia and Herzegovina, in the north-west corner of his Empire. An English traveller in 1875 found the conditions of the peasants still akin to serfdom, made worse by the fact that many of the landowners had adopted the religion of Islam, and they mercilessly exploited the Christian peasantry. He recorded that:

> The Aga [landowner] can break the law with impunity. He is thus allowed to treat his *kinet* [peasant] as a mere chattel. . . . Any land that the kinet may acquire, any house he may have built, any patch of garden that his industry may have cleared among the rocks, the Aga seizes at his pleasure.

Dependent on local bullies for the preservation of his Empire, the Sultan comprehensively disregarded the promises to institute reforms, which he had made at Paris in 1856. In July 1875 his subjects rebelled in Bosnia and Herzegovina, and they won an early success in a skirmish with Turkish forces at Nevesinye.

Retribution seemed certain if the people of Bosnia and Herzegovina could not get outside help. They appealed to the major powers, and Andrassy, the Foreign Minister of Austria-Hungary, enlisted the support of Germany and Russia for the Andrassy Note, to which Britain and France also gave approval. It requested the Sultan to make effective reforms and to guarantee religious toleration. Abdul Aziz agreed to its principles, but ignored it in practice. The rebels struggled on, and the powers sent another note in May 1876, the Berlin Memorandum, urging the Sultan to order a cease-fire – and to make reforms. This time the British Prime Minister, Disraeli, was not associated with the

Memorandum: he was more concerned for the safety of the Turkish Empire than for co-operating with the Europeans. The Turks were encouraged. Abdul Aziz was deposed, and so too was the mad Murad V. By the end of 1876 the Ottoman Empire had a new tough and unscrupulous Sultan, Abdul Hamid II.

Meanwhile the rebellion spread. In early 1876 the Bulgarians joined in, and Serbia and Montenegro declared war on the Turks at the end of June. As usual, the conflict was barbarous. Turkish reinforcements poured into Bulgaria, bent on revenge for the murder of the Sultan's officials. Men, women and children were massacred indiscriminately, and a force of Turkish irregulars known as the Bashi-Bazouks won a special notoriety for savagery. The atrocities brought Gladstone out of retirement in Britain, to thunder against 'the Bulgarian Horrors', and to demand the expulsion of the Turks from the province they had 'profaned', 'bag and baggage'. Disraeli took a different view. He had already sent the British fleet to Besika Bay, more as a warning to Russia than to produce any constructive solution to the Balkan problem. He anticipated, correctly, that Alexander II would not long stand aloof from the slaughter. Russians were already assisting the Serbian army, but the Serbs won little success, and Alexander obtained an armistice for them at the end of October 1876.

No such respite was won in Bulgaria, but the Tsar was still willing to find a solution by conference. With British help the Constantinople Conference met in December. While it was in session Abdul Hamid agreed to a short-lived Turkish constitution (see Section 9.1). This apparent reform helped him to reject almost all other demands by the powers, including self-government for the Bulgarians. When the Conference broke up, he withdrew the constitution within months. Nothing had changed, and the Bulgarians and people of Bosnia and Herzegovina continued to suffer reprisals.

(b) The Russian Intervention

The Tsar declared war on the Turks in April 1877 and advanced through Rumania. Alexander did his best to reassure the British that his intentions were limited, and that he would not interfere with the Straits; and he suggested that the Habsburgs might move into Bosnia. He also addressed a proclamation to the Bulgarians:

> Inhabitants of Bulgaria! The aim of Russia is to build up, not to destroy . . . to pacify and conciliate all races and all denominations in the Bulgarian territory. . . . The arms of Russia will protect all Christians against violence. . . . The life, liberty, honour and property of every Christian will be equally guaranteed, to whatever sect he may belong. . . . Christians of Bulgaria! . . . The hour of deliverance from Mussulman despotism has at length struck.

The Russian armies had to struggle, however. The Turks resisted fiercely at Plevna, which did not fall, to open the way to the liberation of Sofia, until December 1877. The Russians then went on to take Adrianople, where an armistice was arranged at the end of January 1878. The British government, and a considerable portion of the British people, had convinced themselves that this was a war of aggression by the Russians. The Austrians were uneasy too, and there was furious diplomatic activity in Europe, while the Tsar proceeded to impose the *Treaty of San Stefano* on the Turks in March 1878.

The Treaty came near to expelling the Turks from Europe 'bag and baggage'. It left them Adrianople and Salonika and many of the Albanian lands north of Greece and, additionally, Bosnia and Herzegovina, where it was proposed that Russians and Austrians should jointly supervise reforms. Montenegro, Serbia and Rumania were all to profit by gaining additional territories from the Turks, and the Sultan was to cease to call himself the overlord of the Serbs and Rumanians. The Tsar insisted that Rumania must return to Russia the Bessarabian lands at the mouth of the Danube, which had been taken from Russia in 1856, and that Kars and Batoum must be ceded to Russia by the Turks. But the centrepiece of the Treaty of San Stefano was the creation of the state of Bulgaria, as:

> an autonomous tributary Principality, with a Christian Government and a national militia. . . . The Prince of Bulgaria shall be freely selected by the population and confirmed by the Sublime Porte [Sultan], with the assent of the Powers. No member of the reigning dynasties of the great European Powers shall be capable of being elected Prince of Bulgaria.

Turkish rights over Bulgaria were closely defined, and they did not permit the Sultan ever again to send Bashi-Bazouks there. Russia retained a two-year supervision over Bulgarian affairs, though other powers might also be involved in the second year. The size of Bulgaria was such that it stretched from the River Danube to the Aegean Sea.

It was at once assumed in Britain that Bulgaria would give the Russians access to the Aegean and Mediterranean, and that it would somehow become a Russian satellite. The Austro-Hungarian government felt a similar alarm. Before the ink was dry on the Treaty, moves were afoot to alter it. The British brought Indian troops to Malta. The fleet was already lying off Constantinople and could not be sent again, but artists and audiences in British music-halls bellowed in chorus:

> We've fought the Bear before, and while we're Britons true,
> The Russians shall not have Constantinople!

Alexander II gave no sign whatever of intending to take Constantinople, but it was unwise to point out that small detail in the streets of London. The generation of 1878 had quickly forgotten the follies of the Crimean War. The Austrians, however, were less keen than the British appeared to be to rush headlong into a military showdown with Russia, and Bismarck's good offices were enlisted to summon a European conference. Before it met, Britain signed an alliance with the Sultan, promising to protect his territories in Asia against

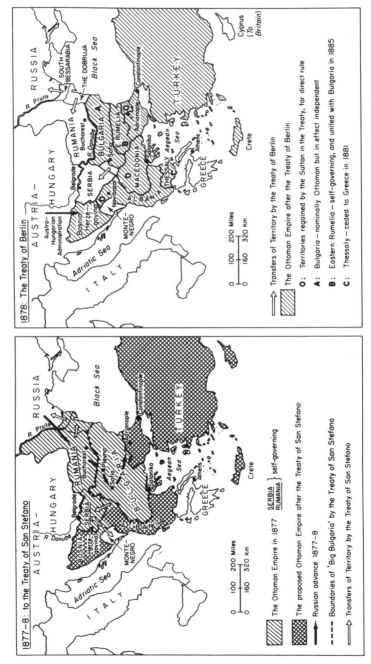

Fig. 15.2 The Break-up of the Ottoman Empire in the Balkans (Phase II)

any future Russian attack. In return, the Sultan made one of his not unusual promises to make 'necessary Reforms', and:

> In order to enable England to make necessary provision for executing her engagement, His Imperial Majesty the Sultan further consents to assign the Island of Cyprus to be occupied and administered by England.

A few days later, the Congress of Berlin met under the chairmanship of Bismarck in June 1878.

(c) The Treaty of Berlin

Bismarck's own interest in the Balkans was limited. His main concern was to restore Europe to a state of quiet as fast as possible. In particular, he wanted to bridge the gap between Austria-Hungary and Russia. France and Italy attended the Congress of Berlin, but neither made much impact. The main problem for Bismarck was Britain, since Disraeli was still intent on taking a tough line with the Russians. Bismarck set himself to play the part of 'an honest broker', to patch up a revised version of the Treaty of San Stefano, and to pacify as many powers as was possible. Bismarck's chairmanship and a variety of earlier agreements, such as that on Cyprus, made it possible for the Congress to complete its work in a month, and the Treaty of Berlin was signed in July 1878.

Fig. 15.3 Delegates at the Congress of Berlin, 1878. Gorchakov (Russia), fifth from the left and seated at the far table; second and third to Gorchakov's left, Salisbury and Disraeli (Britain); the uniformed figure, third to Disraeli's left, Andrassy (Austria-Hungary); next to Andrassy, standing, Bismarck (Germany), who presided over the Congress

Several of the arrangements made at San Stefano remained unaltered. Russia kept its territorial gains, and the total independence of Serbia and Rumania was confirmed. Minor adjustments only were made to the agreed frontiers of Serbia, Rumania and Montenegro, but these included the restoration to the Sultan of Novibazar, so that he could have access by land into Bosnia and Herzegovina from his Albanian properties. Bosnia and Herzegovina remained in the Ottoman Empire in theory, but they were to be occupied and administered by Austria-Hungary, in order to ensure their better government (see page 202). Russia was allowed no part in this administration. Austria-Hungary insisted upon further provisions in the Treaty of Berlin concerning the navigation of the Danube, much as in the Treaty of Paris of 1856 (see page 135), and it was confirmed that the Dardanelles and Bosphorus would remain closed to warships. The Sultan made further promises of reform and of religious toleration, and the French slipped into the Treaty a confirmation of French 'rights' concerning the Holy Places. Greece had briefly declared war on the Turks at the beginning of 1878, but the Greek-Turkish frontier was for the moment left unsettled, pending further negotiation. The outcome of this was that the Sultan ceded a part of Thessaly to the Greeks in 1881.

The centrepiece of the Treaty of Berlin, like that of the Treaty of San Stefano, was the settlement concerning Bulgaria. Article I of the Treaty of Berlin declared:

> Bulgaria is constituted an autonomous and tributary Principality under the suzerainty of His Imperial Majesty the Sultan; it will have a Christian Government and a national militia.

But fundamental changes were made to Bulgaria's boundaries. The south and south-west of the 'Big Bulgaria' (as defined at San Stefano) were restored to the Sultan, thus cutting Bulgaria off from the Aegean Sea. A second part of 'Big Bulgaria', to be known as Eastern Rumelia, was also restored to the Sultan, but a Christian governor was to be appointed here. The Bulgaria which remained was little more than a third of what had been envisaged at San Stefano, and it lay mainly to the east of its capital, Sofia. The changes were primarily intended to be a setback to Russia, but they were in fact a setback chiefly to the Bulgarians: it was almost certain that the changes would give rise to future trouble. Stefan Stambulov emerged as a new strong man in Bulgaria only a few years after the Congress of Berlin, and he seized possession of Eastern Rumelia in 1885. The powers took no action, and Bulgaria and Eastern Rumelia were united. By that time the powers had decided that Bulgaria was not a Russian satellite after all.

The Bulgarians, indeed, had taken up an anti-Russian stance after 1878, showing a determination to be independent of all foreign influences. Tsar Alexander II supported the election of Alexander of Battenberg as the first Prince of Bulgaria, but the Prince was quick to identify himself with Bulgarian rather than Russian interests. Russia disapproved of the annexation of Eastern

Rumelia in 1885, and the Prince was kidnapped in 1886, apparently with Russian connivance, and forced to abdicate. The Bulgarians elected Ferdinand of Saxe-Coburg as their new Prince, but the real power lay with Stambulov, who resolutely resisted Russian influence. There was no thaw in the relations between Sofia and St Petersburg until Stambulov was dismissed in 1894 (and murdered a year later).

The Treaty of Berlin in 1878 was no more successful than the Treaty of Paris of 1856 in providing a lasting settlement of the Eastern Question. The powers had made the same fundamental mistake of propping up the crumbling Ottoman Empire, in preference to risking a substantial increase in the influence of

A BLAZE OF TRIUMPH!

Fig. 15.4 Having maintained the peace, done something to preserve the Ottoman Empire, and collected Cyprus, Disraeli was well satisfied with the outcome of the Congress of Berlin. So too was Punch *in this congratulatory cartoon. Later, there were doubts whether it had been wise to give such British support to the Turks*

Russia. Lord Salisbury, who accompanied Disraeli to Berlin, admitted within a few years that Britain had 'backed the wrong horse'. Bismarck too was worried. The Russians had signed the Treaty of Berlin, but not with enthusiasm, and the coolness between Russia and the Habsburgs weakened his alliance system. In 1879 he felt the need to make the secret Dual Alliance with Austria-Hungary (see Section 15.1(*b*)). Most dissatisfied of all, however, were the peoples of the Balkans. Those who had not yet won their independence from the Turks still intended to obtain it. Those who were free still had territorial objectives, and a new Balkan problem was about to develop, that of rivalry between the Balkan states themselves. When Bulgaria seized Eastern Rumelia in 1885, jealousy led the Serbs to attack Bulgaria from the northwest. The Serbs were beaten at Slivnitza, and they were saved from retribution only by Austria-Hungary. But Serb-Bulgarian hostility now became a regular feature of Balkan affairs, and in the First World War the two countries fought on opposite sides.

15.3   The Ottoman Empire after 1878

Abdul Hamid II rapidly reverted to despotism after his brief flirtation with constitutional rule at the beginning of 1877, and the Ottoman Empire stagnated under government which was deeply conservative. The next major outrage in the Empire occurred in Armenia in 1894. Armenia lay some 500 miles to the east of Constantinople, at the south-east corner of the Black Sea. It was inhabited by some two million Christians who, by 1894, had become restless under the Sultan's rule. Like their co-religionists in the Balkans, they suffered persecution for their faith; and like the nationalities in the Balkans, they wanted their own government. When an uprising occurred at Sassun, Abdul Hamid responded even more fiercely than Abdul Aziz had done in Bulgaria in 1876. Turkish irregulars were unleashed, and racial war was fomented when the Sultan encouraged the Kurds to settle old scores against the Armenians. Now there were 'Armenian Horrors', but this time the great powers did nothing but protest. Nicholas II was new to the Russian throne, and the French refused to support him in any intervention. He was also more interested in Japan's war on China, and was uneasy lest his own Armenian subjects should rebel. In Germany William II had his own reasons for wanting to cultivate good relations with the Sultan – and sent him a birthday present. Unlike Bismarck, the Kaiser had plans for extending German influence in the Middle East. The British, meanwhile, protested vigorously, but they could not restrain Abdul Hamid from carrying out a new massacre in 1896 of several thousand Armenians who lived in Constantinople. All Armenian dissent was crushed.

More blood was spilled in Crete. Christians there had also rebelled against the Ottoman Empire by the end of 1894. There was a movement for union with Greece and, by 1896, the unrest developed into open warfare in which

Greek forces were involved. The Sultan's strategy was the same as in Armenia – to massacre all enemies. The powers found it difficult to agree on any common policy and, again, the German Kaiser was anxious to avoid offending the Turks. The Sultan officially declared war on Greece in April 1897 and began the reconquest of Thessaly, but Britain and France were now intent on imposing a settlement, prodded by Nicholas II, who speculated on the possibility of seizing Constantinople. The upshot was an arrangement, forced on the Sultan by Britain, France, Russia and Italy, whereby Crete remained in the Ottoman Empire, but had self-government under the supervision of the Greek King George. In effect, Crete was as good as lost to the Sultan, and it was formally united with Greece in 1913.

Abdul Hamid provoked even his Turkish subjects to revolt in 1908. A movement of Young Turks developed, eager to introduce western liberalism into the Ottoman Empire, and supported by certain officers in the army. Their uprising began with a mutiny among troops in Macedonia. It spread quickly to Turkey itself and, for the second time, Abdul Hamid granted a constitution. All adult males were given the right to vote for a parliament. Censorship was lifted, and renewed guarantees were given to religious and racial minorities. The Sultan's good intentions lasted for less than a year, but long enough for the parliament to meet. In 1909 he attempted a counter coup, and was promptly deposed, in favour of his brother, Mohammed V. Under Mohammed, the Young Turks quickly lost their liberalism, and the government of the Ottoman Empire continued much as before. The only major change was the acceleration of the disintegration of the Empire.

Austria-Hungary was alarmed in 1908 lest the Young Turks should somehow reinvigorate the Ottoman Empire. Bosnia and Herzegovina were incorporated in the Habsburg Empire. At the same time, the Bulgarians renounced Turkish overlordship, and Ferdinand of Saxe-Coburg proclaimed himself the Tsar of Bulgaria in 1908, having ruled as its Prince since 1887. Italy struck three years later, seizing Tripoli, Cyrenaica, Rhodes and the Dodecanese Islands from the Turks (see Section 12.2(d)). In 1912 the independent Balkan states then united together to tear to shreds what remained of the Ottoman Empire, west of Constantinople.

15.4 Ferment in the Balkans 1908–13

(a) The Balkan League

The last Obrenovic ruler of *Serbia*, King Alexander, was murdered along with his wife, Queen Draga, in 1903. His successor was King Peter Karadjordjevic, a descendant of Black George (see page 41). Peter brought a new urgency to the Serbian interest in freeing fellow-Slavs from alien rule. Relations between Serbia and Austria-Hungary had already deteriorated since 1885, when the Habsburgs had helped to rescue the Serbs from their reckless war against

Fig. 15.5 The Balkans, 1908 – a French cartoon. While Abdul Hamid struggled to keep his throne in Turkey, Franz Joseph of Austria-Hungary annexed Bosnia-Herzegovina and Tsar Nicholas II continued to seek influence in Bulgaria

Bulgaria; and Habsburg-Serb relations were particularly strained in the 1890s over the 'Pig War', when the Hungarian border was closed to imports of Serbian pigs. The closure partly resulted from Franz Joseph's displeasure with Serbia's shifting alignment, away from Austria-Hungary and towards Russia. The Habsburg annexation of Bosnia and Herzegovina in 1908 angered Serbia further, and it added to the Habsburgs' South Slav problem (see Sections 13.3 and 13.4). The annexation also vexed the Russians, who tried in vain to get together a European conference, where they might bargain for compensation for the Tsar and for Serbia.

Meanwhile, the fall of Stambulov in *Bulgaria*, and the accession of Nicholas II in Russia in 1894, helped to improve Bulgarian-Russian relations. When Bulgaria and Serbia temporarily drew together as allies in 1904, they both looked to Russia for support:

> The two allied states hereby promise to submit to the final decision of His Imperial Majesty the Tsar of All Russians, all of those controversies which they are not able to decide among themselves.

At the same time they asserted as their guiding principle, 'The Balkans for the Balkan nations'.

Greece was a third Balkan nation with ambitions. The Greeks had already made some progress in expanding the Kingdom from its 1832 boundaries, obtaining the Ionian Islands from Britain, winning Thessaly in 1881, and half-winning Crete in 1897. But they could not dislodge the Turks from Macedonia in 1902–3 when, along with Serbia and Bulgaria, Greece gave cautious support to Macedonian uprisings. It was only a matter of time before further efforts were made to free Macedonia and Albania, the last major Turkish possessions in the Balkans. When the Habsburgs annexed Bosnia and Herzegovina, Serbia's interest in Albania quickened. Bulgarians were still determined to recover all that had been snatched away at Berlin in 1878, and Russia, smarting under the rebuff of 1908, was willing to encourage them. The result was the *Balkan League* of 1912, in which Bulgaria, Serbia, Greece, and Montenegro, came together in a series of alliances and military conventions. They vigorously asserted their solidarity and common interest in freeing the Balkans from foreign powers, but what they underestimated was that, while it was easy to agree on hostility to the Ottoman Empire, it would be less easy to reconcile their own conflicting ambitions when it came to dividing the spoils. Rough divisions were nevertheless agreed, and Russian arbitration was mentioned again, should problems arise. But that, too, overlooked the fact that other major powers were uncertain to stand idly by.

(b) The Balkan Wars

The First Balkan War began in October 1912. Montenegro was the first to declare war on the Turks, and the other members of the League quickly became involved. Still reeling under the attack of the Italians in 1911 (see page 187), the Turks staggered under the new onslaught, but the Sultan was shrewd enough to appeal for the mediation of the great powers. Before the end of 1912 a conference assembled in London, to work out a settlement which was internationally acceptable. In the Balkans all but the Greeks agreed to an armistice, though Bulgaria soon had second thoughts and renewed the war. Bullied by the powers, all the belligerents were eventually persuaded to sign the *Treaty of London* at the end of May 1913. The Turks had to make sweeping concessions:

> His Imperial Majesty the Sultan cedes to Their Majesties, the Allied Sovereigns, all the territories of His Empire on the continent of Europe west of a line from Enos on the Aegean Sea to Midia on the Black Sea, with the exception of Albania.

The 'exception of Albania' infuriated the Serbs. Possession of Albania would have given Serbia an Adriatic coastline, but the major powers had meddled again. Their intention was to set up an independent Albanian state. From the Habsburg point of view, this would be a setback to Serbia. From the Italian point of view, an independent Albania was likely to be weak enough to be exploited by Italians. The British and French believed that Albanians were an identifiable people, entitled to be free. But the new Albania at once plunged into chaos, with six rival governments during the next 18 months.

The 'exception of Albania' had repercussions throughout the Balkans. There was now great rivalry among the members of the Balkan League to share out the other territories which the Sultan had surrendered. Thwarted of Albania, Serbia now intended to drive deep into Macedonia, and even demanded Salonika in order to have a port on the Aegean Sea. With the Greeks reaching northwards the Bulgarians, who had done much of the fighting in the recent war, were frustrated. Disillusioned again with the Russians, who had done little to protect Bulgarian interests, Tsar Ferdinand sought support from Austria-Hungary, and he recklessly launched an attack on the Serbs and Greeks at the end of June 1913.

This was the beginning of the Second Balkan War. Rumania joined in, scenting the possibility of expanding at Bulgaria's expense. And the Sultan thought it an opportunity too good to miss if he were ever to recover anything in the Balkans. Bulgaria was thus at war with Serbia, Greece, Montenegro, Rumania, and the Turks. The odds were overwhelming, and the Bulgarians were forced to sign the *Treaty of Bucharest* in August 1913. Fig. 15.6 shows that Bulgaria was left with an Aegean coastline, but without a major port. It also shows that Rumania nibbled away the southern Dobruja in north-eastern Bulgaria, and the Turks recovered possession of Adrianople. Serbia and Greece pushed the Bulgarians out of most of Macedonia.

The Treaties of London and Bucharest, therefore, still left festering wounds in the Balkans. Serbia was embittered by the creation of Albania. Bulgaria was embittered against all its neighbours. The Ottoman Empire had lost almost all its Balkan possessions, and attention seemed certain now to begin to focus on the Habsburg Empire, where subject races were still not free. But nationalism was no longer simply a matter of liberating subject peoples from multinational empires. Nationalist ambitions brought the new Balkan states into conflicts among themselves, and they inevitably looked for supporters among the major powers. The next phase in the development of the Balkans was entangled in the First World War, but the shape of it could already be detected after the Treaty of Bucharest. Bulgaria was now violently anti-Russian as well as anti-Serbian, and it was not surprising when Bulgaria joined the First World War in 1915 on the side of Germany and Austria-Hungary. The Turks also joined the Germans, partly as a result of the German friendship which William II had consistently offered since the fall of Bismarck, and partly because of the ancient enmity with Russia. Russia, on the other hand, had become the champion of Serbia whose differences with Austria-Hungary precipitated the First World War in 1914 (see page 201 and Section 17.4). Rumania, like Serbia, had ambitions against the Habsburgs as well as a feud with Bulgaria: in 1916, Rumania joined the war against the Central Powers (Germany, Austria-Hungary, Bulgaria and the Ottoman Empire). Greece manoeuvred in support of its own ambitions, but the Greeks too went to war against the

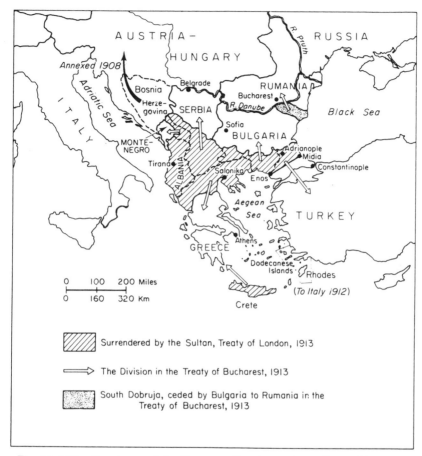

Fig. 15.6 The Break-up of the Ottoman Empire in the Balkans (Phase III)

Central Powers in 1917. Montenegro had assisted Serbia from the outset in 1914, but the Kingdom was overrun by the Austrians and, when the war ended, Montenegro was merged into Jugoslavia. Albania alone opted for neutrality, but that made little difference. The country staggered through the war in a state of almost total confusion, and foreign armies tramped across its soil. The Italians intended to establish themselves there but, like so many ambitions in the Balkans, they were frustrated by the powers when the war ended (see Section 12.3(a)). Mussolini later set to work steadily to infiltrate Albania, and he was finally able to conquer it in 1939 (see Section 24.3(c)). By 1913, however, the Ottoman Empire in the Balkans had been shattered. Five years later, the Habsburg Empire suffered a similar fate (see Sections 13.5 and 20.1(d)).

Further Reading

Clayton, G. D.: *Britain and the Eastern Question*. Hodder and Stoughton (London, 1971).

Geiss, I.: *German Foreign Policy, 1871–1914*. Routledge and Kegan Paul (London, 1976).

Langer, W. L.: *European Alliances and Alignments, 1871–90*. Alfred Knopf (New York, 1950).

Vucinich, W. S.: *The Ottoman Empire, Its Record and Legacy*. Anvil (Dublin, 1965).

Documentary

Anderson, M. S.: *The Great Powers and the Near East, 1774–1923*. Edward Arnold (London, 1970).

Medlicott, W. N. and Coveney, D. K.: *Bismarck and Europe*. Edward Arnold (London, 1971).

Exercises

1. Bismarck's 'most difficult problem lay in reconciling the conflicting ambitions in the Balkans of Austria-Hungary and Russia' (page 231). Explain and illustrate this statement.

2. Study the cartoons in this Unit on pages 233, 241 and 244. Which *one* of them do you consider showed *least* understanding of the historical matter to which it referred?

3. List in one column the terms of the Treaty of San Stefano, and in a second column the terms of the Treaty of Berlin (Sections 15.2(*b*) and (*c*)). Add a paragraph to explain how the Treaties differed, and what was the importance of the differences.

4. (*a*) Summarize *each* of the Balkan Wars of 1912–13 under the headings: Causes; Events; Results.

   (*b*) What further ambitions did the independent Balkan states still have in 1914, and how do these help to explain the sides they took in the First World War (see Fig. 17.1)?

5. Write a paragraph on *each* of the Figs. 3.1, 15.2, and 15.6, to explain what is shown of the changes in the Ottoman Empire.

6. Why did the Young Turks try 'to introduce western liberalism into the Ottoman Empire' (page 243)? Read Section 22.3, and then compare the aims and successes of Mustapha Kemal with those of the Young Turks.

Overseas Empires and European Imperialism

16.1 Empires Old and New

(a) Colonial Empires before 1871

Europeans had begun to seize possessions in other continents as far back as the fifteenth century. Explorers such as Columbus and Vasco da Gama discovered new sea routes and 'new' worlds and, as the knowledge of the Europeans grew, so too did their ambition to control the lands and peoples that they had found. The first discoveries and settlements were made by the Portuguese and the Spaniards, but the French, Dutch and English (the nations with Atlantic coastlines) were quick to join the scramble to discover and to possess. Curiosity and a lust for excitement provided some of the impetus for this outward movement of Europeans, but there were more powerful motives. Greed was one of them. Europeans always hoped that the new lands would yield fabulous riches, especially in the form of gold and silver, pearls and precious stones. National rivalry speeded up the process of discovery and conquest: there was fear that the riches might be discovered by another power, and thus add to its wealth and strength in Europe. Religion was another powerful motive, since European Christians believed they had a duty to convert those peoples who knew nothing of Christ. And there was rivalry between Catholics and Protestants, each eager to teach heathen peoples the 'right' Christian faith. On the other hand, religious persecution in Europe sometimes drove European families to look on places outside Europe as places of refuge, to which they might flee to live their own lives.

From the outset, therefore, Europeans developed certain attitudes to the non-European world which were to persist into the twentieth century. At the root of these attitudes was European arrogance. Europeans seldom doubted their own superiority. The non-Europeans with whom they first came into contact were seldom a match for them in fighting, since European weapons were far more deadly. Nor were the non-Europeans so consistently ruthless. Indeed they often welcomed the white strangers who arrived in their lands. Conquest was therefore possible, but the next step was to exploit the resources of the conquered lands. Where precious metals and stones existed, as they did in the Aztec and Inca civilizations in the Americas in the sixteenth century, they were commonly looted. But such prizes were exceptional and, over the years, the economies of the non-European lands were developed, primarily to serve the needs of the European mother countries. The overseas possessions were expected to produce the tropical crops which could not be grown in Europe, and eventually to provide the minerals and raw materials for European industries which could not always be found in Europe. Vast numbers of African slaves were carried callously across the Atlantic, to work on the plantations of the West Indies and the American mainland, and to serve the interests of their European masters. The overseas colonies produced and sold to their mother country what the mother country needed, and the colonies had to buy from the mother country what they themselves needed. This pattern was also reflected in the societies of the overseas possessions. European values were imposed, and local traditions were often ignored, sometimes even despised. Authority rested with white men, although European social divisions were likely to be perpetuated in the colonial societies. Non-Europeans, however, were looked down on even by the poorest whites, some of whom would often have been dumped overseas as outcasts from European society. The overseas possessions and their native inhabitants were regarded, more often than not, simply as the property of the mother country.

By 1815, therefore, there was already a long history of European empire-building, and certain significant changes had already taken place. The USA fought for and obtained its independence from Britain in 1783 and, by 1815, the Spanish empire in America was on the point of collapse (see pages 22–3). Portuguese Brazil became independent in 1825 (see page 38). These successful independence movements were largely the work of the descendants of Europeans who had settled overseas and grown away from their domineering and interfering mother countries. The overseas empires which remained, with the exception of British Canada, had comparatively few European settlers. They were ruled by the officials of the mother countries, and were still ruled generally on the basis of the attitudes outlined above. In the peace settlement of 1814–15, the British empire was enlarged – the reward the British chose for their part in the defeat of the French and Napoleon I (see page 11). With the loss of the Americas, European overseas empires in 1815 were comparatively small, but a new great expansion took place by 1914.

In fact the bulk of this expansion, and especially the carving up of Africa, took place after 1871. Before that date, the British developed colonies of white settlement in Australia and New Zealand and in southern Africa; and the Boers in southern Africa, of Dutch descent, pushed further inland in an effort to escape from British control. The French seized Algiers in 1830, and began the colonization of Algeria. Otherwise the empires of 1815 were not much extended, and it even seemed possible that European enthusiasm for empire-building might have declined. Nevertheless, the British seized Aden in 1839 and Hongkong in 1842, and they built up a presence in Malaya and Singapore, while steadily consolidating their grip on India. Napoleon III also showed ambition overseas: he consolidated the French control of Algeria, annexed Cochin China, but met only defeat in Mexico (see Section 6.2(*d*)).

Criticisms of overseas empires were already being voiced. They were called expensive and troublesome, and it was suggested that they were millstones round the necks of their mother countries. One of his fellow-countrymen complained to the British Governor-General of India in 1817 of the effect of British rule on the Indians:

> Foreign rulers have treated the natives with violence and often with great cruelty, but none has treated them with so much scorn as we.... It seems to be not only ungenerous, but impolitic, to debase the character of a people fallen under our dominion.... [The] advantages [of British rule] are dearly bought. They are purchased by the sacrifice of independence, of national character, and of whatever renders a people respectable.

It was not until the twentieth century that colonial nationalist movements won popular support, and became irresistible, but earlier outbreaks of protest against foreign rule were not uncommon. Foreign rule was likely to be resented, as it was in Europe by those who endured it. The Indian Mutiny occurred in 1857–8, with a heavy cost in human lives. The basic attitudes of Europeans to overseas empires had not changed much, however. They still wanted cheap food and raw materials, and markets in which to sell their own products. They still believed in the superiority of European civilization; and they were still more powerful than most non-Europeans, except for the USA. The lessons they had learned in the Americas had made Europeans a little more cautious, but they continued to rule their colonies mainly for the benefit of the mother countries. Europeans had learned, however, that *formal imperialism* (the annexation and government of colonies) was not the only way to achieve their objectives. The British controlled parts of India through native rulers, with whom they made deals. An *informal imperialism* developed in many parts of the world, whereby local rulers collaborated with the Europeans. Such rulers granted trading privileges and rendered other services, such as ensuring the safety of European merchants, prospectors, missionaries and travellers. Where friendly and orderly systems existed, Europeans saw no immediate need for setting up formal colonies. Thus the French were able to pursue their interests in Egypt without annexing it, and they built the Suez Canal there in 1869. The British did business in Malaya, while possessing only scattered settlements in Malacca, Penang and Singapore. The direct annexation of more British colonies only occurred when there seemed to be no acceptable informal alternatives – when, for example, the British seized Aden and Hongkong, and undertook the conquest of the Punjab.

(b) The 'New' Imperialism

A renewed interest in the building of formal empires developed after 1871, especially in Africa and in the Far East. This was due in part to the emergence of new nation states in Europe. Both Italy and Germany looked on colonies as status symbols, as the essential badges of great powers (see Sections 12.2(d) and 10.2(c)). The French Third Republic also pursued an expansionist policy (see Section 11.3(*e*)), and the British did not intend to be left behind. It was these four powers which showed the greatest interest in empire-building, but Leopold II, the King of the Belgians, demanded the Congo, and both Russians and Japanese coveted Manchuria and Korea (see Section 14.5). The centuries-old objectives of the colonizing powers persisted in this new phase of imperialist activity. One such objective was to extend European civilization, to carry what Rudyard Kipling referred to as 'the White Man's burden'. Idealists saw it as a mission: the Europeans would bring to areas which they regarded as primitive, the 'benefits' of European rule, such as Christianity, education and medicine, economic development and modern technology, and the social organization and administrative expertise of Europe. But it was not simply a cultural crusade, of course. The self-interest of the European nations was seldom far below the surface.

What that self-interest was is not easy to identify. Some politicians saw it largely in terms of prestige. William II was obsessively jealous of the size of the British empire, and he wanted a German empire. Crispi was eager for an Italian empire in Africa, to help in making Italy a great power. On the other hand, it is unlikely that Bismarck held William II's view, and not all Italians shared Crispi's enthusiasm: The British, for their part, took a special interest in overseas bases. Britain relied heavily on its trade routes, and bases could be used as coaling-stations and as centres for the development and protection of trade routes. The building of the Suez Canal shortened the route to India, where Britain had long-standing interests, and thus it seemed important to Disraeli in 1875 to buy the major portion of the shares in the Suez Canal Company. Having got them, it now seemed important to defend the Canal. It was partly for this purpose that Cyprus was acquired in 1878 (see page 239), but that was not enough. After 1881, Britain demanded a supervisory role over Egypt. The involvement in Egypt led on to the involvement in the Sudan, whence flowed the waters of the Nile, which were so vital to Egypt. Thus, expansionist activities tended to produce their own chain effects, leading the colonizing powers to expand still further in the pursuit of their interests.

It was commonly assumed that the European nations had an economic interest in empire, but this too is difficult to identify and to evaluate. Europeans hoped that their colonies would provide cheap supplies, and they hoped to find secure markets for their exports. The introduction of tariffs made it more difficult to sell goods to fellow-Europeans in the last decades of the nineteenth century and, when goods could not be sold, unemployment was likely to follow, and that could in turn threaten social stability. It seemed reasonable to assume that surplus goods could be sold in a country's colonies. In theory, therefore, colonies would supply cheap food and raw materials, and they would buy the surplus products of European industry. But many of the colonies which were gained after 1871, especially in Africa, were not rich in minerals, and they could provide only limited quantities of the cheap supplies Europeans wanted. Moreover, the poor peoples in the majority of the colonies lacked purchasing power with which to buy European manufactured goods.

Fig. 16.1 British businessmen cashed in on the popular interest in adventure and empire-building and, in this case, on the prestige of Henry Morton Stanley, intrepid explorer

Writing of British affairs, J. A. Hobson put forward a further economic argument in 1902 in *Imperialism*. He pointed to the profits made by industrialists and businessmen, and he argued that they had surplus capital to invest. He further argued that this surplus capital was invested overseas rather than at home, since greater profits could be made overseas. There was some truth in this argument with regard to Egypt and to southern Africa. Rudolf Hilferding published *Finance Capital* in Vienna in 1910, and he argued similarly that surplus capital led capitalists to demand overseas colonies of their governments, in order to have areas in which they might invest profitably. In 1916 Lenin wrote *Imperialism, the Highest Stage of Capitalism*, violently attacking capitalism as an exploiting system. In a preface, added to the work in 1920, Lenin asserted:

Capitalism has grown into a world system of colonial oppression and of the financial strangulation of the overwhelming majority of the population of the world by a handful of 'advanced' countries. And [the] 'booty' is shared between two or three powerful world plunderers armed to the teeth [America, Great Britain, Japan].

In Lenin's view the development of capitalism was responsible both for empires and the First World War. But he did not confine his definition of 'empires' and 'imperialism' merely to formal colonies and empire-building. Indeed the USA never acquired a large colonial empire at all, yet he named 'America' as the first of the 'world plunderers'. The rich, capitalist and imperialist states, he argued, exploited not only their colonies but their poor neighbours, such as Portugal and Cuba. Nor did Lenin claim that economic explanations of imperialism were wholly sufficient in themselves, though he had no doubt that capitalism produced imperialism, and that the basic motives for empire-building were economic – that colonies resulted from the pressures on governments of capitalists eager to invest overseas, and of powerful business interests.

There can be no single explanation of why the powers scrambled for colonies after 1871, and no common explanation will fit all the colonizing powers in Europe. The argument that colonies were created in order to export capital, which had been generated by industrialization, is not convincing. France built an empire second only to that of Britain, but a good deal of French capital was invested not in the empire but in Russia. Britain invested heavily abroad between 1871 and 1914, but well over half of the British investments were in the USA, Canada, Australia and southern Africa, and not in the new colonies. Moreover, France was less industrialized than Germany, though the German empire was smaller than the French; and Italy clamoured for colonies, without itself being heavily industrialized or possessing surplus capital for export. Italy, indeed, was almost unique among the colonizing powers, in having a surplus population to export rather than surplus capital.

Nor is there much evidence to support the idea that colonies in this period brought great economic benefits to the mother countries. The Germans seemed to pay little attention to economic benefit in 1890, when they agreed to surrender many of their colonial claims in east Africa and Zanzibar to the British, in exchange for possession of far from prosperous Tanganyika, and of the island of Heligoland in the North Sea, which would be useful to the German navy. Hobson showed how little Britain gained from the sale of exports to the British colonies. And the cost of administering the French and German empires almost certainly exceeded the income received from them, both by governments and private businesses. On the other hand, there was always hope for future profits, perhaps from the discovery of minerals or from the exploitation of other resources; and, in the meantime, the annexing of a colony would keep it out of the hands of rival Europeans.

There was certainly growing public interest in overseas empire in the late nineteenth century. The press carried stories of the achievements of explorers who were opening up new areas, especially in Africa. It was not only business-men who put pressure on governments to acquire colonies. Bismarck came under pressure from the German Colonial Society, itself a product of the German nationalism that he had encouraged (see page 151). There were many Europeans, such as missionaries, doctors, teachers and scientists, who were eager to find out more about the world, and who felt a sense of duty to serve it. Sometimes the politicians themselves gave a lead. Ferry in France and Joseph Chamberlain in Britain were men with an enthusiasm for empire. Sometimes the politicians simply responded to pressure, hoping like Bismarck, perhaps, that they would win votes. But what was common in the age of imperialism after 1871 was a strong sense of rivalry between the European nations, reinforced by the belief that a nation's greatness could be seen in the size of its possessions. Lord Rosebery, a British Liberal, declared: 'That greater pride in Empire which is called Imperialism . . . is a larger patriotism.' For 'larger patriotism' he might have said 'nationalism', and it was this, perhaps, which best accounted for the renewed enthusiasm for colonies after 1871. This illustration in an English children's book of 1876 splendidly caught the spirit of the times (below). It shows Queen Victoria, who had just been proclaimed the Empress of India; behind her throne stands a turbaned Indian subject and, in front of her, half bowing, the diminutive figure of the German Emperor, William I.

HER MOST GRACIOUS MAJESTY.

Our Queen and our Empress
Is greater and wiser
Than all foreign monarchs,
Including "der Kaiser."

Fig. 16.2

William II, a later Kaiser, regarded it as a personal, indeed as a national insult, that Queen Victoria – to her own obvious delight – reigned over an empire on which the sun never set, whereas his own empire outside Europe was quite tiny by comparison.

16.2 The Expansion of Empires after 1871

(a) The Scramble for Africa

Two scientific discoveries paved the way for the white man's conquest of Africa. The developing use of quinine in the second half of the nineteenth century enabled the whites to resist the malarial mosquito; and the invention, by Richard Gatling in 1862, of a ten-barrelled machine-gun made it almost impossible for Africans to resist European forces. Europeans still knew little of the interior of Africa in 1871. There had long been Europeans on the coast of Africa, and British and Boers had begun to push inland in the south (see Fig. 16.4). But Africa was still 'the dark continent', and it was still probed only tentatively. Mungo Park explored the Upper Niger before 1805, and Burton and Speke reached Lake Tanganyika in 1854. Livingstone began missionary work in Bechuanaland in 1840, discovered the Victoria Falls in 1855, and went on to explore widely from Angola to Mozambique. A new exploration began when Henry Stanley set out in search of Livingstone. Stanley found the missionary-explorer near Lake Tanganyika, and then he himself went on to explore the River Congo in the mid-1870s. He later published his observations in *Through Darkest Africa*, but in the meantime he reported enthusiastically on the probability that important minerals could be found around the Congo. Europeans showed considerable interest in these adventures. None was more interested than Leopold II, the King of the Belgians, and Leopold founded the International Association of the Congo in 1878, with a view to further exploration. That stimulated the French, who hastened to lay claim to their own share of Equatorial Africa. The French also seized Tunisia in 1881, thwarting the Italians, who were driven to look for territories elsewhere (see Section 12.2(*d*)). A year later the British occupied Egypt in response to anti-European rioting, and the Egyptian administration was brought under British control. Interest in Africa was growing rapidly. Germans arrived in east Africa, and the British and Portuguese were alarmed lest Belgian and French activities should encroach on their earlier settlements in west Africa. Governments inevitably

Fig. 16.3 Official transport for a white man, Nigeria 1912. Overseas empire almost always meant the subordination of non-whites to Europeans

became involved in African affairs in the wake of explorers, missionaries and traders.

Bismarck was anxious to avoid international conflicts. The Berlin Conference of fifteen nations was therefore arranged, and it assembled in November 1884. General agreement was reached on the suppression of slavery in Africa, although slavery had ceased in the British empire in 1838, and other European nations had gradually followed suit (e.g. the French abolished slavery in 1848). Further agreements were reached on the free navigation of African rivers, and on the rights of individual nations to claim parts of the continent by 'effective occupation'. At the same time, the Europeans promised not to exploit the native Africans. The powers recognized the Congo Free State, whose trade was to be 'free' to all of them, and which was provided with access to the sea. Leopold became the king of the Free State. He made extensive personal profits by dealing in ivory and rubber, but so many criticisms were made of his misgovernment of the Congo that the Belgian government took charge of it in 1908. Belgium thus ruled an African colony 80 times larger than Belgium itself.

The Berlin Conference was rather like the firing of the official starting-pistol for the partitioning of Africa. A scramble followed as the powers rushed to stake out their areas of 'effective occupation'. Much of the running for the British was made by chartered companies, such as the British South Africa Company, founded by Cecil Rhodes, and the Royal Niger Company, but the British government was never far behind. Africans who resisted were crushed. The British, for example, won wars against the Ashanti, the Matabele and the Zulu; and they eventually conquered the Sudan when General Kitchener defeated the Dervishes at Omdurman in 1898, taking revenge for their earlier victory over General Gordon in Khartoum. When the claim of one European nation clashed with that of another, lines were drawn on the map with an almost total disregard for their effects on the ground. It was more important for Europeans to avoid wars among themselves, than to consider whether such arbitrary international divisions split the African tribes. The partitioning of Africa was therefore carried through with remarkably few conflicts among the European nations, for all their intense rivalry. The whole of Africa had been staked out by 1914, except for Abyssinia (see page 186) and Liberia. In 1822 Liberia had been designated by the Americans as a refuge for freed American slaves, and it had existed as an independent state since 1847, watched over by the USA. It was a watch which came to involve the near-domination of the country by the American Firestone Rubber Company.

(b) The Far East

China seemed, at first sight, to offer Europeans similar opportunities to those in Africa. The Manchu Empire was desperately weak. By 1871, the British had seized Hongkong, and the Portuguese had a lease of Macao; and China had been forced to open various treaty ports to European traders. After 1871

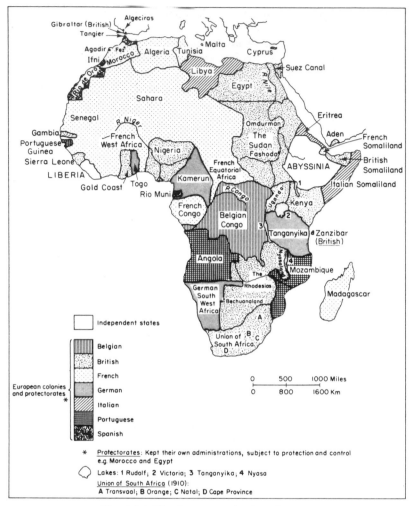

Fig. 16.4 The Division of Africa by 1914

European influence in China continued to grow, and new threats to the north-east of China were launched by Russia and Japan (see Section 14.5). The controversy surrounding Port Arthur whetted the appetites of France and Germany: France took control of Kwang Chow while Germany had control of Kiao Chow and the Shantung Peninsula and, not to be outdone, the British hastened to secure a base at Wei-hai-wei. The Portuguese had, meanwhile, annexed Macao. One result of these encroachments was an outburst of Chinese anti-European and anti-Christian protest, which had come to a head in the Boxer Rising of 1900 – so called since the Rising was spearheaded by the

Society of Harmonious Fists. European legations and missions were attacked, and several hundred were killed, including a representative of the German Reich. A relief force of Europeans, Americans and Japanese occupied Peking, took retribution and restored order, and a separate German force arrived later to exact its own reprisals.

The Europeans did not partition China, however. The USA strongly opposed partition, insisting on an 'open door' for the trade of all nations. But the Europeans did not need to partition China. China had a central government which, whatever its weaknesses, was prepared to collaborate and to grant concessions; and this, along with their bases on the coast, satisfied most of the ambitions of the European nations. Russian ambitions were thwarted by

Fig. 16.5 A German cartoon: the figure of War looms over the pack of European nations scrambling over China. A Japanese dog can be seen behind the Russian (Russland). The American dog (right background) remains aloof, a reference to the US Open Door Policy: the USA did not wish China to be divided into formal colonies

Japan, and Japan pursued its own policy of nibbling away at the Manchu Empire. The Manchu dynasty was overthrown by the Chinese Revolution in 1911, but it took far longer for China to rid itself of the influence of foreigners.

Outside China the powers proceeded with colonial expansion. On the Asian mainland, the British expanded the Indian empire to include Burma in 1886, and they consolidated their hold on Malaya. The French made headway in Indochina. Cochin China was already a colony, and protectorates were now established in Annam, Tonkin, Laos and Cambodia. The mainland did not offer much further scope, and Siam was able to retain an uneasy independence after yielding to the British claim on Burma and the French claim on much of Indochina. But a scramble developed for the unclaimed islands in the Pacific, with the British leading the way by annexing the Fiji Islands in 1874, and the French completing the annexation of Tahiti in 1881. German merchants found Samoan trade profitable and, after 1884, the Germans too began to collect Pacific islands. William II was especially enthusiastic, but he was also furious when the British protested at his designs on Upolu in western Samoa. He wrote angrily to Queen Victoria about this squabble over:

> a ridiculous island which can't be worth a pin to England compared with the thousands of square miles she annexes right and left every year without encountering any protest.

But the USA was also involved in the Samoan Islands, and the Samoa Convention of 1899 arrived at an agreement for their division between Germany and the USA, while Britain took compensation in Tonga and the Friendly Islands. Germany was also able to buy the Caroline Islands and the Marianas from Spain, and to seize the Marshall Islands. By 1914 the gathering up and allocating of the islands was complete, but the area had not been left entirely to the Europeans. The USA now had a considerable presence in the Pacific, and had taken the Philippines from Spain during a brief war which had erupted in 1898, originally over the Spanish misgovernment of Cuba in the West Indies. Japan had also reached as far south as Formosa.

16.3 Colonial Conflicts

The expansion of colonial empires after 1871 was accomplished with no war between Europeans except the Boer Wars of 1881 and 1899–1902, between Britain and the Boer descendants of the early Dutch settlers in southern Africa. The Boers (referred to more commonly in the twentieth century as Afrikaners) were finally defeated in 1902, after almost a century of argument about the rights of the British to rule over them. Yet, even then, the Boers could have claimed to be the winners, since Britain granted self-government to South Africa in 1910 with the status of a Dominion, which came to mean almost total independence within the next 20 years. South Africa was a Union of four states, Cape Colony and Natal (with substantial British populations)

Fig. 16.6 A French cartoon of 1898. 'What big teeth you have,' says the French Red Riding Hood. 'All the better to eat your biscuit,' replies the British Wolf. And the British took Fashoda

and the Transvaal and Orange Free State (with Boer populations); from 1910 onwards South Africa always had Boer governments and Boer prime ministers. They were, of course, white men's governments, and the vast majority of black Africans in South Africa were excluded from participation in politics.

In the 1890s the German Kaiser encouraged the Boers and annoyed the British over such episodes as that of the Kruger Telegram, and with his anti-British criticisms during the Second Boer War (see pages 162–3). But matters never escalated beyond a verbal exchange of fire. The same was true of the other conflicts which arose during the scramble for empire. At the same time, however, colonial rivalries added to the tensions which were growing in Europe. Individual crises were resolved by agreements, as that over Samoa was resolved in the Samoan Convention of 1899. But the cumulative effect of these crises was twofold: they added to the bitterness between nations in Europe, and they created an over-confident belief that crises could always be resolved. The crises that arose over the French penetration into Morocco in the early twentieth century were, indeed, resolved. But that which arose in 1914 over the assassination at Sarajevo led to war. It is impossible to measure precisely how much the colonial squabbling among the Europeans had contributed to the war fever which gripped Europe in the summer of 1914.

The quarrel between Britain and France over the Fashoda Incident in 1898 contributed little, except insofar as it helped to persuade the British to begin to look for allies. It arose from an epic march by Captain Marchand at the head of a French expedition. He came from French Equatorial Africa and, when he reached the Upper Nile at Fashoda in the Sudan, he ran up the French flag. Unfortunately Kitchener was also on his way up the Nile with a British expedition, which had just defeated the Dervishes at Omdurman. Anglo-French relations became tense, but the French eventually agreed to give up their claims in that part of Africa. Marchand was 'rewarded' with another epic march, back the way that he had come, to be fêted as an intrepid explorer when he returned to French territory. The Fashoda Incident had raised the delicate question of French honour, however. When Britain and France made the Entente Cordiale in 1904 (see Section 17.1), the British tactfully changed Fashoda's name to Kodok, to help the French to forget the whole affair.

The disputes over Morocco were more serious, and they inflamed Franco-German relations. In the Entente Cordiale, the British indicated that they would not object to French ambitions in Morocco, the French on their part accepting Britain's privileged position in Egypt. William II did object, however. Morocco was an independent country, and the Kaiser hoped to demonstrate that Germany's opinion was more important than Britain's. He called at Tangier during a Mediterranean cruise, and loudly upheld the independence of the Sultan of Morocco against French infiltration. The matter was taken to an international conference at Algeciras (Spain) in 1906, but William was dismayed when only Austria-Hungary supported the German argument. Britain and Russia supported France, arguing that administrative reform and better policing were needed in Morocco, and Italy and the USA agreed, though keeping a lower profile. The vast General Act of the Conference of Algeciras (with 123 Articles) legislated for reforms in Morocco, while upholding the Sultan's independence only in theory. The United States government issued its own additional declaration, asserting the intention:

> to contribute towards assuring to all nations the fullest equality in Morocco in the spheres of trade, treatment and prerogatives, and to facilitate . . . reforms . . . [for] a general well-being, based upon complete cordiality of foreign relations and an internal administrative stability.

A further Moroccan dispute arose in 1908, when the French arrested three German deserters from the Foreign Legion, who had sought protection from the German consulate in Casablanca. This matter was referred to the International Court, which had been established at the Hague in 1901 (see Section 23.1). The Court upheld the French. In 1909, anxious to try to pacify the Germans, France signed a Moroccan Agreement, declaring that France had:

resolved to safeguard the economic equality [in Morocco] and consequently not to hinder the German commercial and industrial interests.

The Germans had always claimed to be pursuing only economic interests in Morocco, and they now affirmed that Germany:

recognizing . . . that the particular interests of France there are closely bound up with the consolidation of order and internal peace, has decided not to impede these interests.

But the matter was still not ended. France was determined to get a firmer grip on Morocco. In 1911 French troops occupied Fez, the country's northern capital. The Kaiser promptly challenged the French again. He argued that this was a breach of the Algeciras Act, and a German gunboat, the *Panther*, arrived at Agadir, allegedly to protect German interests. That annoyed the British. Lloyd George, the Chancellor of the Exchequer, speaking at the Mansion House, warned the Germans, and chose to involve in the affair Britain's 'place and her prestige'. There followed several months of sabre-rattling and tense negotiation, before France and Germany signed the Moroccan Convention in November 1911. The German government at last backed down and, in return for a French guarantee of 'economic opportunity' in Morocco, it declared that:

it will not hinder the action of France with a view to lending its assistance to the Moroccan Government for introducing all the . . . reforms of which there is need. . . . [If] France were to take steps to specify and extend her control and protection, the German Imperial Government . . . will not raise any obstacle.

At last the way was clear. France made almost the whole of Morocco a French protectorate in 1912. A strip of the northern coastline was given to Spain. Germany meanwhile saved face by obtaining two strips of the French Congo, which were added to the German colony of Kamerun.

These agreements settled the last major confrontation between Europeans before 1914 about their colonial empires, although there was some international criticism of Italy, when that country grabbed Libya in 1912 (see Section 12.2(*d*)). The First World War was fought in part in the German colonies, both in Africa and in the Pacific, and new arrangements were made for these territories when the War ended.

Further Reading

Betts, R. F.: *The False Dawn: European Imperialism in the Nineteenth Century*. University of Minnesota Press (Minnesota, 1976).

Chamberlain, M. E.: *The Scramble for Africa*. Longman (Harlow, 1974).

Gollwitzer, H.: *Europe in the Age of Imperialism, 1880–1914*. Thames and Hudson (London, 1969).

Halladay, E.: *The Emergent Continent: Africa in the Nineteenth Century*. Ernest Benn (London, 1972).

Moore, K.: *Kipling and the White Man's Burden*. Faber (London, 1968).

Oliver, O. and Atmore, A.: *Africa since 1800*. Cambridge University Press (Cambridge, 1972).

Wolfe, M.: *The Economic Causes of Imperialism*. John Wiley (Chichester, 1972).

Wright, P.: *Conflict on the Nile* (Fashoda). Heinemann (London, 1972).

Documentary

Gardiner, L. R. and Davidson, J. H.: *British Imperialism in the Late Nineteenth Century*. Edward Arnold (London, 1968).

Exercises

1. (*a*) Referring to Fig. 16.4, list the possessions in Africa by 1914 of (*i*) Britain, (*ii*) France, (*iii*) Germany, and (*iv*) Italy.

   (*b*) Explain why Abyssinia was still independent in 1914.

2. Write a short definition of *imperialism*. Compare your definition with that in the Glossary on page 434.

3. (*a*) What economic reasons were there for European imperialism in the late nineteenth century (Section 16.1(*b*))?

   (*b*) Why is it difficult to find a single or even simple explanation 'why the powers scrambled for colonies after 1871' (page 254)?

   (*c*) What, in your opinion, was the chief reason why the powers scrambled for colonies at this time? How would you support your argument?

4. Explain how Fig. 16.2 on page 255 was intended to influence young readers, and what it reveals of attitudes in English schools in 1876. How far would such an illustration be acceptable in a present-day schoolbook?

5. Compare the activities of the great powers in China after 1871 with their activities in Africa (Section 16.2). Account for the different results of these activities.

6. Identify *three* colonial disputes involving Germany in the years 1890–1914 (Section 16.3), and write a paragraph on *each*. After re-reading Section 10.2(*c*), state what evidence these disputes provide that 'William was obsessed with strength' (page 163).

7. Read Section 17.1, and explain (*a*) how colonial disputes between France and Britain were settled, and (*b*) how colonial disputes between France and Germany strengthened the Anglo-French Entente.

Unit Seventeen

The Great Powers 1890–1914

17.1 Alliances and Ententes

The Germans renewed the Triple Alliance with Austria-Hungary and Italy in May 1891, this time for 12 years. In July William II visited London, vainly fishing to add Britain to the Alliance. But the damage had already been done to Bismarck's structure of alliances (see Section 15.1(*b*)). William had severed Germany's ties with Russia, and a more significant visit in July 1891 was that of the French fleet to Kronstadt. It paved the way for a Franco-Russian Entente in the following month. What Bismarck had always feared now rapidly came about. The Entente was followed by military conventions which clearly identified the enemy the French and Russians had in mind:

> If France is attacked by Germany, or by Italy supported by Germany, Russia shall employ all her available forces to attack Germany. If Russia is attacked by Germany, or by Austria supported by Germany, France shall employ all her available forces to fight Germany.

The Russian fleet visited Toulon in October 1893 and, by the end of the year, the two governments had turned the Entente into a binding Franco-Russian Alliance. It was confirmed in 1899, and was strengthened in 1912 by a naval convention. Within three years of Bismarck's retirement, Europe thus became divided into two armed camps. The Franco-Russian Alliance was supposedly secret, but even William II could not fail to notice the increasing friendliness between Paris and St Petersburg, and the flow of French capital into Russia.

Britain was the one major power not yet committed. British policy had been explained both to Bismarck and the Kaiser in the years 1889 and 1891 as the avoidance of entangling commitments. But colonial clashes in the 1890s such as the Kruger Telegram (see page 162) and Fashoda (see page 262) persuaded the British of the dangers of total diplomatic isolation. Joseph Chamberlain explored the possibility of an Anglo-German entente in 1898, and the two powers went as far as to make a secret agreement to divide the Portuguese territories in Africa, if the Portuguese empire were to collapse. William II visited London again, but the Second Boer War poisoned relations and Germany's naval expansion angered the British. First one drew back, then the other. William II wanted to make the British sweat before obtaining his favour and, by the end of 1901, Britain's patience had run out. Sylvester Viereck later commented in *The Kaiser on Trial* that:

> Anglo-German relations did not resemble a pattern but a series of patchwork quilts sewn together by a platoon of demented seamstresses.

The Kaiser had discarded another of Bismarck's principles. After allowing Russia to go over to France, he now allowed the British to slip away too.

The British made a firm alliance with Japan in 1902 in the hope of safeguarding their interests in the Far East (see page 228). After that, they looked again for some agreement in Europe, but it was France to which they now turned. Edward VII visited Paris in 1903 and he whipped up some popular enthusiasm on both sides of the Channel. In April 1904 a series of conventions was signed to settle Anglo-French colonial problems. One dealt with west and central Africa and with Newfoundland. Another dealt with Madagascar, Siam and the New Hebrides. A third concerned Egypt and Morocco, the effect of which was that France would not obstruct the British in Egypt and Britain would not obstruct the French in Morocco. Together the conventions amounted to the Entente Cordiale. Unlike the Anglo-Japanese Alliance, the Entente did not include firm commitments of support against any third power. It was simply a settlement of matters in dispute, a clearing of the air. But it was a clear indication that Britain's relations with France were now more cordial than its relations with Germany. In 1907 Britain made a similar Entente with Russia, France's ally, again avoiding firm commitments. The preamble made it clear that the Entente aimed only to settle differences:

> His Majesty the King of the United Kingdom . . . and His Majesty the Emperor of All the Russias, animated by the sincere desire to settle by mutual agreement different questions concerning the interests of their States on the Continent of Asia, have determined to conclude Agreements destined to prevent all cause of misunderstanding between Great Britain and Russia.

The 'Agreements' respected the independence of Afghanistan and of Tibet, and they allocated spheres of British and Russian influence in Persia.

Fig. 17.1 shows that there were thus fundamental changes in the alignments of the powers of Europe after the retirement of Bismarck. It also shows that Britain made no binding alliances with France and Russia until after the First World War began. But it was nevertheless true that the Anglo-French Entente hardened in the years between 1904 and 1914. Britain supported France firmly in the Moroccan crises (see Section 16.3), and from early in 1906 military conversations were held between the British and French high commands, to try to agree some joint strategy if war with Germany were to occur. The talks were merely exploratory, and still no firm commitments were made, but they were extended to naval strategy in 1912. At that time, Edward Grey, the British Foreign Secretary, wrote to the French ambassador to confirm that they did not involve specific commitment:

> Such consultation does not restrict the freedom of either Government to decide at any future time whether or not to assist the other by armed force. . . . Consultation

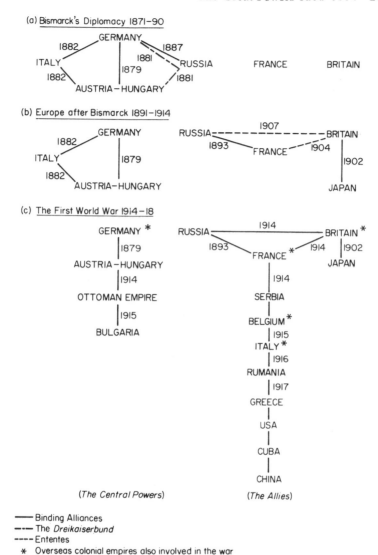

Fig. 17.1 The Alignments of the Great Powers

between experts is not . . . regarded as an engagement that commits either Government to action.

Such was the theory. In practice, the British navy patrolled the North Sea and the French navy patrolled the Mediterranean, watching over their joint interests and, however much the British might have pretended otherwise, the

Anglo-French Entente was close to being at least an unwritten alliance by 1914.

17.2   Killing Power

Alliances and ententes divided Europe into camps. The vast majority of Europeans hoped that disputes between the camps would be settled by negotiation, but there were two further dangerous ingredients in the mixture. One was the anxiety of governments to negotiate from strength, which led them to increase their armed forces. The other was the belief that war might not only sometimes be necessary, but that it even had 'grandeur'. Treitschke wrote about 'the moral force' of war, and asserted:

> Anyone with a knowledge of history realises that to expel war from the universe would be to mutilate human freedom. . . . War must be conceived as an institution ordained of God.

Few Europeans agreed wholeheartedly, but no government was prepared to renounce war as an instrument of policy, however much politicians might hope to avoid it. In 1898 Nicholas II suggested a conference to discuss the limitation of armaments, and 26 nations met at the Hague in the spring of 1899. Little was done about armaments, though certain weapons were condemned. A similar Hague Conference met in 1907, with equally small results. The British pressed in vain for a reduction of Germany's naval programme. One small step was taken towards international co-operation, however: the Permanent Court of Arbitration was set up at the Hague in 1901 (see Section 23.1).

Britain alone among the European powers had not adopted compulsory military service by the beginning of the twentieth century. As a result, the continental powers possessed not only substantial peacetime armies, but they had also vast reserves of men with military training – for example, six million, four million and two million reservists respectively in Russia, Germany, and Austria-Hungary. The powers also had equally formidable stocks of weapons, both of small arms and of artillery; and the killing-power of these weapons grew steadily with technological improvement. Rapid-fire guns had already been used in colonial wars; and howitzers and mortars were now being perfected, to hurl explosive shells in a rain of death and devastation, and to increase the deadliness of the traditional artillery. The destructive power of twentieth-century weapons was particularly evident at sea. The navy which Tirpitz constructed for Germany was led by vast steel dreadnoughts, armed with twelve-inch guns of unprecedented power which were mounted in revolving turrets (see page 161). Furious competition followed between Germany and Britain, as each sought to build more dreadnoughts, and more lighter warships, and to make them ever more destructive. Nor did other nations intend to be left behind. By 1914 the five major sea-going powers of Europe

Fig. 17.2 Developing technology increased the killing power of European armies: an artist's sketch of a howitzer, manufactured by Krupp of Essen and displayed at an exhibition of 1867

(Britain, Germany, France, Russia and Italy) had built some 50 dreadnoughts, and half as many again were under construction. Even Austria-Hungary had two dreadnoughts. The powers also had almost 100 older battleships which were available for service, as well as nearly 800 cruisers and destroyers. Submarines were multiplying too. There were 200 available for action, of which France had the largest fleet. For those who shared Treitschke's belief in the grandeur of war, such vast arsenals were always a temptation to submit quarrels to the test of battle. But the arms race itself was a source of ill-will and of tension. It excited public opinion, and it inflamed national passions. Britain had a Navy League as early as 1895, and Tirpitz soon afterwards set up the *Flottenverein* (Naval Association), to stimulate popular interest in naval programmes. British and Germans eagerly kept the score of dreadnoughts. By 1909 British music-hall audiences enthused to the chant of: 'We want eight, And we won't wait.' Yet more ingredients were thus being mixed. The camps were armed to the teeth, and popular nationalism, stirred by the cheap press and inflamed by economic rivalry, was beginning to focus hatred on emotional issues – Alsace-Lorraine in France, the naval race in Britain and Germany, the South Slav problem in Austria-Hungary. When war came in 1914 a German poet helped to focus nationalism and hatred still more sharply:

Hate by water and hate by land; Hate of the heart and hate of the hand;
We love as one; we hate as one; We have but one foe – England.

Fig. 17.3 HMS Dreadnought, *launched in 1906: this new battleship with a speed of 21 knots and 10 twelve-inch guns brought new killing power to naval warfare, while the building of 'dreadnoughts' added a costly new dimension to national rivalries*

17.3   A Crescendo of Crises

The decade before 1914 saw a variety of crises, which seized the newspaper headlines and added to the stockpile of national grievances. But the crises which occurred up to and including 1913 were all resolved without fighting between the major powers. The crises in Morocco were eventually settled in 1912 to the satisfaction of both France and Germany (see Section 16.3). The crises in the Balkans led to the Treaty of Bucharest in 1913, which no major power had plans to overturn (see Section 15.4). Not one of these crises explains why the powers went to war in 1914. That each crisis passed seemed to argue, indeed, that the international statesmen had mastered the art of settling problems without resort to war, and that it was only the minor states, such as Serbia and Bulgaria, which solved their disputes by fighting. At the same time, however, each crisis added to the list of scores which might one day be settled. A mythology developed that one power had been slighted by another power, that one power had been robbed of its due and that another power had gained an unfair advantage. Every major power in Europe could compile its own list of injustices, and almost all had unfulfilled ambitions. Russia had still not won an ice-free port, had been rebuffed in the Far East by Japan, and had been generally frustrated in the Balkans. Austria-Hungary had annexed Bosnia and Herzegovina, but had not eliminated Russian influence in the Balkans, nor ended the alleged threat from Serbia to the Habsburg authority over the South Slavs. France had not recovered Alsace-Lorraine, and had had to struggle to overcome German opposition to make headway in Morocco. Britain had not been able to stop the Germans building dread-noughts, and the British could recall numerous occasions when the Kaiser had insulted them. Italy suffered general frustration, and still laboured to be recognized as a great power. There was competition for markets and competition in tariffs, just as there had been competition for colonies, while there were still unclaimed overseas territories over which to compete. At the same time, however, innumerable agreements had papered over the difficulties, like that of 1906 when Italy, Britain and France agreed to leave Abyssinia independent.

In British eyes, William II, the German Kaiser, was both menacing and ridiculous. William had strong views on the influence he thought that Germany was entitled to exercise, and he regularly suspected plots against the Reich. In particular, he suspected a plot of encirclement, though he himself bore some responsibility for the development of the Triple Entente, of which he complained (see Section 10.2(c)). William in turn was regarded with deep suspicion by the British. He was eager to build a railway from Berlin to Baghdad, and it was begun in 1899 although still uncompleted in 1914. The British saw the railway as a threat to their interests in the Middle East, perhaps even a threat to India. The project was part of the Kaiser's obsession with the Orient – an obsession which Bismarck always deplored. A strange friendship grew between the Kaiser and the Sultan (see Section 15.3), and William pictured himself as the European defender of Islam, for example in Morocco. His colonial and commercial ambitions spread further than the Moslem world, however, but he failed to match his ambitions with tactfulness. In 1908 the Kaiser gave an interview to the *Daily Telegraph*, and showed the same lack of caution that he had earlier shown over the Kruger Telegram. He told the paper's readers that although he himself was friendly towards Britain, the German people were not. The interview offended the British government, but it also offended powerful forces inside Germany and, after 1908, the Kaiser's influence on German foreign policy declined. More ruthless forces came to control German policy – the German officer Korps and the Prussianized establishment, many of whom were far more inclined than the Kaiser to share the martial inclinations of Treitschke. They had the backing of the German army and navy, a combined force which Balfour, formerly a British Prime Minister, described in 1912 as 'that marvellous instrument of warfare'. It was the support of these German interests that proved decisive in 1914, when they encouraged the reckless eagerness of the government of Austria-Hungary to attempt to crush Serbia. The new crisis over the assassination at Sarajevo

COPYRIGHT EXPIRES.

GERMAN TAR. " 'WE DON'T WANT TO FIGHT, BUT, BY JINGO, IF WE DO,
          WE'VE GOT THE SHIPS, WE'VE GOT THE MEN, WE'VE GOT THE MONEY TOO.' "
JOHN BULL. " I SAY, THAT'S *MY* OLD SONG."
GERMAN Tar. "WELL, IT'S MINE NOW."

Fig. 17.4 A Punch *comment on Anglo-German naval rivalry, March 1909. Germany, it seemed, was aiming to take over Britain's nineteenth-century role as Europe's foremost naval power*

developed into a confrontation which could not be settled by the diplomacy which had de-fused crises in the past.

17.4   From Sarajevo into the Abyss

The Archduke Franz Ferdinand and his Czech wife Sophie were shot in Sarajevo on 28 June 1914. Both died of their wounds within a quarter of an hour. On the following morning *The Times* carried the headline:

AUSTRIAN HEIR SHOT. DOUBLE ASSASSINATION. BOMBS AND BULLETS IN SARAJEVO.

The Times also reported that:

The perpetrator was arrested. He is a young printer, 20 years of age, Nedjeliko

Gabrinovitch by name, and a native of Herzegovina, belonging to the Serb Orthodox faith. . . . [He] was seized by the crowd and severely mauled.

The assassin was, in fact, Gavrilo Princip, a member of the secret society of Young Bosnia, and his weapons had been supplied by the Black Hand, a secret society in Serbia. The Black Hand was organized by Colonel Dimitrievitch, and its aim was to bring about the union of all Serbs by a ruthless campaign of violence. The murder of Franz Ferdinand was no chance event. It had been callously contrived, and Dimitrievitch had trained the Young Bosnia murder squad before turning them loose. This involvement of Serbians, however much it was unofficial and unsupported by the Serbian government, meant that the 'South Slav question' was not simply an internal problem of the Habsburg Empire (see Section 13.3). The roots of the question were clearly in Serbia.

Serbia alone was unlikely to be a match for the Habsburg Empire, but Serbia could expect support from Russia (see Section 15.4). Franz Joseph's government was therefore initially cautious, though public opinion in Vienna, in Budapest, and throughout the Empire, was outraged at the murders. The key to what would happen next lay in Berlin. The Dual Alliance of 1879 tied Germany firmly to the Austro-Hungarian Empire in the event of a Russian attack on the latter. Europe held its breath while Berlin and Vienna decided on the next move. More than three weeks passed before the apparent calm was shattered when, on 23 July, a Habsburg ultimatum was delivered to Serbia. The Serbian government was required to renounce all propaganda directed against Austria-Hungary, to suppress all such propaganda within Serbia, and to dismiss all officials associated with it. It was to report the measures taken to Vienna, and:

Fig. 17.5 An Austrian military-post stamp, issued in Bosnia in 1917, commemorating the assassination of the Archduke Franz Ferdinand and Sophie at Sarajevo

to accept the collaboration in Serbia of representatives of the Austro-Hungarian Government for the purpose of suppressing the subversive movement directed against the territorial integrity of the [Habsburg] Monarchy.

Austria-Hungary gave Serbia forty-eight hours in which to reply.

The Serbians accepted most of the Habsburg terms, but they asked that others be referred to the Court of Arbitration at the Hague, or to an international conference. They could not agree to the policing of Serbian affairs by Austro-Hungarian 'representatives', as had no doubt been foreseen. Vienna was bent on war, and the ultimatum was little more than a formality. The Serbian reply was brushed aside; Austro-Hungarian troops were mobilized, and war was declared on Serbia on 28 July. At the eleventh hour William II and Bethmann-Hollweg made a last-ditch effort to put on the brakes, but there were stronger forces than they in Berlin, and the military high command could be relied on to support – even to encourage – Austria-Hungary. Russia mobilized on 30 July in support of Serbia, ignoring German warnings. German forces were mobilized, and the Reich declared war on Russia on 1 August. Russia had meanwhile requested French help under the Franco-Russian Alliance of 1893, so French forces were mobilized, and Germany declared war on France on 3 August. Thus the powers hurtled into the abyss of the First World War, and only Italy drew back from the brink, declaring itself neutral on 1 August. Britain hesitated, but the agonizing in London ended when the Germans invaded Belgium on 4 August, seeking a swift route to Paris, to fulfil the Schlieffen Plan and quickly to eliminate France and the western front. Whatever obligations Britain might have had to France, Asquith's government had no doubt that Britain had an obligation to defend Belgium under the Treaties of London of 1839 (see pages 47–8). Britain declared war on Germany at midnight on 4 August, after an afternoon and evening during which the British ambassador in Berlin tried vainly to persuade the Germans to evacuate Belgian territory. The ambassador saw Bethmann-Hollweg, who deplored the fact that:

> just for a scrap of paper Great Britain was going to make war on a kindred nation who desired nothing better than to be friends with her.

There was no way in which Bethmann-Hollweg could now divert the German military machine, even had he wished to. For the British, Belgium provided a simple and moral justification for joining a war from which it would have been difficult to remain aloof anyway. During the rest of August, further declarations of war followed, Britain on Austria-Hungary, Austria-Hungary on Belgium, and so on, spreading the plague.

17.5   Why was there a War? War Aims

When the war began it was greeted by enthusiastic crowds in almost all the

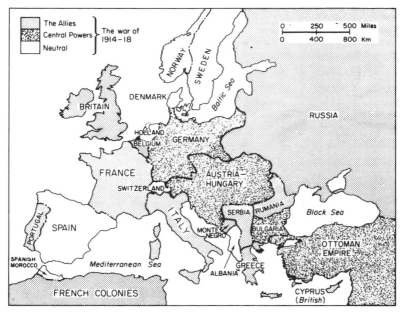

Fig. 17.6 Europe in 1914

capitals in Europe, but it was by no means clear for what the various nations were fighting. It was not until towards the end of the First World War that Allied war aims were defined, especially by Woodrow Wilson, the American President, and by Lloyd George (see page 292 and Section 18.7). Austria-Hungary had, perhaps, the most specific objective in the crushing of Serbia which, it was hoped, might in some way help to solve the South Slav problem. But the nations as a whole seemed to have become enmeshed in an act of collective lunacy in the pursuit of national honour. Each nation persuaded itself that it had scores to settle, and each hoped somehow to profit from the war, if only by weakening its rivals. The illusion was widespread that the war was 'necessary', primarily to 'stop' an enemy. But few nations could point to a specific territory which they hoped to secure. France was almost unique in being able to focus on the precise goal of recovering Alsace-Lorraine.

The events which followed the assassination at Sarajevo explain *how* war came about. It is far more difficult to explain *why* war came about. Some factors must obviously be taken into account. The existing alliances trapped their members, and they made it difficult to draw back from the brink of the abyss. The arms race had also accustomed many Europeans to thinking in terms of military solutions. There was a failure of diplomacy: little or no machinery existed for eleventh-hour peacemaking, though it should not be forgotten that conferences, such as that at Algeciras, had been summoned to deal with earlier crises. That no such conference was summoned in 1914 pointed to the lack of a will to peace. Nations, instead, rushed to honour their commitments with an apparent eagerness – all except Italy. Almost all the powers were at war within a fortnight of the Habsburg ultimatum to Serbia. What is difficult to explain is why there existed this apparent readiness to fight.

Marxists have argued that capitalism (and imperialism) made conflict inevitable, since European economies and societies were now based on a fierce competitiveness. Competition was certainly a strong driving force in Europe. There had been competition for colonial empires, competition for markets, and competition in building armed forces, doubtless to the satisfaction of the manufacturers of weaponry. But businessmen as a whole had little reason to welcome war, which would disrupt national economies and international trade. An economic explanation of the outbreak of war in 1914 is by no means convincing. On the other hand, the years of competition had also been years in which a broader nationalism developed steadily. In its simplest form, nationalism meant the desire to be free from foreign control, or the desire to unite one people into one nation. Once these goals had been attained, however, it was not a great step for nationalism to evolve into the desire for national greatness, and into the desire for national supremacy. Such supremacy could readily require a fierce response to alleged insults and humiliations, a response rooted in the conviction that it was 'necessary' to demonstrate the nation's power. It may be argued, therefore, that nationalism drove European nations to war in 1914 – a more aggressive and more virulent nationalism, indeed, than that of which Metternich and his contemporaries had already shown deep suspicion a century earlier.

Article 231 of the Treaty of Versailles in 1919 (the 'War Guilt Clause') appeared to place the blame for the war on 'the aggression of Germany and her allies' (see Section 20.1(c)). Although it was Austria-Hungary which delivered the first ultimatum, the support of Germany was vital to the Habsburgs. Moreover, the German military machine was renowned not only for its killing power, but also for its influence in the government of Germany. The younger Moltke (nephew of the Moltke who had retired in 1888) had succeeded Schlieffen as the Chief of Staff in 1906. Moltke believed that the German invasion of Belgium, in ruthless pursuit of the Schlieffen Plan, was strategically desirable:

> An advance through Belgium would force the French back into their interior. . . . It should be preferred, because there one can count on quicker progress.

This was military thinking, elevating matters of strategy above considerations of the diplomatic repercussions. The existence of the Plan and its rapid implementation both bore witness to the militarism of the Reich. But the military ambition combined with political and economic ambition. Many Germans believed with the Kaiser that Germany should have a world role, similar to that of the British. Many also believed that the basis of Germany's strength should lie in *Mitteleuropa* (Middle Europe), the European heartlands.

The extension of German political and economic supremacy in these heart-lands would further strengthen the Reich, and this supremacy could perhaps be forged during the upheaval of battle. Without the will to war in powerful circles in the German Reich, the Austro-Serbian quarrel might have been localized.

The fact remains, however, that other countries were willing to fight too. War seemed to offer to Nicholas II an opportunity to rally to his monarchy the many dissident elements in Russia, and to enhance tsarist prestige. But Russia also had genuine anxieties about the Balkans. The crushing of Serbia might Germanize the area, since Bulgaria and the Ottoman Empire were pro-German and the Kaiser was building the Berlin-Baghdad Railway. France and Britain, meanwhile, set great store by their national honour and reputations. All believed, of course, that it would be a short war, soon to be resolved around the conference table, after a suitable display of strength. The Austro-Prussian and Franco-Prussian Wars had seemed to demonstrate that modern wars would be sharp and short, and it was a popular illusion in 1914 that the conflict would be 'over by Christmas'. But once the First World War had begun, that too took control over the nations involved in it. Edward Grey, at the British Foreign Office, took a more sober and more realistic view when, on the eve of the British declaration of war, he observed:

The lamps are going out all over Europe; we shall not see them lit again in our lifetime.

The war lasted for four bloody years, and it destroyed much of the Europe of the nineteenth century.

Further Reading

See **Further Reading** for Unit Fifteen.

Bridge, R.F.: *The Coming of the First World War*. Historical Association (London, 1983).
Joll, J.: *The Origins of The First World War*. Longman (Harlow, 1986).
MacIntyre, D.: *The Great War, Causes and Consequences*. Blackie (Glasgow, 1979).
Parkinson, R.: *The Origins of World War One*. Wayland (Hove, 1970).
Petrie, C.: *The Drift to World War, 1900–14*. Ernest Benn (London, 1969).
Thomson, G. M.: *The Twelve Days*. Secker and Warburg (London, 1964).
Trainor, L.: *The Origins of the First World War*. Heinemann (London, 1974).
Turner, L. C. F.: *Origins of the First World War*. Edward Arnold (London, 1970).

Documentary

Assassination at Sarajevo (Jackdaw Wallet). Cape.

Exercises

1. Why did France and Russia make an alliance (Section 17.1), and how were the terms of their agreement, quoted on page 265, important in 1914 (Section 17.4)?
2. Referring to Fig. 17.1 on page 267, trace the development of alliances and ententes in the period 1871 to 1914.

3. Explain to what the cartoon on page 272 refers, and why both Tirpitz and William II could equally well have been drawn by the cartoonist as the dancing sailor.

4. 'A Crescendo of Crises' (Section 17.3). Write paragraphs on *each* of *four* crises (*two* of them concerning the Balkans) in the years 1900–13, showing how *each* crisis had a peaceful outcome.

5. Why was *each* of the following countries apparently willing to go to war in 1914: Austria-Hungary; Germany; Russia; France? How did the history of Europe during the last hundred years suggest that the war would be a short one?

6. Bearing in mind your definition of *imperialism* (Unit Sixteen, Question 2), what did Lenin mean when he called the First World War 'an imperialist war'?

Unit Eighteen

The First World War

18.1 The Failure of the Schlieffen Plan

Germany was at war on two fronts from 3 August 1914. Russian troops invaded East Prussia, advancing on Germany from the east. To the west, the Germans struck towards France through Belgium and, to stiffen the resistance to the Kaiser's army, British troops landed on the continent on 8 August. It seemed essential that, for a quick German victory, the Kaiser's forces should march into Paris within a matter of weeks, in order to close down the Western Front and to turn the whole might of the German war-machine against the Tsar, who was already mobilizing millions of Russian peasants. The Schlieffen Plan provided a formula for just such a German strategy. By-passing the French defensive fortresses along the borders of Lorraine and Alsace, and attacking through Belgium and Luxemburg, the Germans expected to move rapidly into north-eastern France. They would then drive forward, both to the west and to the east of Paris, to encircle both the city and the French front-line troops. This, the Germans assumed optimistically, would cause the French to surrender. And the British, since they had insisted on joining the war, would be persuaded to negotiate a peace.

The Germans began to encounter difficulties even before the end of August. They took Brussels on 20 August, but the British delayed them a few days later at Mons. The Russians won a victory at Frankenau in East Prussia at about the same time. The British were forced to retreat from Mons, and the Russians were routed in a fierce struggle at Tannenberg. Nevertheless the Germans had to commit more troops to the Eastern Front earlier than the High Command would have wished, and progress in the West was clearly slowing down under the harassment of Belgians, British and French. Moltke also became alarmed lest his forces should become fragmented, some to the west of Paris and some to the east of the city. The Schlieffen Plan was therefore modified. Von Kluck's forces on the German right wing were brought closer to the rest of the army (see Fig. 18.1), and any attack on Paris would now have to be launched from the north and east. The Germans reached the River Marne, but the advance had already begun to falter. They crossed the River in September, but a counter-attack by the French General Joffre drove them back almost immediately. In mid-September the Germans dug in along the line of the River Aisne. Their trenches were over 70 miles short of Paris.

The Germans had also been held at Ypres by the end of November, and this prevented them from taking the Channel ports to cut off reinforcements from

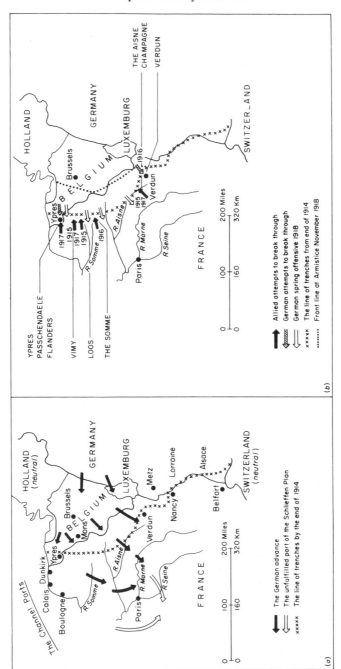

Fig. 18.1 The Western Front (a) The Failure of the Schlieffen Plan (b) the War of Attrition: some major engagements

Britain. The bloodshed had already been horrendous, but all that had been achieved on the Western Front was something near to stalemate. Moltke was dismissed for his failure to bring the German victory which the Schlieffen Plan had appeared to promise, but the Plan had never taken full account of the determination to resist, which both the Belgians and French showed, and of the speed with which British forces went into action. For their part, the French had learned their lessons from Bismarck's wars, and they used their railway system to great advantage in rapidly deploying their forces.

The Russians had also moved more quickly than the Germans had expected. After the Battle of Tannenberg and further struggles around the Masurian Lakes, the Russians were driven from East Prussia. But German troops were needed to help the Habsburgs to stem the Russian offensive in Galicia, and the German war-machine was forced to divide its energies between the various theatres of war. The Habsburgs were not forceful allies and, in these early stages of the war, Austria-Hungary found it was by no means easy even to crush Serbia. By the end of 1914 it seemed that almost everywhere the nations had now become committed to a long struggle. In the west, the war of movement had come to a halt, and the war of attrition had begun. Pulverized by artillery, mown down by machine-guns and entangled in barbed wire, the soldiers in the many miles of trenches on the Western Front were about to endure savage and horrendous warfare on an unprecedented scale. Far from being 'over by Christmas', the war had only just begun to show its true nature.

THE GREAT WAR OF 19——.

Major. "It's pretty certain we shall have to fight 'em in the course of the next few years."
Subaltern. "Well, let's hope it'll come between the polo and the huntin'."

Fig. 18.2 Punch *made a forecast of the war in June 1909, but the war much outlasted any polo and huntin'*

18.2   The Eastern Front and the Defeat of Russia

Within a month of the start of the war in 1914, Britain, France and Russia signed the Pact of London, agreeing not to make peace separately. Geography nevertheless determined that they would fight separate wars, Britain and France mainly in the West, Russia in the East. The Ottoman Empire became involved in the war on the side of the Central Powers in November 1914 and, in 1915, the British attempted to open a supply route to Russia through the Dardanelles, seeking now to open the Straits, which in the past they had so often wanted closed. But the attempt did not succeed. British and Australasian troops landed on the Gallipoli peninsula in April 1915, and they persevered in the enterprise throughout the year, but the troops had to be evacuated in January 1916. Like many campaigns of the war, the expedition was a costly failure. Russia remained to a large extent isolated from its Allies, almost always desperately short of supplies, though not of manpower.

The first Russian onslaught on East Prussia in 1914 caused such panic among the Germans that they recalled General Paul von Hindenburg from retirement to take charge of the Eastern Front, assisted by General Ludendorff. The Russians had a million and a half men in the field, but Hindenburg and Ludendorff turned the tide. For the Russians, the war on the Eastern Front became a long and costly struggle to keep the Central Powers – mainly the Germans – at bay. In August 1915 the retreating Russians had to abandon Warsaw and, shortly afterwards, they were driven from Poland, which the Germans proceeded to declare independent. In 1916 the Russians nevertheless mounted an offensive, responding to an appeal by their Allies that they should distract the Germans from the Western Front. General Brusilov launched the offensive in June, and he won early successes against the Austro-Hungarian forces. Rumania was sufficiently encouraged by his progress rashly to declare war on the Central Powers, but Hindenburg rushed German reinforcements to the Galician front, and once more turned the tide. The Tsar lost half a million men – killed, wounded or taken prisoner. The Russians again retreated, and the Germans also swept into Rumania and entered Bucharest, its capital, before the end of the year.

The succession of defeats, the heavy casualties, and the apparent hopelessness of the war against far better equipped German forces, increased the discontent within Russia. In February 1917 Nicholas II was overthrown. The Tsar had unwisely made himself the Commander-in-Chief of the Russian forces in 1915, but he had as little to show for his military leadership as for his political leadership (see Section 14.4). For a time the Provisional Government, which took over from Nicholas in Russia, continued the war, and Kerensky fondly hoped that a victory would increase his prestige. A new offensive in the summer of 1917 was successful only momentarily. The Russian forces began to disintegrate, and the Bolsheviks increased their propaganda for peace. In October 1917 Kerensky and the Provisional Government were overthrown by a Bolshevik coup, and Russian resistance was virtually at

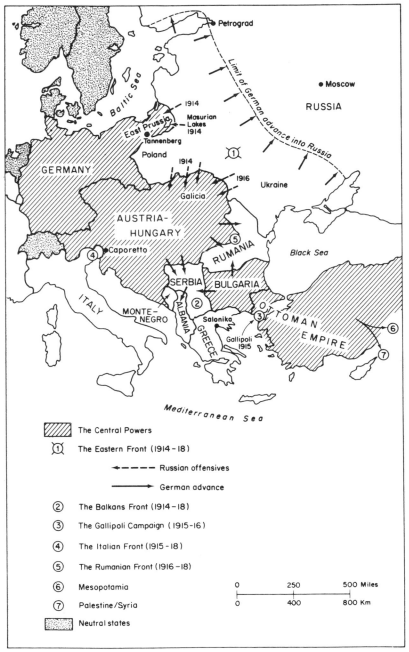

Fig. 18.3 The Theatres of War in Eastern Europe

an end. An armistice was signed in December, and peace was formally concluded in the *Treaty of Brest-Litovsk* in March 1918 (see Section 19.2(*d*)).

Russia had been soundly defeated, and the war had helped both to bring down the tsarist system and to bring into power the world's first communist government (see Section 19.i). At Brest-Litovsk, the Germans exacted a heavy price for the peace. The war on the Eastern Front had ended with German forces deep inside Russia, almost at the gates of Petrograd though still distant from Moscow, and already in control of the Ukraine. Perhaps more important for the Germans, however, was that they could now transfer forces to the Western Front, where the outcome had yet to be decided. In preventing this for more than three years, 1 700 000 Russians had died.

18.3   The Western Front and the Defeat of Germany

(*a*) 1914–15

By the end of 1914 General Falkenhayn, Moltke's successor, badly needed a new plan. The failure of the Schlieffen Plan left both sides firmly entrenched, but with little immediate hope of breaking through the enemy defences (see Section 18.1 and Fig. 18.1). Advances were now measured in yards rather than in miles. Since it seemed impossible to outmanoeuvre the enemy, it became an end in itself to kill him. The armies on the Western Front did not lack killing-power, but they now searched for new decisive weapons. In 1915 the Germans resorted to the use of poison gas and, a year later, the British sent tanks into battle. Meanwhile, the trenches stretched from the Belgian Coast to Switzerland, and the methods were constantly refined whereby the enemy could be maimed and slaughtered. The trenches were also constantly replenished with new men – human sacrifices with whom the generals dreamed of achieving the breakthrough, a breakthrough which remained stubbornly out of reach.

Equally stubbornly, the generals planned and ordered one attack after another. In 1915 the British attacked at Neuve Chapelle, Aubers Ridge and Loos, and their French Allies attacked at Champagne and Vimy, and then at Champagne and Vimy again. The sum total of all their effort was no more than to drive the Germans back into new trenches, and to conquer a mile or two of devastated ground. The Germans attacked near the northern end of the line of trenches, and fought the second bloody battle at Ypres – again to no avail. Searching for new ideas, the British opened the Gallipoli Front (see page 282), and they replaced their Commander-in-Chief on the Western Front, substituting Douglas Haig for John French. It was not an imaginative note on which to end the year 1915. Haig, Joffre and Falkenhayn entered 1916 with hardly any plan at all, except to send their troops on suicidal missions against the enemy trenches.

Fig. 18.4 A British propaganda cartoon dropped in Germany by balloon during the First World War. It suggests suffering by the German people under the burden of the militarism of Crown Prince William and Hindenburg

(b) 1916

Falkenhayn came up with what served for a Plan in 1916. In February the Germans began the massive bombardment of Verdun. Hoping to lure the French into its defence against a massive onslaught, Falkenhayn thought that he could 'bleed the French white' and then, perhaps, march forward towards Paris over the corpses. The French defence of Verdun was entrusted to Henri Pétain, who vowed: 'they shall not pass'. The battle raged around the city for some four months, and the Germans slaughtered over 300 000 Frenchmen. Almost 300 000 Germans were also lost in the action: the bleeding was not confined to the French. Falkenhayn decided to abandon the assault.

As the struggle for Verdun ended, a new major offensive was launched by the British on 1 July – the Battle of the Somme. Haig, too, had devised what served as a Plan, and he wrote to his wife on the eve of battle: 'I feel that every step in my plan has been taken with divine help.' In his diary, he observed:

The weather report is favourable for tomorrow. With God's help I feel hopeful. The wire has never been so well cut.

But any hope of a breakthrough had already been jeopardized by a massive artillery bombardment of the German positions, blasting innumerable craters to be filled with rainwater, which would soon make the Somme a sea of clinging mud. Haig's Intelligence Officer was no more than realistic when he commented:

> We do not expect any great advance. . . . We are fighting primarily to wear down the German armies and nation.

It was on the Somme that the British introduced their tanks. They lumbered forward at little more than two miles an hour, only to stick fast in the oozing mud or, if they could move at all, to trundle off in the wrong direction. Haig stuck to his 'plan' for almost five months, hurling his men against the German lines. An Australian lieutenant described these men:

> We are lousy, stinking, ragged, unshaven, sleepless. I have one puttee, a dead man's helmet, another dead man's gas protector, a dead man's bayonet. My tunic is rotten with other men's blood, and partly spattered with a comrade's brains.

There was no shortage of dead men. When the 'plan' was finally abandoned, the British and their Allies had lost well over half a million troops. By the end of the year, Asquith had resigned, and Lloyd George took office as Prime Minister in Britain, the man, it was thought, to win the war.

The French and Germans meanwhile re-shuffled their military commanders. Joffre gave way to Nivelle, and Falkenhayn gave way to Ludendorff, fresh from his successes on the Eastern Front.

(c) 1917

Nivelle's plan for victory was to break through the German lines on the River Aisne. His campaign gained less than a mile, and the French lost over 100 000 men. French troops mutinied, and Nivelle was quickly replaced by Pétain. While Pétain, with difficulty, restored French morale, executing more than 50 ringleaders of the mutiny in the process, the burden of the war on the Western Front fell mainly on the British and the troops of the British Empire. The Canadians were particularly prominent in a successful assault on Vimy Ridge, which drove the Germans back for several miles. But there was still no prospect of a major breakthrough. The Germans built new defences east of the Somme, the Hindenburg Line, which even an assault by tanks, now more expertly used at Cambrai late in 1917, could do little more than dent.

The major offensive in 1917, however, was launched by Haig at Ypres, in an effort to reach the German submarine bases in the Belgian ports. Once more the attack was bogged down in mud, and once more there was heavy slaughter, especially around the village of Passchendaele. Some half a million men were killed to no avail, almost equal numbers of British and Germans. By the end of

Fig. 18.5 A German strategic conference in 1917 – Hindenburg, the Kaiser and Ludendorff. The problem was always the same: how to break through the enemy lines

1917 the line of trenches had hardly moved from the position of three years earlier.

The most important change in 1917 was that the USA had declared war on Germany in April, incensed by the activities of German submarines, and linked with the British cause, partly by emotional ties but also by economic interests. President Wilson was further incensed by German intrigue in Mexico. Germany's Foreign Minister, Artur Zimmerman, had sent a telegram to the German Minister in Mexico, urging him to pursue an alliance with the Mexicans. The British intercepted the Zimmerman Telegram and quickly made its contents known in Washington. The overthrow of the Tsar in Russia also made it possible for the Americans to claim that it was now a war 'to make the world safe for democracy'. Thus, Wilson went to war against Germany, in spite of his earlier election campaign to keep the United States neutral. It took time to raise US forces, however, and they made little impact on the Western Front during 1917. Nevertheless the first Americans under General Pershing had arrived in June, and this influx of new troops seemed certain to be a serious threat to the Germans, if they could not now end the war quickly.

(d) 1918

The defeat of Russia enabled the Germans to strengthen their forces in the West (see Section 18.2). In Germany itself supplies were running low as the result of the Allied naval blockade, and it was now essential to strike before it became too late. In March 1918 Ludendorff launched the Spring Offensive. The assault was frenzied, spearheaded by specially trained stormtroopers. The Germans smashed through the British lines on the Somme, then broke through in Flanders. They dislodged the French from the River Aisne, and advanced on the Marne, until Paris was almost within reach of the Kaiser's artillery. At last, the Allies appointed a single supreme commander, and entrusted to Ferdinand Foch the task of halting Ludendorff. As had happened in 1914, the German advance was checked on the Marne, and the Spring Offensive came to a standstill. When they had finally made a breakthrough, the Germans had neither the manpower nor the equipment to sustain it.

Foch immediately went over to the offensive, and the Germans began to retreat. They were now prevented from digging-in in trenches, which had enabled them to hold on in the past. The Allied advance made effective use of tanks, and American manpower began to make itself felt. The Germans fell back along the whole line from the Channel coast to Verdun. By the end of September Ludendorff had to inform Berlin that he could no longer stem the Allied advance. A month later, he resigned and took refuge in Sweden.

It was not only on the Western Front that the Central Powers were collapsing. Germany's allies were in trouble, and in Germany itself the Kaiser's regime was crumbling amid shortages, widespread discontent, and violent protests (see Section 10.2). There seemed to be no alternative but to sue for peace, and an armistice was signed to take effect at eleven o'clock on the morning of 11 November.

When the fighting ceased, German troops had been driven from most of France, but they still held almost all of Belgium and Luxemburg. German soil

Fig. 18.6 The ruins of the Cathedral of Notre Dame at Albert on the Somme. France and Belgium were loud in their demands for reparation for such devastation at the end of the First World War

had not been invaded, and the illusion was later fostered in Germany by Ludendorff, Hitler and those who sought to profit from it, that Germany had not been defeated at all, but had been 'stabbed in the back' by malcontents at home and a conspiracy of Jews and socialists. They could not have invented a more absurd epitaph for the millions who had suffered and died during the four years of horror on the Western Front.

18.4 The Land War in Other Theatres

Germany's overseas possessions were attacked by the Allies almost as soon as the war began in Europe. Those in *the Pacific* were overrun quickly, mainly by the Japanese. Those in *Africa* were able to offer a stiffer resistance, but the Kamerun, Togoland, and South West Africa fell before the end of 1915, the last of them to South African troops. German East Africa was also eventually overrun, although General Lettow-Vorbeck kept a German resistance alive in Africa until the war had ended in Europe.

Apart from fighting off Russian attacks on Galicia, Austria-Hungary's main war effort was directed towards *the Balkans*. It took more than a year to overcome Serbia, but Bulgaria joined the Habsburgs in 1915, and the Allied foothold in the Balkans was limited to the port of Salonika. A declaration of war on Austria-Hungary by Rumania in 1916 opened a new front, but Rumanian forces were soon routed. The Rumanians sued for peace, but rejoined the war in November 1918 so as to share in the fruits of the Allied victory. Meanwhile, Greece joined the Allies in 1917 and took part in the Allied advance northwards from Salonika during the closing stages of the war. The successes which the Habsburgs had earlier achieved in the Balkans had been won only with difficulty, and with the help of their allies, not least the troops sent from Germany. When those troops were withdrawn in 1918, Serbia was liberated by the Allies, and the military setbacks helped to hasten the crumbling of the Habsburg Empire (see Section 13.5).

Yet another front was opened in 1915 when *Italy* joined the Allies, lured into the conflict by the promise of gains dangled in the Treaty of London (see Section 12.3(*a*)). The Italian war effort was directed to invading the Habsburg Empire from the south-west, but no great headway was made and, when German reinforcements arrived on the front, the Italians were routed at Caporetto. Towards the end of the war the Italians were able to make a modest advance, though still on their own soil.

The Ottoman Empire, rather like Russia, fought its own war, somewhat cut off from its allies among the Central Powers. The Turks thwarted the Allied attempt to force open the Straits (see page 282), and they battled against Russia in the Caucasus. Fronts were also opened in Mesopotamia, where the British had forces to protect their oil supplies, and in Palestine, where the British co-operated with the Arabs to drive out the Turks. The Turks were defeated in Palestine in 1917 and driven northwards, to be defeated again in

Syria in 1918. By the end of October the Sultan, Mohammed VI, was ready to sue for peace.

The Central Powers had thus been defeated, or driven back, on every front, except for Germany's earlier victory over Russia on the Eastern Front. Bulgaria was the first to make peace, in September 1918. The Ottoman Empire followed. Austria-Hungary ended the war on 4 November, Germany, a week later.

18.5   The War at Sea and in the Air

The defeat of the Central Powers, and especially of Germany, their power-house, owed a good deal to the Germans' inability to dominate the seas. The High Seas fleet which Tirpitz had fashioned (see page 161) proved a great disappointment to the Kaiser. At first the Germans concentrated on attacking the enemy with lone raiders and squadrons. They bombarded Scarborough but, at the end of 1914, German raiders had been sunk in the Pacific, and a squadron had been smashed off the Falkland Islands. Early in 1915 a squadron in the North Sea escaped back to port from an encounter with the British near the Dogger Bank. Not until 1916 did Germany seek a showdown with the British fleet, the culmination of the pre-war naval race between the two powers. Between them, Germany and Britain put some 250 warships into the North Sea in May 1916, 44 of them dreadnoughts, of which Britain had 28 and Germany 16. The engagement took place off Jutland, and its outcome was indecisive, but on 1 June the German fleet headed back to port. The British had lost 14 ships, the Germans 11, and 6000 British sailors were killed to Germany's 2500. Neither navy had convincingly demonstrated its superiority, but the Kaiser never risked his High Seas fleet again.

Yet Germany nevertheless caused grave problems for the Allies by the use of U-boats (submarines). Britain depended heavily on supplies from abroad and on moving its troops about the world by sea, and U-boats took a heavy toll of its shipping. In 1915 a German submarine sank the *Lusitania*, a passenger liner. Over a hundred Americans were among the thousand who died in the disaster, but submarines were too important to the German war effort for their use to be seriously curtailed, in spite of vigorous American protests. The toll of Allied shipping mounted, and by early 1917 the Germans saw 'unrestricted submarine warfare' as their key to victory. It was a forlorn hope. It played a major part in provoking the USA into declaring war on Germany (see page 287), and it thus had grave diplomatic consequences. But the weapon itself became less effective and less damaging to the British war effort. Counter-weapons were invented, such as depth charges. New technology was developed for detecting submerged U-boats, and nets and mines were laid to trap them. Moreover, when Lloyd George insisted on adopting the convoy system (to protect merchant and passenger ships with armed escorts), British losses fell dramatically. By the end of 1917 the U-boat menace had become much less deadly.

Unable to control the seas, Germany could not throttle Britain nor prevent the movement of British troops to the theatres of war. The British, on the other hand, were able to impose an ever-tightening blockade on Germany. The German colonies had quickly been cut off from reinforcements from the Fatherland, and Germany itself could get no supplies from its colonies and very few from anywhere else, except from its conquests in eastern Europe. By the autumn of 1918 the stranglehold on Germany had become extremely damaging.

Aircraft were also used in the First World War. German Zeppelins cruised in the skies, enormous in size, and useful both for observation of the enemy and for bombing missions. As a weapon of terror they were matchless, but their size and slowness combined with their inflammability to restrict their usefulness. Small balloons were much used for observation on the military fronts, but the development of light aeroplanes, armed with machine-guns, added a new spectacle to European warfare in gladiatorial combats between daring pilots. Such conflicts did little to determine the outcome of the war, however, but they provided one more opportunity for the toll of human lives to mount as the First World War went on remorselessly.

18.6 Defeat without Victory

Explaining the need to involve the USA in the war in April 1917, President Wilson told Congress:

> It is a fearful thing to lead this great peaceful people into war, into the most terrible and disastrous of all wars – Civilization itself seeming to be in the balance. But the right is more precious than peace, and we shall fight for the things . . . nearest to our hearts – for democracy, for the right . . . to have a voice in [one's] own government, for the rights and liberties of all nations, for a universal domination of right by . . . a concert of free peoples.

Wilson identified 'the Imperial German Government' as his country's main enemy and, when the guns at last fell silent on 11 November 1918, that government was fast collapsing. There was similar disorder in the crumbling Habsburg Empire, and Russia too was in upheaval. Vast areas of France and Belgium, and other parts of Europe, had been devastated, and European 'civilization' itself had produced a degree of barbarism almost without parallel.

The defeat of the Central Powers was beyond doubt. In the end, Germany had lacked the resources to resist so many and such determined Allied Powers, fighting as it was on numerous fronts, with partners who shared in Germany's suffering but who made little contribution to the winning of the war. For most of Europe, it was a peace of exhaustion. The nations were depleted in man-power, burdened with debt, and sadly demoralized. Only the USA and Japan emerged from the war relatively unscathed. The 'victorious' powers in Europe had suffered deep wounds, from which recovery was sure to be slow, and the 'defeated' nations had been plunged into near chaos. A wave of influenza, sweeping across the world and claiming six million more lives, added to Europe's misery.

Fig. 18.7 Wartime propaganda helped to strengthen the determination to fight, but it would not be easy to set it aside when the war was over. A British view of Kaiser William II, 1917

In January 1918 both Wilson in the USA and Lloyd George in Britain had at last made some attempt precisely to define what the Allies were fighting for (see Section 17.5). There was a broad similarity between Wilson's Fourteen Points and the British War Aims (see Section 18.7, opposite). The self-determination of European peoples, allowing them the right to choose their own governments and national boundaries, and some system whereby to prevent any recurrence of war, were among the general guidelines. And they agreed on certain points of detail: Alsace-Lorraine must be restored to France, Belgium restored, Poland made free, and Italians united with Italy. The Austro-Hungarian Empire was to be broken up; but the problem of Russia was more difficult, and both Wilson and Lloyd George were evasive on how that should be dealt with. They agreed, however, on the need for some sort of international machinery to prevent war, and on the desirability of reducing the level of armaments. Innumerable questions nevertheless still remained to be answered, and the ending of the fighting was bound to be the prelude to the complicated problem of peacemaking.

The war was enormously costly in human life. The total dead numbered over eight and a half million (see Section 18.7, below). Millions more had been maimed and broken. Belligerent governments had spent more than £40 000 000 000 in pursuit of victory, and the cost of devastation was incalculable. From such a holocaust Europe was certain to emerge much changed.

18.7   Appendix: British War Aims; Wilson's Fourteen Points; The Dead

British War Aims outlined by Lloyd George, January 1918:
1. The restoration and independence of Belgium
2. The restoration of Serbia and of the occupied lands of the Allies
3. The restoration of Alsace-Lorraine to France
4. 'Russia can only be saved by her own people'
5. An independent Poland
6. Self-government to the nationalities of Austria-Hungary
7. The union of all Italians to Italy
8. Justice for Rumanians
9. Separate national conditions for the subjects of the Ottoman Empire
10. Self-determination for the German colonies
11. Reparation for injuries in violation of international law
12. The sanctity of treaties to be respected
13. An international organization to limit armaments and reduce the risk of war

Wilson's *Fourteen Points* outlined in January 1918:
1. Diplomacy and treaties to be open
2. Freedom of navigation on the seas
3. The removal of economic barriers between nations
4. The reduction of armaments
5. Colonial problems to be settled with reference to the interests of colonial peoples
6. The evacuation of, and goodwill towards, Russia
7. The restoration of Belgium
8. The restoration of France and the French recovery of Alsace-Lorraine
9. Italian frontiers along the lines of nationality
10. Autonomous development for the peoples of Austria-Hungary
11. Territorial integrity for the Balkan states
12. Autonomous development for the peoples of the Ottoman Empire, and free passage through the Dardanelles
13. An independent Poland
14. An association of nations

The Dead in the First World War

Allies:		Central Powers:	
Russia	1 700 000	Germany	1 773 700
France	1 357 800	Austria-Hungary	1 200 000
Britain/British Empire	908 371	Ottoman Empire	325 000
Italy	650 000		
Rumania	335 706		
USA	116 516		

Total of all belligerent countries:　8 528 831

Further Reading

Gibbons, S. R. and Morican, P.: *World War One.* Longman (Harlow, 1965).
Hawkins, F.: *From Ypres to Cambrai.* Elmfield Press (Leeds, 1973).
Musman, R.: *The First World War.* Chatto and Windus (London, 1968).
Sellman, R. R.: *The First World War.* Methuen (London, 1961).
Taylor, A. J. P.: *The First World War.* Penguin (Harmondsworth, 1966).

Documentary and Maps

The First World War (Exploring History Kit). Macmillan.
Remak, J.: *The First World War: Causes, Conduct, Consequences.* John Wiley (Chichester, 1971).
Sanderson, M.: *The First World War.* HMSO (London, 1987).
Woodget, D.: *Sketch Map History of World War I.* Longman (Harlow, 1976).

Exercises

1. Referring to the maps on page 280, show what were (*a*).the political importance of the Schlieffen Plan, and (*b*) the military importance of its failure.
2. Making use of evidence drawn from Section 18.3, write an account of your experiences in the trenches by the end of 1917 as an ordinary soldier of any one of the warring armies.
3. Why were the Germans defeated on the Western Front during 1918?
4. Explain what you understand by *propaganda*. How do the illustrations on pages 285, 292 and 297 provide examples of propaganda?
5. How do this Unit and Fig. 18.3 support the argument that Germany 'lacked the resources to resist so many . . . Allied powers . . . on numerous fronts, with partners . . . who made little contribution to the winning of the war' (page 291)?
6. In stating their war aims, on what points did Lloyd George and Woodrow Wilson (*a*) agree, and (*b*) differ (Appendix, page 293)?
7. What part did Russia play in the First World War (Section 18.2)? Read Sections 19.1 and 19.2(*d*), and then extend your answer to show how the First World War and its outcome affected events in Russia.

Russia 1917–41: Marxism-Leninism and Stalinism

19.1 Russia in 1917

(a) The Provisional Government

The first revolution of 1917 in Russia overthrew the regime of Nicholas II (see Section 14.4(e) and 18.2). At the crucial moment when strikes and demonstrations occurred in Petrograd in February 1917, the Tsar was deserted by his troops. Whereas they had crushed strikes and riots in the past, most of the Petrograd garrison remained inactive, sympathizing with the crowds who pelted the Tsar's police with lumps of ice. In Trotsky's view this was the key element which turned the demonstrations into a successful revolution against the tsarist system. Trotsky wrote of the soldiers:

> [They] had not the slightest feeling of attachment to the monarchy. They did not want to fight with the Germans, and still less with the Petrograd workers. They hated the ruling class of the capital.

Most of the troops were conscripted peasants and workers who saw themselves as fodder for Russia's war effort against the Kaiser's Germany. They had little of the traditional loyalty to the tsar of the professional soldiers, and the First World War seemed less important to them than the settlement of problems within Russia. Indeed they had little reason to expect victory in the war, and every reason to expect to be killed when they were sent to the front. It was not surprising, therefore, that they greeted the demonstrations with 'relief and rapture', and that:

> thus [there] dawned upon the earth the destruction of the Romanov monarchy.

Yet almost no preparations had been made for the government of Russia without the Romanovs. The revolution had occurred suddenly, without planning. A Provisional Government was hastily set up, consisting of a committee of some of the members of the Fourth Duma, led by Prince Lvov.

From the outset the Provisional Government was aware that it had only limited authority. It made considerable progress in liberalizing Russia, in freeing political prisoners and allowing freedom of speech and of the press. But major problems, such as that of redistributing the land to the peasantry (and the difficult question of compensation for the landowners), were generally shelved until such time as a constituent assembly could be elected, and a new constitution drafted. In the meantime the war continued against the Central Powers, since the members of the Provisional Government believed they had obligations to their Allies, and some of the members, such as Alexander Kerensky, hoped to gain prestige by winning victories which Nicholas II had been unable to win. Hardly any members of the Government had experience of ruling, and the problems they inherited were enormous. They were also faced with the consequences of their own liberalism, for political opponents were given the freedom to attack the Government.

It seemed likely that Russia was about to catch up with western Europe in establishing some sort of liberal democracy. Josef Stalin was among the Bolsheviks who returned to Petrograd from exile in Siberia in March 1917; and at that time, *Pravda*, the Bolshevik newspaper, was inclined to welcome the revolution and to encourage the Provisional Government. In Marxist terms, it seemed that this was Russia's 'bourgeois revolution', which would create a democracy and promote capitalist economic development. Most of the Bolsheviks in Petrograd believed that this was an essential prelude to the proletarian revolution which, on some probably distant day, would establish socialism. In April Lenin returned to Petrograd from exile in the west. He promptly denounced the Provisional Government, and demanded both an immediate peace and the immediate redistribution of land to the peasants. In his *April Theses*, he argued that the bourgeois phase could be cut short, and that Russia could go straight on to the proletarian revolution. The Petrograd Bolsheviks, including Stalin, were sceptical, but Lenin painstakingly won over a majority of them, and he received strong support from Leon Trotsky (who had not previously been a Bolshevik), when he too arrived in Russia from exile in the USA. It was one thing to agree on the principle of a second revolution, but to achieve the revolution needed planning and organization. Lenin's conviction grew that the soviets could be made the instrument of the second revolution.

When the Provisional Government took power, the Petrograd Soviet of deputies, representing workers, peasants and soldiers, also began to meet regularly (see page 225). The first intention of the Soviet was to keep a watchful eye on the Government, to ensure that it did not neglect the interests of the masses. It issued its own newspaper, *Izvestia*, and soviets were quickly set up elsewhere, and then linked in regional and national congresses. Broadly speaking, the Provisional Government tended to represent the middle classes, and the soviets represented the masses. But comparatively few members of the soviets had any intention of overthrowing the Government of Lvov. Nevertheless they put pressure on that Government, so that in the spring of 1917 it recruited more socialist members and made some attempt to move closer to the people. Kerensky was a member both of the Government and of the Petrograd Soviet. In the first cabinet, he was the Minister of Justice, but he became the Minister of War in May, and replaced Lvov as Prime Minister in

July. Kerensky's intention was to bring about a liberal democracy in Russia. He rejoiced in the revolution which had overthrown the Tsar, and declared:

> Our slogan shall be 'liberty, equality, fraternity'. In the name of these things the great miracle has happened, the miracle fashioned out of the blood and sufferings of generations.

Lenin, however, offered a different slogan, and demanded 'Bread, Peace and Land'. The Bolsheviks worked industriously to win majorities in the Petrograd Soviet and other soviets, and when the majorities began to be achieved, Lenin produced a further slogan: 'All Power to the Soviets'.

Kerensky constantly argued that Russia must continue the war; that the members of the Provisional Government were 'merely guardians' of power until a constituent assembly could be elected on a wide franchise, and that major problems, such as that concerning 'land', must be postponed until Russia had a properly-elected government. The war continued to take its toll of Russian lives (see Section 18.2). The constituent assembly was postponed several times as the Government grappled with the problem of elections in such a vast country where little electoral machinery existed. The peasants

Fig. 19.1 The Bolsheviks consistently condemned the war of 1914–18 as an imperialist war. This Bolshevik poster showed War, the Church and the Aristocracy riding on the shoulders of the masses

waited impatiently for that share of the land which they believed was rightly theirs. Frustration grew, especially when Kerensky, like the Tsar, called for patience, greater effort, increased productivity, and low wages, so that profits might generate capital for future development. It seemed to many Russians that the Bolsheviks offered a more urgent policy to redress their grievances. But even the Bolsheviks were moving too slowly for some Russians. In July there was an uprising in Petrograd which claimed 400 lives (the worst bloodshed of the year), and which the Government, the Soviet, and the Bolsheviks, had all been unable to prevent. The Government, however, seized the opportunity to arrest Bolshevik agitators, and Lenin fled to Finland.

A new problem faced the Government in August. General Kornilov had his own ideas for dealing with agitators, and he intended to move loyal troops into Petrograd and to hang all the trouble-makers. The workers paralysed Kornilov's communications, and his plans came to nothing. But Kerensky lost support over the Kornilov episode since, at least in its early stages, he had appeared to encourage the General's scheme. Kerensky's government was now in increasing difficulties and, in a desperate effort to rally support, the Prime Minister summoned in quick succession a right-wing State Conference, a left-wing Democratic Conference, and a Council of the Republic (of intellectuals). Elections for the Constituent Assembly were also announced for December. The continuation of the war and the continued postponement of land redistribution counted for more with the masses than did Kerensky's concern for constitutional manoeuvres. His own liberalism had led to the freeing of the Bolsheviks he had arrested and, by October, his power was slipping away.

(b) The Bolshevik Coup

The Bolsheviks began to dominate the Petrograd Soviet during September, and Trotsky was appointed President of the Soviet. In October the Bolsheviks had a majority when the Congress of Northern Soviets assembled and, when the Congress set up a Military Revolutionary Committee, Trotsky was appointed to lead it. By this time the Bolsheviks had also won considerable successes in municipal elections in cities such as Moscow. Lenin had returned to Petrograd from Finland on 10 October, though he insisted on remaining in hiding. It was already doubtful whether the Bolsheviks did not have more authority in Petrograd than did Kerensky and, indeed, Lenin claimed that the Bolsheviks were already in control, arguing his case in a pamphlet, *Can the Bolsheviks Retain State Power?* Kerensky, however, had not yet been driven away, and some dramatic event seemed to be called for. The timing of the event was decided by the fact that the All-Russian Congress of Soviets, a national meeting of delegates from soviets throughout the country, was due to meet late on 25 October. It was not certain that the Bolsheviks would have a majority in this Congress, and Lenin was anxious to show the delegates that the Bolsheviks were in complete control of the capital. He wrote excitedly on the

Fig. 19.2 Some of the troops of the Provisional Government in the Winter Palace in Petrograd after the abdication of Nicholas II, 1917

evening of 24 October:

> We must at all costs, this very evening, this very night, arrest the government, having first disarmed the officer cadets. . . . We must not wait. We may lose everything.

This was what Trotsky and the Military Revolutionary Committee were waiting to hear. At two o'clock on the morning of 25 October, they went into action, seizing key positions in Petrograd. By mid-afternoon, Lenin was no longer in hiding, and he told the Petrograd Soviet:

> Now begins a new era in the history of Russia. . . . One of our routine tasks is to end the war at once. . . . We shall win the peasants' trust with a single decree which will annihilate landed property. . . . We have the strength of a mass organization that will triumph over everything and bring the proletariat to world revolution.

But Kerensky's government still held the Winter Palace and, at nine o'clock that evening, the *Aurora* fired the shot to signal the start of operations against these headquarters. Eisenstein, for the Russian film industry, later represented a dramatic attack on the Palace but, in fact, it was taken easily. Neither at the Palace nor elsewhere did the Bolsheviks meet significant opposition, and the coup was almost bloodless. Kerensky had already escaped in a car of the United States embassy, and other ministers were arrested without difficulty. When the All-Russian Congress of Soviets met at eleven o'clock, Lenin informed the delegates that the Bolsheviks were now ruling in their name. 'All Power to the Soviets' turned out in practice to mean 'All Power to the Bolsheviks'. On 26 October,* the Congress agreed to the appointment of a council of ministers, the Soviet of People's Commissars (Sovnarcom), of which Lenin was the Chairman and in effect the Prime Minister. Trotsky became Commissar for Foreign Affairs, and Stalin was Commissar for Nationalities.

What was remarkable about the Bolshevik coup was the general absence of resistance to it. It took a week's fighting to gain control of Moscow, and there were local struggles elsewhere. Kerensky himself made a feeble attempt to recapture Petrograd, which ended in a minor skirmish when he could raise only a few hundred troops. But the Bolsheviks' rivals, KDs, SRs and Mensheviks, seemed to have been paralysed (for parties in Russia, see Fig. 14.3). The elections to the Constituent Assembly were allowed to continue, however. The Bolsheviks won some 10 million votes, the SRs over 17 million, while the KDs collected almost 2 million and the Mensheviks rather fewer. The Assembly met in January 1918, though the KDs, as a bourgeois party, were disqualified. and excluded. The 175 Bolshevik delegates were supported by 40 left-wing SRs, but they were still opposed by over 300 SRs. After only brief hesitation, the Bolshevik government declared the Assembly unnecessary, and dismissed it. The Congress of Soviets, it was asserted, was an adequate parliament. The election to the Constituent Assembly was the only free election which Russians have been allowed. They gave a majority to the SRs, but it may be argued with some justification that the SRs were neither a coherent party nor united behind a coherent policy: they were certainly given no opportunity to show whether they could have formed an effective government. The vote for the KDs, although not necessarily the sum total of the support which Kerensky might have gained in the Assembly, hardly suggested that Russians as a whole regretted his departure.

In the All-Russian Congress of Soviets, the Bolsheviks, it had turned out, had a wafer-thin majority, but that was enough for them to consolidate their grip on all the organs of power. Much of the parliamentary authority of the Congress was delegated to a Presidium (standing committee), which the Bolsheviks controlled. They also took control of local soviets, the instruments for municipal and district government. By the middle of 1918, when the last left-wing SRs were outlawed, Russia was a one-party state, with the Bolsheviks exercising the 'dictatorship of the proletariat' – a dictatorship on behalf of the proletariat, for the purpose of carrying out the socialist transformation of the country. In 1918, the Bolsheviks adopted the name 'Communists'. All power in Russia now rested with the Communist Party, and in particular with its leader, Vladimir Lenin. Lenin's adaptations of Marxism to fit the special circumstances in Russia (Marxism-Leninism) had brought to power the world's first communist government, but problems and contradictions remained. Russia had all but by-passed the bourgeois revolution which, Marx

---

* The dates in this Unit have so far been according to the old Russian calendar. Subsequent dates are those of the rest of Europe, which the Bolsheviks adopted.

had argued, would unwittingly prepare the way for the communist revolution. As J. Carmichael put it, Lenin had:

> replaced the traditional Marxist formula that . . . economics determines politics by the Leninist formula . . . that political power may succeed in determining economics.

Fig. 19.3 Lenin (wearing cap and with his overcoat slung over his shoulders), photographed in Red Square, Moscow, May 1919

19.2   Russia under Lenin 1917–24

(a) Promises and Contradictions

Only loyal members of the Communist Party were interested in ideology, in the writings of Marx and Lenin's adaptations from them. Most of the Russians who had supported the Bolsheviks wanted active reforming government, and the delivery of what appeared to have been promised: Bread, Peace and Land – a higher standard of living, peace with the Central Powers, and the allocation of more land to the peasantry. Having tasted freedom during 1917, many Russians were also eager to keep it. The Bolsheviks certainly intended to be active. Within days of seizing power, they began to issue a flood of decrees. The Decree on Land began the process of transferring to the poor the lands of the monarchy, the Church, and the estate owners. The Decree on Peace prepared the way for negotiations with Germany. Other decrees ordered a comprehensive system of social insurance, and the nationalization of banking, foreign trade, and major industries. Mortgages were cancelled; private inheritance and the private possession of land in towns were forbidden. There was little government machinery, however, with which to carry out grand plans, and the Russia the Bolsheviks had taken over had already been disrupted by the war and by revolution. The economy was on the rocks, and the new upheavals made conditions worse. To deal with the problems of rampant inflation, the Bolsheviks repeated the mistakes of former governments by printing more money. Workers seized control of their factories, often bringing them to a standstill for lack of managerial skills. Peasants seized possession of land. Soaring prices, shortages of all sorts, and administrative confusion, led to speculation and black-marketeering and a plague of banditry and anarchism. Sedition and sabotage became widespread, the work of those who resented communist government and wished to overthrow it.

Lenin believed that the first priority of the Bolsheviks must be to stay in power and, throughout 1918, his government tightened its political grip. The Commission to Fight Counter-Revolution (the *Cheka*) had been set up at the end of 1917. Its first duties were to deal with drunkenness, speculation, and crime in general, but its staff grew to 30 000 and it became a formidable political police force, for use against all kinds of opposition to the government. Felix Dzerzhinsky, the leader of the Cheka and a veteran Bolshevik, defended the organization as a necessity:

> [It] must take into account only one thing, the victory of the revolution over the bourgeoisie, so the Cheka must defend the revolution and conquer the enemy even if its sword falls occasionally on the heads of the innocent.

When the Cheka was wound up in 1922, its place was taken by another similar instrument for political control, the GPU which, in its turn, was the ancestor of Stalin's NKVD.

The abolition of all parties except the Communist Party, strict censorship, the Cheka, and the total control of political activity, left no room for opposition to Lenin's government except that which was 'illegal', and Russia drifted into civil war during 1918. A new constitution was agreed by the Congress of Soviets in July 1918, but it made no fundamental changes: power at all levels still rested firmly with the Communist Party. Russia was now to be known as the Russian Soviet Federal Socialist Republic (RSFSR). The capital had been moved from Petrograd to Moscow. The SRs, meantime, continued the terrorist activities they had used against the tsars, assassinating some Bolshevik leaders, and wounding Lenin himself in August 1918. The Cheka struck back with a 'red terror'. The brief freedom which Russia had known in 1917 had been extinguished and, having determined to keep power at all costs, the Communists were forced to rule with an iron hand.

Civil War and the Wars of Intervention were one result of the Communists' unpopularity. But perhaps a greater problem for Lenin's government was that of the Russian peasantry. The promise of 'Land' had swung many peasants to the side of the Bolsheviks in 1917–18, but 'Land' to the peasants meant private property, the chance to make private profit and perhaps to become a *kulak*, a rich peasant-employer. The peasants in the main had bourgeois capitalist ambitions, but the Party they had helped to bring to power stood for the community and for equal shares. When the Civil War was won, it would still remain for Lenin's government to deal with this fundamental contradiction of the Bolshevik revolution.

(b) Civil War: the Wars of Intervention

Hostile generals, such as Kornilov, had already begun to organize opposition to the Communists before the end of 1917. White (anti-Bolshevik) governments were set up by the summer of 1918 at Archangel, Omsk and Samara. They rallied support from the many sections of Russian society who opposed communism, but their general intention to restore something of the old society and their close association with landlords did not endear them to the masses. The peasant risings which occurred in the years 1918 to 1921 had little connection with the Whites and, although Admiral Kolchak proclaimed himself the ruler of all Russia in November 1918, the Whites were far from united, and their forces were never large. Against their enemies the Communists expanded the Bolshevik Red Guards into the Red Army, which was led brilliantly by Trotsky. United in defence of Lenin's government, the Communists struck outwards from their power bases in Moscow and Petrograd, and the Whites were routed. Kornilov was an early casualty, killed while leading a Cossack uprising. Kolchak was taken and executed in 1920. By the end of 1920, when General Wrangel was defeated in the Crimea, the Whites had been crushed. There were many atrocities on both sides during the civil war, and the war added both to the bitterness and the dislocation in Russia. But, when it ended, the Communists remained firmly in power, and there was little further organized opposition to their rule.

Nevertheless, Lenin's government had seemed for a time to be in great peril, since not only Russian dissidents but also many outside powers had given support to the Whites. The Allies were angered by Lenin's determination to withdraw from the war against Germany, and troops arrived in Russia from Britain, the USA and Japan. Before long they were joined by French and Germans. The powers also poured in supplies to help the Whites, eager to overturn a communist regime which, with its adherence to Marxist doctrines, seemed to threaten their own capitalist societies. Russian Marxists argued that the powers came in search of opportunities to exploit Russia's economy, to mine its minerals, and to secure commercial privileges, and the argument was not without truth. But the powers were also trying, rather unsuccessfully, to collect the loans which they had made to Nicholas II, and which the Bolsheviks had repudiated, and to rescue something of the investments they had formerly made in Russia. Their intervention was half-hearted, however, and they made little attempt to take part in the fighting of the Civil War. In spite of lavish equipment from the foreign powers, the Whites lost the war, and the foreign troops drifted away. By associating the Whites with foreign interference, the

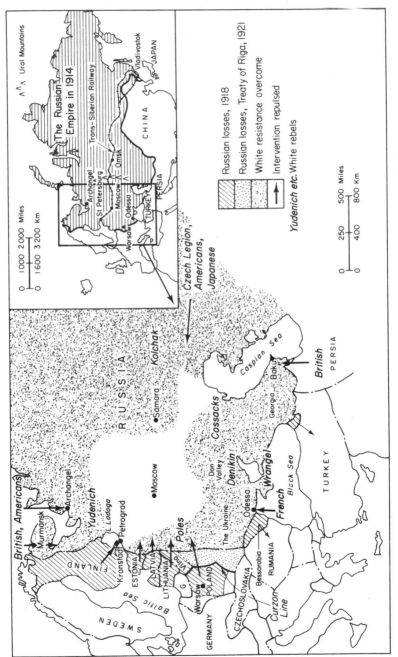

Fig. 19.4 Civil War and the Wars of Intervention in Russia 1918–21

powers perhaps even helped the Communists to triumph. When the powers withdrew, they had recovered neither their loans nor their assets and, if they had hoped to restore the Romanovs to the Russian throne, that hope had also been frustrated. Nicholas II and his family had vanished, presumably murdered by the Bolsheviks in Ekaterinburg.

In 1920, however, Poland had also sought to profit at Russia's expense. Seeking to extend the Polish frontier eastwards, the Poles advanced as far as Kiev. The Red Army turned the tide, and chased the Poles almost to Warsaw. The French then sent General Weygand to help the Poles, and the Communists were halted. By the *Treaty of Riga* of March 1921, Russia had to surrender to Poland much of White Russia and the Ukraine, lands which Stalin recovered in 1939 when he made a deal with Hitler (see Section 24.4(*b*)).

March 1921 was also the month of the Kronstadt rising. The sailors of the Kronstadt base had formerly been among the most zealous Bolsheviks, but they now raised the cry, 'Soviets without Communists'. They were routed in 10 days of ferocious struggle but this, said Lenin, was 'the flash that lit up reality'. The Communists had remained in power throughout the upheavals of civil war, intervention, war with Poland, and now the rebellion of former supporters, but the evidence of discontent was too massive to be ignored: policy had to be modified to win more friends for the regime and, above all, it was necessary to take urgent steps to repair Russia's shattered economy.

(c) The Problem of the Peasantry

The first measures the Bolsheviks had taken after seizing power had been intended to transform Russia almost overnight. The Supreme Council of National Economy (*Vesenkha*) had been set up to organize a planned economy, and numerous other measures had attempted to create an egalitarian society, with a strong emphasis on duty to the community rather than on self-interest. Lenin was almost naïvely optimistic. In January 1918 he told the Congress of Soviets:

> The victorious proletariat looks out on a land that has now become a public good, and it will be quite able to organize the new production and consumption on socialist lines. . . . From now on, all the marvels of science and the gains of culture belong to the nation as a whole, and never again will man's brain and human genius be used for oppression and exploitation.

But he had reckoned without the disruption of civil war and without the peasants. The latter wanted neither central planning, nor an equality which cast them in the role of producers of food to be given, without profit, to their 'brothers' in the towns. By the summer of 1918 government policy was taking the form of *War Communism*, bringing all economic activity under government control. This control extended to small industries and workshops. The peasants were regimented, their surplus crops requisitioned. An army of officials appeared, to press the producers to work harder for the common good and to discipline unco-operative peasants. Lenin justified the policy not simply on ideological grounds, but by referring to the crisis of the Civil War. The sullen resentment of the peasants and the near-breakdown of the economy, however, had already brought acute problems before the Kronstadt sailors rebelled in 1921. The peasants produced little, and they hid their surpluses when there were any. Famine claimed far more lives than were lost in fighting and forced the Bolsheviks to pay more heed to the wishes of the producers.

Fig. 19.5 The Bolshevik promise of 'Bread': food was often desperately short in Russia in the years of upheaval. This photograph shows a meal organized in the village of Novaya Sloboda, for people who were still desperately poor

During 1921 piecemeal relaxations were made of the government's economic policy, but not of its political policy. Lenin hoped that the relaxations would allow time for the Russian masses to be educated, to understand and to accept true communism. In the meantime, some limited concessions to capitalism were made. Peasants were allowed to sell their surplus crops after tax; some private trading was permitted, and small firms were restored to private ownership. Incentives and bonuses were introduced. But the large industrial enterprises, foreign trade and the major banks, remained in government hands, and trade unions were under the Communist Party's guidance. The *New Economic Policy* (NEP) was, therefore, a policy of only limited concessions, but it allowed some pursuit of private profit, and it permitted the emergence of *Nepmen*, small capitalist businessmen. It also pacified the peasants, encouraging them to produce and to dream of being kulaks. The NEP did much to restore stability, but it was not until about 1926 that the Russian economy again reached the production levels of 1913.

Lenin referred to the NEP as a 'strategic retreat', but he never abandoned the ultimate goal of creating a communist state. It would take time, and the problem would be handed on to his successor. In 1921 he told a Party conference:

> We hoped . . . to found state industries and organize distribution on a communist basis in a country that was petit-bourgeois. Life has shown that we made a mistake. A succession of transition periods such as State Capitalism and Socialism was required to prepare, through many years of preliminary work, the transition to Communism.

The years of the NEP were the first such transition period. Lenin died in 1924 and did not live to see the next phase, which began when Stalin abolished the NEP in 1928.

Meanwhile, Lenin's government had continued to try to promote better social conditions for Russians. Working hours were reduced and a campaign was begun to achieve adult literacy. The achievements were limited, however, since the legacy of the Romanovs would take decades to repair. Disruption and the civil war further delayed progress. But plans were made, and priority was given to improving communications and to developing electrification. When Lenin died the climate had been created in which constructive work could begin to take effect. A new constitution had also been introduced in 1923, making Russia a federal state, the Union of Soviet Socialist Republics (the USSR or Soviet Union). The constitution was largely the work of Stalin, and it carefully safeguarded the authority of the Communists. The Congress of Soviets remained the national law-making body, together with its Presidium, to which much of its authority was delegated. The committee of ministers continued to exercise the executive power. All adults were allowed to vote for a local soviet, but elections to the higher levels were indirect. Above all, though the constitution omitted to state it, the Communist Party remained the only one which was permitted.

(d) Foreign Policy

The promise of 'Peace' was fulfilled by Lenin's government when the Treaty of Brest-Litovsk was signed in March 1918. Trotsky negotiated with the Germans, but they drove such a hard bargain that he thought the terms unacceptable. The Germans had made massive inroads on Russian soil (see Section 18.2), and Lenin insisted that the Treaty must be signed:

> The soldiers have voted against the war. They have voted with their feet by running away.

Russia was forced to surrender control of the Baltic Provinces (Estonia, Latvia and Lithuania), of Poland, of Finland, and of the Ukraine. Kars and Batoum were also ceded, to Turkey. This was a fifth of the former tsarist empire and about a quarter of its population, some 46 million. The Germans intended that the Ukraine should be a German puppet state and granary, and they further demanded an indemnity from Russia of 3000 million roubles. Confident that communist revolutions were about to occur across Europe, Lenin thought the Treaty would soon be invalid.

In fact Germany was defeated before the end of 1918, and the Russians were able to re-take much of the Ukraine and to cancel the indemnity. But the Bolsheviks were shut out from the peace conference in Paris (see Section 20.1), which confirmed the independence of the Baltic Provinces and of Finland. Poland also retained its independence, and gained further territory from Russia in the Treaty of Riga (see page 305). Romania also benefited from the upheavals in Russia, to seize Bessarabia (see Fig. 19.4).

For some short time after the Treaty of Brest-Litovsk, Lenin continued to believe that communist seizures of power were imminent in western Europe. But the Spartacists failed in Germany (see Section 21.3(a)), and Bela Kun's communist regime in Hungary was short-lived (see page 325), so that it became obvious that, as a communist power, Russia would remain exceptional. Ideology demanded that the Bolsheviks should continue to pay lip-service to the idea of world revolution to overthrow capitalism, but Lenin's government was cautious. It gave no effective support to a brief soviet in Persia. In practice, there was little alternative but to concentrate on the survival of the Russian communist state, and to build commercial links with the outside world. Lenin began to make trade pacts with capitalist powers in 1921, as part of the NEP and with the encouragement of Britain. By the end of 1921 Russia had signed commercial treaties with 14 foreign governments.

Nevertheless the outside world remained deeply hostile to Russia. Trading arrangements did not necessarily mean political recognition of the Marxist government. At the Genoa Conference of 1922, Russia continued to refuse payment of the debts of the Romanovs; but the Conference had an unexpected outcome, when Russia and Germany signed the Treaty of Rapallo (see page 389). This was a breakthrough for Lenin, since Germany was the first major power to recognize the legality of his government. Article III of the Treaty declared:

> Consular and diplomatic relations between Germany and the Federal Soviet Republic shall be resumed immediately.

Other major powers were slower to recognize Communist Russia, but 1924 brought recognition from Britain and France and, eventually in 1933, from the USA.

Trotsky gave up his post as Russia's Foreign Minister in order to take charge of the Red Army during the Civil War. Georgi Chicherin, once a tsarist minister, became the new Commissar for Foreign Affairs in 1918 and, until 1930, Chicherin concentrated on creating an orthodox Ministry in which foreign powers could have confidence. It was Chicherin who negotiated the Treaty of Rapallo, and he had considerable success in winning the respect of the capitalist powers. But the existence of the Comintern (the Third Socialist International) was a cause for confusion about Russian foreign policy. The

Comintern came into being in 1919, to co-ordinate and to spread international communism. It owed much to the organization of Gregori Zinoviev, who had been in exile with Lenin at the start of 1917, and it sometimes seemed that Russia had two foreign policies: that of Chicherin, and the more subversive policy of Zinoviev. Within a year of the Treaty of Rapallo, the Comintern was trying to foment revolution in Germany, but the Treaty nevertheless survived. It seems that neither under Lenin nor under Stalin was the Comintern ever allowed seriously to undermine Russia's more peaceful foreign policy, and it was abolished in 1943 in an effort to please Russia's allies in the war against Nazi Germany. The defence of the Russian revolution was always more important to Lenin and Stalin than the promotion of revolutions in other countries.

Fig. 19.6 Lenin photographed at a meeting of the Third International (the Comintern), March 1919. The Comintern made ritual noises about world revolution, but both Lenin and Stalin pursued cautious foreign policies

19.3   The Power Struggle

The attempt on his life in 1918 left Lenin much weakened, and he died in January 1924 at the age of 54, to be remembered with devotion by millions. His body was embalmed, and Petrograd was renamed Leningrad. He was much troubled in his later years by the problems of the transition to full communism in Russia, and by the growth of bureaucracy in the country; and he was also worried by the question of his successor. The choice seemed to lie between Trotsky and Stalin. Both Stalin and Trotsky had given good service to the Bolshevik revolution, but, in Lenin's view, both had weaknesses. He referred to Stalin as 'the crafty Georgian', and suspected him of personal ambition. Lenin was always indifferent to personality and to his own self-interest, and he questioned whether Stalin could be equally disinterested. On the whole, Lenin preferred Trotsky, but had misgivings about Trotsky's over-whelming self-confidence.

Stalin was of peasant birth. His enthusiasm for Bolshevism landed him in Siberia, but he returned to edit *Pravda* when Nicholas II was overthrown, became the Commissar for Nationalities and then, in 1922, the Secretary-General of the Communist Party. As Commissar, he did much to hold together the union of states during the turbulence of 1918–20; and as Secretary-General, he organized a loyal party, strong in his own support.

Trotsky, on the other hand, was a late recruit to the Bolsheviks. Before 1917 he had leaned towards the Mensheviks, but was always something of an individualist, careless of creating personal support, and interested in causes rather than his own career. More than anyone Trotsky had been the executive figure of 1917, winning Russia for the Bolsheviks. From being Commissar for Foreign Affairs, he had then become Commissar for War, and successfully organized and led the Red Army. He might have been the Chairman of Sovnarcom, instead of Lenin, had he not stood down, lest the fact that he was a Jew might have stirred up anti-semitism against the Bolsheviks.

Stalin had little of Trotsky's interest in intellectual argument, but he had a talent for political in-fighting. When Lenin died, a coalition of Stalin, Zinoviev and Kamenev manipulated the Party to prevent Trotsky's election to the leadership. Stalin mobilized support for his own policy of 'Socialism in One Country' in preference to Trotsky's ambitious advocacy of 'World Revolu-tion'. His policy of making Russia economically self-sufficient, consolidating the revolution, and avoiding foreign entanglements, seemed safer to many Russians than Trotsky's enthusiasm for colourful adventures. Nevertheless Stalin did not hesitate later to implement many of Trotsky's plans for the economic development of Russia, once Trotsky himself had been suitably discredited. In 1927 Stalin was able to secure Trotsky's expulsion from the Communist Party and, two years later, from Russia. In 1940 Trotsky was murdered in Mexico by a Stalinist agent, an act which finally silenced his continuous criticisms of Stalin's direction of Russian affairs.

Other rivals to Stalin's power were also removed. Zinoviev and Kamenev were disgraced in 1927, branded as supporters of Trotsky for urging rapid industrialization and an attack on the kulaks, the policies Stalin himself was soon to adopt. By 1928 Stalin's authority was supreme. However unwillingly, Lenin had created a political system that was almost a personal dictatorship, and that system had now, indisputably, been inherited by Stalin.

19.4   Russia under Stalin

(a) Socialism in One Country

1928 was also the year in which the NEP was abandoned and the first of Russia's Five Year Plans was launched. The change of policy was designed to resolve several problems. The peasants were again creating difficulties. Angered by the lack of consumer goods on which to spend their profits, many were producing too little food or refusing to sell what they did produce, so that Russia was once more threatened with famine. The bourgeois ambitions of the peasants continued to rankle with the Communists, and the time seemed to have come to move forward to the collectivization of agriculture, which Lenin had envisaged. Collectivization could also lead to more efficient farming, making use of mechanized equipment; and this in its turn, with grain being sold abroad, could produce the capital which Russia desperately needed in order to industrialize. This, then, was the thinking behind Stalin's Five Year Plan, and the Plan of 1928 was followed by others in 1933, 1937, and after the Second World War.

The emphasis was on planning by a central authority, *Gosplan*, the descendant of Vesenkha. In industry there would be massive concentration on capital goods which might generate future wealth, and ambitious production targets would be set for all major enterprises. Hydro-electric power plants were to be built with maximum speed, to provide power for further expansion. At the same time, the private holdings of the peasants were to be merged into collective farms, and the collectives were to achieve the output targets set for them by the planners. Industry would produce tractors and agricultural machinery. The grain produced by more efficient agriculture would be exported; and the foreign earnings would buy more advanced industrial plant and expertise. Stalin claimed that it was a matter of survival:

> We are fifty or a hundred years behind the advanced countries. We must make good this lag in ten years. Either we do it or they crush us.

Russians were driven forward with an energy which amounted to frenzy. Tremendous effort was demanded from the labour force, and the industrial workers at least responded impressively. They acted partly from fear of savage punishment, but they were also encouraged to 'socialist competition' by incentives and rewards. Outstanding workers were honoured as *Stakhanovites*, named after a miner who cut over 100 tons of coal in a single shift in 1935. By 1939 almost half of the industrial workers were Stakhanovites.

Table 19.1 shows how Russian output increased in the 1930s as the result of economic planning and relentless pressure on the labour force. The industrial labour force grew steadily, augmented by some 25 million peasants, shaken out of the villages in the reorganization of agriculture, and increased by the direction of labour by the planners. By the end of the 1930s Russia was second

Table 19.1　Russian Industrial Production 1928–37

	National income (hundred million roubles)	Electricity (hundred million Kwhs)	Coal (million tons)	Steel (million tons)	Oil (million tons)
1928	24.4	5.1	35.4	4.0	11.7
1932	45.3	13.4	64.3	5.9	21.4
1937	96.3	36.2	128.0	17.7	28.5

Adapted from A. Nove, *An Economic History of the USSR*. Penguin (Harmondsworth, 1969).

only to the USA in its industrial production. Huge new power stations had been built on rivers such as the Dnieper. There were vast new steel plants at Magnitogorsk and elsewhere, and new rail links such as the Turkestan-Siberian had been constructed. In spite of the sacrifices that were demanded of them, Russians had a new pride in their country, and 'Hero of Socialist Labour' was an honour which many of them coveted.

One of the many sacrifices Russians had to make was to continue with very few consumer goods. The production of woollen cloth actually fell from 1928 to 1932, and it increased only slowly in the later 1930s. Some attempt was made after 1932 to boost the production of footwear and cotton cloth, but the intentions in the Third Plan to manufacture more consumer goods were frustrated when the danger from Nazi Germany made it necessary to give priority to armaments.

There were some 25 million peasant landowners in Russia in 1928. They farmed over 97 per cent of the country's agricultural land; a few collectives and state farms accounted for the rest. Traditional in their ways and lacking capital, most of the peasants farmed inefficiently. In 1928 they produced only 30 000 tons of grain for export. Collectivization was vital to Stalin's plans, and he was determined to carry it through; but the cost was a heavy one. The kulaks resisted fiercely, and the peasantry as a whole had little enthusiasm for merging their holdings into collective farms. Ideologically collectivization would bring the peasants into line with the socialist society, but that was not what the peasants wanted; and they had little interest in the mechanization which could make the large collective farm (the *kolkhoz*) an efficient productive unit. Stalin first tried cajolery. Then he launched a savage attack on the kulaks, whose ruthless extermination reached a peak in 1930. He considered the destruction of the kulaks as a class to be one of his greatest triumphs. Thereafter the government proceeded by a mixture of incentives and penalties and, by 1935, more than 94 per cent of the agricultural land had been collectivized. Each kolkhoz sold some 90 per cent of its produce to the state at a fixed price, and it could draw on a pool of machinery and equipment from the district tractor station. Members of the kolkhoz were allowed to keep their homes and small private plots, so that in the end the NEP was not entirely dead; but the principal income of the peasants now came from a share in the profits of the collective.

Fig. 19.7 A peaceful midday meal on a collective farm in the Ukraine in the 1930s, but Russian agriculture was collectivized only after struggle and great brutality

In 1935 the output of grain was nevertheless little different from what it had been in 1928; and even in 1931, the best intervening year, it had been possible to export only five million tons of grain. Rural society had been revolutionized, but the peasants remained sullen and unco-operative. Many had slaughtered their livestock rather than contribute their animals to the kolkhoz and, in 1935, the national stock of cattle, sheep and goats was much diminished. The number of tractors grew steadily and the output of fertilizers soared, but agricultural output continued to lag behind the targets set in the Five Year Plans. Although the grain harvest of 97 million tons in 1937 was well above average, it was still well below the target. But the yields of grain, meat and milk in 1939 were much higher than they had been in 1913, and collectivization was by then slowly beginning to pay dividends. The policy had been brutal and lingering resentment remained for generations to come, but Russia now had more than 240 000 collective farms and almost 4000 state farms, and the private peasant occupier had all but vanished. The rural population had also fallen to 114 million, compared with 120 million in 1926, while the urban population had risen from 18 per cent to 33 per cent of Russia's total population.

Russians had some compensations for their hardship as part of the policy of Socialism in One Country. Against the tyranny and the terror, which claimed millions of lives, may be set the social organization which cared for Russian workers in a variety of ways. About 20 million Russians were members of trade unions, which played an important part in supervising a labour code, dealing with their welfare. State health services and social security provisions were extensive. The Constitution of 1936 laid down the right to pensions in old age and to benefits during sickness, although there was not always the money to pay them. Unemployment was virtually unknown in Russia, at a time when it was rampant in the capitalist states. There was emphasis too on education, especially in science and for the children of the workers, and efforts continued to achieve adult literacy. Illiteracy was reduced from about 50 per cent when Lenin died, to below 20 per cent when the Second World War began. In 1934 a campaign was launched to ensure that all children received four years' elementary education, with a seven-year secondary education to become universal as soon as the resources were available. In general, attention was concentrated on basic priorities, such as minimum standards of foodstuffs, and of housing. After that, whatever wealth was generated by the Russian economy must be invested for the future, and none could yet be spared for luxuries, nor even for the modest consumer goods which were often taken for granted in the west of Europe.

(b) Stalinism

Stalin's government demanded total obedience from the Russian people. Those who opposed the system were simply eliminated, as were the kulaks. Russians were subjected to an unending Terror, and they lived in constant dread of the NKVD, which took over the policing functions of the OGPU in 1934. But even loyal members of the Communist Party were not safe. Stalin conducted the Purges against his rivals and potential rivals. The downfall of Trotsky and his then supporters was followed by a new Purge in 1933 and then, in 1936, a further attack was mounted which virtually destroyed all who remained of the Bolsheviks of Lenin's day. In a series of spectacular trials, the accused often 'confessed' their guilt, and even asked for death, in order to purify the communist system. Zinoviev and Kamenev were among the victims (see Section 19.3). Having purged the party of all possible rivals, Stalin turned on the Red Army. Marshal Tukhachevsky was shot, with seven other military leaders and thousands of lesser men. No hostile peasant, soldier or worker was too unimportant to escape Stalin's savagery. His terrorism was similar to Hitler's in the same period and, at times, it was even anti-Jewish. Such was the brutality of the regime that Stalin's wife committed suicide in 1932.

There was no freedom of expression whatsoever in Stalin's Russia. Stalin's verdict was final in everything. He dictated to scientists, writers, artists and composers, pronounced official verdicts on works such as Shostakovich's Fourth Symphony, and imposed his own version of Soviet Culture, to serve his own version of the national interest. He also drafted a new Constitution in 1936, making a hollow pretence that his government was a sort of democracy.

Everyone over the age of 18 could vote by secret ballot, but they voted for a single candidate, whom the local soviet selected from the suggestions put forward by official organizations such as trade unions. Russia's parliament, the Supreme Soviet, was divided into two houses: the Soviet of the Union, representing the people in proportion to population, and the Soviet of Nationalities, representing the individual states which made up the USSR. But real power continued to remain with the Communist Party, and especially with its Central Committee, whose members were often much the same as those of the Council of Ministers. Within the Central Committee, an inner group, the *Politburo*, exercised the greatest power. Stalin continued to be the Secretary-General of the Party, and thus personally controlled the whole apparatus. The Constitution included paper guarantees of human liberties, but they counted for nothing when such liberties came into conflict with the wishes of Stalin. Until his death in 1953, Communist Russia was Stalin's Russia. Stalin had added new dimensions to Marxist-Leninism: the personality cult, and the savage tyranny of Stalinism.

(c) Foreign Policy

Chicherin was replaced as Russia's Foreign Minister in 1930 by Maxim Litvinov. Until Hitler came to power in Germany in 1933, Russian foreign policy continued to be largely isolationist, playing little part in international affairs in spite of the bellowings of the Comintern. Recognition and commercial contacts were all that Russia sought, and the Russians remained sceptical about the usefulness of the League of Nations, and about the sincerity of the capitalist powers who talked regularly about disarmament but achieved little of it. The rise of Hitler created alarm in Russia, however, since Hitler made no secret of his contempt for the Slavonic peoples of eastern Europe, of his hatred of communism, and of his violent anti-Semitism. Litvinov was a Jew, and it was partly due to his influence that Russia joined the League of Nations in 1934, seeking to co-operate with the west against the menace of Nazi Germany. With Hitler in power, the Treaty of Rapallo lapsed, but Russia found a new friend in France in 1935, drawn together by a common anxiety about the changes in Germany. (International relations in the 1930s will be considered further in Section 23.4 and Unit Twenty-four.) Disappointed in his dealings with the west, Stalin removed Litvinov in favour of Molotov, and a dramatic attempt was made to come to terms with Hitler in 1939. The Nazi-Soviet Pact of that year enabled the Soviet Union to avoid immediate entanglement in the Second World War, but it postponed the showdown only temporarily. Nazi Germany launched Operation Barbarossa against the Soviet Union in 1941, and the communist system was severely tested in four years of savage warfare – the Great Patriotic War, from which Russia emerged victorious and Stalin emerged both as a national hero and as an international statesman, the leader of one of the super powers in the changed world after 1945. Socialism in One Country had enabled the Soviet system, unlike that of the tsars, to survive the ultimate test of total war.

Further Reading

Bassett, J.: *Socialism in One Country, USSR 1924–57*. Heinemann (London, 1978).

Carmichael, J.: *A Short History of the Russian Revolution*. Thomas Nelson (Sunbury on Thames, 1964).

Hayes, D. and Gregory, F. H.: *Stalin*. Wayland (Hove, 1977).

Jackson, N. C.: *Russia in the Twentieth Century*. Pergamon (Oxford, 1977).

Kochan, L.: *Lenin*. Wayland (Hove, 1974).

Kochan, L.: *The Russian Revolution*. Wayland (Hove, 1971).

Morgan, M. C.: *Lenin*. Edward Arnold (London, 1971).

O'Connor, P. S.: *The Russian Revolution and Its Aftermath*. Heinemann (London, 1968).

Pearson, R. C.: *Revolution in Russia*. Harrap (London, 1975).

Roberts, E. M.: *Stalin, Man of Steel*. Methuen (London, 1968).

Robottom, J.: *Modern Russia*. Longman (Harlow, 1969).

Williams, B.: *The Russian Revolution, 1917–21*. Blackwell (Oxford, 1988).

Wood, A.: *The Russian Revolution*. Longman (Harlow, 1978).

Documentary

The Russian Revolution (Jackdaw Wallet). Cape.

McCauley, M.: *Stalin and Stalinism*. Longman Seminar Studies (Harlow, 1983).

Stacey, F. W.: *Lenin and the Russian Revolutions*. Edward Arnold (London, 1968).

Stacey, F. W.: *Stalin, and the Making of Modern Russia*. Edward Arnold (London, 1970).

Exercises

1. Write *two* accounts of Kerensky's administration in Russia in 1917 (Section 19.1), one from the point of view of a liberal supporter, the other from the point of view of a Bolshevik.

2. What evidence can you find in Section 19.1, (*a*) to uphold, and (*b*) to dispute, the claim that the Bolsheviks had sufficient popular support to justify their seizure of power in Russia in 1917?

3. Making use of the Index in this book as well as of this Unit, write outline biographies of (*a*) Lenin, and (*b*) Trotsky. Compare what you have written with similar biographies in A. W. Palmer's *Dictionary of Modern History, 1789–1945* (Penguin).

4. Why did the Civil War and the Wars of Intervention occur in Russia? How does Fig. 19.4 illustrate the problems faced by the Bolsheviks at this time? Why did the Bolsheviks defeat all their enemies?

5. Why were the peasants a 'problem' for the Bolsheviks, and how was the problem dealt with (*a*) by Lenin (Section 19.2(*c*)), and (*b*) by Stalin (Section 19.4(*a*))?

6. How far do the statistics in this Unit and in the Tables on pages 312 and 334 support the argument that Stalin had achieved success in his economic policies by 1938? What reservations would you have about this opinion?

7. Write *two* letters, as if from *either* a Russian peasant or a Russian industrial worker in 1937, expressing your views on twenty years of communist rule, one for publication in a Russian newspaper, the other freely expressing your views.

8. What do you understand by the terms given in the title of this Unit: (*a*) *Marxism–Leninism*; (*b*) *Stalinism*?

Unit Twenty

Europe after the First World War

20.1 The Peace Settlement

(a) The Peace Conference, Paris 1919

In agreeing to the armistice on 11 November 1918 (see Section 18.3(*d*)), Germany agreed to make certain interim concessions, among which were the surrender of railway stock and many weapons of war, the evacuation of occupied territory, and the cancellation of the Treaties of Brest-Litovsk and Bucharest, at which Germany had appeared to have won victory over Russia and Rumania. The blockade of Germany continued, since it still remained to make the final peace settlement. The peace conference assembled in Paris in January 1919, only two months after the fighting had stopped. Nowhere more than in Paris, however, was the atmosphere charged with hatred of the Germans. Four years of war had taken an enormous toll of French lives and property, and most of the advice which flooded over the peacemakers at the conference was 'to make Germany pay'. Lloyd George, the British Prime Minister, reported something of the pressures under which the statesmen worked, with 'stones clattering on the roof and crashing through the windows, and sometimes wild men screaming through the keyholes'. The French at least believed that one of the principal purposes of the conference was to humble Germany still further, and to complete its humiliation.

Much more than the punishment of Germany was at stake, however. The peacemakers had to re-draw the map of Europe, and to deal with other Central Powers as well as Germany; they aimed to lay the foundations of everlasting peace. The war aims, which had already been discussed, provided some guidelines by which to proceed (see Section 18.7), but the task was huge. Nevertheless the statesmen felt the necessity to work quickly, partly because they needed to turn their attention to urgent problems at home. In the circumstances the extent of their achievement was remarkable, and it was hardly surprising that the settlement they produced was not without flaws. Not only had they to grapple with vast problems, but they had to overcome divisions among themselves. Decision-making was confined to the victorious Allies (the USA, Britain, France, Italy and Japan), and the conference was dominated by the Council of Ten, to which each of them contributed two members. But the key figures, and the men who took many of the decisions in private discussions, were President Wilson of the USA, Lloyd George, and Clemenceau, the French Prime Minister who presided over the conference. They worked without representatives from Russia, since they could hardly invite Bolsheviks to Paris at the same time as they were trying to overthrow them in Russia (see Section 19.2(*b*)). Some consultation with the Bolsheviks did take place, however – well away from Paris.

Lloyd George had been re-elected as Prime Minister of Britain at the end of 1918. Wartime propaganda and a heated election campaign, in which there was talk of hanging the Kaiser and squeezing the Germans 'until the pips squeaked', left Lloyd George with no alternative but to give some support to peace terms which would humble Germany, what he called 'a stern peace'. At the same time, however, he appealed for 'a peace which will be just but not vindictive', and he worked hard for a constructive settlement. The myth developed that he was in some ways a go-between, who tried to mediate between the idealism of Wilson and the fury of Clemenceau. Wilson posed as the enlightened non-European, able to rise above the petty squabbles of the European states, but he was convinced that German militarism must be punished. Lloyd George therefore received little support from the Americans when he tried to scale down the level of reparations to be imposed on Germany. Wilson, on the other hand, got a good press as the pioneer of the League of Nations and a self-proclaimed man of strong principles, whereas Lloyd George was always a controversial figure, with the capacity for attracting a bad press. Yet Lloyd George was also an enthusiastic founder of the League and, indeed, it owed a great deal to the preliminary work of Eric Drummond, its first Secretary-General, and of other British officials. Had the personalities of the men been different, there might have been a closer partnership between Lloyd George and Wilson and, in consequence, a less revengeful and more coherent peace settlement. But Wilson often appeared self-righteous and intolerant of his colleagues and, even when his ideas were sound, their merits were often obscured by the manner in which he defended them. He was also unable to carry American opinion with him for a commitment to the League of Nations and to world peace, and the electoral defeat of the Democrats, the party led by Wilson, meant that the USA never, in fact, joined the League.

Both Wilson and Lloyd George had frequently to give way to Clemenceau. With justification, Clemenceau pointed out that the recent war had not been fought on American or British soil. Twice in his lifetime, Clemenceau had seen German armies in France, and his first concern was to ensure that that did not happen again. He wanted compensation for the French, and guarantees against the revival of German aggression. Already nicknamed 'the Tiger', Clemenceau was a formidable old man at the peace conference, almost a man obsessed. Orlando, the Italian Prime Minister, carried much less weight, but he too had his obsessions, arising from an anxiety to get the best deal possible for Italy. Not only Orlando but the Italian nation, too, were disappointed with the outcome of his efforts. It was significant that not one of the peacemakers, Wilson, Clemenceau, Lloyd George or Orlando, much longer retained the support of their own countrymen; electors, it seemed, pronounced a harsh verdict on their efforts. The Japanese, meanwhile, concluded that they had been treated contemptuously at the conference by the whites, and that they

Fig. 20.1 The Big Three at the Paris Peace Conference: Lloyd George, Clemenceau and Wilson photographed in June 1919

had encountered racial discrimination. The Russians and some Marxist historians, moreover, have seen the peace as a capitalist plot, as much aimed at Russia as at Germany and its allies. Other historians have also been adversely critical, yet the settlement was nevertheless constructive in many ways.

(b) The Principles of the Peace Settlement

The underlying aim of the settlement was to avoid future war in Europe. It seemed sensible, therefore, to try to solve the problems which had caused past wars, and to set up international machinery to cope with future crises. Clemenceau argued that German aggressiveness was the greatest danger to European peace, so that priority must be given to crippling the German State. But there was also general agreement that the empires on the continent of Europe had been at the root of many past problems, and that the peacemakers should encourage the nation states into which, after their collapse, the Habsburg and Ottoman Empires had fragmented. Most of the lands already lost by Russia remained free. The peacemakers aimed to act wherever possible on the principle of self-determination, at least in Europe: people should be allowed the right to determine their own futures, their nationalities, and the states to which they should belong. Local opinion was tested by plebiscites where that seemed desirable. At the same time, the European peacemakers did not neglect self-interest. It was inevitable, therefore, that many of their decisions resulted from compromises rather than from the unswerving pursuit of this or that principle.

Clemenceau was in any case less concerned with broad principles about self-determination, than with the achievement of a new balance of power, which would be weighted permanently against the Germans. He insisted that Germany must be weakened gravely, but there was conflict between the French and their Allies as to the lengths to which punishment and weakening should be carried. Germany and the Central Powers were to make some reparation for wartime destruction, and they were to be well-nigh disarmed; and the peace terms were dictated to the defeated powers, since they were not permitted to negotiate. The Germans, and in particular Hitler, were thus always able to argue that, whatever the merits or otherwise of the terms, the Paris settlement was an imposed peace, a *Diktat*, and a humiliation.

The Central Powers, especially Germans and Hungarians, argued too that dual standards were applied when the peacemakers implemented the principle of self-determination. The peacemakers busily removed from the new German Republic pockets of non-Germans, and they deprived Germany of its overseas empire. German minorities, on the other hand, were left within neighbouring states such as Poland and Czechoslovakia, and many Magyars were similarly left outside the boundaries of Hungary. In such cases, the peacemakers were not simply acting vindictively, since it was no easy task to define boundaries and to resolve conflicting claims, and there were other factors to be taken into account, such as ensuring that Poland had access to the sea. Such access was bound to leave a German minority within Poland. The German minority in Czechoslovakia lived in the Sudetenland, and Germans complained about this too. But the Sudeten Germans had never lived in Germany. Before 1914 they were subjects of the Habsburg Empire and, when Czechoslovakia was established, it was considered sensible that the Sudetenland should be part of the new state, to provide a defendable frontier and a useful basis for economic development. Comparatively few areas of Europe were deliberately taken as booty, though Italy had hoped to take more than it achieved. Britain and France nevertheless took control of extensive colonial properties from Germany and the Ottoman Empire. These were mandated territories, to be held in trust until the inhabitants were ready for independence, and to be supervised by the League of Nations (see page 334). To the defeated powers, such an arrangement could well appear to be little more than a cloak for annexations. But in reconciling aims which were a mixture of idealism, punishment, and self-interest, the peacemakers inevitably produced a settlement in which all were interwoven.

There was even some confusion about the precise purposes for which the

League of Nations was founded (see Section 23.2). There were two schools of thought. One favoured a 'narrow' League, concerned merely to prevent future war. The other envisaged a 'broad' League, which would combine with this function more varied services to mankind and would seek to promote economic and social well-being. The result was another compromise, leaning towards the 'broad' League, but rooted in the League's Covenant which dealt too sketchily with what could well be the crucial questions in the future. The Covenant was vague, for example, on how the League would deal with aggression by a major power which was determined not to abide by the rules of civilized international behaviour. It was too eagerly assumed at the Paris conference, that only small powers would be so irresponsible as to be a future threat to peace. The French had misgivings, of course. Ideally France wanted everlasting guarantees of support against Germany from the USA and Britain. Suspecting – rightly as it turned out – that these would not be forthcoming, Clemenceau tried both to cripple Germany and to find alternative security in the League, only to achieve neither effectively. Yet it was an achievement to create the League of Nations: to make it a successful organization was the responsibility of future statesmen. The 26 Articles of the Covenant were written as the first 26 Articles of each of the Treaties made at Paris for the defeated powers, though the latter were not immediately allowed to join the League, membership being apparently regarded as a privilege.

The terms to be imposed on the Central Powers were worked out, and in due course were signed at a number of former palaces in the vicinity of Paris. Thus the Paris peace settlement consisted of a number of separate treaties. Germany was dealt with in the Treaty of Versailles; Austria in the Treaty of St Germain, and Hungary in the Treaty of Trianon; Bulgaria in the Treaty of Neuilly; Turkey in the Treaty of Sèvres. We will now examine how the defeated powers were dealt with in these Treaties. (Summaries of the Treaties will also be found in the Appendix to this Unit on pages 336–7.)

(c) The Treaty of Versailles

The Treaty of Versailles was signed in June 1919. Two German delegates signified the German acceptance of the terms which were imposed. An eyewitness observed:

> They are deathly pale. They do not appear as representatives of a brutal militarism. The one is thin and pink-eyelidded: the second fiddle in a Brunswick orchestra. The other is moon-faced and suffering.

And when they had signed:

> Suddenly from outside comes the crash of guns thundering a salute. It announces to Paris that the Treaty of Versailles has been signed by Dr Müller and Dr Bell.

The Treaty was certainly the 'stern' peace which Lloyd George thought was justified, but it is questionable whether it was sufficiently vindictive to justify the frenzy of hatred and self-pity with which Hitler later taught Germans to regard it. In all, it contained 440 Articles, of which Article 231, the so-called War Guilt Clause, was perhaps the most controversial:

> The Allied and Associated Governments affirm, and Germany accepts, the responsibility of Germany and her allies for causing all the loss and damage to which the Allied and Associated Governments and their nationals have been subjected as a consequence of the war imposed upon them by the aggression of Germany and her allies.

The intention behind the Article was to introduce and support the section of the Treaty which dealt with reparations, but it was later used by German propagandists to argue that Germany was improperly alleged to have caused the First World War, and was unjustly punished for it.

How much financial reparation Germany should pay was not immediately dealt with by the Treaty. The question was referred to an Allied Reparation Commission, whose arithmetic took until 1921 to complete, when the figure of £6600 million, plus interest, was reached. In practice, Germany would have to supply goods to this value over a period of time to compensate the Allies for 'the loss and damage'. Large areas of France and Belgium had been ravaged by the war. France had lost over a quarter of a million houses. Thousands of factories had been wrecked and looted, mines flooded, and farmland blasted and polluted to the point of uselessness: and much of this was wanton destruction, wrought when the Germans had finally been forced to retreat. On the other hand, the war had not been fought on German soil, and the French had no doubt but that reparation was justified. Yet reparations became a constant source of friction in the 1920s, and a destabilizing factor in the European economy (see page 328).

The Germans considered that the terms of the Treaty of Versailles were quite severe enough even without reparations. The European territories which Germany lost can be seen by reference to Fig. 20.2 and the summary of the Treaty in Section 20.3. The Allies had no hesitation in restoring Alsace-Lorraine to France, and they considered it essential to give Poland access to the Baltic through the acquisition of West Prussia and Poznania. Poland also gained part of Upper Silesia, and small areas of land were transferred to Belgium, to Denmark and, eventually, to Lithuania. The influence of Lloyd George, however, led to the holding of plebiscites in areas where nationality seemed to be in doubt, and these plebiscites enabled Germany to keep part of Schleswig, most of Upper Silesia and almost all of East Prussia. Germany was deprived of the port of Danzig and, for the time being, of the Saar, both of which were placed under the supervision of the League of Nations. The profits of the Saar's coal industry would go to the French, but there would be a plebiscite in the area after 15 years, to enable the Saarlanders to determine their own future. Germans pointed out that the effect of these arrangements was to rob them of almost half their iron production, 16 per cent of their coal output, 15 per cent of their agricultural yields and, overall, some 10 per cent of their industrial capacity: yet they would have to pay reparations out of what remained. They also argued bitterly that Sudeten Germans were not allowed a plebiscite but, under another treaty, were being merged into Czechoslovakia. Hitler was later to fan their grievances into nationalist frenzy, and his determination to recover the Polish Corridor to the Baltic precipitated further war in 1939 (see Section 24.3 and 24.4).

Overseas, the German empire was dismantled, and German trade was further handicapped by the loss of many treaty rights, such as those which had existed in China. The Germans therefore complained bitterly of the economic effects of the Treaty of Versailles. Clemenceau found such economic handicaps gratifying, but he was even more anxious to cripple the German war machine. The German army was limited to 100 000 men; the air force was

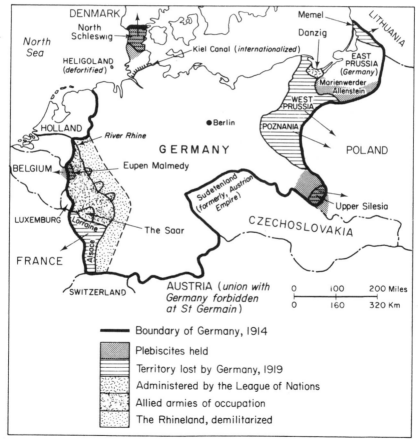

Fig. 20.2 Germany: The Treaty of Versailles

abolished, and little was left of the navy, which was never again to have submarines. (German naval vessels were to have been handed over to the Allies, but many were scuttled at Scapa Flow.) The naval fortifications on Heligoland were destroyed. West of the Rhine, and in three bridgeheads east of the river, the Allies placed armies of occupation, to remain for 15 years. For over 30 miles east of the Rhine, there was to be a permanent demilitarized zone, void of German troops and fortifications, to be a safety buffer for the protection of France and Belgium. This was a compromise for Clemenceau, since he would have preferred the Rhineland to be totally divorced from Germany. One further limitation was imposed on Germany, however: at no time in the future was the German State to be united with Austria.

(d) The Treaties of St Germain and Trianon

The new Republic of Austria signed the *Treaty of St Germain* in September 1919. By that time, the break-up of the Habsburg Empire was an accomplished fact. Indeed, Czechoslovakia had already been admitted to the Paris Peace Conference. Fig. 20.3 and the summary in Section 20.3 show how the Habsburg Empire was fragmented. Austria accepted limitations on its armed forces and made a few small payments in kind by way of reparations, and it agreed to the ban on any future union with Germany. But Austria was now a small and far from wealthy republic, and further severe impositions would be inappropriate. The greatest blow to the Austrians was the loss of the South Tyrol to Italy since, they argued, the area included German-speaking peoples. A plebiscite, however, saved southern Carinthia from being added to the Croatian lands, which were merged into Jugoslavia.

Italy was by no means satisfied with the gains made in the Treaty of St Germain. The South Tyrol, Trentino and Istria were only part of what had been promised in the Treaty of London of 1915 (see Section 12.3(a)). But Wilson had not been party to the Treaty of London, and the peacemakers had now to settle the conflicting claims of Italy and of the South Slavs who were given nationhood in Jugoslavia. Orlando could exert no great influence on the peace conference, and Italy was left to nurse its ambitions east of the Adriatic. They were ambitions in which Mussolini was in due course to show considerable interest.

The signing of the *Treaty of Trianon* was delayed until June 1920. What was left of Hungary was in a state of upheaval. Bela Kun seized power there early in 1919 and set up a communist government. Later in the year he was defeated by counter-revolutionaries, who were assisted by Rumania and Czechoslovakia. Kun fled to Russia, where he perhaps perished as a victim of Stalinism in the 1930s. Hungary became something of a fascist dictatorship under Admiral Horthy, the so-called Regent for the former Emperor Charles, who was conveniently prevented from recovering the Hungarian throne. Horthy submitted to the Treaty of Trianon, which left Hungary much reduced in size, with limited armed forces, and with a small liability for reparations. Horthy complained that some three million Magyars were now under alien rule, many of them in Rumania, and at the end of the 1930s he was to throw in his lot with Hitler.

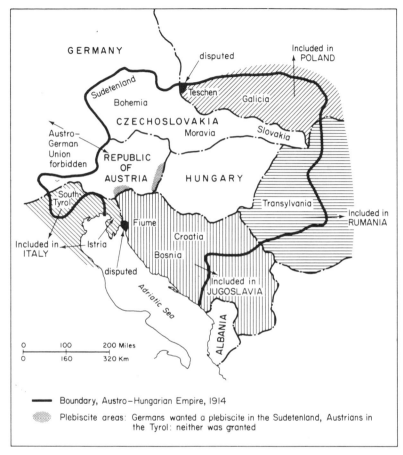

Fig. 20.3 The Former Austro-Hungarian Empire: The Treaties of St Germain and Trianon

(e) The Treaty of Neuilly

Bulgaria signed the Treaty of Neuilly in November 1919 and, like the other Central Powers, had to contribute to reparations and cut down its armed forces – in Bulgaria's case, to 33 000 men. Small areas of land were ceded to

Jugoslavia and to Greece, including the seaport of Dedeagach, but there was minor consolation in the south-east where territory was gained from the Turks. Alone among the Central Powers, Bulgaria retained its monarchy. Tsar Ferdinand abdicated in favour of King Boris. President Wilson had claimed that the First World War had been fought to make the world safe for democracy, and the peacemakers hoped that democracy would help to make Europe stable and peaceful. But Bulgaria saw nothing of it.

(f) The Treaty of Sèvres

The *Treaty of Sèvres* of August 1920 stripped the Ottoman Empire of its Arab lands to the south, and left the Turkish government with no more than a toehold in the Balkans, around Constantinople. Virtually expelled from Europe and Arab states such as Syria, Sultan Mohammed VI was left only as the ruler of the barren and mountainous area of Anatolia (Asia Minor, modern Turkey), and even in Anatolia the Greeks held Smyrna and the Italians held Adalia. The Treaty, moreover, sought to solve the long-standing problem of the Straits of the Dardanelles and Bosphorus by internationalizing them. Article 37 declared that the Straits:

> shall in future be open, both in peace and war, to every vessel of commerce or of war . . . without distinction of flag;

and Articles 38 to 48 set up an international 'Commission of the Straits' to 'ensure the freedom of navigation provided for in Article 37'.

The Turkish sultanate could not survive such a blow to its prestige. Mustapha Kemal, who had commanded Turkish troops at Gallipoli, led a nationalist uprising, in protest both at the Treaty and at the weakness of Mohammed's government in submitting to it. Even before the Treaty was signed, Kemal had set up a revolutionary government in Ankara. In 1921 the Italians were chased from Adalia and, a year later, the Greeks were forced to leave Smyrna. Kemal then turned towards the Straits, and the international Commission promptly began to disintegrate. The French and Italians withdrew from it, and only Lloyd George was in favour of making a stand against this abrupt overturning of the peace settlement. The British garrison at Chanak was ordered to stand firm, but Lloyd George could win little support either internationally or in Britain. The Chanak Crisis was defused when the British commander, General Harington, came to terms with Kemal in the Armistice of Mudania in October 1922. The Turkish sultanate was abolished in the following month. In due course the Turkish Republic was set up which Kemal ruled, virtually as a dictator, until his death in 1938 (see Section 22.3).

The agreement made at Mudania was the basis for a revised peace which the powers signed with Turkey in July 1923, the *Treaty of Lausanne*. (The terms can be compared with those of the Treaty of Sèvres in the summaries in Section

20.3.) Much of the earlier Treaty of Sèvres was confirmed, but there were no longer foreign bases and troops in Anatolia, and Kemal even recovered East Thrace in the Balkans, from the Greeks. The 'freedom of transit and of navigation . . . in the Strait of the Dardanelles, the Sea of Marmora and the Bosphorus' was confirmed, but the Turks themselves were left to supervise the traffic. Moreover, alone among the Central Powers, Turkey was relieved of the payment of reparations and of limitations on its armed forces. In an attempt to forestall future conflict between Turks and Greeks, some transfers of population took place.

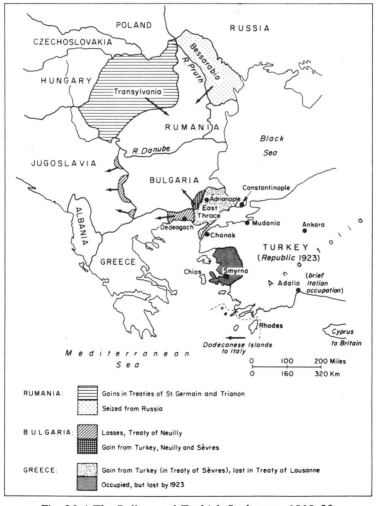

Fig. 20.4 The Balkan and Turkish Settlement, 1919–23

(g) The Paris Peace Settlement: an Assessment

Except for the revision at Lausanne, the treaties of the Paris settlement were all signed before the autumn of 1920. The peacemakers worked energetically and hopefully, if not always confidently. They left the Allied Reparation Commission to persevere with its arithmetic and a Conference of Ambassadors to deal with the loose ends of the settlement, until the League of Nations was fully operational. In such a vast settlement it was only to be expected that there would still be argument about detail, but it was ominous that violence was so often used to secure solutions. Italy still wanted Fiume, and an untidy scramble for possession of it eventually resulted in its seizure by Mussolini (see page 188). Czechoslovakia came to blows with Poland over Teschen early in 1919, and the Conference of Ambassadors settled the issue in favour of the Poles. The Poles went to war with Russia in 1920 to secure additional lands to the east (see page 305), and in the same year seized Vilna from Lithuania. Lithuania grabbed Memel from the hands of the League in 1923 and, in that year too, the French occupied the Ruhr in an attempt to extract reparations from Germany (see pages 348 and 390).

The treaties were therefore being revised almost before their ink was dry; and, where they were not revised, there was sometimes brooding discontent which did not augur well for the future. The Germans were the most discontented of all, many eager to convince themselves and Europe in general that the Treaty of Versailles was vindictive. But the victors were also dissatisfied: the French were uneasy, obsessed with fears, which the British thought tiresome, of a German revival; the Italians alleged that they had been cheated. Not directly involved in the settlement, the Russians regarded it as a hostile conspiracy which robbed them of lands such as the Baltic Provinces, now independent nation states. Some of the new states, however, were not really nation states at all but, like Czechoslovakia and Jugoslavia, were unions of peoples, so that there was still room for argument about nationalities and ideal boundaries.

J. M. Keynes, the economist, vigorously attacked the settlement in 1919 in his *Economic Consequences of the Peace*, prophesying that reparations would bedevil the European economy for years to come. There was room for argument about the severity of the reparations, and there was no doubt that they caused economic disruption; but they did not cripple Germany as Clemenceau had wished them to do. Reparations were cancelled during the financial crisis of 1931–2. By that time Germany had paid only about a quarter of the sum demanded and it had received more than was paid in foreign loans, most of which were never repaid. The League of Nations meanwhile arranged loans to assist Austria and Hungary so that, in the end, the defeated powers received more in aid than they paid in reparations. It may be argued whether the peace settlement was just in imposing reparations to compensate the victors, but it cannot be argued that reparations crippled the defeated.

There was, of course, shrill criticism of reparations from Hitler and the

Nazis. But the Nazis were determined to reject the whole of the Treaty of Versailles, and their opposition to the Treaty was not in itself evidence of an unfair or unwise peace. As early as 1920 the Nazis made clear their attitude:

> We demand the union of all Germans to form a *Grossdeutschland* on the basis of the right of self-determination of nations. We demand equality of rights for the German people in its dealings with other nations, and the abolition of the Peace Treaties of Versailles and St Germain.

The Nazis, however, also maintained that Germany had not lost the war, but that it had been stabbed in the back by a conspiracy of democrats, communists and Jews. Their claims merited little respect. There was more truth in the arguments of moderate Germans, that the settlement's principle of self-determination was not applied consistently to the Germans. Against this, it may be remembered that the peacemakers were forced to work in an atmosphere charged with hatred, which fed on the horrors of the First World War, and that they had to attempt to reconcile numerous conflicting interests.

Fig. 20.5 A prophetic comment on the Paris Settlement in a cartoon by Will Dyson, with its forecast of future conflict for the '1940 class'. Clemenceau, the Tiger, leading Wilson, Orlando and Lloyd George from the Conference

Much of the criticism which was aimed at the peacemakers could more properly have been aimed at the later statesmen, who showed greater concern for their alleged grievances than for constructive effort to consolidate the peace. Too many leaders, such as Mussolini, showed enthusiasm for national self-interest, rather than for international law. Clemenceau had perhaps set a poor example, working above all in the peace settlement for the interests of France. But he became disillusioned. His own pessimism was later reflected in his memoirs, and in the title he gave to them: *The Grandeur and Misery of Victory*. In due course it became fashionable to explain the outbreak of a further European war in 1939 in terms of the alleged injustices of the Treaty of Versailles, but the aggressiveness of Nazi Germany offers a more obvious explanation. Later events, indeed, showed that the peacemakers had been guilty, most of all, of misplaced optimism. There was only limited support in Europe after 1920 for democracy and for international co-operation, and the main weakness of the settlement of 1919–20 lay not in the victimization of the defeated, but in the defencelessness of the small states, which had been created hopefully from the wreckage of the former Empires. Without a stronger and better supported League of Nations than the peacemakers had managed to construct, the small states proved too tempting to the bullies of Europe, and too weak to be able to resist them (see Units Twenty-three and Twenty-four).

Table 20.1   European Production and Consumption

Production	1913	1920	1930
Agriculture (million tons)			
Wheat	36	26	38
Oats	28	24	26
Basic Industries (million tons)			
Coal	575	474	559
Pig-iron	41	20	39
Steel	40	26	43
Merchant shipping built	2.9	2.7	2.4
Expanding Industries			
Paper (million tons)	6	4	9
Cement (million tons)	20	11	33
Rayon (thousand tons)	—	20	130
Consumption			
Electricity (billion kwhs)	30	53	113
Petroleum (million tons)	6	8	20
Rubber (thousand tons)	60	70	230

(Adapted from *Purnell's History of the Twentieth Century*)

20.2 European Society and the Economy

Europe's rising population was checked only temporarily by the First World War, by the influenza epidemic which followed it, and by the further upheavals such as those in Russia. The rate of increase nevertheless slowed down in the twentieth century. In 1921 Russia had a population of about 150 million. At the same time there were some 65 million Germans, 41 million British, 40 million French, and 35 million Italians.* Developing technology, improved nutrition, and advances in medicine (which included the discovery of penicillin in 1928) helped to increase the population but, more than that, they also brought rising standards of living and a better quality of life.

Progress was not, of course, uniform throughout Europe. Eastern Europe continued to be less industrialized and poorer in general than western Europe, although the rapid industrialization of Russia occurred in the 1930s (see Section 19.4(a)). Changes also occurred in the pattern of economic development. Table 20.1 shows that, compared with the output of 1913, basic industries such as coal-mining, steel-production and ship-building, had not much changed by 1930. Areas which had once prospered on the activities of these basic industries were now sometimes in decline, like the mining and ship-building areas of Britain. On the other hand, new industries had grown rapidly with a new technology, so that new industrial centres flourished in the manufacturing of vehicles, in the production of chemicals and in electrical engineering. New sources of power were also exploited, such as electricity and oil. Trade was nevertheless hindered by economic nationalism, the pursuit of national economic interests. Tariff barriers obstructed imports, and Europeans after the First World War were regularly short of international currencies. Europeans needed desperately to sell to the USA, both to pay their war debts and to earn dollars with which to make purchases, but the USA itself erected tariff barriers against foreign competitors. Frustrated in their exports, European nations such as Britain and Germany were unable to employ many of their workers; both Britain and Germany found it impossible to reduce unemployment below the million mark in the 1920s. Many of the unemployed were those who had previously worked in the basic industries. When the Depression set in after 1928 unemployment soared almost universally.

There was a general movement after the First World War towards a greater government involvement in the lives of Europeans. Russia was Europe's only communist state, but totalitarian regimes – which shared something of the Russian interest in economic planning and social organization – mushroomed (see Unit Twenty-two). In the democracies, socialist parties were now firmly established, and they helped to promote extensive political debate about the extent to which governments should intervene in such matters as the organization of national economies, the promotion of educational opportunity, and the

---

* Compare the figures for 1938 in Table 20.2. By 1939 Europe's total population was about 540 million.

Fig. 20.6 The quickening pace of change after the First World War: traffic in the Strand, London, July 1928. Yet Britain and Germany each had a million unemployed, and an even deeper depression was imminent

protection of citizens against misfortune by welfare legislation (see Unit Twenty-one). On the whole, however, the democracies were still reluctant to adopt extensive government interventionism, and more determined movements in this direction had to wait until after the Second World War. In the inter-war years, the democracies continued in general to uphold capitalist economies and societies, which were still firmly based upon private enterprise, though that enterprise tended to be organized in ever larger units. For the middle classes and the élites, the period was one of growing prosperity, but the other side of the coin was widespread unemployment in the working classes, a social evil which governments piously condemned, but did little to eradicate. The vote was commonly extended, however, in the years after the First World War, and women were often among those who were enfranchised. Norway and Denmark had already given a lead in this direction, and the Bolsheviks proclaimed the equality of the sexes in Russia in 1917. Votes for women followed quickly in Britain, Germany, Austria and elsewhere, though women in France and Italy had to wait until after the Second World War to be enfranchised.

In spite of growing urbanization and the general fascination of Europeans with industry, there was no neglect of agriculture. Agricultural labour forces tended to shrink, but output was maintained by greater efficiency and, in many countries, by mechanization. The fascist states strongly emphasized the virtues

THE PARLIAMENTARY FEMALE.

Father of the Family. "COME, DEAR; WE SO SELDOM GO OUT TOGETHER NOW—CAN'T YOU TAKE US ALL TO THE PLAY TO-NIGHT ?"
Mistress of the House, and M.P. "HOW YOU TALK, CHARLES! DON'T YOU SEE THAT I AM TOO BUSY. I HAVE A COMMITTEE TO-MORROW MORNING, AND I HAVE MY SPEECH ON THE GREAT CROCHET QUESTION TO PREPARE FOR THE EVENING."

Fig. 20.7 Punch *poured scorn on political rights for women and female members of parliament in this cartoon of 1853. After the First World War, the political emancipation of females proceeded steadily, however*

of self-sufficiency, elevating economic nationalism to even greater importance, and the support of the peasants was often important politically. The agricultural areas of Europe were, therefore, sometimes prosperous. But wealth continued to be distributed very unequally. There were inevitably social tensions between those who prospered, and those who earned only low wages or could find no work at all. Social conflict often led to bitter political conflict, more so on the continent than in Britain. The Bolshevik success in Russia encouraged those who believed that salvation and social justice could be found in communism and, throughout the 1920s, there was a strong working-class vote in Germany for the Communist Party. Such support alarmed the middle classes, the business interests and the peasants. Not uncommonly these more conservative elements in society preferred a Mussolini-like 'strong man', to be a bulwark against the left. Conservative fears of communism also joined hands with the nationalism which was rampant in Europe – and which the peacemakers at Paris had appeared to encourage with their pursuit of national self-determination. Horthy in Hungary, Kemal in Turkey, Pilsudski in Poland and, more grotesque than any of them, Hitler in Germany, were only a few of the dictators who came to power in Europe during the inter-war period. The number of states which, like France, persevered to maintain democratic government was steadily eroded.

Europeans continued to assume their natural right to dominate most of the globe in vast colonial empires. The British and French still held the largest overseas empires after 1918, but Belgium, Holland, Portugal, Spain and Italy

Table 20.2   Population and Wealth 1938

	Population (millions)	National income (£s million)	Per capita income (£s)
Soviet Union	167	6 300	38
Germany	68	6 700	99
Britain	48	4 700	99
Italy	44	1 400	32
France	42	2 100	50
Poland	35	600	18

(Adapted from *Purnell's History of the Twentieth Century*)

also remained confident mother countries. It was one of Germany's grievances that it had been forced to forfeit its colonial empire in the Treaty of Versailles, and the Italians continued to regret that their empire was not as large as they would have wished. The mandated territories (the former German and Ottoman colonies now ruled by powers such as Britain and France) were defined in the Covenant of the League of Nations as:

> inhabited by peoples not yet able to stand by themselves under the strenuous conditions of the modern world, [where] there should be applied the principle that the well-being and development of such peoples form a sacred trust of civilization.

But it seemed to be assumed that the appropriate 'civilization' was that of the Europeans. Nor was there much evidence in the post-1918 colonial empires, that Europeans yet seriously contemplated their abandonment or that they had ceased to regard them as status symbols and as buttresses to their own economies. The British made half-hearted efforts to consider how best to advance the 'development' of colonial peoples, but even these small efforts were hardly matched by those of other powers. In the 1930s Mussolini decided that Italian East Africa should be expanded by the conquest of Abyssinia, and the 'civilization' the Italians brought to Abyssinia was that of the tank, the flame-thrower and poison gas.

Indeed, European civilization had led to gross barbarism in the war of 1914–18 and, in little more than 20 years, it was to plunge the continent into a further massive conflict of national passions and assertive ideologies. For all its self-confidence, early twentieth-century Europe was in ferment, and the arts began to reflect the competitiveness, violence and unease of European society. There was rioting in Paris in 1913 when Stravinsky's *Rite of Spring* was first performed, but its savagery was only a pre-echo of the coming war. Strident dissonance and syncopated rhythms changed the character of much European music and the death of Puccini in 1924 marked the passing of the age of romantic opera, Composers, poets and artists increasingly shattered the

Fig. 20.8 An East German stamp of 1961, commemorating the contributions of Marx, Engels and Lenin to socialist struggle

composure of Europeans with unorthodox works, which fled from the comfortable, romantic and often elegant forms of the nineteenth century. They seemed to conspire in challenging Reason, as if in rebellion against known and respected values. D.H. Lawrence and James Joyce seemed to introduce a new irrationality into literature. Cubists such as Georges Braque and Picasso shocked the art world, and the Surrealists, among them Salvador Dali, shocked it even more. In Berlin, Berchtold Brecht and Kurt Weill collaborated to present violent and unorthodox stage productions, which poured scorn on the society of the Weimar Republic and infuriated the Nazis as a communist-Jewish assault on the Fatherland. Wherever freedom of expression was allowed, European society and all its traditions seemed to be under attack from a disaffected intelligentsia, yet the artists were themselves simply a part of the new age of uncertainty and turmoil. In totalitarian societies, however, the arts were enlisted in the service of the regime: in Russia, they had to serve the revolution and, in general, they remained staidly conventional, glorifying the workers' struggle in literature, music, paintings and on film. In Nazi Germany art was almost monolithic, ponderously devoted to the worshipping of heroes and to the gigantic presence of the Nazi regime, with more than a touch of Wagnerian grand opera. Hitler himself was fascinated by fire and flames, and here too was a pre-echo of coming war.

Yet for most Europeans the wireless and the cinema, the growing number of motor cars and the development of air travel, seemed to confirm that it was an age of progress as well as of protest. Europeans in general had never been richer and, for those who could afford them, there were diversions in plenty to distract their attention from the economic misfortunes of the unemployed and the impoverished, and from the international and ideological conflicts of the politicians.

Table 20.3   The Increase in Radio Listening

	Wireless licences issued (millions)		Wireless sets declared (millions)
	Germany	Britain	France
1931	4.0	4.3	—
1933	5.1	6.0	1.3
1935	7.1	7.4	2.6
1937	9.1	8.5	4.2
1939	13.7	8.9	5.0

(Adapted from D. S. Landes, *The Unbound Prometheus*. Cambridge University Press (Cambridge, 1970).)

20.3   Appendix: Summaries of the Peace Treaties

The Treaty of Versailles (28 June 1919) (see Fig. 20.2)
1.   The Covenant of the League of Nations
2.   German territorial losses:
     to France: Alsace-Lorraine
     to Belgium: Eupen-Malmedy (after plebiscite, 1920)
     to Denmark: North Schleswig (after plebiscite, 1920)
     to Poland: West Prussia and Poznania; and part of Upper Silesia (after plebiscite, 1921)
     to Allied control and League of Nations: Danzig (Free City); Saar (for 15 years, profits to France); Memel (seized by Lithuania)
     to Allied Powers as mandated territories: East Africa (Britain); Cameroons and Togoland (divided between Britain and France); South-West Africa (South Africa); Samoan Islands (New Zealand); New Guinea (Australia); Marshall Islands (Japan)
3.   Loss of trading concessions in China, Egypt and elsewhere
4.   Demilitarization: Rhineland and Heligoland demilitarized; armed forces limited; army of occupation west of the Rhine and in bridgeheads east of the Rhine at Cologne, Coblenz and Mainz
5.   Article 231 (see page 322), and undertaking to make reparation
6.   Cancellation of Treaties of Brest-Litovsk and Bucharest, and German withdrawal from all occupied territory
7.   Independence of Austria 'shall be inalienable': no union. Germany recognizes 'the complete independence of Czechoslovakia'

The Treaty of St Germain (10 September 1919) (see Fig. 20.3)
1.   The Covenant of the League of Nations
2.   The fragmentation of the former Habsburg Empire:
     (a) Austria and Hungary separate states with no control of other lands formerly within the Empire
     (b) New states from these lands: Czechoslovakia and Jugoslavia (latter including pre-war Serbia)

    (c) Parts of former Empire to Poland (Galicia), to Rumania (Transylvania), to Italy (South Tyrol, Trentino, Istria)
3. Definition of boundaries of southern Carinthia by plebiscite
4. Union of Austria with another country forbidden
5. Armed forces limited
6. Undertaking to make reparation

The Treaty of Trianon (4 June 1920) (see Fig. 20.3)
1. The Covenant of the League of Nations
2. Hungary accepts the break-up of the Habsburg Empire; Hungary reduced in size
3. Armed forces limited
4. Undertaking to make reparation

The Treaty of Neuilly (27 November 1919) (see Fig. 20.4)
1. The Covenant of the League of Nations
2. Bulgarian territorial changes:
    Losses: to Jugoslavia, areas of west Bulgaria; to Greece, western Thrace including Dedeagach
    Gains: from Turkey, areas to south east of Bulgaria
3. Armed forces limited
4. Undertaking to make reparation

The Treaty of Sèvres (10 August 1920) (see Fig. 20.4)
1. The Covenant of the League of Nations
2. Turkey's territorial losses and the fragmentation of the Ottoman Empire:
    to Greece: East Thrace and Adrianople and numerous islands such as Chios
    to Bulgaria: lands on Bulgaria's south-eastern frontier
    to Italy: Rhodes and the Dodecanese Islands (seized in 1911–12)
    to Britain: Cyprus (occupied since 1878)
    to Britain (as mandated territories): Palestine, Iraq, Transjordan
    to France (as mandated territory): Syria, including Lebanon
    to independent governments: Arab states such as Hedjaz and Arabia
3. The occupation of Anatolia (i.e. what remained of Turkey); to Italy, Adalia; to Greece, Smyrna and a surrounding area for five years when a plebiscite would be held; garrisons of British, French, Italian and Greek troops
4. International control of the Straits (see pages 326–7)

The Treaty of Lausanne (24 July 1923) (see Fig. 20.4)
1. Territorial changes in the terms of the Treaty of Sèvres: Turkey regains East Thrace and Adrianople, Smyrna and Adalia
2. Demilitarization of Greek-Turkish frontier in the Balkans
3. Turkish control of the Straits (see page 327)
4. No limitations on Turkey's armed forces and no undertaking to make reparation
5. Confirmation of the other terms of the Treaty of Sèvres

Further Reading

Bloncourt, P.: *The Embattled Peace, 1919–39*. Faber (London, 1968).
Bruce, M. G.: *From Peace to War, 1918–39*. Thames and Hudson (London, 1967)

Mowat, C. L.: *Lloyd George.* Oxford University Press (London, 1966).
Taylor, A. J. P.: *From Sarajevo to Potsdam.* Thames and Hudson (London, 1966).

Documentary and Miscellaneous

Barker, B.: *Versailles: The Peace and After* (History Replay). Blackwell (Oxford, 1979).
Brandon, L. G.: *John Maynard Keynes.* Edward Arnold (London, 1972).
Remak, J.: *The First World War: Causes, Conduct, Consequences.* John Wiley (Chichester, 1971).

Exercises

1. Who were the main peacemakers of 1919–20, and how in their aims did they (*a*) agree and (*b*) differ?
2. 'Much more than the punishment of Germany was at stake' (page 317). Explain and illustrate this statement about the peace settlement of 1919–20.
3. Making use of Section 20.1(*c*), Fig. 20.2, and the Appendix to this Unit, describe how the Treaty of Versailles dealt with Germany. Write *two* commentaries on the Treaty, one from the point of view of an informed and moderate German, the other from the point of view of a Nazi supporter of Hitler.
4. Making use of Section 20.1(*d*), Fig. 20.3, and the Appendix to this Unit, describe how the Austro-Hungarian Empire was broken up in the peace settlement of 1919–20. How does the history of the Austro-Hungarian Empire (Unit Thirteen) suggest that this change was necessary?
5. Referring to Sections 20.1(*f*) and 22.3 and Fig. 20.4, explain why and how the Treaty of Sèvres was soon revised.
6. How did the peace settlement of 1919–20 fulfil the war aims of Lloyd George and Woodrow Wilson (Section 18.7)?
7. What regrets for the past, and what hopes for the future, would you have had as a citizen of Europe in 1919? Refer in your answer to Europe as a whole and to the specific continental state in which you might have lived.

Unit Twenty-One

The Struggle for Democracy

21.1 Optimism and Obstacles

In April 1917 President Wilson told the United States Congress, 'The world must be made safe for democracy.' Democracy, it was assumed, meant a parliamentary system of government, with government responsive to the wishes of the electorate. The USA, Britain and France (and lesser powers among the Allies such as Belgium and Italy) had long ago established such a system. In these countries, the influence of peoples over their governments was growing steadily. With piecemeal amendments to the constitutions and the extension of the right to vote, the parliamentary systems were becoming ever more democratic. The Central Powers, on the other hand, had remained more authoritarian, dominated by monarchy and narrowly based élites. When the Allies defeated the Central Powers in 1918, it seemed that not only had Europe been 'made safe for democracy', but that constitutional and democratic government had proved its superiority over other systems of government. Germany and Austria, in defeat, hastened to adopt democratic constitutions, following the example of the USA and France and setting up republics, without kings. Monarchies survived elsewhere in Europe, for example in Britain, Belgium and Italy, but they were much reduced in power, mere shadows of the European monarchies of the eighteenth and early nineteenth centuries. After 1918 it seemed certain that power would rest with prime ministers and cabinets rather than with kings and councils, and it seemed that the ideal system of government, appropriate to postwar Europe, was one in which two or more political parties competed to win support from enlarged electorates.

There already existed another system in Europe in 1918, however. The Russian Revolutions had destroyed an outdated monarchy, but they had created a one-party state. The Bolsheviks claimed that this too was a democracy, a people's democracy, and the constitutions of 1918, 1923, and 1936, provided many of the trappings of democratic organization. But Russians could vote only for members of the Communist Party. They could do little to change their government, and they were kept in line by various instruments of terror. Russia in 1918 was fast becoming a totalitarian state, where power resided less with the people than with the ruling élite, who had appointed themselves the representatives of the people – what Lenin called 'the dictatorship of the proletariat' (see Sections 19.2 and 19.3).

In the years between 1918 and 1939 totalitarian states became commonplace in Europe but only the Russian state was ruled by communists. The democratic states had feared at first that totalitarianism would be spread by communist revolutions, for example in Germany (see pages 346–7) and in Hungary (see page 324). But it was right-wing nationalist movements which proved more successful than communism, and which swept through central and southern Europe. As early as 1920 Admiral Horthy was in power in Hungary and, two years later, Mussolini seized office in Italy (see Sections 12.3 and 22.2). They were the forerunners of many non-communist dictators, and they provided early evidence that it was too soon for democracy to prosper on most of the continent of Europe.

The weakness of the democracies, and the opportunity for would-be dictators, was that democratic politicians in Europe showed little ability to solve persistent economic problems, and to heal social divisions. Lloyd George declared in 1918 that his intention was to make Britain 'a fit country for heroes to live in' but, all over Europe, 'heroes' returning from the war found that re-arranged frontiers in a world 'made safe for democracy' did little to improve their lives. The short-lived boom, when wartime shortages were made good, barely lasted into the 1920s, and it soon became apparent that the postwar economies could not guarantee substantial incomes nor full employment (see Section 20.2). There was widespread social unrest. Turbulence in Germany threatened to strangle the Weimar Republic at birth, and there were numerous strikes in Britain, France, Italy, and elsewhere. Disillusionment spread

Fig. 21.1 The Soldiers Sailors Self Support Society; ex-servicemen in London reduced to the role of pedlars, photographed in February 1920. Disillusionment came rapidly when war veterans found themselves unemployed

rapidly – with the peace, with capitalism, and with democracy.

Europe after 1918 soon provided a favourable breeding-ground for would-be dictators. Europeans were more aware of their grievances than in earlier times, and they demanded redress for their discontents – tangible progress which would do something towards compensating for the sacrifices of the First World War. Cheap newspapers competed for an expanding mass market, and the invention of the wireless made possible communication with the masses on a scale previously unknown. The number of licences for wirelesses in Britain rose from about one and a half million in 1925 to almost nine million in 1940 (see Table 20.3). Such mass media and growing basic literacy provided new opportunities for those who sought followings, while the general level of education did little to equip the masses to evaluate shrewdly the programmes put before them. Unscrupulous politicians could exaggerate grievances for their own ends, and they could manufacture threats and exploit disillusionment. Such was Hitler's strategy in Germany, trading on the alleged need to overturn the Treaty of Versailles and to save Germans from their 'enemies', and thriving on the publicity his Nazi supporters obtained. Democracy allowed a dangerous freedom to such demagogues, just as Kerensky had allowed a dangerous freedom to the Bolsheviks in Russia during 1917. Where democracy was firmly rooted, as it was in Britain and in the USA, this was less important than in the many parts of Europe where democracy had no roots, and where people had still to be convinced of its virtues. Europeans wanted rapid results after 1918 – full employment, increasing prosperity, and the solution of their problems – and when such results were not produced by parliamentary democracy, few nations were prepared to cling to a democratic constitution with the dogged perseverance of the French. Many nations preferred the Italian example, snatching impatiently at the offer from a demagogue of 'strong government'. One after another, the states of central and southern Europe succumbed to dictatorships, whose theme, in varying degrees, was action, violence and fervent nationalism.

The supporters of democracy often found themselves squeezed between two forces, each of them representing authoritarianism. Industrial workers tended to prefer the authoritarianism of communism, but the middle classes and peasant proprietors preferred the authoritarianism of fascists and similar nationalists. On top of disillusionment came fear. The middle classes and peasants feared the egalitarian doctrines of communism and they looked, therefore, for the 'strong government' which could (or which claimed that it could) both save them from Marxism, and solve the problems democracy was too weak to solve. Mussolini, Hitler, and Franco in Spain, all fed on such fears. By 1939 democratic systems survived only in Britain, France, and certain smaller countries such as Belgium, Switzerland and the constitutional monarchies of Scandinavia. Other countries had surrendered to authoritarianism with hardly a struggle, although the Weimar Republic had battled through the 1920s in Germany, and Czechoslovakia had kept democracy alive in central Europe until it was destroyed by Nazi invasion early in 1939.

21.2   The French Third Republic 1918–40

(a) The Political Framework

The Third Republic in France successfully weathered the storms of the First World War. When the War ended the Republic was almost half a century old (see Unit Eleven). Wartime controls were quickly dismantled, and France plunged back into a not unfamiliar political confusion. From 1917 to 1940 French democracy produced 44 different governments and called on more than 20 different prime ministers. But Frenchmen neverthless clung to the constitution, coped with each new crisis as it arose, and retained their reputation as the leaders of continental liberalism.

The immediate postwar years were dominated by nationalist fervour and anti-Germanism. Clemenceau had become Prime Minister for the second time late in 1917. He steered France to victory in the First World War, and presided over the peace settlement at Paris which followed (see Section 20.1). But he was overthrown in January 1920, when many Frenchmen had begun to believe that the peace settlement had brought inadequate rewards. At this time, right-wing groups were strongest in French political life, united in the *Bloc National*. The Bloc would not tolerate weakness towards Germany, and anti-Germanism culminated in the French invasion of the Ruhr in 1923 in an effort to extract reparations (see page 348). By this time Raymond Poincaré was Prime Minister, a veteran of the right wing, who had been elected President of the Republic in 1913 and had held that office for seven years. The results of the occupation of the Ruhr were disappointing, and the Bloc lost ground. Poincaré remained Prime Minister until well into 1924, and he formed further governments from 1926 to 1929. But the more dominant influence in foreign policy was now that of Aristide Briand, Poincaré devoting more attention to economic reorganization and the stabilization of the franc.

Briand was also a veteran of French politics, but his early associations had been with socialism. Between 1909 and 1929 Briand headed 11 governments, two of them during the First World War. He had been expelled from the Socialist Party in 1906 (see page 174), but he remained an internationalist, and his influence in foreign policy was directed towards reconciliation with Germany and towards international co-operation. He controlled French foreign policy from 1925 to 1932, and was one of the principal sponsors of the Kellogg-Briand Pact of 1928 (see page 393). By 1932, however, a new generation of politicians was emerging in France. Clemenceau had retired after 1920 and died in 1929. Poincaré was eclipsed after 1929, and Briand died in 1932.

The years 1929 to 1936 were years of great political instability in France, with some 20 ministerial crises. The new generation of politicians proved skilful in political manoeuvring, but they revealed few qualities of statesmanship. These were the circumstances in which countries such as Italy had abandoned democracy, but even the Stavisky Affair did not overturn the Third Republic. Stavisky was a shady financier whose 'suicide' in 1934, it was widely suspected, was a political murder to conceal the corruption of politicians and of the police. Riots broke out, and there was a call for a general strike. Fascist squads and communists staged demonstrations and counter-demonstrations, and condemned the Republic. Political and financial scandals were not new in France, but the Stavisky Affair coincided with dangerous economic and social unrest, and with acute political weakness. The Depression was producing spreading distress. There was anxiety about the rise of the Nazis in Germany, and a succession of brief governments offered only feeble answers to urgent questions. Daladier's government of January 1934 lasted for only nine days, and the system seemed near to breakdown. Paris rioters tried to break into parliament, and the streets echoed with demands for 'strong government', either communist or fascist. But French democracy continued to show a remarkable capacity for survival. Gaston Doumergue collected together a broad coalition government in which almost all parties were represented. It took emergency powers and ruled by decree. The Republic was preserved, and new elections were held in the spring of 1936.

The parties of the left drew together at these elections in a Popular Front of Radicals, Socialists and Communists. Similar left-wing coalitions before 1914 had united on a policy of anti-clericalism. The cement of this union was anti-fascism, and the Front won a sweeping electoral victory. The Communists declined to hold office, but Léon Blum, the leader of the Front, formed a government of the other reforming parties, and he was the first Socialist to hold office as the Prime Minister of the Republic. Blum was succeeded by Chautemps, the leader of the Radicals, in 1937, and the government of the Popular Front lasted into 1938. It achieved successes in curbing the activities of French fascist organizations, but fell apart early in 1938. Blum's effort to revive it resulted only in a brief government of about a month which fell in April 1938. Edouard Daladier then took office with a ministry of Radicals, and remained in power until March 1940. It was Daladier who, anxious to keep France out of war over the Sudetenland crisis, attended the Munich Conference (see Section 24.3(a)). But war with Nazi Germany came nevertheless in 1939 and, when Daladier resigned, the Germans were poised for a full-scale attack on the French Republic. Paul Reynaud, his successor, governed for only three months and then stepped down in favour of Marshal Pétain.

Pétain was an old man of 84, but he still carried the prestige he had won during the First World War. It helped to give him the authority to make a humiliating surrender to the Germans on behalf of France in June 1940, when the French forces had apparently been routed. Pétain took the title 'Head of the French State', and presided over the Vichy governments of Laval and Darlan in southern France. In 1940 the Germans occupied only northern France and the west coast. The Vichy regime kept some token independence in exchange for a commitment to right-wing and fascist policies, but it was never more than a Nazi puppet. Among Frenchmen it drew support only from fascist sympathizers and the right-wing groups, which the Popular Front had sought to smash in 1936–7. And even the Germans distrusted it, extending their occupation to the whole of France in 1942. Darlan was assassinated in that year and, when France was liberated by the Allies in the closing stages of the war, the Vichy leaders fled. Laval and Pétain were later condemned for treason; Laval was shot, and Pétain was imprisoned.

The Third Republic lasted, in theory, until a new constitution inaugurated the Fourth Republic in 1946. As Frenchmen had always feared, the greatest threat to French democracy had come not from within France but from German conquest. When the Nazis in their turn were overthrown, French democracy was promptly re-born.

(b) French Policy

The French economy was basically well-balanced in the years 1918 to 1939. Agriculture continued to prosper and to employ large numbers of Frenchmen. In comparison with the years before 1914, French basic industries were expanded, and new industries developed for the mass production of consumer goods. France was less dependent on foreign trade than were Britain and Weimar Germany, and unemployment was consequently less of a problem. In fact France had a shortage of manpower in the 1920s, and over a million foreign workers were needed. When the Depression struck it was comparatively slow to take effect in France, and its results were less severe than in Britain and Germany. The weakness of the French currency was more of a headache for French politicians than was unemployment, and vigorous government action was needed in the 1920s to stabilize the franc. Industrial relations, on the other hand, were often turbulent. The French Communist Party was founded in 1920, and the Communists set up the *Confédération Générale du Travail Unitaire* (CGTU) to rival the existing federation of trade unions, the CGT (see page 175). Social divisions plagued France as they plagued other countries, but French society, like French democracy, nevertheless refused to disintegrate, and every crisis was weathered.

From time to time, governments undertook energetic programmes of reform. The early years after 1918 were devoted to economic reconstruction, to repairing wartime devastation, and to re-equipping industry and agriculture. In the late 1920s Poincaré concentrated on overhauling government finances and on securing the franc. Social insurance schemes were introduced in 1928 and family allowances were added in 1932, which the government hoped might help to increase the French population. But no government matched that of Blum and the Popular Front in its enthusiasm for reform. The Popular Front carried through an extensive programme in 1936–7. The working week was reduced to 40 hours, and holidays with pay were introduced. A legal framework was provided for wage bargaining, in an effort to make industrial relations less anarchic. There were further measures of social security, which included old-age pensions and greater assistance to the unemployed. The Bank of France was placed under closer state supervision, and some measures of nationalization were carried out. Not all of the reforms survived, however. The 40-hour week was an early casualty when France lurched into a new financial crisis, brought on by a trading deficit and declining gold reserves. It was necessary to devalue the franc as a further consequence. Even so, the economic and social record of the Third Republic in the inter-war years compared favourably with that of most European states, in spite of the frequent political confusion. There were undoubtedly wasted years, like those of the early 1930s, and there was some decline in the quality of French politicians after the passing of men such as Clemenceau, Poincaré, and Briand. But the weakness of France was perhaps then more apparent in its foreign policy, than in the French economy and in its society.

As a major power, France was naturally involved in almost all of the international problems in the period 1918 to 1941, the history of which we will consider in Units Twenty-Three and Twenty-Four. The French were obsessed with the problem of their own security (see Section 20.1(b)). When the USA withdrew from the League of Nations and Britain refused to underwrite French security, France searched desperately for other safeguards. From 1919 to 1923, policy was directed towards the enfeeblement of Germany. At Locarno, Briand initiated a new policy, based on an optimistic and idealistic pursuit of reconciliation and goodwill. But the French persistently refused to disarm, unwittingly stoking the fires of those German nationalists who argued that it was humiliating to Germans to be disarmed, while France had not followed suit. The coming to power of the Nazis in Germany, and German rearmament, followed quickly on the death of Briand, and France once more plunged into gloom. The fortifications of the Maginot Line were hastily completed to shield France's eastern frontier, and the French continued to wrap themselves in a cocoon of treaties and alliances. Alliances had already been made with Czechoslovakia, Poland and Jugoslavia, and a new Treaty of Mutual Assistance was signed with the Soviet Union in 1935. Yet France was still unwilling to risk confrontation with Nazi Germany, and the French continued to brood on the lack of firm guarantees from Britain and the USA. In 1938 Daladier preferred to trail meekly behind Neville Chamberlain to Munich (see Section 24.3(a)) rather than to honour France's commitment to Czechoslovakia. Since the death of Briand, nervous twitching had taken the place of a coherent and positive French foreign policy; and when, comforted at last by the partnership of Britain in a guarantee of Polish integrity, a belated attempt was made to restrain the Germans in 1939, France was trapped in a new German war. The Germans stormed into northern France, advancing through Belgium as they had done in 1914 and demonstrating the irrelevance of the Maginot Line, which did not protect the Franco-Belgian frontier. The Nazis marched into Paris in June 1940. The obsessive search for security had led to no security at all. In 1919 Clemenceau had done his best to fashion to peace settlement in the interests of France, but it took only 20 years of apprehensive diplomacy, and almost total disunity among the democracies, for France to suffer a greater humiliation than any it had suffered in recent centuries.

21.3   Weimar Germany

(a) The Democratic Republic and the Alternatives

Friedrich Ebert, a Social Democrat, was left to preside over the provisional government in Germany in 1918, when William II abdicated and the Imperial system collapsed (see page 160). A National Constituent Assembly met in Weimar in February 1919, to work out the details of a democratic constitution. Ebert was elected the first President of the Weimar Republic, and the details of the constitution were completed during the summer of 1919. In the following year the government moved from Weimar to the German capital, Berlin. By that time the first elections had produced a vote of confidence in the democratic republic. An overwhelming majority of the votes were cast for the moderate political parties, almost 40 per cent of them for the moderate socialists. On the other hand, no single party had an overall majority and, like governments in France and in liberal Italy, the governments of the Weimar Republic were coalition governments.

On paper, the Weimar constitution provided Germany with an almost perfect democracy. Elections to the Reichstag, the lower house of parliament, were to be held at intervals of not more than four years, on the basis of universal suffrage, the secret ballot, and a system of proportional representation. Governments would be formed on the basis of majority support in the Reichstag, the Chancellor (prime minister) of such governments being answerable to the Reichstag, and thus to the people. An upper house of parliament, the Reichsrat, had delaying powers similar to those of the British House of Lords, but the Reichsrat was made up of representatives of the German states, such as Prussia and Bavaria, according to population. The head of state in the Republic was the President, whom the people elected at seven-year intervals. The constitution included guarantees of human rights, and it also provided for the holding of plebiscites to make known the wishes of the people on matters of particular importance. Article 48 of the constitution, however, tried to anticipate national emergencies by providing exceptional powers for the President:

> The Reich President may, if the public safety and order . . . are considerably disturbed or endangered, take such measures as are necessary to restore public safety and order. If necessary, he may intervene with the help of the armed forces. For this purpose he may temporarily suspend . . . the Fundamental Rights.

Here was a toe-hold for a return to authoritarianism in Germany, of which Hitler was later to make use.

Germans had had little experience of democracy before 1919, and not all Germans were convinced of the virtues of democratic government. The first elections gave some ten per cent of the seats in the Reichstag to extremist nationalists. Outside parliament there were authoritarian forces who were prepared to back their own opinions with violence. Communists wanted a revolution similar to that of the Russian Bolsheviks. Various groups of nationalists wanted strong government and a stand against Germany's alleged enemies. Such nationalists associated the Weimar Republic with the Treaty of Versailles, and they equated democracy with socialism and liberalism, and weakness. They imagined they could detect Jewish and communist conspiracies to enfeeble the German Reich. The years 1919 and 1920 were therefore turbulent.

The Communists struck first, with the uprising of the Spartacus League in Berlin in January 1919. Soviets were set up in Berlin and in the Baltic ports and, for a time, revolutionary sailors even held Ebert prisoner. In Bavaria, Kurt Eisner proclaimed an independent socialist state. The leaders of the Spartacists, Karl Liebknecht and Rosa Luxemburg, were murdered by counter-revolutionary forces, and the uprising in Berlin collapsed. Eisner too was assassinated. The communist seizure of power in Germany, which Lenin had confidently expected, had not materialized and, in the 1920s, the German Communist Party (the KPD) was more concerned to win seats in the Reichstag, than to promote a revolution.

Meanwhile, the Republic was attacked from the right and by the *Freikorps* – self-appointed vigilante groups, dedicated to 'order' and anti-communism. Many of the Freikorps members were restless ex-servicemen, embittered by military defeat, by the collapse of the Imperial system, and by the Treaty of Versailles. They despised democracy. After skirmishing for some time with the communists and with other enemies whom they identified somewhat arbitrarily, they tried to seize control of Berlin in March 1920, as a preliminary to restoring the monarchy. They were supported by remnants of the German army, some of whom wore swastikas on their helmets, and the government was forced to flee to Dresden. The attempted coup became known as the *Kapp Putsch* after the leader of the nationalists, Wolfgang Kapp. The government called for a general strike, and the working classes paralysed Berlin. Kapp abandoned his coup after only four days. He was sent to prison, where he died in 1922, but the government was too weak to punish most of his supporters, including Ludendorff, and a general pardon was issued for them in 1925.

The Weimar Republic was seldom free from lawlessness during its early years. The courts showed reluctance to punish right-wing extremists, and it was obvious that nationalist sympathies remained strong in various sections of society, including the judiciary, the civil service, the military, and the teaching profession. There were further spasmodic riots by communist-inclined workers, and counter-blows by the right. Munich, and Bavaria generally, became a breeding-ground for fascist groups and for militant anti-semitism. The Republic was plagued by assassinations, such as that of Walter Rathenau in 1922, the Jewish Foreign Minister who negotiated the Treaty of Rapallo with Communist Russia. But the democratic system survived and there was hope that, given time, the Weimar Republic might begin to flourish. The postwar years had shown that it was the most acceptable to Germans of the various alternative systems of government which were canvassed.

(b) Crises and Policy

The Republic needed successes with which to consolidate its hold on public opinion. Born in defeat and forced in 1919 to accept the Treaty of Versailles, it was not difficult for enemies of democracy to argue that the Weimar system was a symbol of the national humiliation. As early as 1920, elections showed that there was a tendency for votes to be transferred from the moderate supporters of democracy to more extreme groups, both nationalist and communist. The shifting coalition governments of the early years did little to inspire confidence, and there were ominous signs of economic ills. Reparations had to be paid, but it was difficult to find markets for exports, and the mark (the German currency) was consequently weak. In a short-sighted effort to solve immediate problems, the German government recklessly printed more money. In 1914 four marks were equivalent to an American dollar, but 7000 marks had become the dollar exchange rate by the end of 1922. With prices soaring and the mark wobbling, the economy was already in peril. The faltering German economy alarmed the French and Belgians, and they had already been annoyed by Germany's sluggishness in making reparation.

The upshot was the occupation of the Ruhr by French and Belgian troops in January 1923. An eye-witness reported their arrival in Essen:

> At their head . . . five parti-coloured cars. From these grim-looking cars, of which the occupants were invisible, stood out the muzzles of the machine-guns, a silent threat to the sullen crowd (see page 390).

Nothing could have done more to infuriate German nationalists and to embarrass the Weimar Republic. Chancellor Cuno advised the workers in the Ruhr to boycott the invaders, and to withhold the production from which the occupying forces intended to collect reparations. The workers were punished by the French with mass arrests, and the French struck a further blow by imposing an economic blockade on the Ruhr and on much of the Rhineland. The disruption was fatal to the mark. By July 1923, 160 000 marks were needed in exchange for a dollar. By November the figure soared to 4 200 000 000 000. Printing presses could not keep pace with the changes, as bank notes and postage stamps were printed and overprinted with ever crazier figures. It was easier to resort to barter than to try to keep up with the useless flood of paper money. Savings became worthless and, for shopping, a suitcase was needed rather than a purse. The French stayed stubbornly in the Ruhr for more than two years, but they gained hardly any benefit from their exploit. Meanwhile, the Weimar Republic struggled to survive the crisis.

A rash of plots threatened to overthrow the Republic by force. There was a communist rising in Hamburg, but it was suppressed by the police. Nationalists were quick to reaffirm the connection between democratic government and national humiliation, but Ebert acted more positively than the right-wing malcontents. He summoned Gustav Stresemann to form a broad coalition government in August 1923, to replace the discredited administration of

Fig. 21.2 Evidence of Germany's hyper-inflation: a Thousand-Mark banknote of December 1922, quickly overprinted with a Milliard (one thousand million). Money and savings became worthless, and confidence in the Weimar Republic declined sharply

Wilhelm Cuno, and to save the Republic. Bavarian nationalists launched their intended coup too late, and the *Munich Putsch* of November 1923 ended ignominiously. The Putsch was organized, with considerable incompetence, by Adolf Hitler. Like the Kapp Putsch, it had the backing of Ludendorff, now more than ever convinced that betrayal, rather than military defeat, had lost Germany the First World War. The intention was to take control of Bavaria, to march on Berlin, and to create the Nazi state. But the demonstrators were routed by the Bavarian police, and sixteen of Hitler's followers were killed. Hitler was sentenced to five years in prison. In later years, the Nazi martyrs were honoured, and the blood-splashed flags of the Putsch were cherished. The episode was commemorated on postage stamps, and what had been a squalid and barely significant skirmish was built up into a glorious milestone in Nazi history.

Stresemann had become the leader of the National Liberals in 1917. The party was renamed the People's Party in 1919, and it commanded the loyalties in the 1920s of over two million voters. Stresemann remained Chancellor for only a few months before the end of 1923, but he continued to be the dominant figure in German politics until his death in 1929. He served as Foreign Minister and worked for reconciliation, but his importance was also that of a stabilizing force. From August 1923 the fortunes of the Weimar Republic began to improve. The threat of civil war was averted and the industries of the Ruhr resumed production. Reparations were paid regularly, with the help of

Fig. 21.3 A stamp of Nazi Germany, 1935, commemorating 9 November 1923 when the Nazis tried to seize power in the Munich Putsch

the Americans under the Dawes Plan, and the French were appeased. In 1924 the new currency of the Reichsmark was introduced, and the Reichsbank was reorganized. Slowly the Republic began to enjoy a measure of prosperity, and its prestige grew with the Locarno Treaties and with Germany's admission into the League of Nations.

The Republic was nevertheless not undamaged by the inflation of 1923. The middle classes, whose savings had been wiped out, remained deeply suspicious of democratic governments. In the election of December 1924 nationalist parties won 24 per cent of the votes cast and 117 seats in the Reichstag, of which 14 were won by Hitler's Nazis, in spite of the fiasco at Munich. The Social Democrats, the largest German party throughout the 1920s, gained 26 per cent of the votes and 131 seats. Among the smaller parties, the KPD won 45 seats, almost matching the 51 won by the People's Party. It was important for the moderate parties to check the drift of support to the extremists, and useful progress was made before the next election of 1928. From 1923 to 1928 Wilhelm Marx of the Centre Party was Chancellor for much of the time, and more stable government produced economic and social improvements. Foreign capital, especially from the USA, made economic expansion possible, and unemployment was reduced, though not below a million workless. Unemployment insurance was introduced in 1927, and improved machinery for the settlement of disputes helped to reduce industrial strife. Public works were undertaken extensively and, with rising employment and increased purchasing power, there were real advances in the standard of living. The moderates reaped some benefit in the election of 1928. The Social Democrats increased their seats to 153, and the nationalist representation fell to 85, of which the Nazis held 12 seats. The People's Party also suffered losses, however, and so

Fig. 21.4 A group of German communists photographed at the beginning of the 1930s. The communists alone provided determined resistance to the Nazis. The working model held aloft here would demonstrate a thump on the head of a Nazi when the string was pulled

too did the Centre Party, while working-class support for the KPD remained firm, the Communists raising their representation from 45 to 54.

The further period of consolidation which the Republic needed was not forthcoming. Already in 1928 there were grounds for concern. Foreign trade had started to slacken, and German farmers were dismayed by falling prices as markets became over-stocked. The Depression deepened in 1929, and a double disaster occurred in October. Stresemann died suddenly and, in the USA, the Wall Street Crash occurred, when the value of shares plunged on the American stock exchange. The German revival had been heavily dependent on American loans, but the loans were already drying up and American financiers now clamoured for repayment. Germany had dwindling capital with which to finance production and, at the same time, shrinking markets increased the problems of selling exports. The Young Plan quickly reduced the burden of reparations, spreading their payment over almost 60 years from 1929, but it did not go far enough. The financial crisis spread from the USA to Europe. The repayment of loans was demanded, preferably in gold. The strain was too much for *Credit Anstalt*, the Austrian Bank, which had to close in May 1931. Driven to panic by their losses in Austria, creditors put pressure on other banks. There was a swift loss of confidence in Germany, and the Reichsbank tottered. Reparations were suspended. They were not paid again, and in 1932, they were in effect cancelled at the Lausanne Conference.

The Weimar Republic was nevertheless in deep trouble. Unemployment increased rapidly. In 1932 six million Germans were without work. The insecurity of the Reichsbank also revived fears of another financial catastrophe like that of 1923, though the problem was now different, in that it was one of deflation and depressed prices, not of inflation. Old prejudices and the old suspicions of democracy were revived, and with the economic crises came political crisis. At this moment, the Republic was denied what it most needed – a stable and respected government. Chancellor Müller resigned in March 1930, when the Social Democrats opposed his intention of cutting unemployment benefits to balance the government's budget. He was replaced by Heinrich Brüning of the Centre Party, but a new period of instability had begun. Table 21.1 shows how a succession of elections showed the weakening faith of the German electorate in the moderate supporters of democracy.

Table 21.1   Seats in the Reichstag

	Elections				
	May 1928	September 1930	July 1932	November 1932	March 1933
Moderate Parties					
Social Democrats	153	143	133	121	120
Democrats	25	20	4	2	6
Centre	62	68	75	70	73
People's Party	45	30	7	11	4
Extremist (Left-wing)					
KPD (Communist)	54	77	89	100	81
Extremist (Right-wing)					
Nationalists	73	41	40	51	52
NSDAP (Nazis)	12	107	230	196	288

(c) The Nazi Destruction of the Republic

Adolf Hitler was born an Austrian in 1889. Contemptuous of Habsburg inefficiency, he joined the German army in 1914, and he remained in Germany when the war ended. He became a member of the German Workers' Party in Munich in 1919 and soon rose to its leadership. The party was renamed the National Socialist German Workers' Party (NSDAP), known for the sake of brevity as the Nazis. Hitler had less interest in socialism than some of his fellow-members, but he revelled in the party's fanatical nationalism and anti-semitism. He felt shame and bitterness for Germany's defeat in 1918, for which it was essential to find scapegoats. The Party put forward a Twenty-Five-Points programme in 1920, of which the last Point ran:

That all the foregoing requirements may be realized, we demand the creation of a strong central power of the Reich.

Hitler had no sympathy with anything weak, and his principal aim was to achieve power. The Reich could then be purged of all those elements which, in his view, weakened it: Jews and non-Aryan immigrants, democrats, liberals, and communists – 'the November Criminals' who had accepted, even connived at, defeat in 1918. Only then could Germany fulfil its destiny and confront its enemies, among whom France and Russia attracted his special venom.

Hitler's first attempt to seize power failed miserably, and the result of the Munich Putsch of 1923 was his imprisonment. But it also brought the Nazis publicity, and 14 seats in the Reichstag in 1924. Hitler spent little more than a year in prison before his early release. While in jail, he began work on his book *Mein Kampf* (My Struggle), developing, though hardly clarifying, his philosophy and hatreds. When he emerged from prison, his Party was poised to develop its machinery and its theatrical trappings. The Brownshirts (the SA, *Sturmabteilung*) developed their skills in thuggery, and gained more publicity. The Party élite, men like Hess, Goebbels and Goering, orbited around their leader. No opportunity was missed to denigrate the Weimar Republic, and to preach the doctrine of German greatness. But the German people were not as yet a receptive audience and, during the comparative prosperity of the late 1920s, the Nazis could do little but wait, and prepare. The crises which developed from 1928 onwards opened a new chapter in Nazi history. The 1930 election was made turbulent by the open violence of Nazis, communists, and other malcontents, and the Nazis won over 100 seats. But Hitler achieved greater personal stature when he contested the presidential election of 1932.

In 1925 von Hindenburg had been elected President. Although well over 80, he sought re-election in 1932 and defeated Hitler only on a second ballot, at which Hitler collected over 13 million votes. The Nazi leader was now a national figure. The Republic, moreover, was crumbling. Hindenburg was senile, his name alone a comfort to Germans who craved security. The President was befuddled by the intrigues that surrounded him, of politicians, of army officers, of landowners and of industrialists. He was dismayed by the daunting economic problems yet, with a Reichstag in which no party had a clear mandate to govern, it was Hindenburg's duty to appoint governments and, if necessary, use the emergency powers conferred by Article 48 of the constitution. Hindenburg was not his own man. General von Schleicher lurked behind the Presidency, influencing events on behalf of the army but more especially on behalf of himself. In 1932 Schleicher withdrew support from Brüning, and the aristocratic Franz von Papen became Chancellor. Papen held two elections in quick succession, in a vain search for support after he had been repudiated by the Centre Party, to which he previously adhered. It was in the first of these elections (July 1932) that the Nazis became the largest party in the Reichstag. Papen relied heavily on the President's emergency powers, but he lost office in December 1932, when Schleicher himself took the Chancellorship. Papen at once intrigued to oust him. Papen was prepared to do a deal with Hitler; Hindenburg was persuaded to agree to it. In January 1933 Hitler was appointed Chancellor, with Papen his Vice-Chancellor. Imagining that he would be able to manipulate Hitler for his own ends, Papen had in fact signed the death warrant of the Weimar Republic. A Chancellor had been appointed whose first mission was to destroy German democracy. Yet Hitler had come to power legally as the leader of a party with substantial – though not majority – support in the Reichstag. Like Mussolini, he first presided over a cabinet in which his own followers were in a minority. An excited Goebbels nevertheless wrote in his diary:

> It is almost like a dream . . . a fairy tale. . . . The new Reich has been born. Fourteen years of work have been crowned with victory. The German revolution has begun!

The economic and political crises which occurred after 1929, and the inadequacy of Hindenburg, had provided the Nazis with the opportunity to gain power; and Hitler himself had shown considerable skill in political manoeuvring in these crucial years. But the foundations of the Nazi success had been laid earlier. Throughout the 1920s the Nazi Party had built up a dedicated membership and a fanatical organization, and the liberalism of the Weimar Republic enabled the Nazi Party to achieve publicity, both for its programme and for its often violent defence of alleged German interests against 'the enemy'. The programme was vague enough to be flexible and, after 1929, Hitler was quick to sense that it would pay dividends to underplay the Party's interest in socialist reform, and to emphasize its right-wing concern for order and the protection of property. The Party could make little headway in industrial areas, where the workers showed an increasing attachment to communism. But it could play on the fears of Marxism, which the support for communism aroused elsewhere. By 1932 the Nazis won much genuine support, mainly among the lower middle classes and the peasantry, who feared for their status and for their property, should the workers grow too powerful. The roots of democracy were still not deep in Germany, and the Republic gave little confidence to Germans fearful of economic collapse or of a communist takeover. Economic difficulties and the tangled politics of the Republic also caused much confusion, and it was not difficult for the prejudiced and ill-educated to believe the highly-coloured Nazi tales of conspiracies and treachery by Jews and their collaborators. It was tempting, moreover, to put faith in a superman, who claimed to have all the answers which would sweep away problems and conjure up national regeneration through strong government. What the Nazis intended to do to cure German ills was hardly clear, but they successfully projected the image of a party of action, dedicated to ridding the country of seditious forces and to restoring German greatness. Such an image made a strong appeal to the petty bourgeoisie, and to other sections of German society, where the suspicion persisted that since 1918 Germany had been humiliated, and that democracy was a recipe for incompetence. The elections of 1932 showed that a third of German society was prepared to trust the Nazis, and that was enough to ensure the failure of the struggle for democracy in Germany.

The transition from democracy to totalitarianism began when Hitler persuaded his cabinet that a new election should be held in March 1933. The campaign was a vicious one. Rival parties were handicapped, their meetings broken up, supporters battered and newspapers muzzled. The Nazis whipped up an atmosphere of crisis: Germany was in danger, and its enemies, especially the communists, were plotting its overthrow. The Reichstag went up in flames – evidence, the Nazis alleged, of the communist plot. But the election results were hardly satisfying for the Nazis. They still obtained less than 44 per cent of the total vote, and needed the support of the 52 Nationalists in Parliament to obtain a majority. (The Reichstag had 647 members at this time.) A bare majority was not enough, however. A two-thirds majority was needed to pass the Enabling Law, by which Hitler intended to give his government almost unlimited powers for four years. The 81 KPD representatives were therefore expelled. Further intimidation was practised, and only the Social Democrats dared to vote against the Enabling Law 'For the Removal of the Distress of the People and Reich', a last vain protest against dictatorship.

The Nazis could now carry through what Goebbels had termed 'the German revolution'. All power was consolidated in the hands of the Party and, in July 1933, all other parties were outlawed, and Germany became a one-party state. A further election was held in November 1933, when over 92 per cent of German voters registered approval of the Hitler regime and, in the absence of any other candidates, the Nazis won all the seats in the Reichstag. When Hindenburg died in August 1934, Hitler proclaimed himself the 'Führer of the German Reich', and the Weimar Republic was formally buried.

21.4 The Lesser Democracies

The Germans, in fact, persevered longer with democracy after 1918 than did many states in central and southern Europe. Democracy scarcely gained a foothold at all in Hungary, Rumania, and Bulgaria. Mussolini came to power in Italy in 1922 and, at the same time, Mustapha Kemal was creating a near-dictatorship in Turkey. Pilsudski staged a military coup in Poland in 1926 and, by the end of the 1920s, not much was left of democracy in Portugal, Lithuania, Jugoslavia and Albania. During the next decade, Estonia, Latvia and Greece also turned to dictatorships.

Spain had succumbed to dictatorship in 1923, when Primo de Rivera seized power, expressing the exasperation of the military with democratic confusion. But when Primo retired, an attempt was made to return to democracy in the early 1930s. Civil war followed in 1936, and a new dictatorship was born under Franco (see Section 22.5). Franco was brought to power partly by the support of Mussolini and Hitler. Elsewhere, where democracy had survived, Hitler

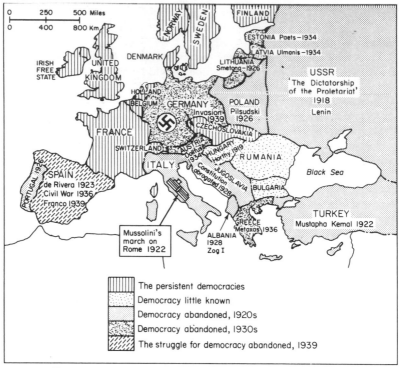

Fig. 21.5 The Eclipse of Democracy in Europe 1918–39

acted as its executioner. In 1938, he destroyed democracy in Austria. The Austrian Republic had struggled through the 1920s and the Depression. Chancellor Dollfuss suspended the constitution in 1934, but he was assassinated; democracy lingered for a few years more in the face of much Nazi harassment, until German troops marched into Vienna and the *Anschluss* was effected (see Section 24.2). Shortly afterwards, the Germans destroyed democracy in Czechoslovakia.

Czechoslovakia had adopted a democratic constitution on the French model in 1920. The state proved remarkably stable, in spite of a mixture of nationalities (seven million Czechs, over three million Germans, two million Slovaks, and substantial minorities of Hungarians and Ruthenians). Tómàš Masaryk served as President until 1935, when he was succeeded by Eduard Beneš, who had hitherto been Foreign Minister. With a prosperous industrial base and political stability and continuity, Czechoslovakia fulfilled many of the ambitions of the peacemakers of 1919. Except for a quarrel with Poland over Teschen in 1919, its external relations were peaceful and constructive. The total population was only 14 million, however, and the presence of over three million Germans in the Sudetenland provided Hitler with a grievance. Viol-

Fig. 21.6 Tómàš Masaryk, President of Czechoslovakia until 1935, and Eduard Beneš, his successor, honoured on Czech stamps in 1945. Masaryk and Beneš preserved democracy in Czechoslovakia until the country was overrun by the Nazis

ence triumphed. Czechoslovakia was abandoned by its allies in 1938, and the Sudetenland was incorporated into Germany. Czechoslovakia began to disintegrate under further German pressure, and it ceased to exist when the Nazis marched into Prague in 1939 (see Sections 24.3(a) and (b)).

Democracy endured in Scandinavia in the inter-war years. Finland had seized independence from Russia during the upheavals of 1917, and a democratic constitution was adopted two years later. Finland was a republic, while the other Scandinavian countries (Sweden, Norway and Denmark) had monarchies; but they all retained liberal institutions. Many Scandinavian governments, like the socialist administrations in Sweden, were both efficient and progressive. The countries had a general history of stability, and stability encouraged the growth of prosperity. In spite of the Depression, the Scandinavian populations showed little enthusiasm for either communism or fascism. Elsewhere on the continent, the constitutional monarchies of the Netherlands and of Belgium, and the republican constitution of Switzerland, also proved resistant to more authoritarian movements: Dutch, Belgians and Swiss continued to prefer liberalism to totalitarianism. In 1921 the Irish Free State became independent of British government, and the Irish, too, successfully adopted a democratic constitution.

It seems unlikely that the traditional institutions were ever in serious danger in Britain in the inter-war years, in spite of severe economic difficulties and less than dynamic political leadership. The General Strike of 1926 passed without bloody conflict, and social tensions were contained within the democratic system. The British Communist Party dated from 1920, but it showed no enthusiasm for violent revolution even though, unlike the German KPD, it

Fig. 21.7 King Gustav of Sweden, a constitutional ruler in a country where democracy survived. Gustav, at the far end of the table, photographed at an outdoor luncheon with gramophone music playing through the loudspeaker. He reigned from 1907 to 1950

could not win parliamentary seats. In the 1930s the British Union of Fascists came into existence under the leadership of Oswald Mosley. Mosley marshalled his visions of *The Greater Britain* in book form, and the uniformed strutting and saluting of his Blackshirts was in imitation of the models he admired in Fascist Italy and Nazi Germany. But like their counterparts in Belgium and elsewhere, British Fascists remained only a noisy rabble. The disorders they created in east London echoed the early activities of Mussolini's Squadristi and of Hitler's Nazis, but they bore no political fruit, and the British Fascists were a spent force by 1939. By that time, however, the democracies which had survived in Europe were about to face a new peril. Not content with the rape of Czechoslovakia, Nazi Germany was cultivating a further grievance – against the Poles, whom Britain and France were pledged to protect (see Section 24.4).

Further Reading

Hiden, J. W.: *The Weimar Republic*. Longman (Harlow, 1974).
Holland, P.: *Twentieth-Century France*. Oxford University Press (London, 1965).
Johnson, D.: *The Inter-War Economy in Western Europe*. Harrap (London, 1973).
McKenzie, J. R. P.: *Weimar Germany, 1918–33*. Blandford (Poole, 1971).

Smith, D. A. G.: *Left and Right in Twentieth-Century Europe*. Longman (Harlow, 1970).
Snyder, L. L.: *The Weimar Republic*. Anvil (Dublin, 1966).
Tint, H.: *France since 1918*. Batsford (London, 1970).
Tint, H.: *Modern France*. Hamish Hamilton (London, 1966).
Yass, M.: *The Great Depression*. Wayland (Hove, 1970).

Documentary

Cranfield, G. A., Dalton, B. J. and Stambrook, F. G.: *Select Documents*. McGraw-Hill (Sydney, 1966). Includes German affairs 1918–39.

Exercises

1. Define *each* of the following terms: *communism; democracy; the proletariat; a totalitarian state*. Compare what you have written with the definitions in the Glossary on pages 433–6.
2. Was the Third Republic in France any more stable after 1918 (Section 21.2(*a*)) than before 1914 (Section 11.3)? Why did it survive until 1940?
3. Study Table 21.1 and explain the reasons for the changes it shows in the support for extremist parties in Germany.
4. Explain *each* of the terms, *inflation* and *depression*, and show how the first weakened the Weimar Republic in 1923, and the second weakened the Weimar Republic after 1929.
5. Why and how did Hitler become Chancellor of Germany, and what did Goebbels mean by 'fourteen years of work' (page 354)?
6. 'The Weimar Republic had battled through the 1920s' (page 341). 'The Germans, in fact, persevered longer with democracy after 1918 than did many states' (page 355). Outline the history of the Weimar Republic (Section 21.3), and explain why the author has used the words 'battled' and 'persevered'.
7. Why did not more Europeans 'prefer liberalism to totalitarianism' (page 358) in the years 1918 to 1939?

Unit Twenty-Two

The Dictatorships

22.1 Nationalism and Fascism

It was a characteristic of the dictators who rose to power in Europe in the inter-war years that they cherished the ideal of national strength. Many were carried to power on a tide of discontent and frustration with existing systems of government, which had proved 'weak'. Some came of a military background, like Kemal in Turkey, Primo de Rivera in Spain, and Pilsudski in Poland, considering it their destiny to impose a military discipline on government, and to develop the national spirit. They aimed to promote respect, both for authority and for the nation. Mussolini and Hitler, on the other hand, had had little military experience except among the rank and file of the First World War. But they elevated the notion of national greatness to even greater heights, dominating the European stampede to what Mussolini called 'Fascism' (see Section 12.3(*b*)). The essence of Fascism, in Mussolini's view, was the powerful state:

> The keystone of the Fascist doctrine is the conception of the State, of its essence, its purposes, its ends. For Fascism the State is an absolute, before which individuals and groups are relative. . . . The Fascist State organizes the Nation, but then leaves sufficient margin to the individuals. . . . The judge of such things cannot be the individual but only the State.

Behind the high-flown theories, however, lurked a quite simple idea. The subjects of the nation should obey the leader, who would embody both political authority and the national glory. Mussolini called himself *Il Duce*; Hitler called himself *Der Führer*; and Franco called himself *El Caudillo*. And the obedience they demanded was summarized in the oath required of members of the Italian Fascist Party:

> In the name of God and of Italy, I swear to execute the orders of Il Duce and to serve with all my powers, and, if necessary, with my blood, the cause of the Fascist Revolution.

Expressed even more briefly, Italian Fascism was based on the slogan, 'Mussolini is always right.' German Fascism, Nazism, was briefer still: 'Heil Hitler'.

Although both Mussolini and Hitler wrote extensively to elaborate their political philosophies, Fascism never achieved the intellectual stature, nor even the coherence, of Marxism. Fascist philosophy was a rag-bag of ideas based on the admiration of force, on theories of national and racial superiority, on selective views of history and on mystical beliefs in destiny. Fascists were fiercely anti-communist, but they made no claims to support capitalism. They opposed the class war and sometimes sought, as in the Italian Corporate State, to create a partnership between classes in the interests of national greatness. They believed in active government and in radical measures to deal with problems such as unemployment, and their policies could sometimes be vaguely socialist. Hitler called his movement National Socialism, though the socialism was little in evidence after 1929. It is a matter for controversy how widely the label 'Fascist' can be applied among the inter-war dictators, and in recent years the word has tended to become a rather meaningless term of abuse. Strictly, it should be applied only to Mussolini's regime, and to the movements, such as the British Union of Fascists, which sought to imitate it. Nor did the nationalist fervour of the inter-war dictators make all of them expansionist in the way that Mussolini and Hitler were expansionist. Kemal, Franco and many of the lesser dictators, recognized both the limitations of their nations and the dangers of foreign adventure, and they confined their activities to domestic organization. But however Mussolini might try to define the 'sufficient margin' for 'individuals', it was a characteristic of all the dictatorships that they abandoned the liberal concern for individual rights, which was essential in the democracies.

22.2   Fascist Italy

(a) The Fascist State

Mussolini quickly consolidated his power once he became the Prime Minister of Italy in 1922 (see Section 12.3(b)). The *Fasci* operated as a sort of private army to do his bidding. The monarchy imposed no restraints on the Prime Minister and, after the election of 1924, Mussolini had control of Parliament. Giacomo Matteotti, the outspoken socialist author of *The Fascists Exposed*, was murdered in that year, and it grew increasingly dangerous to obstruct the Fascist Grand Council which ran the Fascist organization. Fascists took control of key appointments and, in 1926, all political opposition was outlawed. The Italian parliament consisted only of Mussolini's stooges and, in 1928, electors could do no more than accept or reject the entire list of Fascist candidates, which the Grand Council authorized. Most chose to accept. A few years later, Mussolini further expounded the doctrine of Fascism:

> The Fascist conception of the State is all-embracing; outside of it no human or spiritual values may exist, much less have any value. Thus understood, Fascism is totalitarian.

The Fascists claimed that class warfare was the evil product of Marxism and unnecessary. At first they strongly supported private enterprise, but increasingly, although not always consistently, they turned in the 1930s to government economic controls. At the heart of the system lay the Corporations, and the state became the Corporate State. The Corporations were based on occupations and, within them, the Fascists brought together employers, managers and workers. They were subject to government supervision, under a Ministry of Corporations. The normal functions of trade unions were suspended; strikes and lock-outs were forbidden, and disputes were to be resolved by state officials. On the surface, the Corporate State provided a recipe for co-operation and progress but, in practice, it extended the authority of the Fascists. The Corporations were used to muzzle opposition, but they were frequently both inefficient and corrupt, and they did little to promote either harmony or economic expansion. Nevertheless in 1939 the Italian Parliament was replaced by a Chamber of Fasces and Corporations, pursuing the illusion of partnership between Party and the nation.

Illusion was the life-blood of the Fascist state. It thrived on propaganda, and the brilliance of Mussolini was proclaimed until he believed it himself. Under the leadership of 'the Sawdust Caesar', Italy gave the appearance of bustling efficiency. Party members in their black shirts saluted and paraded and made speeches. A censored press and radio created the illusion of dramatic and exciting achievement. Trains (some of them) ran to time, school-teachers wore uniform, and Italian society was organized as never before. Even sport was organized and regimented for the glory of the regime. A chief referee of Italian football in Rome presided with a golden whistle. There was no room for opposition and criticism, and Italians lost not only their freedom but their grip

Fig. 22.1 Benito Mussolini, in the lead as befitted Il Duce *and always the showman. This photograph of 1937 shows the* Duce *demonstrating the Roman Marching Step, loyally imitated by his Fascist followers, for the benefit of a German audience. But he had been impressed by the German goose-step, which he now intended to introduce into Italy*

on reality. Bent on recreating the Glory of Ancient Rome, Fascist Italy became a play-house, enacting the tragi-comedy that Italy under the Fascists was a great power. On the other hand, the regime avoided the excesses of Stalinism and of Nazism. Until Mussolini came under the spell of Hitler at the end of the 1930s, Fascism showed little evidence of anti-semitism, although Mussolini himself was inclined towards anti-semitism. Italian Fascists practised thuggery against dissidents, but incompetence and corruption rather than massive terror were the hallmarks of their regime. Mussolini was a bully-boy, but he lacked the self-discipline and capacity for hard work necessary to be a systematic tyrant. He was merely an unpredictable and theatrical one whose physique and character quickly degenerated.

The Fascist state made one important advance in 1929, settling the long-standing problem of relations with the Papacy. By the Lateran Treaties, Pius XI agreed to recognize the Italian government and to heal the long feud (see Section 12.2(b)). Grateful for this blessing on his regime, Mussolini gave official recognition to the Catholic religion, accepted the authority of the Church over Italian morals, and paid compensation for the lands the Papacy had long ago lost to the Italian state.

(b) The Great Illusion

Disappointment with the performance of the Italian economy had been an important factor in the downfall of liberal Italy. The Fascists hoped to create a more dynamic economy; but their vision of a self-sufficient and thriving economy, which could support a forward foreign policy, was not realistic. Italy lacked minerals and fuel, and it had too little foreign currency to buy supplies for rapid expansion. Volpi made the situation worse in 1925, when he revalued the lira at too high a level while trying to stabilize the currency. It was already difficult to market Italian exports, and the revaluation made them expensive and uncompetitive. Unemployment rose, and wages were depressed. In the early 1930s the Depression intensified the problem, and the Italian government ceased to publish the relevant statistics, apparently believing that a problem hidden was a problem solved.

Too often the Fascists showed a preference for propaganda and prestige projects rather than thorough planning and basic development. An economic revolution like that in the Soviet Union was out of the question, however, given Italy's meagre resources. The output of capital goods remained disappointing, in spite of the further development of hydro-electric power, the electrification of railways and the increases in production which followed the outlawing of strikes. But propaganda made the most of what achievement there was, and the impressive draining of the Pontine Marshes for agriculture was immortalized. At other times there was more noise than substance. Mussolini dramatized the 'Battles' his government fought. The 'Battle for Grain' did produce a greater output, but much of it was obtained on land more suited to fruit-growing. The 'Battle for Births' was similarly over-dramatized.

With high unemployment, Italy hardly seemed to need a larger population except perhaps to swell the armed forces. Nevertheless, the 'Battle' was fought, and taxes were imposed on bachelors to harry them into marriage and parenthood. Impressive new motorways (the *autostrade*) were built, along with fine public buildings such as railway stations and sports stadiums, and an earnest campaign was undertaken to reconstruct ancient monuments to remind Italians of the glories of Rome. Such ventures helped to encourage tourism and they gave an appearance of grandeur, but they did little to reduce unemployment and even less to generate real wealth. The government's concern for its subjects' welfare did not go far beyond the building of blocks of flats, and some limited measures of assistance to large families. The grandeur of public buildings and nostalgia for the ancient past did nothing to make the south less poverty-stricken, though the Fascists did make useful efforts to curb the activities in southern Italy of the Mafia and the Neapolitan Camorra (see Glossary).

In 1939 Mussolini had to admit to Hitler that Italy was 'not ready', in spite of a binding alliance, to fight alongside Germany. In foreign policy, as in his illusions about Italian economic growth, Mussolini's ambitions tended to run ahead of his capacity to fulfil them. 'I adore war,' he declared. 'War is to men what childbirth is to women'. The first of Ten Commandments issued to the Fascist youth organizations stated:

> Know that the Fascist and in particular the soldier must not believe in perpetual peace.

But war is expensive, and Mussolini found it difficult to finance major campaigning. He dreamed of a great Italian empire which would dominate the Mediterranean (*Mare Nostrum* – Our Sea), and he wanted to create a greater empire in east Africa than that which he had inherited. But he had to choose his victims with care and proceed with caution, lest his resources become overstretched. In the 1920s he seized Fiume and bullied Greece, and contented himself with the role of an important statesman at Locarno and in international councils (see Section 23.3). Until the mid-1930s, in fact, he often appeared to be a supporter of peace and stability. But his threadbare domestic policy called for distractions abroad and, by 1935, his eyes were fixed on Abyssinia (see Section 23.4(*c*)). The Abyssinian conquest gave him further delusions of grandeur, and Italy became inseparably linked in foreign policy with Nazi Germany. With growing confidence, Mussolini seized Albania in 1939, but he hesitated when Germany went to war with Britain and France. He was not 'ready' for such a conflict until June 1940, when France seemed to be already defeated and he hoped to get a share of the Nazi booty. He had over-reached himself, however, and Italy's involvement in the Second World War proved utterly disastrous (see Unit Twenty-Four). The Commandments to the young Fascists had continued:

> Discipline is the soul of armies; without it there are no soldiers, but only confusion and defeat. . . . One thing must be dear to you above all: the life of Il Duce.

Italian soldiers in the Second World War, however, proved no more effective than in the First World War. Their morale was sapped. Italy was invaded and, in the clamour to surrender, the Fascist regime collapsed. The Duce himself was later murdered by his fellow-countrymen, who no longer shared his visions of greatness.

22.3 The Turkish Republic and Mustapha Kemal

Mustapha Kemal had a more realistic appreciation of what was possible than had Mussolini. His first major achievement was the renegotiation of the Treaty of Sèvres at Lausanne (see Section 20.1(*f*)). He was elected President of the new Turkish Republic in October 1923, and the Republic soon became a one-party state in the grip of Kemal's Republican People's Party. After Lausanne, Kemal concentrated on authoritative government and modernization in Turkey, and he avoided dangerous foreign ambitions. Indeed, Kemal's was a fiercely non-expansionist nationalism, and he actually welcomed Turkey's loss of its Arab territories. In 1934, by general agreement, he took the title Atatürk, 'The Father of Turks'. His policy was to carry through a social and an economic revolution, which inevitably brought him into conflict with the supporters of tradition, and of the Islamic religion. He kept himself in power by relying on the army, and by riding roughshod over the opposition. Although he toyed with the idea of making the political system more democratic, it seemed more urgent that firm government should first cure Turkey of its reputation as 'the sick man of Europe'.

Europeanization seemed to Kemal to hold the key to modernization. He attacked the Islamic religion, which tied the state to the past. The Caliphate was abolished in 1924, and the Church was thus deprived of its watching brief over Turkish affairs. Four years later Turkey became a completely secular state, politics being divorced from religion, when Islam ceased to be the established religion in the country. Kemal also attacked other traditions, and the outward symbols of the old society were outlawed. It became illegal to keep harems, for women to be veiled, and for men to wear the fez. Western dress, the metric system and the western alphabet were introduced, along with the western weekend. The overhaul of the legal system led to new laws which abolished polygamy and which authorized civil marriage and divorce: Kemal aimed to revolutionize society, starting with the emancipation of women. Traditionalists were enraged, but Kemal was not without supporters. Madame Ferid Tek recalled in 1938:

> From the first we Turkish women were wholeheartedly Kemalist. The peasant, the bourgeois, the intellectual, all took the sacred cause passionately to heart.

She probably exaggerated, but the peasantry gained extensively from the redistribution of Church lands, and many could appreciate the social benefits of reform. Education was expanded and it was made free. Health services were

Fig. 22.2 Mustapha Kemal, the nationalist President of the Turkish Republic 1923–38. Kemal was eager to modernize his country but he had none of the expansionist ambitions of Mussolini

improved, and a system of social insurance was introduced. Banking and trade were encouraged as part of the drive towards a stronger economy.

Kemal had little interest in ideology, whether fascist or communist, but he recognized the advantages of state intervention in the economy. The Turkish state took control of the railways and of certain important industries, such as sugar production. In 1933 Kemal borrowed ideas from the Soviet Union, and introduced a Five-Year Plan. The government allocated funds for industrial development, which it protected by tariffs, and more scientific farming was encouraged, often through co-operatives. The results were not spectacular, since the available funds were limited and Turkey lacked both minerals and expertise. But Kemal's Turkey was more progressive and more efficient than the Turkey of the sultans, and it benefited from the new-found stability of honest, though ruthless, government.

Abroad Kemal sought constructive trade agreements rather than conquests. The Turks accepted the arbitration of the League of Nations when a dispute arose over Mosul in 1926, developing from a British claim to what they alleged was a part of the mandated territory of Iraq. Six years later Turkey became a member of the League. Turkish support was regularly given to condemnations of aggression throughout the 1930s, but the Turks were also careful to avoid entanglements. When Kemal died in 1938 he was succeeded by the Kemalist

Ismet Inönü, who kept Turkey out of the Second World War and presided over a further transition within the Republic – to parliamentary government.

22.4 Nazi Germany

(a) The Nazi State

The Enabling Law suspended the Weimar constitution for four years but, in effect, it abolished it (see Section 21.3(c)). In 1934 the Nazis went on to abolish the separate parliaments of the individual states within the Reich, such as Prussia. They also began to devour their own kind: the SA (*Sturmabteilung*) was destroyed on the night of 30 June 1934, the 'Night of the Long Knives'. The Brownshirts of the SA included potential rivals to Hitler; they also included party members who took the socialist pretensions of the Nazis more seriously than Hitler did. The SA antagonized the German military, who saw the Brownshirts as a rival force to the army. The Nazi élite, therefore, disposed of a variety of persons they no longer needed or trusted. In a night of murder, the victims included Ernst Röhm of the SA, Gregor Strasser (a Nazi who had too many scruples), and von Schleicher, the political manipulator. Some 400 perished in the purge. From now onwards, Hitler relied on the fanatical SS (*Schutzstaffel*), the Blackshirts who were organized by Himmler, a sadistic ex-school-teacher. Von Papen's life was spared, but he was forced to retire from office, and a final obstacle to the Nazis was removed when the aged Hindenburg died in August 1934. Hitler proclaimed himself *Führer*, combining in himself the offices of Chancellor, President, and military Commander-in-Chief. The remnants of the SA were merged into the *Wehrmacht*, the German army. A secret police force was developed, the *Gestapo*, to strike terror into all enemies of the Nazi regime, and this too, like the SS, came under the leadership of Himmler. The Reichstag had already been reduced to an assembly of loyal Nazis, cheering and saluting on cue, and Nazi officials had steadily taken over all political appointments. Trade unions were abolished, and a fierce censorship blotted out all criticism. As Minister of Propaganda, Goebbels distorted all truth in the service of the Nazi state, and an overwhelming majority of intimidated and deluded Germans gave approval to the changes in a plebiscite, held before the end of 1934. By this time, all power lay with the Nazis and, above all, with the Führer.

The regime was not unopposed but, in the face of Nazi ruthlessness, opposition could not be effective. The Catholic Church made a Concordat with Hitler as early as 1933, agreeing in effect that neither the Church nor the government would interfere with the other. But the Nazi persecution of the Jews proved too much for the Papacy and, in 1937, Pius XI condemned Hitler's doctrines in the Encyclical, *Mit Brennender Sorge* (With Burning Anxiety). The Lutheran Church was equally uneasy, and opposition was expressed by a group of Lutherans led by Pastor Niemöller. But for all those who defied the SS and the

Gestapo, the regime established concentration camps, which filled up steadily with humanitarians, liberals, democrats, socialists, and communists. Meanwhile, the masses and the more timid were brainwashed in a massive campaign of indoctrination. Above all, the Nazis concentrated on the youth of Germany. Apart from strictly controlled education in schools, the *Pimpfen* (Little Fellows) catered for children from the age of six to ten, rallying them with the slogan, 'Clench your teeth, boys; endure!' By the age of 10 the Little Fellows were expected to have acquired much 'important' knowledge, such as the history of Hitler and of the Nazis, the terms of the Treaty of Versailles, and the strategic targets in enemy countries. At 10 they could graduate to the *Jungvolk* for further preparation in Nazism, and they could go from the Young Folk into the *Hitler Jugend* at the age of 14, as a finishing school in fanaticism. Nor were girls neglected since, alongside the Hitler Youth, there existed the *Bund der Deutschen Mädeln* where German Girls could learn to appreciate the importance of becoming the mothers of soldiers of the Reich. Mussolini and Stalin also had their youth organizations, but they hardly matched the Nazis in their thoroughness. The children became agents of the state, keeping watch for any evidence of disloyalty, even among members of their own families. This was more important to the Nazis than any academic achievement, for the Nazis

Fig. 22.3 The Night of the Long Knives, 30 June 1934: David Low, a British cartoonist, comments on the purge of the SA, whose leaders wanted the Nazis to honour their socialist promises. Hitler, Goering (in a Wagnerian image) and the diminutive Goebbels are branded as the murderers, with the support in the background of the German army

despised intellectualism. Indeed, the number of university students fell dramatically.

Thus the German nation was mobilized in the service of the Nazis. The nation was to be made great, to fulfil its destiny as the nation of the *Herrenvolk*, the master race. First, the nation had to be purified, and purged of those, such as the Jews, who were said to pollute the race. As the Nazi Programme had asserted as early as 1920:

> None but those of German blood, whatever their creed, may be members of the nation. No Jew, therefore, may be a member of the nation.

The Nuremberg Laws of 1935, 'for the Protection of German Blood and Honour', deprived Jews of their rights as German citizens. A virulent campaign was launched to vilify and to humiliate the Jews. About half a million Jews lived in the Reich. Their businesses were boycotted, and they were dismissed from employment. Jews were required to wear a distinguishing patch on their clothing, in order to single them out for ostracism and ridicule. Julius Streicher, who became known as the Jew-Baiter, emerged as the Nazi organizer of persecution. In 1938, however, the initiative was taken by the SS General Heydrich, and there was a night of wanton destruction – called 'Crystal Night', because of the vast number of smashed windows. Jewish shops and houses were devastated, over 100 synagogues were burned and, in a

Fig. 22.4 Hitler, Hindenburg and Goering, an ill-assorted trio, photographed in August 1933 at a rally to celebrate the victory at Tannenberg in 1914. Hindenburg died twelve months later, and Hitler was able to make himself the Führer

vicious new pogrom, Jews were marched to the concentration camps in their thousands. When Poland was invaded in 1939, millions more Jews were exposed to the Nazi fury and, three years later, Hitler embarked on the 'Final Solution', a policy of genocide aiming to wipe out the Jewish race from German and German-seized territories. Some six million Jews perished at the hands of the Herrenvolk, almost three million of them in Poland, and a million in the Soviet Union, which the Germans invaded in 1941. This Holocaust was the true face of Nazism: racial hatred carried to the furthermost extremes of human cruelty.

(b) The Third Reich

Hitler chose to call his regime 'The Third Reich'. Economic strength was necessary for the Reich to achieve greatness and, like Mussolini, Hitler aimed at self-sufficiency, an *Autarky* based on what Germans themselves could produce, and on what they could plunder from the lands to which they claimed they were entitled. In the Depression years after 1929 the Nazis had promised to solve German economic problems, and they adopted the interventionist policies which were common to many dictatorships. Production was boosted wherever possible. Rejecting disarmament as soon as he achieved power, Hitler encouraged the manufacture of munitions. German scientists were set to work to find alternatives for the substances Germany was obliged to import, such as rubber, petrol and wool, and a new range of *ersatz* (substitute) commodities was produced. By 1938 Nazi Germany was the richest state on the European continent (see Table 20.2, page 334), but the Nazi achievement was only a modest one, given the foundations on which the regime built, and Germany's resources in expertise, manpower, and minerals. In fact the national economy was flawed. The government committed a large proportion of the national income to maintaining its armed forces (see Table 22.1(*a*)) and to extending its own bureaucracy. The balance of payments was far from healthy, and the continuing need for imports helped to provide an incentive for territorial expansion, since stolen imports would not need to be paid for. (Germany's share of world trade fell from 10 per cent in 1929 to 8 per cent in 1938.) On the surface, the Nazis had reduced unemployment, however. By 1937 the total of jobless had fallen from six to one million, but many of those who found employment did so in non-productive occupations. They were absorbed into the armed forces and the Nazi bureaucracy, and some simply took the places of ousted Jews.

There was, nevertheless, economic planning, similar to that in the Soviet Union. Government money was made available to expand industry and agriculture, and to encourage exporters. The government also kept a tight control over prices and wages, and the President of the Reichsbank, Dr Schacht, kept a watchful eye on Germany's currency. The munitions industry and extensive public works, among them the building of the *autobahnen*, helped to stimulate the economy and to spread a measure of prosperity. It was

WER EIN VOLK RETTEN WILL
KANN NUR HEROISCH DENKEN

Fig. 22.5 Nazi slogans with a philatelic souvenir sheet: Ein Volk, Ein Reich, Ein Führer *(One People, One State, One Leader);* Wer Ein Volk Retten Will . . . *(He who wishes to save a people can only think heroically). This sheet was 'postmarked' at Vienna shortly after the* Anschluss

government policy to make social improvements. State health services were expanded. Slums were demolished, to be replaced by better housing with controlled rents. But the Nazi economic and social policy was always the servant of ideology. Workers were regimented. The *Kraft durch Freude* (Strength through Joy) movement provided them with sports facilities, subsidized holidays and controlled leisure activities. The *Volkswagen* was intended to become the people's car, readily available to all workers when sufficient wealth was generated, and when such rewards had been earned by loyalty (see Table 22.1(*c*)). Parades and torchlight processions brought colour to drab lives (and also attracted a useful income from tourists), but at an early stage in the history of the regime many books had been burned to deprive Germans of unsuitable literature: the Nazis never felt it desirable that their subjects should think for themselves. Any form of disruption was punished. The Labour Front took the place of trade unions, seeking to produce the social harmony and co-operative effort at which Mussolini aimed through the Corporations. In a sense, the Nazis aimed to create a classless society, much as did the communists in the Soviet Union, yet the Nazi élite was as dominant as the Soviet

Communist Party. Unlike the Russians, however, the Nazis believed fanatically in racial superiority. Classlessness among the Herrenvolk was but a stepping-stone to the domination of lesser peoples by the Herrenvolk.

Hitler did not disguise his ambitions in eastern Europe. Germans, he believed, were entitled to *Lebensraum*, the living-space and elbow-room which was essential to German development. He considered that Slavs and east European people in general were, like the Jews, inferior people. It was at their expense that, in 1920, the Nazis demanded:

> land and territory for the nourishment of our people and for settling our surplus population.

At the same time, the Nazis were intent on destroying the peace settlement of 1919, and on extracting the maximum mileage from alleged injustices to Germany. From the outset the Nazi state was geared to militarism, to rearmament, and to substantial armed forces. From 1933, therefore, the rise of Nazi Germany was the dominant factor in the international history of Europe (see Section 23.4 and Unit Twenty-Four).

22.5   The See-Saw in Spain

Both Portugal and Spain arrived, by 1939, at dictatorship rather than democracy. In Portugal Antonio Salazar became Prime Minister in 1932, with ideas for a 'New State' to replace the old, whose history of parliamentary government and military interventions had proved disappointing. He borrowed ideas for the Corporate State from Mussolini, and for the one-party state from dictators in general; and he ruled until his retirement in 1968 with a government which showed many similarities to fascism.

Spain, meanwhile, had ended the nineteenth century in defeat, routed by the USA in a brief war in 1898 which ended with the loss of Spain's remaining possessions in the Americas (Cuba and Puerto Rico) and in the Pacific (the Philippines and Guam). Little was left of the Spanish empire but Rio d'Oro, and a claim to a part of Morocco. In spite of periodic upheavals, however, a system of constitutional monarchy survived in Spain itself, much influenced by the Catholic Church and the military. Spain remained neutral during the First World War, but it was not unaware of developments elsewhere in Europe. Spanish communists were quick to try to imitate the Bolsheviks, and there were widespread disturbances and strikes at the beginning of the 1920s. The upshot was a coup by Primo de Rivera, who dismissed the Spanish Parliament and, with the approval of the Church, of the landowners, of the army, and of King Alfonso XIII, imposed authoritarian rule from 1923. Some modernization and economic reorganization were undertaken, but the Depression brought new strains. Primo retired and Alfonso permitted elections in 1931. The monarchy itself was a casualty, since there was an overwhelming vote in

Table 22.1 Aspects of the Economy of Nazi Germany

(a) **Production of Armaments Index (Germany)**

1933	2
1934	2
1935	4
1936	6
1937	9
1938	20
1939	25
1940	44
1943	100

(b) **Production of Crude Steel** (million tons)

Year	Germany	Britain	France
1913	14.3*	7.8	3.5
1929	18.4	9.8	9.7*
1939	22.5	13.4	7.9*

* including Lorraine

(c) **Registered Motor Vehicles** (millions)

Year	Germany	Britain	France	Italy	USA
1913	0.09	0.21	0.13	—	1.26
1930	0.68	1.52	1.46	0.29	26.53
1938	1.82	2.42	2.25	0.47	29.44

Adapted from D. S. Landes, *The Unbound Prometheus*. Cambridge University Press (Cambridge, 1970).

support of republicanism, and Alfonso XIII went into exile. He had reigned for some 46 years.

The new Republic launched a vigorous assault on Spain's traditional institutions, spurred on by its success over the monarchy. President Zamora and his Prime Minister, Manuel Azaña, intended to carry out a social revolution, to reduce the power and privileges of landowners, and to weaken the influence of the Church and of the military. But it was difficult to get a parliamentary majority for resolute action. The vested interests were strongly entrenched, and regional rivalries hindered national policy. The election of 1931 had shown support for republicanism and socialism, but in 1934 there was a swing to the right and almost at once the new government began to undo Azaña's work. New political forces had emerged, a pro-Church party under Gil Robles

Fig. 22.6 General Franco, inspecting a guard of honour of the revolutionary forces at Burgos, a day after he had proclaimed himself Spain's Head of State

and the *Falangists*, a party with many similarities to the Italian Fascists, which was founded by José Primo de Rivera, the son of the dictator. The workers resorted to violent protest in pursuit of anarchist and communist revolution, and the army struck back brutally. Zamora ordered new elections for 1936 as Spain appeared to be becoming ungovernable. Left-wing parties united in a Popular Front, similar to that led by Blum in France, and they won a narrow victory over a similar coalition of the right – of Falangists, the Church, the army and the landlords. But the politics of the Cortes began to seem irrelevant. Catholic churches were attacked; the peasants seized land, and the workers demonstrated in support of communism. Reprisals by the army and extensive bloodshed only added fuel to the flames. Azaña took over the Presidency, but the divisions were too deep to be healed. Two contending sides emerged: the Republicans, supporting the social revolution and proclaiming the title to rule of the Popular Front, and the Nationalists, bent on restoring order and much that was traditional. The result was the Spanish Civil War, when General Franco, the Chief of Staff, invaded Spain with military units from Morocco, and proclaimed himself the Head of State in October 1936. A year later, borrowing from the example of Mussolini and Hitler, Franco styled himself *El Caudillo*.

By the end of 1936 the Nationalists had won control of much of west and north Spain, and had laid siege to Madrid. Spain became a battleground for ideologies. Mussolini and Hitler gave support to Franco and to the Falangists, recognizing in the Nationalists fellow-fascists. Stalin gave fitful support to the

Republicans, hoping that the outcome might be success for Spanish communists. But Stalin was not prepared to hazard the security of the Soviet Union, and his commitment was less than whole-hearted, as likely to consist of food and advice as of men and weapons. The democracies adopted a policy of non-intervention, and they set up a non-intervention committee of considerable irrelevance in London. Volunteers on the other hand flocked to Spain, principally to fight against fascism in the International Brigades. Communists, socialists, liberals, and democrats, rallied to the Popular Front, but their aims were varied and imprecise. They quarrelled among themselves, and even communists dissipated their energies in debates about Stalinism and Trotskyism. The Civil War lasted, nevertheless, for three vicious years but, in the end, the Republicans were no match for the Nationalists, some 50 000 Italians, and the German *Luftwaffe*.

The Nationalists won about half of Spain in 1936 but they were checked in the following year, when they made little progress except against the Basques in the far north. Guernica, the centre of Basque culture and by no means a military target, was razed by the Luftwaffe, whose master, Hermann Goering, used the war in Spain to perfect the new technique of dive-bombing. An eye-witness reported that, after the bombing of Guernica:

> fighting machines swooped low to machine-gun those who ran in panic from the dugouts. Many were killed as they ran. A large herd of sheep being brought in to market was also wiped out.

In 1938 Franco's forces cut through the middle of Spain and reached the Mediterranean coast. Madrid was besieged again and Barcelona was forced to surrender at the beginning of 1939. The Republican resistance crumbled. Stalin withdrew support and the International Brigades disintegrated. In March 1939 Madrid capitulated and the war ended, having taken three-quarters of a million lives. Franco established his dictatorship, presiding over a strongly right-wing regime.

Franco's regime was essentially Spanish, a Catholic dictatorship of Falangists and other Nationalists, dedicated to anti-communism and to upholding the interests of the Church, of the army, and of privileged groups such as landowners, financiers and industrialists. There was a brutal, political police force, and the regime certainly bore traces of fascism. But, like Kemal, Franco had no ambitions for foreign conquest. He thanked Mussolini and Hitler for their assistance, and sent a token force of Spaniards to plague the Russians during 1942, but he resolutely refused to become further involved in the Second World War, and Spain remained neutral. The Spanish parliament was re-convened during the War, but it had little power and, in 1947, Franco was declared Chief of State for life. Like Salazar's Portugal, Franco's Spain had internal stability, but it carried little weight in international affairs. When Mussolini and Hitler were dead, Salazar and Franco lived on as uncomfortable reminders of the inter-war fascism which Europeans would have preferred to forget. Franco ruled until his death in 1975, seven years after the retirement of Salazar.

22.6   The Lesser Dictatorships

Alone among the small states created after the First World War, Czecho-slovakia proved both prosperous and stable (see pages 356–7). The others turned to various systems of authoritarian government as they grappled with a multitude of problems, and periods of steady economic development were usually brief. Few of the states rested on solid economic foundations, and many of them lacked a substantial, liberal-minded middle class, such as might have been expected to show strong attachment to democracy. They turned, therefore, to those who posed as 'strong men' and upholders of order against confusion. But there was little evidence that these authoritarian governments as a whole were able to achieve much. The small states remained as they had been from the outset, tempting and almost defenceless neighbours to the greater powers of Europe.

The Baltic states escaped from the Russian Empire in 1918. Lithuania turned to a nationalist dictator, Antanas Smetona, in 1926, and the Depression and increased economic difficulties prodded Estonia and Latvia in a similarly authoritarian direction in the 1930s. Their independence was not destined to last, however. When the Second World War had already begun, and when Stalin was determinedly searching for security for the Soviet Union, the Russians repossessed the states in 1940, and incorporated them in the USSR (see Section 24.5(*b*)).

The states of southern Europe and the Balkans remained restless after 1918. The drawing of the Balkan frontiers had left discontented minorities. A movement for Macedonian independence plagued Bulgaria, and Croats were still inclined to believe that they should have had their own national independence when the Habsburg Empire broke up, rather than being merged into Jugoslavia. Jugoslavia was the peacemakers' answer to the South Slav problem. In some ways, the new state was an enlarged Serbia, under the Serbian royal family, the Karadjordjes. Its first name was cumbersome but descriptive – the *Kingdom of Serbs, Croats and Slovenes*. Rivalry between the races created instability and, in 1929, King Alexander established what was, in effect, a royal dictatorship, soon afterwards naming his Kingdom, Jugoslavia. He was murdered in 1934 by Croatian dissidents. Succeeding governments adopted an increasingly pro-German stance, until an anti-Nazi coup occurred in 1941, when Jugoslavia was promptly invaded by the Germans.

Other states had also moved towards fascism and towards collaboration with Nazi Germany. Horthy ruled *Hungary* from 1920, and he became a German ally in the Second World War. In *Rumania*, the monarchy provided poor leadership and politicians were notoriously corrupt. King Carol II paid little attention to the wishes of the people in appointing his ministers in the 1930s.

Fig. 22.7 The self-styled King Zog of Albania with some of the ladies of his court in national costume. Mussolini seized Zog's throne for Victor Emmanuel III of Italy in 1939

His governments were usually right-wing and anti-semitic. A new constitution in 1938, and the dominance of the Party of National Rebirth, made little difference, and the country drifted steadily towards fascism and an alliance with the Nazis against the Soviet Union. *Bulgaria* staggered along a similar path. Until 1923 King Boris combined his monarchy with a curious peasant dictatorship led by Alexander Stamboliisky, whose rule in the interests of the peasantry produced a right-wing backlash, and resulted in his own murder. Boris then appointed a succession of royal nominees, while the turbulent Macedonian Revolutionary Organisation carried out a wave of assassinations. Military leaders took control of affairs in 1934, and Bulgaria subsequently collaborated with Nazi Germany. Boris kept his throne long enough to help the Germans to invade Jugoslavia in 1941.

Albania, meanwhile, adopted a republican constitution in 1925, only for the first President of the Republic to proclaim himself King Zog three years later, and thereafter to rule as a virtual dictator. But Albania was high on Mussolini's shopping list. The country became economically dependent on Italy; the Albanian army was Italian-trained, and Mussolini laboured to ensure that Albanians would have little power to resist an Italian takeover. He judged that the time was ripe in April 1939. King Zog was put to flight and Albania was handed to Victor Emmanuel as a new trophy to the glory of Italian Fascism.

Mussolini also had ambitions in *Greece*. There had been a struggle in Greece during the First World War between King Constantine and Eleutherios

Venizelos. Venizelos finally succeeded in linking Greece to the Allies in the war against the Central Powers, and Constantine was forced to abdicate in 1917. He returned to the throne in 1920, only to lose it again, and a republic was proclaimed in 1924. Venizelos was similarly in and out of office, until he was forced to flee from Greece after an attempted coup in 1935. In that year the monarchy was again restored, but King George II almost at once installed a fascist-type dictatorship led by General Metaxas. Mussolini invaded in 1940, but he had quickly to call for help from the Germans. By the end of 1941, almost the whole of the Balkans was under Nazi domination.

Poland had a population of more than 30 million people. It was sandwiched between Germany and Russia, and it faced the problem after 1918 of unifying areas which had recently been ruled by Germans, by Russians, and by the Habsburg Empire. The country had also suffered wartime devastation, and it would take time to build a healthy economy. Natural resources were not extensive, and there was a high level of unemployment from the outset. The Poles first intended to fashion a democratic republic, and Poland was represented at the peace conference in Paris in 1919 by Paderewski, the pianist-prime minister. The constitution worked badly, however. There were too many small political parties in the Polish parliament, and many of them represented only sectional interests. As in Weimar Germany, the multiplicity of parties was encouraged by an electoral system based on proportional representation. Paderewski's government fell even before the end of 1919, and it was followed by further short-lived administrations. In 1923 Poland suffered from inflation, and economic and political disappointments paved the way for a coup. Jozef Pilsudski marched on Warsaw in 1926, to set the political house in order. Pilsudski was a veteran Polish nationalist, and he had led Poland's forces in the war against Russia in 1920–1. From 1926 to his death in 1935, he was virtually a dictator. His regime was not entirely illiberal, and elections continued to be held; but opposition was curbed, and strict censorship was imposed. Stability and continuity were the first considerations in the appointment of ministers. The Depression nevertheless brought new strains, and more than 20 per cent of the Polish labour force was unemployed. Pilsudski's death led only to the rule of other military leaders, whose viciousness came near to provoking civil war.

Poland began by setting a poor example in international affairs, and by resorting to violence in pursuit of national ambitions – over Teschen, Vilna and the frontier with Russia. By 1925, however, Poland sought security in alliance with France. Pilsudski warned of the dangers of the growth of Nazism in Germany and, as late as 1936, Jozef Beck, whom Pilsudski had appointed Foreign Minister, reaffirmed that the Poles would stand by the French alliance if France were prepared to resist Hitler's remilitarization of the Rhineland (see Section 23.4(*d*)). France was not prepared to resist. By 1938 the Poles showed more interest in adjusting their own frontiers at the expense of Czecho-slovakia, than in further encouraging the French to resist the Nazis at Munich (see Section 24.3(*a*) and (*b*)). But Nazi ambitions turned towards Poland itself in 1939, and Beck obtained British as well as French guarantees of support. The Poles were in a dilemma, however. To the west of Poland lay Nazi Germany, and to the east of Poland lay the Soviet Union. The Poles had no wish to see Soviet forces coming westwards even to contain Nazism and, indeed, this was perhaps an insuperable barrier, at the time of the Munich Conference, to an effective Russian defence of Czechoslovakia. The Poles adamantly refused to allow Russian troops again to set foot on Polish soil: they had too many recollections of their earlier history. Polish fears were nevertheless realized in August 1939. When the Nazi-Soviet Pact was signed it contained secret clauses to allow Russian troops to occupy eastern Poland if the Germans were to attack Poland from the west. The Polish state was thus overrun in September 1939, and war in Europe began when Britain and France honoured their pledges to the Poles, and declared war on Nazi Germany (see Section 24.4).

In the event, the democracies went to war in support of a state where democracy was non-existent, which had itself shown only a patchy respect for international law, and which, by its hostility to the Soviet Union, had handicapped their efforts to deter the Nazis by the threat of coalition.

Further Reading

See **Further Reading** for Units Twelve and Twenty-one
Bayne-Jardine, C.: *Mussolini and Italy*. Longman (Harlow, 1966).
Berwick, M.: *The Third Reich*. Wayland (Hove, 1971).
Blinkhorn, M.: *Mussolini and Fascist Italy*. Methuen (London, 1983).
Cassells, A.: *Fascist Italy*. Routledge and Kegan Paul (London, 1969)
Catchpole, B.: *Twentieth-Century Germany*. Oxford University Press (London, 1965)
Elliott, B. J.: *Hitler and Germany*. Longman (Harlow, 1966)
Gibbs, J.: *The Spanish Civil War*. Ernest Benn (London, 1973)
Gregory, F. H.: *Goering*. Wayland (Hove, 1974)
Kedward, R.: *Fascism in Western Europe, 1900–45*. Blackie (Glasgow, 1972)
Mandle, W. F.: *Fascism*. Heinemann (London, 1968)
Musman, R.: *Hitler and Mussolini*. Chatto and Windus (London, 1968)
Palmer, A. W.: *Yugoslavia*. Oxford University Press (London, 1964)
Pullar-Smith, M. A.: *Hitler and Mussolini*. Blackie (Glasgow, 1979)
Snellgrove, L. E.: *Franco and the Spanish Civil War*. Longman (Harlow, 1965)
Weber, E.: *Varieties of Fascism*. Anvil (Dublin, 1964)

Documentary

Browne, H.: *Spain's Civil War*. Longman Seminar Studies. (Harlow, 1983).
Gregory, D.: *Mussolini and the Fascist Era*. Edward Arnold (London, 1968)
Hewison, A.: *The Spanish Civil War*. Edward Arnold (London, 1973)
Phillips, D. M.: *Hitler and the Rise of the Nazis*. Edward Arnold (London, 1968)

Exercises

1. (*a*) Summarize the various ways in which Mussolini and his supporters themselves defined Fascism (Sections 12.3 (*b*), 22.1 and 22.2).
   (*b*) What further definitions have been added by the author of this book?
   (*c*) How would you yourself define the term?
2. Bearing in mind the previous history of governments in Italy (Unit Twelve), arrange in two separate columns the advantages and disadvantages to Italians of Mussolini's domestic policies. What overall conclusions can you draw from these columns?
3. 'Kemal's Turkey was more progressive and more efficient than the Turkey of the sultans' (page 366). Explain and illustrate this statement.
4. Study the cartoon on page 368. Explain (*a*) to what the cartoon refers, and (*b*) what attitudes to Nazism on the part of the cartoonist are most clearly suggested.
5. In what ways does Section 22.4 show that the Nazis after 1933 (*a*) gained almost total control over the lives of Germans, and (*b*) achieved only limited success in their economic policies?
6. Write *two* letters from the point of view of a German who had earlier voted for the Social Democrats, expressing your views of life in Germany under the Nazis by 1938, one for publication in a German newspaper, the other to be sent secretly to friends outside Germany.
7. What divisions existed in Spanish society in the 1920s and 1930s? How did these divisions lead to civil war, and which sections of Spanish society supported Franco's bid to become El Caudillo?

The Struggle for International Co-operation and Peace

23.1 Before the First World War

Europeans stepped gingerly before 1914 towards a degree of international co-operation, but they stopped well short of establishing permanent peace-keeping machinery to prevent war. Instead, they sought to make war less barbaric, though the First World War showed the measure of their failure. Jean Dunant, a Swiss, witnessed the carnage at the Battle of Solferino (see page 108), and the Red Cross movement was begun as a result of his compassion for the wounded. The Red Cross Convention laid down regulations for the treatment of war-time casualties, including those of the enemy, and this Convention was accepted by many European governments in 1864. The Red Cross then grew steadily. It spread to the USA in 1881 and eventually became worldwide. Further Conventions were signed, extending the influence of the Red Cross to war at sea in 1907 and, when the movement had proved itself invaluable during the First World War, to prisoners of war and to the protection of civilians. In 1917 the International Committee of the Red Cross was awarded the Nobel Peace Prize, an annual prize first made in 1901 under the will of Alfred Nobel.

Nicholas II of Russia also took an initiative towards international co-operation. He suggested a meeting at the Hague in 1899, to consider how best to secure 'real and lasting peace', and to reduce the level of armaments (see Section 17.2). Armaments were not reduced, partly because of strong opposition to the idea from Germany. On the other hand, agreements were reached about the 'rules' of war, and poison gases and explosive bullets were outlawed. The most important decision of the Conference, however, led to the setting up of the Permanent Court of Arbitration in 1901. A panel of judges was drawn up, to whom quarrelling nations could submit disputes which involved 'neither honour nor vital interests'. The Court's authority was thus limited, and it proved irrelevant to the conflicts of major powers (for example in 1914). Nevertheless, it was the forerunner of the Permanent Court of International Justice, which was set up in 1921 under the auspices of the League of Nations.

Nicholas II persevered, and a further Hague Conference met in 1907, this time with representatives from 44 governments. Disarmament was again rejected, however, and it was suggested rather unkindly that it only appealed to the Tsar because he was desperately short of money. In some ways, the Conference even took a step backwards, failing to renew the ban on poison gas

Fig. 23.1 An East German stamp of 1957 commemorating the founding of the International Red Cross by Jean Henri Dunant

and explosive bullets; but further declarations were issued concerning other 'rules' for warfare on land and at sea. Another Hague Conference was planned for 1915, but it was not to meet. By 1915, a new and more terrible war was already demonstrating that what Europe needed was not 'rules' to make warfare respectable, but machinery to prevent wars from occurring.

Europeans were not ready for such machinery before 1914. The period of the congresses which followed the Napoleonic Wars had been short-lived, and the powers had reverted, by the mid-1820s, to the pursuit of national, rather than international interests (see Section 2.2). Thereafter, conferences were sometimes hastily summoned to discuss specific problems and to de-fuse crises, but it could not be claimed that there was a 'system' for keeping the peace. No conference was convened to prevent Europe plunging into war in 1914 (see Section 17.5). The war taught Europeans a lesson, however. Support grew for the setting up of some permanent peace-keeping machinery – what Woodrow Wilson, in his Fourteen Points, called:

> a general association of nations . . . under specific covenants, for the purpose of affording mutual guarantees of political independence and territorial integrity to great and small nations alike.

Thus, the League of Nations was born in 1920.

23.2   The League of Nations

(a) The League's Machinery

The Covenant of the League of Nations was drawn up quickly, and it was incorporated into the postwar treaties made at Paris (see Sections 20.1(*b*) and 20.3). It pledged the members of the League to 'just and honourable relations

Table 23.1   The Machinery of the League of Nations

CENTRAL ORGANS				AUXILIARY ORGANS		
ASSEMBLY	COUNCIL	SECRETARIAT	COURT of JUSTICE	PERMANENT COMMISSIONS	SPECIAL COMMISSIONS	AGENCIES
Annual Meetings for General Supervision Often worked through committees Original Membership: 42 Based on the principle of equality	Quarterly Meetings and Meetings in Crisis Supervising and Co-ordinating Role Original Membership: 4 Permanent (Major Powers) 4 Elected (Lesser Powers)	International Civil Service at Geneva First Secretary-General: Eric Drummond 1919–33	Permanent Court of Justice at the Hague Originally: 11 Judges and 4 Deputy Judges	for DISARMAMENT MANDATES MILITARY AFFAIRS	*Administration* Danzig The Saar *Inquiry* Manchuria 1931 (Lytton)	*Organizations* Health Organization International Labour Organization Organization for Communications and Transit Economic and Financial Organization *Committees for* Child Welfare Drug Traffic Minorities Refugees Women's Rights *Support for* Red Cross Universal Postal Union
CONTROL OF BUDGET	F	I	N	A	N	C	E

between nations', to 'obligations not to resort to war' and to respect for 'international law'. Forty-two states initially joined the League, but it was a major setback to the organization when the USA declined to take up membership: American voters shied away from international entanglements, and they rejected the policy of Wilson and the Democrats in the elections of 1920. The membership of the League grew nevertheless. By 1923 its 54 members included Austria, Bulgaria and Hungary, all of which had been excluded at the outset as defeated Central Powers. Most of the machinery of the League was also in operation by 1923. In the meantime, crises had often been dealt with by the Conference of Ambassadors, of representatives from Britain, France, Italy and Japan, meeting in Paris. Although the Conference was not wound up until 1931, the work of the Ambassadors was limited in 1924 to matters arising from the peace settlement, so that the League of Nations at Geneva thus became the world's principal peace-keeping organization – its function, 'to promote international co-operation and to achieve international peace and security'. (Table 23.1 and the summary of the Convenant in Section 23.5 show how the machinery of the League fitted together.)

The main organs of the League were the Assembly and the Council, with whom rested the principal responsibility for the settlement of disputes. The Permanent Court of Justice continued to sit at the Hague, to deal with disputes of a legal nature, rather than of a political nature. Several Commissions had specific responsibilities, such as the Commissions for Disarmament and Mandates. A variety of organizations and committees reflected the broader interests of the League, for example the International Labour Organization, and committees for refugees and for women's rights. The League additionally took on a modest role in connection with the recent peace treaties, of which the administration of the Saar provided an example. The whole structure was serviced by the Secretariat, whose paid officials pledged their loyalty to the League and to the international community. The underlying intention of the League was not only to prevent future wars, but to promote the well-being of mankind, by international co-operation on an unprecedented scale.

The Assembly was founded on the principle of equality. Each member-nation, regardless of its size, had the right to be heard and to cast an equal vote. The Assembly met annually. It controlled the League's budget, and it had a general authority over all the League's affairs, including the admission of new members and the membership of Committees. At first sight the rules of the Assembly seemed to provide a recipe for paralysis, since decisions had to be unopposed, and one dissenting vote would constitute a veto. But in practice the Assembly worked well, and it made a real contribution to international co-operation. Work was often done in committees and, when final votes were taken, those dissenting frequently abstained in order not to block the will of the majority.

The League of Nations Council was a smaller body than the Assembly. It met at least every three months, and it could be summoned quickly to deal with crises. The original intention in the Covenant was to give permanent seats in the Council to the five major powers who were victorious in 1918, but the withdrawal of the USA left only Britain, France, Italy and Japan with permanent seats, though Germany was added in 1926. Four other members of the Council were to be elected by the Assembly for limited periods, and the first non-permanent members were Belgium, Brazil, Greece and Spain. The number of elected members rose to six in 1922, nine in 1926, ten in 1933, and eleven in 1936. Such growth showed the eagerness of many smaller powers to play their part in international decision-making, but Council decisions also had to be unopposed, and decisions needed to be taken quickly in times of crisis, therefore a larger Council might well be a less efficient one.

The Permanent Court of Justice had 15 judges of various nationalities, to give legal advice to the Council and to hear cases involving international law. The contesting parties in such cases agreed in advance to accept the verdict of the Court, a safeguard against time-wasting. The officials of the Secretariat were also drawn from various nationalities, and an international civil service was developed under the leadership of Eric Drummond, the first Secretary-General of the League, who served until 1933. No such body of officials had existed previously, and it was one of the achievements of the League that it built up a dedicated and efficient force of bureaucrats, committed to international co-operation.

Much constructive work was done in the numerous lesser bodies which helped to make up the League. Since this work was usually undramatic and involved few confrontations between nations, it often went unreported in contemporary newspapers. The International Labour Organization did achieve a measure of publicity, however, partly due to the energy of its first Director, Albert Thomas, a passionate French socialist. But the popular press in particular found little that was newsworthy in the activities of the Health Organization, the Intellectual Co-operation Organization and the Organization for Communications and Transit, though these Organizations worked earnestly to improve the world's standards of health, education and communications. The committees which dealt with women's rights, child welfare, refugees, prisoners of war, drugs, and economic problems, were similarly seldom reported. The League tended to be judged for its successes and failures in dealing with international quarrels, and too little attention was paid to its important work in humanitarian and social fields. Under Thomas, the ILO campaigned zealously to improve working conditions, wages and pensions, and to spread trade unionism. The USA became a member of the ILO, since membership was not restricted to members of the League. Each member of the Organizations sent four representatives to its annual conference and, of these, two represented government and the remaining two, employers and workers. By publicizing advanced practices in relation to employment and by putting pressure on backward states and employers, the Organization was able to improve the lot of millions of the world's workers. The other bodies had similar successes and, at the same time, they were able to harness the contributions to international co-operation of countless individuals, the majority of whom gave their services unpaid.

Article 22 of the Covenant dealt with mandated territories and set up the Mandates Commission, to supervise them and to report to the Council. The mandated territories were the former colonial possessions of Germany and of the Ottoman Empire (see page 334 and Section 20.3). The task of the Mandates Commission was to ensure that they were well governed and prepared for independence. Iraq moved smoothly to independence as early as 1932, having been mandated for a time to Britain. Other mandated territories reached independence more slowly, most of them after the Second World War, when the work of the Mandates Commission had been taken over by the United Nations Trusteeship Council. Progress was sometimes disappointingly slow, but the Mandates Commission carefully collected annual reports and served constantly to remind the mandatory powers of their 'sacred trust'. It was likely that the European powers were also made more aware of the need to apply the general principles of the mandate system to all their colonies, and the British at least began to show a slowly increasing interest in the welfare of their colonial subjects.

The Disarmament Commission encountered more opposition from national interests than did the Mandates Commission. Article 8 of the Covenant pledged member-nations to recognize that:

> the maintenance of peace requires the reduction of national armaments to the lowest point consistent with national safety.

But, like the Hague Conferences before 1914, the Disarmament Commission found that states were not willing to reduce their own armaments and thus set an example. Anxiety about 'national safety' remained too strong (see pages 391–2).

(b) The League's Limitations

The League of Nations suffered from two major handicaps. It lacked teeth with which to bite international wrongdoers, and it lacked a total commitment to it on the part of its members. The lack of teeth had to a large extent been written into the Covenant. The Covenant was drafted hastily, but it was also drafted by optimists, who too readily assumed that future crises would be caused by minor powers, and that such powers would easily be overawed by the pronouncements of the League. Articles 10–17 dealt with the League's responses to aggression; but they did little to anticipate what might be done if a major power insisted on breaking the rules of international good behaviour, and they were vague about dealing with non-members of the League. Hopefully, they assumed that moral disapproval and censure would be enough to bring an erring state into line. If that was not enough, there was provision for economic sanctions (an economic boycott) and, in the last resort, the Council could recommend:

what effective military, naval or air force the Members of the League shall severally contribute to the armed forces to be used to protect the covenants of the League (Article 16).

The underlying dilemma, of course, was that if the League were to raise 'armed forces', it would be threatening to go to war in order to prevent war, and the Council never used this final sanction. Parties to a dispute were not allowed to vote on it, but this was not enough. Those who did vote preferred weak compromises to stern action. Japan was condemned for seizing Manchuria in 1931, but no sanctions were imposed. Italy was condemned some years later for invading Abyssinia, and weak economic sanctions were imposed, only to be abandoned in 1936 when they had little effect. Japan and Italy walked out of the League, and the latter was so discredited that, when the Germans invaded Poland in 1939, the League had become irrelevant to the settlement of international crises. The Covenant had proved too optimistic in the vital area of dealing with aggression.

The Covenant could have been amended, and the rules of the League could

MORAL SUASION.

The Rabbit "MY OFFENSIVE EQUIPMENT BEING PRACTICALLY *NIL*, IT REMAINS FOR ME TO FASCINATE HIM WITH THE POWER OF MY EYE"

Fig. 23.2 Punch showed little confidence in the powers of the League of Nations in July 1920. The 1930s showed that the Moral (Per)Suasion of the League was not enough to deter aggressors

have been sharpened, if the members of the League had been more firmly committed to it. The best opportunity for strengthening the League occurred in 1924. In that year the Assembly enthusiastically considered the Geneva Protocol, a set of proposals to strengthen the machinery for dealing with aggression, which included measures of disarmament, plans for compulsory arbitration in disputes, and a treaty of mutual security. The Protocol might well have been adopted, but the Labour government in Britain was defeated in a general election, and the incoming Conservative government under Baldwin rejected the Protocol as binding Britain too tightly to international obligations. The opportunity was therefore missed. The League continued to lack teeth. It was also handicapped by the absence of the USA and, until 1934, of the Soviet Union, so that the burden of its support fell too heavily on Britain and France. France sought security outside the League, in old-fashioned treaties of alliance; and Britain anxiously sought to avoid all unnecessary commitments. Worse than that, however, Japan, Germany and Italy chose in the 1930s to defy the League rather than to support it, deliberately putting their alleged national interests first, and scorning the very idea of international co-operation for peace. In the face of this defiance, the League of only some Nations could not be expected to deter them effectively. From the outset, however, commitment to the League had been less than total. Its members found little difficulty in declaring support for its principles, but they preferred words to action. The League was as short of money as it was of teeth. Members were reluctant to contribute generously to its budget, and the Assembly persistently showed interest in reducing the costs of international co-operation. In spite of the lessons of the First World War, the nations of Europe still preferred to spend money on weapons, it seemed, than to spend money on the League of Nations. The average annual budget of the League, for all its organs and staff, was little more than five million dollars.

23.3 The 1920s: Decade of Hope

(a) Territorial Alterations

The Paris peace settlement was a remarkably detailed one in view of the speed with which it was accomplished. The details, however, were not universally pleasing, and Section 20.1(g) has already shown that various changes were made to the treaties at the beginning of the 1920s, often by force. Poland in particular showed a readiness to resort to violence in pursuit of its objectives against Russia, Czechoslovakia and Lithuania. Italy, although a permanent member of the League of Nations Council, hardly set a better example of law-abiding behaviour. The government of liberal Italy dislodged D'Annunzio from Fiume which he had seized from Jugoslavia in 1919, but the Italian appetite had been whetted (see page 188). After coming to power in Italy in 1922, Mussolini wasted little time in seizing Fiume again, and this time

Jugoslavia had to accept the Italian occupation. Meanwhile, Mussolini had resorted to force against Greece, to avenge what he chose to consider was an insult to Italy's, and to the Fascists', honour. The Conference of Ambassadors had sent a mission to map the Greek-Albanian border, and an Italian general and four of his staff were shot in a skirmish on Greek territory. Mussolini bombarded and occupied the Greek island of Corfu, pressing a claim for compensation. Rejecting a role for the League of Nations in the matter, Mussolini persuaded the Conference of Ambassadors to order the Greeks to apologize and to pay up. His own bullying behaviour passed without censure. It was an ominous start to Fascist rule in Italy, but Mussolini embarked on a more peaceful course after securing Fiume in 1924 and, although scheming to infiltrate Albania, for some ten years he supported the League and international stability.

The League began to establish its authority. It promoted an international loan to assist Austria through its early economic troubles, and it settled a dispute about possession of the Aaland Islands in 1921. The Islands were awarded to Finland, and Sweden accepted the League's verdict. In 1925 the League again achieved success, when it intervened in a minor war between Greece and Bulgaria which had developed from border incidents. Greece was admonished for aggression, and it was persuaded to withdraw and to compensate the Bulgarians. A year later Turkey accepted the League's ruling on a border dispute with Britain concerning Mosul and, by that time, the League had also made awards in disputes between Colombia and Venezuela, and between Chile and Peru. Significantly, however, it had looked on helplessly when France, a major power, had invaded the Ruhr in 1923.

(b) The Revival of Germany

The Genoa Conference of 1922 met at the suggestion of Lloyd George, primarily to consider the problems of economic reconstruction. The Conference as a whole came to nothing, but it provided the opportunity for diplomatic activity on the sidelines. The British offered the French the prospect of firmer British support for their security, if France would soften its antagonism towards Germany and Russia. The suggestion was rejected in the French parliament, however, and Britain's tentative movement towards a greater involvement in post-war Europe was frustrated. Germany and Russia, on the other hand, drew together. Rathenau and Chicherin moved from Genoa to nearby Rapallo, and surprised Europe with a bilateral treaty (see page 308). The Treaty of Rapallo led to a resumption of German-Russian diplomatic and commercial relations:

> to give each other mutual assistance for the alleviation of their economic difficulties in the most benevolent spirit.

Financial claims arising from the First World War were mutually renounced and, secretly, Chicherin undertook to allow Germany to build and test

Fig. 23.3 Part of the French occupation forces in the Ruhr, photographed outside the railway station at Essen, February 1923. The Germans jeered and refused to co-operate with the invaders

weapons on Russian soil, in defiance of the Treaty of Versailles. The Treaty was strengthened in a further Treaty of Berlin in 1926, and in the further establishment of conciliation machinery in 1929. But the practical results of the Treaty of Rapallo were few: it gave a lift to German morale, and it provided the Bolsheviks with recognition by a major power, but it lapsed when the Nazis came to power in Germany in the 1930s. In 1922, however, it increased French anxieties, since Germany appeared once more to be assuming the role of an international power. Since the Treaty coincided with Germany's falling behind in the payment of reparations, French and Belgian troops invaded the Ruhr in January 1923 (see page 348), and the French remained in stubborn occupation until July 1925 in spite of fierce protests from the USA and Britain. But the occupation was fruitless, and few reparations were collected.

There were further disappointments for the French when Britain rejected the Geneva Protocol (see Section 23.2(*b*) above), but its discussion led to more constructive western policies towards Germany. The Dawes Plan of 1924 made American loans available, enabling Germany to keep up its payments of reparations, and statesmen were ready to look for constructive agreements in 1925. The Foreign Ministers of Germany, France and Britain (Stresemann, Briand and Austen Chamberlain), were men who preferred reconciliation to confrontation. Mussolini was also in a mood to be constructive, and they met in Locarno with representatives from Belgium, Czecho-slovakia and Poland. The outcome was a series of agreements, signed in October 1925, which were intended to:

> bring about a moral relaxation of the tension between nations . . . [and to] help powerfully towards the solution of many political and economic problems in accordance with the interests and sentiments of peoples, and . . . in strengthening peace and security in Europe . . . [to] hasten on effectively the disarmament provided for in Article 8 of the Covenant of the League of Nations.

One of the Locarno Treaties was a Rhineland Pact. Belgium, France and Germany confirmed the sanctity of their boundaries as laid down in the Treaty of Versailles, and they confirmed that the Rhineland would remain demilitarized. The boundaries and the demilitarization were guaranteed by Britain and Italy, and the Pact was to come into force when Germany had been admitted into the League of Nations. A further Treaty of Arbitration bound France and Germany to accept mediation in any future disputes. Germany signed similar Treaties of Arbitration with Belgium, Czechoslovakia and Poland, but significantly avoided accepting the sanctity for all time of its eastern frontiers. Equally significantly, Britain undertook no guarantees in eastern Europe. France, on the other hand, searching relentlessly for as many guarantees as possible, signed Treaties of Mutual Guarantee with both Czechoslovakia and Poland, to complete the Locarno package.

Germany joined the League of Nations in 1926 and it seemed for a time that Europe was entering a new phase of 'peace and security'. In fact the Locarno Treaties were eventually to prove useless. In 1936 Nazi Germany remilitarized the Rhineland and no country upheld the Rhineland Pact (see Section 23.4(d)). (British occupation forces had been evacuated from the Rhineland in 1926, and the French left in 1930.) Two years later France failed to uphold its obligations to Czechoslovakia (see Section 24.3). It could even be argued that the Locarno Treaties weakened the force of the Treaty of Versailles, since Germany's western boundaries could now appear more sacred than its boundaries to the east. The Soviet Union, of course, was not a party to the Treaties, and tended to regard them, like them the League of Nations, as some sort of capitalist conspiracy. It was in an attempt to reassure Russia that Germany signed the Treaty of Berlin, confirming the Treaty of Rapallo. Nevertheless, Locarno gave new hope to Europe and, at least until the death of Stresemann and the onset of the Depression in 1929, Franco-German relations enjoyed something of a honeymoon.

Little came of the hopeful intentions to 'hasten on' disarmament, however. Germany had in general been held to the disarmament clauses of the Treaty of Versailles during the 1920s, but other powers had taken few steps to reduce the level of armaments. There was an agreement in Washington in 1921 to reduce capital ships (battleships and cruisers) by stopping their building for ten years, and by cutting down existing fleets. The USA, Britain and Japan agreed to trim their fleets to a ratio of 5:5:3, and France and Italy agreed each to have slightly more than half of the Japanese total of ships. The USA, Britain and Japan made a new agreement in 1930 in London to cover other warships and submarines, this time in the ratio 10:10:7, but France and Italy undertook no new commitments. More general disarmament remained out of reach. The Disarmament Commission of the League of Nations made no headway before the Locarno Treaties, but a further Conference was summoned in 1926 in the hope of exploiting the new spirit of goodwill. The Commission then laboured for five years without success. Germany constantly reminded the powers that Germany had been disarmed, and it called on them to follow suit. France continued to express its anxieties, and no state was ready to be the first to reduce its own security. Litvinov, Russia's new Foreign Minister in 1930, made a spirited attack on capitalism, and demanded immediate and total disarmament. Such a startling idea was duly rejected after a decent interval in which to consider it. The Commission finally produced a compromise plan at the end of 1930, but that was promptly rejected by Germany and by the Soviet Union.

A new Disarmament Conference of 60 nations met in 1932 with Arthur Henderson as Chairman, a former British Foreign Secretary. That too made little headway. France still wanted further guarantees of security before agreeing to reductions in its forces. The Russians remained sceptical and unco-operative, and the German representatives were handicapped by the unstable political situation in the Weimar Republic. Even if an agreement could be reached, the Conference had doubts about how it might be enforced. The British put forward a plan in 1933, but Hitler had come to power in Germany by that time. The French quibbled about what arms were to be allowed to Germany and, loudly declaring the injustice of the situation to Germans, Hitler withdrew his representatives in October 1933. Germany also withdrew from the League of Nations. There was now no hope of progress. The Nazis began to rearm Germany, and the French hastily completed the Maginot Line to fortify their eastern frontier. The Conference held its last session in 1934. Germany had recovered its status as a major power during the 1920s, but the birth of Nazi Germany clearly indicated that the Locarno honeymoon was over.

(c) Pieces of Paper

The optimism which was based on the Treaties of Locarno turned out to be little more than misplaced faith in pieces of paper. The French search for security produced further pieces of paper. In 1926 France signed a Treaty of Friendship with Rumania, and signed another, in 1927, with Jugoslavia. French fear of Germany was matched by a similar fear of Hungary among the lesser powers of south-eastern Europe, and Czechoslovakia, Jugoslavia and Rumania had busily signed treaties in 1920–1 in the hope of preventing amendments to the Treaties of St Germain and Trianon. This 'Little Entente' was consolidated with further agreements in 1929, but the Entente proved useless when Czechoslovakia fell to the Nazis, and it was dissolved in 1939. The Paris peace settlement, in its pursuit of self-determination, had fragmented Europe into small states which proved no match for a revived and aggressive Germany and, busily as France and the small states themselves stitched together alliances, the fact remained that such alliances were of limited value. They were no substitute for an effective international organization for keeping the peace. After 1930, however, the League of Nations was not effective.

The outstandingly optimistic treaty of the late 1920s was the Pact of Paris of 1928, popularly known as the Kellogg-Briand Pact. It originated with the French: Briand proposed that France and the USA should sign a pact to renounce war. Kellogg, the American Secretary of State, responded enthusiastically, and he suggested opening the pact to many more nations, so that it was eventually signed by 65 states. Germany, Italy, Japan and the Soviet Union were among them. They undertook to:

> condemn recourse to war for the solution of international controversies and [to] renounce it as an instrument of national policy in their relations with one another.

They were fine words, but the Pact said nothing about how the undertakings could be enforced. Indeed the USA was anxious that such entanglements should not be included. Once more the world was satisfied merely to declare good intentions. Japan had 'recourse to war' against Manchuria in 1931, preferring merely to substitute the word 'incident' for 'war' so that its full-scale war against China in 1937 was dubbed 'the China Incident'. Such events, and others for which Europeans were responsible in the 1930s, starkly revealed the hollowness of the Pact of Paris.

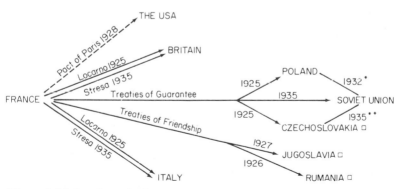

* Russo–Polish Non–Aggression Pact, 1932
** Russo–Czech Treaty of Mutual Assistance, 1935
□ The Little Entente

Fig. 23.4 The French Search for Security

23.4   The Early 1930s: Years of Setback

(a) The Depression

The trade depression at the end of the 1920s shattered whatever confidence was beginning to grow in Europe. Unsold goods accumulated. Production slowed down and in some cases stopped. Unemployment soared, and with little money in the pockets of the unemployed even fewer goods were sold. A financial crisis accompanied the trade depression, threatening banks in Vienna, Berlin and London (see page 351). Political crises developed and governments generally were more concerned with domestic problems than with preserving international peace. National recovery took precedence over international security and, well into the 1930s, governments shrank from taking on additional problems beyond their borders.

Japan's attack on Manchuria in 1931, itself in part a product of Japan's economic problems, created embarrassment among the powers rather than a resolute desire to uphold the principles of the League of Nations. Manchuria was conveniently far away from Europe. The League sent a commission under Lord Lytton to investigate. It made a leisurely journey by sea, and it did not report until October 1932. The League then condemned Japan for aggression, but it showed no inclination to go further than expressing moral disapproval. Japan was not impressed. It withdrew from the League in 1933 and expanded from Manchuria into neighbouring Jehol, though observing a request from the League to call off, for the time being, a further attack on Shanghai. The USA refused to recognize the puppet state of Manchukuo which the Japanese set up in Manchuria, and Henry Stimson, the US Secretary of State, expressed strong disapproval. But the USA, like the European nations, had no intention of imposing economic sanctions on Japan at a time when the Depression was biting deeply into national economies.

The Depression had other results. It helped Hitler to climb to power in Germany (see Section 21.3(c)) and it created problems in Italy which helped to turn Mussolini's mind, like that of the Japanese, to foreign conquest. The democracies, in the meantime, recovered only slowly from their economic problems, and they preferred to keep a low profile in international affairs.

(b) Nazi Germany

Hitler made no secret of his intention to rearm Germany, of his hostility to the Treaty of Versailles, of his contempt for the League of Nations and of his hatred of communism. Nevertheless, he moved cautiously. He consolidated Nazi power within Germany, and reassured Poland in a Non-Aggression Pact in 1934 in which he asserted his support for the Kellogg-Briand Pact. Within months, however, he was intriguing in Austria, hoping that Austrian Nazis would gain control and unite the Republic with Germany. The Austrian Nazis murdered Dollfuss, the Chancellor of the Republic, but their coup was unsuccessful. Mussolini, moreover, moved Italian troops to Italy's frontier with

Austria, and he warned Hitler against meddling further. Kurt von Schuschnigg replaced Dollfuss, and Austrian independence was preserved, while Hitler cautiously drew back (see Section 24.2). The Soviet Union was nevertheless sufficiently alarmed by the rise of the Nazis to take up membership of the League of Nations during 1934, and to renew its own Non-Aggression Pact with Poland, which had been signed two years earlier.

Hitler grew bolder in 1935. At the beginning of the year, the plebiscite was held in the Saar for which provision had been in the Treaty of Versailles. Some 90 per cent of the Saarlanders voted to be reunited with Germany and the reunion was quickly accomplished. Hitler hailed the reunion as a great victory, and it gave him the confidence to announce a policy of conscription and a new programme of rearmament, in defiance of the limitations imposed at Versailles. His policy was condemned at Stresa by Britain, France and Italy. The Soviet Union hastened to make new treaties, exchanging mutual guarantees with France and Czechoslovakia, but barely a month later, in June 1935, Britain concluded the Anglo-German Naval Agreement with the Nazis, apparently approving the expansion of the German navy. Hitler was jubilant. The Agreement gave British consent to a Nazi navy up to 35 per cent of the tonnage of Britain's, and with as many submarines as there were in the British Commonwealth of Nations, if a situation arose which, in Germany's opinion, made that 'necessary'. Such a policy of appeasement, of course, infuriated the French, giving Hitler further cause for satisfaction at divisions among his critics. October 1935 brought yet more comfort to him. In that month Mussolini launched the Italian invasion of Abyssinia, effectively destroying any anti-German coalition.

(c) Mussolini Changes Sides

From the time that he guaranteed the Rhineland Pact in the Treaties of Locarno, Mussolini had been almost a model supporter of international co-operation. He signed the Kellogg-Briand Pact and, in 1933, advocated a pact to preserve peace between Italy, Britain, France and Germany. That pact was never ratified, however. But Mussolini helped to deter Nazi ambitions in Austria in 1934, and he reinforced treaties of friendship with Austria and Hungary at that time. In April 1935 he met with the Prime Ministers of Britain and France at Stresa, and the so-called 'Stresa Front' solemnly condemned German rearmament and intrigues, a condemnation which was echoed by the Council of the League of Nations. The three powers who had met in the Stresa Conference agreed rather vaguely to 'close and cordial collaboration' to maintain peace, and there seemed good reason to believe that Fascist Italy was committed to upholding the principles of the League of Nations.

There was another side to Fascist Italy and to Mussolini, however (see Section 22.2(*b*)). Mussolini had been impressed by Japanese vigour in Manchuria, and he had even been impressed by his own strength when the four divisions sent to the Brenner Pass in 1934 had apparently deterred Hitler. And it was in the nature of Fascism to be ambitious. Mussolini cast covetous eyes on Abyssinia, which lay between the Italian colonies of Eritrea and Somaliland. An earlier Italian attempt to seize Abyssinia had been defeated at Adowa in 1896 (see page 186), a humiliation which Mussolini intended to avenge. A dramatic overseas success could also be useful in distracting the attention of Italians from the repression of the Fascist regime, and from Italy's economic and social problems. In 1928 Mussolini had signed a pact of friendship with Abyssinia, but by the time of the Stresa Conference a dispute had already arisen between them, and Italian troops were assembling – a matter which it hardly seemed tactful to mention at Stresa, when Mussolini was obligingly condemning Hitler. Thirty Italian soldiers had been killed in a skirmish at the end of 1934 at the oasis of Walwal, on the border between Abyssinia and Italian Somaliland. A hundred Abyssinians had also been killed, but Mussolini demanded both the oasis and financial compensation. Haile Selassie, the Emperor of Abyssinia, appealed to the League of Nations for a solution to the problem, but the League advised him to negotiate with Mussolini. Such negotiation was pointless: throughout 1935 the Duce steadily sent troops through the Suez Canal to reinforce his armies in East Africa. On 2 October, he addressed the assembled crowds in Rome in typically bombastic language:

> For many months the wheel of fate turns under the impulse of our calm determination and moves towards this goal. In the last few hours the rhythm has grown swifter; it cannot be stopped. It is not only an army which marches towards its objective. Forty-four million Italians march with this army, all united and alert. Let others try to commit the blackest injustice, taking away Italy's place in the sun.

Fig. 23.5 Haile Selassie, the Emperor of Abyssinia, addressing the League of Nations in 1936. His appeal for effective help against invading Italian armies fell on deaf ears

At that time a quarter of a million Italian soldiers were pouring into Abyssinia. Mussolini the peacekeeper had again become Mussolini the aggressor, and the 'Stresa Front' had received its death-blow. This was perhaps the true face of Italian Fascism. As Mussolini himself put it on a later occasion:

> The Italian character has to be formed through fighting. . . . I shall not leave the Italians in peace until I have six feet of earth over my head.

The League of Nations acted swiftly. Within a week of the Italian invasion, the Council and the Assembly declared Italy an aggressor and decided to impose economic sanctions to deprive the Fascists of supplies. The sanctions did not, however, extend to oil, coal and steel – the very commodities Italy most needed. In any case, Nazi Germany would not apply sanctions, and Austria and Hungary similarly refused to offend their friend. Rumania and the Soviet Union, both of them oil-producing countries, called for an embargo on oil, but that was rejected by Britain and France, and the British continued to allow Mussolini to supply his armies through the Suez Canal. The British and French still cherished lingering hopes that Mussolini might be an ally in deterring Nazi Germany, and for that it would be worth sacrificing Abyssinia, which was of little concern to them anyway. In December 1935 Hoare, British Foreign Secretary, and Laval, the French Prime Minister, came up with a plan to buy back Italian goodwill. Mussolini would be allowed some two-thirds of Abyssinia, including sections to enlarge Eritrea and Italian Somaliland, and much of southern Abyssinia for 'economic expansion and settlement'. For the loss of most of his country Haile Selassie was offered a tiny strip of land, to give Abyssinia access to the sea. The Hoare-Laval Plan was rejected by almost everybody, including Mussolini – who intended to have the whole, not just two-thirds. There was also a public outcry in Britain and France, and both Hoare and Laval were driven from office. Meanwhile, Haile Selassie continued to appeal to the League of Nations for more effective action:

> It is my duty to inform governments of the deadly peril which threatens them. It is a question of trust in international treaties and of the value of promises to small states that their integrity shall be respected. In a word, international morality is at stake.

His words fell, apparently, on deaf ears.

Marshal Badoglio made a triumphant entry into Addis Ababa, the Abyssinian capital, in May 1936. Not surprisingly, Italian tanks and aircraft, poison gas and flame-throwers, had proved more than a match for African rifles and spears, and Italy had lost only about 5000 men. Mussolini told his henchmen:

> One day, the part I have played in the technical direction of the war will be known.

He proudly proclaimed Victor Emmanuel III the new Emperor of Abyssinia, and Haile Selassie went into exile in England. Two months later, the League quietly abandoned the sanctions policy. Anthony Eden, the British Foreign

Secretary, explained to the House of Commons:

> We have to admit that the purpose for which sanctions were imposed has not been
> realised. The Italian military campaign succeeded. . . . His Majesty's Government
> have come to the conclusion that there is no longer any utility in continuing sanctions
> as a means of pressure upon Italy. We have got to comprise within one organization
> the willing collaboration of governments of totally divergent character. I say this to
> give some indication of the nature of the problem, and unless we face it, we cannot
> expect the League in the future effectively to meet these problems.

In fact, the League had now ceased to be effective as a custodian of international morality. Italy withdrew from it in 1937.

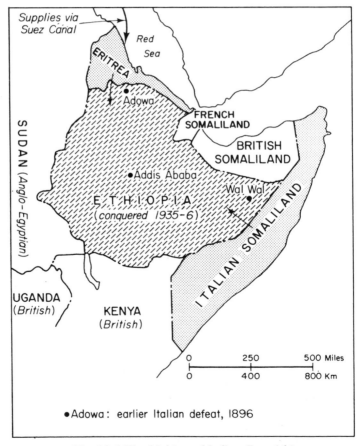

Fig. 23.6 The Making of Italian East Africa

(d) The Rhineland and the Axis

While Mussolini's armies advanced on Addis Ababa, German troops marched into the Rhineland in March 1936. This remilitarization had been forbidden by the Treaties of Versailles and Locarno. The League of Nations condemned the action, but left it to Britain and France to uphold the Rhineland Pact and the guarantees given at Locarno. Mussolini, of course, was too busy elsewhere to uphold the Italian guarantee. The French looked to Britain for encouragement, but Eden told the House of Commons that in 'this difficult period', they should seek 'a peaceful and agreed solution'. He considered it 'our imperative duty to seek by negotiation to restore confidence'. He wanted to 'further Germany's return to the League of Nations', to bring about 'a happier atmosphere', and to go on to discuss disarmament. This was music to Hitler's ears. The Locarno powers negotiated for months and, in the end, did nothing. German troops remained in the Rhineland, and a start was made on building the Siegfried Line to fortify Germany's western frontier. While Nazi propaganda made the most of the Führer's 'victory', voices in the west argued that he had, after all, only put troops on German territory, and that demilitarizing the Rhineland had been unjust anyway. French anxieties mounted but the French, like the British, preferred negotiation to confrontation. For Hitler the Rhineland was been something of a test-case, and he was delighted to find the democracies apparently so weak. They had done nothing effectively to prevent either the conquest of Abyssinia or the remilitarization of the Rhineland, and Churchill commented:

> Mussolini, like Hitler, regarded Britannia as a frightened, flabby old woman, who at the worst would only bluster, and was anyhow incapable of making war.

The Spanish Civil War began in the summer of 1936 (see Section 22.5). Disregarding the policy of non-intervention recommended by the democracies, Italy and Germany sent assistance to the Nationalist rebels. Mussolini was now discovering considerable common ground with Nazi Germany, and he was captivated by the 'fine martial spirit' of the Germans and by their 'heroic philosophy'. Earlier he had expressed contempt for Germans:

> the descendants of people who were illiterate in the days when Rome boasted a Caesar, a Vergil and an Augustus.

Officially this contempt now evaporated, although it never entirely disappeared. Mussolini endeavoured to match the Germans in displays of force. His fancy was captured by an imaginary line between Rome and Berlin, around which Europe would revolve, and which he referred to in 1936 as 'the Axis'. The bond between Italy and Germany was quickly to grow stronger in subsequent years, and to lead to the Pact of Steel in 1939.

By the end of 1936, therefore, Europe was already on the slippery slope which would lead to the Second World War. The League of Nations had been

Fig. 23.7 Mussolini's exploits in Abyssinia distracted international attention from Hitler's remilitarization of the Rhineland. They were also the beginning of Mussolini's change of sides, since after 1935 he grew ever fonder of the Nazis. Goebbels, Hitler and Goering were therefore happy to see Mussolini embarking on his 'Abyssinian Gamble'. A David Low cartoon

discredited. Collective security (the search for security against aggression through mutual support and collective action) had been gravely weakened. Italy had changed sides and abandoned its anti-Germanism. Little had been done to bridge the ideological gap between the western democracies and the Soviet Union, and the democracies themselves were in disarray. The USA concentrated on its own economic recovery from the Depression and continued to avoid international entanglements, although Roosevelt spoke scathingly of Mussolini's bullying strategy in Abyssinia. Between France and Britain there was underlying tension and distrust. France trusted hopefully in its alliances in eastern Europe. Britain put its faith in appeasement, hoping to satisfy specific grievances by negotiation and goodwill. Eden told the House of Commons in 1936: 'It is the appeasement of Europe as a whole that we have constantly before us.' Appeasement was essentially a policy of response, however. The initiative no longer lay with the League of Nations and the democracies. The question now was whether appeasement could be an adequate response to the initiatives of the dictators. Although new members still joined the League of Nations, as Egypt did in 1937, the League was no longer a forum for the great powers, and the effort to build effective peace-keeping machinery had virtually been abandoned. The democracies waited nervously for the Nazis and Fascists to manufacture the next international crisis, and they sought in the meantime to hide the conflict in Spain behind the smoke-screen of pious platitudes about non-intervention.

23.5   Appendix: Summary of the Covenant of the League of Nations

Preamble: 'to promote international co-operation and to achieve international peace and security'

Articles

1   Membership: originally the Allies in the First World War and 13 neutral states. New members to be admitted by the approval of two-thirds of the Assembly

2–6   Basic machinery: the Assembly, the Council, the Secretariat. One vote per member in the Assembly. Five permanent members of the Council (the USA, Britain, France, Italy, Japan) and four members elected by the Assembly, all with one vote each. Decisions in the Assembly and Council to require the support of all members. The subscriptions to the League to be determined by the Assembly

7   League headquarters at Geneva

8–9   The reduction of national armaments. A permanent Commission to advise the Council

10–12   Undertakings to preserve members against aggression, to refer disputes to the Council and not to go to war for three months after arbitration

13–15   Arbitration agreements; methods of arbitration; the Permanent Court of International Justice

16   Breach of the Covenant. Economic sanctions. 'Armed forces to be used to protect the covenants of the League'

17   Non-members to be invited in disputes to accept League obligations. Sanctions against non-members

18–21   Treaties to be made public and to be consistent with the principles of the League

22   Mandated territories; their 'tutelage'; the Mandates Commission, and the supervision of the Council

23–25   Co-operation for the common good, e.g. concerning conditions of labour, colonial subjects, drugs traffic, disease. The League's supervision of bureaux already established. The encouragement of Red Cross organizations

26   'Amendments to this Covenant'

Annex

(a)   Original Members (signatories of the Paris peace settlement): USA (withdrew), Australia, Belgium, Bolivia, Brazil Britain, Canada, China, Cuba, Czechoslovakia, Ecuador, France, Greece, Guatemala, Haiti, Hedjaz, Honduras, India, Italy, Japan, Jugoslavia*, Liberia, Nicaragua, New Zealand, Panama, Peru, Poland, Portugal, Rumania, Siam, South Africa, Uruguay

(b)   Members additionally invited: Argentine, Chile, Colombia, Denmark, Netherlands, Norway, Paraguay, Persia, Salvador, Spain, Sweden, Switzerland, Venezuela

*   Kingdom of Serbs, Croats, Slovenes

Further Reading

See **Further Reading** for Unit Twenty

Gibbons, S. R. and Morican, P.: *The League of Nations and UNO*. Longman (Harlow, 1970).

Hastings, P.: *Between the Wars*. Ernest Benn (London, 1969).

Henig, R.: *Versailles and After, 1919–1933*. Methuen (London, 1984).

Marks, S.: *The Illusion of Peace, 1918–33*. Macmillan (London, 1977).

Smith, D. Mack: *Mussolini's Roman Empire*. Penguin (Harmondsworth, 1979).

Documentary

Henig, R.: *The League of Nations*. Oliver and Boyd (Edinburgh, 1973).

Exercises

1. Study Section 23.2(*a*), Table 23.1 and the Appendix to this Unit. With what undertakings in the Covenant, and with what machinery, did members of the League of Nations aim 'to promote international co-operation and to achieve international peace and security' (page 384)?

2. What criticism of the League of Nations is the cartoonist making on page 387? After reading Sections 23.2 and 23.4(*c*), show how fitting this criticism was in the Abyssinian Crisis.

3. 'The 1920s: Decade of Hope'. How far does Section 23.3 show that this was a suitable title?

4. Making references to Fig. 23.4, describe how the French tried to achieve security in the years 1925 to 1935. Why were they still insecure at the time of the remilitarization of the Rhineland in 1936 (Section 23.4(*d*))?

5. How do Sections 23.3 and 23.4 show that Mussolini's foreign policy from 1922 to 1936 was erratic and unpredictable?

6. Summarize the agreements made at Locarno, and show how they eventually proved useless in 1936. After reading Unit Twenty-four, extend your answer to show that they also proved useless in 1938–9.

7. Explain the cartoonist's view, on page 400, of the 'Central European' significance of 'the Abyssinian Gamble'. How did events show that the cartoonist's view was a shrewd one?

The Coming of the Second World War

24.1 The Anti-Comintern Pacts

Anti-communism was one of the factors which helped to bring together the Axis powers. Germany and Italy pledged their support for the Nationalists against the political left in the Spanish Civil War, in the secret October Protocols of 1936, and Germany and Japan signed the Anti-Comintern Pact in the following month. The Comintern had existed since 1919 for the purpose of spreading international communism, but it had been a rather sleepy revolutionary organization (see Section 19.2(*d*)). The Anti-Comintern Pact was, in fact, a declaration of hostility towards the Soviet Union by the German Nazis and Japanese militarists. They appointed themselves watchdogs against 'the activities of the Communistic International' and claimed to believe that:

> the toleration of interference by the Communistic International in the internal affairs of nations not only endangers internal peace and social welfare, but threatens the general peace of the world.

Japan was a greater threat to the 'peace of the world' than was the Soviet Union. In July 1937 the Japanese launched a full-scale war against China which went on until 1945. In the first year alone 60 million Chinese were uprooted from their homes. Moreover, Germany and Italy were at least as much involved in the Spanish Civil War as was the Soviet Union, while the latter could at least claim to be involved there in support of the legitimate government.

Shortly before the signing of the Anti-Comintern Pact, Mussolini had first spoken of the Rome-Berlin Axis, 'around which can revolve all those European states with a will to collaboration and peace'. It is unlikely that he considered the Soviet Union to be such a state, and it was a logical step for Fascist Italy to join the Anti-Comintern Pact. It was agreed in November 1937 that 'Italy becomes a party to the Agreement against the Communistic International'.

Fig. 24.1 shows how Europe was thus being divided and how, through the Anti-Comintern Pacts, the aggressive powers of Europe were joining hands with the Japanese, the aggressive power in Asia. Germany, Italy and Japan came to be commonly known as the Axis powers. They eventually consolidated their alliance in September 1940, when they signed the Tripartite Axis Pact, promising full support to one another if attacked by any 'Power at present not involved in the European War or in the Sino-Japanese conflict'. At

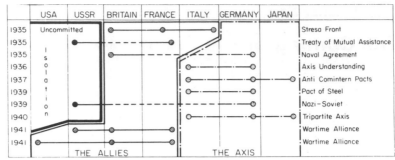

Fig. 24.1 The Origins of the Second World War: Some Treaties and Alliances 1935–45

the same time they confirmed their belief in their right to reorganize Europe and Asia to their own liking:

> The Governments of Germany, Italy and Japan, considering as the condition precedent of any lasting peace that all nations of the world be given each its own proper place, have decided to stand by and co-operate with one another in regard to their efforts in Greater East Asia and the regions of Europe respectively, wherein it is their prime purpose to establish and maintain a new order of things calculated to promote mutual prosperity and welfare of the peoples concerned.

Japan had begun to create the 'new order' in Asia in 1931 with the attack on Manchuria, stepping up the pace in 1937 with war against China. Germany had embarked on an expansionist policy towards the 'new order' in Europe, when Austria was united with the Reich in March 1938.

24.2   The Anschluss

The Republic of Austria had remained democratic in the 1920s, in spite of tension between Vienna and the rest of the country. Vienna leaned towards the Social Democrats and socialist reforms, but there was strong conservatism and anti-socialism elsewhere in the Republic. Nationalists organized the *Heimwehr*, similar to the German *Freikorps*, and Austrian Fascists sought to create a political machine like that of the Italian Fascists. The extremists were contained, however, until the Depression struck the Republic. At that time the *Credit Anstalt* collapsed (see page 351), unemployment mounted and a political crisis developed. Engelbert Dollfuss became Chancellor in 1932, with promises of strong government and curbs upon the socialists. He suspended parliamentary government in 1933 and, in 1934, was in the process of introducing a new Fascist constitution when he was murdered. Dollfuss was an admirer of Mussolini, to whom he looked for his model. His assassins were

Austrian Nazis, admirers of Hitler, who hoped to merge Austria and Germany in defiance of the peace settlement of 1919. Such a merger was unacceptable to Mussolini in 1934, and he moved Italian troops to the Brenner Pass (see Section 23.4(*b*)) to warn Hitler against proceeding further.

For the moment Austria had won a reprieve. Schuschnigg, the new Austrian Chancellor, preserved Austrian independence for four more years but, in the meantime, von Papen arrived in Vienna, with a watching brief as Hitler's personal representative. Mussolini withdrew his objections to a German takeover of Austria during 1936, but Hitler remained cautious until February 1938, when Schuschnigg was requested to visit Berchtesgaden. An interview in the previous November with Lord Halifax, the British Foreign Secretary, had convinced Hitler that British interference was unlikely, and he now felt confident enough to bully the Austrian Chancellor. Schuschnigg suffered a torrent of abuse for the alleged ill-treatment of Austrian Nazis, and he was forced to accept various German demands, one of them that he should appoint the Nazi Seyss-Inquart as the Austrian Minister of the Interior. In spite of threatening German troop movements, Schuschnigg made a last bid for independence, ordering a plebiscite for 13 March to test Austrian opinion concerning the *Anschluss*, the union of Austria and Germany. At once new German demands poured in, and he was forced to step down as Chancellor in favour of Seyss-Inquart. The plebiscite was cancelled and, declaring that he had

Fig. 24.2 Part of the 'new order' imposed by the German Nazis on Europe; Nazis find entertainment in making elderly Jews scrub the streets of Vienna, Austria in August 1938

discovered a communist plot, Seyss-Inquart requested German assistance. German troops invaded Austria and entered Vienna on 12 March 1938. Hitler arrived in Vienna a day later to an ecstatic greeting from Austrian Nazis and welcoming words from Seyss-Inquart:

> In spite of a dictated peace treaty, Germans have found their way to each other. Today the entire German people stand united and indivisible. . . . You, my Führer, are the Leader of the German nation in its struggle for honour, freedom and right.

Austria was rapidly turned into a province of the German Reich under the administration of Seyss-Inquart, and Schuschnigg was imprisoned. The Nazis organized their own plebiscite and, of those who voted, over 99 per cent approved the Anschluss. All possible resistance was eliminated by murder, and by arrests which filled the concentration camps.

No country attempted – other than by lodging verbal protests – to uphold the peace settlement which had forbidden an Austro-German union. France was busy with a domestic political crisis, and Britain chose to take the view that the Austrians appeared to want the union, and that Austrians and Germans were racially similar anyway. Hitler himself acknowledged his debt to Mussolini in a telegram.

> Mussolini – ich werde Ihnen dieses nie vergessen.
> (*Mussolini – I shall never forget you for this.*)

24.3   The Failure of Appeasement

(a) The Sudetenland

With the acquisition of Austria the German Reich now pressed on Czechoslovakia from three sides. Colonel Hossbach recorded that, at a meeting with his military leaders in November 1937, Hitler had referred to the importance of conquering 'Czechoslovakia and Austria simultaneously', as the first aim 'for the improvement of our military political position'. Hossbach also recorded the Führer's view that 'in all probability England and perhaps also France have already silently written off Czechoslovakia'. The Hossbach Memorandum is by no means conclusive proof that Hitler was pursuing a predetermined plan in foreign policy, but his eyes now focused nevertheless on the Sudetenland. The Sudetenland housed some three million German-speaking subjects of the Czechoslovakian Republic, who had formerly been the subject of the Habsburg Empire (see page 356). Though many of these Germans were anti-Nazi Social Democrats, some were Nazis, led by Konrad Henlein, who had been complaining loudly since 1933 of alleged ill-treatment. Like Seyss-Inquart, Henlein had become something of a puppet, manipulated by Hitler and, in 1938, his antics persuaded Britain and France that the Sudetenland question was now an urgent one. Hitler ordered the German army to make ready, but expressed no specific objectives. On the other hand Neville Chamberlain, the British Prime Minister since 1937, concluded that he had a mission to solve the 'problem'. He sent Lord Runciman to Prague in August 1938 to talk with the Czechoslovak President Beneš.

Beneš was willing to make concessions. Runciman appeared to believe that concessions were necessary, and there seemed no obstacle to the granting of self-government to the Sudeten Germans. But Hitler wanted more. Further disturbances were whipped up in the Sudetenland. Hitler condemned Czechoslovakia as an 'artificial state', and insisted that the Sudeten Germans were 'tortured creatures'. He detested the alliance the Czechs had made with the Soviet Union, and he distrusted their alliance with the French, but his own intentions remained unclear, while hinting that 1 October 1938 was some sort of deadline. Chamberlain hastened to Berchtesgaden to talk with the Führer on 15 September.

Chamberlain was anxious, above all, to prevent war; and war could be prevented, he believed, by appeasement. Such a policy seemed sensible and it was, indeed, a traditional British policy. Conflict would be avoided by negotiation and compromise and, ideally, the just settlement of legitimate grievances. Chamberlain was apparently far more aware of German grievances, however, than of those of the Czechoslovakian government, so that appeasement on this occasion came to mean pacifying Hitler. Britain had no alliance with Czechoslovakia as had France, but the French were only too willing for Chamberlain to secure some peaceful solution which would rescue them from the need to go to war to defend the Czechs. The Soviet Union's commitment to defending Czechoslovakia was valid only 'in so far as assistance may be rendered by France' – a clause the Russians had cautiously inserted in the Treaty of Mutual Assistance with Czechoslovakia in 1935 (see page 395). Having met Hitler at Berchtesgaden, Chamberlain agreed with Daladier, the French Prime Minister, that the German Reich should be allowed to take over those parts of Czechoslovakia where the population was more than 50 per cent German. Beneš was merely required to give his consent, which he did under protest, when informed that he could no longer expect assistance from France.

Chamberlain took the plan to Hitler at Godesberg on 22 September. The Führer promptly raised the stakes. He now demanded that the German army should immediately occupy the Sudetenland, and that Czechoslovakia should make further concessions to Hungary and to Poland. Chamberlain relayed the new terms to Beneš, who rejected them. Czechoslovakia prepared to resist, and the French began to mobilize reservists in gloomy expectation of war. In the face of Hitler's new obstinacy, it was a matter of French honour to fulfil their treaty obligations to Czechoslovakia. Britain had no such obligations, but was nevertheless likely to support the French. Chamberlain expressed his own melancholy in a radio broadcast:

> How horrible, fantastic, incredible it is that we should be digging trenches and trying on gas masks here because of a quarrel in a faraway country between people of whom we know nothing.

He determined to make yet another effort. Mussolini's assistance was enlisted by telegram, and Hitler was cajoled into consenting to a further meeting at Munich. It took place on 29 September. Hitler and Chamberlain were joined by Daladier and Mussolini, but the Czechoslovakian delegation had to wait in a nearby hotel to hear what the Big Four had decided, while the Russians were not invited to Munich at all (see pages 378–9). The Big Four decided what Hitler wanted them to decide: the Sudetenland was handed over to Germany, with all the areas the Germans declared were more than 50 per cent German. The Munich Agreement was signed in the early hours of 30 September. German troops began moving in on the following day. An international commission could later hold plebiscites in areas where doubt existed about the predominant character of the inhabitants, and there was a half-hearted guarantee of the rest of Czechoslovakia, which would only take effect when Hungarian and Polish claims had been satisfied.

Before he left Munich, Chamberlain obtained Hitler's signature on another piece of paper. The two leaders asserted that they regarded:

> the Agreement signed last night, and the Anglo-German Naval Agreement, as symbolic of the desire of our two peoples never to go to war with one another again.

They also put their faith in 'the method of consultation' for settling future problems. Chamberlain was warmly welcomed on his return to England. He waved the paper with Hitler's signature. 'I believe it is peace for our time,' he said. By thus publicizing the paper, Chamberlain perhaps hoped to hold Hitler to abiding by it. It is likely that the British public at large shared his optimism, but an anti-Munich minority, both in Britain and France, brooded on the outcome of the Conference. Winston Churchill summed up their criticisms in the House of Commons:

> £1 was demanded at the pistol's point. When it was given, £2 were demanded at the pistol's point. Finally the Dictator consented to take £1.17.6 and the rest in promises of goodwill for the future. . . . All is over. Silent, mournful, abandoned, broken, Czechoslovakia recedes into the darkness.

(b) The Darkness

The Munich Agreement left Czechoslovakia with only two choices: to fight alone, or to submit to the loss of the Sudetenland. Beneš resigned, and Czechoslovakia submitted. Poland took the town of Teschen, settling an old score against its neighbour; and Hungarian claims were largely satisfied when German and Italian arbitrators re-drew the Czechoslovak-Hungarian border. Vital industry and defences had been lost to Czechoslovakia when Germany annexed the Sudetenland, and what had been a stable and prosperous state now began to disintegrate. The new President, Emil Hacha, had to introduce a new federal constitution when the authority of Prague was challenged by Slovaks and Ruthenians. Czecho-Slovakia became almost two separate states,

Fig. 24.3 *The Expansion of Nazi Germany 1935–9*

① The Saar: legitimate plebiscite, 1935 (January)
② The Rhineland: remilitarized, 1936 (March)
③ Austria: the Anschluss, 1938 (March)
④ Sudetenlands: surrendered at Munich, 1938 (September–October)
⑤ Czechoslovakia: invaded, 1939 (March)
⑥ Memel: seized, 1939 (March)
⑦ The Corridor, Danzig, Poland: new invasion and war, 1939 (September)

and Hitler seized the opportunity in March 1939 to demand new rights for any Germans still under Czech rule. He followed up the demand with a new invasion and the occupation of Prague. The Germans promptly imposed their 'new order'. Bohemia and Moravia became a German protectorate. Slovakia became a German puppet state, and Ruthenia was given to Hungary. Czechoslovakia would not exist again until after the Second World War, and the half-hearted guarantees of Munich had proved useless.

(c) The Pact of Steel

Hitler added Memel to his trophies by seizing it from Lithuania less than a week after entering Prague. Moreover, before the end of March 1939, Madrid fell to the Nationalists in the Spanish Civil War. The tide was flowing strongly with the Nazis and their allies, and it reawakened the warlike passions of

Mussolini. Since conquering Abyssinia he had won only minor victories. His submarines preyed on supplies to the Republicans in the Spanish Civil War, and angered Britain and France. But when the matter was discussed at Nyon, it was cautiously agreed simply to patrol the Mediterranean to discourage such unidentified submarines, and not to embarrass Mussolini by branding them Italian. To appease Mussolini further, Italy itself was allowed to police part of the Mediterranean, a curious arrangement which made Mussolini's meddling in Spain all the easier. The Duce also basked in the glory of the role he played at Munich, and of the trophies he was able to secure for Hungary, his ally, at the expense of Czechoslovakia.

By 1939, however, Mussolini wanted a more dramatic success, and he looked to Albania to provide it. Italians had already infiltrated the country (see page 377). Since the Albanian army was Italian-trained, serious resistance to an Italian invasion seemed unlikely, and Mussolini was ready to attack in April 1939. He chose Good Friday for the assault, and Albania was overrun, though not without difficulty. King Zog fled, and Victor Emmanuel was given a new crown.

In the following month, Mussolini cemented his ties with Nazi Germany. Ciano, his Foreign Minister, signed the Pact of Steel. Italy and Germany found an 'inner affinity between their ideologies', and resolved 'to act side by side':

Following this path, marked out for them by history, Germany and Italy intend, in the

Fig. 24.4 The signing of the Pact of Steel, May 1939. Ciano signs for the Italians on the left of the photograph. Ribbentrop (right) signs for the Germans. Hitler (centre) perhaps had doubts about the value of this new alliance

midst of a world of unrest and disintegration, to serve the task of safeguarding the foundations of European civilization.

They dated the Pact 22 May 1939, adding for good measure 'in the XVIIth year of the Fascist Era'. Mussolini was now almost completely under the spell of the German Führer. For others, however, the spell had been broken, and the western policy of appeasement had been abandoned when Hitler imposed his 'new order' on Czechoslovakia.

24.4   The Unsuccessful Threat

(a) The New Guarantees

The policy of appeasement had been based on the assumption that the aggressive powers could be satisfied. It can also be argued that it aimed to buy time. The military in Britain in 1937, and the military in France in 1938, advised the politicians that they were unprepared for a major war. On the other hand, it was assumed that Nazi Germany in particular was well-prepared, an assumption which Hitler always encouraged, whatever the true state of his armed forces (see Table 22.1 (a), page 373). Moreover, the democratic politicians had to take into account public opinion, and there was no certainty that in 1938 the British and French were yet ready to support another major war. They became more ready as the list of aggressions lengthened, and when it was clearly shown that the aggressors accepted concessions only to demand more.

The invasion of Czechoslovakia in March 1939 dismayed Neville Chamberlain. Britain and France were still unwilling to take immediate action against Nazi Germany, but Chamberlain's pride had been injured, and Halifax wanted a strong statement to warn Hitler against any further aggression. Hitler was already discussing the future of Danzig and the question of a route across the Polish Corridor, and Britain hastened to guarantee support for Poland. At the end of March Chamberlain told the House of Commons:

> In the event of any action which clearly threatened Polish independence, and which the Polish Government accordingly considered it vital to resist with their national forces, His Majesty's Government would feel themselves bound at once to lend the Polish Government all support in their power. They have given the Polish Government an assurance to this effect. I may add that the French Government have authorised me to make it plain that they stand in the same position in this matter as do His Majesty's Government.

The French had strengthened their earlier alliance with Poland and, in April, both Britain and France issued similar guarantees of support for the independence of Greece and of Rumania, responding to Mussolini's invasion of Albania. Meanwhile Poland had signed a new treaty of friendship with the Soviet Union at the end of 1938. The lines, it seemed, had been drawn, beyond which the aggressors could not now proceed without a confrontation with the major powers. The threat of force had taken the place of appeasement.

(b) The Soviet Union

During the spring and summer of 1939 the Nazis grumbled ominously about German minorities who were allegedly ill-treated by the Poles, about Danzig, and about 'Lebensraum in the East'. The Poles seemed to be determined to resist Nazi pressure, but they too grumbled about the reluctance of Britain and France to provide money for increasing Poland's defences, and they resisted any suggestion that Russian troops should move westwards in order to protect them against the Germans. The Soviet Union now became a vital factor in deterring the Nazis. The western powers had doubts about Russian strength: recent purges of the Russian armed forces seemed likely to have undermined the Red Army (see Section 19.4(b)). They also had suspicions about communist intentions, but the old fears about a war on two fronts might well help to make the Germans less reckless. Exploratory talks were therefore held between the British, French and Russians, in order to present a united threat of reprisals to the Germans if they resorted to further aggression. There was little sense of urgency in the talks. Western suspicions were matched by the suspicions of Stalin, who resented Russia's exclusion from the Munich Conference, and who claimed to believe that the capitalist powers might be willing to encourage the Nazis to attempt to destroy communism in the Soviet Union. Stalin also resented Poland's refusal to allow Soviet troops to move westwards (see pages 378–9). In May 1939 Molotov replaced Litvinov as the Soviet Foreign Minister, and this seemed to indicate a shift in Russian foreign policy. Litvinov, a Jew, had been fiercely anti-Nazi, and he had favoured co-operation with the west and with the League of Nations. Molotov seemed to have fewer such commitments and by July he was negotiating with both the west and with Nazi Germany.

At first sight it seemed unthinkable that Germany and the Soviet Union might revive the friendship of the Treaty of Rapallo of 1922. The Nazis had constantly shouted their anti-communism. The communists had loudly condemned fascism. But Stalin prized most of all the security of the Soviet Union, and he had no confidence in the capitalist democracies. He wanted, moreover, to recover the lands which Russia had lost in the Treaty of Brest-Litovsk and in the Treaty of Riga. The talks with the west made little headway, but Molotov seemed to have more success with Ribbentrop, the Nazi Foreign Minister. For his part, Ribbentrop could see the advantage of some agreement with the Soviet Union to save Germany from a war on two fronts even if, at a later date, the Führer might still wish to destroy Russian communism. The way was prepared by a German-Russian trade agreement, signed on 19 August 1939, which included credit to the Russians of 200 million Reichsmarks, a useful bait for building Russian industry. Four days later the Nazi-Soviet Non-Aggression Pact was signed by Ribbentrop and Molotov, in the presence of Stalin. Its first Article was a shattering blow to the western hopes of deterring Hitler:

Both High Contracting Parties obligate themselves to desist from any act of violence, any aggressive action, and any attack on each other, either individually or jointly with other Powers.

There was no hope now that Germany could be frightened by the prospect of a war on two fronts. Even more ominously, however, the Pact contained secret Articles. Germany and the Soviet Union agreed, in effect, to carve up Poland:

In the event of a territorial and political rearrangement of the areas belonging to the Polish State, the spheres of influence of Germany and the USSR shall be bounded approximately by the line of the Rivers Narew, Vistula and San.

Germany also gave the Russians a free hand in Bessarabia, and an almost free hand in the Baltic States. Stalin had thus freed himself from the danger of immediate involvement in a major war and, at the same time, he could now recover much that Russia had lost in the years 1917–21 (see Section 19.2(d)). The real victory was Hitler's, however. He had watched Ribbentrop's negotiations with mounting delight. Nothing could now stop the Nazis from moving against Danzig and Poland and, even if they honoured their guarantees to the Poles, Britain and France were too remote geographically to affect the outcome. Hitler reassured the doubters that Nazi supporters would accept the

SOMEONE IS TAKING SOMEONE FOR A WALK

Fig. 24.5 An English comment by David Low on the strange Nazi-Soviet Pact of August 1939 between Stalin and Hitler. Russian oil wells were still coveted by the Germans – just one of the reasons why Hitler broke this Pact in 1941 and launched Operation Barbarossa

Nazi-Soviet Pact and would trust their Führer not to abandon his ultimate aim of destroying communism. The bizarre marriage of convenience between fascism and communism was a temporary expedient and, like many other treaties, it could be broken when the time came to revive the crusade against the Soviet Union. For the democracies, meanwhile, the Pact came as a shock, and Chamberlain soberly observed that it was 'a surprise of a very unpleasant character'.

(c) The Invasion of Poland

Within days of the Nazi-Soviet Pact, Hitler decided to attack Poland. Mussolini sent an urgent last-minute message that Italy was not ready to fight, apparently short of military equipment after squandering it in Spain. The Germans were unperturbed. With a routine lie, Hitler claimed that the Poles had invaded Germany, and a suitable episode was stage-managed by Heydrich with the help of stolen Polish uniforms. The German army began moving into Poland on 1 September 1939, and local Nazis drove the League of Nations High Commissioner from Danzig on the same day, proclaiming its union with the Reich. Britain and France half-appeared to hesitate, but an ultimatum was nevertheless issued that the Germans should withdraw from Polish soil. The Germans took no notice, and Britain and France declared war on 3 September. Chamberlain addressed the House of Commons in the despairing voice of a decent man, almost bewildered by the savage world in which he found himself:

> This is a sad day for all of us, and to none is it sadder than to me. Everything that I have worked for, everything that I have hoped for, everything that I have believed in during my public life has crashed into ruins. . . . I trust I may live to see the day when Hitlerism has been destroyed and a liberated Europe has been re-established.

He did not live so long. He was replaced as Prime Minister in 1940, and died later that year. After the Munich Conference, the British Ambassador in Berlin, Nevile Henderson, had written to Chamberlain:

> Millions of mothers will be blessing your name tonight for having saved their sons from the horrors of war. Oceans of ink will flow hereafter in criticism of your action.

Appeasement did not save Czechoslovakia, and the threat of war did not save Poland from invasion in 1939. And even the declaration of war by Britain and France did not save Poland.

The Germans hurled six heavily armed and highly mobile *Panzer* (armoured motorized) divisions against Poland. The *Luftwaffe* pounded the Poles from the air. In spite of heroic resistance from the Poles, the German advance was rapid, and Warsaw was forced to surrender on 27 September. The Poles experienced the full horrors of Hitlerism: two and a half million of them were taken to Germany for forced labour and two hundred thousand children were taken to be 'Germanized'. Polish Jews went in a steady stream to the concentration camps and, before Poland was liberated, some three million were slaughtered. Meanwhile, the Russians seized their share of Poland before the end of September 1939, and they in their turn deported Poles from eastern Poland, for ideological reasons, and perhaps also for their Jewishness. In 1939 there was not much for Poles to choose between Hitlerism and Stalinism, but the Russians later played a major part in driving the Germans from Poland, and in re-creating a Polish State with a government sympathetic to communism.

24.5   The Second World War

(a) The German Steamroller

German armies on the continent of Europe suffered hardly any setbacks for several years from September 1939. There was a 'Phoney War' in the west until the spring of 1940. Unable to save Poland, Britain and France made plans for fighting the war but, in effect, they waited – for the Germans to make another move. With the Polish question 'settled', the Germans hoped that the democracies might negotiate peace; and the democracies speculated whether the Germans could be persuaded to surrender by a blockade and by starvation. The Dominions of Australia, Canada, New Zealand and South Africa had joined Britain in declaring war on Germany, and so forces were built up while weapons began to pour from the factories. President Roosevelt of the USA supplied equipment to the democracies on a 'Cash and Carry' basis, but there was still a seeming reluctance to get to grips with Nazi Germany.

The situation changed dramatically in April 1940. Germany attacked Denmark and Norway. A month later German armies swept into Belgium, Holland and Luxemburg. They won decisive victories, went round the northern end of the Maginot Line, and poured into France. British and Allied troops were evacuated from Dunkirk in a desperate rearguard action, and German troops entered Paris on 14 June. France accepted defeat a week later (see page 343). Britain was expected to follow suit as soon as the Germans could mount Operation Sealion, the invasion of Britain, but the Nazis were defeated by geography. They failed to win command of the air in the Battle of Britain, and they could not gain control of the seas. Operation Sealion was postponed but Britain, on the other hand, was in no condition in 1940 to strike again at the Nazi stronghold on the continent.

The German successes had meanwhile given courage to Mussolini. Italy joined the war just before the fall of France, looking for easy booty. Mussolini met disaster, however, when he endeavoured to extend the war on his own account. His invasion of Greece brought a Greek counter-attack on Albania, and the Italians urgently needed German assistance. Hungary and Rumania had sympathetic governments who were willing to co-operate with the Axis powers, and Bulgaria agreed to collaborate with them in March 1941. Jugoslavia resisted (see page 376), and so to did Greece (see page 378). The

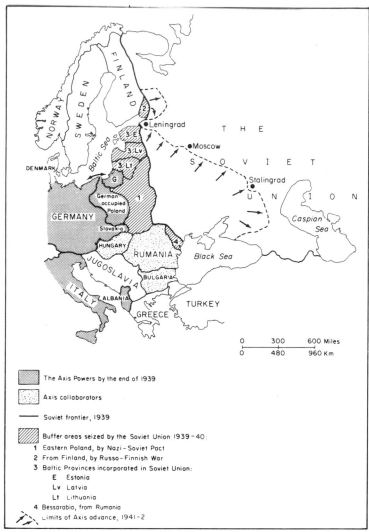

Fig. 24.6 The Soviet Union's European Frontier 1939—42

Balkans were nevertheless under Axis control by the end of May 1941. Sweden and Switzerland remained neutral, but the Nazi steamroller had otherwise crushed the whole of continental Europe except where there were friendly regimes such as Franco's in Spain, and where the Soviet Union was in control.

(*b*) **Operation Barbarossa**

Stalin was later criticized for neglecting to build up Russia's forces after the signing of the Nazi-Soviet Pact, but he busily pushed his frontiers westwards. In addition to eastern Poland, he penetrated the Baltic states and incorporated Estonia, Latvia and Lithuania into the Soviet Union in 1940. He also made demands on Finland, seeking bases and part of the Karelian Isthmus as further protection against a future threat from Germany. The Finns resisted and the Soviet Union went to war in November 1939. The campaign was more difficult than the Russians had expected, and it lasted for more than three months. The western democracies expressed considerable indignation, and even made plans for sending help to the gallant Finns, though none of them came to anything. The League of Nations suddenly stirred in its grave, and spiritedly expelled the Soviet Union from membership for aggression. Finland was nevertheless defeated in March 1940, and Russia demanded further territories as the price of peace.

The Nazi-Soviet Non-Aggression Pact of 1939 had been made for a period of ten years. Nazi Germany broke it in less than two years, when Hitler launched Operation Barbarossa against the Soviet Union in June 1941. He was joined in his new crusade against communism by his fascist allies – Italy, Rumania, Slovakia and Hungary – and by Finland, eager for revenge. Thus began a new savage conflict to impose the Axis 'new order' on Europe. This was a war of annihilation, in which no quarter was given, and 20 million Russians died before it ended. But Nazi Germany too was destroyed, and vast areas of eastern Europe were laid waste.

(*c*) **Global War**

1941 was also the year in which the European war merged with the war in Asia, and the Second World War became global. The Axis powers – Germany, Italy and Japan – strengthened their bonds in the Tripartite Axis Pact in September 1940 (see Section 24.1). But Britain, the Commonwealth, and refugees from the continent of Europe such as the Free French, were also winning support. Roosevelt was re-elected as the President of the USA at the end of 1940, and he at once declared his country's intention to be 'the great arsenal of democracy'. American public opinion was not yet ready for active involvement against the Axis powers, but the Neutrality Laws were being eroded and there was growing sympathy for Britain and for China. Congress agreed to make 50 destroyers available to Britain in return for the lease of bases, and war materials were supplied without the need for immediate payment. In August 1941 Roosevelt met Churchill, who had replaced Chamberlain as the Prime Minister in Britain in May 1940. The meeting took place off the coast of Newfoundland, and the two leaders issued the Atlantic Charter, having:

considered the dangers to world civilization arising from the policies of military domination by conquest upon which the Hitlerite government of Germany and other governments associated therewith have embarked.

The USA was still not directly involved in the war, but the Charter left no doubt where the American sympathies lay and it looked forward to a world where mankind might live 'in freedom from fear and want'. The USA went on to supply war materials to the Soviet Union and to China, and American troops took over from Britain the task of protecting Greenland and Iceland.

The Japanese attacked the United States base at Pearl Harbor on 7 December 1941. US–Japanese relations had steadily deteriorated in recent years and, ambitious to expand in South-East Asia and to secure vital oil supplies from the Dutch East Indies, the Japanese gambled on crippling American naval power in the Pacific, for at least some considerable time. Nevertheless, it brought the USA into the war and, on the following day, Roosevelt addressed Congress:

> I ask that the Congress declare that since the unprovoked and dastardly attack by Japan on Sunday, December 7, a state of war has existed between the United States and the Japanese Empire.

Congress had no hesitation in making the declaration, and Britain too declared war on Japan. For once Hitler honoured a treaty instead of breaking it and, in support of the Axis Pact, Germany declared war on the USA on 11 December, with Mussolini promptly following the Führer's example. Hitler had already persuaded himself that Roosevelt was 'the elect of the Jews', and he saw his new war as a crusade against international Jewry, which he thought was rooted in America. 'The United States already is shooting at our ships,' he protested. In any case, he declared:

> We cannot lose the war! Now we have a partner [Japan] who has not been defeated in three thousand years.

More recent history appeared to have escaped his notice: the USA was also a power which had never been defeated. But the Second World War was now a global war, within which the Nazis pursued their twin ambitions of crushing Russian Marxism and destroying the influence of Jews.

(d) The Defeat of the Axis

The tide began to turn for the Axis in 1942. The Nazi invasion of the Soviet Union ground to a halt after advancing for a thousand miles and more without quenching the will to resist of the Russian people. The Nazis in the end could not take Leningrad, Moscow or Stalingrad, and in 1943 the Red Army began to drive them back. Meanwhile, the Germans and Italians suffered defeat in north Africa, and the Allied invasion of Italy in July 1943 brought the immediate overthrow of Mussolini. Less warlike Italians sued for peace, though

German troops in Italy continued to dispute the Allied advance. In June 1944 the Allies landed in Normandy, and German forces began steadily to be driven from western Europe. Germany itself was now suffering massive bombardment from the air, and its ability to wage war at sea was also rapidly declining. Allied armies advanced relentlessly towards the Reich from east, south and west. Fearful of falling into the hands of the Russians, who were already fighting their way into the city of Berlin, Hitler committed suicide. About the same time, Mussolini was murdered by some of his own countrymen. Germany surrendered unconditionally a week or so later, and 'Victory in Europe' was celebrated on 8 May 1945.

The war in Asia seemed likely to continue much longer. Japan too had been on the defensive since 1942, but Allied armies were still in no position to invade Japan itself. It was an entirely new weapon which brought an abrupt end to Japanese resistance. President Roosevelt had died in April 1945. He was succeeded as President of the USA by Harry S. Truman, who took the agonizing decision in August to unleash the atomic bomb, first against the city of Hiroshima and then against Nagasaki. The Japanese admitted defeat, and the Second World War was over. In all, it had taken almost 40 million lives and, although half the dead were Russians, far from destroying communism, the Nazis had simply goaded the Soviet Union into a massive expansion westwards of its influence. Germany itself, vast areas of eastern Europe and parts of Europe elsewhere lay in ruins. The 'new order' in Europe had turned out to be destruction bordering on chaos.

(e) Nationalism Run to Seed

The tragedy of Europe after 1918 was that there came to co-exist for a time peaceful democratic regimes, whose leaders were horrified by the barbarism of the First World War, and fascist regimes, in which war was still glorified. Mussolini spoke for the latter when he asserted that 'war sets the seal of nobility on those peoples who have the courage to face it.' The peace settlement of 1919–20 had attempted to satisfy national aspirations, but the peacemakers could not have been expected to allow for a more rabid nationalism, which exploited every grievance, dramatized every crisis, and thrived on violence. This was a nationalism which aimed not merely to free fellow-countrymen from foreign rule; it aimed also to dominate inferior peoples. It is highly unlikely that Hitler planned the Second World War in Europe, but it developed from the nature of the Nazi regime, which emphasized violence, preached hatred, demanded *Lebensraum* and economic resources, and linked together traditional German ambitions with Hitler's personal obsessions. There were sections of the German military and of German society – for example among industrialists and financiers – who supported the pursuit of ambitions in central Europe which had been unfulfilled in the First World War. But the Nazis added their fanatical ambitions to destroy communism, and their obsessional hatred of Jews and Slavs. German traditionalists were horrified

Fig. 24.7 Hitler's bunker amid the ruins of Reich's Chancellery, Berlin, 1945. In this underground retreat (entrance on the left), Hitler killed himself

but helpless when it became apparent to what lengths they were willing to go. Like Mussolini, Hitler was carried away by his own rhetoric and his own successes. With increasingly unrealistic confidence, he swept into Poland in 1939, launched Operation Barbarossa in 1941, and finally declared war on the USA.

It is sometimes argued that the Nazis might have been 'stopped' by an earlier demonstration of opposition on the part of the democracies, of the League of Nations, and perhaps of the Soviet Union. This can be no more than speculation. Certainly Germany profited from the division of Europe into small states after 1918, from the weakness of the League of Nations, from the willingness of Britain and France to pursue a policy of appeasement, and from the ideological gulf between the democracies and the Soviet Union. It can be argued, with the benefit of hindsight, that the Nazis were allowed too many opportunities to grow in confidence during the 1930s, while the western democracies and the Soviet Union took care to avoid confrontations. But it was not unreasonable to try to de-fuse crises by negotiations and agreement – by appeasement. Britain and France had no effective help from the USA. They were also distrustful, each of the other, and they both distrusted the Soviet Union, where Stalin's regime seemed as brutal as that of the Nazis. All countries had pressing domestic problems, and in the western democracies politicians could not ignore public opinion. With vivid memories of the First World War, only those who were brainwashed by fascist propaganda could regard further conflict as anything but uncivilized. The diplomacy of the democracies might often appear fumbling, and more might have been done to present a united front against the Nazis and to involve the Soviet Union in collective security. But the Second World War resulted from ambition and from the worship of force on the part of Germany, Italy and Japan. Mussolini spoke for them all when he declared, 'I want to make Italy great, respected and feared.' All three were willing to choose war as their instrument. In the face of this commitment to the use of force, the last resort of the more law-abiding powers was to turn to force in reply. Britain and France reached that point in 1939, the USA in 1941; and the Soviet Union, distrustful of the entire capitalist world, in vain sought its own path to security, only to be caught up in the Nazi War after all. It turned out that, after 1918, the initiative in Europe did not lie with either liberal democracy or with communism. It was Europe's misfortune that it lay with a new and more virulent form of nationalism, buttressed by the ideological gobbledegook of fascism.

Further Reading

See **Further Reading** for Unit Twenty-three
Bayne-Jardine, C.: *World War Two*. Longman (Harlow, 1968).
Carr, W.: *Arms, Autarky and Aggression*. Edward Arnold (London, 1972).
Parkinson, R.: *The Origins of World War II*. Wayland (Hove, 1970).
Ray, J.: *Second World War*. Heinemann (London, 1977).
Rock, W. R.: *British Appeasement in the 1930s*. Edward Arnold (London, 1977).
Stone, R.: *The Drift to War*. Heinemann (London, 1976).
Taylor, A. J. P.: *The Origins of the Second World War*. Penguin (Harmondsworth, 1964).
Yass, M.: *The Home Front*. Wayland (Hove, 1971).

Miscellaneous

Barker, B.: *Origins of the Second World War* (History Replay). Blackwell (Oxford, 1979).

Exercises

1. How do Figs. 24.1 and 24.3 illustrate the various stages in the development of Hitler's foreign policy?
2. 'Mussolini – ich werde Ihnen dieses nie vergessen' (page 406). Why was Hitler by this time so grateful to Mussolini?
3. Write *two* paragraphs expressing opinions about the German occupation of the Sudetenland, one by a supporter of Henlein, the other by an elderly inhabitant of the Sudetenland who remembered with affection the rule of the area by Franz Joseph.
4. Make notes for a speech you would have made in the House of Commons in the debate on the Munich Agreement, having heard Churchill's opinion (page 408).
5. What do you understand by (*a*) 'collective security' (page 400), and (*b*) 'appeasement' (page 400)? Why did both fail in the 1930s?
6. 'There was little sense of urgency in the talks' 'between the British, French and Russians' (page 412). How did this lack of urgency prove to be a matter of grave importance during 1939?

7. Explain what the cartoonist meant to suggest in Fig. 24.5. Why does the caption to this illustration refer to the Pact of August 1939 as 'strange'?

8. Explain what Fig. 24.6 shows of Stalin's foreign policy in the years 1939 to 1941. How far was this policy (*a*) unscrupulous, and (*b*) unwise?

9. Suggest ways in which Mussolini might have attempted to justify to the Italian people his declaration of war on Britain and France in June 1940. How would you as an Italian citizen at that time, have been likely to regard his explanations?

Europe 1815–1941: Retrospect

25.1 Revolution and Evolution

(a) Economy and Society

The writings of eighteenth-century philosophers, the French Revolution which began in 1789, and the two decades of warfare which followed it, shook the foundations of the old Europe. Its restoration could never be total. But the statesmen who met in Vienna in 1814–15 aimed nevertheless to restore and to preserve what they could of pre-revolutionary Europe. The order they re-established was backward-looking rather than forward-looking, but it was amended over the years, and the nineteenth century turned out to be an age of flexibility and considerable change. Opponents of the existing order at first showed a romantic faith in effecting change by revolution, but revolutions in fact brought comparatively few changes. Though revolution itself became almost a tradition by 1848, after that year it lived on only in eastern Europe and especially in Russia. The Russian revolutions of 1917, however, resulted in a system very different from that at which European revolutionaries had aimed in the early nineteenth century. Elsewhere in Europe change came much less from political revolution, than from economic and social evolution. Such change nevertheless transformed the face of Europe.

The continent of Europe was still predominantly rural in 1815. The vast majority of Europeans toiled to extract their living from the soil, and the privileges which the statesmen of the time sought to preserve, were those of the titled élite, of landowners, and of churchmen. Table 25.1 shows how occupations had changed by the 1920s, and such economic changes were inevitably accompanied by social changes. Already in 1815 there was a clamour for reform and for liberties. It came mainly from the bourgeoisie, whose numbers were small but growing. The bourgeois ambition was to increase the influence of the middle classes. They demanded parliamentary systems of government, a host of civil liberties, and opportunities for their own advancement. As the nineteenth century went on, the traditional élites were forced to give way steadily, especially in western Europe. Industrialization, urbanization, and liberalism seemed to march forward hand in hand. As Marx observed, the bourgeoisie challenged the old feudal authorities, and then re-fashioned states in order to entrench in them their own privileges. The sweeping away of feudal restrictions brought some accompanying benefits to the masses, but the new societies still excluded the masses from government, and still denied them opportunities. Throughout the nineteenth century, both peasants and

POLITICS FOR THE MASSES.

Orator. "TAKE THE FIGURES, FORTY-THREE MILLION SEVEN HUNDRED AND FIFTY-THREE THOUSAND EIGHT HUNDRED AND SIXTY-TWO IN 1906, AND SUBTRACT THIRTY-NINE MILLION FOUR HUNDRED THOUSAND SIX HUNDRED AND EIGHTY-SEVEN IN 1907, ALLOWING 1·27 PER CENT. FOR INCREASE OF POPULATION. GENTLEMEN, YOU CAN DRAW YOUR OWN CONCLUSIONS." *Enlightened Audience.* "'EAR, 'EAR!'"

Fig. 25.1 A comment by Punch *(January 1910). With economic and social change in Europe came political change*

industrial workers remained comparatively poor, and comparatively powerless.

The bourgeoisie did not triumph universally in nineteenth-century Europe, however. The ruling élites were by no means dislodged even in Germany where, before the First World War, aristocrats, landowners, and the military remained influential, along with the great new industrialists and financiers. The old order persisted more tenaciously still in the Habsburg and Romanov Empires, where industrialization was less extensive than in western Europe. The pace was quickening, nevertheless, and Russia embarked on comparatively rapid industrialization at the end of the nineteenth century. As a result Nicholas II had to face an angry proletariat and a small disaffected bourgeoisie, as well as the ever-present and embittered Russian peasantry. They all united to overthrow him in 1917, and the bourgeoisie were then too weak to prevent the further revolution of the masses. But in other parts of Europe the bourgeoisie had made more headway against tradition, and the middle classes had themselves become the defenders of the new society. They set their face against the movements of the masses, in the name of free enterprise, individualism, self-reliance, and morality. There thus developed a new class struggle, when the bourgeoisie was challenged by the proletariat.

Socialism provided a philosophy for many of the industrial workers in the later nineteenth century. Socialists demanded 'Equality' as well as 'Liberty', but they were frequently divided as to how they should pursue their goals.

Moderates among them hoped to win parliamentary seats and to overcome the resistance of the bourgeoisie to egalitarianism, in the very assemblies which the bourgeoisie itself had extracted from the more traditional élites. Syndicalists aimed to accelerate social change by massive strikes, first to paralyse and then to subordinate economies to the control of the workers. Others heeded the arguments of Lenin, and continued to plan for revolution, but a revolution of the proletariat, not of nineteenth-century liberals. Most common of all, however, were the outbreaks of industrial unrest, which expressed the frustrations of the labour force but which aimed at piecemeal improvement, rather than at the fundamental transformation of society. Until well into the twentieth century, European economies were seldom regulated by governments, and booms and slumps were left to take their course. The workers, therefore, had to struggle as best they could, to cope with periods of unemployment, and to survive on wages which were often low. The nineteenth century was a liberal age, and the emphasis was on freedom – but for some, that was no more than the freedom to starve.

Table 25.1:   Occupations in the 1920s (percentages)

Country	Agriculture	Industry and Mining	Trade and Transport	Professions and Miscellaneous
Britain	7	48	24	21*
Belgium	19	47	19	15
Netherlands	24	38	22	16
France	25	40	17	18
Switzerland	26	44	17	13
Germany	30	42	17	11
†Rumania	80	8	5	7
†Russia	80	6	3	11

* Britain still had 13 per cent of its population employed in 'personal service', the bulk as domestic servants.

† The figures for Rumania and Russia illustrate the gulf which then existed between eastern and western Europe.

(Adapted from H. Heaton, *Economic History of Europe*. Harper and Row (London, 1965).)

(b) Frontiers and Nationalism

The order which was re-established at Vienna in 1814–15 left many subject peoples, whose demands for freedom were demands not only for parliaments and civil liberties, but for freedom from foreign rule. Nationalists clamoured for their own nation states, such as the French and the Spaniards had long ago achieved, and the dividing line was often blurred in such cases between liberal revolutions and wars of liberation. In general, the nationalist movements were bourgeois movements, which aimed (for example, in Belgium) to achieve freedom from alien control and a liberal constitution. Such movements made piecemeal changes to the map of Europe, as new nation states were born. Many such states were in the Balkans, although national independence in that area seldom led simultaneously to successful constitutionalism. Other peoples discovered their national identities in unification, and Italy and Germany were founded. Alongside the nation states, the surviving Empires of eastern Europe seemed increasingly outdated, although the Habsburgs and Romanovs continued successfully to resist the nationalist ambitions of peoples such as South Slavs and Poles.

The nation states, however, grew more ambitious and competitive. Free enterprise and competition were part of the essence of nineteenth-century liberalism. Most of Europe's industrial development was promoted by private enterprise, and it was spurred on by the desire to make profits. Industrialists, traders, and financiers competed for gains and for prestige, and the nations too absorbed the prevailing philosophy of enterprise and self-help. In the late nineteenth century, the nations protected their own economies with tariffs, and they vied with one another to capture markets and to build colonial empires. As national rivalries grew, they were given a new cutting edge in a frantic arms race, which was itself a source of profit to the manufacturers of weaponry. Nationalism, it seemed, was moving into a more aggressive phase, and for those already free, it was no longer simply a question of liberation or of unification; it was becoming a question of expansion and supremacy.

The many social, economic, and international tensions in Europe combined in 1914 to plunge the continent into war. The war marked the beginning of a new age of violence and impatience, and yet there was considerable continuity in the issues which were at stake. The western democracies saw the conflict as a crusade for liberalism and constitutionalism, to create a world 'safe for democracy'; and they intended the postwar peace settlement to solve the problems of nationalism by liberating subject peoples on the continent of Europe from outdated Empires. Clemenceau, however, glimpsed another view of nationalism, although he seems to have seen it only in the context of Germany. In his view it was necessary to curb Germany's expansionist nationalism. The peacemakers of 1919, themselves bourgeois, aimed at a bourgeois peace. Like the peacemakers at Vienna a century earlier, they aimed to reconstruct Europe according to their own values, so that, with suitable moderation, they based the treaties of 1919–20 on the principles of liberalism and nationalism. Bolshevik Russia played virtually no part in the settlement, and Russia was set aside as an awkward difficulty. Meanwhile, the peacemakers hoped that the Russians – of their own accord, prodded by half-hearted intervention – would somehow return to the liberalism they had briefly glimpsed in 1917.

(c) Ideology and the Masses

By comparison with that of the nineteenth century, twentieth-century Europe appeared violent, strife-ridden, and torn by strident ideological conflict. Yet most of Europe's problems had already existed during the nineteenth century, though masked for some time by much complacency and some callousness, and less publicized before the twentieth-century development of the mass media. On the other hand, twentieth-century Europe was brutalized by the First World War, and governments in unscrupulous hands acquired a new capacity for controlling and dominating the lives of their subjects.

Russia emerged from the First World War as a Bolshevik state. There was no return to the liberalism of the brief Provisional Government. The Bolsheviks preached the philosophy of communist revolution to the rest of Europe, though they took care not to match propaganda with action, lest that should endanger 'Socialism in One Country' – the survival of socialism in the Soviet Union itself. Even so, the Bolshevik success in Russia inevitably encouraged socialist opposition to the bourgeoisie elsewhere, and the class struggle in the democracies was intensified. The struggle fed on the inequalities and inconsistencies of capitalism. In general, the years after 1918 were years of prosperity for the west European bourgeoisie. New technology and mass-production produced an increasing flow of comparatively cheap consumer goods, which enhanced the quality of life for those who could afford them. At the same time, however, trade cycles continued regularly to threaten the livelihood of workers in industries which depended on depressed and vulnerable markets. Unemployment was a persistent problem in capitalist societies, and it added fuel to the underlying social conflicts.

Growing fear added a further ingredient. The workers feared unemployment, and the bourgeoisie feared the workers. The First World War had shaken the nineteenth-century confidence in the inevitability of progress and, at the same time, it had quickened the impatience of those who wanted to share in progress, and to enjoy a better life. In general, it was the confidence of the bourgeoisie which was shaken, and it was the impatience of the proletariat which was quickened. The bourgeoisie now wished to defend the existing order in many parts of Europe. Armies of white-collar workers were anxious to preserve their status, which they assumed should be higher than that of the proletariat. With businessmen, managers, and the professional classes, they feared the egalitarian principles of Marxism, and the propertied classes everywhere – peasants among them – had a horror of socialism and communism. It was largely on these fears that the 'new' illiberal movements were built – movements which, for the sake of convenience, are commonly labelled 'fascist'. Such movements were not without their nineteenth-century precedents, and elements of fascism have been noticed in the activities of Napoleon III and of Boulanger, as well as in the expansionist ambitions of pre-1914 governments. The inter-war fascist movements were anti-communist but also vehemently anti-liberal as well as anti-intellectual (as in Nazi Germany). They could also well be anti-semitic. They rejected the moderation of liberalism and democracy, and they stridently asserted that democracy was too weak and too inefficient to save Europe from communism. But they themselves created an even greater danger to their fellow-Europeans, since they also preached an extremist form of nationalism. Italian Fascists and German Nazis carried nationalism to new lengths: it was no longer a semi-romantic crusade for freedom, but a supremacist movement, linked with a doctrine of racial superiority.

Fig. 25.2 Extremist nationalism and the indoctrination of the young went hand in hand in Nazi Germany to create an illiberal and anti-intellectual threat to civilization. Hitler inspects some of the Hitler Youth. Behind him, hatless, Rudolf Hess, the deputy leader of the Nazis

Against this virulent supremacist nationalism, the liberal democracies at first relied on nineteenth-century traditions of negotiation, flexibility, and compromise; and they did not finally abandon this policy of appeasement until 1939. By that time it had become clear that reasoned argument and agreement offered no protection against fascist ambitions. Only 21 years after the ending of the First World War, Europe plunged into a new abyss. Operation Barbarossa united liberalism and communism against fascism in 1941. It was a strange alliance between the ideological opposites of capitalism and Marxism, but it sufficed to destroy Nazism, the most vicious of the fascist variations. The Second World War involved the masses in conflict as no previous war had done, and it was a salutary lesson for Europeans. Nationalism, they discovered, was not the answer to their problems which it was once thought to have been, and it was a more cautious Europe which emerged from the war in 1945. The League of Nations gave way to the more comprehensive United Nations Organisation, and Europeans soon came to seek their future security in two massive power blocs.

The division between the blocs was the ideological division between capitalism and Marxism. But it was also a division between western and eastern Europe, such as had developed between the liberal industrialized west and the authoritarian agricultural east in the nineteenth century. The west continued to pursue the goals of liberal democracy, with a basically capitalist economy rooted in private enterprise. But national rivalries were now overshadowed by the assumed threat from Marxism. The west looked for protection to the USA, and this time found a readier response than France had found in a similar quest in 1920. The USA became locked into the North Atlantic Treaty Organization, while the west Europeans also sought to co-operate among themselves in associations such as the European Economic Community. Eastern Europe looked for protection to the Soviet Union, and the eastern states developed organizations similar to those in the west, such as the Warsaw Pact and Comecon. The east Europeans also undertook a massive economic and social reorganization, attempting, like Russia, to develop their industries and, to a large extent, to by-pass bourgeois societies in favour of a socialist road to communism. It seemed at first that Europe was thus caught up after 1945 in an even more dangerous rivalry between the super powers, the USA and the USSR. But by the 1970s, the ideological division of Europe had created an almost unprecedented stability on the continent. Two contrasting ideals for society remained – broadly-speaking the liberal and bourgeois in western Europe, and the collectivist and proletarian in eastern Europe – but Europeans on the other hand had apparently set aside the unending squabbles about national frontiers and disputed territories, which were so much a feature of their earlier history.

Some three times as many people lived in Europe at the end of the Second World War as at the beginning of the nineteenth century. It was a feature of European history in this period that the masses grew in importance, particularly during the twentieth century. Education was extended, and universal suffrage eventually came to be the norm. Newspapers began to seek mass circulations, and they adapted their presentation and content accordingly. Mass entertainment became a growth industry, and the mass media in the twentieth century aimed at mass audiences. Producers increasingly catered for the mass market. Something of the old Europe remained, mainly on the southern fringes, but society elsewhere was transformed. Compared with the outside world, Europeans increased greatly in prosperity and, whatever the ideology, expanding wealth meant that the growing numbers of Europeans were nevertheless rich in material terms. The Europe of motor cars and television sets in the mid-twentieth century was far removed from the agricultural and under-developed Europe of 1815, when even the railway was yet unknown. Individualism and craftsmanship were perhaps among the casualties of the transformation, though they had helped to launch the industrial revolution. Technology, mass consumerism and conformism, left little room in twentieth-century Europe for the romanticism of the age of Schubert and Heine. The marked alienation of the young in the later twentieth century, and of dissidents within both of the ideologies, suggested that not everyone believed that material progress had changed Europe for the better.

25.2   European Civilization

The supremacy of Europe in the nineteenth and early twentieth centuries was the product of many factors, but it coincided with a considerable cultural and intellectual achievement on the part of Europeans. Europeans showed both persistent curiosity and a relentless aggressive energy. Industrialization enabled Europeans to dominate the world's markets in the nineteenth century, and developing technology steadily boosted production. One of the by-products of technological change was the increase in the killing power of European weapons, but Europeans had other reasons for believing in themselves than their advancing economies and their armed might. They were developing highly complex societies, with a cultural and intellectual life on a level which they believed was unprecedented. From this stemmed an assumed moral superiority, and the belief that European civilization existed to give a lead to the world.

The cultural achievement of nineteenth-century Europeans was as remarkable as their achievement in other fields. Writers, composers, artists, and architects, were often influenced by their own distinctive national characteris-

Fig. 25.3 'Drill' (physical education) in Freetown, Sierra Leone, c. 1910: schoolgirls at Fourah Bay College. Europeans took it for granted that they should impose their own systems on peoples in other continents

tics, and they showed an imaginativeness and an energy which matched those of scientists, railway engineers and entrepreneurs in all branches of economic activity. The arts flourished and grew ever more adventurous. At the same time intellectuals pursued new learning. They opened up new fields of study, many of them scientific, and they built on all the earlier studies of human experience. At the end of the nineteenth century, radioactivity was one of the new areas of study, and Sigmund Freud was pioneering the study of the workings of the human mind, while others laboured industriously to extend the frontiers of philosophy, of theology, of sociology, and of political ideology. This was the icing on the European cake. Millions of other Europeans were content, however, to reap the material rewards of the 'progress' they had begun to take for granted, and which, it was assumed, would eventually extend to the further millions who still endured a life of toil and poverty. Meanwhile, traders, administrators, soldiers and missionaries, carried elements of Europe's civilization overseas, and imposed them on non-Europeans in Africa and Asia, with a confident unconcern for the civilizations already in existence there.

Only a minority of Europeans – intellectuals, writers, and painters among them – brooded on the contradictions which were developing in European societies. There was a yawning gulf between the prosperous and the poor. The Christian religion and various forms of idealism co-existed with the ruthless pursuit of wealth and power, and with a persistent undercurrent of violence. European nations trod an uneasy path between international agreements and international crises, and it became obvious when war broke out in 1914 that Europeans had not yet solved their own problems. The savagery with which the war was fought, and the mass hysteria about national interests which accompanied it, came as a shock. Competitiveness and aggressiveness had helped to make Europe pre-eminent, but it could now be seen that Europeans had neither outgrown their capacity for quarrelling among themselves and for tearing their continent apart, nor had they outgrown their primitive barbarism, which thrived on the passion for killing and destroying. Revolutions in Russia and upheavals in other parts of Europe followed in the wake of the War. And the callous brutality of Stalinism, together with the genocide practised by the Nazis against the Jews, contrasted sharply with the notion that Europeans had evolved a higher form of civilization. Nineteenth-century 'progress' had led in the early twentieth century to savage war, and to atrocities on an almost unprecedented scale. The Second World War gave further impetus to the disillusionment.

The massive destruction of life and property in the years 1914 to 1945 perhaps at last taught Europeans their lesson, in a final blood-letting. Europeans could no longer assume, almost unthinkingly, that Europe led the world. European colonial empires disintegrated in the years after 1945, and from them scores of new nations were born and old nations were re-born. The world was now dominated by super powers, and the nations of Europe were soon to be heavily outnumbered by the emerging nations of the Third World. For

Fig. 25.4 Belsen, April 1945: what liberating armies found in just one of the Nazi concentration camps. Never again would Europeans be able to take it for granted that they had evolved a higher form of civilization

Europe the period 1815 to 1941 had been a period of remarkable development and of pre-eminence, but in the end it seemed that European civilization had all along contained the seeds of self-destruction. With typical energy, however, Europeans rebuilt after the holocaust of the Second World War. In retrospect, the years 1815 to 1941 may perhaps best be seen as important formative years in the development of contemporary Europe – a Europe prosperous and influential but no longer pre-eminent, a Europe in which two distinct ideologies apparently learned to co-exist, and a Europe proud of its own achievement but, at the same time, chastened by the follies and tragedies of its still recent history.

Glossary

* For further definition, reference should be made to the index of this book.

Aggrandisement   The act of making greater, in power, territory or prestige.
Amnesty   The granting of forgiveness, a pardon, usually to political offenders.
Anarchism   Opposition to government and authority. The rejection of government.
Anti-clericalism   Opposition to the influence of the church and churchmen, especially their influence in politics.
Anti-semitism   Opposition to Jews, and to their economic and political influence.
***Appeasement**   The policy of pacifying, conciliating, and settling grievances by negotiation.
Arbitration   The settlement of disputes through the verdict of a third party.
Assembly   A coming together, meeting. Often used of a parliamentary body, e.g. the French Assembly.
Autarky   A plan for economic self-sufficiency in Nazi Germany.
Authoritarian   Not liberal. Usually applied to stern and repressive attitudes and governments.
Autocracy   Absolute rule by one man: a *dictatorship*.

Balance of Power   A distribution of power (usually between nations) such that no single power or group of allies is pre-eminent. A nation's concept of the ideal balance of power usually meant a balance in which the nation did not feel itself threatened.
'Blood and Iron'   Phrase used by Bismarck about how Germany might be united. Commonly assumed to mean by 'bloodshed and weapons', but perhaps by 'kinship and industrialization'.
Bourgeoisie   The middle classes.
Bund   League or association. After 1815 in Germany, *Confederation*.

Camorra   Secret and terrorist society in Naples, with criminal connections.
Coalition Government   Government by two or more parties, acting together.
***Collective Security**   International security and stability, achieved by joint effort of several countries to deter those seeking to injure their neighbours and to disturb the peace.
Collectivism   A policy of co-operation, community effort and ownership, usually under state direction, in preference to private enterprise.
***Communism**   An egalitaran political philosophy, embracing *collectivism* and rooted in the writings of Karl Marx: dedicated to the well-being of the *proletariat*.
Confederation   A league or union of states. A *federation*, but with weak central government.
Conference   A meeting for discussion, e.g. an international conference.
Congress   Similar to an international *conference*.
Conservative   Inclined to uphold existing institutions. Conservative parties are usually parties of the *right*.
Constituent Assembly   Parliamentary *assembly* for the purpose of drafting a *constitution*.

*Constitution   A system of government, usually with liberal characteristics, such as an *assembly*, and perhaps guarantees of human rights.

Coup d'état   A sudden and illegal change of government; a seizure of power.

Democracy   Rule by the people. A system of government which permits some effective control to the masses.

Despotism   Absolute rule, a *dictatorship*.

Dictatorship   Rule by a dictator, similar to *autocracy*.

Diet   *Assembly*, usually parliamentary, e.g. the Prussian Diet.

Émigrés   Those who fled abroad during the French Revolution, mainly nobles.

*Entente   A friendly understanding, without the specific commitments of an alliance.

*Fascism   A political philosophy and system common in Europe in the period 1918–45 – nationalist, authoritarian, but in some ways radical.

Federation   Union of states into a larger state with a central government, but with each member-state also retaining certain powers.

Feudal   Based on a medieval social organization in which authority was closely linked with the possession of land.

Franchise   The right to vote.

Free Trade   Trade free from restrictions, such as *tariffs*.

*Imperialism   Empire-building, the gaining of colonies, i.e. formal imperialism. Influence and power over other states may also be gained without direct colonization, i.e. informal imperialism.

Indemnity   Often used for a sum of money, a sort of fine, required of one country by another after a war. See *reparations*.

Inflation   Rising prices, with a consequent fall in the value of money.

Isolation   Internationally, being without allies and commitments.

Junkers   East Prussian landowners, noted for their aristocratic and military traditions and, usually, for their anti-liberal opinions.

Laisser-faire   To leave alone: the policy of government not to interfere.

Lebensraum   Living-space, elbow-room. The areas claimed by Nazi Germany as necessary for German development.

Left   A relative term to describe political inclinations. Those to the left are more in favour of reform and change than those with whom comparison is made. Contrast *right*.

Legislation   Laws, or law-making.

*Liberalism   A political philosophy which usually emphasizes liberty, the rights of the individual and parliamentary government.

Mafia   Robber bands which originated in Sicily: a criminal organization.

*Mandates   Mandated territories allocated during the peace settlement of 1919–20, and ruled under the supervision of the League of Nations.

*Marxism   The philosophy of Karl Marx. See *communism* and *socialism*.

Mercantilism   A pre-nineteenth-century economic philosophy and system, based on extensive regulation of trade and economies in general. It included many elements of *protection*.

Multiracial   Concerning many races; see *race*. A multiracial empire includes peoples of many races.

Nationalization   Converting into national property, placing under state ownership as an alternative to private ownership, e.g. the nationalization of railways.

*****Nationalism**   Pride in one's country, with a consequent desire for the country's freedom, the unification of its peoples, and perhaps its pre-eminence.

Nation State   An independent country made up to a large extent of the people of one nationality.

Oligarchy   A system of government by a privileged few.

Ottoman   Turkish.

Plebiscite   A vote by the people on a particular issue.

Pogrom   Systematic plundering and killing, e.g. a Pogrom against the Jews.

Populist   One who seeks to please the people and to represent their interests.

Prerogative   A special privilege or right.

Proletariat   The working masses.

Proportional Representation   The representation of voters in an *assembly* in proportion to their expressed wishes, e.g. 10 per cent of the votes for Party Z should ensure 10 per cent of the seats for Party Z.

Protection   A system of *tariffs* to protect home industries. The opposite of *free trade*.

Race   A group of persons of common descent, of distinctive ethnic stock. Strictly, mankind is divided into five races, e.g. Caucasoids, Negroids. Europeans are Caucasoids, but can be sub-divided, e.g. Nordic, Mediterranean. *Race* is used not uncommonly (though strictly speaking not accurately) for further sub-divisions, similar to nationalities. For example, *multiracial* empires in the nineteenth century included many races/nationalities: the Habsburg Empire included Teutonic, Slavonic and Magyar peoples.

Radical   Enthusiastic for major change, for reform.

Reactionary   Backward-looking, desiring to put back the clock: opposed to change.

*****Realpolitik**   Literally, practical and realistic politics. Commonly used to suggest elements in policy of clear-sightedness, ruthlessness, and perhaps the threat of force.

Reparations   Compensation for injury and damage. Similar to an *indemnity*, but compensation rather than a fine.

Representative Government   Government which represents, and allows effective power to, a wide section of society.

Republic   A state without a monarchy.

Right   A relative term to describe political inclinations. Those to the right are more in favour of tradition and order than those with whom comparison is made. Contrast *left*.

*****Sanctions**   Penalties, methods which put pressure on nations guilty of unpopular acts, e.g. economic sanctions involve penalties on trade.

Secular State   A state relatively free from the political influence of the church and churchmen.

Self-determination   Freedom to choose; commonly used for the freedom of a people to choose their own system of government without foreign interference.

Serfdom   A medieval system of restriction which tied the masses to the land, and to service to their social superiors: an aspect of the *feudal* system.

*****Socialism**   An egalitarian political philosophy, similar to *communism* and *Marxism*, but commonly considered to be less extreme, less revolutionary, more democratic.

Sovereignty   Power, the authority to make the final decision.

Soviet   A council, committee. Since 1905 in Russia, commonly associated with revolutionary purposes.

Spartacists   Members of the Spartacus League in Germany (see page 347). They take their name from a rebel gladiator and slave-leader in ancient Rome.

Status Quo   Loosely, the existing state of affairs. *Status quo ante bellum*: the existing state before the war. Thus, policy may aim to restore the status quo.

Suffrage   The right to vote. Universal (or adult) suffrage: the right of all adults to vote. Manhood suffrage: the right of adult males to vote.

Suzerainty   Final, over-riding authority, but perhaps at some distance.

*****Syndicalism**   The policy of securing political control for the *proletariat* through the medium of trade-union organization. (French *syndicat*: trade union).

Tariffs   Levies (duties, taxes) on imports. See *protection*.

Totalitarian   Permitting no rival parties, involving total control by the authorities.

Ultimatum   A final warning, usually with conditions which must be met lest a threat (e.g. of war) be implemented.

Welfare State   A state with comprehensive social services (e.g. in health) and social security (e.g. insurance against unemployment, old age).

Bibliography

Further Reading has been suggested at the end of each Unit. The following will be found useful on the period as a whole.

International Histories

Brett, S. Reed: *European History, 1900–60*. Murray (London, 1978).
Burnham, C.: *War or Peace*. Batsford (London, 1972).
Haigh, A.: *Congress of Vienna to Common Market*. Harrap (London, 1973).
Hayes, P.: *Modern British Foreign Policy, 1880–1939*. Black (London, 1977).
Joll, J.: *Europe since 1870*. Penguin (Harmondsworth, 1976).
Knapton, E. J. D. and Derry, T. K.: *Europe 1815–1914*. Murray (London, 1965).
Knapton, E. J. D. and Derry, T. K.: *Europe and the World since 1914*. Murray (London, 1967).
Palmer, A. W.: *Dictionary of Modern History, 1789–1945*. Penguin (Harmondsworth, 1964).
Palmer, A.W.: *Dictionary of Twentieth-century History, 1900–1982*. Penguin (Harmondsworth, 1983).
Rundle, R. N.: *International Affairs, 1890–1939*. Hodder and Stoughton (London, 1979).
Seaman, L. C. B.: *From Vienna to Versailles*. Methuen (London, 1972).
Watson, J. B.: *Success in Twentieth Century World Affairs*. Murray (London, 3rd edn., 1984).
Wood, A.: *Europe 1815–1945*. Longman (Harlow, 1964).

Social and Economic Histories

Duffy, M. N.: *The Emancipation of Women*. Blackwell (Oxford, 1969).
Henderson, W. O.: *The Industrialisation of Europe, 1780–1914*. Thames and Hudson (London, 1969).
Huggett, F. E.: *The Land Question and European Society*. Thames and Hudson (London, 1974).
Kemp, T.: *Industrialisation in Nineteenth-Century Europe*. Longman (Harlow, 1969).
Mosse, G. L.: *The Culture of Western Europe, the 19th and 20th centuries*. Murray (London, 1963).
Pollard, S.: *European Economic Integration, 1815–1970*. Thames and Hudson (London, 1974).
Temple, J.: *Mining, An International History*. Ernest Benn (London, 1972).

National Histories

Bury, J. P. T.: *France 1814–1940*. Methuen (London, 1969).
Carr, W.: *A History of Germany, 1815–1945*. Edward Arnold (London, 1979).

Halecki, O., and Polonsky, A.: *A History of Poland*. Routledge & Kegan Paul (London, 1983).
Macartney, C. A.: *The Habsburg Empire, 1790–1918*. Weidenfeld and Nicolson (London, 1969).
Rowbottom, J.: *Russia in Change, 1970–1945*. Longman (Harlow, 1985).
Rowlands, B.: *Modern Italy*. University Tutorial Press (Cambridge, 1972).
Shreeves, W.G.: *Nationmaking in Nineteenth Century Europe*. Nelson (Walton-on-Thames, 1984).
Stephenson, G.: *A History of Russia, 1812–1945*. Macmillan (London, 1969).

Biography

Ayling, S. E.: *Nineteenth-Century Gallery, Portraits of Power and Rebellion*. Harrap (London, 1970).
Ayling, S. E.: *Twelve Portraits of Power*. Harrap (London, 1961).

Map Books

Brown, W. E. and Coysh, A. W.: *Map Approach to Twentieth-Century History*. University Tutorial Press (Cambridge, 1971).
Catchpole, B.: *A Map History of the Modern World, 1890 to Present Day*. Heinemann (London, 1968).
Catchpole, B.: *A Map History of Russia*. Heinemann (London, 1974).
Jones, P. G. D.: *Atlas of European Political History*. Blackie (Glasgow, 1973).
Perry, D. G. and Seaman, R. D. H.: *Sketch Maps in Modern History, 1789–1970*. Murray (London, 1971).
Richards, I., Goodson, J. B. and Morris, J. A.: *A Sketch-Map History of the Great Wars and After*. Harrap (London, 1961).
Taylor, G.: *A Sketch-Map History of Europe, 1789–1914*. Harrap (London, 1936).
Woodget, D.: *Europe 1789–1914. A Sketchmap Textbook*. Longman (Harlow, 1971).

Documentary Collections

Breach, R. W.: *Documents and Descriptions in European History, 1815–1939*. Oxford (London, 1964).
Breach, R. W.: *Documents and Descriptions: The World since 1914*. Oxford (London, 1966).
Firth, C. B.: *From Napoleon to Hitler, Reference Book*. Ginn (Aylesbury, 1946).
Snyder, L. L.: *Fifty Major Documents of the Nineteenth Century*. Anvil (Dublin, 1955).
Snyder, L. L.: *Fifty Major Documents of the Twentieth Century*. Anvil (Dublin, 1955).
Stacey, F. W.: *Britain and Russia from the Crimean War to the Second World War*. Edward Arnold (London, 1969).
Wroughton, J. and Cook, D.: *Documents on World History 1870–1918*. Macmillan (London, 1976).
Wroughton, J. and Cook, D.: *Documents on World History, 1919 to the Present Day*. Macmillan (London, 1976).

Multiple-Choice and Data-Based Testing

Burton, I. F., Moore, Seaman and Watson: *Multiple Choice Practice Items in History*. Chatto and Windus (London, 1973).

Burton, I. F., Moore, Seaman and Watson: *Multiple Choice Testing in History Examinations*. Chatto and Windus (London, 1973).

Clarke, E.: *Objective Tests in O Level History: Europe and the Modern World, 1870–1970*. Murray (London, 1975).

Rayner, E.G., Stapley, R.F. and Watson, J.B.: *Evidence in Question: World Affairs from the Russian Revolution to the Present Day*. Oxford (Oxford, 1984).

Rayner, E. G., Stapley, R. F. and Watson, J. B.: *New Objective Tests in History, 1760–1848: British and European*. Hodder and Stoughton (London, 1974).

Rayner, E. G., Stapley, R. F. and Watson, J. B.: *New Objective Tests in Twentieth-Century History*. Hodder and Stoughton (London, 1974).

Rayner, E. G., Stapley, R. F. and Watson, J. B.: *History in Evidence: Twentieth-Century World Affairs*. Oxford (London, 1980).

Watson, J. B., Rayner, E. G. and Stapley, R. F.: *History in Evidence: European History 1815–1949*. Oxford (London, 1980).

Index

Note: Bold numbers indicate principal references. Italic numbers indicate illustrations and tables. The dates in brackets by the names of rulers are those of reigns. Abbreviations used in this Index: d. = year of death; FWW = First World War; SWW = Second World War.

Aaland Islands, 389
Abdul Aziz (Sultan, 1861–76), 135, 137, 235–6, 242
Abdul Hamid II (Sultan, 1876–1909), 137–8, 236, **242–3,** *244*
Abdul Mejid I (Sultan, 1839–61), 129, 130, 131–2, 135, 137
Aberdeen, Lord, 131
Abyssinia, 182, **186,** 257, *258,* 271, 334, 364, 387, 395, **396–8,** 399, 400, 410
Adalia, 187, 188, 326, *327,* 337
Addis Ababa, 397, *398,* 399
Aden, 250, 251, *258*
Adowa, **186,** 228, 396, *398*
Adrianople, *131,* 236–7, *238,* 246, *247, 327,* 337 (*see* Treaties of Peace)
Aeroplanes, 143, *145,* 291, 335, 375, 397; (SWW) 414, 419
Afghanistan, *227,* 266
Africa: (explorers in) 256–7, 262; (partition of) 151, 178, 185–6, 231, 250, 251, 252, 254, **255–7,** *258,* 262–3, 266, 431; (FWW and mandates) 289 (*see* Mandated Territories)
Agadir, *258,* 263
Agram (*see* Zagreb)
Agriculture, 1, **35–6,** 106, 138, 206, **209–11,** *330,* 423, *425* (*see* individual states); (new technology) 140, 144, 311, 332
Airships, 143
Aisne, River, 279, *280,* 286, 288
Aix-la-Chapelle, Congress of, **19–20,** 25, 58
Akkerman, Convention of, 128
Albania, 187, 188, 201, *247;* (before independence) 43, 237, *238,* 240, 245–6; (in FWW) 203, 247, *283;* (after FWW) *325,* 355, *356,* 364, **377,** 389, **410,** 411; (in SWW), 415, *416*
Alexander I (Tsar, 1801–25), 18, 29, **48–9,** 56–7, **67–9**
  Foreign policy of, 20–2, 23, 43, 68, 193; (at Vienna) 7, *8,* 9–10, 68; (and Holy Alliance) **11–13,** 68
Alexander II (Tsar, 1855–81), 71, 138, **209–14;** (and peasantry) 36, 138, **209–11,** 212–13; (foreign policy of) 117, 118, **134–5,** 201, 226, 231–2, **236–42**
Alexander III (Tsar, 1881–94), **214–15,** 226, 234; (foreign policy of) 163, 185, 234
Alexander of Battenberg and Bulgaria, 234, 240–1
Alexander (King of Jugoslavia, 1921–34), 376

Alexander Obrenovic (King of Serbia, 1899–1903), 243
Alexandra, Tsarina (d. 1918), 215, 221, 224
Alexei, Tsarevich, 224
Alfonso XII (Spain, 1874–85), 126
Alfonso XIII (Spain, 1885–1931), 372–3
Algeciras, Conference of, *258,* 262–3, 275
Algeria, 65, 93, 95, 101, *139,* 178, 250, *258*
Alliances before 1870: (Holy, 1815) *8,* **11–13,** **21,** 68; (Quadruple, 1815) **11, 18–19,** 22; (Quintuple, 1818) 20, 58, 125; (Russo-Turkish, 1833) 71, **129,** 130
Alliances/Alliance System (1871–1914), 155, 163, 179, 185, 201–2, 226, **231–5,** 242, **265–8;** (*Driekaiserbund*) 201, 226, 231, *233,* **234,** *267;* (Dual Alliances, 1879) 201–2, **232,** 234, 242, *267,* **273;** (Triple, 1882) **185,** 187, **233–4,** 265, *267;* (Reinsurance Treaty, 1887) **234,** *267;* (Franco-Russian, 1893) 163, 179, 226, 228, **265,** *267,* 274; (Anglo-Japanese, 1902) 228, 266, *267;* (Anglo-French Entente, 1904) 179, 262, **266,** *267,* 268; (Anglo-Russian Entente, 1907) **266,** *267;* (Triple Entente) 179, **266,** *267,* 271
Alliances (FWW): (Pact of London, 1914) 282; (Treaty of London, 1915) **187–8,** 289, 324
Alliances after 1918, *393, 404;* (Franco-Czech, 1925) 345, 391, *393,* 407–8; (Franco-Polish, 1925) 345, 378–9, 391, *393,* 411; (Franco-Rumanian, 1926) 392, *393;* (Franco-Jugoslav, 1927) 345, 392, *393;* (Little Entente, 1929) 392–3; (Franco-Russian, 1935) 315, 345, *393,* 395, *404;* Russo-Czech, 1935) *393,* 395, 407; (Rome-Berlin Axis, 1936) 399–400, 403 (*see* Pacts, Anti-Comintern, Nazi-Soviet, Non-Aggression, of Steel; and Stresa Front)
Alma, River, *131,* 133
Alsace (-Lorraine), *116,* 121, **123,** 124, 127, 160, 165, 176, 178, 230, 269, 271, 275, 279, 292–3, 322, *323,* 336
Alvensleben, General, 117
Amur, 226, *227*
Anarchism, 147, 174, 175, 184, 198, 213, *217,* 302, 374, 433
Anatolia, 326–7, 337
Ancona, 31
Andrassy, Gyula (d. 1890), 194, 200, 202, 232, 235, *239*
Ankara, 326, *327*

Annam, 260
Anschluss, The, 356 (see Austria, Republic of, Union with Germany)
Anti-clericalism, 433; (France) 59, 62, 172–3, 178, 343; (Piedmont-Sardinia) 107, 183; (Switzerland) 88
Anti-semitism (see Jews): (France) 176–8; (Germany) 315, 347, 352, 427; (Habsburg Empire) 196; (Italy) 363, 427; (Rumania) 376; (Russia) 310, 314
Antwerp, 47
Appeasement, 395, 406–11, 414, 420; (definition) 400, **407**, 428, 433
April Theses, 296
Arakcheyev, General, 68
Arc de Triomphe, 64
Argentina, 23, 50, 144
Aristocracy, 2, 10, 17, 63, 144, 206, 212 (see Landowners, and individual states); liberal-minded, 53, 56, 160, 207
Armenia, 242–3
Arndt, Ernst (d. 1860), 51
Armies, size of, 231, 268 (see individual states)
Artois, Charles of (see Charles X)
Aspromonte, 112, *113*
Asquith, Herbert (d. 1928), 274, 286
Atlantic, The, 140, 249; (Charter) 417
Auber, Daniel (d. 1871), 47
Augustenburg, Dukes of, 117–18
Aurora, The, 299
Ausgleich, The, 123, **193–5**, 198, 200, 202
Australia, Australasia, 144, 250, 254, 336, 401, 415
Austria, Republic of, *204*, 324, *325*, **336–7** (see Peace Settlement, 1919–20, St Germain); (constitution and government) 332, 339, 356; (society and economy) 324, 328, 351, 389; (foreign policy) 384, 397; (union with Germany) *323*, 324, *325*, 336–7, 356, *371*, **394–5, 404–6**, *409*
Austrian Empire before 1867, 2, *12*, 18, *29*, 117, 125 (see Metternich)
Internal: (government and history) 18–19, **24–7, 83–8, 193–4**; (condition and society) 6, 7, 19, **25–6**, 83; (multinational) 13, **24–5**, *26*, 42, 52, 81, **85**, 89, 123, 193, **435**; (peasantry) 25, 26, 83, 84; (population) 36; (provincial diets) 25, 194
Revolutions (1848–9), 18, 27, 30, 73, 74, *75*, **76–88**, 193
Foreign relations (see Alliances before 1870; Italy-Austrian influence; Schleswig-Holstein Question; Wars, Austro-Prussian): (Peace settlement 1814–15 and Congress period) **7–13**, 15, **19–22**; (and German Confederation) 14, 15, **27–30**, 52, **80–2**, 112, 115, **116–19**, 150, 193; (and Ottoman Empire) 23–4, 42, 128, 130, 131, 133, 134
Austrian Netherlands, 15, 46
Austrian Swabia, 15
Austro-Hungarian Empire (1867–1918), 115, 123, 137, **Unit 13**
Internal: (constitution) 196–9 (see Ausgleich); (economy) 138, *141*, 181, 197, 200; (multinational) 185, 195,

196–7, **198–201**, 202, 246, 320, 406; (multinational–South Slav Problem) **201**, 203, 244, 269, 271, **273**, 275, 324, 426 (see Bosnia); (political parties) 196, 200–1; (population) 138, 197, 200; (provincial diets) 196, 198, 200; (society) 144, **196–8, 200–1**
Foreign relations, 185, **201–3**, Unit 15, 262, **Unit 17** (see Alliances, 1871–1914; Eastern Question); (relations with Germany) 155, 201–2, 232 (see Alliances, Dual Alliance); (and Balkans) 201–3, 228, 231–2, Unit 15; (and FWW) 187, 198, 199, 200, 202, **203**, 232, 247, *267*, **271–7**, **Unit 18**, *283*; (armed forces) 268–9
Collapse of, 195, 199, **203–4**, 247, 289, 291, 292–3, 319, 324–5, 336–7, 376
Autarky, 370, 433
Avanti, 184, 185, 190
Axis powers, 403, *416* (see Alliances, Rome-Berlin Axis; Pacts, Anti-comintern and Tripartite Axis)
Azaña, Manuel (d. 1940), 373–4

Bach, Alexander, 193
Baden, *12*, 15, *28*, 40, *87*, *116*, 123, 160; (constitution) 78, 82
Badoglio, Pietro (d. 1956), 397
Baku, 206, *304*
Bakunin, Mikhail (d. 1876), 147, 174, 184, 213, 217
Balaclava, *131*, *132*, 133
Balance of Power: (1815) 10, 13, 27, 125, 433; (Mediterranean) 43–4, 45, 185; (Central Europe) 103, 118, 120, Unit 15; (Balkans) Unit 15; (after 1918) 320; (after 1945) 429
Baldwin, Stanley (d. 1947), 388
Balfour, Arthur (d. 1930), 271
Balkans, The, 201, 226, 228, Unit 15, 277, 289, 293, 378, 416, 426 (see individual states)
Nationalism in and Ottoman rule of, 6, 13–14, 127, 133, 186, 202, Unit 15, 326 (see Eastern Question and Ottoman Empire)
Balkan League, **243–6** (see Wars)
Balloons, *103*, 141, 166, *285*, 291
Baltic Provinces, Russian, 68, 214, *304*, 307–8, 328, **376**, 413, *416*, 417
Bandiera Brothers, 33
Banditry: (Italy) 31, 76, 181, 188; (Russia) 302
Barbary Coast, 20
Barcelona, 375
Bashi-Bazouks, 236, 237
Basques, 375
Batoum, 237
Battle of Britain, 415
Bavaria, *26*, 27, *28*, 40, 45, 49, *116*, 123, 346, 347, 349; (customs union) 51–2; (1848) 78, *86*; (state in German Reich) 151
Bazaine, Marshal, 122
Beck, Jozef, 378–9
Beethoven, Ludwig van (d. 1827), 6
Belgium
United with Holland, nationalism, struggle for independence, 6, 7, 11, 15, 17, 33, **46–8**, 49, 53, 65, 71, 126, 426
History after 1839, 120, 252, 322, *323*, 333,

336, 348, 385, 390, 401; (constitutional ism) 47, 48, 339, 341, *356*, 357, 426; (economy) 46, 48, 138, *141*; (neutrality) **48**, 121; (population and society) 46, 48, 138, 358, *425*
FWW, *267*, **274**, 276, **279–81**, 286, 288, 291, 292–3, 322
SWW, 345
Belgrade, *26*, 41, *42*
Belle Époque, La, 180
Belsen, *432*
Benckendorff, General, 70
Benedetti, Vincent, 120
Beneš, Eduard (d. 1948), 356, *357*, 407–8
Berchtesgaden, 405, 407, *409*
Berlin, *28*, 51, 120, 201, 231, 273, 335, 346–7, 349, 394, 414, 419, *420*; (population) 35, 158; (revolution in) 74, 79–80, *86*
  Conference (1884–5), 178, 231, **257**
  Congress of (1878), 155, 231, 232, *238*, **239–42**, 245
  Memorandum (1876), 235
Berlin-Baghdad Railway, 271, 277
Berlioz, Hector (d. 1869), 56
Berri, Duke of, 58
Besika Bay, 131, 236
Bessarabia, 135, 237, *238*, *304*, 308, *327*, 413, *416*
Bessemer process, *140*
Bethmann-Hollwegg, Theobald von (d. 1921), 156, 159–60, 274
Beust, Count, 194, 196
Biarritz Meeting, 118, 119
Bismarck, Otto von (d. 1898), 105, **115–24**, 142, 162
  Minister-President of Prussia: (domestic policy) 115–16; (foreign policy) 99, 103, 112, 114, **116–23**, 125, 134, 167, 201
  Imperial Chancellor (1871–90), 123, 144, **150–6**, 158, 160, 185; (domestic policy) 124, **150–5**, 159, 160, 183, 184; (foreign policy) 151, **155**, 161, 163, 167, 176, 178, 185, 226, **230–5**, 237, **239–42**, 266, *267*, 271; (and colonies) 151, 155, 178, 234, 252, 254–5, **257**; (retirement and legacy) **155–6**, *157*, 234, 246, 265
Bizet, Georges (d. 1875), 100
Black Hand, The, 273
Blanc, Louis (d. 1882), 63, 91–3
Bleriot, Louis (d. 1936), 143
'Blood and Iron', 105, 114, 433
Bloody Sunday (1905), 217–8, 223
Blücher, Gebhard von (d. 1819), *2*, 4
Blum, Léon (d. 1950), 174, 343, 344, 374
Boers, 250, 256, 260–1 (*see* Wars, Boer)
Bohemia, 24, *26*, 119, *195*, 198–9, *325*, 409; (Diet in) 25; (economy) 196; (1848) **83**, *86*
Bolsheviks, 147, 188, 209, 310, 314, 347; (before 1917) **216**, *217*, 223; (1917–18) 226, **296–300**, 305, *306*, 310, 341 (*see* Communist Parties, Russia)
Bomba, King, (*see* Ferdinand II)
Bonapartism, 14, 58, 64, 91, 93, 100, 165, 167, 171, 176 (*see* Louis Napoleon and Napoleonic Legend)
Bonomi, Ivanoe (d. 1951), 188

Bordeaux, 167, 168, 172
Boris, King of Bulgaria (1918–43), 326, 377
Bosnia, *26*, *195*, 201, **202–3**, 228, **235**, 236, 237, *238*, 240, 243–5, *247*, 271, *325*
Bosphorus, The, *131*, 240, 326–7
Boulanger, Georges (d. 1891), 176, *177*, 178, 427
Boulogne, *63*, 94, *97*, 98
Bourbons (*see* rulers in France, Lucca, Naples, Spain)
Bourgeoisie (*see* Middle Classes)
Boxer Rebellion, 228, 258–9
Brahms, Johannes (d. 1897), 197, 199
Brazil, 23, 38–9, 41, 250, 385, 401
Brecht, Berchtold (d. 1956), 335
Bremen, *28*, 150
Brenner Pass, 394–5, 405
Briand, Aristide (d. 1932), 174, 175, **342**, **345**, 390–1, 393
Britain
  Internal: (constitutional development) 13, 14, 22, 25, 36, 59, 105, 106, 137, 144, 159, 170, 332, 339, 341, 357–8; (economy) 1, 53, 106, 138, *140*, *141*, 144, 156, 188, 254, 331, *332*, *334*, *373*; (economy – trade) 22–4, 44, 52, 125, 128, 138, 144, 151, *156*, 165, 252, 344; (population) *140*, 331, *334*; (society) 1, 53–4, 146, 148, *336*, 340–1, *373*, *425*
  Foreign Policy and Relations, 3–4, 38, 110, 118, 120, 121, 125–35, 185, 232, 234, 235–41, 242, 245–6, Unit 17, **317–30**, 345, 384–5, **388–415**; (1814 Peace and Congress Period) **7–13**, 17, **19–24**, 41; (aid to Belgium) 17, **47–8**, 65, 126; (aid to Greece) **43–5**, 126; (relations with France) 65, 102, 103, 126–35, 179, 185, 232, 266–8, 271, **345**, 358, 389, 390, **395**, **399–400**, 411–12, 420; (and FWW) *267*, **274**, Unit 18; (and Communist Russia) 303, *304*, 308, 379, 412–14, 420–1; (and SWW) 379, 414–19
  Overseas Empire, 6, **11**, 15, *42*, 162–3, 178, 186, 233, 239, 249, **Unit 16**, *267*, 333–4, *398*; (mandates) 320, 336–7, 366, 386
  Navy, 4, 130, 131, **161–2**, 237, 266–7, 268–70, *272*, **290–1**, **391–2**, 395
Broglie, Duke of, 170
Brüning, Heinrich (d. 1970), 352–3
Brusilov Offensive, 203, 223, **282**
Brussels, 47, 176, 279, *280*
Bucharest, *42*, 282 (*see* Treaties of Peace)
Budapest, 89, *194*, 195, 200, 201, 203–4, 273
Bulgaria, 234, *238*; (struggle for independence) 231, **236–40**, 242; (after independence) 240–2, 243, 244–7, 270; (and FWW) 242, 246, *267*, 277, *283*, 289, 290; (after 1918) **325–6**, *327*, 337, 355, *356*, 376, **377**, 384, 389; (and SWW) 377, 415, *416*
Bulgarian Horrors, 236
Bülow, Bernhard von (d. 1929), 156, 159, 161
Bund (*see* Germany before 1871, Confederation)
Bundestag, (German Confederation) 27, 29; (North German Confederation and Reich) 119

Burschenschaften, 27–9
Byron, Lord (d. 1824), 43

Cadets, 216–17, 219, 221, 223, 300
Calabria, *32*, 33
Calatafimi, 110, *113*
Cambodia, 260
Cambrai, 286
Cameroon (see Kamerun)
Camorra, The, 364, 433
Canada, 144, 250, 254, 286, 401, 415
Canning, George (d. 1827), **21–4**, 25, **39**, **43–4**, 69, 126
Canrobert, General, 133
Can the Bolsheviks Retain State Power? 298
Cape of Good Hope, 11
Capital, Investment, 57–8, 62, 99, 181, 189, *208*, 210, 222, 298, 311, 312, 350–1, 366; (foreign investment in Tsarist Russia) 207, 212, 215, 226, 254, 265, 303, 308; (overseas investment) 253–4
Caporetto, 187, 203, *283*, 289
Caprera, 112, *113*, 114
Caprivi, Leo von, 158–9, 163, 234
Carbonari (Italy), **31**, 33, 39, 50, 94; (France) 59
Cardigan, Lord, *132*
Carinthia, 324, 337
Carlos, Don, 37–8
Carlsbad, *28;* (Decrees) 28–9, *30*, 69
Carnot, President (d. 1894), *173*, 174
Carol II (Rumania, 1930–40), 376–7
Caroline Islands, 260
Casablanca, 262
Cash and Carry, 415
Castelfidardo, 111, *113*
Castlereagh, Viscount (d. 1822) **8–13**, 20–2, 23
Catholic Church, 2, 110, **147–8**, 249; (Belgium) 46; (France) 2, 31, **59**, 62, 78, 88, **96**, 98, 101, **102**, 103, 108, 112, 130–1, 148, 171, **172–3**, 175, 178; (Germany) 119, **151–4**, 159, 367 (see Kulturkampf); (Habsburg Empire) 77, 88, 102, 148, 193, 201; (Italy) **31**, 50, 108, 112, 148, **183–4**, 188, 191, *363*; (Piedmont) 106; (Poland) 48, 49; (Spain) 37–8, 148, 372–5; (Switzerland) 88. (See also Education)
Cavaignac, General, 93, 94
Cavour, Camillo de (d. 1861), **106–12**, 116, 145, 181, 182, 187; (policy in Piedmont) 106–7; (external policy) 107–12, 119, 125, 133, 134
Central Powers (FWW), *267*, *275*, 339; (defeat of) 291, 320, 339 (see Austro-Hungarian Empire, German Reich, Bulgaria, Ottoman Empire)
Ceylon, 11
Chamberlain, Austen (d. 1937), 390–1
Chamberlain, Joseph (d. 1914), 255, 265
Chamberlain, Neville (d. 1940), 345, 407–8, 411–12, 414
Chambord, Count of, 60, 169–70
Champagne, *280*, 284
Chanak, 326, *327*
Charles, Emperor (1916–18), 203–4, 324
Charles X (France, 1824–30), 23, 56, 58, **59–60**, 62, 126, 169

Charles XIV (Sweden, 1818–44), 33
Charles Albert (Piedmont-Sardinia, 1831–49), 31–2, 40, 50, **76–7**, *87*, 106, 107
Charles Felix (Piedmont-Sardinia, 1821–31), 31, 39–40
Charter, The (*see* Louis XVIII)
Chartists, 54, *75*, 95
Cheka, The, 302
Chicherin, Georgi, 308, 315, 389
Chile, 389, 401
China, 127, 187, 226, **257–60**, 323, 336, 393, 401, 403 (*see* Boxer Rebellion and Manchuria); (FWW) *267*
'China Incident', The, 393, 417–18 (*see* Wars, Chinese-Japanese)
Chios, *327*, 337
Christian IX (Denmark, 1863–1906), 117
Chrzanowsky, Adalbert, 77
Churchill, Winston (d. 1965), 399, 408, 417–18
Ciano, Galeazzo (d. 1944), 410
Cinematograph, 143, 335
Civil Marriage, 106, 153, 172, 184, 193, 196, 365
Clemenceau, Georges (d. 1929), 171, 175, 176, 177, 342, 345; (Peace Settlement, 1919–20) 317–21, 323–4, 328, *329*, 330
Clothilde, Princess, 108
Coal production, 124, 138, **140**, 156, 197, *208*, 311, *312*, *330*, 331
Cobden Treaty, 99, 100
Cochin China, 101, 250, 260
Collective security, definition, 400, 421, 433
Collectivization of agriculture, 311–13
Colombia, 23, 389, 401
Colonial empires and Imperialism, **Unit 16**, 271, 276, **333–4**, 426, 430–1 (*see* individual states); (motives for colonization) **249–55**
Combes, Emile (d. 1921), 172–3
Comecon, 429
Comintern, The, 147, 308–9, 315, 403 (*see* Pacts, Anti-Comintern)
Commonwealth of Nations, British, 395, 415, 417
Commune, Paris (1871), 145, **167–9**, 171, 219
Communism, 168, **427–9**; (definition, examples) 341, 433; (in Russia) **Unit 19** (*see* Commune, Paris)
Communist Manifesto, The, 89, 146
Communist Parties (*see* Bolsheviks): (Britain) 357; (France) 343, 344; (Germany) 329, 333, **346–7**, 348, 350–1, *352*, 353, 354–5, 357, 368 (*see* Spartacists); Hungary (*see* Kun); (Italy) 188–90; (Russia) 300, 307, 310, 314, 315, 339, 371 (*see* Russia, Communist); (Spain) 372, 374–5
Concordat, (Austria) 193; (France) 173; (Germany) 367 (*see* Italy) (*see* Treaties, Lateran)
Confédération Générale du Travail, 175, 344; *(CGT Unitaire)* 344
Conference of Ambassadors, 328, *384*, 389
Congo, The, (Belgian) 252, 256, 257, *258*; (French) 178, 256, *258*, 263; (Free State) 257
Congresses, (Vienna, 1814–15) **7–15**, 19; (after 1815) 11, 17, 18, **19–24**, 68, 125, 381; (*see* Berlin)

Connell, Jim, 147
Conscription, 268; (Austro-Hungarian) 196; (France) 167, 175; (Prussia, Germany) 115, 150–1, 395; (Russia) 210, 212
Constantine I (Greece, 1913–17 and 1920–2), 377–8
Constantine (Romanov), 46, 69
Constantinople, 41, 42, 131, 132, 234, 237, 242, 243, 326, 327; (Conference, 1876) 236
Constitutionalism, 36, 105, 137, 433 (see individual states):(appeal of) 2–3, 5, 43, 68; (resistance to) 25
Consumer goods, 140–1, 311, 312, 314, 330, 331
Corfu, 389
Corporate State, 361, 362, 371, 372
Corsica, 32, 113, 115
Cossacks, 217, 224, 303
Court, International, 262, 268, 274, 381, 383, 384, 385, 401
Cracow, 9, 12, 15, 28, 86, 88
Credit Anstalt, 351, 404
Crete, 42, 43, 45, 130, 238, 242–3, 245, 247
Crimea, The, 131, 133, 303 (see Wars, Crimean)
Crispi, Francesco (d. 1901), 110, 182–3, 184, 185–6, 252
Croatia, 26, 195, 324, 325: (Diet in) 25; (1848–9) 83, 84, 85, 86, 200
Croats in Habsburg Empire, 24, 26, 200, 203, 376
Cuba, 254, 260, 267, 372, 401
Cubists, 335
Cuno, Wilhelm, 348–9
Curie, Marie and Pierre, 143, 179
Curzon Line, 304
Custozza, Battle of (1848) 77, 84; (1866) 112, 113
Cuza, Alexander, 231
Cyprus, 238, 239, 241, 252, 258, 327, 337
Cyrenaica, 186–7, 243
Czech Legion, 304
Czechoslovakia, 199, 323, 325, 328, 336
   Internal: (history) 341, 356–7, 376; (economy and society) 320, 323, 356, 408–9; (population) 356
   Foreign relations, 323, 324, 328, 345, 356, 358, 378–9, 388, 390, 392–3, 401, 406–9, 410–11, 414
Czechs in Habsburg Empire, 24, 26, 195, 198–9, 201, 203 (see Bohemia)

Daily Telegraph, The, 271
Daladier, Edouard (d. 1970), 343, 345, 407–8
Dalmatia, 12, 15, 26, 195
Danube, River, 202; (navigation of) 134–5, 240
D'Annunzio, Gabriele (d. 1938), 188, 388
Danzig, 9, 12, 15; (after 1918) 322, 323, 336, 383, 409, 411, 412–14
Dardanelles, The, 44, 128, 129–30, 131, 240, 282, 293, 326–7
Darwin, Charles (d. 1882), 147, 148
Daumier, Honoré (d. 1879), 61, 66
Dawes Plan, The, 350, 390
Deák, Ferenc (d. 1876), 194, 200
Decazes, Duke of (d. 1860), 58

Decembrist Conspiracy, 68, 69
Dedeagach, 326, 327, 337
Degeyter, Paul, 147
Democracy: (bourgeois) 3, 137, 287, 291, 339–41, 356, 361, 426 (see Constitutionalism); (people's) 3, 314–15, 339
Denikin, Anton (d. 1947), 304
Denmark, 15, 20, 28, 33, 75, 87, 88, 117–18, 144, 322, 323, 332, 336, 356, 357, 401, 415 (see Schleswig-Holstein Question)
Depression, The (after 1928), 331, 343, 344, 351–2, 356, 357, 363, 370, 372, 376, 378, 391, 394, 400, 404
Depretis, Agostino (d. 1887), 182
Descent of Man, The, 147
Development of Revolutionary Ideas in Russia, The, 69
Devil's Island, 95, 177
Dictatorship of the Proletariat, 300, 310, 339, 356
Diets, 434 (see Austrian Empire and Austro-Hungarian Empire); (Germany) 40, 78 (see Prussia)
Dimitrievitch, Colonel, 273
Disarmament, 268, 293, 320, 323–4, 336–7, 345, 370, 391–2, 399 (see Hague Conferences; Peace Settlement 1919–20; Washington Agreements); (Commission for) 383, 384, 386, 392, 401; (Conference, 1932–4) 392
Disraeli, Benjamin (d. 1881) 235–6, 239–42, 252
Dobruja, The, 238, 246, 247
Dodecanese Islands, 187, 243, 247, 327, 337
Dollfuss, Engelbert (d. 1934), 356, 394–5, 404
Döllinger, Johann (d. 1890), 153
Dostoievsky, Fedor (d. 1881), 71–2, 209
Drang nach Osten, 202
Dreadnoughts, 161, 268–9, 270, 271, 290 (see Jutland)
Dreikaiserbund (see Alliances 1871–1914)
Dreyfus, Alfred (d. 1935), 172, 174, 177–8
Drummond, Eric (d. 1951), 318, 383, 385
Dual Monarchy, 137, 194 (see Austro-Hungarian Empire)
Dunant, Jean Henri (d. 1910), 381, 382
Dunkirk, 415
Dvořák, Antonin (d. 1904), 199
Dzerzhinsky, Felix (d. 1926), 302

Eastern Question (see Ottoman Empire and Russia, Relations with Ottoman Empire): (definition) 13–14, 128; (before 1880) 125, 127–35, 155, 202, 230–2, 235–42; (after 1880) 226, 234, 242–7
Eastern Rumelia, 238, 240–2
East Prussia, 116, 279, 281, 292, 283, 322, 323
Ebert, Friedrich (d. 1925), 346, 347, 348
Economic Consequences of the Peace, 328
Ecuador, 94, 401
Eden, Anthony (d. 1977), 397–400
Education: (religious control of) 46, 59, 96, 153, 172, 184, 193; (state control and expansion) 46, 59, 172, 184, 331, 341, 429 (see Universities); (Bohemia/Czechoslovakia) 199; (France) 59, 62, 96,

172, 175; (Germany) 150, 153, 159, 172, 368–9, 371; (Habsburg Empire) 193, 195, 196, 197, 200; (Holland) 46; (Italy) 183, 184, 362; (Russia) 68, 70–1, 207, 211, 216, 221, 307, 314; (Turkey) 365

Edward VII (Britain, 1901–10), 163, 266

Egypt, 41, 43, 45, 129–30, 178, 251, 252, 253, 256, *258*, 262, 266, 336, 400

Eiffel, Gustave (d. 1923), 176

Eisenstein, Sergei (d. 1948), *218*, 299

Eisner, Kurt (d. 1919), 347

Ekaterinburg, 305

Elba, 3, 4, 7, *12*, 58

Electricity, 140–3, 157, *166*, 307, *312, 330*, 331, 363 (*see* Hydro-electric)

Emancipation of Labour, 216–17

Emancipation of serfs, 1, 144; (Habsburg Empire) 83–4, 85, *86*, 88; (Prussia) 52; (Russia) 1, 68, 138, 207, **209–11**

Émigrés, 59, 60, 434

Ems, *116*, 120; (Telegram) 120

Enabling Law, German, 355, 367

Encyclicals; (*Rerum Novarum*) 148; (*Mit Brennender Sorge*) 367

Engels, Friedrich (d. 1895), 89, *335*

Ententes, definition, 433 (*see* Alliances)

Erfurt Union, 83

Eritrea, 185–6, *258*, 396, 397, *398*

Ersatz commodities, 370

Essen, *158, 269*, 348, *390*

Estonia, *304*, 307, 355, 376, *416*, 417

Ethiopia (*see* Abyssinia)

Eugénie, Empress (d. 1920), 96, 100, 101, 108

Eupatoria, *131*, 133

Eupen-Malmedy, *323*, 336

European Economic Community, 429

Exhibitions, commercial, 100, *166*, *269*

Exiles, 89; (from eastern Europe and Russia) 49, 213, 216, 219, 223, 296, 309 (*see* Siberia); (from France) 95, 169, 173 (*see* Émigrés); (from Italy) 114

Facta, Luigi (d. 1930), 188, 191

Falangists, 374–5

Falk, Adalbert (d. 1900), 153

Falkenhayn, General, 284–6

Falkland Islands, 290

Farini, Luigi, 109, 182

Farouk (Egypt, 1936–52), 45

Fasci di Combattimento, 189–91, 358, 361

Fascism: (definition and ideas of) 98, 189–91, 332–3, 341, **360–1, 419–21**, 427–8, 434; (Austria) 394–5, 404–6; (Britain) 358, 361; (France) 343; (German Nazis) 329, 335, 347, **349**, 350, *351*, **352–5**, 360–1, **367–72**, 419–20, 427–8; (Hungary) 324, 376; (Italy) 185, 188, **188–91**, **360–5**, 396, 428; (Portugal) 372; (Rumania) 377; (Spain) 374–6; (Sudetenland) 406–7

Fascists Exposed, The, 361

Fashoda, *258, 261*, 262, 265

Federati, 31

Ferdinand, Emperor (1835–48), 24, 83–4, *86*

Ferdinand I (Two Sicilies, 1759–1825), 10, 21, 31, 39

Ferdinand II ('Bomba', Two Sicilies, 1830–59), 39, 76, 78, 110

Ferdinand VII (Spain, 1814–33), 23, 37

Ferdinand of Saxe-Coburg (Tsar of Bulgaria, 1887–1918), 241, 243, 246, 326

Ferry, Jules (d. 1893), 171, 172, 178, 255

Feudalism, 3, 26, 56, 83, 434 (*see* Serfdom)

Fez, *258*, 263

Fichte, Johann (d. 1814), 51

Finance Capital, 253

Fiume, 188, *325*, 328, 364, 388–9

Flanders, *280*, 288

Florence, *32*, 112, *113*

Foch, Ferdinand (d. 1929), 288

Formosa, 226, *227*, 260

Fourteen Points, 293 (*see* Wilson, War Aims)

France

Under Napoleon I, 3

Bourbon Rule; 1814–1830, **58–60** (*see* Louis XVIII and Charles X)

Internal: (constitution) 36, 55, 58–60; (economy) 55; (population) 35, 55; (society) 1, 3, 14, 36, 55–6, 58, 59

Relations with other powers, **20–3**, 37, 44, 59, **125–6**; (1815 Settlement) **7–13**, 27

Orleanist Rule, 1830–48, **60–7**, 94–5 (*see* Louis Philippe)

Internal: (constitution) 60–1, 64, 66–7; (economy) 53, 62, 65, 96, 128; (society) 53–4, 57, 61–5

Relations with other powers, 17, 38, **65**, **126–7, 129–30**

Revolutions: (1789) 2, 3, 5, 6, 26, 38, 56, 59, 60, 68, 73, 94, 423; (1830) 29, 31, 46, 49, 56, **60–1**, 71, 98, 126; (1848) 33, 54, 56, 57, 62, **66–7**, 71, 73, 74–6, *86*, **91–3**, 95, 98, 105

Second Republic, 1848–1852, 74–6, *86*, **91–6**, 105 (*see* Louis Napoleon)

Internal: (constitution) 92, 93, 95, 96; (economy) 96; (peasantry) 95; (society) 74, 76, 91–2, 94, 95

Relations with other powers, 78, 96, 102

Second Empire, 1852–1870, 91, **96–104**, 122, 124, *166*, 179 (*see* Louis Napoleon)

Internal: (constitution) 98–9, 105, 106; (economy) 99–100, 127, 165; (society) 97–8, 148

Relations with other powers, 98–9, **101–4**, **120–3**, 127, **130–5**

Culture before 1914, 50, 100, 179–80

Overseas Empire before 1870, 65, 101, 102, 249, 250–1

Third Republic, 1870–1940, **Unit 11, 342–5**

Internal: (constitution) 144–5, 165, 167, **170–1**, 182, 332, 333, 339, 341, **342–4**, 346, 356; (economy) 138, *140, 141*, 144, 156, **165**, 174, 175, 181, 207, 212, 254, *334*, 342, 343, **344–5**, *373*; (monarchy rejected) 169–70, 171, 172; (political parties) **171–2, 174–5, 342–3**, 374; (population) *140*, 144, 165, 331, *334*, 344; (scandals) 171, 174, 176–8, 342–3; (society and reforms) **144**, 165, 168, 171, 174, **175**, 178, 179–80, *336*, 340, **344–5**, *373*,

425; (society and religion) **172–3**, 178, 184
Overseas Empire, 171, **178–9**, 185, 186, 233, 251–2, 254, 256–8, **260**, *261*, 262–3, *267*, 333–4; (mandates) 320, 336–7
Relations with other powers: **178–9**, 230–3, 235, 239–40, 242–3, 246, **Unit 17**, 328, **345**, **388–415**, 429; (armed forces) 269, 391–2, 411; (and Germany before 1933) 155, 171, 175, 178–9, 230–5, **262–3**, 270, 271, 328–9, 342, 345, **348**, 350, **389–92**; (alliances and ententes before 1914) 163, **179**, 226, 228, 262, **265–8**; (FWW) *267*, **274–5**, 276, **Unit 18**; (Peace Settlement 1919–20) **317–30**, **336–7**, 384–5; (alliances after 1918) 315, 320, **345**, 378–9, **391–3**, 400, 411–12 (*see* Alliances); (and Nazi Germany) 171, 343, 344, 345, 378–9, 392, 395, 399–400, 411–12, 420–1 (*see* Stresa); (and Communist Russia) 303–5, 308, 315, 345, 412–14, 420–1 (*see* Alliances, Franco-Russian 1935); (SWW) **343–4**, 345, 364, **414–5**, 419; (Free French) 417
Fourth Republic, 1946–58, 344
Francis I, Emperor (1792–1835), 6, *8*, 11, 19, 24
Francis II (Two Sicilies, 1859–60), 110, 111
Franco, Francisco (d. 1975), 341, 355, *356*, 360–1, **374–6**, 416
Frankenau, 279
Frankfurt, *28*, *30*, *116*, 119; (Parliament 1848–9) 51, *75*, **80–2**, *86–7*, 105
Franz Ferdinand, Archduke (d. 1914) 198, 201, 272–3
Franz Joseph, Emperor (1848–1916), 84–5, *87*, 109, 144, **193–8**, 200, 201, **202–3**, *204*, 231, 232, 244, 273; (relatives) 102, 198 (*see* Franz Ferdinand)
Frederick, Kaiser (1888), 155
Frederick VII (Denmark, 1848–63), 81
Frederick Augustus of Saxony, 8–9, 10
Frederick William III (Prussia, 1797–1840), 8, 11, 29, 30, 40, 51, 52, 71
Frederick William IV (Prussia, 1840–61), 30, **78–83**, *87*, 115, 117
Free Cities, 188, 336; (German) *28*, 150
Free Trade, 5, 46, 106, 138, 151, 181, 293, 434 (*see* Cobden Treaty)
Freikorps, 347, 404
French, John (d. 1925), 284
French Impressionists, 179
Freud, Sigmund (d. 1939), 197, 431
Fürstenbund, The, 82

Gaeta, 77
Galicia, *9*, *12*, 15, 24, *26*, 83, *195*, 281, 282, *283*, 289, *325*, 337
Gallipoli, 282, *283*, 284, 289, 326
Gambetta, Leon (d. 1882), 166–7, 171
Gapon, Georgi (d. 1906), 217, 219
Garibaldi, Giuseppe (d. 1882), 50, 78, *79*, 106, *107*, **110–14**
Gas-lighting, 100, 141–3

Gas, Poison, 284, 334, 381, 397; (gasmasks) 407
Gastein, Convention of, *116*, 118
Gatling, Richard (d. 1903), 256
Geneva, *383*, 384, 401; (Protocol) 388, 390
Genoa, 10, *12*, 15, *32*, 110, *113*; (Conference, 1922) 308, **389**
Georg Ernest of Hanover, 11, 30
George III (Britain, 1760–1820), 10, 13
George IV (Britain, 1820–30, earlier Prince Regent), 4, 13, 25
George II (Greece, 1922–3 and 1935–47), 378
Germany
Before 1871 (Confederation) **10**, 15, 18, 24, *28*, **40**, 52, *75*, 88, 433; (North German Confederation) *116*, **119–20**, 123; (history before 1848) **27–30**, 40, 52–3, 69; (history, 1848–9) 40, 74, *75*, **78–82**, *86–7*, 89, 105; (history after 1849) 83, **115–19**; (economy) 51–3; (peasantry) 51, 80; (population) 35–6; (society) 1, 27, *74*, 80; (nationalism and process of unification) **27**, *29*, 49, **50–3**, 105–6, 112, **115–24**, 120, 123, 166–7, 426
German Reich, 1871–1918, 105, *116*, **121–3**, 125, 127, **Unit 10**, 230
Internal: (and Catholic Church) 148, 151–4, 232; (constitution) 123, 137, **150–1**, 159, **160**, 170, 182 (*see* North German Confederation, above); (economy) 124, 138, *140*, *141*, **144**, **151**, **156–8**, 159, 161, 163, 165, 197, 228, 254; (militarism) 114, *122*, 144, 150, 158, 160, 162, 163, 231, 271, 274, 276, *285*, 318; (nationalism) 150, 160, 161, 163; (naval development) 155, 157, **159**, **161–2**, 235, 254, 265, 268–9, 271, *272*, **290**, 324; (political parties) 151–5, 158–60, 349; (population) 123, *140*, 144; (society) **144**, 150, **158**, 159, 163, 424
Overseas Empire: 151, 155, 157, 161, 230, 251, 252, 254, 255, 256, 258–60, 263, 289, 291, 293, 320, 323, 334, 386
Foreign relations: (*see* Alliances 1871–1914 and Bismarck, foreign policy); (1890–1914) 158–9, **161–3**, 179, 234–5, **262–3**, **Unit 17**; (FWW) 187, 203, *267*, **271–7**, **Unit 18**, **307–8**, 317, 419; ('War Guilt') 276, **322**, 336
Collapse of Reich, **160–1**, 291
Weimar Republic, 1918–1933, 161, **346–55**
Internal: (constitution and government) 332, 339, 341, **346–7**, 349, **353–5**, 367, 378; (economy and society) 322–4, 328–9, 331, *332*, 335, 344, **348–52**, 353, **354–5**, *425*; (inflation) 348–50, 352; (political parties) 349–51, *352*; (population) 331; (unrest) 308, 309, 340, **346–7**, **348–9**, **353**, 355
Foreign relations: (Peace Settlement, 1919–20), **317–24**, (*see* Peace Settlement, Versailles); (policy) 350, **389–93**; (and Communist Russia) 303, 308, 309, 347, 389–90 (*see* Treaties, Rapallo); (and League of Nations) 350, 391–2
Nazi Germany, 1933–1945, 333, *356*,

367–72, 394–400, Unit 24, 427–8 (see Hitler)
Internal: (birth) 354–5, 367, 394; (armed forces) 367, 368, 370, 372, *373*, 375, 392, 395, 411 (see SWW below); (economy and society) *334*, 335, *336*, 367–71, *373*, 419, 427; (population) *334*, 370, 372; (terrorism) 314, 367–8, 369–70, 431–2 (see Jews); (youth movements) 368, *428*
Foreign relations: 330, 341, 357–8, 370, 372, 376–9, 387, 388, 393, 394–5, 399–400, Unit 24; (and Communist Russia) 312, 315, 407, 412–15, *416*; (and Fascist Italy) *362*, 363, 364, 394–5, 397, 399–400, 403–6, 410–11, 415; (SWW) 343–4, 345, 414–19
Collapse of, 419
Gestapo, The, 367, 368
Gilchrist (steel production) *140, 157*
Gioberti, Vincenzo (d. 1852), 50
Giolitti, Giovanni (d. 1928), 183, 184, 187, 188, *189*
Gladstone, William (d. 1898), 236
Godesberg, 407, *409*
Goebbels, Joseph (d. 1945), 353, 354, 355, 367, *368, 400*
Goering, Hermann (d. 1946), 353, *368, 369, 375, 400*
Goethe, Johann (d. 1832), 40, 51
Goito, 77
Goluchowski, Agenor (d. 1921), 193
Gorchakov, Alexander (d. 1883), *239*
Goremykin, Ivan, 219, 220
Gosplan, 311
Gotha Programme, 154
Göttingen, 30
Grandeur and Misery of Victory, The, 330
Gravelotte, 122
Greece
    Nationalism and struggle for independence, 17, 21, 22, 23–4, 41, *42*, 43–5, 49, 53, 71, 126, 128, 129
    After independence, 231, *238*, 240, 242–3, 245–6; (constitution) 129; (FWW) 246–7, *267, 283*, 289, 378; (after 1918) 326–7, 337, 355, *356*, 364, 377–8, 385, 389, 401, 411; (SWW) 415
Greek Orthodox Church, 2, 43, 128, 130–1, 201, 231 (see Russia, religion)
Gregory XVI, Pope (1831–46), 31, 50
Greenland, 418
Grévy, Jules (d. 1891), 170, 176
Grey, Edward (d. 1933), 266–7, 277
Grossdeutschland, 123, 329
Guernica, 375
·Guesde, Jules (d. 1922), 174, 175
Guiana (British) 11; (French) 95, 102
Guizot, Francois (d. 1874), 62, 64, 65–6
Gustav V (Sweden, 1907–50), *358*

Habsburgs, 7, 15, 18, *32*, 40, 80–1, 102, 109, 117, 118, 123, 148, 352 (see Austrian, Austro-Hungarian Empire and Vienna, Court in)
Hacha, Emil, 408

Hague, Hague Conferences, 262, 268, 274, 381–2, 384, 386
Haig, Douglas (d. 1928), 284, 285–7
Haile Selassie (Ethiopia, 1928–74, d. 1975), 396–7
Halifax, Lord (d. 1959), 405, 411
Hambach Festival, 29
Hamburg, *28*, 150, 348
Hanover, 10–11, *12, 28*, 30, 82, *116*, 117, 119; (customs union) 51–2
Hardenberg, Karl (d. 1822), 8, 9
Harington, General, 326
Haussmann, Georges (d. 1891), 100, *101*
Haynau, General (d. 1853), 193
Hegel, Georg (d. 1831), 51
Heimwehr, 404
Heine, Heinrich (d. 1856), 29, 429
Heligoland, 11, *12*, 254, *323*, 324, 336
Henderson, Arthur (d. 1935), 392
Henderson, Nevile, 414
Henlein, Konrad, 406
Herrenvolk, 369–70, 372, 428
Herzegovina, *195* (see Bosnia)
Herzen, Alexander (d. 1870), 69, *217*
Hess, Rudolf (d. 1987), 353, *428*
Hesse, *28*, 119
Hesse-Cassel, 52, 82, 83, *116*
Hesse-Darmstadt, 51, *116*, 123, 215
Heydrich, Reinhard (d. 1942), 369, 414
Hilferding, Rudolf, 253
Himmler, Heinrich (d. 1945), 367
Hindenburg, Paul von (d. 1934), 282, *285*, 286, *287*, 353–5, 367, *369*
Hiroshima, 419
Hitler, Adolf (d. 1945): (before 1933) 341, 349, 350, 352–5, 360, 394; (ideas, philosophy of) 289, 315, 320, 322, 328–9, 335, 341, 353, 354, 360–1, 368–9, 371–2, 394, 406, 418–20; (from 1933, domestic policy) 333, 346, 367–72, *428*; (foreign policy) 123, 323, 325, 355–6, 358, 363, 372, 374–5, 392, 394–400, 403–15; (SWW) 414–20; (suicide) 419, *420*
Hoare-Laval Plan, 397
Hobson, John (d. 1940), 253, 254
Hohenlohe-Schillingfürst, Chlodwig von (d. 1901), 159
Hohenzollern, *116*: (family) 81, 115, 119 (see Prussia, kings)
Holland, 7, *28*, 94, 120, 144, 148, 160, 401; (constitutionalism) 14, 33, 46, 48, *75, 87*, 88, *356*, 357; (overseas empire) 11, 46, 249, 333, 418; (population and society) 46, *425*; (union with Belgium) 11, *12*, 15, 17, 33, 46–8; (SWW) 415
Holocaust, The, 370 (see Germany, Nazi and Jews)
Holstein, *28*, 81, *116*, 117–18 (see Schleswig-Holstein Question)
Holy Land, 101, 130–1, 240
Hongkong, 250, 251, 257
Horthy, Miklos (d. 1957), 324–5, 333, 340, *356*, 376
Hossbach Memorandum, 406
Hugo, Victor (d. 1885), 100
Humbert, King of Italy (1878–1900), 183, 184, *186*

Hungary, 26 (see Austrian Empire, Austro-Hungarian Empire, and Ausgleich); (Diet in) 25, 85; (1848–9) 18, 83, **85–8,** 130, 193; (1867–1918) 196, **200–1**; (economy, society, population) 144, 200
Independent after 1918: 308, 320, **324–5,** 328, 333, 336–7, 340, 355, *356,* 376, 384, 392, 397, 407, 408–10; (SWW) 376, 415, *416,* 417
Hydro-electric power, 311, 312, 363

Ibrahim Pasha (d. 1848), 43, 44
Iceland, 418
Idées Napoléoniennes, Des, 63–4, 94
I.G. Farben, 157
Imperialism, definition, 251, 254, 255, 276, **434** (see Colonial empires and Imperialism)
Imperialism, 253
Imperialism, the Highest Stage of Capitalism, 253–4
India, 250, 251, 252, 255, 260, 271, 401
Indochina, 178, 260
Industrialization, 1–2, **35–6,** 54, 138, **140–3,** 144, 146, 154, **156–8,** 165, 181, 196, 206–7, *208,* 214, 250, 310, **311–12,** 331, **423–5,** 430 (see individual states, economies)
Inequality, 1, 17, 138, 145–7, 333, 335, 427, 431 (see individual states, societies)
Influenza epidemic, 292, 331
Inkerman, *131,* 133
Innsbruck, *26,* 83, *86*
Inönü, Ismet (d. 1973), 367
International, The: (First) **146–7,** 154; (Second) 147; (Third) 147 (see Comintern)
International Brigades, 375
Internationale, The, 147
International Labour Organization, *383,* 384, **385**
Ionian Islands, 11, *12, 42,* 45, 245
Iraq, 337, 366, 386
Ireland, Irish, 46, *140,* 147: (Irish Free State) *356,* 357
Iron production, *52,* 53, **140,** 156, 157, *208, 330*
Isabella II (Spain, 1833–68), **37–8,** 65, 120, **126,** *127*
Iskra, 209, **216,** *217*
Islam, 13, 43, 128, 235, 236, 271, 365
Istria, 188, 324, *325,* 337
Italia Irredenta, 115, 185, 187–8
Italy
  Before 1861, 7, 10, *12,* 13, 18, 24, **30–3,** **39–40,** 49, 99; (Austrian influence in) *12,* 15, 24, **30–3,** 50, **76–8,** 83, 89, 193; (nationalism) 6, 31–3, **49–50,** 105, 115, 123; (peasantry) 31, 50, 76; (population) 36; (society) 31, 33; (revolutions) 21, 31, 33, **39–40,** 65; (revolutions 1848–9) 50, 74, *75,* **76–8,** 83, *86–7,* 88–9, 106, 107; (process of unification and war of independence) 102, 105, **106–15,** 181, 426
  Liberal (1861–1922), 105, **112–15,** 125, **Unit 12,** 340, 342
    Internal: (armed forces) 269; (constitution and government) 112, 144–5, 181, **182–5,** **188–91,** 332, 339, 341, 346, 355 (see Socialism, Italy); (corruption) 182;

(economy) 138, *141,* **181,** 182, 183, 184, 185, 188, 363; (population) 138, 181, 200, 254, 331; (society) 144, 181, 182–4, 340 (see Catholic Church, Italy)
    Overseas Empire, 178, **185–7,** 228, 243, 251, 252, 254, 256, *258,* 263, *267,* 333–4
    Foreign relations: **185–8, 233–4,** 239, 243, 245–6, 262, 265, *267,* 271, 388, 391; (FWW) 185, **187–8,** 203, 247, *267,* 274, 276, *284,* **289,** 292–4, 365; (Peace Settlement, 1919–20) 317, 318, 320, 324, *325,* 326, 318, **337,** 384–5, 401
  Fascist (1922–1943), **360–5,** 428 (see Mussolini)
    Internal: (government) 361; (population) *334,* 363–4, 396; (religion) 363; (society and economy) *334,* **361–5,** *373,* 396
    Overseas Empire, 364, **396–8**
    Foreign relations: **364–5,** 387, 388, 392–3, **395–8, 403–4**; (SWW) 364–5, 415–19; (collapse) 418–19
Izvestia, 296

J'Accuse, 177
Jacobins, 60
Japan: (before 1914) 226–8, 252, 258–60, *267,* 271; (FWW) *267,* 289, 291, 303; (after FWW) 254, *304,* 317–9, 336, 384–5, 387, 388, 391–3, **394,** 395, 401, **403–4**; (SWW) **417–19**
Jaurès, Jean-Léon (d. 1914), 174
Jellacic, Josip, 84–5
Jena, 27
Jesuits: (in France) 59, 172; (in Germany) 153
Jews (see Anti-semitism): (Austria) *405;* (France) 176–8; (Germany) 20, 289, 329, 335, 347, 353, 354, 367, **369–70,** 372, 419, 431; (Poland) 370, 414–15; (Russia) 70, 206, 214, 221, 225, 310, 315, 370, 412; (USA) 418
Joffre, Joseph (d. 1931), 279, *284,* 286
John VI (Portugal, 1816–26), 38
John, Archduke, 80–1, *86*
Johnson, Andrew (d. 1875), 102
Joseph II, Emperor (1765–90), 24
Juarez, Benito (d. 1872), 102
Jugoslavia, 201, 247, 324, *325, 327,* 328, 336–7, 355, *356, 376;* (foreign relations: Fiume) 188, *325,* 388–9; (foreign relations and SWW) 345, 376, 377, 392, *393,* 401, 415
June Days (France 1848), *86,* 93, 100, 168
July Monarchy, 60, (see Louis Philippe)
Junkers, 115–16, 144, 150, 159, 434
Jutland, 290

Kamenev, Lev (d. 1936), 310, 314
Kamerun, *258,* 263, 289, 336
Kant, Immanuel (d. 1804), 51
Kapital, Das, 146
Kapp Putsch, 347, 349
Karadjorje family, 376; (Black George) 41, 243; (Peter) 243
Kars, *131,* 134–5, 237
Kemal, Mustapha (d. 1938), **326–7,** 333, 355, 360–1, **365–7,** 375

Kerensky, Alexander (d. 1970), 221, 282, 296–300, 341
Keynes, John M. (d. 1946), 328
Khartoum, 257
Kiao Chow, 258
Kiel, *116;* Canal, *323*
Kiev, 69, 305
Kingdom of Serbs, Croats, Slovenes, 376 (*see* Jugoslavia)
Kipling, Rudyard (d. 1936), 252
Kitchener, Herbert (d. 1916), 257, 262
Kleindeutschland, 123
Kluck, General von, 279
Kolchak, Alexander (d. 1920), 303, *304*
Kolowrat, Count, 18, 24
Konia, 129
Körber, Ernst von (d. 1919), 196
Korea, 226, *227*, 228, 252
Kornilov, Lavr (d. 1918), 298, 303
Kossuth, Louis (d. 1894), 26, **85**, 88
Kotzebue, August von (d. 1819), 28
Kronstadt, 265, *304*, 305, 306
Kruger Telegram, 162, 261, 265, 271
Krupp manufacturing, 157, *158, 162, 269*
Krupskaya Lenin, 216
Kulaks, **222**, 302, 306, 310, **312**, 314
Kulturkampf, The, 151, **152–4**, 155, 172, 232
Kun, Bela (d. 1939), 308, 324
Kutaya, Convention of, 129
Kwang Chow, 258

Lafayette, Marquis of (d. 1834), 60
Laibach, Congress of, **21**, 31, 38
Lamartine, Alphonse de (d. 1869), 65, 91, 92, 93
Landowners, **1–3**, 5, 25, 35–6, 49, 55, 59–60, 137, **144**, 189, 194, 200, 206, 210–11, 221, 222–3, 372–5, 423 (*see* Aristocracy and individual states, societies)
Lassalle, Ferdinand (d. 1864), 154
Lateran Treaties (*see* Treaties, Miscellaneous)
Latvia, *304*, 307, 355, *356*, 376, *416*, 417
Lauenburg, 117–18
Lausanne, Conference of (1932), 352; (*see* Treaties of Peace)
Laval, Pierre (d. 1945), 343–4, 397
Law of: (Associations) 172, 175; (Convents) 106–7; (Guarantees) 183; (Separation) 173
League of Nations, 22, 330, **382–8**, 394, 428; (Covenant) **321**, 334, 336–7, 366, **382–7**, 391, **401**; (creation of) 293, 318, **320–1**, 328, 382; (machinery of) 320, 381, *383,* **384–6**; (membership of) 315, 318, 321, 345, 350, *383*, **384**, 385, 387–8, 394, 400, **401**, 417; (work of) 322, *323,* 326, 328, 336–7, 366, 387, 414, 417, 434; (work, peacekeeping role) **388–9**, 393, **394**, 395, **396–8**, 399–400, 420
Lebensraum, 372, 412, 419, 434 (*see* Hitler, foreign policy)
Ledru-Rollin, Alexandre (d. 1874), 65, 93
Legitimacy, **10**, 15
Legitimists, French, 62, 91, 93
Legnago, 77
Leipzig, *2*, 28, 216

Lena goldfields, 223, *227*
Lenin, Vladimir (d. 1924): (before 1917) 216, 219, 252; (ideas about revolution) 69, 89, 146, 209, 219–20, 309, *335*, 347, 425; (and FWW) 174, 254, *257,* 307; (1917–1924) 252–3, **296–310**, 311; (brother Alexander) 214
Leningrad, **309**, *416*, 418
Leo XIII, Pope (1878–1903), **148**, 154–5, 172, 184
Leopold of Saxe-Coburg, King of Belgians (1831–65), 45, **47–8**
Leopold II (Belgium, 1865–1909), 252, 256, 257
Leopold, Duke of Tuscany (1824–59), 76
Leopold of Hohenzollern-Sigmaringen, 120
Lesseps, Ferdinand de (d. 1894), 176, 178
Lettow-Vorbeck, General, 289
L'Extinction du Paupérisme, 94
L'Humanité, 174
Liaotung Peninsula, 226, *227*, 228
Liberalism: (definition and examples) **5**, 48, 73, 80–1, **137**, 196–7, 211, 214, 243, 295–6, 354, 361, 423, 426, 427, 429, 434, (*see* Constitutionalism; Revolutions); (appeal of) 2–3, 27, 36, 37, 50, 53, 71, 98, 105, 216, 357; (fear of) 5, 6, 18–19, 27–31, 69, 148
Liberia, 257, *258*, 401
Libya, 186–7, *258,* 263
Liebknecht, Karl (d. 1919), 347
Lieven, Madame de, 25
Limburg, 47–8
Lisbon, 39, 41
Lisle, Rouget de (d. 1836), *57*
List, Friedrich (d. 1846), 51
Lister, Joseph (d. 1912), 143
Literature, 179, 209, 335 (*see* individual writers)
Lithuania, *304*, 307, 322, *323*, 328, 336, 355, *356*, 376, 388, *409, 416*, 417
Litvinov, Maxim (d. 1951), 315, 392, 412
Livingstone, David (d. 1873), 256
Lloyd George, David (d. 1945), 154, 263, 340, 389: (and FWW) 275, 286, 290; (War Aims of) **292–3**, 317; (and Peace Settlement) 317–21, 322, 326, *329*
Locarno (*see* Treaties, Miscellaneous)
Loi Falloux, 96, 172
Lola Montez (d. 1861), 78
Lombardy, *12*, 15, 18, *26, 28, 32*, 39, 40, 102; (1848–9) 76, 77, *86–7*; (liberation of) **108–9**, *113*
London, 142, 143, 146, 199, 237, 265, *340*, 358, 375, 394; (population) 35
Convention of, 1840, 130; 1841, 130 (*see* Straits Convention)
Naval Agreement, 392 (*see* also Treaties)
Loos, *280*, 284
L'Organisation du Travail, 63, 93
Loris-Melikov, Mikhail, 213
Lorraine, economy of, 157, 165, *373* (*see* Alsace-Lorraine)
Louis XVI (France, 1774–92), 3, 55, 60
Louis XVII (France, d. 1795), 55
Louis XVIII (France, 1814–24), **55–6**, **58–9**; (restoration) 3, 7, *14*, 55, 58; (Charter) 3, 5,

13, 36, **55**, 56, 58, 61; (foreign relations) 20, 125–6
Louis, Archduke, 24
Louis Bonaparte, 94
Louis Napoleon (d. 1873): (before 1848) 62, **63–5**, 78, **94–5**, 97, 101, 102, 176; (1848 and Presidency) 76, 78, 86, 91, **93–6**, 97 as Emperor Napoleon III (1852–70): 91, **96–104**, 105, 117, *121*, 127, 167, 170, 215, 250, 427: (domestic policy) **98–100**, 106; (relations: with Germany) 99, 101, 102–3, 114, 117, **118–22**; (with Italy) 99, 101, 102, 103, **107–9**, 110, 112, 119; (with Mexico) 99, 101, **102**, 103, 250; (with Russia) 101–2, 103, **130–5**
Louis Philippe, King of the French (1830–48), 46, 56, **60–7**, 71, 74, 76, 80, *86*, 91, 93, 94, 105, 170; (corruption and finance) 61, 62, 65, *66, 127*; (foreign relations) 31, **47, 65, 126–7, 129–30**, 131
Lucca, *12, 32*
Luddites, 54
Ludendorff, Erich von (d. 1937), 160, 282, 286, *287*, 288–9, 347, 349
Ludwig I (Bavaria, 1825–48), 78, *86*
Ludwig II (Bavaria, 1864–86), 232
Lusitania, SS, 290
Luxemburg, *28*, 47–8, 120: (FWW) 279, *280*, 288; (SWW) 415
Luxembourg, Rosa (d. 1919), 347
Lvov, Prince Georgi (d. 1925), 224, 295–6
Lyons, 62, 168
Lytton Commission, *383, 394*

Macao, 257, 258
Macedonia, *238*, 243, 245, 246, 376, 377
MacMahon, [Patrice] de (d. 1893), 167, 170
Madagascar, 178, *258*, 266
Madrid, 41, 374–5, 409
Mafia, 364, 434
Magenta, 108, *113*
Maginot Line, 345, 392, 415
Magnitogorsk, 312
Magyars, 24, *26*, 83, 85, 193, 199, **200–1**, 203, 320, 325, 435 (*see* Hungary)
Mahler, Gustav (d. 1911), 197, 199
Mahmud II (Sultan, 1808–39), 41, 43, 44, 128, 129
Malaya, 250, 251, 260
Malta, 11, *12, 32*, 237, *258*
Manchukuo, 394
Manchuria, 226, *227*, 228, 252, *383*, 387, 393, **394**, 395, 404
Mandates, definition, **334**, 434; Mandated Territories, 320, **336–7**, 386
Mandates Commission, *383*, 384, 386, 401
Manin, Daniele (d. 1857), 76–8, 89
Marchand, Jean (d. 1934), 262
March Laws, Hungarian, 85, *86*
Maria II (Portugal, 1826–53), 39, 126
Marianas, The, 260
Marie-Louise (d. 1847), 15, *32*
Markets, competition for, 22–3, 252, 271, 276, 426 (*see* Trade)
Marne, River, 279, *280*, 288

Marsala, 110, *113*
Marseillaise, The, 56, *57*
Marshall Islands, 260, 336
Martignac, Jean (d. 1832), 59
Martov, Jules, 216, *217*
Marx, Karl (d. 1883), 89, **145–7**, 154, 168, 300–1, *335*, 423, 433, 434
Marx, Wilhelm (d. 1936), 350
Marxism, Marxists, 2–3, **89, 145–7**, 148, 174, 184–5, 196, 209, 213, 214, **216–17**, 276, 296, 300, 303, 319, 341, 354, 360, 361, 418, 427, 428–9, 434 (*see* Communism, Communist Parties, Socialists)
Marxism-Leninism, **300–1**, 315 (*see* Lenin)
Masaryk, Tómàš (d. 1937), 199, 203, 356, *358*
Mass production, 141, 427, 429
Masurian Lakes, 281, *283*
Matteotti, Giacomo (d. 1924), 361
Mauritius, 11
Max, Prince, 160
Maximilian, Archduke (d. 1867), 102, 198
May Laws, Prussian, 153
Mazzini, Giuseppe (d. 1872) 50, 77–8, 107, 110, 114
Mecklenburg, *28, 116*
Medicine, 141, 143, 331
Mediterranean Agreements (1887), 185, 234
Mehemet Ali (Egypt, 1805–48), 41, **43–5**, 65, 71, 126, **129–30**
Mein Kampf, 353
Memel, *323*, 328, 336, 409
Menelek II (Ethiopia, 1889–1913), 186
Menshekov, Alexander (d. 1869), 131, 133
Mensheviks, **216**, *217*, 300, 310
Mentana, 112
Meshersky, Count, 215
Mesopotamia, *283*, 289
Messina, 76, 110, *113*
Metaxas, John (d. 1941), *356*, 378
Metternich, Clemens (d. 1859), 2, **Unit 2**, 35, 38, 42, 43, 44, 47, 71, 125, 276; (Peace Settlement 1814–15 and Congress Period) **8–13, 19–24**, 52; (policy in Austrian Empire) **24–7**, 193; (policy towards Germany) **27–30**, 40, 52, 78; (policy towards Italy) **30–3**, 39, 40; (philosophy) 18–19; (overthrow 1848) 18, 19, 76, 79, **83, 86**
Metz, 122, 230, *280*
Mexico, 23, 287, 310; (Napoleon III in) 99, **102**, 198
Michael, Grand Duke (d. 1918), 225
Middle classes, **1–3, 5**, 13, **18**, 35–7, 53–4, 73–4, 89, **144–5**, 146, 332–3, 341, 376, **423–5**, 427; (Belgium) 46, 48; (Britain) 2, 144; (France) 2, 36–7, 55–6, 59–65, 92–3, 144; (Germany) 350, 354; (Habsburg Empire) 25, 84, 194, 199; (Holland) 48; (Italy) 31, 33, **39–40**, 144, 183, 191; (Portugal) 38; (Russia) 56, 144, 207, 221, 223, 296; (Spain) 37–8; (Turkey) 365
Miguel (Portugal, 1828–34), 38–9
Milan, *26, 32*, 50, 76, 77, *113*, 184, 189
Millerand, Alexandre (d. 1943), 174, 175
Minsk, 216
Missionaries, 65, 179, 251, 255, 257, 431
Mitteleuropa, 276–7

Modena, *12*, 15, 18, 31, *32*, 40, 76, 108, **109**, *113*
Mohammed V (Sultan, 1909–17), 243
Mohammed VI (Sultan, 1917–22), 290, 326
Moldavia, *26*, 41, *42*, 43, 71, 128, 131–3, 135, 231
Molotov, Vyacheslav (d. 1986), 315, 412
Moltke, Helmuth von (the Elder, d. 1891), 118, 119, 120–1, 125, 156, 166, 276
Helmuth von (the Younger, d. 1916), 276, 279, 281, 284
Monroe Doctrine, The, 23, 102, 126
Mons, 279, *280*
Montenegro, *12*, *42*, 231, 236, 237, *238*, 240, 245–6, *247*; (FWW) 247
Moravia, *26*, *195*, 198, *325*, 409
Morea, The, *42*, 43
Morocco, *139*, 179, 186, *258*, 261, **262–3**, 266, 270, 271, *275*, 372, 374
Moscow, 56, 57, 206, 208, 218, 219, 226, *227*, *283*, 284, 298, 300, *301*; (1812) 6, 58, 68, 209; (Russian capital) 302, *416*, 418
Moslems (*see* Islam)
Mosley, Oswald (d. 1980), 358
Mosul, 366, 389
Motor vehicles, 142–3, *145*, 331, *332*, 335, 371, *373*, 429
Motorways, 364, 370
Mudania, 326, *327*
Mukden, *227*, 228
Müller, Hermann, 352
Münchengrätz Meeting, 71
Munich, *28*, 347, 352, *409*; (Putsch, 1923) **349**, *350*, 353; (Conference 1938) 343, 345, 378–9, **408**, 409, 410, 412, 414
Murad V (Sultan, 1876), 236
Music, 179, 197, 199, 209, 334–5 (*see* individual composers)
Mussolini, Benito (d. 1945) (*see* Fascism, Italy; Italy, Fascist): (before 1922) 185, **189–91**, 360; (becomes Prime Minister) 182, **191**, 340, 354, 355, 361; (Fascist ruler) *190*, 330, 341, **360–5**, 368, 370; (foreign relations) 186, 188, 247, 324, 328, 334, 355, **364–5**, 374–5, 377–8, **388–9**, 390–1, **394–400**, **403–6**, 408, **410–11**, 414, 419–21; (SWW) 414, 415–19; (overthrow of) 418–19

Naples, *32*, 49, 110, 112, *113*, *142*; (Bourbon rule in) 10, 15, 39, 76; (revolutions) 20–1, 33, 39, 47, 77, *86*, (*see* Two Sicilies)
Napoleon I, Emperor (1804–14), 93–4, 125, 173; (conquests) 6, 8, 9, 38, 46, 50, 68, 94, 102, 129, 209; (Hundred Days) 7, 55, 58; (overthrow and captivity) 2, **3–4**, 6, 7, 11, 18, 20, 28, 52, 58 (*see* Bonapartism; Napoleonic Legend)
Napoleon II (d. 1832), 94
Napoleon III (*see* Louis Napoleon)
Napoleonic Legend, The, 64, **94**, 96–8, 101
Narodniks, 212–13, 214, 216–17
Narodnovoltsy, 213, 214, *217*
Nationalism, definition and ideas, **6**, 246, 255, **276**, 333, **360–1**, **419–21**, 425–6, 428, **435**; (appeal of) 2, 6, 25, 27, 36, 73, 198–9, 269, 341, 347, 374–5; (independence move-

ments) **40–9** (*see* individual states); (in colonial empires) 251
National Guard, 92–3, 168
National Society, 109, 110
National System of Political Economy, 51
National workshops, 91–3
Nation states, 137, *139*, 231, 251, 328, 425–6, 435
Navarino, *42*, 44, *45*, 128
Nazism (*see* Fascism, Germany; Germany, Nazi)
Nemours, Duke of (d. 1896), 47
Netherlands (*see* Holland)
Nevesinye, 235
New Economic Policy, **306–7**, 308, 311, 313
Newfoundland, 266, 417
Newspapers, 141, 341, 385, 429; (and FWW) 201; (pressure by) 254, 269, 270
New Zealand, 250, 336, 401, 415
Ney, Michel (d. 1815), 58
Nezib, 129
Nice, 102, 103, 108, 119, 110, *113*, 127
Nicholas I, Tsar (1825–55), 34, **49**, 57, **69–72**, *134*, 209, 212; (foreign relations) 18, 22, 43–5, **71–2**, *75*, 83, **85**, *87*, 101, **128–34** (*see* Wars, Crimean)
Nicholas II, Tsar (1894–1917) 34, **215–25**, 303; (domestic policy and opposition to) 209, **215–23**, 298, 424, (*see* Russia, Revolutions); (foreign relations) 179, 217, 223, 226, **228**, 242, 243, 244–6, 266, **268**, 277, 296, **381**; (overthrow of) 215, **223–6**, 282, 287, 295, **305**, 424
Niemöller, Martin (d. 1984), 367
Nigeria, *256*, *258*
Night of the Long Knives, 367, *368*
Nightingale, Florence (d. 1910), 133
Nihilists, 213
Nikolsburg, Truce of, 119
Nivelle, Robert (d. 1924), 286
Nobel Peace Prize, 381
North Atlantic Treaty Organization, 429
North German Confederation (*see* Germany)
Norway, *12*, 15, **33**, 46, 332, *356*, 357, 401, 415
Novara, 77
Novibazar, *238*, 240
Nuremberg, *28*, 51; Laws, 369
Nyon, Conference of, 410

Obrenovic, Milos, 41
October Manifesto, *217*, **218–19**, 221
Octobrists, *217*, 221
Odessa, *218*, 219, *304*
Offenbach, Jacques (d. 1880), 100
Oil, *208*, 289, *312*, *330*, 331, 397, *413*, 418
Okhrana, The, 208, 216
Ollivier, Emile (d. 1913), 99
Olmütz, 84; (1850 'Humiliation') 83, 115, 119
Omdurman, 257, *258*, 262
'Open Door' policy, 259
Operation: (Barbarossa) 315, *413*, **417**, 420, 428; (Sealion) 415
Orange, William of (*see* William II, Netherlands)
Ordinances of St Cloud, 60
Origin of Species, The, 147

Orlando, Vittorio (d. 1952), 187–8, 318, 324, *329*
Orleanists, 93, 167, 170, (*see* Louis Philippe)
Orsini, Felice (d. 1858), 107–8
Otto I (Greece, 1832–62), 45
Ottoman Empire, *12*, 13, *26*, *42*, *75*, 88, *238*, Unit 15, 271; (condition of) 13, 41, 128, 129, *130*, 135, 137, 202–3, 226, 231, 235, 242–3, 366 (*see* Eastern Question); (constitutionalism) 138, 236, 242, 243; (rebellions against: by Bulgarians) 231, 235–40; (by Greeks) 17, 21, 23–4, 41, 43–5, 71, 128, 129, 137, 231; (by Serbs) 41–2, 43, 71, 128, 137, 231; (war with Italy), 186–7; (FWW) 246–7, *267*, 277, 282, *283*, 289–90 293–4; (after FWW) 319, 320, 326–7, 334, 337, 386 (*see* Turkey; *see* also Russia and Ottoman Empire; Balkan League)
Oudinot, General, 78
Owen, Robert (d. 1858), 36

Pacts: (Anti-Comintern) 403–4; (Kellogg-Briand, Paris) 342, 393, 394, 395; (Nazi-Soviet) 315, 379, *404*, 412–3, 417; (Non-Aggression, German-Polish 1934) 394; (Non-Aggression), Russo-Polish, 1932) *393*, 395, 411; (of Steel) 399, *404*, 410–11; (Tripartite Axis) 403–4, 417–18
Paderewski, Ignaz (d. 1941), 378
Palacky, Francis (d. 1876), 83
Palatinate, *28*, *116*, 120
Palermo, *32*, 110, *113*
Palestine, *283*, 289, 337
Palmerston, Viscount (d. 1865), 45, 47–8, 78, 88, 102, 103, 108, 109, 117, 126–7, 129–30
Panama Canal, 174, 176
Papacy, The, 13, 108–9, 147–8 (*see* Concordats; Papal States; (authority eroded) 106–7, 147–8, 172–3, 181, 183
Papal Infallibility, 114, 148, 153, 183
Papal States, The, *12*, 15, 31, *32*, 40, 50, 78, 94, 109, 110, *113*, 148, 181 (*see* Patrimony; Romagna; Umbria); (1848–9), 76, 77–8; (liberation of) 108, 110–11
Papen, Franz von (d. 1969), 353–4, 367, 405
Paris, 3, *4*, 58, 65, 94, 99, 108, 115, *143*, 147, *166*, 171, 176, 178, 266, 274, 317, 334, 343, 345, 384; (population) 35, 57, 100, 158, 179; (modernization) 100, *101*; (revolutions in) 56, 60, 62, 66, 74, *86*, 91–3, 95; (1870–1) *103*, 120, 122, 123, 166–9 (*see* Commune; (FWW) 279–81, 285, 288; (SWW) 415 (*see* also Peace Settlement, 1919–20)
Parma, *12*, 15, 18, 31, *32*, 76, 108, 109, *113*
Passchendaele, *280*, 286
Pasteur, Louis (d. 1895), 100, 143, 179
Patrimony of St Peter, *32*, 112, *113*
Paul I, Tsar (1799–1801), 56
Peace Settlement, Vienna (1814–15), 6–15, 17, 18, 24, 47–8, 68, 125, 250, 423, 425, 426
Peace Settlement, Paris (1919–20), 188, 308, 317–30, 333, 336–7, 342, 345, 372, 378, 382, 384, 388, 393, 405, 406, 419, 426, 434
Treaty of Versailles (1919), 276, 321–4,

328–9, 330, 334, 336, 341, 347, 348, 368, 390, 391, 394–5, 399
Treaty of St Germain (1919), 321, 324–5, *327*, 328, 336–7, 392
Treaty of Neuilly (1919), 321, 325–6, *327*, 337
Treaty of Trianon (1920), 321, 324–5, *327*, 337, 392
Treaty of Sèvres (1920), 321, 326–7, 337, 365 (*see* Treaties of Peace, Lausanne)
Pearl Harbor, 418
Peasantry, 1, 36, 144, 146, 171, 181, 184–5, 200, 235, 333, 341, 354, 365, 377, 423, 427 (*see* individual states); (uprisings of) 54, 73, 183, 208, 209, 211, 212–13, 218
Pedro IV (Portugal, 1826; Brazil, 1822–31), 38–9
Peking, 259
Pellico, Silvio (d. 1854), 50
Penicillin, 331
People's Will, 212, *217*
Perovskaya, Sofia, 213
Persia, *227*, 266, 308, 401
Pershing, John (d. 1948), 287
Peru, 389, 401
Peschiera, 77
Pestel, Pavel, 68, 69
Pesti Hirlap, 85
Pétain, Henri (d. 1951), 285, 286, 343–4
Petrograd, 224, *283*, 284, 295–300, 302 (*see* St Petersburg and Leningrad); (Soviet) 296–9
Philike Hetaireia, 43
Philippe Albert, 170
Philippe Egalité (d. 1793), 60
Philippines, The, 260, 372
'Phoney' war, 415
Picasso, Pablo (d. 1973), 335
Picquart, Colonel, 177
Piedmont-Sardinia, 10, *12*, 15, 31, *32*, 50, 89; (constitutionalism) 39–40, 76, 77–8, *86*, 88, 106; (revolutions to 1848) 21, 33, 39, *75;* (development and authority after 1848) 89, 105, 106–12, 114, 133, 147–8, 201 (*see* Cavour; Victor Emmanuel II)
'Pig War', 244
Pilsudski, Jozef (d. 1935), 333, 355, *356*, 360, 378
Pius VII, Pope (1800–23), 31, 40
Pius IX, Pope (1846–78), 40, 50, 76, 77–8, *79*, *86*–7, 96, 102, 106, 110, 114, 148, 153–4, 172, 181, 183–4, 193 (*see* Papal Infallibility)
Pius X, Pope (1903–14), 173, 184
Pius XI, Pope (1922–39), 363, 367
Plebiscites, 435; (of Louis Napoleon) 95, 96, 98, 99, 145; (in Italy) 109, 111, *113*; (Peace, 1919–20) 320, 322–4, *325*, 336–7, 395; (Weimar Republic) 346; (of Hitler) 367, 395, 405–6, 408
Plehve, Vyacheslav von (d. 1904), 215
Plekhanov, Georgi (d. 1918), 214, 216, *217*
Plevna, 236, *238*
Plombières Meeting, 108, 112
Pobedonostsev, Konstantin (d. 1907), 214, 215
Poincaré, Raymond (d. 1934), 342, 345
Poland
 Before 1815, 8–9
 Kingdom of, 9–10, *12*, 15, 34, 48–9, 68, 144,

214, 282; (nationalism and rebellions in) 6, 41, 47, **49**, 65, 71, 88, 102, **117**, 118, 138, **212**, 426; (peasantry) 49
Independence regained, 282, 292–3, 307–8, 322, *323*, *325*, 336–7, 378
Republic after 1918: (government and history) 333, 355, *356*, **378–9**; (population) *334*, 378; (society and economy) 320, *334*, **378**; (foreign relations) *304*, **305**, 308, 328, 345, 356, 358, **378–9**, 388, 390, *393*, 394, 401, 407, 408, *409*, 411, **412–15**; (SWW) 345, 370, 387, **414–15**, *416*, 420
Poles, 70; (in Habsburg Empire) 24, *26*, 204
Polignac, Jules de (1847), 59–60
Polish Corridor, *409*, 411
Pomerania, 10, *12*, 15
Pontine Marshes, 363
Popolo D'Italia, Il, 189
Popular Fronts; (in France) 343, 374; (in Spain) 374–5
Population, European, 1, **35–6**, 138, **140**, **143**, **331**, *334*, 429 (*see* individual states); (urban) **35** (*see* Urbanization)
Port Arthur, 226, *227*, 228, 258
Portugal, *12*, 14–15, 33, 65, 254; (history of) **38–9**, 355, *356*, **372**, 375–6, 401; (constitutionalism) 38–9, 126; (rebellions in) 20–1, 22, 38–9, 126; (overseas empire) 6, 23, 38–9, 41, 249, 250, 256–8, 265, 333
Posen/Poznania, *9*, 322, *323*, 336
Potemkin, Battleship, *218*, 219
Potsdam, 80
Pottier, Eugene, 147
Prague, *26*, 60, 83, *86*, 198, 200, 203, 357, 407–9; (University of) 198, 199
Pravda, 296, 310
Primo de Rivera (d. 1930), 355, *356*, 360, **372**
Princip, Gavrilo (d. 1918), 273
Proletariat, 89, (*see* Working classes)
Propaganda, 142, 160, 273, *285*, *292*, *297*, 318, 322, 362, 363, 399, 420, 427
Protection, 5, 46, 138, 271, 331, 426, 434, 435, 436; (in France) 175; (Germany) 51, 150, **151** (*see* Zollverein); (Italy) 183; (Russia) 208; (Turkey) 366; (USA) 331
Prussia
   Before 1871, *12*, *28*, 103, 125, (*see* Frederick William III and IV; William I; Bismarck); (constitution, Diet, Landtag) 30, 78, 79, 81, *86*–7, 88, **115–16**, 119, 151, 193; (economic development) 51–3 (*see* Zollverein); (1848) 30, 75, **78–81**, *86*–7; (foreign relations) 3, **7–13**, *15*, 20, 22, 23, 47, 109, 130, 131, 144; (and German Confederation) 27–30, 51–2, 79–83; 89, 105, **116–19**
   State in united Germany, 150–1, 153, 346, 367
Pskov, 225
Puccini, Giacomo (d. 1924), 334
Punch, *63*, *67*, *97*, *111*, *127*, *134*, *145*, 156, *157*, 162, *233*, *241*, 272, *281*, *333*, *387*, *424*
Putilov steelworks, 206, *207*

Quadrilateral, The, 77, 102, 108, 109, *113*
Quinine, 255

Radetsky, Josef (d. 1858), 76–8, 83
Radio, 143, 335–6, 341, 362, 407
Raglan, Lord (d. 1855), 133
Railways, 1, 2, 35, **140**, 143, 429; (Britain) 1, 35, 51; (France) 35, 62, 93, 98, 100, 175, 197, 281; (Germany) 35, **51**, 121, 123, *140–1*, 150, 156 (*see* Berlin-Baghdad Railway); (Habsburg Empire) 25, 35, 138, 197, 200; (Italy) 106, 138, *142*, 362, 363; (Prussia) 35; (Russia) 57, 206, *208*, 211–12, 218, 224, 312 (*see* Trans-Siberian, Turkestan-Siberian Railways); (Turkey) 366
Rasputin, Gregori (d. 1916), 224
Rathenau, Walter (d. 1922), 347, 389
Realpolitik, definition, 118, 435; (examples) 123, 125
Red Army, 303–5, 308, 314, 412, 418–19
Red Cross, 125, **381**, *382*, *383*, 401
Red Flag, The, 147
Redcliffe, Stratford de, 131
Redemption payments, 210, 215, 218
Reflections on Violence, 175
Reform Banquets, 65–6
Refrigeration, 141, 144
Reichsbank, 150, 351–2, 370
Reichsrat: (planned by Metternich) 25; (Habsburg after 1848) 193, 194, 195, **196–8**, *199*, 200; (in Weimar Republic) 346
Reichstag: (Austrian) 84, *86*; (Hungarian) 195, 200–1; (German, 1871–1918) 119, 145, 151–5, 158–60, 161, 163; (German after 1918) **346**, **350–1**, *352*, 353–5, 367; (Fire) 355
Religious toleration: (France) 55, 173; (Holland) 46; (Italy) 183; (Ottoman Empire) 240, 243; (Poland) 48
Reparations after FWW, *288*, 307–8, 318, 320, **322**, 323, **328**, 336–7, 342, **348–52**, 389, 390, 434, 435
Republic of St Mark (*see* Venice, Republic)
Revolutions of 1848–9, 17, 33–4, 38, 54, 57, 71, **Unit 5**, 130, 423; (summary) *86*–7; (*see* individual states)
Reynaud, Paul (d. 1966), 343
Rhineland: (Prussian) 9–10, *12*, 15, *28*, *116*, 153; (after 1918) *323*, 324, 336, 348, 378, **391**, **399**, *400*, 409
Rhodes, 187, 243, *247*, *327*, 337
Ribbentrop, Joachim von (d. 1946), *410*, 412–13
Ricasoli, Bettino, 109, 182
Richelieu, Duke of (d. 1822), 20, 58
Rio d'Oro, *258*, 372
Risorgimento, 11, 106
Robles, Gil (d. 1980), 373
Röhm, Ernst (d. 1934), 367
Romagna, The, *32*, 109, *113*
Romanovs, The, 56, 72, 208, 212, 214, 215, 224, 225, 226, 295, 307, 308 (*see* Tsars by name: Alexander; Nicholas)
Romanticism, definition, **5–6**; (appeal and decline of) 27, 29, 31, 33, 43, 47, 49, 65, 73, 78, 88, 89, 106, 114–15, 146, 335, 423, 429; (survival in Russia) 71–2, 88, 212, 423
Rome, 100, 110, 111; (Republic 1849) 77–8, *79*, *87*, 110; (French garrison in) 78, 96,

102, 112, 144; (capital of Italy) 112, *113*, 114, 181, 396; (March on Rome) 191
Roon, Albert von (d. 1879), 115, 118, 120, 125, 156, 166
Roosevelt, Franklin D. (d. 1945), 400, 415, 417–19
Roosevelt, Theodore (d. 1919), 228
Ruhr, The, 156, 349; (French occupation of) 328, 342, **348**, 389, **390**
Rumania, **135**, 137, 144, 201, 202, 231, 237, *238*, 240, 246, *304*, 308, 324, *325*, *327*, 337, 355, *356*, **376–7**, 392, *393*, 397, 401, 411, *425*; (and FWW) 203, 246, *267*, 282, *283*, 289, 293–4, 317; (and SWW) 415, *416*, 417
Rumanians, 43; (in Habsburg Empire) 24, *26*, 85, 201
Runciman, Walter (d. 1949), 407
Russia
   Tsarist rule (*see* Tsars by name: Alexander I, II, III; Nicholas I, II)
   Internal, government: (government and history) 33–4, 56–8, **67–72**, *75*, 137–8, **Unit 14**; (the Dumas) 207, *217*, **218–21**, 223, **224–5**, 295; (political parties and groups) 211, 212–13, 214, **215–17**, **219**, **221**; (revolutionaries) 147, 208–9, 211, *217*, 223, 291 (*see* Bolsheviks; Romanticism, survival in Russia); (1905 Revolution) 215, **217–20**, 224, 228
   Internal, economy and society, 56, 57–8, 69, 72, 138, *140*, *141*, 144, 165, 197, **206–8**, 209–10, 211–12, 214–15, 221, 223–4, 424; (peasantry) 1, 36, 49, 56, 57, **70–1**, 144, **206–7**, 208, **209–13**, 214–16, *217*, 218–21, **222–3**, 279, 295–8, 424; (population) 57, *140*, 206, 210, 222; (religion) 2, 56, 57, 68–9, 70, 128, 130–1, 214, 217, 221, 223, 224, *297*; (armed forces) 268–9
   Foreign relations, 28, 47, **71**, **127–35**, **226–8**, Unit 15, 252, 258–60, 262, **Unit 17**; (Peace Settlement, 1814–15) **7–13**, **15**; (and Ottoman Empire) 13, 17, **23–4**, **41–5**, 71, **127–35**, 202, 226, 232, 234, **235–42**, 243, 244–7, 271; (and FWW) 203, 221, 223–5, 229, **273–4**, **Unit 18**, 295, 317, 319. (*See also* Alliances; Poland, Kingdom)
   Revolution, February 1917, 209, 2̃4–6, 282, 295, 339, 423–4, 426, 431; (Provisional Government) 224, 282, **295–8**, 341, 427
   Revolution, October 1917, 188, 282–4, **298–301**, 310
   Communist Rule, **Unit 19**, 331, 333, 335, 427, 429
      Peace Settlement after FWW, 292–3, 301, 317–8, 328, 426
      Civil War, Wars of Intervention, 302, **303–5**, 306–8, 318, *327*, 331
      Constitutions, 299–300, 302, 307, 310, 314–15, 332, **339**; (police forces) 302
      Society: (peasantry) 299, 301–3, **305–7**, **311–13**; (population) 313, 331, *334*; (religion) 301
      Recognition of, 308, 315, 390
      Under Lenin **300–10**, *356;* (economy and

society) 302, 303, 305–7, 308, 314, *425*; (foreign relations) 301, 305, **307–9**, 347, 388, 389–90
      Under Stalin, **310–15**, Unit 24; (economy and society) 310, **311–14**, 331, *334*, 363, 366, 368, 370; (purges and terror) 302, 311, 312, 313, **314–15**, 324, 415
      Under Stalin, Foreign Relations, 310, **315**, 345, 376, 391, 393, **395**, 397, 400, 411, **412–15**, *416*; (and League of Nations) 315, 388, 391, 392, 395, 412, 417; (and Nazi Germany) 312, 315, 379, 395, 403, 407–8, **412–15**, 420–1; (and SWW) 315, 370, 375, *416*, **417–19**, 421
Ruthenians, in Habsburg Empire, 24, *26;* in Czechoslovakia, 356, 408–9

Saar, The, 156, 322, *323*, 336, *383*, 384, 395, *409*
Sadowa, *116*, 119, 120, 194
St Helena, 4, 94
St Petersburg, 44, 56, 57, 69, 115, 138, 206, *207*, 209 (*see* Petrograd; Winter Palace); (revolutionary activity in and Soviet) 216, 218–20, 225; (Congress of, 1825) 22; (Protocol of, 1826) 44
St Simon, Duke of (d. 1825), 62–3
Sakhalin, *227*, 228
Salazar, Antonio (d. 1970), 372, 375–6
Salic Law, 117
Salisbury, Lord (d. 1903), *239*, 242
Salonika, 237, *238*, 246, *247*, *283*, 289
Salzburg, 15
Samoan Islands, 260, 261, 336
Sanctions, definition, 386–7, 435; examples, 394, 397–8, 401
Santo Domingo, 23
Sarajevo, *195*, 198, 201, 261, **271–3**, 275
Sardinia, 181 (*see* Piedmont-Sardinia)
Saxe-Coburg, 45, 47
Saxe-Weimar, 27
Saxony, 8, 9, *12*, 15, 28, 52, 82, *116*, 117, 119; (state in German Reich) 151, 156
Savoy, *12*, 15, *32*, 102, 103, 108, 109, *113*, 127
Scapa Flow, 324
Schacht, Hjalmar (d. 1970), 370
Schiller, Friedrich von (d. 1805), 6, 40, 51
Schleicher, Kurt von (d. 1934), 353–4, 367
Schleswig, 81, *116*, 117–18, 322: (North) *323*, 336
Schleswig-Holstein Question, *28*, *75*, **81–2**, **117–18**, 119, 120
Schlieffen, Alfred von (d. 1913), 162, 276; (Plan) 162, **274**, 276, **279–81**, 284
Schönbrunn, Convention of, 231–2
Schuschnigg, Kurt von (d. 1977), 395, 405–6
Schutzstaffel (SS), 367, 369
Schwarzenberg, Felix (d. 1852), 84–5, 193
Scutari, *131*, 133
Sebastopol, *131*, 131, 134, 209, 228
Sedan, 99, 100, *121*, **122**, 166
Self-determination, **292–3**, **320**, 329, 333, 393, 435–6
Serbia, *26*, 44, 49, 71, 202, 226, 231, *238*; (history of) **41–2**, 43–5, 53, 128, 201, 236, 237, 240, 242, **243–7**, 270, **336**, 376; (and FWW)

147, 201, 203, 242, 246, **273–5**, 276, 281, *283*, 289, 293. (*See* Jugoslavia)
Serbs in Habsburg Empire, 24, *26*, 85, 201 (*see* Austro-Hungarian Empire, South Slav)
Serfdom, definition, 436 (western Europe) 1, 2, 5; (eastern Europe) 1, 56, 68, 70–1 (*see* Emancipation)
Seyss-Inquart, Artur von (d. 1946), 405–6
Shanghai, 394
Shostakovich, Dmitri (d. 1975), 314
Siam, 260, 266, 401
Siberia, *227*; exile in, 69, 71, 212, *213*, 216, 223, 296, 310
Siccardi Laws, 106
Sicily, *32*, 39 (*see* Two Sicilies); (revolutions) 73, 76, *86*, 183, 184; (Garibaldi in) 110, *113*
Siegfried Line, 399
Silesia, *28, 52*, 54, *116*, 119, 156; Upper, 322, *323*, 336
Simon, Jules (d. 1896), 170
Singapore, 250, 251
Sinope, *131*, 132
Six Articles, 29
Slavery: (Negro) 2, 250, 257; (Slave Trade) 10, 250
Slavophils, 216–17
Slivnitza, 242
Slovakia, *325*, 409, *416*, 417
Slovaks in Habsburg Empire, 24, *26*, 199, 201; in Czechoslovakia, 356, 408
Slovenes in Habsburg Empire, 24, *26, 201*
Smetana, Bedrich (d. 1884), 199
Smetona, Antanas, *356*, 376
Smyrna, 326, *327*, 337
Socialism, definitions and examples, 91, **146–7**, 331–2, 361, 424–5, 427, 429, 436 (*see* Communism; Marxism); (before Marx) 36, 63, 146; (in Austria) 404; (France) 91–3, 94, 96, 100, 145–6, 165, 168, 171, **174–5**, 176, 184, 342, 343; (Germany) 105, 145–6, 151–2, **154–5, 158–60**, 184, 289, 346, 350, *352*, 367, 368; (Habsburg Empire) 196–7, 203; (Italy) 105, 183; **184–5**, 188–91; (Russia) 147, 212, 214, **216–17**, 219, 221, 296–300, 307, 312; (Serbia) 147; (Spain) 373–5; (Sweden) 357
'Socialism in One Country', 310, 311–14, 315, 427
Socialist Revolutionaries (SRs), 212, 216–17, 219, 221, 223, 300, 302
Society, European, **1–6**, 17, **35–6**, 137–8, **144–7**, **332–6**, (*see* individual states)
Sofia, 236, *238*, 240, 241
Solferino, 108, *113*, 125, 381
Somaliland, 185–6, *258*, 396, 397, *398*
Somme, River, *280*, **285–6**, 288
Sonderbund, The, 88, 126
Sorel, Georges (d. 1922), 175, 179
South Africa, 160–1, *258*, 289, 336, 401, 415 (*see* Boers)
South Slavs, 376 (*see* Austro-Hungarian Empire)
South West Africa, *258*, 289, 336
Soviets, **219–20, 296–300**, 436 (*see* St Petersburg and Petrograd); (outside Russia) 308, 347
Soviet Union, 307 (*see* Russia, Communist)

Sovnarcom, 300, 310
Spain, *12*, 14–15, 33, 39, 65; (history of) **37–8**, 102, 120, **126**, 355, *356*, **372–6**, 385, 401, 416; (constitutionalism) 37–8, 126; (monarchy) 15, 37, 59, 120, 126, 372–3; (revolutions) 20–1, 22, 23, **37–8**, 126, 374; (revolutions: Civil War) 355, *356*, **374–5**, 399, 400, 403, 409–10, 414 (*see* Franco); (overseas empire) 6, 11, 20, **22–3**, 37, 41, 249, 250, *258*, **260**, 263, 333, **372**
Spartacists, 308, **347**, 436
Speransky, Mikhail (d. 1839), 67–8
Spiritual Pre-eminence of the Italians, 50
Stakhanovites, 311
Stalin, Joseph (d. 1953): (before 1924) 296, 300, 307, **310**; (power struggle) 309–10; (after 1927) 307, **311–15**; (foreign policy) 309, **315**, 374–5, 376, **412–14, 417–19**
Stalingrad, *416*, 418
Stalinism, **314–15**, 324, 363, 375, 415, 420, 431
Stamboliisky, Alexander (d. 1923), 377
Stambulov, Stefan (d. 1895), 234, 240–1, 244
Stanley, Henry (d. 1904), *253*, 256
State insurance schemes: (Britain) 154; (France) 344; (Germany) 155, 183, 350; (Habsburg Empire) 197; (Italy) 183; (Russia) 223, 301, 314; (Turkey) 366
Stavisky Affair, 342–3
Steam power, 1, 100, **140**, *141*, 142 (*see* Railways); (steamships) 100. 106, 140
Steel production, **140**, 156, 157, *158*, 206, *208*, *312*, *330*, 331, *373*
Stein, Heinrich von (d. 1831), 52
Stimson, Henry (d. 1950), 394
Stolypin, Peter (d. 1911), 206, 220–3
Strasbourg, 94, *97*, 98, 178, 230
Straits, The, (*see* Dardanelles); Straits Convention, 130, 135
Strasser, Gregor (d. 1934), 367
Strauss, Johann (d. 1899), 197
Stravinsky, Igor (d. 1971), 334
Streicher, Julius, (d. 1946), 369
Stresa Front, *393*, **395–7**, *404*
Stresemann, Gustav (d. 1929), 348–9, 352, 390–1
Strossmayer, Josef (d. 1905), 201
Students, 48–9, 88 (*see* Burschenschaften; Universities); (Austrian) 83–4; (German) 51, 105
Sturmabteilung (SA), 353, 367, *368*
Stuttgart, 82
Submarines, 269, 286–7, **290**, 324, 392, 410
Sudan, The, 179, 252, 257, *258*, 262
Sudetenland, The, 320, 323, *325*, 343, 356, 357, **406–8**, *409*
Suez Canal, 176, 178, 251, 252, *258*, 396, 397
Surrealists, 335
Sweden, 10, *12*, 15, **33**, 288, *356*, 357, *358*, 389, 401, 416
Switzerland, 10, *12*, 15, *28*, 126, 144, 204, 401, 416, *425*: (constitutionalism) *86*, **88**, 341, 357
Syllabus of Errors, 148
Syndicalism, definition, 174, **175**, 436; examples, 184, 425
Syria, 43, 45, 129–30, *283*, 290, 326, 337

Tahiti, 65, 260
Talleyrand, Charles de (d. 1838), 7, 9, 10
Tanganyika, 254, *258*
Tangier, *258*, 262
Tanks, 284, 286–8, 397
Tannenberg, 279, 281, *283*, 369
Tariffs (*see* Protection)
Tchadeyev, Peter, 72
Tchaikovsky, Peter (d. 1893), 209
Tchernaya, 107, *131*
Telegraphy, 141, 143
Telephones, *142*, 143
Teschen, *325*, 328, 356, 378, 408, *409*
Thessaly, *238*, 240, 243, 245
Thiers, Adolphe (d. 1877), 60, 62, 96, 129–30, **167–9**, 170
Third World, 431
Thomas, Albert (d. 1932), 385
Thomas (steel production), *140*, 157
Thorn, *9*, *12*, 15
Thrace, 327, 337
Through Darkest Africa, 256
Thyssen manufacturing, 157
Times, The, 133, 272
Tirpitz, Alfred von (d. 1930), 161, 268–9, 290
Tisza family, 200
Tobacco riots, 76, *86*
Todleben, Count, 133
Togo(land), 289, 336
Tolstoy, Leo (d. 1910), 209
Tonkin, 260
Toulon, 265
Towns (see Urbanization, and towns by name)
Trade, 22–4, 44, 100, 106, 127, 128–9, 138, *156*, 157, 161, 165, 179, 251, 257, 276, 344, 351–2, 370, 394, *425* (*see* Depression; Exhibitions; Markets; Open Door policy; Treaties, Trade)
Trade unions, *53*, 146, 148, 385, 425, 436 (*see* Working-class Organizations); (in France) 62, 100, **175, 344**; (Germany) 155, 367, 371; (Italy) 183, 190, 362; (Russia) 221, 225, 306, 314, 315
Transjordan, 337
Trans-Siberian Railway, 214, **226,** *227*, 228, *304*
Transylvania, *26*, 85, *195*, 201, *325*, *327*, 337
Treaties
  of Alliance (*see* Alliances)
  of Peace: *Paris, 1814*, **7**, 10; *Paris, 1815*, **7**, 10; *Vienna, 1815*, **6–13, 15**, 48; *Adrianople, 1829*, *42*, 44, 128–9; *Paris, 1856*, 102, 107, **135**, 209, 231, 235, 240, 241; *Tientsin, 1858*, 127; *Zürich, 1859*, 109; *Vienna, 1864*, 117–18; *Prague, 1866*, 112, *113*, **119**, 201; *Frankfurt, 1871*, **123**, 165, 167, 230; *San Stefano, 1878*, **237,** *238*, 239–40 (*see* Berlin); *Shimonoseki, 1895*, 226, 228; *Portsmouth, 1905*, 228; *London, 1913*, 245–6, *247*; *Bucharest, 1913*, 246, *247*, 270; *Bucharest, 1918*, 317, 336; *Brest-Litovsk, 1918*, 284, **307–8,** 317, 336, 412; *Riga, 1921, 304,* 305, 308, 412; *Lausanne, 1923*, **326–7, 337**, 365. (*See* Peace Settlement for Treaties of 1919–20)

Miscellaneous: *London, 1827*, 23–4, **44;** *London, 1831*, 47; *Unkiar Skelessi, 1833*, 71, **129**, 130; *London, 1834*, 126; *London, 1839*, **47–8**, 274; *London, 1852*, 117; *Berlin, 1878* (*see* Berlin); *Rapallo, 1922*, **308**, 309, 315, 347, **389–90**, 391, 412; *Locarno, 1925*, 345, 350, 364, **391**, 392, *393*, 395, 399; *Berlin, 1926*, 390, 391; *Lateran, 1929*, **363;** *Anglo-German Naval, 1935*, **395, 404**, 408. (*See* also Pacts; London Naval Agreement; Washington Agreements)
Trade, 308, 315, 366, 412 (*see* Cobden Treaty)
Treitschke, Heinrich von (d. 1896), 160, 161, 268, 269, 271
Trieste, *26*, *113*, 115, 185, 188, 201
Trinidad, 11
Tripoli, 186–7, 243
Troppau, Congress of, **20–1**, 38, 126; Protocol of, **20**
Trotsky, Leon (d. 1940), *217*, 219, 224, 295, **298–300, 303**, 307, 308, **309–10,** 314, 375
Truman, Harry S (d. 1972), 419
Tsushima, Straits of, *227*, 228
Tukhachevsky, Mikhail (d. 1939), 314
Tunisia, *139*, 177, **178, 185,** 233, 256, *258*
Turin, *32*, 106, 111, 112, *113*
Turkestan-Siberian Railway, 312
Turkey, 188, 326–7, 333, 355, **365–7,** 389; (Turkey before 1918 and Turkish Empire, *see* Ottoman Empire)
Tuscany, *12*, 15, 18, *32*, 40, 108, **109,** *113*, 181; (1848–9) 76, 77, *87*
Two Sicilies, Kingdom of, *12*, 31, *32*, **39**, 108; (1848–9) 76; (united with Piedmont) 110–12, 181 (*see* Naples; Sicily)
Tyrol, *113*, 115, 185, 188, 324, *325*, 337

Ukraine, The, *283*, 284, *304*, 305, 307–8, *313*
Ulmanis, Karlis, *356*
Ultras, French, 58, 60 (*see* Charles X)
Umbria, *32*, 111, *113*
Unemployment, 73, 93, 94, 100, 252, 425; (after 1918) 188, 314, 331–2, 335, 340, 344, 350, 352, 363–4, 370, 378, 394, 404, 427 (*see* Depression)
Union of Liberation, 216–17
United Nations Organization, 428; Trusteeship Council, 386
Universities, 40, 46, 49, 200 (*see* Prague; Vienna); (German) 27–30, 40, 48–9, 153, 369; (Russian) 68, 69, 70, 208, 214
Urbanization, 1, **35–6, 57**, 138, **144**, 158, 165, **313**, 332, 423
Uruguay, 50, 401
USA, The, 94, 102, 228, 250, 254, 259–60, 262, 296, 299, 308, 339, 341, 372, 381, 385, 388, 390, 401, 429 (*see* London Naval Agreement; Monroe Doctrine; Pacts; Kellogg-Briand; Washington Agreements; presidents by name): (economy) 140, 144, *156*, *208*, 251, 257, 287, 291, 312, 331, 351, *373*, 400 (*see* Depression; Wall Street); (economic aid to Weimar Germany) 350–1, 390; (encourages nationalism) 6, 23, 24, 41;

(and Napoleon III) 101, 102; (FWW and Peace Settlement) 188, *267*, 287–8, **290–4**, 303, *304*, **317–30**, 345, 384, 385; (1930s and SWW) 394, 415, 417–21
USSR, The Union of Soviet Socialist Republics, 307 (*see* Russia, Communist)
Uvarov, Count, 70

Varna, *131*, 133
Vatican, The, 114, 183–4; Decrees (1870), 148
Venetia, *12*, 15, 18, *26*, *28*, *32*, 39, 40, 77, *86–7*, 102, 187; (liberation of) 108, 109, **112**, *113*, **118–19**, 181, 193
Venezuela, 389, 401
Venice, *26*, *32;* (Republic 1849) 73, 76–8, 85, *86–7*, 88
Venizelos, Eleutherios (d. 1936), 378
Verdi, Giuseppe (d. 1901), 100, 110
Verdun, *280*, **285**, 288
Verona, 55, 77, 109, *113*; Congress of, **21–2**
Versailles, 122–3, 172 (*see* Peace Settlement, 1919–20, Versailles)
Vesenkha, 305, 311
Vichy government, 343–4
Victor Emmanuel I (Piedmont-Sardinia, 1802–21), 31, 39
Victor Emmanuel II (Piedmont and Italy, 1849–78): (King of Piedmont) 77, 106, 107–12, *113*, 116; (King of Italy) 112, 182, 183
Victor Emmanuel III (Italy, 1900–46), 183, 191, 377, 397, 410
Victoria (Britain, 1837–1901), 10, 30, 47, 255, 260
Vienna, *8*, 18, 25, *26*, 27, 38, 119, *194*, 195–7, 200–1, 203–4, 231, 253, 273, 356, *371*, 394, 404–7 (*see* Peace Settlement, 1814–15; Treaties of Peace); (Habsburg court in) 57, 193, 197–8; (population) 35, 158; (revolution in) 74, 83, **84**, 85, *86*, 89; (University) 83, *84*, 197
Vienna Note (1853), 131
Vilagos, 85, 193
Villafranca, Truce of, 109
Villèle, Jean (d. 1854), 58–9
Vilna, *304*, 328, 378
Vimy, *280*, 284, 286
Vittorio Veneto, 187
Viviani, René (d. 1925), 165
Vladivostok, 226, *227*, 228, *304*
Volkswagen, 371
Volturno, River, 111, 112, *113*
Vorparlament (*see* Frankfurt Parliament)

Waldeck- Rousseau, René (d. 1904), 171, 172, 174, 178
Wallachia, *26*, *42*, (*see* Moldavia)
Wall Street Crash, 351
Walwal oasis, 396, *398*
War Communism, 305
Wars
 Before 1871: *American Independence, 1775–83*, 60, 250; *Revolutionary and Napoleonic, 1792–1815*, **6**, 10, 14, 60, 68, 94, 133, 250, 283, 423; *Russo-Turkish, 1828–9*, 41, 44, 71, 128–9; *Piedmontese-*

Austrian, 1848, 76–7, *86*; *Prussian-Danish, 1848*, 82, *86*; *Piedmontese-Austrian, 1849*, 77, *87*; *Russo-Turkish, 1853–6*, 71; *Crimean War, 1854–6*, 72, 101–2, 103, 107, 125, 127, **131–5**, 193, 209, 226, 231, 237; *Italian Independence, 1859*, 101, 102, **108–9**, 110; *Danish, 1864*, 117; *Austro-Prussian, 1866*, 99, 112, **118–19**, 120, 201, 277; *Franco-Prussian, 1870–1*, 38, 99, 101, 103, 112, 114, **120–3**, 135, 166–8, 172, 179, 201, 230, 277
 1877–1913: *Russo-Turkish, 1877–8*, 232, **236–9**; *Boer, 1881*, 260; *Serb-Bulgarian, 1885*, 242, 243–4; *Chinese-Japanese, 1894*, 226, 242; *Greek-Turkish, 1897*, 243; *Spanish-American, 1898*, 260, 372; *Boer, 1899–1902*, 162–3, 260–1, 265; *Russo-Japanese, 1904–5*, 212, 217, **228**, 271; *Italian-Turkish, 1911–12*, 186–7, 243, 245; *Balkan Wars, 1912–13*, **245–6**
 First World War, 1914–18: (outbreak of) 147, 163, 185, 187, 223, 226, 246, 261–2, **272–7**, 431; (the War) 14, 22, 42, 160, 174, 179, 180, 198, 203, 232, 242, 246–7, 263, 266, **Unit 18**, 297, 329, 334, 360, 381–2, 388, 419, 420, 426, 427; (opposing sides) *267*, *275*; (neutrals) *275*, *280*, *283*, 372; (Western Front) **279–81**, 282, **284–9**, 318, 322; (Eastern Front) 279, 281, **282–4**, 286, 287, 290, 296–7, 303; (other theatres) 282, *283*, 284, **289–90**; (naval war) 287, **290–1**; (armistices) 290, 317, 353; (casualties and cost) **293–4**, 331, 341, 431
 After 1918: *Russo-Polish, 1920–1*, *304*, 305, 328, 378; *Chinese-Japanese, 1937–45*, 393, 403–4 (*see* also Manchuria); *Russo-Finnish, 1939–40*, 417
 Second World War, 1939–45: 309, 364–5, 370, 375, 376–9, 399, *404*, **415–21** (*see* Chinese-Japanese, 1937–45); (outbreak in Europe) 315, 323, *329*, 330, 379, 387, *409*, 414–15, 421, 428; (neutrals) 367, 375, 416; (cost) 417, 419, 431–2
Warsaw, *9*, 49, *86*, 88, 204, 282, 305, 378, 414; Grand Duchy of, 8, *9*
Warsaw Pact, 429
Wartburg Festival, 27–9
Washington Agreements, 391–2
Waterloo, 3–4, 7, 58
Water supply, 100
Weaponry, 125, *140*, 143, 162, 248, 256, **268–9**, 275, 276, 334, *373*, 375, 388, 397, 426, 430 (*see* Disarmament; Dreadnoughts; Submarines; Tanks); (FWW) 281, 284, 286, 287, 290–1; (SWW) 414, 419
Wei-hai-wei, 258
Weill, Kurt (d. 1950), 335
Weimar, *28*, 40, 356
Weimar Republic (*see* Germany, Weimar)
Wellington, Duke of (d. 1852), 4, 8, 21–2, 44
West Indies, 102, 250, 372
West Prussia, 322, *323*, 336
Weygand, Maxime (d. 1965), 305
What Is to be Done?, 216
William I (Prussia and Kaiser, 1861–88): King

of Prussia, 115, 118–19, 120; Kaiser, *122*, 123, 150, 152, 155, 160, 201, 231, 255
William II, Kaiser (1888–1918), 152, **155–6**, *157*, **158–63**, *197*, *287*, 288, 290, *292*; (external policy) **161–3**, 226, 234–5, 242–3, 246, 252, 255, 260–1, **262–3**, **265–6**, **271**, 274, 276–7; (abdication and exile) **160**, 318, 346
William I (Netherlands, 1815–40), 33, 46–8
William II (Netherlands, 1840–9), 47, 48
Wilson, Woodrow (d. 1924), 188, 339, 384; (FWW) 275, 287, **290**; (War Aims of) **292–3**, 317, 382; (and Peace Settlement, 1919–20) 317–21, 324, 326, *329*
Windischgrätz, Alfred (d. 1862), 83–5, 89
Windthorst, Ludwig, 153
Winter Palace, The, St Petersburg, *70*, 217, 299
Wireless (*see* Radio)
Witte, Sergei (d. 1915), 214–15, 219, 220, 226
Women's rights, *142*, *333*, 365, *383*, 384, 385; (voting rights) 137, 315, **332**
Working classes, 3, 5, 35, **73–4**, **89**, 332, 341, 385, 423–5, 427; (in France) 60, **62**, **168–9**, 344; (Germany before 1918) 152, 154–5; (Germany after 1918) 333, 347, 348, 351, 354, 370–1; (Habsburg Empire) 83–4, 196–7; (Italy) 188–91, 363–4; (Spain) 372–5; (Russia) 206–9, 214–15, 217–20,

221, 223, 224–5, 295–9, 302, 311–14 (*see* Soviets)
Working-class organizations, *52*, *53*, **53–4**, **145–7** (*see* Trade Unions)
Wrangel, General (d. 1928), 303, *304*
Württemberg, *28*, 51, *116*

Young Bosnia, 273; Young Czechs, 198; Young Germany, 29; Young Ireland, *75*, Young Italy, 29, **32–3**, 50; Young Ottomans, 137; Young Turks, 138, 243
Young Plan, The, 351
Ypres, 279, *280*, 284, 286
Ypsilanti, Alexander (d. 1828), 43
Yudenich, Nicolai (d. 1933), *304*

Zagreb, *26*, 85, *195*, 200, 201, 203
Zamora, Alcalá (d. 1949), 373–4
Zanzibar, 254, *258*
Zemstva, 211, 212, 214–15, *217*, 221
Zeppelins, 143, 291
Zimmerman Telegram, 287
Zinoviev, Gregori (d. 1936), 309, 310, 314
Zog (Albania, 1928–39, d. 1949), *356*, 377, 410
Zola, Émile (d. 1902), 177, 179
Zollverein, The Prussian, **51–3**, 150; (other) 51–2